OLE 2 Programmer's Reference

VOLUME ONE

Working with Windows™ Objects

PUBLISHED BY
Microsoft Press
A Division of Microsoft Corporation
One Microsoft Way
Redmond, Washington 98052-6399

Library of Congress Cataloging-in-Publication Data
Microsoft OLE 2 programmer's reference.
p. cm.
Includes index.
Contents: Contents: v. 1. Introduction and API reference -- v. 2. Creating programmable applications with OLE automation.
ISBN 1-55615-628-6 (v. 1). -- ISBN 1-55615-629-4 (v. 2)
1. Windows (Computer programs) 2. Microsoft Windows (Computer file) I. Microsoft Corporation. II. Title: OLE 2 programmer's reference.
QA76.76.W56M52325 1993
005.4'3--dc20 93-36458
CIP

Printed and bound in the United States of America.

3 4 5 6 7 8 9 AG-M 9 8 7 6 5

Distributed to the book trade in Canada by Macmillan of Canada, a division of Canada Publishing Corporation.

Distributed to the book trade outside the United States and Canada by Penguin Books Ltd.

Penguin Books Ltd., Harmondsworth, Middlesex, England
Penguin Books Australia Ltd., Ringwood, Victoria, Australia
Penguin Books N.Z. Ltd., 182-190 Wairau Road, Auckland 10, New Zealand

British Cataloging-in-Publication Data available.

Printed in the United States of America.

Contents

About This Book

OLE 2 Programmer's Reference, Volume 1: Working with Windows Objects

The *Object Linking and Embedding Programmer's Reference, Volume 1: Working with Windows Objects*, provides a complete reference to the extensible application protocol known as OLE (Object Linking and Embedding). While OLE can run on other platforms, such as Windows NT and the Apple Macintosh system, the focus of this book is around applications that use the Microsoft Windows operating system, version 3.1.

To get the most out of this book, you should be familiar with:

- The C/C++ programming language concepts.

  While not a prerequisite for programming OLE, the inherent properties of C++ can make a difference in programming OLE.

  To aid in moving from C to C++, Microsoft provides sample OLE applications written in C to mimic and teach the object-oriented principles behind C++ and OLE.
- The Microsoft Windows programming environment, version 3.1 or later. The OLE protocols are implemented through dynamic-linked libraries (DLLs) that are used in conjunction with other Microsoft Windows programs.

How This Book Is Organized

The following sections summarize the book's contents:

Part 1 About OLE

Chapter 1 "Overview," introduces the basic concepts of OLE and presents a high-level overview of the design principles behind OLE, including the component object model and an introduction to common interfaces. Illustrations are used to show the architecture of and the relationship between component objects.

Chapter 2 "Programming Considerations," describes guidelines on a variety of subjects that pertain to the implementation of OLE in a general sense. This chapter also discusses implementation issues specific to container applications that deal with compound documents.

Chapter 3 "Registering Object Applications," describes that portion of the registration database that pertains to the registration of object applications. Information is provided regarding the entry and modification of database keys as well as addressing some OLE 1 compatibility issues.

Chapter 4 "User Interface Guidelines," describes the visual and interactive interfaces that support component objects. Where appropriate, illustrations are provided to show the details of dialog boxes and OLE concepts where they concern the end user of the OLE application.

Part 2 Reference Information

Chapter 5 "Component Object Interfaces and Functions," covers much of the functionality that forms the underlying foundation on which OLE 2 is built. The **IUnknown** interface, from which all other interfaces inherit, plus the object-class creation interface, **IClassFactory**, is described in this chapter. This chapter also describes issues such as reference counting (the mechanism used to keep track of valid objects), error handling, and the marshaling of pointers across process boundaries.

Chapter 6 "Compound Document Interfaces and Functions," describes most of the interfaces and functions that form the heart of compound document functionality. This chapter covers the **IOleObject** interface, the interface that exposes basic embedding functionality. Also covered is **IOleClientSite**, the interface that allows an embedded object to communicate with and request services from its embedding container.

Chapter 7 "Data Transfer/Caching Interfaces and Functions," describes the interfaces and functions that support displaying and rendering objects, caching presentation data for objects, and setting up advisory connections to keep applications informed of changes made to OLE objects.

Chapter 8 "Linking Interfaces and Functions," describes the interfaces that enable linked objects to be tracked and kept current to their source data, as well as API functions for creating application-specific instances of these OLE-provided interface implementations.

Chapter 9 "Persistent Storage Interfaces and Functions," describes the OLE object storage model and the interfaces and API functions that support storing and retrieving objects to and from disk and memory.

Chapter 10 "In-Place Interfaces and Functions," describes the interfaces that support activating objects within the context of their container application; activation could be editing, play, or any of the actions an object is capable of providing to the user.

Chapter 11 "Drag and Drop Interfaces and Functions," describes the interfaces that will need to be implemented to enable users to selectively drag and drop objects from one application to another, or to iconic representations of target devices, such as a printer or fax.

Chapter 12 "Compatibility with OLE 1," describes interfaces and functions that allow objects created by an OLE 1 object application to be embedded in and linked to by OLE 2 containers. OLE provides these capabilities by means of a built-in compatibility layer in the core code that include a set of API functions for conversion.

Chapter 13 "Concurrency Management," describes interfaces and functions that allow OLE applications to correctly deal with user input while processing one or more calls from OLE or the operating system. OLE calls, when made between processes, are categorized as synchronous calls, asynchronous notifications, and input-synchronized calls.

Appendixes

Appendix A "Object Handlers," describes the basics of object handlers, a library of interfaces and functions that provide services on behalf of OLE object applications while an object is in its loaded state, eliminating the need to start the object application. The following types of object handlers are discussed: the default object handler, custom handlers, and DLL object applications.

Appendix B "Data Formats for Properties and Property Sets," describes the standard data format that can be used to store information that is accessible across applications. This standard format allows outside applications to access and manipulate information such as the storage of character formatting properties in a word processor or the rendering attributes of an element in a drawing program.

Appendix C "Creating Distribution Disks," describes issues related to the distribution of your OLE application. It lists the files that *must* be included on your distribution disk(s), discusses special considerations for OLE application distribution, and concludes with a discussion of special considerations for distribution of OLE server applications.

Notational Conventions

The following typographical conventions are used throughout this book:

Typographical Convention	Meaning
Bold	Indicates a word that is a function name, method name, structure name, data type, or other fixed part of the Microsoft Windows and OLE Application Programming Interface. For example, **OleSave** is an OLE-specific function. These words must always be typed exactly as they are printed.
Italic	Indicates a word that is a place holder or a variable value. For example, *ClassName* would be a place holder for any OLE object class name. Function parameters in API reference material will be in italic to indicate that any variable name can be used. In addition, italics is used to highlight the first time use of OLE terms and to emphasize meaning.
UPPERCASE	Indicates filenames and paths as well as constants. For example, C:\WINDOWS\SYSTEM\OLE2.H is an MS-DOS path and filename. WM_DESTROY is a Windows constant.
`monospace`	Indicates source code and syntax spacing. For example:

```
typedef struct _APPSTREAM
{
  OLESTREAM      olestream;
  int            fh;
} APPSTREAM;
```

Note Much of the interface syntax in this book follows the variable-naming convention known in programming jargon as Hungarian notation where variables are prefixed with lower-case letters that indicate their data type. For example, *lpszNewDocname* would be a long pointer to a zero-terminated string named *NewDocname*. See *Programming Windows* by Charles Petzold for more information about Hungarian notation.

For More Information

For more information about the Microsoft Windows programming environment, consult the documentation in the *Microsoft Windows Software Development Kit for Microsoft Windows, version 3.1*. Another good source is *Programming Windows* by Charles Petzold.

For more information about C/C++ programming, consult the documentation in Microsoft C/C++, version 7.0.

For information about Microsoft Windows NT, see the *Microsoft Windows NT Software Development Kit*.

The *OLE 2 Programmer's Reference, Volume 2: Creating Programmable Applications* describes OLE Automation, a way to manipulate an application's objects from outside that application. OLE Automation uses OLE's common object model, but may be implemented separately from the rest of OLE. Using OLE Automation, you can:

- Create applications that expose objects to programming tools and macro languages.
- Create and manipulate objects exposed in one application from another application.
- Create tools that access and manipulate objects. These tools can include embedded macro languages, external programming tools, object browsers, and compilers.

Inside OLE 2 by Kraig Brockschmidt shows you, by example, exactly how to build OLE 2 applications from scratch as well as how to convert existing applications. It provides a tutorial and a strong set of example programs on disk that you can incorporate into your own programs.

P A R T 1

About OLE

CHAPTER 1

Overview

What is OLE 2?

Object Linking and Embedding (OLE) Version 2 is a technology that enables developers to create sophisticated and extensible applications that operate across multiple platforms and conform to the programming model for future versions of the Windows operating system. OLE is the first step in presenting applications as a collection of independently installable components.

OLE enables users to manipulate information in an intuitive manner, using an environment that is more “document-centric” and less “application-centric.” Users can create *compound documents* with data, or *objects*, of different formats, and focus directly on the data rather than on the applications responsible for the data. The data can be *embedded* within the document, or *linked* to it, so that only a reference to the data is stored in the document.

OLE facilitates application integration by defining a set of standard *interfaces*, groupings of semantically related functions through which one application accesses the services of another. The concept of exposing functionality through interfaces makes OLE an open, extensible system. It is open in the sense that anyone can provide an implementation of a defined interface and anyone can develop an application that uses it. It is extensible because new or extended interfaces can be defined and integrated into existing applications without requiring changes to existing code. Applications that can implement or access the new interfaces can exploit them while continuing to operate with other applications through the older interfaces. Interfaces can be implemented within a single process in Dynamic Linked Library (DLL) objects or across processes in EXE objects. Applications can take advantage of built-in functionality provided by OLE, or they can either add to it or fully replace it as best suits their needs.

The set of OLE services can be viewed as a two tier hierarchy. The lower level contains the infrastructure services; basic services that provide the means by which features can be implemented and used. The infrastructure services include interface negotiation, memory management, error and status reporting, interprocess communication, structured storage, and data transfer. Application features are those services that benefit the end user; the features comprise the upper level of the OLE service hierarchy. Some of the features that are currently available include compound document management, in-place activation, programmability, and drag and drop operations. Because OLE is open and extensible, others will be added by developers as needs are recognized.

Figure 1-1 illustrates the relationship between the infrastructure services and the features. As discussed above, each service and feature represents one or more interfaces made up of semantically related functions.

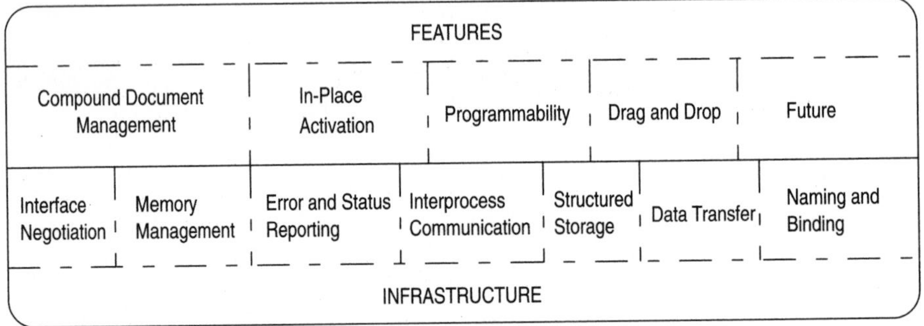

Figure 1-1. OLE as a layered architecture.

The rema5inder of this chapter provides an overview of the OLE 2 architectural model. The chapter begins with a discussion of the *Component Object Model*, the object-oriented programming model that is the basis for the OLE infrastructure. A brief description of the infrastructure services follows and more detailed information can be found in the particular reference chapter dedicated to describing the interfaces that support each service. The rest of the chapter introduces compound documents and topics associated with them. These include the differences between linked and embedded objects, the various roles an application can play in compound document creation and management, and the components that provide communication between applications.

Component Object Model

The Component Object Model specifies how objects interact within a single application or between applications. A *component object* conforms to this model, implementing and using the interfaces that support object interaction. Implementing component objects is a matter of style. They can be implemented using C++ classes, for example, or C structures. Component objects can be independent, stand-alone entities or be composed of other objects. Using a composition technique known as *aggregation*, a new object can be built using one or more existing objects that support some or all of the new object's required interfaces.

This technique enables the new object to appear as a seamless whole rather than as a collection of independent parts. Aggregation is explained in detail in the Programming Considerations chapter.

The Component Object Model defines the following:

- the concept of an interface by which a client of a service communicates with the provider of that service. The service provider, whether it is implemented in a DLL or an EXE, is referred to as the *object*.
- an architecture by which objects can support multiple interfaces, providing a way for potential clients to query an object about support for a specific interface.
- a reference counting model for object management that permits simultaneous use of objects by multiple clients. It also provides a way to determine when an object is no longer in use and can be safely destroyed.
- a mechanism by which memory passed between clients and objects can be allocated and freed.
- a model for reporting error and status information.
- a mechanism for allowing objects to communicate transparently across process boundaries
- a mechanism by which a specific object implementation (DLL or EXE) can be identified and dynamically loaded into the running system. The implementation may be local or remote and the difference is handled transparently.

The Component Object Model is the key to OLE's extensible architecture, providing the foundation on which the rest of OLE is built. Each of the mechanisms described above is supported by one or more interfaces. Figure 1-2 below provides an alternate way of looking at Figure 1-1. The infrastructure is divided into the services supported by Component Object Model (interface negotiation, memory management, error and status reporting, and interprocess communication) and other basic services built on the model. The feature set is divided into two groups: those that are currently provided and features that might be available in the future.

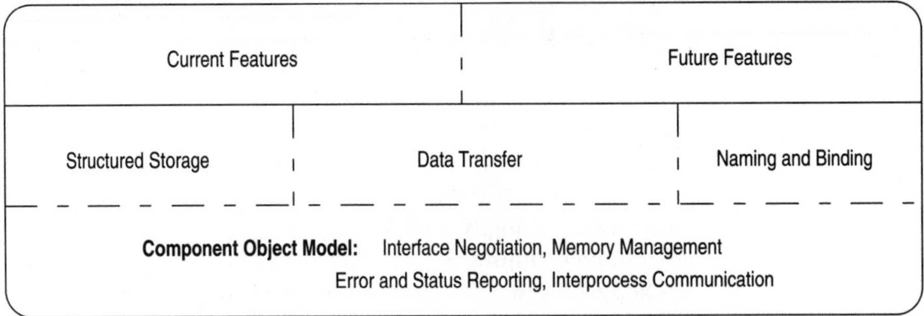

Figure 1-2. Component Object Model as OLE's foundation layer.

Interfaces

Interfaces are the binary standard for component object interaction. Each interface contains a set of functions that defines a contract between the object implementing the interface and the client using it. The contract includes the name of the interface, the function names, and the parameter names and types. Under this contract, the object must implement all of the functions defined for that interface and the implementations must conform to the contract.

Clients use pointers to reference interface instances, obtaining them either when the object is instantiated or by querying the object. An interface pointer points to an array of function pointers known as a *virtual table (VTBL)*. The functions that are pointed to by the members of the VTBL are called the *methods*, or *member functions*, of the interface.

Figure 1-3 shows the run-time representation of an interface instance. A variable supplied by the client of the component object points to the object's VTBL pointer that points to the VTBL instance. The component object contains, in addition to the VTBL pointer, private data that cannot be used by the object's client. Each function pointer in the VTBL points to the actual method implementation.

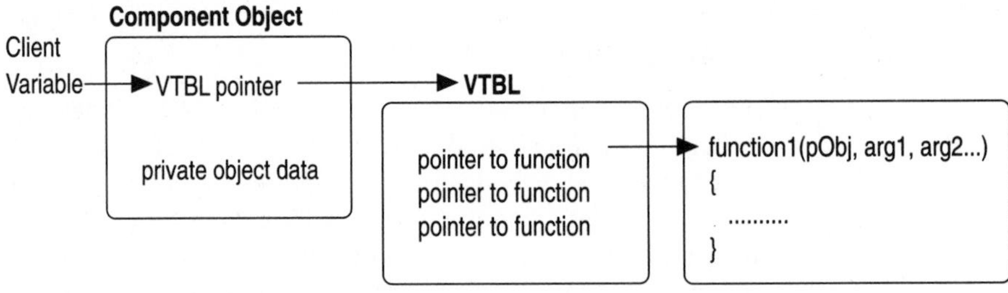

Figure 1-3. OLE interface model.

Interfaces, using C++ terminology, are abstract base classes that specify behavior in a general manner with no implementation. Interfaces are defined by OLE to be "pure virtual", which means without implementation specified here. OLE provides implementations for the interfaces that support the Component Object Model and other pieces of the infrastructure as well as for some of the interfaces that support application features. Applications typically implement some of the infrastructure interfaces, such as those that support data transfer, and some of the feature-specific interfaces. Also, if an OLE implementation of a particular interface is somehow unsuitable, an application can provide its own unique implementation, either adding onto what OLE has provided or completely replacing it.

The following illustration, Figure 1-4, shows all interfaces available to OLE applications by functional area. The Component Object Model interfaces are placed in the center of the diagram because they provide the foundation on which all other interfaces are built. The Component Object Model interfaces support the services described above in the Component Object Model section. For example, **IUnknown** provides the reference counting model and **IMalloc** supports memory management.

All interface names are prefixed with either "*IOle*" or "*I*." Interfaces that begin with "*IOle*" provide services relating to compound document management; those that begin with "*I*" provide services that are more general in nature. For example, **IOleObject** contains methods used by a client of an embedded or linked compound document object. **IOleObject** is implemented and used only by applications that participate in compound document management. **IDataObject**, however, contains methods that are used by all applications. These methods provide the means by which data of any type is transferred.

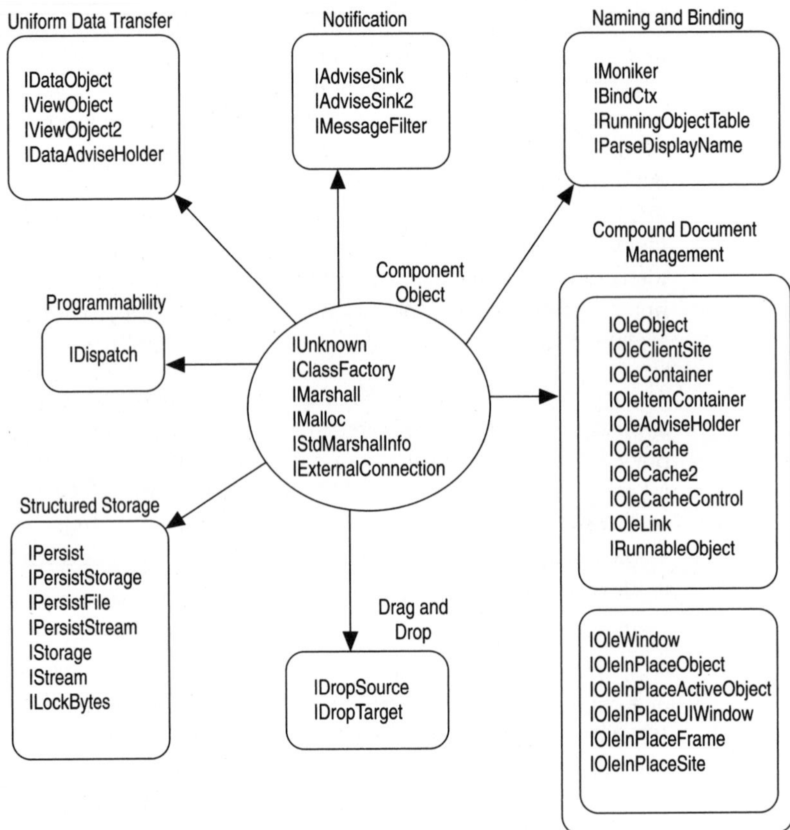

Figure 1-4. Functional area view of OLE.

Interface Negotiation

Objects use interfaces through a mechanism known as *interface negotiation*. Each interface has a globally unique *interface identifier (IID)* by which it is known at run time. The IID allows a potential client to dynamically determine, via a call to **IUnknown::QueryInterface**, the capabilities (i.e. supported interfaces) of other objects.

IUnknown::QueryInterface is the method that allows clients of objects to query for and obtain pointers to needed interfaces. **IUnknown** is implemented by all component objects because it is the base interface from which all other OLE 2 interfaces are derived. Given the interface pointer *pInterface1*, a caller can invoke *pInterface1->QueryInterface* to get pointers to other interface implementations that are supported by the object supporting the interface pointed to by *pInterface1*. The caller passes the *IID* of the desired interface to **IUnknown::QueryInterface**, which then returns either a NULL pointer, signifying that the interface is not supported, or a valid pointer to the interface.

Note Even though **IUnknown** is the OLE base interface, it is possible to implement or use an interface that does not derive directly from it. If an interface is implemented in an object containing an implementation of another interface that does derive from **IUnknown**, it is possible to request the new interface using **QueryInterface** by passing it a pointer to the derived interface.

There are two strategies for obtaining interface pointers in OLE applications. Some applications acquire all the interface pointers they will use over the lifetime of the application at initialization time. These applications typically store copies of the pointers with the objects that make calls to the interfaces' methods. Other applications postpone the acquisition of interface pointers until an interface is needed. These applications do not store pointer copies. The interface pointer is used and then released.

Reference Counting

Reference counting is keeping a count of each instance of a pointer to an interface that is derived from **IUnknown**. Reference counting ensures that an object is not destroyed before all references to it are released. Objects are kept alive if there are one or more references to one or more of their interfaces. Under no circumstances is an object to be deleted when its reference count is not zero. The reference counting mechanism enables independent components to obtain and release pointers to a single object with no coordination required.

The rules for accurate reference counting and suggestions for optimization are described in the chapter, "Component Object Interfaces and Functions."

Memory Management

OLE uses two kinds of memory: local application task memory, and shared (between processes) memory. Each kind of memory has a different memory allocator implementation. All task (non-shared) memory allocated by the OLE libraries and by object handlers is allocated using either an application-supplied allocator or a default allocator provided by OLE when the application does not provide its own. The application controls how memory is actually allocated, and benefits from the improved efficiency that results from not being required to allocate copies of data to pass as parameters to OLE functions. This allocation method results in improved robustness during failures because the task memory is owned by an application and freed by Windows when the application terminates.

Shared memory is used much less frequently in OLE than is task memory. The primary use of shared memory is to optimize data copying that might otherwise result in a remote procedure call. If the caller knows that the data it is allocating will be passed as a parameter to a remote method call, allocating it in shared memory will be more efficient.

The management of memory allocated for pointers to interfaces is handled by the reference counting mechanism described above. Managing the memory for parameters to functions or methods that are passed between processes is handled by a universal convention adopted by OLE, whereby the caller and callee agree on the allocation and deallocation of memory for the function parameter. OLE parameters to functions are defined as either *in* parameters, *out* parameters, or *in-out* parameters. For each parameter type, the responsibility for allocating and freeing of resources is as follows:

Parameter Type	How It Is Allocated and Freed
In Parameter	*In* parameters are both allocated and freed by the caller. Either the task or the shared allocator can be used to allocate the parameter.
Out Parameter	*Out* parameters are allocated by the callee using only the task allocator; they are freed by the caller. If the *Out* parameter is memory that is allocated using the standard OLE allocators, it must be freed using **IMalloc::Free**.
In/Out Parameter	*In/Out* parameters are initially allocated by the caller using only the task allocator; they are freed and reallocated by the callee if necessary. As with *out* parameters, the caller is responsible for freeing the final returned value.

Note These memory management conventions apply only to public interfaces and APIs. Memory allocation internal to applications does not need to be done this way.

Pointers passed as *in* parameters are temporarily owned in that the data pointed to can be inspected and possibly modified, depending on the semantics of the function. To hold data longer than a call's duration (for example, storing it in a global collection), the data must be copied.

Regarding error handling, if a function containing an *out* parameter returns an error result, the *out* parameter must be set to a value that can be cleaned up without any effort by the caller. Pointer *out* parameters must be explicitly set to NULL. *In-out* parameters should be left untouched when the function returns an error, thereby remaining in the state set by the caller.

Error and Status Reporting

Most OLE interface methods and API functions return result handles, HRESULT, that comprise a severity code, context information, a facility code, and a status code. The returned HRESULT can be interpreted at two levels. At the simplest level, zero indicates success and nonzero indicates failure or nonsuccess. At a more complex level, the nonzero value can be examined to determine a more detailed reason for the failure.

In the current release of OLE 2, HRESULTs do little more than wrap the status code. In future releases, however, HRESULTs will be transparently enhanced to convey more information about the error and where it occurred.

The tables listing interface method return values in the following reference chapters specify status code constants that incorporate information about the facility, severity, and status. For example, STG_E_MEDIUMFULL is returned when there is no space left on a storage device. The STG prefix indicates the storage facility, the E indicates that the status code represents an error, and the MEDIUMFULL provides specific information about the error.

Success codes are defined when the interface's designer ships that interface (that is, makes it public). Although success codes cannot be altered, error codes can be changed by the designer of the interface. At the present time, most interfaces have been designed by Microsoft, but in the future, other developers will design and ship interfaces.

More details about the HRESULT structure and strategies and suggestions for error handling can be found in the "Component Object Interfaces and Functions" chapter.

Interprocess Communication

OLE uses a lightweight remote procedure call (LRPC) communication mechanism based on posting messages or events to window handles to transfer data between processes. The communication mechanism is referred to as "lightweight" because, at present, it only handles communication between processes on one machine. In the future, communication will be across machines. LRPC is not a protocol because there is no need for a conversation between the communicating processes. Data is simply sent to a predefined space in memory.

The sending and receiving of interface parameters across process boundaries, referred to as *marshaling* and *unmarshaling*, is the job of *proxy* and *stub* component objects. Every interface has its own proxy object that can package method parameters for that interface. On the receiving side, there is an interface-specific stub object that unpackages the parameters and makes the required method call.

A proxy manager exists to establish connections to the LRPC channel and to load and unload proxy objects as needed. In most cases, callers of interface methods are not affected when calls cross a process boundary.

Several component object interfaces manage the marshaling and unmarshaling process. For more information about this process and how it works, see the "Component Object Interfaces and Functions" chapter.

Dynamic Loading of Object Implementations

One of the key features of the Component Object Model is that a client of a component object can locate the code that is responsible for the object and dynamically load it into a running system. By associating each component object with a *class identifier* (CLSID), OLE can match the CLSID with the code containing the implementation of the associated object. Once it is loaded, OLE makes a call to the object implementation to retrieve an instance of the specific interface requested by the client.

Data Transfer Model

OLE's data transfer model allows users to transfer data uniformly with a drag and drop operation, a copy/paste operation, or programmatically. The data transfer model is supported by the **IDataObject** interface. By implementing **IDataObject**, an application can provide data to be pasted or dropped in a variety of formats across a range of mediums. By obtaining a pointer to an **IDataObject** implementation, an application can call **IDataObject** methods to query for appropriate formats and mediums, set up data advises, and send or receive the actual data.

OLE associates two types of data with a compound document object: *presentation data* and *native data*. The presentation data is needed to render the object on an output device, while the native data is needed for editing. There are data formats that are used to describe both types of data. Applications that copy to the clipboard or that can act as drag sources publish formats that best describes the source data. These can be standard formats (such as CF_METAFILEPICT), private formats, or OLE formats. OLE formats support the creation of compound document objects so one or more of these formats must be available to create a linked or embedded object.

Non-OLE applications that copy data to the clipboard do not offer OLE data formats; data transfers remain unchanged. In an analogous way, OLE 1 applications offer the OLE 1 set of clipboard formats that can be understood by OLE 2 applications. OLE 2 sources offer OLE 2 clipboard formats and the OLE system then synthesizes additional corresponding OLE 1 formats. Some source applications might not follow the rules of offering preferred formats first. A target application pasting from such a source might end up with a non-typical result.

Structured Storage Model

OLE's structured storage model specifies how data is saved and retrieved from storage. In this model, multiple streams are multiplexed onto one underlying file (or byte array) so this layer looks like a file system directory tree; a file system within a file. There are two types of objects in a file system: directories and files. The structured storage model has two equivalent types of objects: storages and streams. A storage object is analogous to a directory in that each storage may contain nested storages and streams. Stream objects are analogous to files. The structured storage model enables objects to control their own storage, loading directly from and saving directly to disk.

Storage objects are binarily compatible across all OLE-supported development platforms. OLE writes information to an object's storage so that the information can be read on other platforms. All supporting data that OLE stores about an object is converted as needed on each platform.

Figure 1-5 shows the hierarchical nature of the structured storage model. A container creates the root storage object needed to store the document. The document's outermost storage object is referred to as the *root* storage object. Root storage objects, like all storage objects, can be marshaled from one process to another. The root storage object in Figure 1-5 contains a stream for OLE data and one or more streams for native data. The two embedded objects have storage objects with their own streams for OLE and native data.

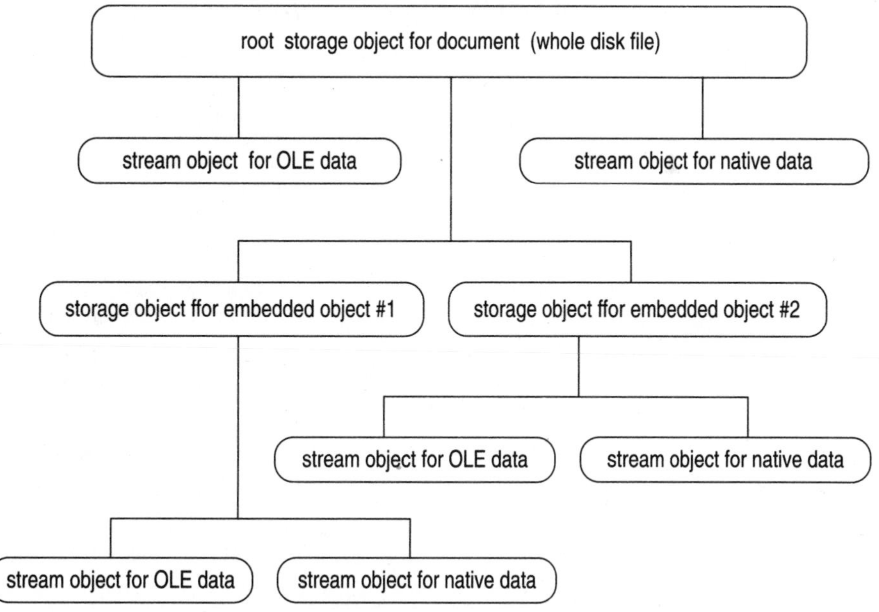

Figure 1-5. Hierarchy of the OLE structured storage model.

Compound Document Management

A *compound document* is a document within a *container application* that seamlessly integrates data of different formats, such as sound clips, spreadsheets, text, and bitmaps. Each piece of integrated data, referred to as a *compound document object,* is created and maintained by its *object application.* End users feel as though they are using a single application, with all the functionality of each of the object applications. Therefore, rather than being concerned with managing multiple object applications, they focus solely on the compound document and the task being performed.

A compound document object is a specific type of component object. In addition to using the component object interfaces, container and object applications that deal with compound document objects implement and use a set of interfaces for creating and managing compound documents. There are various types of container and object applications and the type relates to the features offered by the application. The type determines the specific set of interfaces to be implemented. For example, container applications either can be pure containers, providing sites for compound document objects, or linking containers that allow other containers to link to their embedded objects. Object applications can support linking to file-based objects only or linking to portions of their file-based objects, referred to as *pseudo objects.*

The following table describes the types of OLE applications:

Application Types	Description
Pure Container	Contains linked and embedded objects within its documents. Does not allow other applications to link to its data.
Link Container	Contains linked and embedded objects within its documents. Allows other applications to link to its embedded objects.
Simple Object Application	Creates object(s) that can be embedded or linked. Allows linking only to the whole object.
Pseudo Object Application	Creates object(s) that can be embedded or linked. Allows linking to whole object and to selections of data.
Link Object Application	Cannot create object(s) to be embedded in a container (is not insertable). Acts as a link source only.
Container/Object Application	Creates object(s) that can be embedded or linked and can embed or link objects within its documents.

Linking vs. Embedding

Users can create two types of compound document objects: *linked* or *embedded*. The difference between the two types lie in how and where the actual source data comprising the object is stored. This, in turn, affects the object's portability, its method(s) of activation, and the size of the compound document.

When an object is linked, the source data, or *link source*, continues to physically reside wherever it was initially created, either at another point within the document or within a different document altogether. Only a reference, or *link*, to the object and appropriate presentation data is kept with the compound document. Linked objects cannot "travel" with documents to another machine; they must remain within the local file system or be copied explicitly.

Linking is efficient and keeps the size of the compound document small. Users may choose to link when the source object is owned or maintained by someone else because a single instance of the object's data can serve many documents. Changes made to the source object are automatically reflected in any compound documents that have a link to the object. From the user's point of view, a linked object appears to be wholly contained within the document. In addition to simple links, it is possible to get arbitrarily complex by nesting links and combining linked and embedded objects.

In the case of an *embedded object*, a copy of the original object is physically stored in the compound document as is all the information needed to manage the object. As a result, the object becomes a physical part of the document. A compound document containing embedded objects will be larger than one containing the same objects as links. However, embedding offers several advantages that might outweigh the disadvantages of the extra storage overhead. For example, compound documents with embedded objects can be transferred to another computer and edited there. The new user of the document need not know where the original data resides because a copy of the object's source (native) data travels with the compound document.

Embedded objects can be edited, or activated, in place. This means all maintenance of the object can be done without leaving the compound document. Because each user has a copy of the object's source data, changes made to an embedded object by one user will not effect other compound documents containing an embedding of the same original object. However, if there are links to this object, changes to it will be reflected in each document containing a link.

Architecture

Several component objects participate to enable compound document interaction. The *object handler* is a piece of object-specific code loaded in the container's space so that communication is by function call rather than remote messaging. The object handler services container requests that do not require the services of the object application, such as requests for drawing. The object handler, therefore, is needed only if the object and container applications are not in the same process space. When implemented as a DLL, the object application can handle all container requests by function call.

OLE provides a default object handler that object applications can use. For object applications that require special behavior, a custom handler can be implemented that either replaces the default version or uses it to provide selected default behavior. Object handlers are described in more detail in the following section.

When an object is embedded in a container application, data flows both from the container application to the object application and from the object application to the container application. Proxy and stub objects facilitate the transfer of the data across process boundaries as described earlier in the Interprocess Communication section. Data flowing from the container to the object application always goes through the object handler. When data flows from the object application, however, there are two possible routes using these remoting objects on either side of the process boundary. Data can flow directly either to the container application or to the object handler.

Figure 1-6 shows the flow between applications for an embedded object. The more general term, LRPC Remoting, is used in this diagram for the proxy and stub objects. The object handler is a composite, or aggregate, object made of three pieces: a remoting piece, a controlling piece, and a cache. Notice that the container and object applications, as well as the object handler, can access the structured storage for the compound document.

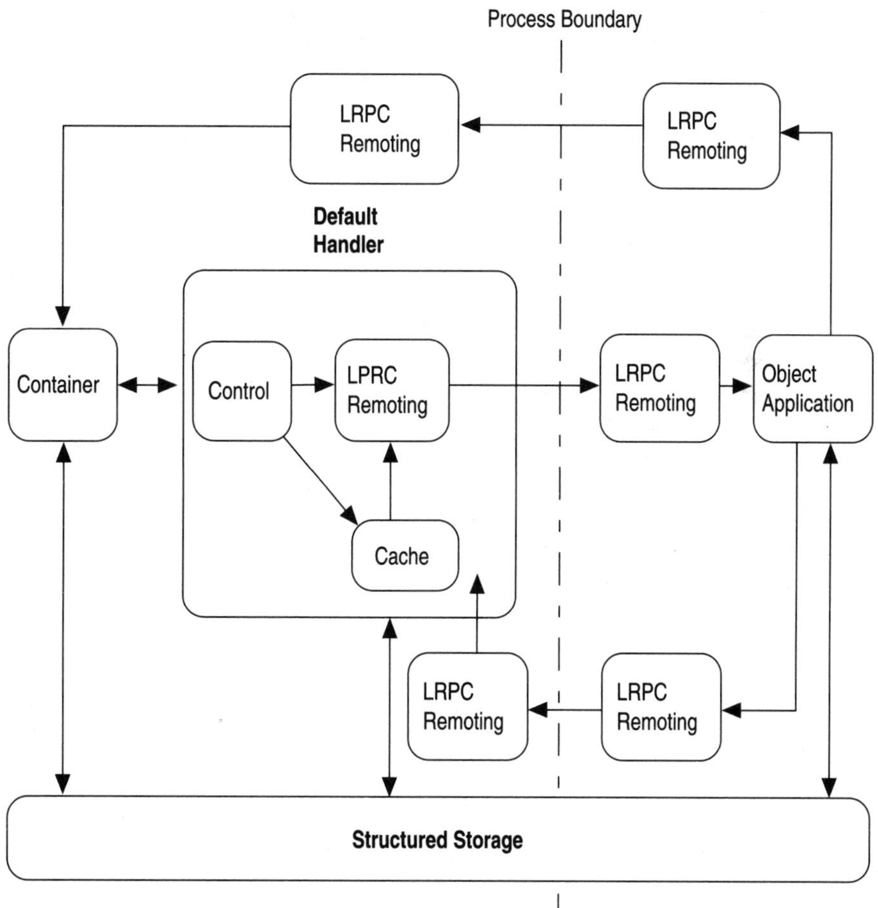

Figure 1-6. Data flow for an embedded object.

Figure 1-7 illustrates the flow of a linked compound document object whose link source is in a separate process. For linked compound document objects, OLE instantiates a component object referred to as the link object. The link object and the object handler are instantiated in the container's process space. However, only the link object has access to the compound document's storage. Rather than holding a pointer to the object handler as is the case with embedded object, the container of a linked object holds a pointer to the link object. When the linked object in the container is activated, this link object initiates the *binding* process whereby the link source application is located and run.

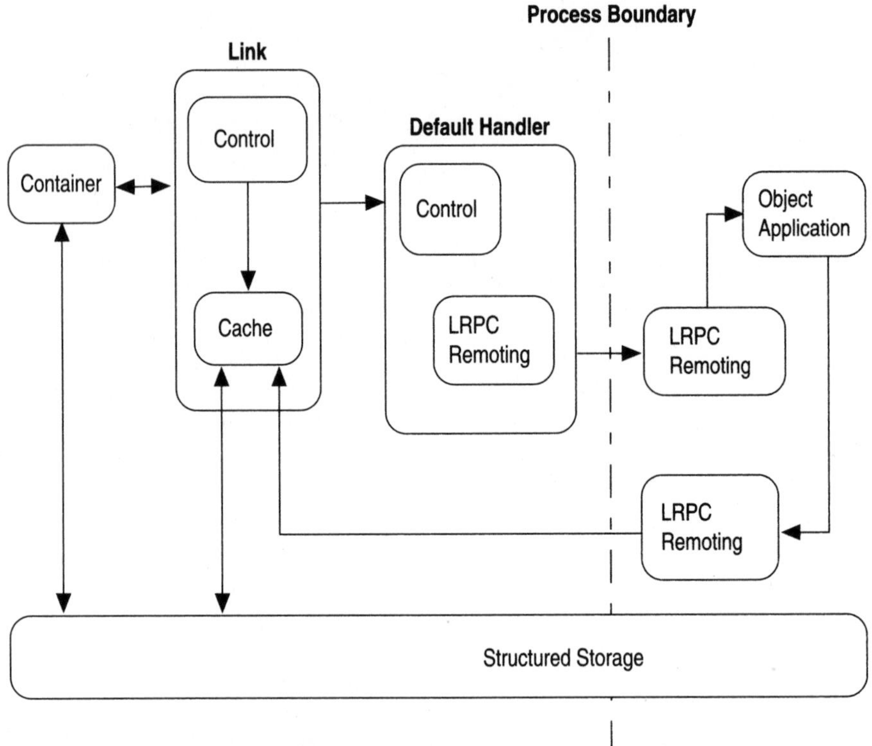

Figure 1-7. Data flow for a linked object.

Both of the preceding illustrations describe the compound document architecture when a container application and object application reside in separate processes. Object applications can be written either as a separate task in a separate process space (.EXE), providing services to containers remotely, or as a dynamic linked library in the container process space (.DLL), providing services to containers through local function calls. Object application executables that run in a separate process space are referred to as *local servers*. Object applications that run in the container's process space are referred to as *in-process servers*.

When an object application is implemented as an in-process server, it replaces the majority of functionality provided by the object handler. Implementing the object application in-process does not preclude it from using some or all of the services provided by the default object handler. The remoting object may or may not exist. However, if there is a remoting object, OLE is not affected by its existence.

Figure 1-8 shows the flow for in-process servers and container applications.

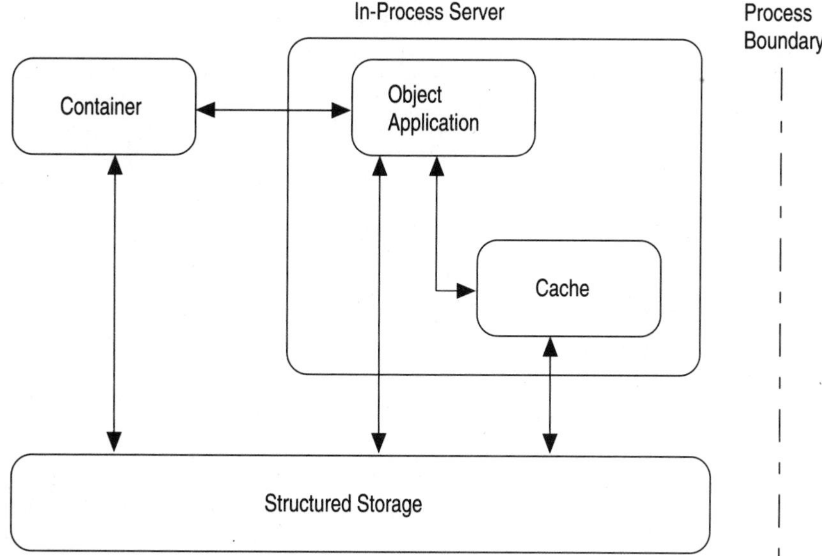

Figure 1-8. Data flow for an in-process server.

Object Handlers

The object handler provides a partial implementation of a particular object class. Object handlers are dynamically loaded into a container's address space so that communication is by function call rather than remote messaging.

The object handler is an aggregate object, a composite object made up of a remoting piece for marshaling and unmarshaling interface parameters across the process boundary, the cache, an optional link object, and a controlling object that coordinates between the pieces. There is a one-to-one relationship between an object class and its handler. An object handler is unique to an object class. Once instantiated, it is not possible to interchange or share a handler between object classes. When used for a compound document, the object handler implements the container-side data structures when objects of a particular class are accessed remotely.

The object handler can be structured in one of the following four ways shown in Figure 1-9.

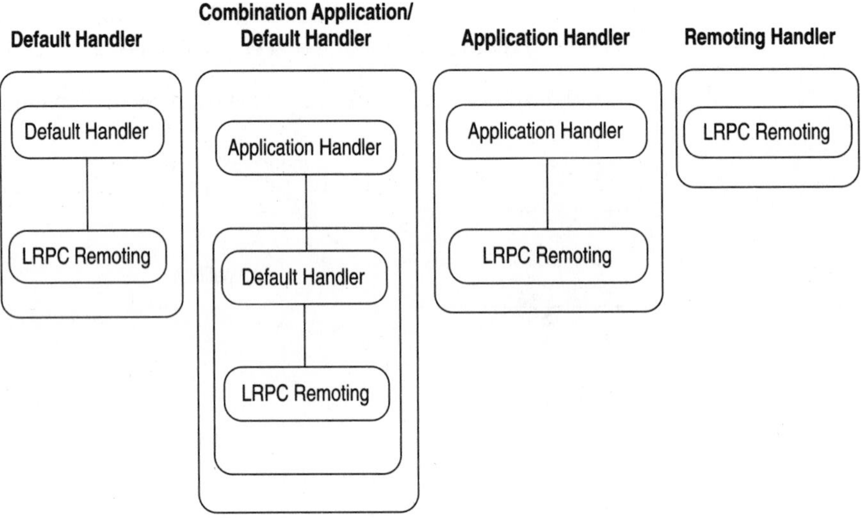

Figure 1-9. Structures of object handlers.

The default handler, an implementation provided by OLE, is used by most applications as the handler. An application implements a custom handler when the default handler's capabilities are insufficient. A custom handler can either completely replace the default handler or use parts of the functionality it provides where appropriate. In the latter case, the application handler is implemented as an aggregate object composed of a new control object and the default handler. Combination application/default handlers are also known as *in-process handlers*. The *remoting handler* is used for objects not assigned a CLSID in the system registry or that have no specified handler. All that is required from a handler for these types of objects is to pass information across the process boundary.

Figure 1-10 shows how objects communicate through interfaces across process boundaries using the default and remoting handlers. Object A's private functions make calls to Object B's interface methods. Similarly, Object B's private functions make calls to Object A's interface methods. The communication between the two objects is maintained through the handler. Object A uses a remote handler because it has no assigned CLSID, whereas Object B uses the default handler. The remoting part of the object handler packages parameters in each function call into a known format and sends them to the appropriate object.

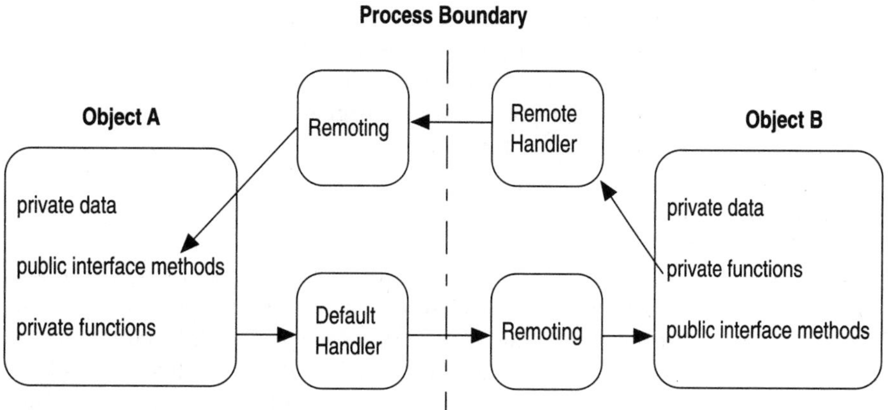

Figure 1-10. Component objects using interfaces.

Link Objects

The link object is a component object that is instantiated whenever a linked compound document object is created or loaded. The link object manages the naming of linked objects and the tracking of link sources. Object naming is accomplished through a mechanism known as a *moniker*. A moniker is a conceptual handle to the linked object at the source of the link that can be persistently stored with the container. Similar to a pointer in programming languages, the moniker can be bound, or dereferenced, to locate and load the object to which it refers.

The important properties of a moniker are:

- A moniker's representation is opaque to applications. Monikers are to name components what OLE is to data formats.
- Applications can compose (concatenate) and decompose a moniker without knowing its syntax. This allows an application to give a composite moniker that describes, for example, a range within a spreadsheet. The application is able to do this without recognizing the syntax name by which the spreadsheet is known.
- OLE defines a set of moniker (component) types that provide standard ways for applications to participate in naming support. The main type is the item moniker. An item moniker is an encapsulation of an item name that can be composed with other monikers, which encapsulate other names, such as path names. Item names are strings assigned by the object or container.

When a running application contains data to which another application can potentially create a link, the application names the data by creating a moniker.

When a linked compound document object is created, the instantiated link object acts like an in-process server. For example, when the user of the container activates the linked object with a double-click, the link object locates and launches the appropriate object application so that editing (or other supported verbs) can be initiated.

Cache

The *cache* is responsible for transferring an embedded object's data from storage to memory and back to storage, where it is persistently saved. OLE provides an implementation of the cache used by OLE's default object handler and the link object. The cache stores data in formats needed by the object handler to satisfy container draw requests. When an object's data changes, the object sends a notification to the cache so that an update can occur.

Container Applications

Container applications are the compound document object's consumer, providing storage, a place for object display, and access to this display site, referred to as the *client site*. Containers can be pure containers that simply hold embedded and linked objects, or more sophisticated containers that allow other containers to link to their embedded objects. Combination container/object applications can be used to embed and link to objects created by other applications as well as to create and service their own class(es) of objects.

The following table lists the interfaces that are implemented by container applications of various types. The interfaces that support drag and drop operations and in-place activation are included. If an application does not support these features, the interfaces need not be implemented. Only two of the interfaces are required: **IOleClientSite** and **IAdviseSink. IOleClientSite** is the primary interface by which a container provides services to the compound document object. **IAdviseSink** supports the flow of notifications between an object and its container. Other interfaces are implemented to provide additional functionality. The table includes only derived interfaces; it is implied that all inherited interfaces are used or implemented along with those that are derived.

Pure Container	Link Container	Container/Object
IOleClientSite	IOleClientSite	IOleClientSite
IAdviseSink	IAdviseSink	IAdviseSink
IAdviseSink2	IAdviseSink2	IAdviseSink2
IMessageFilter	IMessageFilter	IMessageFilter
IOleInPlaceSite	IOleInPlaceSite	IOleInPlaceSite
IOleInPlaceFrame	IOleInPlaceFrame	IOleInPlaceFrame
IDataObject	IDataObject	IDataObject

Pure Container	Link Container	Container/Object
	IClassFactory	IClassFactory
	IDropSource	IDropSource
	IDropTarget	IDropTarget
		IPersistStorage
		IOleObject

Container applications are typically structured so that particular interfaces are grouped together in an object. These groupings are shown in Figure 1-11. The **IOleInPlaceFrame**, **IClassFactory**, and **IMessageFilter** interfaces are each implemented in a separate object, instantiated once per application instance. At the document level, there is an object that exposes **IPersistFile** and **IOleItemContainer** to support linking to embeddings and **IDropTarget** to allow data to be dropped onto the document window. There is an additional data transfer object to support clipboard and drag and drop operations that exposes **IDropSource** and **IDataObject**. The container site object contains the required interfaces, **IOleClientSite** and **IAdviseSink**, and **IOleInPlaceSite**.

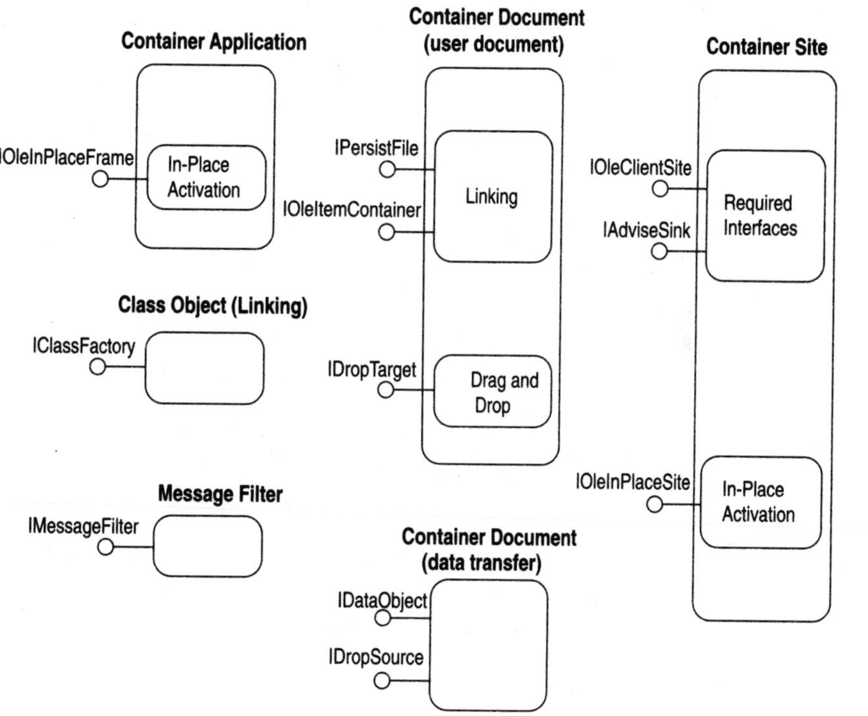

Figure 1-11. Interface groupings for a container.

Object Applications

Object applications create embedded or linked objects at the request of the user working with a compound document in the container. Because some object applications act as containers also, this could be the same application. Object applications are responsible for creating one or more objects of a specific class. Microsoft Paintbrush is an example of a single-object application; Microsoft Excel is an example of a multiple-object application.

Object applications must provide a persistent representation of each object and one or more presentations for the container's use. Object applications also supply user interface and editing capabilities.

Object applications can allow linking to file-based documents or to pieces of data within those documents. When linking to pieces of data is allowed, the object application is said to support *pseudo objects*. These pseudo objects implement the same interfaces as the registered objects that are supported.

The following table lists the interfaces that object applications of various types typically implement.

Simple Object Application	Pseudo Object Application	Link Object Application
IOleObject	IOleObject	IOleObject
IClassFactory	IClassFactory	IClassFactory
IDataObject	IDataObject	IDataObject
IMessageFilter	IMessageFilter	IMessageFilter
IPersistFile	IPersistFile	IPersistFile
IOleInPlaceObject	IOleInPlaceObject	IOleInPlaceObject
IOleInPlaceActiveObject	IOleInPlaceActiveObject	IOleInPlaceActiveObject
IDropSource	IDropSource	IDropSource
IDropTarget	IDropTarget	IDropTarget
IPersistStorage	IPersistStorage	IOleItemContainer
	IOleItemContainer	

Some object applications are referred to as *mini servers*. A mini server is one that cannot run as a stand-alone application—it is always run from another application. Mini servers, with their simplified user interface, can only support embedded objects and they cannot open or save files independently. Microsoft Draw is an example of a mini server. A mini server is useful to create when limited functionality is required or when there is a predefined partnership with specific containers.

Object applications can support either one document per application instance or multiple documents per application instance.

When a single document interface (SDI) application is running and a user tries to create an object, a new instance must be launched to service the request. When a multiple document interface (MDI) application is running and a user tries to create an object, the application creates a new document within the instance that is already running. MDI applications are capable of servicing both a container and a user simultaneously.

Object applications, like container applications, structure their implemented interfaces so that the interfaces that make sense to be grouped are implemented within the same object. Figure 1-12 shows the typical structure of an object application. As with container applications, there are two types of document objects: one for the user document and one for data transfer, which exposes **IDataObject** and **IDropSource**. However, in object applications, the user document object also implements **IDataObject** and a variety of other interfaces. The pseudo object is implemented only if the object application supports linking to selections of data.

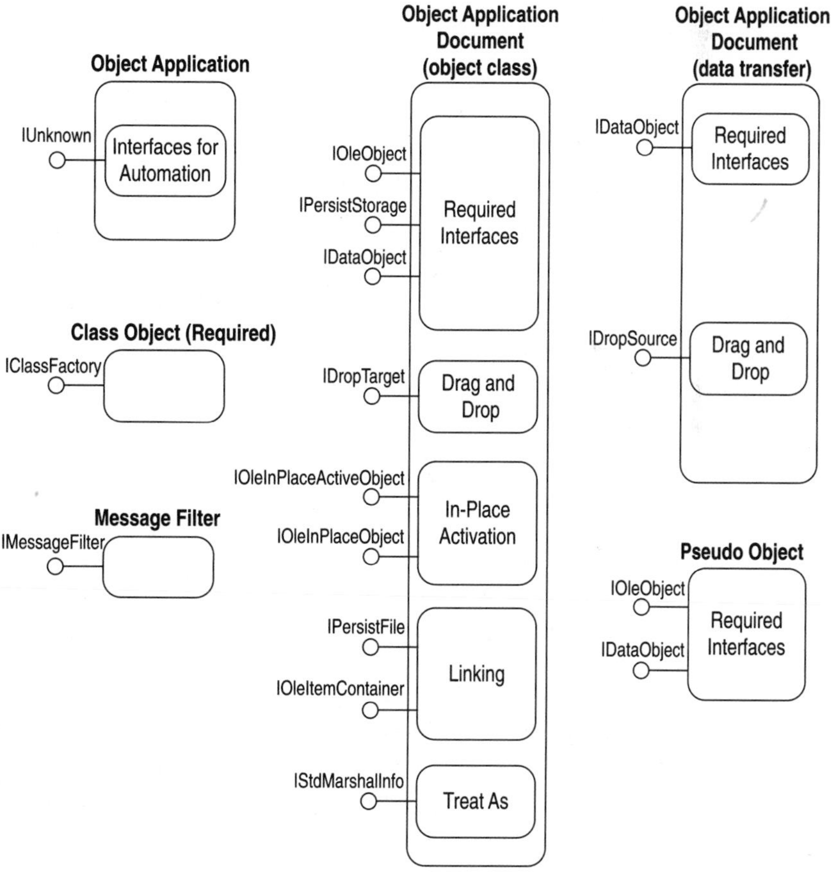

Figure 1-12. Interface groupings for an object application.

Object States

The states of a compound document object apply to the object once it has been created by an object application and embedded or linked in a container. A compound document object's state describes the relationship between the object in its container and the application responsible for its creation. Compound document objects have three states: *passive*, *loaded*, and *running*. The loaded and running states are referred to as *active* These object states do not correlate with the end user object states described in the chapter called, "User Interface Guidelines."

The compound document object states are described as follows:

Object State	Description
Passive	The compound document object is not selected or active. It is in its stored state (on disk or in a database).
Loaded	The object's data structures created by the object handler are in the container's memory. The container has established communication with the object handler and there is cached presentation data available for rendering the object. Calls are processed by the object handler.
Running	The object application is running. It is possible to edit the object, access the object's interfaces, and receive notification of changes. The objects that control remoting have been created. The object handler delegates calls to the real object (in the object application).

Figure 1-13 shows the three states and the method calls that cause an object to transition from one state to another.

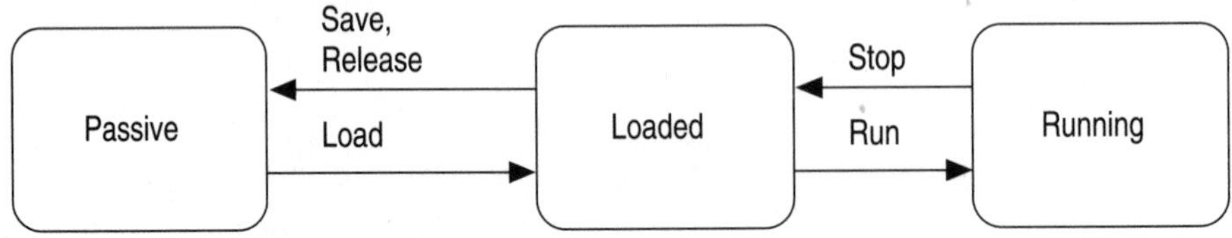

Figure 1-13. States of an embedded object.

Figure 1-14 shows the relationship between a container for an embedded object, its object handler, and its executable object application as the object transitions to each of the three states. In-process servers have no object handler in the container process; it is up to the server to keep track of its state (loaded vs. running).

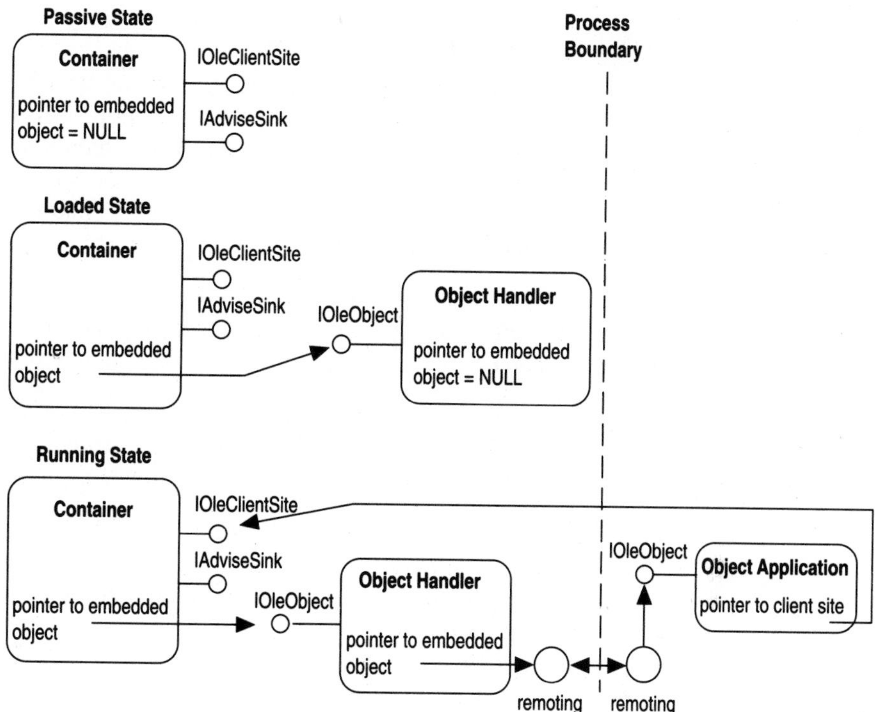

Figure 1-14. States of an embedded object.

Entering the Loaded State

When an object enters the loaded state, the in-memory structures representing the object are created so that operations can be invoked on it. The object's handler or in-process server is loaded. This process, referred to as *instantiation,* occurs when an object is loaded from persistent storage (a transition from the passive to the loaded state) or when an object is being created for the first time.

Internally, instantiation is a two-phase process. An object of the appropriate class is created, after which a method on that object is called to perform initialization and give access to the object's data. The initialization method is defined in one of the object's supported interfaces. The particular initialization method called depends on the context in which the object is being instantiated and the location of the initialization data.

Entering the Running State

When an embedded object transitions to the running state, the object application must be located and run so that the object application's services can be utilized. Embedded objects are placed in the running state either explicitly through a request by the container, such as a need to draw a format not presently cached, or implicitly by OLE as a side effect of invoking an operation, such as when the user of the container double-clicks the object.

When a linked object transitions into the running state, this process is known as *binding*. *Binding* involves first locating the object data before the object application can be located and run.

At first glance, binding a linked object appears to be no more complicated than running an embedded object. However, the following points complicate the process:

- OLE allows a link to refer to objects (and possibly parts of objects) that are embedded in other containers. This implies a potential for nested embeddings. The link must include sufficient information to allow it to locate the object inside the other container(s). This information is maintained through the use of monikers, the naming mechanism described earlier. Typically, an object's moniker is part of a filename (path) concatenated with a series of item name parts. During binding, names are reduced before the steps in binding take place; this allows for important functionality such as link tracking and user aliases to be implemented transparently.
- Because linking permits multiple references to a given object, it is possible that the object may already be running, in which case OLE binds to the running version rather than running another copy. At any point in the containment hierarchy, OLE might be able to bind to an already running object.
- Running an object requires accessing the storage area for the object. When an embedded object is run, OLE is given a pointer to the storage during the load process, which it passes on to the object application. However, for linked objects, there is no standard interface for accessing storage. The object application may use the file system interface or another mechanism.

OLE manages the binding process for applications. For more information see the chapter "Linking Interfaces and Functions."

Entering the Passive State

Object closure forces an embedded or linked object into the passive state. It is normally initiated from the object application's user interface, such as when the user selects the File Close command. In this case, the object application notifies the container, who releases its reference count on the object. When all references to the object have been released, the object can be freed. When all objects have been freed, the object application can safely terminate.

A container application can also initiate object closure. When the container wants to close an object, it releases its reference count after optionally completing a save. Containers may want to release objects when they are deactivating after an in-place activation session, thereby allowing the user to click outside the object without losing the active editing session.

CHAPTER 2

Programming Considerations

While detailed application-specific information is beyond the scope of this publication, this chapter contains some helpful guidelines for developing OLE applications. Information is provided on variety of subjects that pertain to the implementation of OLE in a general sense. However, the major part of the chapter discusses implementation issues m ore specific to applications that act as containers dealing with compound documents.

You should read through this chapter for any information appropriate to your current programming task.

Designing Component Objects

Component objects contain one or more interface implementations and data that is specific to the object. The data is private and inaccessible from outside the object, while the interface implementations are public and can be accessed through pointers.

Because interfaces are a binary standard, interface implementation is language independent. However, C++ is the preferred language because it supports many of the object-oriented concepts inherent in OLE. Using a procedural language such as C involves extra work, as is summarized below:

- VTBLs must be initialized explicitly either at compile or run time. VTBLs should be unchangeable; once a VTBL is initialized with function pointers, those pointers should remain unchanged until the application shuts down. VTBLs in C++ are declared as constants to prevent them from being modified inadvertently. However, in C there is no way to ensure that a VTBL will remain unchanged.

  OLE provides a mechanism that allows C developers to choose how their VTBLs should be declared. If you want to declare constant VTBLs, place the following statement before the *#include* statement for the "ole2.h" header file:

  ```
  #define CONST_VTABLE
  ```

- Each method requires a pointer to the object that owns the method. With C++, all members are implicitly dereferenced off the *this* pointer. With C, there must be an additional first parameter passed to each method that is a pointer to the interface in which the method is declared.
- Methods in C++ can have identical names because methods are actually known by a name that is the result of concatenating the method name to the class name. Methods in C must have a unique name to designate the object with which they are associated.

For example, the following C++ code sample defines an implementation of **IUnknown::QueryInterface**. The method name is **QueryInterface** and there are two parameters: a REFIID and a pointer to where to return the requested interface instance.

```
CUnknown::QueryInterface (REFIID riid, LPVOID FAR* ppvObj);
```

A similar C implementation would require a more complex name and an additional first parameter to indicate the object owning the method:

```
IUnknown_Doc_QueryInterface (LPUNKNOWN pUnk, REFIID riid,
    LPVOID FAR* ppvObj);
```

The following sections demonstrate how to declare a component object in a few typical ways: using C nested data structures, C++ nested classes, and C++ multiple inheritance. The demonstration object, called *CObj*, derives from **IUnknown** and supports two interfaces that also derive from **IUnknown**, **InterfaceA** and **InterfaceB**. *CObj's* private data includes a pointer to another component object in the application (*m_pCDoc*), a count of all the external references to the object (*m_ObjRefCount*), and pointers to two interfaces implemented by other component objects and used by *CObj* (*m_pOleObj* and *m_pStg*). All object members use the *m_* prefix to make it easy to distinguish between member variables and other variables.

Component Objects: C Nested Structures

C interface implementations comprise data structures nested within the object's data structure. Each interface structure contains a VTBL pointer as its first member (*pVtbl*), a pointer to the object (*pCObj*), and a count of the external references to the interface (*m_RefCount*). The order of the members in the interface structures is identical to facilitate code sharing.

```
typedef struct CObj {
    ULONG                          m_ObjRefCount;
    LPSTORAGE                      m_pStg;
    LPOLEOBJECT                    m_pOleObj;
    struct CDOC   FAR *            m_pCDoc;
```

```
    struct InterfaceA  {
  {
        LPVTBL                          pVtbl;
        struct CObj FAR *               pCObj;
        ULONG                           m_RefCount;
    } m_InterfaceA;

    struct InterfaceB {
        LPVTBL                          pVtbl;
        struct Obj FAR *                pCObj;
        ULONG                           m_RefCount;
    } m_InterfaceB;

} COBJ;
```

Component Objects: C++ Nested Classes

The next example shows how the same object is declared and initialized using the C++ nested class approach. As in the C example, the nested class declaration includes one data structure for each interface and four private data members: an object-level reference count, two interface pointers, and a pointer to the enclosing object. The private implementations of the **IUnknown** methods are called by the implementations declared for the derived interfaces. For each interface implementation, there is a structure containing a public constructor and destructor, private declarations of the interface methods, a private pointer to *CObj*, and an interface-level reference counter for debugging purposes. To allow the nested interface classes to access the private members of the outer class, each interface class is made a friend of the outer class.

The benefits of implementing with C++ nested classes lie in the ability to include initialization code and method implementation inline. However, inline declaration is for the convenience of illustration and is not required.

```
class FAR CObj  {

private:
    ULONG                           m_ObjRefCount;
    LPSTORAGE                       m_pStg;
    LPOLEOBJECT                     m_pOleObj;
    CDOC FAR *                      m_pCDoc;

public:
    CObj();
    ~CObj();

    struct CUnknown : IUnknown
{
  private:
    ULONG           m_RefCount;
```

```
    CObj FAR *      m_pCObj;

  public:
    CUnknown(CObj (pCObj)
    { m_pCObj = pCObj; m_RefCount = 0; }
    HRESULT QueryInterface(REFIID riid, LPVOID FAR * ppvObj)
    ULONG AddRef(void) { return ++m_ObjRefCount; }
    ULONG Release(void);
}
friend CUnknown;
CUnknown m_Unknown;

struct InterfaceA : InterfaceA
{
  private:
    ULONG           m_RefCount;
    CObj FAR *      m_pCObj;

  public:
    CInterfaceA(CObj *pCObj)
    { m_pCObj = pCObj; m_RefCount = 0; }
    HRESULT QueryInterface(REFIID riid, LPVOID FAR * ppvObj)
    ULONG AddRef(void) { return ++m_ObjRefCount; }
    ULONG Release(void);
    HRESULT MethodA1(LPVOID FAR * ppvObj);
    HRESULT MethodA2(DWORD dwArg);
}
friend CInterfaceA;
CInterfaceA m_InterfaceA;

struct InterfaceB : InterfaceB
{
  private:
    ULONG           m_RefCount;
    CObj FAR *      m_pCObj;

  public:
    CInterfaceB(CObj *pCObj)
    { m_pCObj = pCObj; m_RefCount = 0; }
    HRESULT QueryInterface(REFIID riid, LPVOID FAR * ppvObj)
    ULONG AddRef(void) { return ++m_ObjRefCount; }
    ULONG Release(void);
    HRESULT MethodB1(void);
    HRESULT MethodB2(DWORD dwArg1, DWORD dwArg2);
}
friend CInterfaceB;
CInterfaceB m_InterfaceB;
```

Component Objects: C++ Multiple Inheritance

The next example illustrates the use of C++ multiple inheritance. There are two disadvantages to using multiple inheritance with OLE. First, it is not possible to have an interface-level reference count. For more information about reference counting, see the section entitled "Reference Counting" in the "Component Object Interfaces and Functions" chapter. Second, there is the potential for confusion over the interpretation of the class statement. A standard C++ multiple inheritance declaration implies the "is a" relationship where an object inherits implementations. In OLE, however, interfaces are attributes of the object and implementations are not inherited.

The main advantage to using multiple inheritance lies in its simplicity. Only the prototypes for each of the interface methods are listed; no interface data structures or class definitions are necessary.

Because both InterfaceA and InterfaceB inherit from **IUnknown**, **IUnknown** does not need to be explicitly listed in the class statement and a single implementation of the **IUnknown** methods (**QueryInterface**, **AddRef**, and **Release**) is sufficient.

```
class FAR CObj : public InterfaceA, public InterfaceB
{
private:
    ULONG                        m_ObjRefCount;
    LPSTORAGE                    m_pStg;
    LPOLEOBJECT                  m_pOleObj;
    CDOC FAR *                   m_pCDoc;

public:
    CObj();
    ~CObj();

    HRESULT QueryInterface(REFIID riid, LPVOID FAR * ppvObj)
    ULONG AddRef(void) { return ++m_ObjRefCount; }
    ULONG Release(void);

    HRESULT MethodA1(LPVOID FAR * ppvObj);
    HRESULT MethodA2(DWORD dwArg);

    HRESULT MethodB1(void);
    HRESULT MethodB2(DWORD dwArg1, DWORD dwArg2);
};
```

Aggregation

An aggregate is an object like any other object in that it implements one or more interfaces. Internal to the aggregate, the implementation of certain interfaces is actually provided by one or more contained objects. Users of the object are unaware of this internal structure. They cannot tell and do not care that the object is an aggregate: aggregation is purely an implementation technique.

Figure 2-1 shows an aggregate object consisting of a control object that implements Interface A and Interface B, and a noncontrol object, which implements Interface C. All these interface implementations are exposed publicly, as indicated by the line and circle extending to the outside of the aggregate.

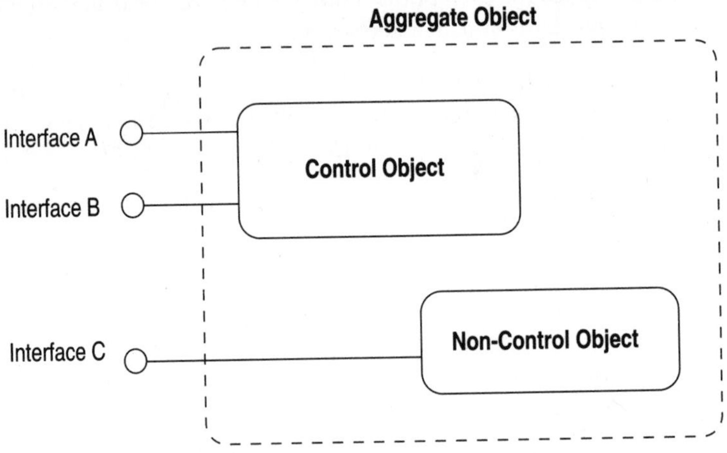

Figure 2-1. Aggregate Containing Two Internal Objects.

In the aggregation model, the *control object* forms the aggregate's personality and determines how it operates, making decisions about which interfaces are exposed outside of the object and which interfaces remain private. The control object has a special instance of the **IUnknown** interface known as the *controlling unknown.* The controlling unknown is always implemented as part of the new code written when the aggregate is put together from other objects.

The other objects can be implemented at any time. These noncontrol objects can be instantiated separately or as part of the aggregate. However, if these objects are to aggregatable, they must be written to cooperate with the control object by forwarding their **QueryInterface**, **AddRef**, and **Release** calls to the controlling unknown. A reference count for the aggregate as a whole is maintained so that it is kept alive if there are one or more references to any of the interfaces supported by either the control or noncontrol objects.

It is possible for an object to call a method that may cause the object to be released. A technique known as artificial reference counting can be used to guard against this untimely release. The object calls **IUnknown::AddRef** before the potentially destructive method call and **IUnknown::Release** after it. If the object in question is aggregatable, it must call the controlling unknown's implementations of **AddRef** and **Release** (*pUnkOuter*->**AddRef** and *pUnkOuter*->**Release**) to artificially increment the reference count rather than its own implementations. Refer to the "Component Object Interfaces and Functions" chapter for more information about reference counting.

When shutting down, aggregatable objects should either not attempt to use their *pUnkOuter* pointer or should set *pUnkOuter* to their own **IUnknown** implementation.

It is possible for an object to make a call to a method that may cause the object to Figure 2-2 shows how the coordination between the control and noncontrol object works. The control object exposes the controlling unknown, Interface A and Interface B. The noncontrol object supports Interface C. All three interfaces derive from **IUnknown**.

The control object holds a pointer to the noncontrol object's **IUnknown** implementation so it can call the noncontrol methods when appropriate. The noncontrol object holds a pointer to the controlling unknown for the same reason. The pointer to the controlling unknown is supplied when the noncontrol object is instantiated. Whereas the controlling unknown is available to the outside, as is indicated by the line and circle identifying it extending past the bounds of the aggregate, the noncontrol object's **IUnknown** implementation works locally and is not obtainable from outside the aggregate. It is called solely by the controlling unknown to obtain instances of the noncontrol interfaces, such as Interface C, to expose to the outside.

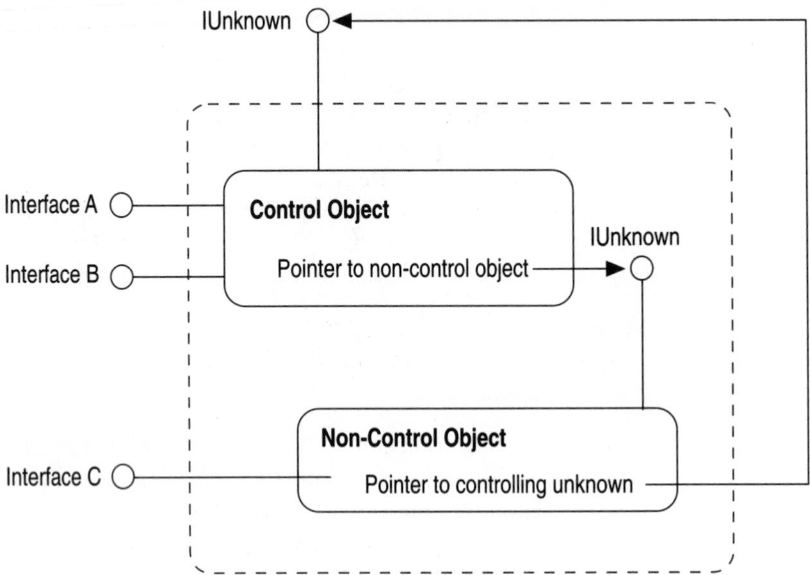

Figure 2-2. Internal Structure of an Aggregate.

Aggregation is entirely optional and designing for it is an optional decision to be made for each object. However, providing support for aggregation costs little in time and complexity. The reward is larger than the cost in that it enables the effective reuse of interface implementations. The key in implementing an aggregate object is making the correct delegation decision in both the aggregated and non-aggregated situations.

The following code example is an aggregate object implemented using C++ nested classes. The constructor takes as an argument the pointer to the control object's **IUnknown** implementation, or controlling unknown. If this pointer is NULL, indicating that the new object is not being aggregated, the *m_pUnkOuter* member is set to the address of *m_Unknown*, the local implementation of **IUnknown**. If **pUnkOuter** is not NULL, indicating that the new object is being aggregated, *m_pUnkOuter* is set to *pUnkOuter*. The **InterfaceA** implementations of the **IUnknown** methods forward their calls to the controlling unknown implementations. The controlling unknown **IUnknown** implementations manage queries for interfaces for the aggregate and maintain a master reference count.

```
class cAggregateObj
P
public:
    CAggregateObj(LPUNKNOWN pUnkOuter);
    ~CAggregateObj();

    HRESULT CreateObj(REFCLSID rclsid, REFIID riid,
                        LPVOID FAR * ppvObj);
```

```
private:
    struct CUnknown : IUnknown
    {
        CUnknown(CAggregateObj FAR * pAgg)
        { m_pAgg = pAgg; }

        HRESULT QueryInterface(REFIID riid, LPVOID FAR * ppvObj)
        ULONG AddRef(void) { return ++m_ObjRefCount; }
        ULONG Release(void);
      private:
        CAggregateObj FAR * m_pAgg;
    }
    friend CUnknown;
    CUnknown m_Unknown;

    struct CInterfaceA : InterfaceA
    {
        CInterfaceA(CAggregateObj FAR * pAgg)
        { m_pAgg = pAgg; }

        HRESULT QueryInterface(REFIID riid, LPVOID FAR * ppvObj)
        { return m_pAgg->m_pUnkOuter->QueryInterface
            (riid, ppvObj); }
        ULONG AddRef(void) {return m_pAgg->m_pUnkOuter->AddRef();}
        ULONG Release(void)
        {return m_pAgg->m_pUnkOuter->Release();}

        HRESULT MethodA1(LPVOID FAR * ppvObj);
        HRESULT MethodA2(DWORD dwArg);

      private:
        CAggregateObj FAR * m_pAgg;
    }
    friend CInterfaceA;
    CInterfaceA m_InterfaceA;

private:
    ULONG                    m_ObjRefCount;
    LPUNKNOWN                m_pUnkOuter;
    LPSTORAGE                m_pStg;
    LPOLEOBJECT          m_pOleObj;
}
```

Grouping Interfaces

Interface relationships are based on the ability to successfully obtain interface pointers by using **IUnknown::QueryInterface**. Although interface implementors are advised to design objects in such a way that many interfaces are accessible from many other interfaces, there is generally no guarantee to an interface user, that a specific interface is accessible from another interface. This means that given one interface, it usually cannot be assumed that **QueryInterface** returns a pointer to a second interface because implementations of **QueryInterface** are application-specific.

There are three ways in which two interfaces can be related. For example, consider Interfaces A and B in the following list:

1. Given a pointer to Interface A, it **should** be possible to obtain a pointer to Interface B. Interface A and Interface B are managed by a single reference count. OLE defines the following interfaces that fall in this category:
   - **IOleObject, IDataObject, IViewObject, IOleCache, IOleInPlaceObject,** and **IPersistStorage.** If the object is a link, **IOleLink** should also be available.
   - **IPersistFile** and **IOleItemContainer**
   - **IOleClientSite** and **IOleInPlaceSite**
2. Given a pointer to Interface A, it **must not** be possible to obtain a pointer to Interface B. Interface A and Interface B can be managed by either a single reference count or separate reference counts. **IOleInPlaceActiveObject** and **IOleInPlaceObject** fall in this category. **IStorage** and **IStream**, typically implemented by OLE, also fall in this category.
3. Given a pointer to Interface A, it might be possible to obtain a pointer to Interface B, depending on the implementing application. Interface A and Interface B can be managed by a single reference count. Clients of the interfaces **cannot** assume it is always possible to obtain the same set of interfaces in this category from all implementing applications. The decision to group these interfaces is up to the implementor, and there is no guarantee they will be implemented in the same manner by all applications.

All OLE interfaces not mentioned as belonging to the first or second groups belong to the third type. These interfaces can be grouped in a manner that works best for the application. It is wise to implement interfaces together whenever possible, because it leads to greater flexibility and interconnectivity. Implementing interfaces together implies they are within a single object supported by one piece of memory. The interfaces share one **IUnknown::QueryInterface** implementation that recognizes all related interfaces. Pointers to the interfaces are managed by a single reference count.

An object that has multiple groups of interfaces, each managed by its own reference count, is kept alive if there is at least one reference to any interface in one of the groups.

For interfaces that cannot be implemented together, there are two possible approaches. They can be implemented either in separate objects, or in a single object that manages the interfaces independently. In the single object approach, there can be one **IUnknown::QueryInterface** implementation or several, depending on the number of interface groups in the object. In the single **QueryInterface** implementation, explicit steps must be taken to return pointers only to related interfaces.

Common Reference Counters, Pointers, and Flags

The following tables include suggestions for data members for application, document, and site objects that might be included in most container or object applications. Only the more widely used members have been listed; applications that support custom features such as in-place activation may have additional data members. Also not included in these tables are pointers to interfaces that may be used either temporarily or throughout the lifetime of the application.

The following table lists data members that may be useful for an application-level object.

Data Member	Type	Application Type	Use
m_cRef	**ULONG**	All	Reference count for application.
m_cDoc	**ULONG**	All	Total count of open documents (ones that are visible to the user and invisible data transfer documents).
m_fUserCtrl	**BOOL**	All	Count to control lifetime of application on behalf of user.
m_dwRefClassFac	**DWORD**	Object applications and containers that support linking	Value returned by **CoRegisterClassObject**
m_fOleInitialized	**BOOL**	All	Indicates whether **OleInitialize** was called.
m_cfFormat1, 2, ...	**UINT**	All	OLE 2 clipboard formats.

Data Member	Type	Application Type	Use
m_arrFormatetc	**FORMATETC**	All	Array of formats offered in clipboard copy and supported in **IDataObject::GetData**.

The following table contains suggestions for document level object data members:

Data Member	Type	Application Type	Use
m_cRef	**ULONG**	All	Reference count for document.
m_cLock	**ULONG**	All	Lock count for document; useful for debugging. These locks are not strong enough to warrant reference counts, because they can be arbitrarily broken by the user closing the application (File Exit).
m_fObjClosing	**BOOL**	All	Flag to guard against recursive close call.
m_dwDocType	**DWORD**	All	Type of document; for example, uninitialized, embedded, etc.
m_fObjDestroying	**BOOL**	All	Flag to guard against recursive destroy call.
m_dwRegROT	**DWORD**	All	Key if document is registered as running
m_nNextObjNo	**ULONG**	Containers	Next available object number for storage name.
m_fShowObject	**BOOL**	Containers	Indicates whether to show object.
m_cPseudoObj	**ULONG**	Object applications	Count of pseudo objects.
m_dwStorageMode	**DWORD**	Object applications	Indicates state during save.
m_szAppName	**char**	Object applications	Name of application.
m_szObjName	**char**	Object applications	Name of object in container.
m_clsidTreatAs	**CLSID**	Object applications	CLSID to pretend to be.
m_typeTreatAs	**LPSTR**	Object applications	User type to pretend to be.

The following table contains suggestions for site objects in containers.

Data Member	Type	Use
m_cRef	**ULONG**	Reference count for site.
m_szStgName	**char**	Name of storage object.
m_fObjWinOpen	**BOOL**	Indicates whether object window is open. If open, need to shade object.
m_fMoniker	**BOOL**	Indicates if a moniker is currently assigned.
m_dwDrawAspect	**DWORD**	Current display aspect.
m_fDoGetExtent	**BOOL**	Indicates extents may have changed.
m_fDoSetExtent	**BOOL**	Indicates object was resized when not running.
m_sizeInHimetric	**SIZEL**	Extents of object in himetric units.
m_dwLinkType	**DWORD**	Indicates type of link: automatic or manual.
m_lpszShortType	**LPSTR**	Short type name of OLE object.

Implementing OLE Applications

This section focuses on the implementation tasks that pertain to OLE container and object applications. Where implementation differs depending on the type of application, these differences are described. The implementation tasks can be grouped as follows:

- Tasks that apply to all applications.
- Tasks that apply to applications serving a specific role.
- Tasks that apply to applications supporting a specific feature.

The following table lists these tasks with the action(s) that typically cause the state to be entered:

Application Task	User Action
Starting an application	User launches application directly or by double-clicking an object in a container.
Opening a document	User selects the File New or Open command.
Activating a linked or embedded object (open mode or in place)	User double-clicks object or selects a verb from the object's Edit menu.
Creating a linked or embedded object	1. User selects the Insert Object command. 2. User copies data to the clipboard and selects the Paste or Paste Link command. 3. User drags and drops data.
Saving a linked or embedded object	User selects the File Save, Save As, Close, or Exit command.

Application Task	User Action
Closing a document	User selects the File Close or Exit command.
Closing an application	User selects the File Exit command.

Starting OLE Applications

The following list of tasks are performed by OLE applications before they display their main window and enter the message processing loop. These tasks are described in greater detail in the following sections.

- Enlarge the application's message queue to more efficiently handle LRPC processing.
- Verify that the correct registry information is in the system registration database. (Containers that do not support linking to embedded objects do not need to do this.)
- Check the application's compatibility with the OLE libraries.
- Initialize the OLE libraries.
- Register the **IMessageFilter** interface implementation to manage concurrency.
- **C-based applications only:** Initialize the OLE interface VTBL data structures.
- Register the clipboard data formats.
- Determine how the application was started.
- Register the application's class object(s), if required.
- Initialize any flags and variables used to maintain the state of OLE objects and/or interfaces.

Enlarging the Application Message Queue

The OLE LRPC mechanism is based on the Windows **PostMessage** API. When the user of an object in one application calls an object's interface methods, it generates an LRPC that is really a **PostMessage** from one application process to another. To properly handle the LRPC **PostMessage** calls, it is recommended that all OLE 2 applications call the Windows **SetMessageQueue** API and specify a minimum size value of 96 messages for their application queues. Failure to enlarge the queue could cause the OLE libraries to fail or reject some LRPC calls.

Because **SetMessageQueue** destroys any existing messages that might exist in the application message queue, the call to **SetMessageQueue** should be the first call the application makes within its **WinMain** function.

Verifying Entries in the Registration Database

On start up, a stand-alone object application should verify that the path for its EXE and handler are correct in the system registration database. If the information is incorrect or not present, the object application should automatically update it; Otherwise the application will not be found should a user try to activate an object belonging to that application. In addition, an EXE should also check the paths for its own handlers and in-process object application DLLs (a DLL installed with the application). Mini object applications should do these same steps before they exit.

For more information on registering object applications in the registration database, see the chapter "Registering Object Applications."

Verifying Build Version Compatibility of OLE Libraries

Refer to "**OleBuildVersion**" and "**CoBuildVersion**."

Initializing the OLE Libraries

Refer to "**OleInitialize**."

Initializing the Interface VTBL Data Structures—C Only

A C-based OLE application typically implements its interfaces as nested data structures. Interface data structure initialization involves allocating memory and setting each member to an initial value. These structures can be allocated and initialized in any order but, it is required that the **IUnknown** and **IClassFactory** interface structures be initialized *before* registering a class of object(s).

Applications written in C *must* explicitly initialize each interface VTBL. Typically the VTBLs are initialized as part of creating the application object's frame window, before the window is shown to the user. Initializing the VTBLs involves setting each of the VTBL pointers to the appropriate method implementation.

The following code sample illustrates how a C program might initialize the **IUnknown** VTBL. The **IUnknown** interface is implemented in a data structure nested in *MyObject*. The members of the VTBL are set to the application's unique implementations of the **IUnknown** methods, **IUnknown_MyObj_QueryInterface**, **IUnknown_MyObj_AddRef**, and **IUnknown_MyObj_Release**.

```
myUnknownVtbl.QueryInterface = IUnknown_MyObj_QueryInterface;
myUnknownVtbl.AddRef = IUnknown_MyObj_AddRef;
myUnknownVtbl.Release = IUnknown_MyObj_Release;
pMyObject->m_Unknown->pVtbl = &myUnknownVtbl;
```

Determining the Start-Up Method

Because an application's set of initialization tasks is affected by its method of start-up, an OLE application must determine whether it was started by a user or as part of activating a linked or embedded object. To determine how it was started, an application parses the command line to see whether the **/Embedding** option has been specified. Its presence indicates that OLE has started the application on behalf of a container of an embedded or linked object. The absence of the **/Embedding** option indicates that the user is in control.

Note Applications should check for both **/Embedding** and **-Embedding** whenever they check for the command-line options. Although this manual refers to **/Embedding**, either option is valid.

How an application initializes itself depends on whether **/Embedding** [*filename*] is present on the command line:

- A multiple-use application started with the **/Embedding** option on the command line registers its class object(s), providing OLE with a pointer to the **IClassFactory** interface; single-use applications do not register their class object. The application frame window is kept hidden until either **IOleObject::DoVerb** (with an *iVerb* parameter value of OLEIVERB_SHOW) is called for an object application or **IOleClientSite::ShowObject** is called for a container.

  The presence of **/Embedding** *filename* indicates the application is being started to service a file-based linked object and the filename references the linked file. In this case, the application should load the file and register it in the running object table—but not make it visible. An application started with **/Embedding** *filename* might or might not need to register its class object(s), depending on the type of class object. Single use class objects should not be registered; multiple use class objects must be registered.

- An application started by the user creates either an untitled document or, if a filename is specified, a document initialized to the contents of the specified file. The application window is made visible immediately. Because an SDI application can only work with one user document at a time, it does not register its class object(s). An MDI application registers its class object(s), indicating that multiple objects can be handled or created.

For more information on creating and opening documents, see "Opening Compound Documents," later in this chapter.

Registering Class Objects and Object Classes

Refer to "**IClassFactory::CreateInstance**."

Locking an Application in Memory

Refer to "**CoLockObjectExternal**."

Opening Compound Documents

Note The information presented in this section assumes an application is saving its native data using the OLE structured storage model. While there is no prerequisite for using structured storage, using it can simplify solutions to storage needs.

For an overview of the OLE storage model, see the chapter, "Persistent Storage Interface and Functions."

A user typically initiates the opening of a compound document by choosing the File New command for new documents or the File Open command for existing documents. The tasks an application has to perform to open existing documents and new ones are the same, except for the added of step of loading an existing document into memory.

Before making an open compound document visible, container applications must complete the following tasks:

- Allocate memory for the document object, using a class or a structure, and initialize its members.
- Lock the application object in memory.
- Create and register a file moniker, if linking to the file is supported.
- Open an **IStorage** object.
- Load the data (for existing documents only).
- Change the user interface as appropriate.
- Register as a drop target (if applicable).
- Show the document to the user and set the document's dirty flag, as appropriate.
- If the document was opened by the user, lock the document in memory.

Initializing the Document Structure

Before allocating memory for a new document object, SDI applications check to see whether there is a document already open that needs to be saved. If there is and the document has changes, the application should prompt the user to save the document. An MDI application can open a new document while others are open. For more information on closing a document, see "Closing OLE Compound Documents," later in this chapter.

The type of document being opened determines the user interface changes needing to be made, if any. For example, when the user opens a new untitled document in an MDI object application started with **/Embedding**, the application needs to change its user interface menus. When saving a document, applications check the document type in order to call the correct save routine. For information on saving OLE documents, see "Saving OLE Compound Documents," later in this chapter.

To help keep track of the document type and how it is being initialized, applications can define and use constants similar to the following:

Document Type	Description
DOCTYPE_UNKNOWN	A newly allocated document object exists but has not been initialized with application data yet.
DOCTYPE_NEW	A new document was created by the user by means of the File New command. The document is initialized as an untitled document. The usual user interface for user documents is displayed.
DOCTYPE_FROMFILE	The document was initialized from an existing file using the File Open command (or by using **IPersistFile::Load** being called when binding a link source).The normal user interface for user documents is displayed.
DOCTYPE_EMBEDDED	The document was initialized as an embedded compound document object using the **IStorage** opened by its container. The usual user interface is replaced with the modified user interface for an embedded object.
DOCTYPE_FROMSTG	The document is initialized using data from the **IStorage** provided by using **IPersistStorage::Load**. The usual user interface for user documents is displayed

The document type is initially set to DOCTYPE_UNKNOWN because the actual document type is not known until the document object is initialized with data.

Applications should keep track of references to its document object in a data member of the object. To guard this object from accidental destruction while it is being initialized, the reference counter should be intentionally incremented at the beginning of the initialization process. When initialization is complete, the counter can be decremented.

This technique is known as *artificial reference counting* and is explained more fully in the chapter called "Component Object Interfaces and Functions."

This document level reference counter can work in conjunction with a corresponding counter in the application object. To guarantee the application is not accidentally closed while the document is open, it is wise to increment both counters.

Creating and Registering File Monikers

Applications that allow containers to link to their file-based documents must create a file moniker to represent the open document and register the moniker in the running object table. The file moniker is created by calling **CreateFileMoniker**, passing in the document's complete path. To register the moniker, make the following two calls: **GetRunningObjectTable** to retrieve a pointer to the running object table and **IRunningObjectTable::Register** to complete the registration. Refer to the "Linking Interfaces and Functions" chapter for more information about monikers and the running object table.

Opening IStorage Objects

Refer to "Opening IStorage Objects" in the "Persistent Storage Interfaces and Functions" chapter.

Loading Objects

Refer to "Loading Objects from Storage" in the "Persistent Storage Interfaces and Functions" chapter.

Changing the User Interface

An application sets the title of the document window either to the name of the file from which the document was initialized or to an untitled document name.

If an SDI object application started with **/Embedding** opens a document, the File New and File Open commands are disabled and the File Save and File Exit commands are replaced with the File Save Copy As and File Exit and Return to <*container document*> commands. The File Save Copy As command enables a user to save an embedded object in a document other than its containing document.

An MDI object application started with **/Embedding** makes the same user interface changes as does an SDI object application, except these changes are made when the document window changes from a user-opened document to one needed to service an embedded object. Also, an MDI object application does not disable the File Open and File New menu items.

Registering a Document for Drag and Drop

Application windows that can accept dropped data must register as valid drop targets by calling **RegisterDragDrop**, passing a pointer to their **IDropTarget** implementation. The object exposing the **IDropTarget** interface must have at least one external reference lock on it. Without an external lock, the object is in an unstable state and might be destroyed prematurely. Calling **CoLockObjectExternal** just before the document is made visible to the user and before **RegisterDragDrop** is called safeguards the object.

Showing the Document and Setting the Dirty Flag

The application needs to make the document visible to the user and set a flag to indicate whether data has changed since it was last saved to storage. For a document opened with **/Embedding**, the document dirty flag should be set to TRUE to ensure the container always gets the most up-to-date representation of the object.

Figure 2-3 shows the state of an MDI document object opened by OLE. This document object is the data source for a linked object in a container. OLE opened the document via a moniker bind operation. (Had the document been opened by the user in an SDI application, the class object would not have been registered.) The reference counts for the objects are stored in the data member *cRef.* As shown, the document and application objects have a reference count of one, reflecting the external reference held by the stub managers. The stub managers keep track of the total number of external references (leftmost number) to the objects and how many of those references are strong (rightmost number).

The class object has a reference count of two: the one that OLE holds on the object on behalf of the class factory table registration, and the pointer reference to the object's **IClassFactory** interface.

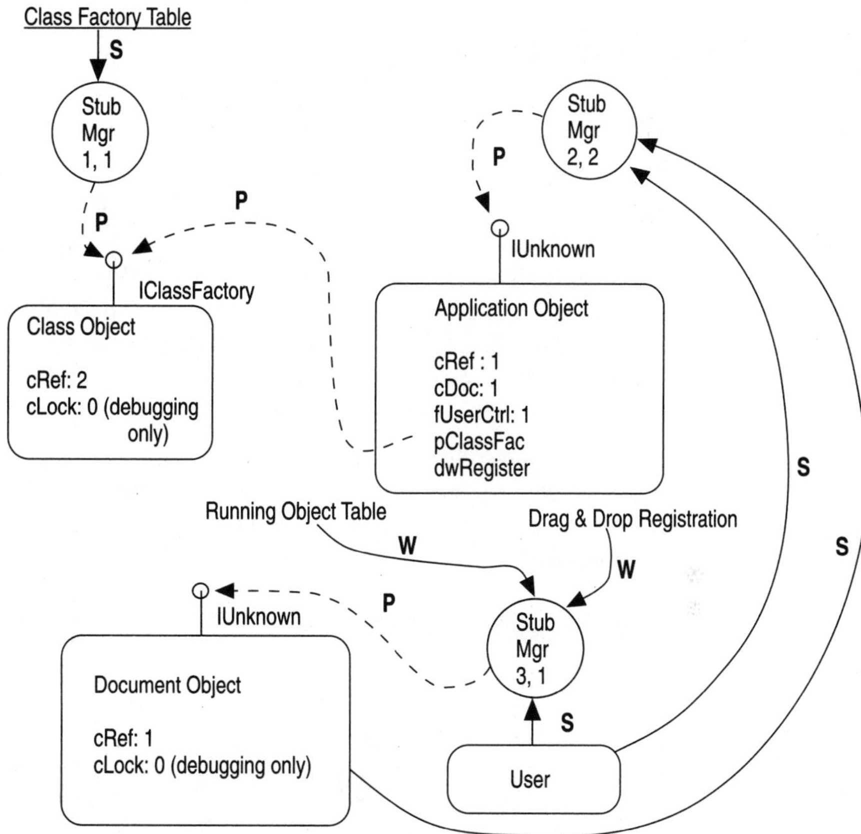

Figure 2-3. Document object created during a file moniker bind operation.

Documents created or opened by the user should set their dirty flag to FALSE. To explicitly lock the document in memory on behalf of the user, the application calls **CoLockObjectExternal** (*pUnk*, TRUE, NULL).

Using the Insert Object Dialog

The Insert Object dialog box, which is accessed from the Edit menu, allows a user to create a new or embedded object from either a default object application object or a file.

The Insert Object dialog, provides two options for creating objects: Create New and Create From File. The Create New option creates an embedded object from a list of registered object application object types. When the Create New option is selected, a list of currently registered objects is displayed from which the user can choose. The helper function **OleUIInsertObject** from the sample user interface library can be called to display the dialog box, accept the user's selection, and optionally go on to create the necessary object.

The Insert Object dialog is displayed in Figure 2-4. The Create From File option, when selected, creates either a new embedded object from a file or a link to a file if the Link check box is chosen.. The Display as Icon check box allows the object to be inserted as an icon.

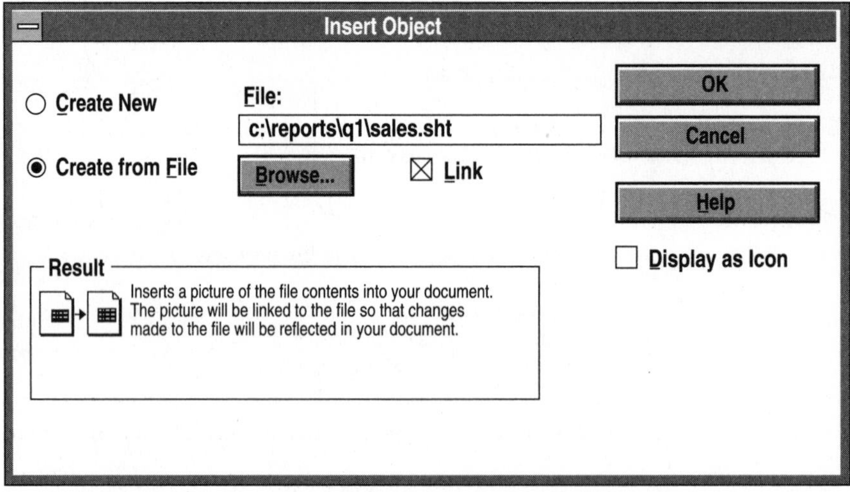

Figure 2-4. Insert Object dialog for creating an object from a file.

The implementation of the three options is identical from the container's point of view, with one exception. A different OLE creation API function is called for each option. The container performs the following steps:

1. Display the Insert Object dialog box and allow the user to make a selection.
2. Allocate a storage object and allocate and initialize the container site.
3. Depending on the user's selection, call the appropriate OLE creation API.
4. Set up advisory connections between the object application and the newly initialized container site.
5. Integrate the object into the container document.
6. Make the object visible.
7. Mark the document as changed.

Calling OLE to Create the Object

OLE provides several helper functions for creating embedded and linked objects. As noted above, depending on the option selected by the user, a different OLE creation function is called.

The following table lists the OLE creation functions used with the Insert Object dialog and provides a brief description:

OLE Object Creation Function	Type of Object Created
OleCreate	New embedded object.
OleCreateFromFile	Embedded object from a file.
OleCreateLinkToFile	Linked object to a file.

The OLE creation functions take several parameters, among them the CLSID of the object being created, the name of the file (if appropriate), the interface ID to be returned, the render option for cache initialization, and a pointer to the container's **IOleClientSite** interface. The typical container sets the render option to OLERENDER_DRAW, indicating that the compound document object should determine the formats to cache.

Containers, if they choose, can implement the functionality provided in the creation helper functions. However, most developers will want to use these functions to minimize errors and speed implementation.

If preferred, containers can implement this functionality in a different way. The function calls made in **OleCreate** and the purpose of each call is listed in the following table in the order in which they are made:

Object Creation Function Called	Purpose of Call
CoCreateInstance	Creates a class object for the object to be created and returns a pointer to that class object (**IClassFactory** interface).
IClassFactory::CreateInstance	Allocates and initializes the new object.
IOleObject::SetClientSite	Passes a pointer to the container's **IOleClientSite** interface to the object.
IPersistStorage::InitNew	Passes a pointer to the storage object.
OleRun	Runs the object and initializes the cache if a cache has been requested.

Setting Up Advisory Connections

When the OLE creation function returns, the container registers to receive either OLE notifications and data or view notifications. Typical compound document containers that rely on OLE to draw their embedded and linked objects register for OLE and view notifications. Containers handling the caching of their own presentation data can register for data notifications rather than view notifications. These containers pass OLERENDER_NONE in the render option in the call to the OLE creation function and then call **IUnknown::QueryInterface** asking for the **IOleCache** interface, creating the cache(s) needed with the **IOleCache** methods.

The following table indicates the interface methods that should be called to set up notification registration and the type of notifications handled by each method:

Interface Method Called	Type of Notification Registered For
IViewObject::SetAdvise	Registers for view notifications.
IOleObject::Advise	Registers for OLE notifications.
IDataObject::DAdvise	Registers for data change notifications.

When containers are finished registering, they call **IOleObject::SetHostNames** to inform the object of the name in the container. The object is made visible with a call to **IOleObject::DoVerb**.

Activating Objects

Activation refers to invoking a particular operation, or verb, available for a compound document object when it is selected in its container. The operations can be invoked on both embedded and linked objects. Activation requires that the compound document object be in the running state so the object application is available to supply the requested operation. The process of getting the object into the running state is known as *binding*. Because binding is handled by OLE, it is transparent to containers and object applications.

An embedded object is activated when the user selects a verb from the Edit or popup menus or double-clicks the object. The container makes a call to **IOleObject::DoVerb**, and the object application either activates the object in place or in a separate window in the object application process space, as is appropriate. Binding an embedded object involves locating and running the object application with the object data passed from the container.

From the container's perspective, activating a linked object is the same as activating an embedded object. However, the internal process required to activate the link source is much different from the process for activating an embedded object. When a linked object is bound, each of the pieces that make up the link source's moniker, typically a generic composite moniker, is evaluated. When the binding process is complete, the link source's application, if not already running, is forced into the running state.

Linked objects must be edited in their original source application. This usually implies that the linked object is to be edited in a separate window rather than in place. The use of the separate window makes it clear that an edit process is occurring, which is important because changes made to a linked object might potentially impact others. However, if the link is to an embedded object whose object application supports in-place editing, the embedded object is to be edited in place. Other types of activation, such as play or rewind, can also be done in place.

Activating an Embedded Object

Binding an embedded object involves locating and running the object's object application using the unique CLSID stored with the object. The object application is invoked with **/Embedding**, indicating it is being launched to support an OLE operation. For information on initializing an object application for OLE operations, see "Starting OLE Applications," earlier in this chapter.

Figure 2-5 shows what happens after a container makes a call to **IOleObject::DoVerb** to activate an embedded object. The site for the embedded object in the container has a pointer to one of the object's interfaces in the object handler, typically **IOleObject**. The object handler is responsible for locating and starting the object application. A pointer to the object in the object application is stored in the object handler.

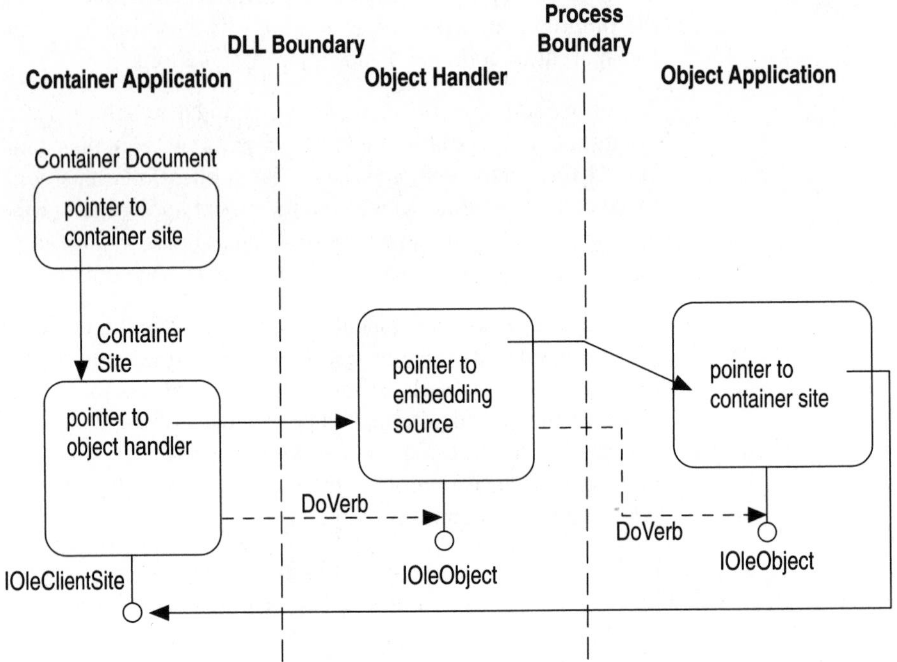

Figure 2-5. Relationship between an embedded object, the object handler, and the object application.

An object application's implementation of **IOleObject::DoVerb** for activating in open mode is quite simple: **IOleObject::DoVerb** determines which of the supported verbs have been requested and then initiates the action required. The object returns OLEOBJ_S_INVALIDVERB if the verb is invalid.

Activating a Linked Object

The link source for a linked object can be a file-based document, a selection of data within a document, an embedded object, or a selection of data within an embedded object. Each of these link sources is represented by a moniker that is itself made up of one or more monikers of the following types:

- *item moniker*: a null terminated string for naming an item or object.
- *file moniker*: a wrapper for the path name in the native file system (always the leftmost piece in a generic composite moniker).
- *generic composite moniker*: a concatenation of two or more monikers. A generic composite moniker is made up of one file moniker and one or more item monikers.

The following table briefly describes the types of monikers typically assigned to link source data:

Link Source Type	Type of Moniker
Document stored in a disk file.	File moniker.
Range of data within a document that might or might not be explicitly named by the user (pseudo object).	Generic composite moniker comprised of a file moniker and an item moniker to represent the pseudo object.
Part or all of an embedded object (either within the same container or in a different container)	Generic composite moniker comprised of a file moniker and two item monikers, one for the object in the container and one for the data in the object application

A pseudo object is created when a link is made to a selection of data within a document. Pseudo objects are not associated with an identifiable storage location. The pseudo object is assigned a generic composite moniker consisting of the file moniker for its document and an item moniker for the data range. Figure 2-6 shows the typical components of a generic composite moniker.

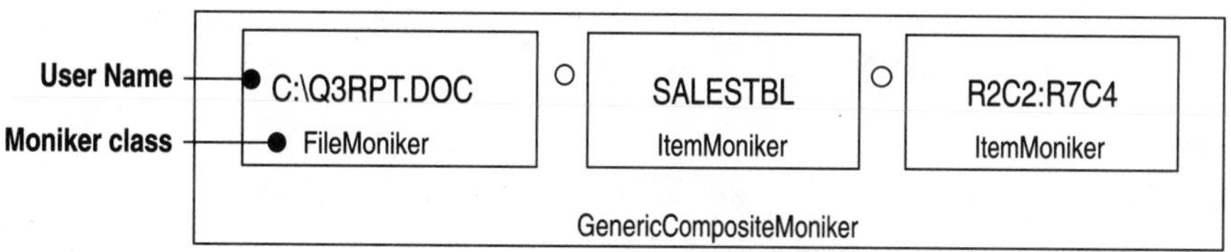

Figure 2-6. Components of a Generic Composite Moniker.

Figure 2-7 shows what happens after a container makes a call to **IOleObject::DoVerb** to activate a linked object. Except for the insertion of the OLE link object between the container site and the object handler, the flow of control for linked objects is identical to the flow of control for embedded objects. The OLE link object's implementation of **IOleObject::DoVerb** initiates the moniker binding process.

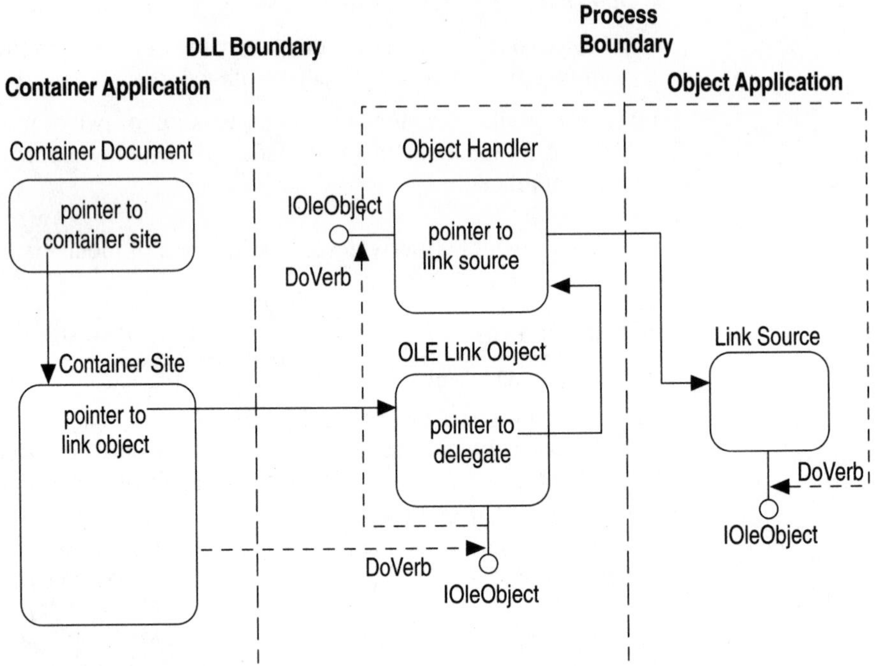

Figure 2-7. Relationship between a linked object, the OLE link, the class handler, and the object application.

Figure 2-8 illustrates how editing a link to an embedded object that is typically edited in place might appear to the user. Two containers are involved, one to hold the linked object and the other to hold the embedded object. When the user double-clicks the linked object, the moniker for its link source is bound. This starts the object application for the embedded object. Because the object application's **IOleObject::DoVerb** implementation supports in-place editing, the link source is edited in place within its embedding container.

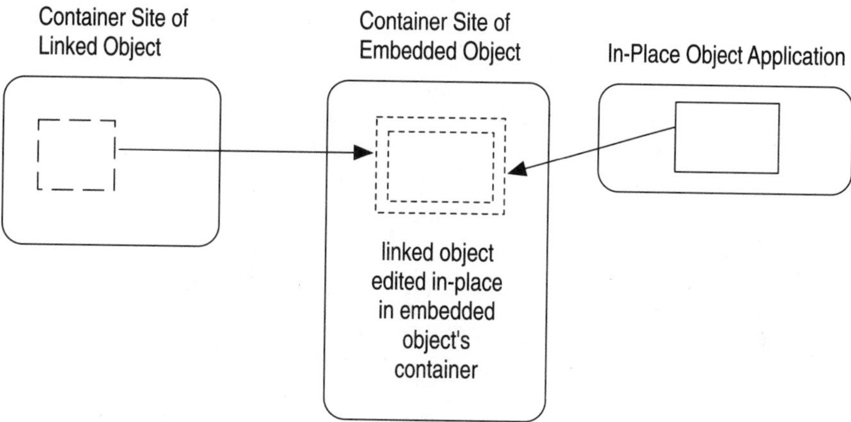

Figure 2-8. Editing a link to an in-place embedded object.

Binding a File Moniker

When a file moniker is bound, the running object table is checked first to see whether the object is already running. If it is, the file moniker then binds to the running object. If the object is not currently running, the OLE function **GetClassFile** is called to determine the object class associated with the file. There are three strategies **GetClassFile** uses to determine the object class. If the file is a compound file, the class is read directly from the compound file. If compound files are not used, **GetClassFile** looks in the registration database and checks the registered file type patterns against the data stored in the file. If these two strategies fail, the class is determined from file's extension.

GetClassFile runs the appropriate object application, if it is not already running, and then calls **IPersistFile::Load** to open the file and **IClassFactory::CreateInstance** to instantiate the object.

Binding an Item Moniker

An item moniker requires the **IOleItemContainer** interface of the object to its left to bind. **IOleItemContainer** is implemented by all object applications that allow linking to pseudo objects and all containers that allow linking to embedded objects. When the item moniker gains access to the interface, **IOleItemContainer::GetObject** is called to locate and run the object represented by the item name and to return a pointer to one of the object's interfaces. The caller passes the item name, a value that indicates the amount of time the caller is willing to wait for the object, an interface identifier, and a place to return the object. The object application's implementation of **IOleItemContainer::GetObject** returns the pointer to an active pseudo object. The container's implementation of **GetObject** returns a pointer to an interface belonging to the running object. **GetObject** cannot be recursive; it must get the object and then return.

Binding a Generic Composite Moniker

Binding a generic composite moniker involves binding all its pieces. The process starts with the rightmost piece, typically an item moniker. OLE locates and loads the object represented by the item moniker by calling **IOleItemContainer::GetObject,** and then initiates binding on the piece to the left. This process is repeated until the binding of the leftmost moniker, a file moniker, causes the object application to be run (if it is not already running). The file containing the link source is opened and loaded, and the link source is placed in the running state.

Verifying Links

IOleItemContainer::IsRunning provides an application with a way to determine whether an object identified by a specific name is running. Determining the state of a link source is important for maintaining active link connections.

Containers call **IOleObject::IsUpToDate** to find out whether they have the most up-to-date data. Linked objects can be outdated if the document containing the link source has changed. If **IOleObject::IsUpToDate** returns FALSE, containers of manual links that are connected can get updated data by calling **IOleLink::GetBoundSource** to get a pointer to the link source. The container can then call **QueryInterface** on the returned pointer asking for a pointer to **IDataObject**. **IDataObject:GetData** can then be called to get the most up-to-date data.

Using an Object's Verbs

Verbs are the set of operations supported by a particular object. The set of object-specific verbs can differ for each object type because different verbs make sense for different objects. For example, a sound object's verbs displayed to the user might include play, rewind, and edit, while a text object might only support edit. An object application registers a set of object-specific verbs in the registration database for each type of object supported. These user-selectable verbs are assigned sequentially positive values, beginning with 0 for the primary verb (in order to maintain compatibility with OLE 1 containers).

Compound document objects must also register and support a set of special OLE verbs. (These verbs are not to be confused with those that appear on the Edit and popup menus for the user to select.) The OLE verbs have a predefined meaning and value for each supported object. The OLE verbs include OLEIVERB_PRIMARY, OLEIVERB_SHOW, OLEIVERB_OPEN, OLEIVERB_HIDE, and a few other verbs that apply only to in-place activation. Refer to the discussion of **IOleObject::DoVerb** in the "Compound Document Interfaces and Functions" reference chapter for detailed information about verbs.

OLE verbs are typically invoked programmatically and are registered in the registration database. OLEIVERB_PRIMARY has a value of 0; the other OLE verbs have negative values in sequential order beginning with -1. Refer also to the chapter on "Registering Object Applications."

Managing Notifications

Notifications are callbacks generated by an object when it detects a change. Containers and other clients of an object register to receive notifications of interest by setting up an advisory connection to the object. Through this connection, the object undergoing the change notifies the advisory sink. Some of the changes that can cause a notification to be sent include renaming of the object, saving the object to persistent storage, closing the object, changing its view, and so on. Notifications ensure that a container has the most up-to-date information about its embedded and linked objects.

There are three types of notifications: OLE (or compound document), data, and view. The OLE notifications include OnRename, OnSave, OnLinkSrcChange, and OnClose. Containers and other objects interested in receiving OLE notifications call the object's **IOleObject::Advise** method, passing it a pointer to its **IAdviseSink** interface implementation. (Advise connections are not saved with objects.) The **IAdviseSink** interface is implemented by all objects interested in receiving notifications of any type.

An extension of **IAdviseSink**, **IAdviseSink2**, is implemented by objects that are interested in receiving OnLinkSrcChange notifications. Each type of notification maps to one of the methods in **IAdviseSink** or **IAdviseSink2**. For example, when an object application is saving an embedded object, it generates an OnClose notification that causes the container's **IAdviseSink::OnClose** method to be called.

Notification registration is handled by methods in three different interfaces. To register for OLE notifications, an object calls **IOleObject::Advise.** To register for data change notifications, an object calls **IDataObject::DAdvise**. To register for view notifications, an object calls **IViewObject::SetAdvise**. **IDataObject** and **IOleObject** are implemented by the object application and object handler; **IViewObject** is implemented by the cache object.

The five types of notifications are described below:

Notification	Description
OnRename	Sent when the object application's full moniker is initially set or changed. (OLEWHICKMK_OBJFULL is passed as a parameter to **IOleObject::SetMoniker**). Tells the OLE link object to update its moniker. Containers can ignore this notification.
OnSave	Sent when the object application saves the object. If the ADVF flag ADVFCACHE_ONSAVE was specified, tells the OLE link object or object handler to update its cache.
OnClose	Sent when the object application is closing the object. Tells an OLE link object to release its pointer to the bound link source. Containers can revert the storage to ensure that uncommitted changes are flushed.
OnViewChange	Sent when the object's view (presentation) has changed. Containers need to redraw. Can be sent when the object is in either the running or loaded state.
OnDataChange	Sent when the object's data has changed. Cache might need updating. Linked objects with manual links do not update the cache with OnDataChange.
OnLinkSrcChange	Sent by the OLE link object when it receives the **OnRename** notification from the link source (object) application. The link object updates its moniker and calls **IAdviseSink2::OnLinkSrcChange**

There are a few other methods related to notification registration. **IDataObject::DUnadvise** and **IOleObject::Unadvise** remove a registration; **IDataObject::EnumDAdvise**, **IOleObject::EnumAdvise**, and **IViewObject::GetAdvise** list the registrations currently in effect for the object.

Managing Notification Registration

An object application must manage registration requests, keeping track of who is interested in which notifications and sending those notifications when appropriate. OLE provides two component objects to simplify this task: the OleAdviseHolder for OLE notifications and the DataAdviseHolder for data notifications.

The OleAdviseHolder, created with a call to the OLE API function **CreateOleAdviseHolder**, is an object provided by OLE that implements the **IOleAdviseHolder** interface. **IOleAdviseHolder** contains methods for managing registration requests and sending notifications to **IAdviseSink** sites.

The DataAdviseHolder is an object provided by OLE that implements the **IDataAdviseHolder** interface and is used to manage data notifications. Applications can call the OLE API function **CreateDataAdviseHolder** to instantiate a DataAdviseHolder.

When an object application uses one of the advise holder objects, a call to one of the registration methods in **IOleObject** or **IDataObject** results in the corresponding function being called in the advise holder object. For example, the following implementation of **IDataObject::DAdvise** illustrates the use of the DataAdviseHolder to handle data change notification registration:

```
HRESULT IDataObject_DAdvise(
        LPDATAOBJECT        pThis,
        FORMATETC FAR*      pFormatetc,
        DWORD               advf,
        LPADVISESINK        pAdvise,
        DWORD FAR*          pdwConnection )
{
    HRESULT hrErr;
    LPDOC pDoc=((struct CDocDataObjectImpl FAR *)pThis)->pDoc;
    *pdwConnection = NULL;

    if (pDoc->m_pDataAdviseHldr == NULL && CreateDataAdviseHolder
         (&pDoc->m_pDataAdviseHldr) != NOERROR)
            return ResultFromScode(E_OUTOFMEMORY);
    else  {
        hrErr = pDoc->m_pDataAdviseHldr->pVtbl->DAdvise(
            pDoc->m_pDataAdviseHldr,
            (LPDATAOBJECT)&pDoc->m_pDataObject,
            pFormatetc,
            advf,
            pAdvise,
            pdwConnection    );
        return hrErr;
    }
```

Among the parameters passed to **IDataObject::DAdvise** is a group of flags, the *advf* parameter in the above example, that controls the advisory connection. These flags are also used with the **IOleCache** methods. The value for the parameter is taken from the enumeration **ADVF**; one or more of these values (or-ed together) can be used.

When a caller specifies ADVF_PRIMEFIRST as the *advf* parameter, **DAdvise** immediately sends an OnDataChange notification, thus enabling the caller to get the data immediately.

A possible scenario for setting these flags involves a user selecting the Display as Icon check box in the Paste Special dialog. The object is requested with the DVASPECT_ICON aspect value that causes an icon to be placed in the cache. When a data change notification is set up, the caller could specify ADVF_NODATA | ADVF_ONLYONCE | ADVF_PRIMEFIRST in its call to **IDataObject::DAdvise**. The result would be that the only one data change notification would ever be sent and no data would be sent with it. The ADVF_NODATA value can be used whenever the caller does not want OLE to update the cache.

Notification Flow

Notifications originate in the object application and flow to the container by using the object handler. If the object is a linked object, the OLE link object intercepts the notifications from the object handler and notifies the container directly.

All containers, the object handler, and the OLE link object register for OLE notifications. The typical container also registers for view notifications. Data notifications are usually sent to the OLE link object and object handler. A special purpose container, such as a container that renders the data itself (instead of calling the OLE helper function **OleDraw**), might want data notifications instead of view notifications. For example, an embedded chart container with a link to a table can register for data notifications. Because a change to the table affects the chart, the receipt of a data notification would direct the container to call **IDataObject::GetData** to get the new tabular data.

Figure 2-9 shows the notification flow from an object application to an embedded object container that has registered for OLE and view notifications. The solid lines represent memory pointers; the dotted lines represent notifications. Note that the notifications go directly to the **IAdviseSink** interface. Data notifications sent to the object handler are forwarded to the appropriate cache element in the object handler's cache object. If a container has registered for view notifications rather than data notifications, the cache generates an OnViewChange notification it sends to the container site.

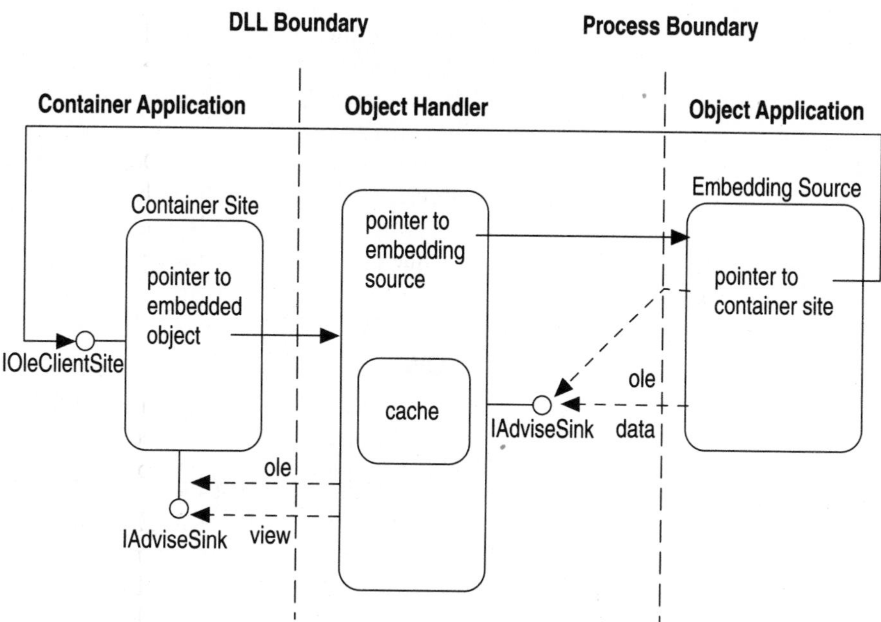

Figure 2-9. Notification flow for an embedded object.

For a linked object, the flow is slightly different. Instead of holding a pointer to the object handler, the container points to the OLE link object. The OLE link object points to its delegate, the object handler. There is no pointer from the object application back to the container site. The object application, or link source, sends data and OLE notifications to the object handler which in turn sends them on to the OLE link object. The OLE link object generates a view notification it sends to the container, if it has registered for view notifications, and a link source change notification, if appropriate. Figure 2-10 shows the flow for a linked object.

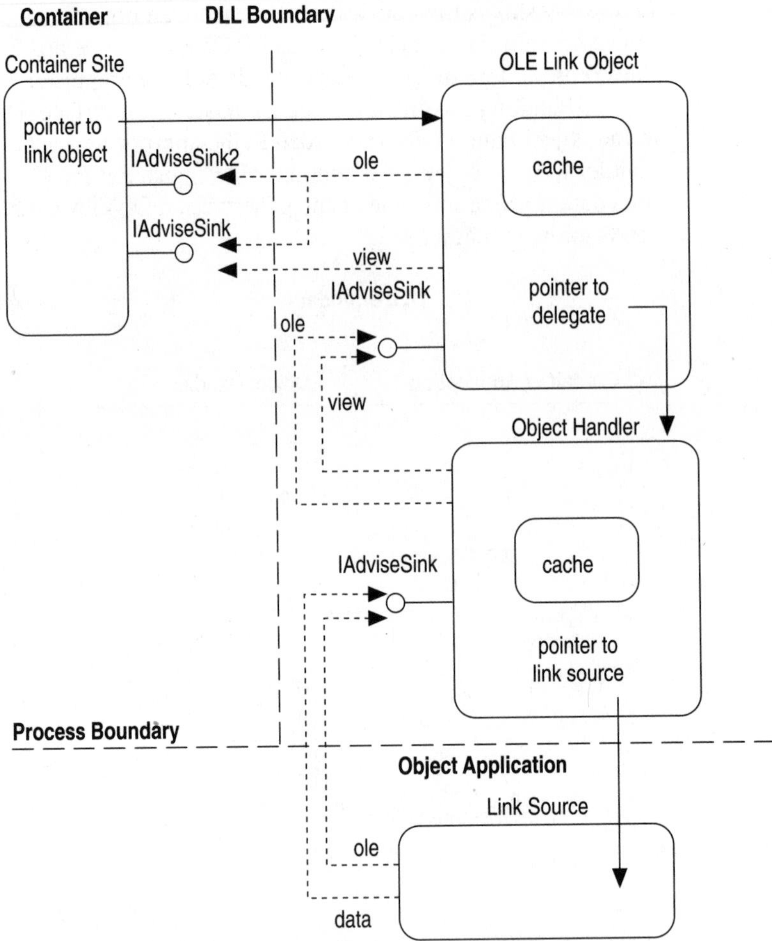

Figure 2-10. Notification flow for a linked object.

Figure 2-11 shows how notifications are sent to container sites in separate container applications. The container sites contain linked objects that are linked to the same link source. Note that each container has its own OLE link object and object handler within its process space. Figure 2-11 introduces the advise holders to keep track of the advisory connections. The OleAdviseHolder manages OLE notifications; the DataAdviseHolder manages data notifications.

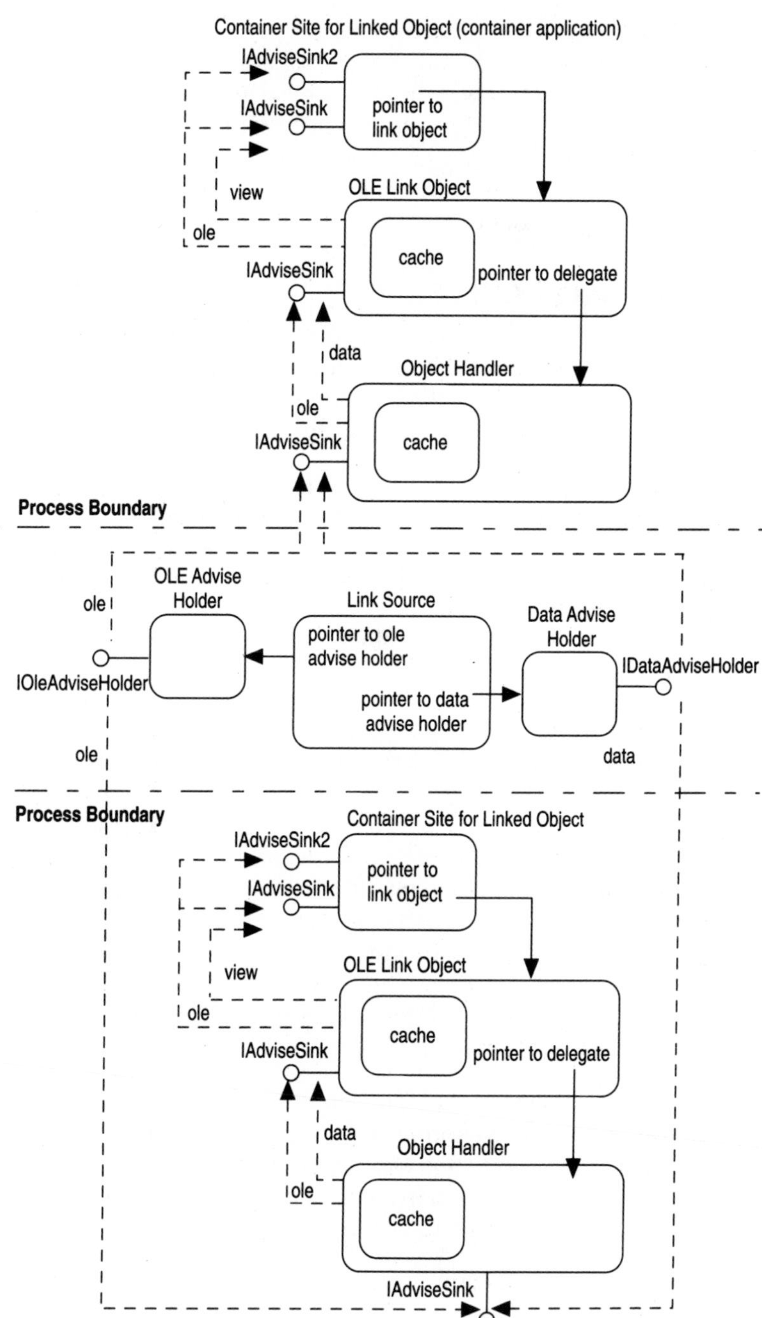

Figure 2-11. Notification flow to separate container processes.

Notifications can be synchronous or asynchronous. With synchronous notifications, the remoting object responsible for marshaling the data across the process boundary waits for a response from the remoting object on the other side of the boundary before returning control back to the object that sent the notification. With asynchronous notifications, the remoting object does not wait for a response before returning. For more information about the types of method calls in OLE, refer to the chapter called "Concurrency Management."

Sending Notifications

Object applications determine the conditions that prompt the sending of each specific notification and the frequency with which each notification should be sent. When it is appropriate for multiple notifications to be sent, it does not matter which notification is sent first; they can be sent in any order.

Each notification maps to one or more conditions. The following table lists the common conditions that generate each notification. The view and link source change notifications are not included because object applications do not send them.

Condition in Object application	Notification Generated
User selects Close	OnClose
User selects Save or Save As	OnSave
Document or Pseudo Object name first assigned or changed	OnRename
Object's data changed	OnDataChange

The timing of notifications affects the performance and coordination between an object application and its containers. Whereas notifications sent too frequently slow processing, notifications sent too infrequently result in an out-of-sync container. Notification frequency can be compared with the rate at which an application repaints. Therefore, using similar logic for the timing of notifications (as is used for repainting) is wise.

Object applications that support linking to ranges need to consider how pseudo objects are to be informed of the need to send notifications. For example, when a document is saved, the OnSave notification must be sent to both the container sites of the standard objects and the container sites of the pseudo objects. Two approaches can be considered:

- Any change in the document causes a notification to be sent to all container sites for all pseudo objects in the document.
- A mechanism can be implemented for determining the specific pseudo object affected by a change. Notification is sent only to the container sites of the those affected.

Some object applications disable the sending of notifications for an extended period of time so certain operations are not interrupted. Notification requests are placed in a queue, and when the operation completes, these pending notifications are sent. For example, a graphic object application can ensure that the repainting of its image is not interrupted; notifications are not sent until the repaint operation has completed.

There are a few considerations for object applications that implement pseudo objects to support linking to ranges. If such an object application supports the queueing of notifications, a mechanism to queue pseudo object notifications must be implemented. Notifications must be sent to all pseudo object container sites when the OnRename and OnSave conditions arise.

Receiving Notifications

A container is responsible for registering for notifications and responding if necessary after a notification is received. Containers register to receive notifications when a new embedded or linked object is created and when an object is loaded.

The **IAdviseSink** interface implementation dictates the necessary response for each notification. **IAdviseSink** is implemented by containers, the OLE link object, and the object handler; and each implementation is different. For example, the OLE link object's implementation of **OnRename** updates the moniker for a linked object, but the object handler and container versions of **OnRename** do nothing.

A container that does not use OLE's caching support registers for data change notifications. If a container receives data notifications, its implementation of **IAdviseSink::OnDataChange** could post an internal message or invalidate the rectangle for the changed data by calling the Windows function **InvalidateRect** and then wait for a WM_PAINT message. It is not valid to call **IDataObject::GetData** within **OnDataChange**. Calling **GetData** would result in a synchronous call nested inside of an asynchronous call.

OnViewChange handles view and extent changes. To handle extent changes, set a flag in **OnViewChange** called *fDoGetExtent* to TRUE and then call **InvalidateRect** to force repainting. In the drawing code, insert the following functionality:

```
if (fDoGetExtent)  {
    fDoGetExtent = FALSE;
    GetExtent(&newExtents);
    if (newExtents are different)
        relayout the contents.
}
draw the object
```

Containers can postpone receiving view notifications so an operation, such as printing, can continue uninterrupted. A call to **IViewObject::Freeze** causes view notifications to be queued until **IViewObject::Unfreeze** is called.

Saving OLE Compound Documents

Users typically initiate a document save by selecting the File Save or File Save As commands. An SDI object application opened with **/Embedding** also offers the File Save Copy As command, which is used to save the embedded object in a file that is separate from its containing document's file. Saving an object with the File Save Copy As command does not break the connection to the object's container application.

Note Unlike OLE 1 object applications, OLE 2 object applications do not need a File Update command to update changes made to an open OLE 2 embedded object. The changes are automatically reflected in the object's container document. However, if the object application is going to support OLE 1 objects, they need to support the Update command. For more information on OLE user interface recommendations, see the chapter on "OLE User Interface Guidelines."

When saving untitled documents, OLE applications need to create a new file moniker for the document and register it in the running object table. If the untitled document had a temporary file moniker registered in the running object table, this temporary moniker must be revoked by calling **IRunningObjectTable::Revoke**.

File Save As Command

To save a document using the File Save As command, an OLE application performs the following tasks:

- Prompt the user for the filename in which to save the document. If the user cancels the save operation, leave the document object initialized in the state it was in before the user chose the save operation.
- Set the document's title to that of the filename specified by the user.
- If linking is supported, create and register a new file moniker for the document in the running object table. Destroy and revoke the registration of the document's temporary file moniker (if it exists).
    - **Object application only:** Notify all linking containers and/or pseudo objects that the document has been renamed by calling **IAdviseSink::OnRename**. Direct all pseudo objects to notify their registered linking clients. Each pseudo object sends a notification in a similar fashion by calling **IAdviseSink::OnRename** for each of its registered sinks or **IOleAdviseHolder::SendOnRename**.

- **Container only:** Notify all compound document objects that have monikers assigned that the document's moniker has changed by calling **IOleObject::SetMoniker**. If the container is a top-level container, this is done when the container's filename changes.

- Open the specified file in which to save the document as an OLE compound file by calling **StgOpenStorage**.
- Open a stream in the open **IStorage** object and save the object's CLSID by calling **WriteClassStg**. Save the object's user type name and clipboard data format by calling **WriteFmtUserTypeStg**. (When saving an embedded object, the object application does not call **WriteClassStg**; it is called automatically when the container calls **OleSave** to save the object.)
- Open as many streams as needed to write the document's native data.
- **Container only:** If the document contains objects, save them as child **IStorage** objects of the opened **IStorage** instance.
- **Object application only:** If the object application loads all of its native data into memory, it can release the pointer to its open **IStorage** object. However, a container, even if it loads all of its native data into memory, *cannot* release its **IStorage** pointer because it must keep the storage object open at all times so its loaded embedded objects have access to their storage.
- Reset the document's dirty flag.

Setting the Filename of the Document

An OLE object application started with **/Embedding** does not have a File Save As command; instead, the File Save As command is replaced with the File Save Copy As command. In a File Save Copy As operation, the application does not reinitialize the document object to the file in which the document is being saved, because this would break the connection with the object's container application. This model is different from OLE 1.

After getting the name of the file from the user, an OLE application sets the document's title to the filename specified by the user.

Opening an IStorage Object

IStorage objects can be opened in one of two access modes: direct or transacted. In *direct* mode, the changes to the **IStorage** are committed immediately with no chance of undoing the changes. In *transacted* mode, the **IStorage** is opened in a buffered state, whereby changes are saved to temporary files until they are committed with a call to **IStorage::Commit**.

The access mode can be combined with the ability to read and write to the **IStorage**, and to deny others the right to do the same.

StgCreateDocfile uses its *grfMode* parameter (a set of flags) to control how the **IStorage** object is created and subsequently accessed. Valid values for *grfMode* are taken from the following constants defined in STORAGE.H:

```
#define STGM_DIRECT             0x00000000L
#define STGM_TRANSACTED         0x00010000L

#define STGM_READ               0x00000000L
#define STGM_WRITE              0x00000001L
#define STGM_READWRITE          0x00000002L

#define STGM_SHARE_DENY_NONE        0x00000040L
#define STGM_SHARE_DENY_READ        0x00000030L
#define STGM_SHARE_DENY_WRITE       0x00000020L
#define STGM_SHARE_EXCLUSIVE        0x00000010L

#define STGM_PRIORITY           0x00040000L
#define STGM_DELETEONRELEASE 0x04000000L

#define STGM_CREATE         0x00001000L
#define STGM_CONVERT        0x00020000L
#define STGM_FAILIFTHERE 0x00000000L
```

The *grfMode* parameter values are meant to be used together. Only one value from each of the five groups of flags can be specified at one time. As an example, the following combination of flag values opens the **IStorage** in transacted mode, with read and write access granted to the caller and write access denied to all other objects:

```
STGM_TRANSACTED | STGM_READWRITE | STGM_SHARE_DENY_WRITE
```

Except for the root **IStorage**, each **IStorage** object and its contained **IStream** object(s) are always opened in the context of some other open **IStorage** object. Child **IStorage** objects inherit the access mode of the parent; thus, the child **IStorage** object can only be opened in a more restrictive mode.

Writing OLE Data to IStorage

OLE uses one or more **IStream** objects for saving information about the document in the root **IStorage** object. This information includes the object's CLSID, which is written to the root **IStorage** object using **WriteClassStg**. Note that an object application launched to service an embedded object does not save the object's CLSID. The object's container saves this in an **IStream** of the object's **IStorage** element. OLE also saves the moniker of a linked object, the clipboard data format of the document's native data, and the user type name by calling the **WriteFmtUserTypeStg** function.

Writing Native Data to IStorage

Before it can write its native data to an **IStream** instance in the root **IStorage** object, an application must create a stream; this is done by calling the **IStorage::CreateStream** method. After creating the **IStream** object, the application calls the **IStream::Write** method to write its data to the **IStream** instance.

Saving Compound Document Objects to IStorage

Consider the compound document illustrated in Figure 2-12. The root **IStorage**, *pStg1* contains nested embedded objects, which also contain nested embeddings. For simplicity, the streams are represented by the small circles.

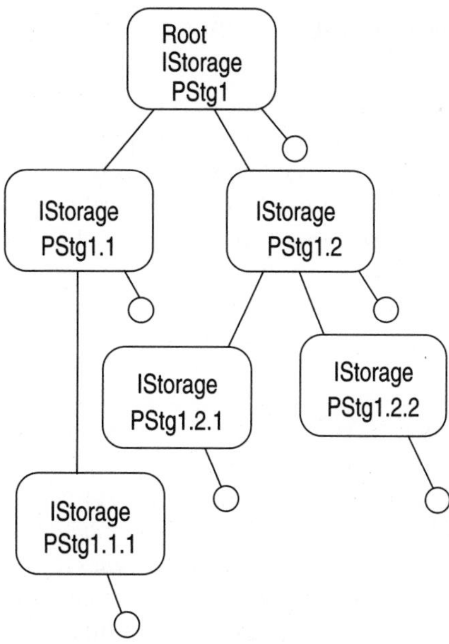

Figure 2-12. Saving a compound document object.

To save its contained embeddings, the top-level container must do the following tasks:

1. Call **OleSave** on the **IStorage** object of each immediate embedded object, passing the **IStorage** object a pointer to where the object is to be saved. The object then recursively calls **OleSave** on any of its nested embeddings.

   OleSave first calls **WriteClassStg** to save the object's CLSID before calling the object handler's **IPersistStorage::Save** method. (Usually, the object handler is the OLE-provided default handler.) The default handler's implementation of **IPersistStorage::Save** first saves the object's presentation cache and then calls **IPersistStorage::Save** on the running object to save the native data.

   Finally, **OleSave** calls **IStorage::Commit** on the **IStorage** object to commit the changes back one level to the transaction state of the root **IStorage** object.

2. After the return from **OleSave**, the top-level container must call **IPersistStorage::SaveCompleted** on the immediate embedded objects to return them and any of their nested embeddings to the normal storage mode. Unless this is done, the object is left in the no scribble mode it was put in when **OleSave** called **IPersistStorage::Save**. Because of this, **SaveCompleted** should be called immediately on the object after the return from **OleSave** to put the object and any of its nested embeddings back in the normal storage mode with full read and write access.

Note **IPersistStorage::SaveCompleted** is always called on the **IStorage** object that contains the object; it is a call that recurses to all currently loaded or running embedded objects. Should **SaveCompleted** fail, the object(s) does not return to normal storage mode. In this case the container should back out any changes that have been committed and instead try to save the object following the recommendations for saving an object in low-memory situations. See "Saving Objects in Low Memory," later in this chapter.

Saving a linked object is no different from saving an embedded object. To save a linked object that is not loaded or running, **IStorage::CopyTo** can be used. When an object is in the loaded or running state, **OleSave** should be called because it saves all changes.

OleSave and **IPersistStorage::Save** use the *fSameAsLoad* flag to determine whether the storage object that the object is being saved to is the same one from which the object was loaded. The value of *fSameAsLoad* can be combined with the value of the *pStg* passed to these functions to determine the save routine being used to save the compound document, as shown in the following table:

Value of *fSameAsLoad*	Value of *pStg* passed to IPersistStorage:: SaveCompleted	Save Routine to call
TRUE	NULL	File Save
FALSE	*pStg*	File Save As
FALSE	NULL	File Save Copy As

A container should save both the document's native data stream and any information on behalf of the compound document object, including the following data:

Data Saved on Behalf of a Compound Document Object	Description
m_szStgName	Stores the name of object's persistent **IStorage** element.
m_fMonikerAssigned	Keeps track of whether or not a moniker was assigned to the compound document object.
m_dwAspect	Determines how to display the object when it is later loaded into memory: as an embedded object, a thumbnail representation (appropriate for browsing tools), an iconic representation, or as a sequence of pages (as if the object had been printed).

Handling Monikers

Saving an untitled document requires that the application revoke the temporary file moniker created and registered for the untitled document, if any.

If a linking container established links to an object application's untitled document and then shuts down before the object application saves the untitled document, the links to the untitled document are broken. To repair the links, the user needs to use the Edit Links dialog. For this reason, some applications might not allow linking to untitled documents.

Notifying Linking Clients of File Moniker Changes—Object application Only

When the file moniker to a document changes, OLE object applications need to notify all registered linking clients. A linking client must have previously registered to receive change notifications by calling the **IOleObject::Advise** and/or **IDataObject::DAdvise** methods, as appropriate. To notify the linking clients, the object application calls the OLE-provided **IOleAdviseHolder::SendOnRename** method.

Notifying Pseudo Objects of Moniker Change—Object application Only

Just as they notify linking clients of a change in the document's file moniker, OLE object applications that support linking to pseudo objects must notify the registered linking clients that the pseudo object's file moniker has changed. Again, the application can use the OLE-provided implementation of the **IOleAdviseHolder** and **IDataAdviseHolder** interface to notify the linking clients of the file moniker change.

Notifying Compound Document Objects of File Moniker Change—Containers only

A container that supports linking to its embedded objects must notify each of its linking containers that the file moniker used to represent its document has changed, either when the document is saved for the first time or when it is saved to a new file. Otherwise, all links to the container's embedded objects are broken.

To notify an embedded object of its document's moniker change, containers call the **IOleObject::SetMoniker** method, passing in the new moniker and a flag that specifies the name of the object's container has changed (OLEWHICHMK_CONTAINER). Calling **IOleObject::SetMoniker** on a running object forces the object to revoke its currently registered moniker from the running object table and register the new moniker.

Resetting the Document's Dirty Flag

After saving the document, applications reset their dirty flag on the document to FALSE. However, if the document is being saved as the result of a File Save Copy As operation, the flag is not reset.

File Save Command

Saving a document with the File Save command follows the same logic as File Save As, except when saving documents with File Save, the application does not need to prompt the user for the name of the file or call the routines that create and register new monikers.

To save a document using the File Save command, OLE applications perform the following tasks. For a discussion of these tasks, see the preceding section, "File Save As Command."

- Open the specified file in which to save the document as a compound file.
- Open as many **IStream** instances as needed to save the OLE information to the document's root **IStorage** object, including the CLSID, user type name, and clipboard data format.
- Save the document's native data to the root **IStorage** object.

- If the document contains objects, save them as child **IStorage** instances to the open root **IStorage** object. After saving all objects, call **IPersistStorage::SaveCompleted** on each **IStorage** object to return it and any of its nested embeddings to the normal storage mode.
- Reset the document's dirty flag.

Saving to Temporary Files

A document saved to a compound file can choose to implement its save functionality by doing a complete save to a temporary file residing in the same directory as the original. After the temporary file has been created, the original file is deleted, and the temporary one is renamed to have the name of the original. As far as the object is concerned, the process of saving documents this way works in three steps:

1. The object's container calls **IPersistStorage::Save**. This call temporarily removes the object's right to scribble into its storage; putting the object into the no scribble storage mode. While in this mode, the object cannot write to its storage object, although it can read from it. Thus, the duration of the no scribble storage mode should be kept to the absolute minimum.
2. The container does whatever it needs to do to safely retain the changes the object saved. Usually, containers call **IStorage::Commit**.
3. The container returns the object to normal storage mode by calling **IPersistStorage::SaveCompleted**.

Notice that in either normal or no scribble storage mode an object can hold on to its open **IStorage** instance. With OLE compound files, the object application also has the actual disk file open. Unfortunately, under MS-DOS, a file cannot be deleted or renamed while is open, preventing the application from doing a full save operation. To solve this problem, an object can be put into the hands-off storage mode, which is similar to but somewhat more severe than the no scribble storage mode. In this mode, the object *must* release the **IStorage** instance it owns. If the object is also an OLE container, it recursively causes any of its loaded or running objects to enter the hands-off storage mode. When the object returns to the normal storage mode, its container gives the object back its storage pointer.

To put an object into the hands-off storage mode, the container calls the **IPersistStorage::HandsOffStorage** method. To return the object to its normal storage mode, the **IPersistStorage::SaveCompleted** method is called with a *pStg* to the object's **IStorage** instance. The contents of the just-passed *pStg* are guaranteed to be identical to the contents of the *pStg* that the object had but which was revoked in the call to **IPersistStorage::HandsOffStorage**. Thus, the object does not have to do a full reload; it only needs to reopen any substreams in the normal storage mode.

Note Calling **IPersistStorage::Save** *always* causes the object to enter the no scribble storage mode. This is done to guarantee that low-memory saves work while ensuring efficiency in the high-memory cases. Thus, every call to **IPersistStorage::Save** *must* be followed by a call to **IPersistStorage::SaveCompleted** to return the object and any of its child **IStorage** objects to the normal storage mode. In addition, the container can make an intervening call to **IPersistStorage::HandsOffStorage**, which is useful for implementing the application's File Save As routine.

From the perspective of a client of an object, the hands-off storage mode is very similar to the no scribble storage mode. In neither mode can the client expect anything at all to work on the object. From the object's perspective, in no scribble storage mode the object can read but not write to its **IStorage** instance; in hands-off storage mode, it clearly can no longer read from the **IStorage**.

Saving Objects in Low Memory

Often an object is asked to save itself in low-memory situations. Conceptually, this can be thought of as doing a File Save As operation. For example, suppose there is a root document in a file and all the changes to its embedded objects have been saved, but not yet committed at the document level, as shown in Figure 2-13:

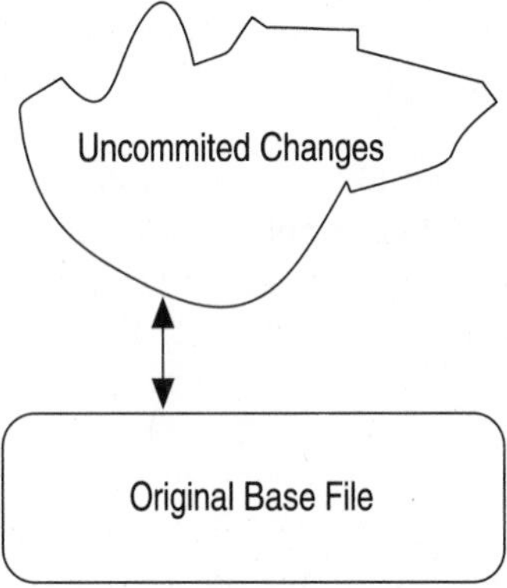

Figure 2-13. State of an unsaved object in a low-memory situation.

Here, the uncommitted changes are those written to the compound file that have yet to be committed. In low-memory situations, an application needs to be guaranteed a way to save its compound document to a new base file without consuming any new memory, as shown in Figure 2-14.

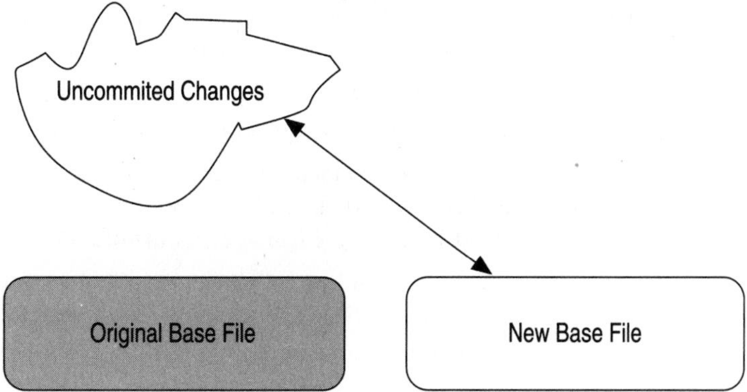

Figure 2-14. Saving objects to a new base file in low-memory situations.

The new base file is a copy of the original file. The uncommitted compound file changes are now associated with the new file; the old file is inaccessible. If an **IStorage::Commit** is now made, the changes go to the new file. In this situation, **IStorage::Commit** is guaranteed to work without consuming additional memory.

When saving compound documents in this manner, it is recommended that any loaded or running embedded objects be in the hands-off storage mode, which simplifies the implementation of this low-memory save operation in compound files.

When saving an object in low-memory situations, the following interface methods are guaranteed to work:

IStream::Read	**IStream::Write**
IStream::SetSize	**IStream::Seek**
IStream::Commit	**IStream::Revert**
IStream::AddRef	**IStream::Release**
IStorage::QueryInterface	**IStorage::SetClass**
IStorage::SetStateBits	**IStorage::Commit**
IStorage::Revert	**IStorage::AddRef**
IStorage::Release	**IRootStorage::QueryInterface**
IRootStorage::AddRef	**IRootStorage::Release**
IRootStorage::SwitchToFile	

Full Save Operations

▶ **To do a full save of a document, an application completes the following steps:**

1. The object creates and opens a temporary destination file in direct mode.
2. The container then creates the appropriate **IStorage** instances for each object, also using direct mode for these storage objects.
3. The container then asks each loaded or running embedding to save to the new storage by calling **IPersistStorage::Save** (*pStg*, FALSE).
4. If the object's **IStorage** instance was opened in transacted mode, the container then writes the root level document's data to the compound file and flushes the root storage object by calling **IStorage::Commit**.

   If any of these steps fail for low memory reasons, the container should back each object out by calling **IPersistStorage::SaveCompleted** (NULL) and try to save the document using the sequence of steps for saving in low-memory situations.
5. Once the data is in the new file, the container calls **IPersistStorage::HandOffStorage** on each object and releases the **IStorage** instance that the root document is holding on to. This then allows the container to delete the original file and to rename the new one to be the old name.
6. The container reloads each object by calling **IPersistStorage::SaveCompleted** (*pStgNew*).

If any errors occur after the data is saved in the new file but before completion, error handlers need to note that some objects are either in the no scribble or hands-off storage mode and need to be returned to the normal storage mode eventually.

Doing a Full Save in Low Memory

▶ **To do a full save in low memory, a container does the following steps:**

1. Ask each object to save to its current **IStorage** by calling **IPersistStorage::Save**(*pStg*, TRUE). Objects are responsible for ensuring that this operation works without consuming additional memory.
2. Commit the storage of each of the objects by calling **IStorage::Commit** to percolate the changes out to the next transaction level.
3. Write any changes made to the root-level document to the appropriate streams immediately contained within the root **IStorage** instance.
4. Put each object in the hands-off storage mode by calling **IPersistStorage::HandsOffStorage** on the object.
5. Close any streams the root-level document might be holding on to.
6. Call **IRootStorage::SwitchToFile**(*lpszNewFile*) to switch the files.

7. Call **IStorage::Commit** on the root **IStorage** instance to commit the new file. This **Commit** can safely be done using STGC_OVERWRITE, which reduces the size of the final file.
8. After the data is in the new file, close and delete the original file before renaming the new one to the old name. Then reattach the objects by calling **IPersistStorage::SaveCompleted**(*pStgNew*).
9. Reopen any root-level streams.

The error handling cautions for doing a full save in high memory apply to the low-memory case as well.

The Save As case is the same, except the container need not bother with deleting the original file and renaming the new one.

Backing Out of a Save As

In the File Save As sequence, a container recursively calls **IPersistStorage::Save** followed by a call to **IPersistStorage::SaveCompleted** on its contained embedded objects. However, suppose the Save As operation cannot be completed. In this case, some of the objects will be holding on to a storage object in the new location, while some are holding on to the old location. There are two things a container can do to get the objects that have been saved to back out:

1. The container can ask these objects to "Save As" back to their original location. This is slow, but might be an acceptable solution for the container, especially if this scenario happens infrequently.
2. The container can close and reload the object from the original location. If the object is loaded, this has no visible effect on the user; however, if the object is running, this closes the object on the user's screen.

Incremental Save Operations

Incremental saves are somewhat less complicated, because the presence of transactioning and the lack of a need of a new temporary file makes things easier. Incremental saving assumes that the root **IStorage** object is open in transacted mode.

▶ **To do an incremental save, the container does the following tasks:**

1. Ask each object to save to its current **IStorage** by calling **IPersistStorage::Save** (*pStg*, TRUE). This is guaranteed by contract with the object not to fail for lack of memory.
2. Commit the storage of each of the objects by calling **IStorage::Commit** to percolate the changes out to the next transaction level; compound files are guaranteed that this works in low memory.
3. Write any changes made to the root-level document to the root **IStorage** instance. As with objects, the root document is responsible for ensuring this works in low memory.
4. Call **IStorage::Commit** on the root **IStorage** instance to commit the compound file.
5. Return the object to their normal storage mode by calling **IPersistStorage::SaveCompleted** (NULL).

Supporting Link Updating

Applications that act as file-level link sources can better handle all cases of manual links and nearly all cases of automatic links by setting the change time in the running object table to the time of the file's last save. The following pseudo code can be implemented after the save:

```
if registered in the running object table
    get time of saved file in FILETIME format
    get a pointer to the running object table (pROT)
    call pROT->NoteChangeTime(dwRegister, &filetype)
    call pROT->Release()
```

To get the time of the saved file:

```
#include <dos.h>
struct _find_t fileinfo;
_dos_findfirst(<filename), _A_NORMAL|_A_HIDDEN|_A_SUBDIR|_A_SYSTEM,
    &fileinfo)
CoDosDateTimeToFileTime(fileinfo.wr_date, fileinfo.wr_time, pfiletime)
```

Closing OLE Compound Documents

On shutdown, an SDI application will have only one open document to close while an MDI application might have many documents to close. To close a document, OLE applications do the following tasks:

- Check the open document(s) for changes. If a file-based document has changed, prompt the user to save the document; otherwise, do nothing. If an embedded object has changed, tell the object's container to save it.
- Safeguard both the application and document objects from premature closing by intentionally incrementing the objects' reference counters.
- Revoke the registration of the document's moniker from the running object table.
- If the document is the source for the data on the clipboard, flush the clipboard.
- Hide the document window and unlock the document on behalf of the user. If the application supports drag and drop operations, revoke the document as a drop target.
- **Object application only:** Force all pseudo objects to close.
- **Object application only:** Send a final OnDataChange to all clients that have registered to receive data notifications when the object stops running (ADVF_DATAONSTOP). After sending the notification, release the DataAdviseHolder.
- **Object application only:** Send an OnClose advisory notification to all registered containers; after sending it, release the OleAdviseHolder.
- **Container only:** Force all loaded embedded and linked objects to close.
- To guarantee the document object has been freed of all external and pointer references, call **CoDisconnectObject**.
- Release the intentional reference count on the document and application objects. When the document object's reference count goes to zero, destroy the object.

Checking Documents for Changes

When closing documents, an application should ensure that its application and document objects are prevented from accidentally closing. To guard the objects, an application intentionally increments the reference counts on these objects. The reference counts remain until all other external memory pointers have been released.

Application shutdown begins by first checking all open documents to see whether there are changes that need to be saved. If the application was started by the user, it should prompt the user to save any changes made to the document. This model is different from OLE 1, where the application prompted the user to save the object in its container.

If the document is dirty, the object application should check to see whether or not OLE opened the document. If the document was opened by OLE, the object application should call the container's **IOleClientSite::SaveObject** method to save the object. Otherwise, the object application should prompt the user to save the changes made to the document.

Closing Pseudo Objects—Object Application Only

Object applications that support linking to pseudo objects need to close the pseudo objects as part of closing the open document(s). The object application also needs to send an OnClose notification to all registered linking containers of the pseudo object, telling them the pseudo object is being closed. Upon receipt of the OnClose notification, the linking container is automatically disconnected from the pseudo object. This disconnection is done by the OLE Link object, which is part of the container's object handler. To forcefully close any connections to its pseudo object, the object application can call the **CoDisconnectObject** function.

Closing Loaded Objects—Container Only

To forcefully close all loaded objects—including links and embeddings—containers can call **CoDisconnectObject**. The container passes to **CoDisconnectObject** a pointer to one of the interfaces being maintained on behalf of the object. Usually, this is a pointer to the **IUnknown** interface.

Note Care should be taken when calling **CoDisconnectObject** because it forcefully closes all objects. An application should not call **CoDisconnectObject** to routinely disconnect and release an interface pointer to an object; instead, it should call the object's **IUnknown::Release** method. **CoDisconnectObject** should only be called by the process that manages the object and only when that process wants to exit.

Hiding the Document Window

As the last part of closing a document, the application hides the document's window from the user. At the time of hiding the window, the application needs to revoke the document's registered file moniker from the running object table and take control of the document away from the user. (If the application supports drag and drop operations, it also unregisters itself as a drop target.)

As was discussed earlier in the section, "Opening Compound Documents," applications that support linking to pseudo objects create and register a file moniker for every document they open. Registering the file moniker results in a weak reference lock being placed on the document object on behalf of the registered moniker. Before the document can be closed, this moniker should be revoked from the running object table by calling the **IRunningObjectTable::Revoke** method, passing it the *dwRegister* token returned by the **IRunningObjectTable::Register** method when the moniker was registered.

Note Registering a moniker in the running object table results in a weak reference lock being placed on the document which is not strong enough to keep the document object alive should all the other external connections be released. Still, the application should release the moniker from the table before closing the document.

If the object application activated the object in a window in the object application process space, it must call **IOleClientSite::OnShowWindow** (FALSE) to tell the container to remove the hatching around the open object.

When there are no more documents visible to the user and the application is not under user control, the application should hide its application window. This leaves the application in a hidden, running state. Only when the application object's last external reference is freed, does the application actually shut down. This step is most critical for MDI applications.

Taking Control Away from the User

If the document was visible to the user when closing on shutdown, the application takes control of the document away from the user. To free this external user reference, the application calls **CoLockObjectExternal** (*pDoc*, FALSE, TRUE).

Sending Close Notifications—Object Applications Only

When closing a document, an object application sends a final OnDataChange notification to all clients registered with the ADVF_DATAONSTOP flag, telling them the object has stopped running. After sending the notification, the object application releases its **IDataAdviseHolder** pointer.

The object application also sends an OnClose advisory notification to all registered containers telling them it is shutting down. The object application then releases its **IOleAdviseHolder** interface pointer.

For more information on sending notifications, see "Managing Notifications," earlier in this chapter.

Releasing Reference Locks

Just as **CoLockExternal** (*pDoc*, FALSE, TRUE) was called to release the external reference on behalf of the user, the application needs to call **CoLockObjectExternal** (*pApp*, FALSE, TRUE) to release the lock on the application made when the document was first created.

Closing Scenarios

How an OLE container or object application was started and subsequently used affects the closing of the application. There are three scenarios around which applications can be closed:

- The user started the container or object application and initiated application shutdown by choosing the File Exit command or the system Close command.
- The object application was started by means of **Embedding** to service a linked or embedded object. Application shutdown was initiated by the container calling the **IOleObject::Close** method.
- The object application was started to service a linked or embedded object. Application shutdown was initiated by the user choosing the File Exit command or the system Close command.

The procedure for closing an application started by the user is the same for both object application and container applications; the sequence of shutdown tasks begin with the application object. However, for an object application started with /**Embedding**, shutdown is initiated by the object's container application and begins with the document object.

The following sections describe each of these scenarios in greater detail.

Closing an Application With the File Exit Command

Figure 2-15 shows the state of an MDI object application at the time the user initiated program shutdown by choosing the File Exit command (the application was started explicitly by the user).

Note While Figure 2-15 is representative of an MDI object application, the scenario is also applicable to SDI object applications, except that SDI object applications do not register their class of object(s) in the class factory table.

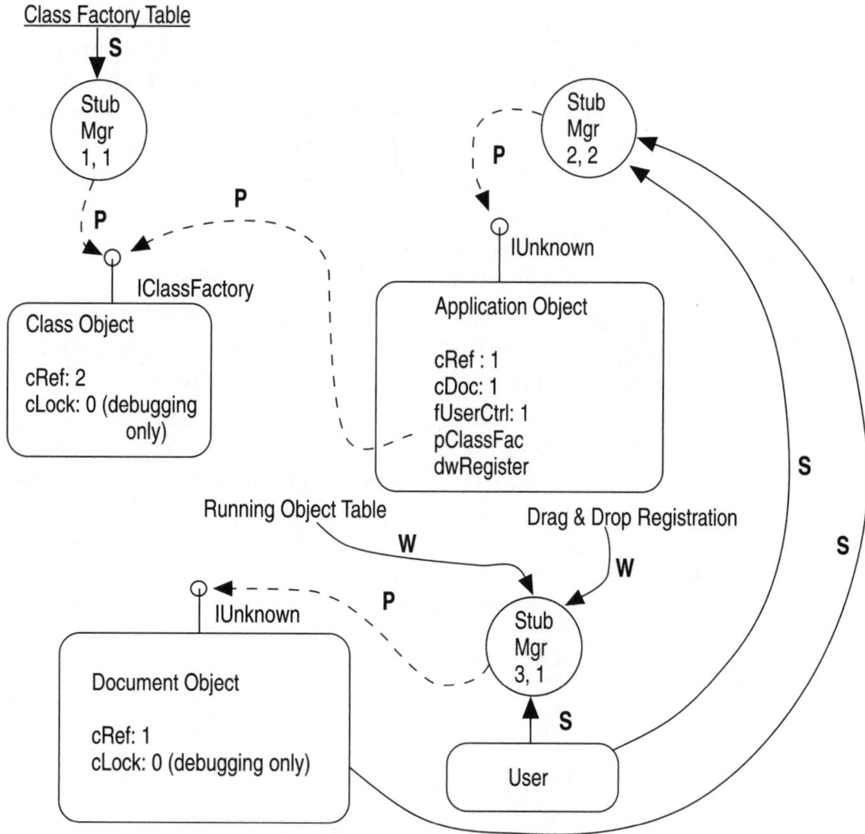

Figure 2-15. MDI object application shutdown initiated by user choosing File Exit command.

As shown in Figure 2-15, the application object's reference count is one, which reflects the reference on behalf of the stub manager. The document object also has a reference count of one on behalf of the user opening the document. (If a data transfer object had been created during a Copy/Paste operation, the clipboard object would also maintain similar reference counts.)

Closing an application with the File Exit command starts a sequence of shutdown events beginning with the application object. Upon receiving the WM_CLOSE command, the application object begins shutdown by first closing the open document. After the document has been saved, the document's moniker is revoked from the running object table, the document window is hidden, the document is unregistered as a drag and drop target, and control of the document is taken away from the user from the user. These acts cause the document object's reference counter to be decremented to zero. Only when the reference count goes to zero, can the document be safely destroyed.

After destroying the document object, the application object's reference count maintained on behalf of the document object is released, leaving the object application in the state shown in Figure 2-16.

Note The scenario described around Figure 2-16 reflects an MDI object application with one open document; it is possible there could have been multiple document objects to close. Each open document in an MDI application would have been reflected in the application object's application and document reference counts.

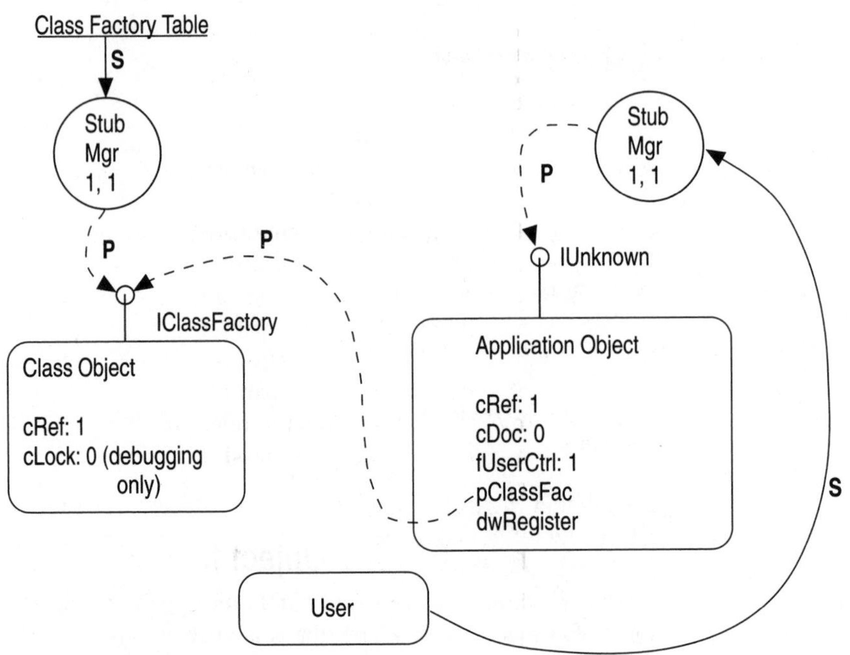

Figure 2-16. MDI object application after closing open document.

After all documents have been closed, the application object removes control of the application from the user and hides the application frame window. Figure 2-17 shows the state of the application immediately after control of the application is removed from the user.

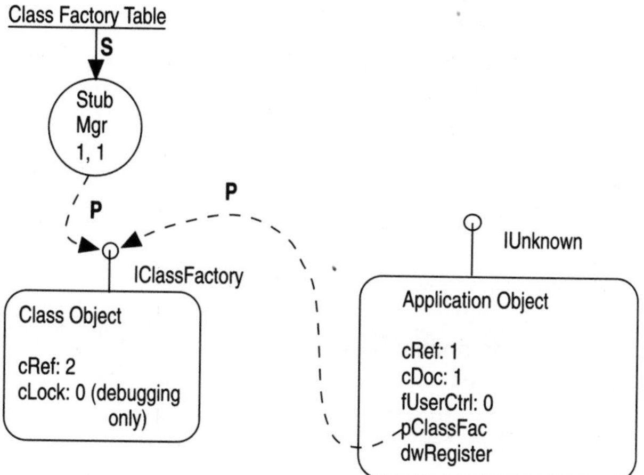

Figure 2-17. Object application after removing user control.

After calling **CoLockObjectExternal** (*pApp*, FALSE, TRUE) to remove control from the user, the application object's reference count is generally zero. When this count reaches zero, the application calls its destructor routine. Because **CoLockObjectExternal** was called with *fLastUnlockReleases* set to TRUE, the application object is freed when control is removed from the user and there are no outstanding external references. As part of its destructor routine, the application should call **CoRevokeClassObject** to release the class object from the class factory table and then release the **IClassFactory** interface pointer. This destroys the **IClassFactory** object.

Closing an Embedded Object from its Container

Figure 2-18 shows the state of an SDI object application started to service an embedded object. Because the object is visible, the user controls the lifetime of the running embedded object but not the application itself. The embedded object, in turn, holds the application alive.

Application shutdown is forced by the object's container calling **IOleObject::Close** on the loaded object. (If the embedding container were to simply release the object, the application would not necessarily shutdown.)

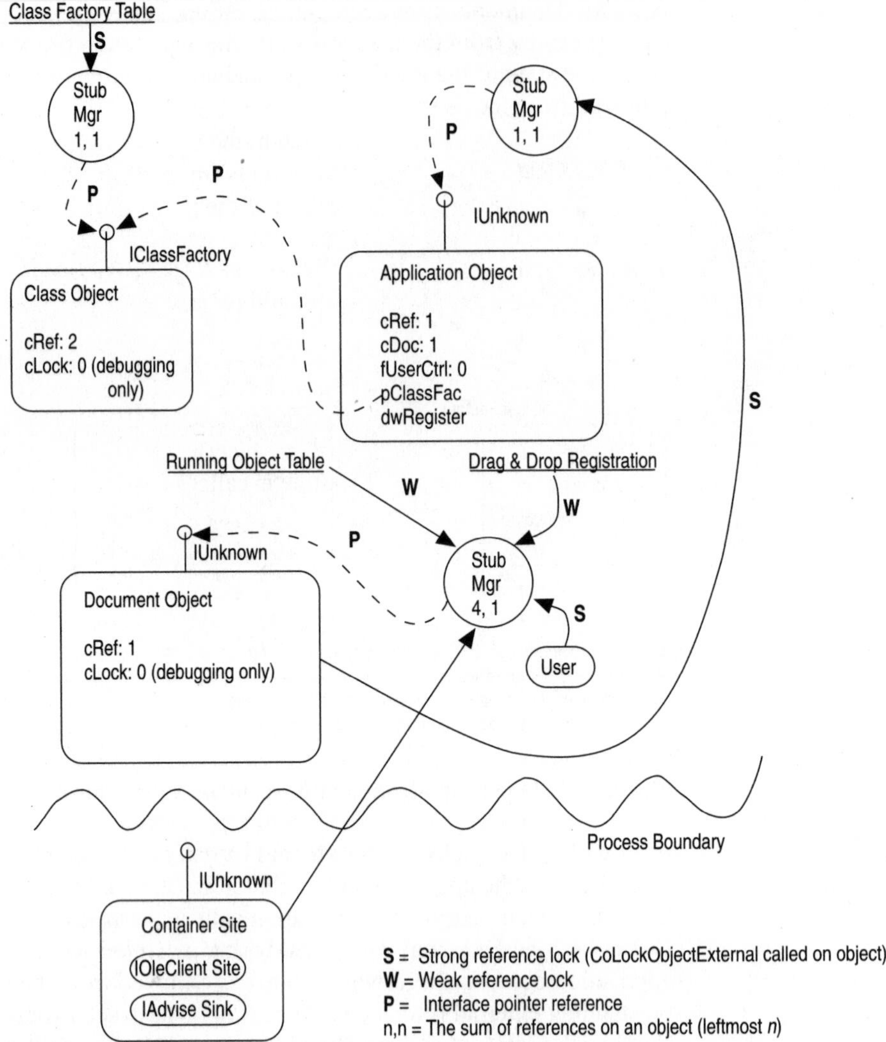

Figure 2-18. SDI object application at the time the object's container called IOleObject::Close.

As shown, the document object has a *cRef* of one on behalf of the document being visible to the user. The application object has a *cRef* of one on behalf of the open document. Because the user is not in control of the application or document, the *fUserCtrl* flag is FALSE on the application object.

The embedding container initiates shutdown by calling the **IOleObject::Close** method on the running OLE object. Closing begins with the open document object instead of with the application object as is done when the user explicitly initiates shutdown by using the File Exit command.

As part of closing, the document object closes all open pseudo and embedded objects before revoking the document's registered moniker from the running object table. Only when all external connections are disconnected does the document object receive its final release. To release the reference, the document object sends an OnClose notification to the container, telling it the document is being closed. The OnClose notification is first received by the object handler in the container's process. Upon receipt of the notification, the handler disconnects its LRPC connection to the running object application document, and then forwards the notification on to advisory sink in the container. On receiving the OnClose advisory, the container should revert the OLE object's **IStorage** to flush any uncommitted changes.

In conjunction with sending the OnClose notification, the document object calls **CoDisconnectObject** to forcefully disconnect any existing external connections to the document. Once the document object's reference count goes to zero, the document object's destructor routine is called and the document is destroyed.

Note Because any changes made to the open document would have already been saved by the time of sending the OnClose notification, an object application can safely call the **CoDisconnectObject** function to release all references to the object.

After the document object has been destroyed, the application object's *cDoc* reference count maintained on behalf of the document object is released. If this was the only open document and the user was not in control of the application, the application would have one *cRef* reference count remaining on behalf of the registered class object. To release its class object, the object application calls the **CoRevokeClassObject** function as part of calling its destructor routine.

MDI Object Application Considerations

If the user creates a new untitled document or opens a file-based document in an MDI application started to service a linked or embedded object, the application object sets its *fUserCtrl* flag to TRUE. On a shutdown initiated by the container application calling **IOleObject::Close**, the loaded OLE object would first be closed. After the document object's destructor routine is called, control of the shutdown process is passed to the application object. This leaves the application in a state similar to that of an application started by the user. Because the user is in control, the application would not shut down until the user chose the File Exit or system Close commands.

Closing Data Transfer Objects

How the data transfer object is destroyed depends on how application shutdown was initiated: by the user choosing the File Exit command or by the container calling **IOleObject::Close** on its loaded object. If the object is being closed by the user, the object is responsible for closing the clipboard data object and flushing it of any data pertaining to the application.

When a container calls **IOleObject::Close** to initiate shutdown on an object application document that is the source for a data transfer object, the object application's document object flushes the clipboard of data pertaining to the document.

To empty the clipboard, an application calls **OleFlushClipboard** if it is desirable to have all hGlobal-based formats and OLE 1 compatibility formats remain on the clipboard. Otherwise, **OleSetClipboard**(NULL) can be called.

Closing OLE Applications

As part of application shutdown, OLE containers and object applications do the following tasks. These tasks are described in the following sections.

- Safeguard the application against premature shutdown by intentionally incrementing the reference count on the application object.
- Close all open documents. For more information on closing open compound document objects, see "Closing OLE Compound Documents," earlier in this chapter.
- Flush the clipboard of any data object pertaining to the application. (Object applications usually flush the clipboard when closing the document that is the source of the clipboard data.)
- If the user had control, release the external reference lock on behalf of the user and hide the application frame window.
- To ensure that all references to the application have been freed, call **CoDisconnectObject** on the application object.
- When the reference count on the application object transitions to zero, destroy the application object, freeing all application-specific structures from memory.
- Close the OLE libraries.

Safeguarding the Application Object

On initiating application shutdown, applications should take precautions to ensure they are not exited until all shutdown procedures have been done. To safeguard itself, the application can increment *cRef*, which controls the lifetime of the application. This reference count remains until all other counted references to the application object have been released. Only after all other references have been released, does the application release the reference count.

Hiding the Application Frame Window

If the user has control of the application after the document and clipboard data transfer objects have been closed, release user control of the application by calling **CoLockObjectExternal** (*pApp*, FALSE, TRUE) on behalf of the user. After releasing this last external reference on behalf of the user, hide the application frame window from the user for the remainder of the shutdown process.

Upon return from **CoLockObjectExternal**, the application's destructor routine is called. As part of its destructor's routine, the application should revoke the registered class factory object from the class factory table. This is done by calling **CoRevokeClassObject**, passing in the *dwRegister* token returned by **CoRegisterClassObject**.

Closing OLE Libraries

After the application has exited its main **GetMessage** loop, the final step in the shutdown process is to close the OLE libraries initialized at program startup.

To close the libraries, an application calls the **OleUninitialize** function. This function *must* be the last call made to the libraries on behalf of the application.

To guard against **OleUninitialize** being called if **OleInitialize** was never called, applications can set a flag as part of initializing the libraries. Before calling **OleUninitialize**, the application checks the flag to ensure that the libraries were properly initialized.

Converting Mapping Modes

In Microsoft Windows, mapping modes define how numbers relating to object sizes are to be passed and interpreted. OLE uses only one mapping mode, which is HIMETRIC. The other mapping modes include ENGLISH, METRIC, TWIPS, and PIXELS (with ISOTROPIC and ANISOTROPIC being PIXEL modes). When working with the visual presentation of OLE data, it is important to be aware of the mapping mode that OLE uses and how this mapping mode affects an application.

The mapping modes communicate physical sizes. For example, if an application using HIMETRIC is to display a line ten centimeters long, the number of units would be 10,000. However, the line drawn on the screen would be ten centimeters long, regardless of the size of the video display area. The printed output would also be a line ten centimeters long.

Note For those applications that use a mapping mode other than HIMETRIC, the sample user interface library provides some functions that can be used to convert objects to and from HIMETRIC units.

Because people read display screens from a greater distance than they do printed copy, most applications written for Microsoft Windows display text in a larger size than they print it, using what is commonly referred to as *logical resolution.* For example, a ten-point font is easy enough to read on the printed page, but generally appears too small on a screen for comfortable reading. To afford more comfortable viewing, applications typically expand the size of the displayed text to some logical size. Using this approach, a column of text that is physically six inches wide might be eight inches wide on the screen, yet still print as a six-inch column.

While this display enlargement scheme works well from the user's point of view, a problem can occur when pasting objects into container documents. It is possible to lose the correct size ratio between the pasted object and the text owned and displayed by the container. The result is that the container's text is scaled up for readability but the pasted object might not be. Consequently, applications must preserve the relative size and position of text and objects, meaning that if text uses logical resolution, it should scale objects accordingly.

In the examples shown in Figure 2-19, a chart object has been pasted from a source application that uses physical size into documents of two different containers that use logical resolution for display of the text. The container displaying the object on the left has scaled up the chart object to the logical size of the adjacent text to maintain the object/text size ratio.

That is, it has been enlarged from its physical size by an amount that maintains its proportion to the text of the container document. In the document on the right, the application displays the chart object at its physical size, with no scaling to logical resolution for display. Both documents print with the correct object-to-text-size ratio.

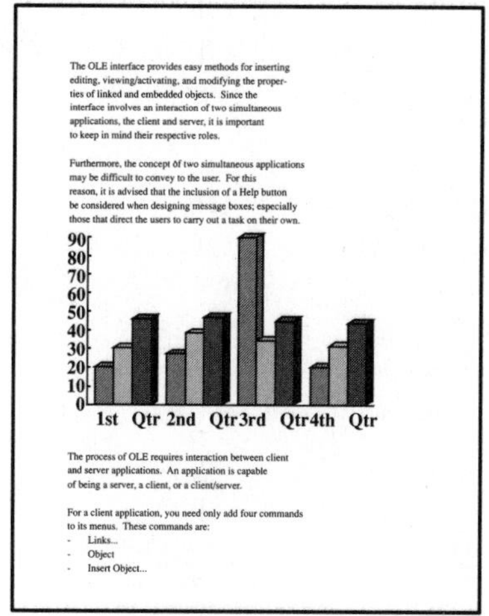

USING LOGICAL RESOLUTION

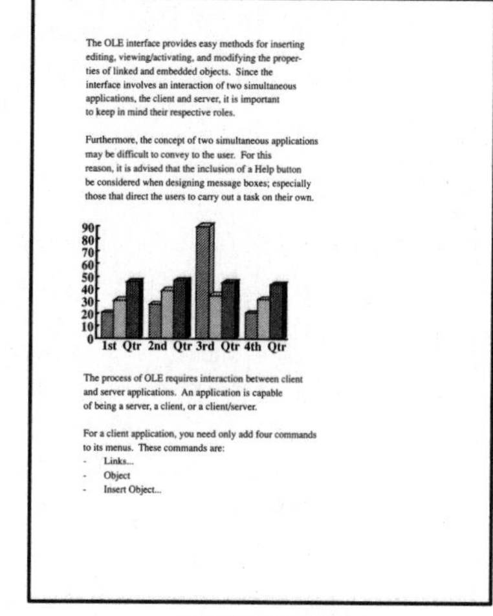

USING PHYSICAL SIZE

Figure 2-19. Object sized in logical and physical resolution.

In OLE, the units for specifying the size of drawn objects is HIMETRIC, which means object sizes are in physical units. However, containers need not use the MM_HIMETRIC mapping mode to draw pasted objects to the display, but should rather map objects to the screen in the same manner as text. That is, if the container application displays text to the screen using a mapping mode that enlarges it, objects should be mapped to the display in the same manner. Using the same mapping mode for both the text and objects is required to establish the correct object-to-text ratio as shown in the document on the left side of Figure 2-23. Because most Windows applications use logical resolution for this type of display mapping, it is suggested that OLE containers also use logical resolution and set up their mapping modes and coordinate transforms accordingly. This allows objects to be moved from one application to another without changing their displayed size.

CHAPTER 3

Registering Object Applications

This chapter describes that portion of the registration database that pertains to the registration of object applications. Information is provided regarding the entry and modification of database keys as well as addressing some OLE 1 compatibility issues.

Your installer/setup program needs to add items to the user's registration database file, REG.DAT, located in the Windows subdirectory if it is to perform any of the three following types of installations:

- Installing an object application.
- Installing a container/object application.
- Installing a container application *that allows linking to its embedded objects.*

In all three cases, you must register OLE 2 library (DLL) information as well as application-specific information.

Note For information about the reading and writing of registration database entries, refer also to "Object Class Conversion and Emulation Functions" in the chapter "Component Object Interfaces and Functions."

Registering Application-Specific Information

To register information about your specific object application in the registration database, it is recommended that you create a *registration entry file* and, during installation or setup, run:

```
REGEDIT.EXE /s YYYY.REG
```

where YYYY.REG is the name of your entry file.

Note For complete information on the registration entry file and how to register your object application by making entries this file, refer to "Creating the Registration Entry File."

Running REGEDIT with a silent switch (**/s**) appends the entries in the registration entry file into REG.DAT on the user's hard disk. At the end of the setup/install operation, use the SHELL.DLL registration APIs (as described in the *Microsoft Windows Programmer's Reference*) to update the entries (server, default icon, local server, InProcServer, InProcHandler) pointing to the location where you installed your application/handlers on the user's hard disk.

Layout of the Registration Database File

Syntax

Keys in the registration database file (REG.DAT) are case insensitive, while values in it are case sensitive. The names of the keys are not localized (altered for non-English versions of the application being installed), although user-type names (all forms) and verb names are localized for language considerations.

Commas are used to separate values into individual items. This convention is not localized (just as WIN.INI keys and values are not localized).

Note In the registration database (and also in the registration entry file) the numerical value of the class identifier (CLSID) is *always placed between "curly" braces*, such as in {12345678-9ABC-DEF0-C000-000000000046}. The braces are not shown in the CLSID notations in the following paragraphs, but are implied.

All digits in the CLSID are in uppercase hex notation with no spaces; this format is the same as the OSF DCE standard. (Refer also to "Creating New CLSIDs & IIDs")

In addition, by using **StringFromCLSID** to convert the CLSID into a string of printable characters, different CLSIDs always convert to different strings.

Similarly, IID is a shorthand notation for an interface identifier. As with the CLSID, the required surrounding braces are not shown in the examples. **StringFromIID** can be used to produce an IID string.

Numbers that appear as keys (usually on the left side of an = sign) are always decimal. Numbers on the right side (values) can be either decimal or hex but hex values must be preceded by 0x such as 0xABC123. Negative numbers are always in decimal (for example, -1).

A clipboard format is represented as a number if the format is built into Windows (value < 0xC000) and as a string if it is not. The string is translated into a number by using **RegisterClipboardFormat**. (This number can be converted back into the string using **GetClipboardFormatName**.)

Programmatic Identifiers

Every OLE 2 object class that is to appear in an Insert Object dialog box (hereafter referred to as an "insertable class") must have a programmatic identifier or *ProgID*. This string uniquely identifies a given class. Additionally, the ProgID is the "class name" used for an OLE 2 class when placed in an OLE 1 server (container).

The ProgID string must:

- Have no more than 39 characters.
- Contain no punctuation (including underscore). The only exception is that it may contain one or more periods.
- Not start with a digit.
- Be different from the class name of any OLE 1 application, *including the OLE 1 version of the same application*, if there is one.

Relative to the conversion process, it is important to note that there are two kinds of ProgIDs. One depends on the version of the object application (version dependent) and the other is version independent. The version-dependent ProgID is the string used when OLE 1 is trying to contact OLE 2 by using DDE. Version-dependent ProgID-to-CLSID conversions must be specific, well defined, and one to one.

An example of version-independent ProgID usage is when a container application is to create a chart or table with a toolbar button. In this situation, the application could use the version-independent ProgID to determine the latest version of the needed object application.

The **CLSIDFromProgID** and **ProgIdFromCLSID** functions can be called to convert back and forth between the two representations of the class identifier. These functions use the registration database to perform the conversion.

The ProgID-to-CLSID conversion is done by using the ROOT\<*ProgID*>\CLSID key. The reverse translation is done using the ROOT\CLSID\<*clsid*>\ProgID subkey. This means that the ProgID subkey under ROOT\CLSID\<*clsid*> is version dependent.

The version-independent ProgID is stored and maintained solely by application code. When given the version-independent ProgID, **CLSIDFromProgID** returns the CLSID of the current version. **CLSIDFromProgID** works on the version-independent ProgID because the subkey, CLSID, is the same as for the version-dependent one.

The ProgID must *never* be shown to the user in the user interface. If you need a short human-readable string for an object, call **IOleObject::GetUserType**(USERCLASSTYPE_SHORT, *lpszShortName*).

The ProgID Key and Subkeys

Note In the registration database examples that follow, **boldface** indicates a literal standard key or subkey, *<italics>* indicates an application-supplied string or value, and ***<boldface-italics>*** indicates an application-supplied key or subkey. In the first example, "OLE1ClassName," "OLE1UserTypeName," and "CLSID" are all supplied by the application.

As previously described, OLE 2 classes that belong in the Insert Object dialog box each have a ProgID. The value assigned to this key is the human-readable name that is displayed in the dialog box; it should be the same as the "*MainUserTypeName*" of the class. If this class is insertable in an OLE 2 container, the ProgID key must have an immediate subkey named **Insertable** and it must have no value assigned to it.

Note Because OLE 2 provides a built-in OLE 1/OLE 2 compatibility layer, it will be rare that an OLE 2 class that is insertable in an OLE 2 container will not be insertable in an OLE 1 container.

If a particular class is insertable in an OLE 1 container, the "ProgID" *root* key will contain a **Protocol\StdFileEditing** subkey with appropriate subkeys **Verb**, **Server**, and so on, as in OLE 1. The **Server** that should be registered here is the full pathname to the executable file of the OLE 2 object application. An OLE 1 container uses the path and executable file names to launch the OLE 2 object application. The initialization of this application, in turn, causes the OLE 2 compatibility layer to be loaded. This layer handles subsequent interactions with the OLE 1 client (container), turning them into OLE 2-like requests to the OLE 2 application. An OLE 2 object application need take no special action beyond setting up these registration database entries for its objects to be insertable into an OLE 1 container.

The ProgID key and subkeys appear in the registration database as shown in the following example, where "**<*Progid*>**" is the key, and "**Insertable**," "**Protocol**," "**StdFileEditing**," "**Verb**," and so on are subkeys.)

```
<Progld> = <MainUserTypeName>
Insertable  // class is insertable in OLE 2 containers
Protocol
    StdFileEditing  // OLE 1 compatibility info; present if, and only if, objects of this class are
                    // insertable in OLE 1 containers.
        Server = <full path to the OLE 2 object application>
        Verb
            0 = <verb 0>     // Verb entries for the OLE 2 application must start with zero as the
            1 = <verb 1>     // primary verb and run consecutively.
CLSID = <CLSID>  // The corresponding CLSID. Needed by GetClassFile.
Shell  // Windows 3.1 File Manager Info
    Print
    Open
    Command = <appname.exe> %1
```

To summarize, any root key that has either an **Insertable** or a **Protocol\StdFileEditing** subkey, is the ProgID (or OLE 1 class name) of a class that should appear in the Insert Object dialog box. The value of that root key is the human-readable name displayed in the Insert Object dialog box.

The CLSID Key and Subkeys

Most of the OLE 2 object application information is stored in subkeys under the **CLSID** *root* key (unlike OLE 1 in which all information is kept immediately under the root). As a result, only classes explicitly intended to be user-visible appear when the registration database editor, REGEDIT.EXE, is run in the nonverbose mode. This can be significant for product support purposes.

The immediate subkey of the **CLSID** *root* key is a string version CLSID. Subkeys of this version of the CLSID include indications of where the code that services this class is found. For more information about converting the CLSID, see **StringFromCLSID**. For other related information see LocalServer, InprocServer, and InprocHandler under "CLISD Key Entry."

A major portion of the **CLSID** information is used by the default OLE 2 handler to return various information about the class when it is in the loaded state. Examples of this include the **Verb**, the **AuxUserType**, and the **MiscStatus** entries.

The **Insertable** subkey appears under both this key and the **Progid** key.

```
CLSID

    <CLSID> = <Main User Type Name>
      LocalServer = <path to exe>// local (same machine) server; see "Server =" under ProgID key.
      InprocServer = <path to dll> // in process server; relatively rare for insertable classes.
      InprocHandler = <path to dll>    // in process handler. "OLE2.DLL" for the default OLE 2
    handler
      Verb         // info returned in IOleObject::EnumVerbs().
          verb number = <name, menu flags, verb flags>
      // several examples follow:
               0 = &Edit, 0, 2  // primary verb; often Edit; on menu; possibly dirties object,
                                 // MF_STRING | MF_UNCHECKED | MF_ENABLED == 0.
           1 = &Play, 0, 3  // other verb; appears on menu; leaves object clean
          -3 = Hide, 0, 1   // pseudo verb for hiding window; not on menu, opt.
          -2 = Open, 0, 1   // pseudo verb for opening in sep. window; not on menu, opt.
          -1 = Show, 0, 1   // pseudo verb for showing in preferred state; not on menu, opt.
      AuxUserType   // auxiliary user types (main user type above)
          <form of type> = <string>    // See IOleObject::GetUserType(); for example:
          2 = <ShortName>    // key 1 should not be used
          3 = <Application name>  // Contains the human-readable name of the application. Used
    when
                 // the actual name of the app is needed (for example in
                 // the Paste Special dialog's result field) Example: Acme Draw
      MiscStatus = <default>  // def status used for all aspects; see IOleObject::GetMiscStatus
          <aspect> = <integer>     // exceptions to above;  for example:
              4 = 1           // DVASPECT_ICON = OLEMISC_RECOMPOSEONRESIZE
      DataFormats
          DefaultFile = <format>   // default main file/object format of objects of this class.
          GetSet  // list of formats for default impl. of EnumFormatEtc; very similar
                 // to Request/SetDataFormats in OLE 1 entries
              <n> = <format ,aspect, medium, flag>// in this line,
                 // n  is a zero-based integer index;
                 // format is clipboard format;
                 // aspect is one or more of DVASPECT_*, -1 for "all";
                 // medium is one or more of TYMED_*;
                 // flag is one or more of DATADIR_*.
                 // three examples follow:
              0 = 3, -1, 32, 1          // CF_METAFILE, all aspects, TYMED_MFPICT,
                 // DATADIR_GET
              1 = Biff3, 1, 15, 3      // this example shows
                 // Microsoft Excel's Biff format version 3,
                 // DVASPECT_CONTENT,
                 // TYMED_HGLOBAL | TYMED_FILE |
                 // TYMED_ISTREAM | TYMED_ISTORAGE,
                 // (DATADIR_SET | DATADIR_GET)
              2 = Rich Text Format, 1,1,3
```

```
Insertable  // when present, the class appears in the Insert Object dialog.
            // (not present for internal classes like the moniker classes)
ProgID = <ProgID>        // the programmatic identifier for this class.
TreatAs = <CLSID>        // see CoGetTreatAs()
AutoConvertTo = <CLSID>        // see OleGetAutoConvert()
Conversion              // support for Change Type dialog box
    Readable
        Main = <format,format,format,format, ...>
    Readwritable
        Main = <format,format,format,format, ...>
DefaultIcon = <path to exe, index>   // parameters passed to ExtractIcon
Interfaces = <IID, IID, ...>    // optional. If this key is present, then its values are the
        // totality of the interfaces supported by this class:if the IID is not in this list, then the
        // interface is never supported by an instance of this class.
VersionIndependentProgID = <VersionIndependentProgID>
```

The Version-Independent ProgID Key and Subkeys

The application must register a version-independent programmatic identifier in the "Version-Independent ProgID" *root* key. This key provides a constant name, referred to as the *MainUserTypeName*. It is used with macro languages and refers to the currently installed version of the application's class. The *MainUserTypeName* must correspond to the name of the latest version of the object application.

```
<VersionIndependentProgID> = <MainUserTypeName>
    CLSID = <CLSID>   // the class id of the newest installed version of that class
    CurVer = <ProgID> // the ProgID of the newest installed version of that class
```

In additon to the above entry, you should add the following entry to the the **CLSID** *root* key.

```
CLSID
    <CLSID> = <Main User Type Name>
        VersionIndependentProgID = <VersionIndependentProgID>
```

The File Extension Key

If your OLE 2 application can handle requests from the Windows 3.1 File Manager, create the file extension *root* key shown in the following example of the registration database file.

```
<.ext> = <ProgID>      // used by File Manager and by GetClassFile (and thus File Monikers)
```

The (Non-Compound) FileType Key and Subkeys

Entries under the FileType key are used by the **GetClassFile** function to pattern match against various file bytes in a non-compound file. FileType has *CLSID* subkeys, each of which has a series of subkeys 0, 1, 2, ... whose values contain a pattern that, if matched, should yield the indicated *CLSID*. See also **GetClassFile**.

```
FileType        // used by GetClassFile()
    <CLSID>
        <n> = <offset, cb, mask, value>  // Offset and cb are limited to 16 bits. Offset can
                //be negative for file end.
                // As above, offset and byte count are decimal unless preceded by "0x", in which
                // case they are hex. The mask and the pattern are always hex and cannot be
                // preceded by "0x". Mask can be omitted, implying a value of all ones.
                // An example:
        0 = 0, 4, FFFFFFFF, ABCD1234 // This requires that the first 4 bytes be AB CD
                                     // 12 34, in that order,
        1 = 0, 4, FFFFFFFF, 9876543  // or requires that they match 9876543.
        2 = -4, 4, , FEFEFEFE        // The last four bytes in the file must be FEFEFEFE
```

The New Interface Key and Subkeys

If your application adds a new interface, the Interface key must be completed for OLE 2 to register the new interface. There needs to be one IID subkey for each new interface.

```
Interface
    <IID> = <textual name of interface>  // for example: "IOleObject"
        ProxyStubClsID = <CLSID   >  // Used internally by OLE 2 for interprocess
                // communication.
        NumMethods = <integer>      // Number of methods in the interface.
        BaseInterface = <IID>     // Interface from which this was derived. Absence
            // of key means IUnknown. Key present but empty value means derived
            // from nothing.
```

OLE 1 Compatibility Subkeys

To handle two-way compatibility, the OLE 2 compatibility layer creates OLE 2-style entries for OLE 1 classes it discovers and places them under the CLSID key. When installing an OLE 2 object application on a system that contains an OLE 1 version of the same application, it might be necessary to add "AutoConvertTo" or "TreatAs" subkeys to the *original* OLE 1 application portion of the registration database. For more information, see "When the OLE 1 Version is Overwritten."

```
CLSID
    <CLSID> = <OLE1UserTypeName>  // This is an entry auto-generated by OLE 2 for an OLE 1 class.
        OLE1Class = <OLE 1 class name>  // This entry is created the first time an object of that class
                                        // is inserted in an OLE 2 container.
        ProgId = <OLE 1 class name>  // Allows OLE 2 to convert CLSID back to an OLE 1 class name
```

OLE 1 Application Entries

When an OLE 1 class is inserted into an OLE 2 container for the first time, a new subkey, **CLSID**, is added *to the original OLE 1 registration information* by the OLE 2 compatibility layer. The value given to this key is a CLSID assigned by OLE 2 to this OLE 1 class as shown in the following portion of the registration database file.

```
<OLE1ClassName> = <OLE1UserTypeName>
    Protocol
        StdFileEditing
        Verb
    CLSID = <CLSID>
```

Registration Database Example

The following illustration shows the portion of the registration database, as viewed with REGEDIT, that contains the entries created by the install/setup program for an OLE 2 object application. The entries shown in this example are actually a result of running REGEDIT.EXE with a registration entry file made up of the specific lines described in "Creating the Registration Entry File." For information about running REGEDIT.EXE, refer to "Registering Application-Specific Information."

Note Due to use of REGEDIT, some subkey entries may appear in reverse order after registration.

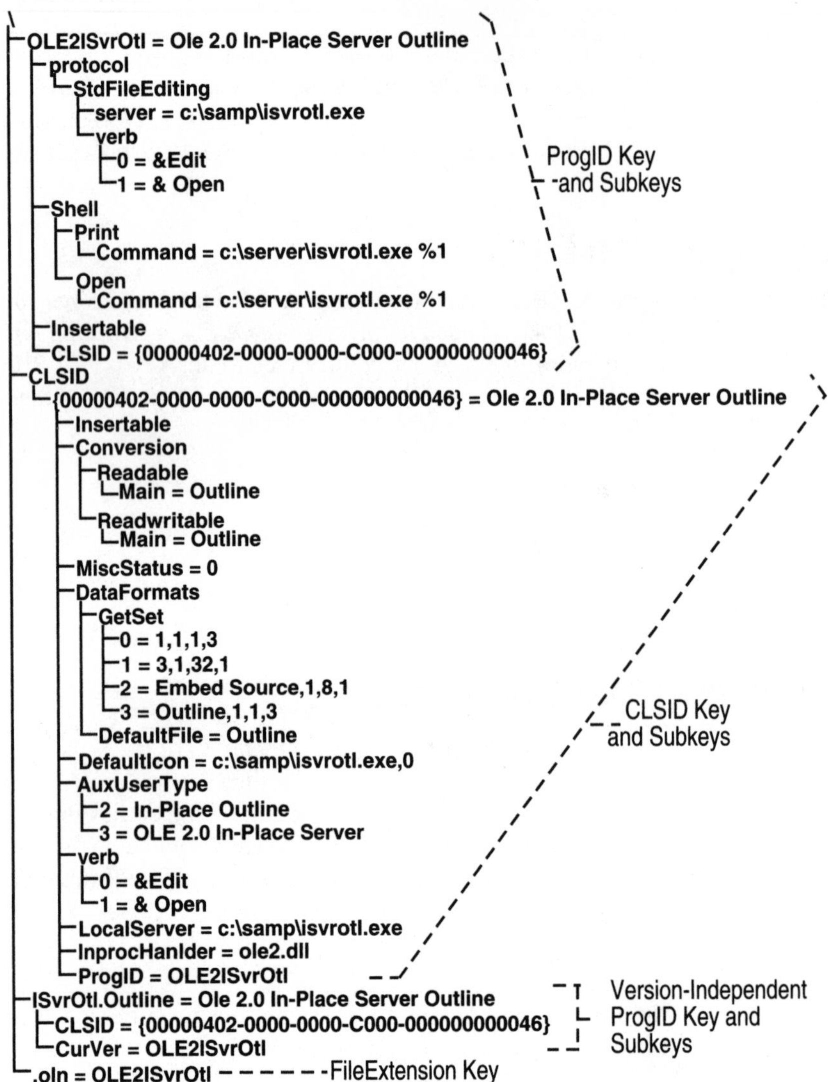

Creating the Registration Entry File

The following paragraphs present examples of the HKEY_CLASSES_ROOT statements that make up the registration entry file. This file is used to modify the registration database file (REG.DAT). For information about running REGEDIT.EXE, refer to "Registering Application-Specific Information."

The registration entry file is a text file containing a single-line entry for each key/value to be stored in the registration database. The key and the value must be separated by an equal sign surrounded by spaces.

At the left side of the equals signs in the examples that follow, the "OLE2ISvrOtl" (ProgID for "Ole 2 In-Place Server Outline" application) should be replaced by the ProgID string that you use for your own application. For information about ProgID construction rules, refer to the "Programmatic Identifiers" section of this chapter. Also, the CLSID used in the examples {00000402-0000-0000-C000-000000000046} should be replaced by the CLSID you use for your application.

ProgID Key Entry

The values of each key in the example below are used for registering the "Ole 2 In-Place Server Outline" sample application. You need to set these values as required and used by your application.

Human-Readable String Subkey Entry

The entry to register the human-readable string (long form), such as that used in The Insert New dialog box, is as follows. The recommended maximum length for the string is 40 characters.

```
HKEY_CLASSES_ROOT\OLE2ISvrOtl = Ole 2 In-Place Server Outline
```

Information for OLE 1 Applications Subkey Entries

To maintain OLE 1.0 compatibility, include the following OLE 1.0 information. The "server" key entry should contain a full path to the application. The entries for verbs must start with 0 as the primary verb and be consecutively numbered.

```
HKEY_CLASSES_ROOT\OLE2ISvrOtl\protocol\StdFileEditing\server =
c:\samp\isvrotl.exe
HKEY_CLASSES_ROOT\OLE2ISvrOtl\protocol\StdFileEditing\verb\0 = &Edit
HKEY_CLASSES_ROOT\OLE2ISvrOtl\protocol\StdFileEditing\verb\1 = &Open
```

Windows 3.1 Shell Subkey Entries

These entries are for Windows 3.1 shell printing and file open usage. They should contain the path/filename of the object application. The examples below contain simple entries only; more complicated ones could include DDE entries.

```
HKEY_CLASSES_ROOT\OLE2ISvrOtl\Shell\Print\Command = c:\svr\isvrotl.exe %1
HKEY_CLASSES_ROOT\OLE2ISvrOtl\Shell\Open\Command = c:\svr\isvrotl.exe %1
```

Insertable Subkey Entry

This entry indicates that the object application should appear in the Insert New... dialog box's list box when used by OLE 2 container applications.

```
HKEY_CLASSES_ROOT\OLE2ISvrOtl\Insertable
```

Entry Point Subkey

This entry points to the application's OLE 2 information in the registration database. To assign a CLSID for your application run the GUIDGEN.EXE found in the \TOOLS directory of the OLE 2 Toolkit.

```
HKEY_CLASSES_ROOT\OLE2ISvrOtl\CLSID = {00000402-0000-0000-C000-000000000046}
```

CLSID Key Entry

CLSID (Object Class ID) Subkey Entry

Use the following statement to create your *CLSID* subkey under the **CLSID** key in the registration database. To obtain a CLSID for your application, run the GUIDGEN.EXE found in the \TOOLS directory of the OLE 2 Toolkit.

```
HKEY_CLASSES_ROOT\CLSID\{00000402-0000-0000-C000-000000000046} = Ole 2 In-Place Server Outline
```

Note The subkey entries described in this "CLSID Key Entry" section are subkeys to your CLSID subkey. (Not all possible subkeys are described.)

LocalServer Subkey Entry

This subkey designates where the application is located. The LocalServer subkey has the same value as the "OLE2ISvrOtl\protocol\StdFileEditing\server" key and should contain a full path name. The entry can contain command line arguments. Note that OLE 2 appends the "-Embedding" flag to the string, so the application that uses flags will need to parse the whole string and check for the -Embedding flag.

```
HKEY_CLASSES_ROOT\CLSID\{00000402-0000-0000-C000-000000000046}\LocalServer = c:\samp\isvrotl.exe
```

InprocHandler Subkey Entry

This subkey designates whether the application uses a custom handler. If no custom handler used, the entry should be set the database to OLE2.DLL as shown in the following example.

```
HKEY_CLASSES_ROOT\CLSID\{00000402-0000-0000-C000-000000000046}\InprocHandler = ole2.dll
```

Verb Subkey Entry

The verbs to be registered for the application must be numbered consecutively. The first value after the verb string describes how the verb is appended by AppendMenu API call. See the *Windows 3.1 SDK* documentation for details.

The second value indicates whether the verb will dirty the object. It also indicates whether the verb should appear in the menu (as defined by OLEVERBATTRIB_). For more information, see the **IOleObject::EnumVerbs** method.

Verb 0: "Edit", MF_UNCHECKED | MF_ENABLED, no OLEVERATTRIB flags

```
HKEY_CLASSES_ROOT\CLSID\{00000402-0000-0000-C000-000000000046}\Verb\0 = &Edit,0,0
```

Verb 1: "Open", MF_UNCHECKED | MF_ENABLED, no OLEVERATTRIB flags

```
HKEY_CLASSES_ROOT\CLSID\{00000402-0000-0000-C000-000000000046}\Verb\1 = &Open,0,0
```

AuxUserType Subkey Entry

This key describes the short and actual human-readable names of the application. See also **IOleObject::GetUserType**. The short name is used in the menus, including pop ups, and the recommended maximum length for the string is 15 characters. A short name example follows.

```
HKEY_CLASSES_ROOT\CLSID\{00000402-0000-0000-C000-000000000046}\AuxUserType\2 = In-Place Outline
```

The long human-readable name of the application is used in the Results field of the Paste Special dialog box. This string should contain the actual name of the application (such as "Acme Draw 2.0").

```
HKEY_CLASSES_ROOT\CLSID\{00000402-0000-0000-C000-000000000046}\AuxUserType\3 = Ole 2 In-Place Server
```

MiscStatus Subkey Entry

Use the following statement to set the MiscStatus subkey. Refer to the **IOleObject::GetMiscStatus** method description for information on the different settings.

```
HKEY_CLASSES_ROOT\CLSID\{00000402-0000-0000-C000-000000000046}\MiscStatus = 0
```

DataFormats Subkey Entry

The DataFormats subkey lists the default and main data formats supported by the application. This entry is used by the **IDataObject::GetData**, **IDataObject::SetData** and **IDataObject::EnumFormatEtc** methods.

The values defined in the following example entry are CF_TEXT, DVASPECT_CONTENT, TYMED_HGLOBAL, and DATADIR_GET | DATADIR_SET.
See "Layout of the Registration Database File" for other examples.

```
HKEY_CLASSES_ROOT\CLSID\{00000402-0000-0000-C000-000000000046}\DataFormats\GetSet\0 = 1,1,1,3
```

The values defined in the following entry are: CF_METAFILEPICT DVASPECT_CONTENT, TYMED_MFPICT, DATADIR_GET.

```
HKEY_CLASSES_ROOT\CLSID\{00000402-0000-0000-C000-000000000046}\DataFormats\GetSet\1 = 3,1,32,1
```

The values defined in the following entry are: 2 = cfEmbedSource, DVASPECT_CONTENT, TYMED_ISTORAGE, and DATADIR_GET.

```
HKEY_CLASSES_ROOT\CLSID\{00000402-0000-0000-C000-000000000046}\DataFormats\GetSet\2 = Embed Source,1,8,1
```

The values defined in the following entry are: 3 = cfOutline, DVASPECT_CONTENT, TYMED_HGLOBAL, and DATADIR_GET | DATADIR_SET

```
HKEY_CLASSES_ROOT\CLSID\{00000402-0000-0000-C000-000000000046}\DataFormats\GetSet\3 = Outline,1,1,3
```

The following example entry declares the default File Format supported by this application to be CF_OUTLINE

```
HKEY_CLASSES_ROOT\CLSID\{00000402-0000-0000-C000-000000000046}\DataFormats\DefaultFile = Outline
```

Insertable Subkey Entry

The Insertable entry indicates that this application should appear in the Insert New... dialog box's list box when used by OLE 2 container applications. Note that this is a duplicate entry of the one above but is required for future use.

```
HKEY_CLASSES_ROOT\CLSID\{00000402-0000-0000-C000-000000000046}\Insertable
```

ProgID Subkey Entry

Every insertable object class has a "programmatic identifier" or ProgID. For information on the creation and syntax of programmatic identifiers, see "Programmatic Identifiers" earlier in this chapter.

```
HKEY_CLASSES_ROOT\CLSID\{00000402-0000-0000-C000-000000000046}\ProgID = OLE2ISvrOtl
```

Conversion Subkey Entry

Conversion information is used by the Convert dialog box to determine what formats the application can read and write. The comma-delimited file formats are indicated by a number if it is one of the predefined clipboard formats defined in WINDOWS.H. A string is used for indicating when the format is not one defined in WINDOWS.H (private). Note that in this case the readable and writeable format is CF_OUTLINE (private).

An entry to register a file format that the application can read (convert from) is shown below.

```
HKEY_CLASSES_ROOT\CLSID\{00000402-0000-0000-C000-000000000046}\Conversion\Readable\Main = Outline,1
```

An entry to register a file format that the application can read and write (activate as) is shown below.

```
HKEY_CLASSES_ROOT\CLSID\{00000402-0000-0000-C000-000000000046}\Conversion\Readwritable\Main = Outline,1
```

DefaultIcon Subkey Entry

The DefaultIcon subkey provides default icon information for iconic presentations of objects. This entry contains the full path to the executable name of the object application and the index of the icon within the executable. Applications can use this information to obtain an icon handle with **ExtractIcon**.

```
HKEY_CLASSES_ROOT\CLSID\{00000402-0000-0000-C000-000000000046}\DefaultIcon = c:\samp\isvrotl.exe,0
```

Version-Independent ProgID Key Entry

The ProgID key describes the version-independent programmatic ID used for this class (for more information, see "Programmatic Identifiers"). The following example statements show that "Ole 2 In-Place Server Outline" is the version-independent ProgID for the CLSID {0000402-0000-0000-C000-000000000046}.

```
HKEY_CLASSES_ROOT\ISvrOtl.Outline = Ole 2 In-Place Server Outline
HKEY_CLASSES_ROOT\ISvrOtl.Outline\CLSID = {0000402-0000-0000-C000-000000000046}
HKEY_CLASSES_ROOT\ISvrOtl.Outline\CurVer = OLE2ISvrOtl
```

File Extension Key Entry

The file extension key registers the file extension of the file created by your application. The value of the key is the application's ProgID, which in this case is "OLE2ISvrOtl."

```
HKEY_CLASSES_ROOT\.oln = OLE2ISvrOtl
```

Registering OLE 2 Libraries

The OLE 2 libraries require that many internal interfaces be registered in the registration database. Therefore, if your installation program installs the OLE 2 libraries on a machine that does not have them already, it should register OLE 2 specific information by running

```
REGEDIT.EXE /S OLE2.REG
```

to register the OLE 2 internal interfaces in the REG.DAT file.

Also, if your installation/setup program has overwritten older versions of the application on the user's hard drive, run the `REGEDIT.EXE /S OLE2.REG` entry mentioned above.

If your installation program does not install OLE 2 libraries because it found more recent libraries on the user's drive, it should not register the OLE 2 interface information.

Note When checking the version stamp (using VER.DLL) on existing OLE 2 libraries to determine whether or not to replace them on the user's hard drive, do so on a file-by-file basis.

Accommodating OLE 1 Versions of the Object Application

Whenever the OLE 1 version of an object application is superseded by an OLE 2 version and the OLE 2 version is to be installed in the user's system, such as when upgrading, two basic situations can arise:

- An OLE 1 version of the application is present on the user's system and the installation process overwrites the OLE 1 executable with the OLE 2 version.
- An OLE 1 version of the application is present on the user's system and the user chooses not to overwrite it with the OLE 2 version.

Note Even if the OLE 1 object application is not present on the user's system, it is recommended that the install/setup program for the OLE 2 object application register the application as being able to service its OLE 1 objects. To do this, follow the guidelines presented under "When the OLE 1 Version is Overwritten," plus, add the following entry to the *root* of the registration database:

<OLE 1 class name>/CLSID = *<CLSID of OLE 1 application>*

When the OLE 1 Version is Overwritten

When the OLE 1 object application is replaced by the OLE 2 version, do the following to the registration database (REG.DAT). (For the purpose of illustration, the OLE 1 object application is referred to as Ole 1 In-Place Server Outline while the OLE 2 version is Ole 2 In-Place Server Outline, as shown in the dialog box illustrations that follow).

1. Register Ole 2 In-Place Server Outline in the REG.DAT file as previously described.
2. Modify (with your install/setup program) the *original* registration database entries of Ole 1 In-Place Server Outline by changing the executable path to point to the Ole 2 In-Place Server Outline executable.

For example, the Server subkey for the OLE 1 executable, named **svrapp.exe** in this example, changes from

OLE1ISvrOtl\Protocol\StdFileEditing\Server = svrapp.exe

to

OLE1ISvrOtl\Protocol\StdFileEditing\Server = isvrotl.exe where **isvrotl.exe** is the name of the OLE 2 object application.

Note The following steps, 3 and 4, are mutually exclusive.

---

3. If there is to be automatic conversion of Ole 1 In-Place Server Outline objects to the Ole 2 In-Place Server Outline format when saved, create or modify the following registration database entries:
   a. Modify the *original registration database entry* of Ole 1 In-Place Server Outline by changing the "Value of the ProgID = Main User Type Name" key of the registration database to Ole 2 In-Place Server Outline.

      For example, where **OLE1ISvrOtl** is the ProgID of the OLE 1 application,

      OLE1ISvrOtl = Ole 1 In-Place Server Outline

      becomes

      OLE1ISvrOtl = Ole 2 In-Place Server Outline
   b. Set the "AutoConvertTo = CLSID" subkey entry for Ole 1 In-Place Server Outline *under the CLSID key* (not under the original OLE 1 entries at the root of the registration database) to the CLSID of Ole 2 In-Place Server Outline. (See also "OLE 1 Compatibility Entries"

      CLSID\{CLSID of OLE 1 app.}**AutoConvertTo** = {CLSID of OLE 2 app.}

Note You can obtain the CLSID of the OLE 1 object application for inclusion in registration entry file by calling **CLSIDFromProgID**.

---

c. Modify the *original registration database entry* of Ole 1 In-Place Server Outline by setting the verbs to those of Ole 2 In-Place Server Outline.

For example, change

OLE1ISvrOtl\Protocol\StdFileEditing\Verb\0 = &Edit

to

OLE1ISvrOtl\Protocol\StdFileEditing\Verb\0 = &Edit

OLE1ISvrOtl\Protocol\StdFileEditing\Verb\1 = &Open

4. If the user is allowed to open Acme Draw 1.0 objects and save them back to disk in the Acme Draw 1.0 format:

a. set the "TreatAs = CLSID" entry to the CLSID of Ole 2 In-Place Server Outline using the following form.

CLSID\{CLSID of OLE 1 app.}**TreatAs** = {CLSID of OLE 2 app.}

b. Set the Ole 1 In-Place Server Outline verbs to those of Ole 2 In-Place Server Outline as described in the preceding step 3.

When the OLE 1 Version is Not Overwritten

When the OLE 1 object application (Ole 1 In-Place Server Outline) is *not* replaced by the OLE 2 version (Ole 2 In-Place Server Outline), but the user is allowed to open Ole 1 In-Place Server Outline objects with Ole 2 In-Place Server Outline and save them back to disk in the Ole 1 In-Place Server Outline format, set the "TreatAs = CLSID" entry (Ole 1 In-Place Server Outline's portion of the registration database) to the CLSID of Ole 2 In-Place Server Outline (as in step 4 above).

If the OLE 1 version of the application is not overwritten, or if the user does not want to set the "Treat As" option, register the OLE 2 version as a separate and new application.

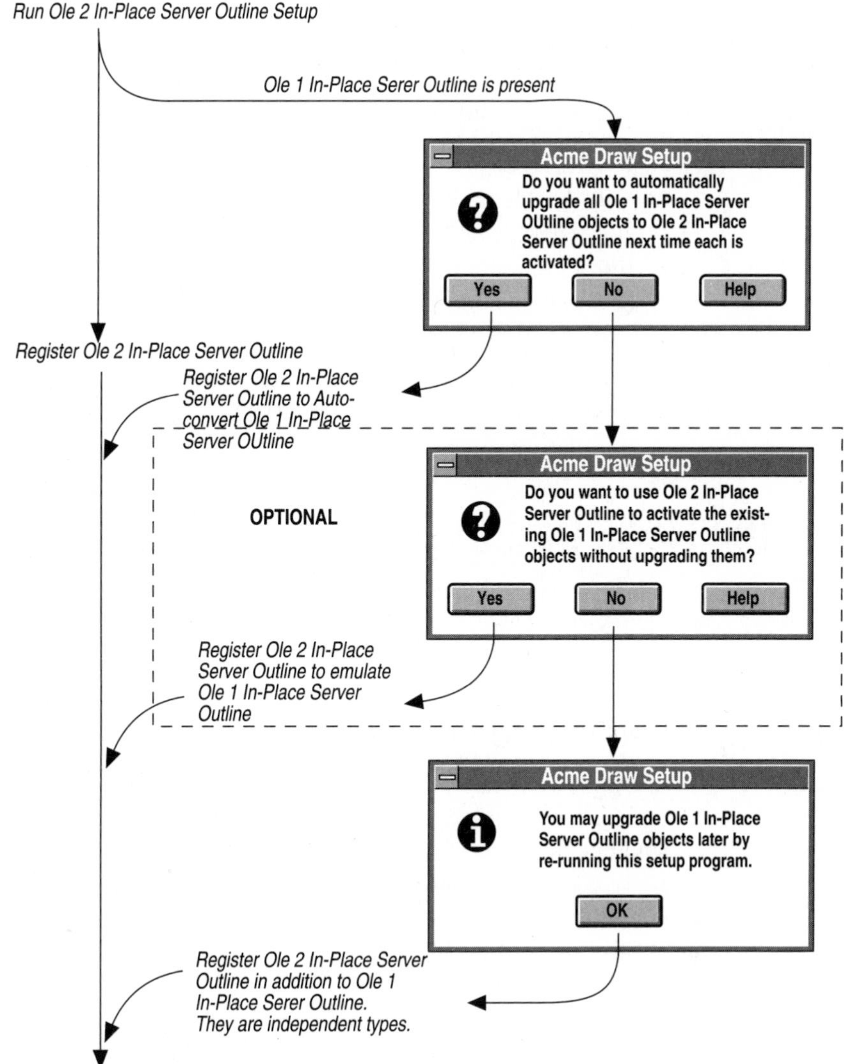
Run Ole 2 In-Place Server Outline Setup
Ole 1 In-Place Serer Outline is present
Acme Draw Setup
Do you want to automatically upgrade all Ole 1 In-Place Server OUtline objects to Ole 2 In-Place Server Outline next time each is activated?
Yes
No
Help
Register Ole 2 In-Place Server Outline
Register Ole 2 In-Place Server Outline to Auto-convert Ole 1 In-Place Server OUtline
OPTIONAL
Acme Draw Setup
Do you want to use Ole 2 In-Place Server Outline to activate the existing Ole 1 In-Place Server Outline objects without upgrading them?
Yes
No
Help
Register Ole 2 In-Place Server Outline to emulate Ole 1 In-Place Server Outline
Acme Draw Setup
You may upgrade Ole 1 In-Place Server Outline objects later by re-running this setup program.
OK
Register Ole 2 In-Place Server Outline in addition to Ole 1 In-Place Serer Outline. They are independent types.

Figure 3-1. Installing a new version of a server application.

Checking Registration During Runtime

The application should check its registration at the application load time, noting three particular issues:

- If the CLSID(s) that the application services are not present in REG.DAT, the application should register as it does during the original setup.
- If the application's CLSID is present, but has no OLE 2-related information in it, the application should register as it does during the original setup.
- If the path containing server entries (LocalServer, InprocServer, DefaultIcon entries) do not point to the location in which the application is currently installed, the application should rewrite the path entries to point to its current location.

Using the Registration Database for Localization

It is possible to address a pair of product-localization issues by inserting a key in the registration database. This key, described below, allows functions to return a specified string instead of a default value or "Unknown."

Specifying Unregistered Verbs

It is possible to have OLE 1 object applications (servers) registered in the registration database with no specified verbs. In such cases, the application has a single implied verb that is understood to be "edit" by OLE 1 containers. When an OLE 2 application calls **IOleObject::EnumVerbs** (or **OleRegEnumVerbs**) on an object of this class, one verb is enumerated. By default, the name of the verb is "Edit." To avoid having the string "Edit" as the enumerated verb, a key can be included in the registration database. This key is

\Software\Microsoft\OLE1\UnregisteredVerb = <*verbname*>

(where *verbname* is the value that will be returned from the enumeration) and allows for localization of the default verb to a specified string to accommodate a specific language.

Note Do not attempt to register a verb (under ProgID\Protocol\StdFileEditing) for an application that did not register the verb itself.

Specifying Unknown User Types

The OLE 2 default handler's implementation of **IOleObject::GetUserType** first examines the registration database by calling **OleRegGetUserType**.. If the object's class is not found in the database, the User Type from the object's **IStorage** is returned. If the class is not found in the object's IStorage, the string "Unknown" is returned. By inserting the

\Software\Microsoft\OLE2\UnknownUserType = *<usertype>*

key in the registration database, **IOleObject::GetUserType** returns the value of the string specified by *<usertype>*. This string can be localized for a different language user-type name, instead of using the "Unknown" string, for the User Type.

CHAPTER 4

User Interface Guidelines

To benefit fully from OLE's integrated nature, it is necessary to understand and subscribe to a common user model, even though it is physically possible for OLE objects and containers to implement any user interface supported by the OLE protocol. This chapter specifies and illustrates the user model and explains the user interface implementation guidelines for OLE. The goals of the OLE user interface include the following:

- To express a unified model of compound document composition and interaction that allows users to efficiently accomplish tasks.
- To fully exploit the integration power of OLE 2 using current user-interface frameworks and mechanisms.
- To establish a sound user model of compound documents that meets current application needs and that gracefully leads to more data-centric systems in the future.

Note In general, the concepts in this chapter are a superset of the principles set forth for the implementation of OLE 1. However, there are some major differences in the capabilities of OLE 1 and OLE 2. One of the most crucial is the ability of the OLE 2 user interface to perform in-place activation, sometimes referred to as visual editing. Whereas OLE 1 required an object to be edited in its original application window, OLE 2 enables the user to activate and manipulate an object from within the document containing it. OLE 2 makes this possible by presenting an object's commands and tools within the container document's window. As a result, the conceptual model of containment is no longer compromised by the need to remove objects from the document for editing.

In-place activation is the typical way to manipulate objects in OLE 2, although the user may still edit in a separate window. Therefore, OLE 2 objects usually set some kind of in-place activation as their primary action (or verb), but may also provide the option to open separately, as required by OLE 1 objects.

Simply put, a user creates and manipulates various types of information (objects) that reside in a containing document. As a user focuses on a particular object, its corresponding commands and tools become available, allowing the user to interact with the object directly from within the document (in-place activation). Objects may be transferred within and across documents and still retain their full-featured editing and operating capabilities. In addition, information may be connected so that changes in one object are automatically be reflected in another (linking).

Object Type

An OLE object, as portrayed to the user, is a unit of information that resides in a document and whose behavior is constant no matter where it is located. The object's intrinsic behavior is defined by the object itself rather than being determined by the document that holds it. The user may interact with an object as a whole (by using OLE verbs and container commands), or with its contents (by engaging its proper tools such as those provided by its object application). Objects may be nested arbitrarily within other objects; objects may be moved, copied, or linked from one location to another.

An object's type is the human-readable form of its class and conveys the object's behavior or capability to the user in dialog boxes and menu commands throughout the OLE 2 interface. **CorelDRAW! 3.0 Drawing** would be a typical example. The object's type is not meant to imply its storage format. Two different object types may use the same storage format (such as **.bmp** or **.rtf** file formats), but their types are distinct if they are handled by different object applications. An object's type is expressed as a string (maximum of 40 characters) in one of the three recommended forms below:

- *<brandname> <application>* [*<version>*] *<data type>*
  for example, **Ami Pro 2.0 Document**.
- *<brandname-application>* [*<version>*] *<data type>*, for cases when the brandname and application are the same
  for example, **WordPerfect Text**.
- *<brandname> <application>* [*<version>*], for cases where the application sufficiently describes the item
  for example, **Microsoft Graph 3.0**.

As shown in the following list, the four components of the type name convey wide range of useful information to the user:

- *<brandname>*: communicates product identity and differentiation.
- *<application>*: indicates which object application is responsible for activating the object.
- *<data type>*: suggests the basic nature or category of the object (such as drawing, spreadsheet, or sound) and should be a maximum of 15 characters.
- *<version>*: when there are multiple versions of the same basic type, a version number is necessary to distinguish types for purposes of upgrading.

These object type names provide users with a precise language for referring to objects. Because object type names appear throughout the OLE interface, users become conscious of an object's type and its associated behavior. The full type name (also referred to as *<descriptive type name>* in the Status Bar Messages at the end of this chapter) should be used in dialogs, messages, and status lines.

Because of the restrictions on the length of type names, only their *<data type>* should be used in menus (both pull-down and pop-up), title bars, and in the list pane of the Links dialog box. The data type is considered to be the short form of the full type name (referred to as *<shortform>* in the "Status Bar Messages"). If a short form name is not available for an object (because it is an OLE 1 object or the string was simply not registered), the full type name should be used instead. For example, an **Ami Pro 2.0 Document** is referred to simply as a "Document" in menus, title bars, and in the list pane of the Links dialog. All dialogs that display the full type name must allocate enough space for 40 characters in width. Likewise, dialog boxes must accommodate 15 characters when using the short-form name.

Class Registration

An object type is also called an object class, particularly as it relates to the registration database. When an object class is registered, such as during the installation of the object application that supports its class, the installation program should first determine whether a previous version of the same class already exists in the registration database (REG.DAT) file. If a previous version does exist, the user has the option of upgrading all older version objects to the new version automatically the next time each is activated. If a previous version is not detected, the new version is simply registered without prompting the user.

Note Refer also the chapter that describes "Registering Object Applications" for more information.

When appropriate, a message should point out any important differences between object versions to help the user decide whether or not to upgrade. If the user elects to upgrade all of the older objects, the older version is replaced by the newer one in the registration database. From that point on, previous version objects activate with the new version of the application and are saved in its format.

Optionally, the new object application can offer to emulate the older version's objects without actually converting them to the new format. This enables a user to use the features of the new object application while maintaining the object in its old format for as long as possible. However, if the user makes use of a particular feature of the new object application that cannot be accommodated by the old type's format, the user should be prompted with the option of abandoning such edits and staying within the old format or keeping the edits and accepting the necessary conversion to the new format. If the user specifies no upgrading or emulating, the new object application is registered in addition to the old one, and the two are considered to be completely independent types. The user may rerun the installation program any time later to respecify version-upgrading options.

Figure 4-1 illustrates the decision tree and recommended dialog boxes for installation of an object application named **Acme Draw 2.0**.

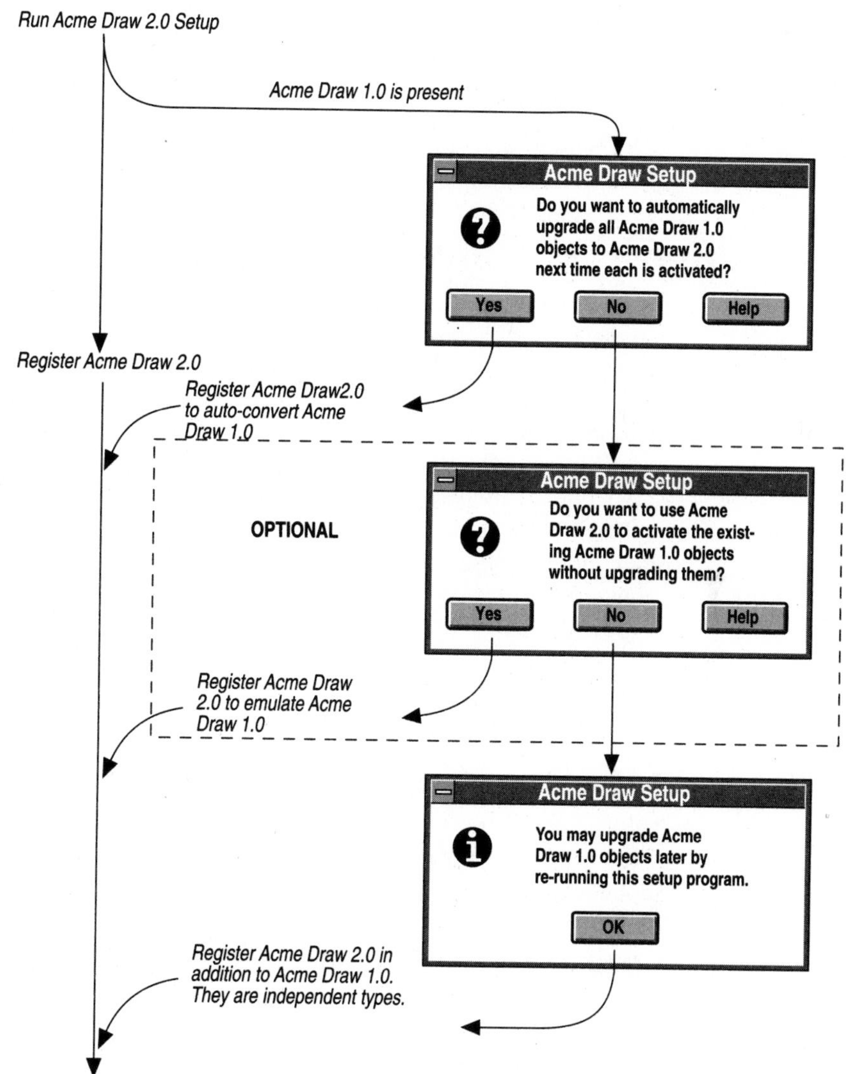
Run Acme Draw 2.0 Setup
Acme Draw 1.0 is present
Acme Draw Setup
Do you want to automatically upgrade all Acme Draw 1.0 objects to Acme Draw 2.0 next time each is activated?
Yes
No
Help
Register Acme Draw 2.0
Register Acme Draw2.0 to auto-convert Acme Draw 1.0
OPTIONAL
Acme Draw Setup
Do you want to use Acme Draw 2.0 to activate the existing Acme Draw 1.0 objects without upgrading them?
Yes
No
Help
Register Acme Draw 2.0 to emulate Acme Draw 1.0
Acme Draw Setup
You may upgrade Acme Draw 1.0 objects later by re-running this setup program.
OK
Register Acme Draw 2.0 in addition to Acme Draw 1.0. They are independent types.

Figure 4-1. Installing a new version of a object application.

As part of the class registration procedure, a setup program may register a list of data formats, such as **.tif**, **.eps**, **.xls**, that the object application is capable of reading and activating, as well as a list of formats it is capable of writing. These formats are discussed further in the following sections and are listed in the registration database.

Objects and Other Object Applications

Although an object is normally activated by the object application corresponding to its class in the registration database, this is not always the case. By comparing the lists of data formats registered in the database with other types of object applications, an application can determine which other object types a newly registered application is capable of converting and emulating. For example, if a newly registered application reads and writes objects saved in the **.tif** format and an existing object application writes objects in the **.tif** format, the new object application can convert objects saved by the existing application. The Convert dialog box, as shown in Figure 4-4, provides users with the means to convert and emulate object types.

There are three specific situations in which an existing object is not activated by the object application corresponding to its class in the registration database, each of which is discussed in the following sections.

Activating an Object Having an Upgraded Version

If the user activates an object whose application version has been reassigned to a newer version, the object is activated by launching and is saved by the new object application.

Converting an Object from One Type to Another

Permanently converting an object from one type to another is frequently necessary. To do so, the user selects the object and, using the Edit/Object submenu, chooses Convert.... The result of these steps is the appearance of the Convert dialog box, which allows the user to select the Convert to: option button. This button displays a list of other types (classes) to which the object may be converted. It is selected by default when Convert is chosen using the menus or if the selected object's type is registered in the database. This list of other object types is composed of all types that have registered themselves as capable of reading the selected object's format. (The list does not guarantee that a reverse conversion is possible).

The list of object types also contains the selected object's current type. This enables the user to change to Display As Icon without necessarily converting the selection's type. If a new type is chosen from the list and the dialog box selection is committed, the selected object is immediately and silently converted to the new type. (If the object was opened, the container closes it before performing the conversion.) If, however, the Convert dialog box resulted from an attempt by the user to edit an unregistered object, the new type application should immediately activate after the Convert dialog box and the actual conversion take place as part of loading the object.

Emulating Different Object Types

Because users will be exchanging OLE documents between different machines, it will be common for them to receive an object and not have the object application necessary to activate it. In addition, users may want to use other than default applications with their own objects to exploit unique editing features of a particular object application. The Convert dialog box also supports these situations.

By choosing the Activate as: option button in the Convert dialog box, the subset of types capable of emulating (reading and writing) the selected object are displayed in the Object Type list box. This button is chosen by default if the object's type is not registered. The remaining types, which are only capable of conversion, do not appear. When the user chooses a type and responds Yes to the resulting message box, every object of the selected object's type is activated as an object of the "emulating type." This provides an alternate type to be used thereafter. This means that these objects take on the alternate type's verbs in the Edit Object submenu and are activated by using the alternate application. However, they still keep their original type name throughout the entire user interface because they continue to be stored in their original type's format. Since the alternate application does not actually convert the objects, they can continue to be exchanged among users in their original type. (Behind the user interface, this dialog box registers the alternate application for the selected object's type in the database. As a result, the emulation applies only to a particular machine; each machine will activate the type with the particular object application registered in its own database.)

An Error dialog box, which provides immediate access to the Convert dialog box, should appear when a user attempts to activate (double click) an unregistered object type. Additionally, the user may *voluntarily* access the dialog through the Edit / Object > Convert... command (the only command available for an unregistered object since its verbs are unknown).

Because the Convert dialog box can be invoked at any time, the user may respecify an alternate type whenever necessary. Even if there are no conversions or alternate types available for the selected object's type, the Convert dialog box should still be available as a means of simply respecifying the icon of the object. The Result help text elaborates on the outcome of the conversion and emulation options. The following table outlines the Result text that should be used within the Convert dialog box.

When an *embedded* object is selected...

Function	Result Text
Convert to Original Type	The selected <*original type*> will not be converted.
Convert to Original Type + Display as Icon	The selected <*original type*> will not be converted. It will be displayed as an icon.
Convert to Different Type	Permanently changes the selected <*original type*> to a <*selected type*>.
Convert to Different Type + Display as Icon	Permanently changes the selected <*original type*> to a <*selected type*>. It will be displayed as an icon.

When a *linked* object is selected...

Function	Result Text
Convert to Original Type (only)	The selected <*original type*> will not be converted.
Convert to Original Type (only) + Display as Icon	The selected <*original type*> will not be converted. It will be displayed as an icon.

When either a *linked or embedded* object is selected (Display As Icon - disabled) ...

Function	Result Text
Activate as Original Type	Every <*original type*> will be activated as a <*selected type*>.
Activate as Emulating Type	Every <*original type*> will be activated as a <*selected type*>, but it will not be converted.

Figures 4-2 and 4-3 show how these cases are handled on a system that has three registered object applications, Acme Draw 1.0, Acme Draw 2.0, and Megasoft Draw 1.0. Beginning at the point "Select an Acme Draw 1.0 object," the user would normally follow the straight down path of activation and deactivation. However, if Acme Draw 1.0 is replaced by Acme Draw 2.0, or if the user wants to convert or emulate Acme Draw 1.0, the appropriate alternate routes are taken.

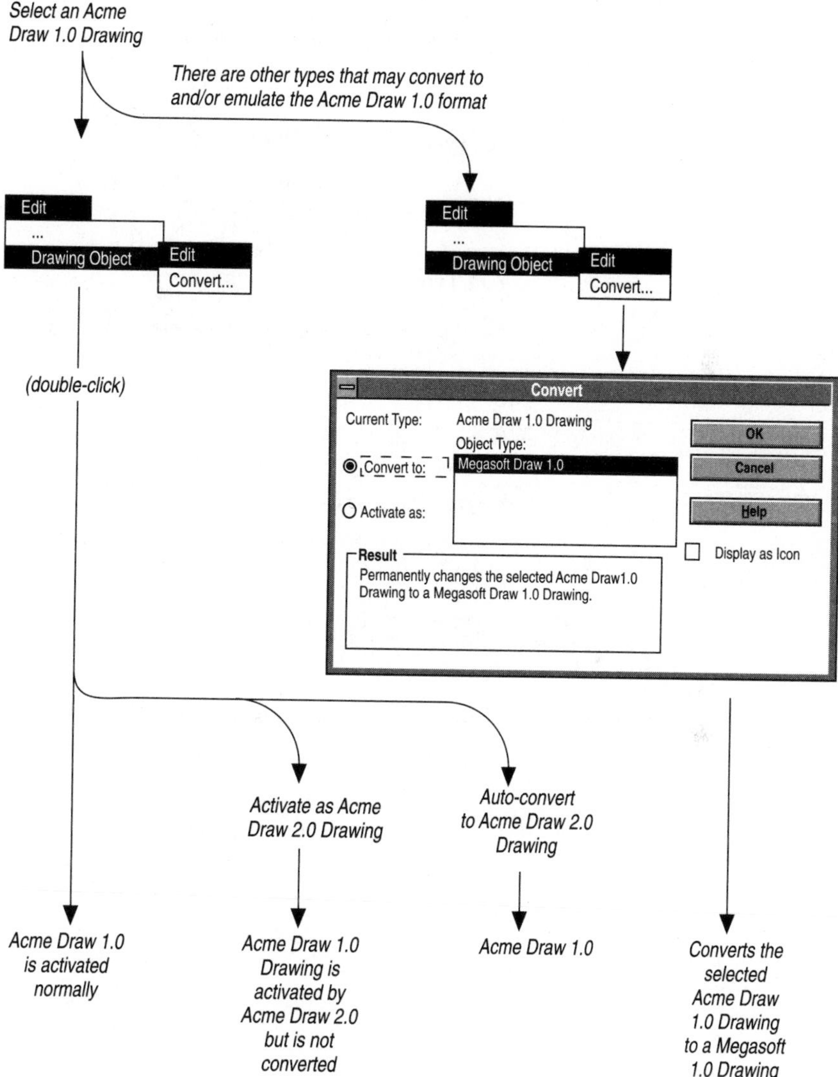

Figure 4-2. Upgrading and converting object types.

Figure 4-3 shows the result of trying to activate an unregistered ProDraw 1.0 drawing and the ensuing Error and Convert dialog boxes. Note that in this example both Acme Draw 2.0 and Megasoft Draw 1.0 are possible conversions of the ProDraw 1.0 drawing, but only Megasoft Draw 1.0 is a legal emulating type. Figure 4-4 shows the recommended dialog boxes referred to in Figures 4-2 and 4-3.

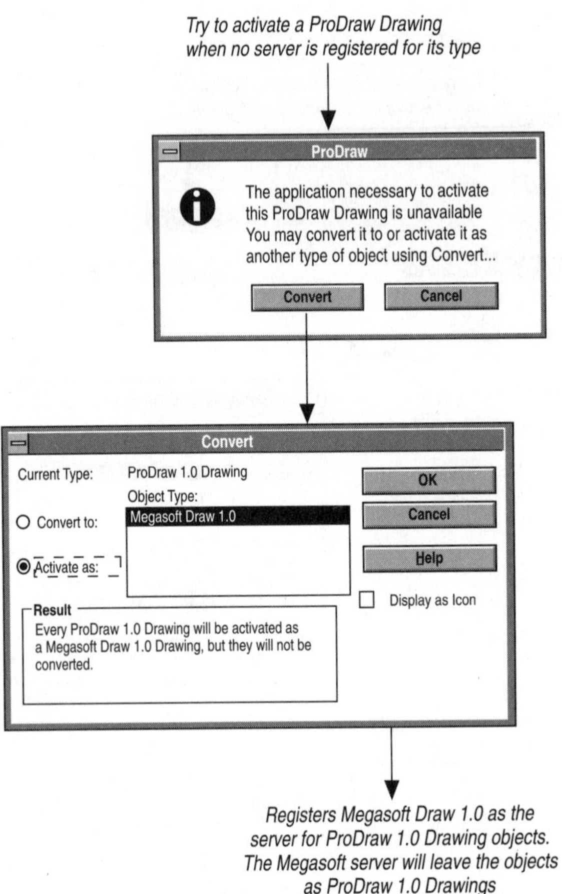

Figure 4-3. Emulating object types.

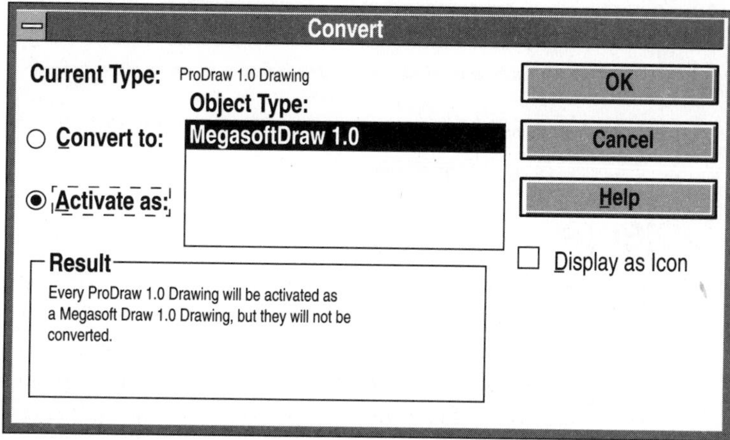

Figure 4-4. The Convert dialog box.

A user who specified activation of all Acme Draw 1.0 objects as Acme Draw 2.0 objects could have done so either 1) while running the Acme Draw 2.0 setup program or 2) at any point afterward using the Activate As: option in the Convert dialog box. If the user makes use of features unique to Acme Draw 2.0 that cannot be accommodated in the Acme Draw 1.0 format, the warning message shown in Figure 4-5 should be given at the moment the object is deactivated (when using an in-place application) or closed (using an open application).

Selecting Yes performs the conversion and saves the object with all of its changes intact. Selecting No discards certain changes to preserve the object in Acme Draw 1.0 format. This dialog box should be issued not only with different versions of the same type, but also with competitor type emulations that can incur a loss of data or compromise the integrity of the object's image when being saved in the emulating type's format.

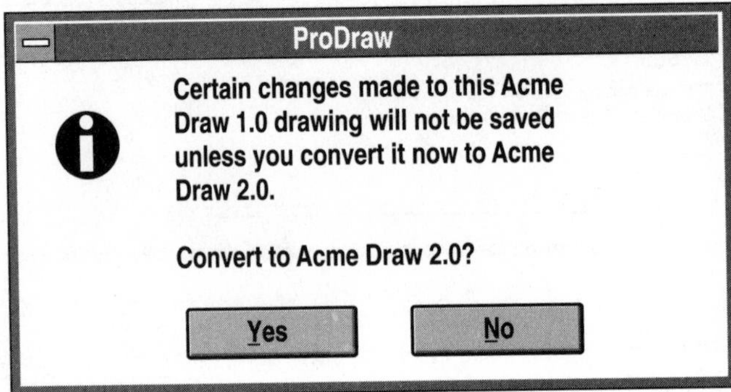

Figure 4-5. Possible warning message for emulation data loss.

Creating Objects

Users can create objects either from existing objects or from "scratch." When creating objects from existing objects, users can either modify a copy of an existing object of the same type (class) or convert an object from one type to another using the Convert dialog box, as discussed in the preceding section. Converting spreadsheet cells to a word processor table is an example of this.

To create new objects, OLE 2 provides the Insert Object dialog box. Using this dialog box enables the user to create new objects by:

- embedding an object of a selected class (type). See Figure 4-6.
- inserting a file as an embedded object. See Figure 4-7.
- inserting a file as a linked object. See Figure 4-8.

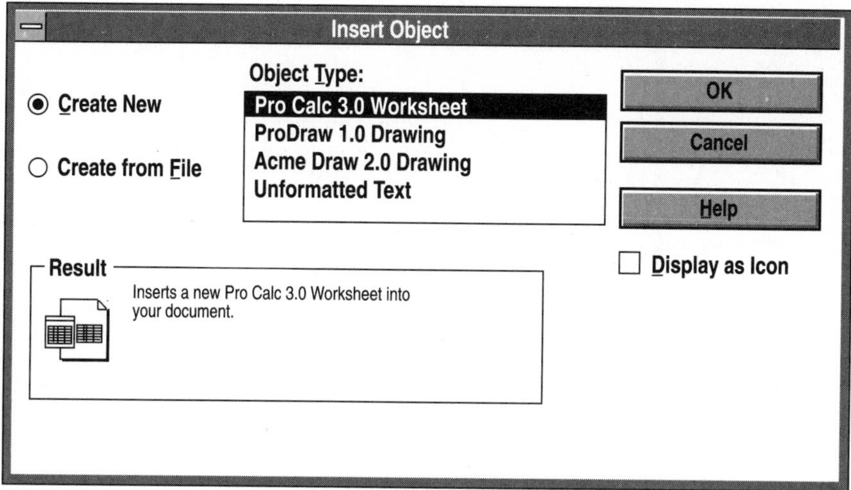

Figure 4-6. The Insert Object dialog box, embedding an object of a selected class.

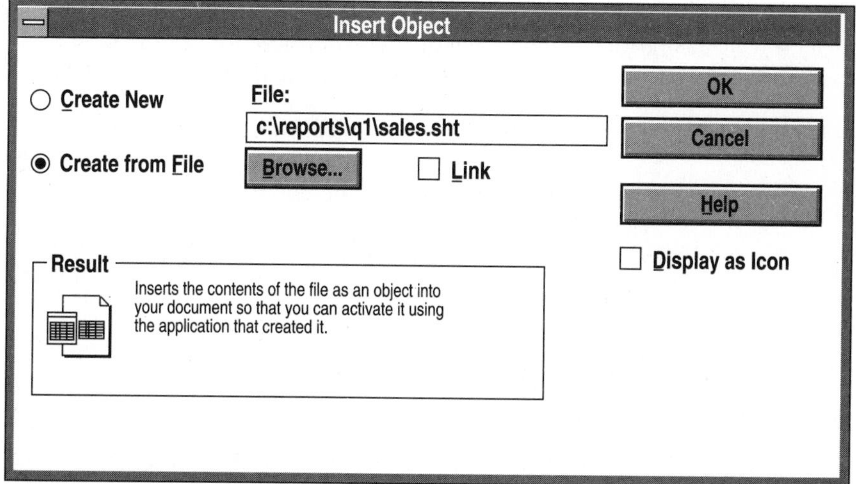

Figure 4-7. The Insert Object dialog box, inserting a file as an embedded object.

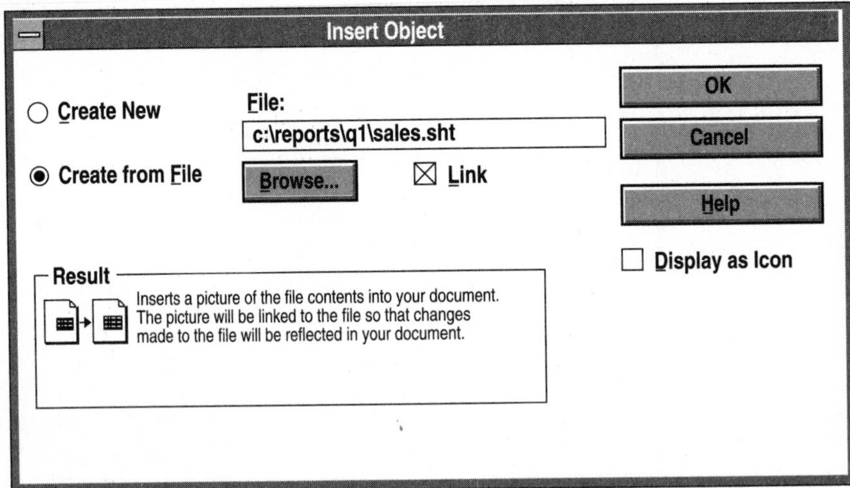

Figure 4-8. The Insert Object dialog box, inserting a file as a linked object.

Access to this dialog box is provided by an Insert Object... command, so it should be placed within the menu responsible for instantiating or importing new objects into the document. If no such menu exists, use the Edit menu.

The user can embed a new object by choosing a type from the Object Type list box and selecting OK. Certain types of new objects might make use of the current selection in the container document and build themselves accordingly. For example, an object created by an application whose function is to create charts might assume an appearance that reflects the values of data contained in a selected word processor table.

To ensure predictable insertion behavior, use the following guidelines.

- If a newly inserted object is *not* based on the current selection, the selection should be replaced by the new object, effectively pasting over it.
- If the new object is to remain linked to the current selection, the new object should be inserted in addition to the selection. It thenbecomes the new selection.
- If the object is based on, but will not remain linked to, the selection, it is up to the new object's application whether or not to remove the given selection. Whether it is more meaningful to replace or add depends on the specific use of an object type.

The user can also link to an existing file as an object by checking the Link check box. Leaving it unchecked embeds the file as an object. When the user selects the Create from File option button, the Object Type list box is replaced with a File text box and a Browse command button because the Object Type list box is unrelated to the file options.

The embedded or linked file specifies the class of the inserted or linked object. The Result box contains text describing the final outcome of the insert operation to the user.

Function	Result Text
Create New	Inserts a new <*object type name*> into your document.
Create New as Icon	Inserts a new <*object type name*> into your document as an icon.
Create From File	Inserts the contents of the file as an object into your document so you can activate it by using the application that created it.
Create From File as Icon	Inserts the contents of the file as an object into your document so you can activate it using the application that created it. It will be displayed as an icon.
Create From File + Link	Inserts a picture of the file contents into your document. The picture will be linked to the file so that changes to the file will be reflected in your document.
Create From File as Icon + Link	Inserts an icon into your document that represents the file. The icon will be linked to the file so that changes to the file will be reflected in your document.

Whether the inserted object is new or already exists, the user can specify to insert it as an icon by selecting the Display as Icon check box as shown in Figure 4-9. If the user has chosen a non-OLE file for insertion, it may only be inserted as an icon, effectively "packaging" the file.

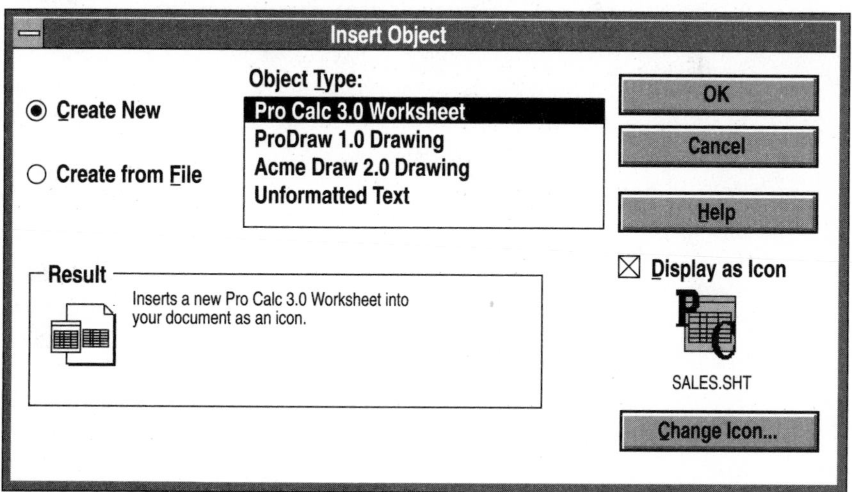

Figure 4-9. The Insert Object dialog box, displaying an object as an icon.

Because a newly created object does not exist in another file, it can be inserted only as an embedded object. Only objects created from existing files can be inserted as linked objects.

When the user selects the Display as Icon check box, the icon appears beneath the check box and the Change Icon... command button is enabled. The Change Icon... command button provides the Change Icon dialog box, as shown in Figure 4-10, that allows the user to choose another icon and optionally give it a label. A related discussion about OLE 2 and the Packager is presented later in this chapter.

In the Change Icon dialog box, the current icon is the one presently assigned to the object, persisting with the object even if it moves to other machines. The default icon is determined by the object's type and is the same as the application's default icon.

The From File: option in this dialog box enables the user to pick an icon from a file. The From File: text box is prefilled with the pathname of the current icon. This text box is parsed and checked for a legal path when the focus moves to some other dialog box element. Once the icon is chosen and the dialog box is committed, the chosen icon becomes the current icon.

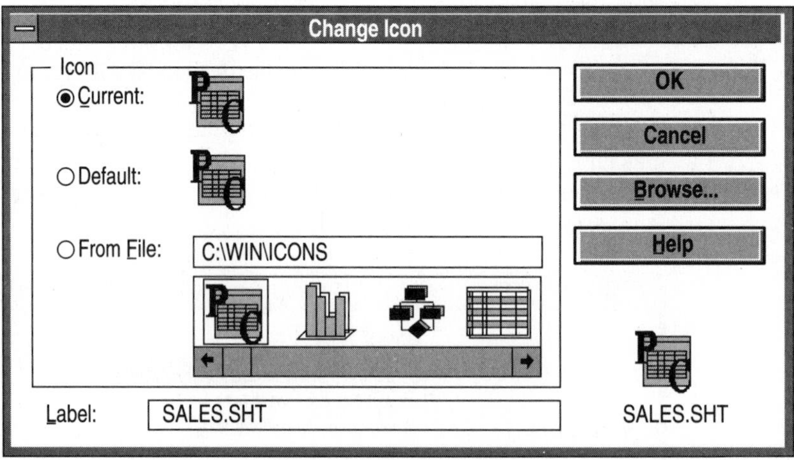

Figure 4-10. The Change Icon dialog box.

The Convert dialog box, described earlier and shown in Figure 4-4, contains a Display as Icon check box that can be used to change an object's icon at any time. When this dialog box is invoked for an object that already has an icon assigned, it is handled as a user-chosen icon. This means the dialog box does not automatically change it to the default icon of the new type after the conversion.

If the user decides to adopt the default icon of the new conversion type, it is done by returning to the Change Icon dialog box and choosing the Default icon option button When this is done, the Convert dialog box dynamically displays the appropriate icon of the selected type in the Convert type list.

If an item is embedded as an icon (by means of Paste Special, Insert Object, or drag/drop from the File Manager), its default label should be one of the following:

- For an OLE object, the label should be the short form of its type name (for example, Picture, Worksheet, and so on).
- For an OLE object that has not registered a short form name, use its full type name (such as Microsoft Paintbrush Picture, Microsoft Excel Worksheet)
- For an item that is not associated with an OLE class, the label is simply "Document."

If an entire file is linked into a container as an icon by using Insert Object Create from File + Link or by transfer from the File Manager, its default label is the source file's *<filename>.<extension>* name in lower case (for example, source.xls). If a portion of a document is linked as an icon by using the Paste Special dialog box its default label should be formed from the display name of the link source. In general, the display name of a link source may have a completely arbitrary syntax. Consequently, the following algorithm for determining the default label is inherently heuristic. It is suggested, however, that the default label be formed as follows.

1. From the end of the display name of the link source, scan for the last and second-last occurrence of the following characters:

   \ / ! :

   The label should be formed from the display name starting at the penultimate scanned-for character through the end of the string.
2. If this scan does not consume the whole display name, the first line of the label should begin with "...". Following this, the portion of the display name between the penultimate and ultimate scanned-for characters (inclusive) should be displayed.
3. The second line of the label should contain the portion of the display name that follows the ultimate scanned-for character.

The occurrence of only one scanned-for character should be handled in the obvious way. Further, if the entire label fits on one line, do not break it into pieces. It is acceptable for applications to display the full name of the link source, although the above algorithm produces more pleasing results.

In general, the label should be no more than two lines, and each line should be no wider than 10 uppercase W's in the rendered font. The text of each line should be centered beneath the icon image. The label of an icon persists with the object as it is transferred between containers and can only be changed afterward by using the Change Icon dialog box.

After an in-place object has been inserted, its application becomes active. If the inserted object appears in an open application, an opened-style hatch rectangle appears in the container, similar to the open selected object shown in Figure 4-16, until an image from the object application is available for an update.

Note Applications can also display buttons in their control bar that insert objects directly. Such buttons function in the same manner as the Insert Object dialog box.

States and the Visual Appearance of Objects

With the availability of in-place editing, OLE enhances the conceptual structure of a compound document by exposing the entire hierarchy of containment in a single window. OLE 1 handles two kinds of objects, the container (or client) and the embedded objects it contains. That the contained objects themselves might also contain embedded objects is of no consequence; because they are not accessible to the container, it is not necessary to consider embedded objects as containers themselves. In OLE 2, however, the open object becomes the root of a hierarchy of embedded objects, each of which may be a container of another object (or objects). For example, a word processor document can contain a range of cells from a spreadsheet program, which in turn contains a chart representing the values contained in those cells. The chart is accessible from within the word processor document even though the chart's container is the range of spreadsheet cells. Figure 4-11 illustrates this concept.

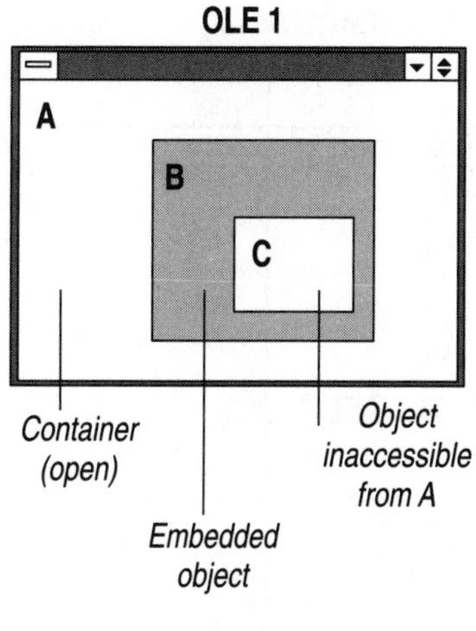

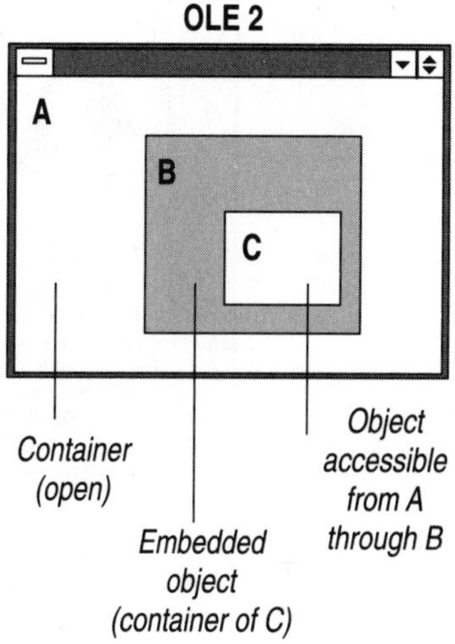

Figure 4-11. OLE 1 and OLE 2 object hierarchies.

As the user navigates through the object hierarchy within a document, OLE objects assume different states and appearances. An OLE object may be:

- inactive
- selected
- active
- open

The following sections discuss each of these states and their differences.

The Inactive State

An object is said to be inactive when it is neither active nor part of a selection. It is displayed in its presentation form, which is usually conveyed through its cached metafile description. A user may want to know whether an object is embedded or linked without being required to interact with it. Container applications should provide a Show Objects command that places a single pixel wide black *solid border* around the extent of an embedded object and a *dotted border* around linked objects as shown in Figure 4-12.

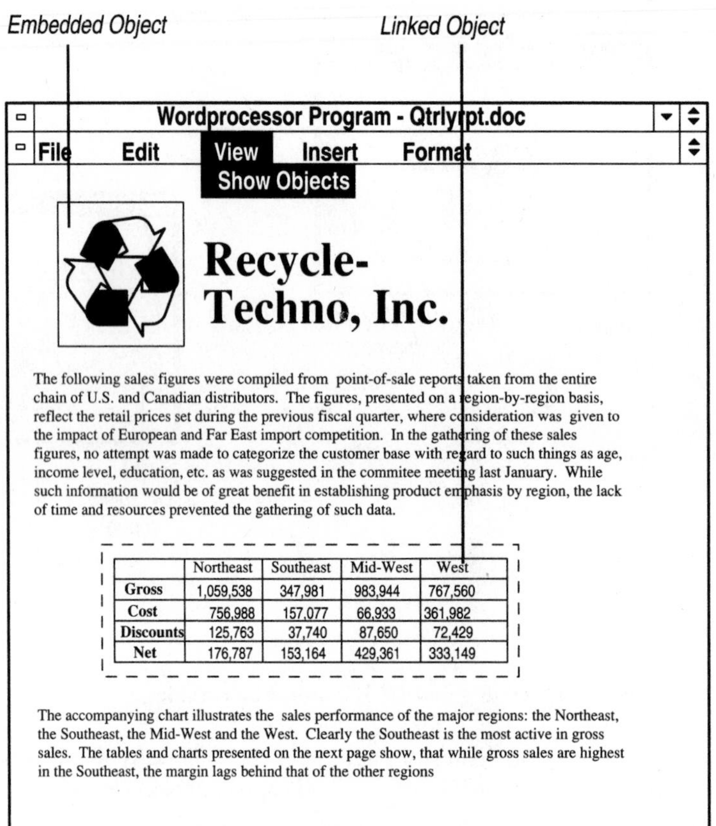
Embedded Object
Linked Object
Wordprocessor Program - Qtrlyrpt.doc
File
Edit
View
Insert
Format
Show Objects
Recycle-
Techno, Inc.
The following sales figures were compiled from point-of-sale reports taken from the entire chain of U.S. and Canadian distributors. The figures, presented on a region-by-region basis, reflect the retail prices set during the previous fiscal quarter, where consideration was given to the impact of European and Far East import competition. In the gathering of these sales figures, no attempt was made to categorize the customer base with regard to such things as age, income level, education, etc. as was suggested in the commitee meeting last January. While such information would be of great benefit in establishing product emphasis by region, the lack of time and resources prevented the gathering of such data.
Northeast Southeast Mid-West West
Gross 1,059,538 347,981 983,944 767,560
Cost 756,988 157,077 66,933 361,982
Discounts 125,763 37,740 87,650 72,429
Net 176,787 153,164 429,361 333,149
The accompanying chart illustrates the sales performance of the major regions: the Northeast, the Southeast, the Mid-West and the West. Clearly the Southeast is the most active in gross sales. The tables and charts presented on the next page show, that while gross sales are highest in the Southeast, the margin lags behind that of the other regions

Figure 4-12. The effect of the Show Objects command.

If the container application cannot guarantee that a linked object is up to date with its source (because an automatic update was unsuccessful or the link is manual), the dotted border should appear in the Windows disabled-text color (typically gray), suggesting the link is potentially out of date. Only the container document's first level objects should be bordered. For example, if the Show Objects command was chosen from an outer-level container, only those objects that are directly embedded would be bordered; nested objects would not be bordered. These borders should be distinct from the visual appearance given to the other object states.

An inactive object may be selected by single clicking anywhere within its extent, or it may be double clicked to perform the action named by its primary verb.

The Selected State

An object is selected when the user clicks it or when it is included in a selection of multiple objects. An object is selected (and deselected) and rendered according to the normal highlight rules of its container. When the object is selected, object-specific operations can be performed on it using the verbs associated with the object. The container application retrieves the verbs from the registration database. When the object is selected, as shown in Figure 4-13, the container may supply handles (for resizing) that affect the object as a unit in relation to the container. It is recommended that resizing an OLE object, while it is selected, results in a scaling operation.

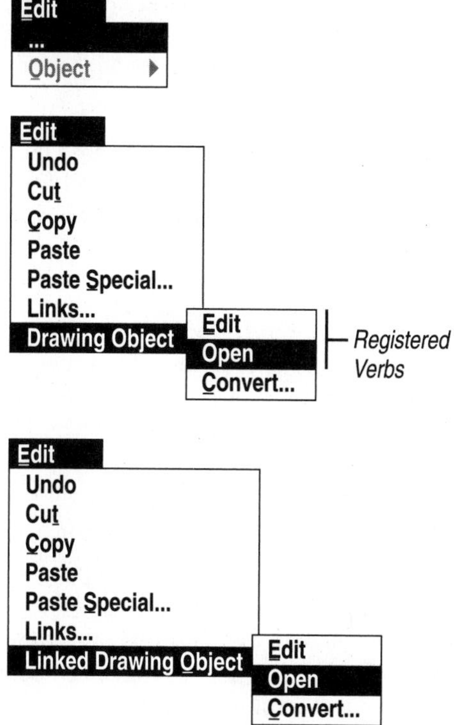

Figure 4-13. A selected OLE object.

When an object is selected, but not as part of a multiple selection, any of its registered verbs may be applied. For example, the verbs Edit and Open activate and open the object, respectively, but verbs such as Play might operate and leave the object in the selected state. Any number of single clicks simply reselects the object, while clicking outside the object deselects it.

Verbs that are meaningful only for certain states of the object should be enabled and disabled appropriately. For example, a media object that has Play and Rewind as verbs should disable Rewind when the object is already at the beginning. Similarly, if an object has two verbs, Edit (for in-place editing) and Open (for opened editing), Edit should be disabled when the object is open, because the object cannot directly achieve the in-place active state without first closing.

The Active State

OLE objects may enter an active state in which the user may interact with the object's contents in-place, using the container document's window for the menus of its object application and for its interface controls. The user can make an object active either by performing its appropriate verb (Edit), double clicking it (the primary verb will be Edit for many objects), or selecting the object and pressing ENTER. If the ENTER key is already used by the container application, then ALT+ENTER is recommended.

When an object becomes active, its application's menus and interface controls are grafted into the containing document's window and apply over the extent of the active object as shown in Figure 4-14. Frame adornments appear outside the extent of the object, and thus may temporarily cover neighboring material in the document.

The active object and its frame adornments are surrounded by a black diagonal hatch border as an indication of the active state and to suggest the area of focus. The hatch-pattern border consists of right-ascending diagonal four-pixel lines with three transparent pixels between the lines (as shown in Figure 4-17). Because the border is translucent, underlying material shows between the diagonal lines. The hatch border is considered to be part of the object's layout; consequently, it is the object's pointer that appears when over the border.

In the active state, the object takes on the appearance that is best suited for its own editing. Frame adornments such as table gridlines, handles, scroll bars, as well as other editing aids may be shown with the object. Figure 4-16 shows row/column headers as adornments to the object, an active worksheet. Scroll bars could be included if the object is large and scrolling is needed to show the entire object in its viewport.

Clicking the hatch pattern (and not the resize handles) should be re-interpreted by the object as clicking just inside the edge of the border. The hatch area is effectively a click slop zone that prevents inadvertent deactivations and makes it easier to select the contents of the object that lies right along its edge.

Because the container may be set at a view-scale (zoom ratio) that the object cannot match to perform in-place activation, the object should instead open into a separate window. If the object does not support an open mode, it should not respond to the verb but issue an appropriate error message.

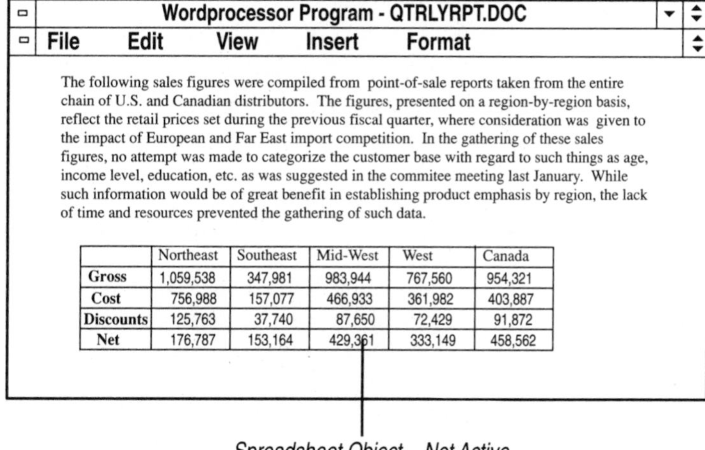

Wordprocessor Program - QTRLYRPT.DOC
File Edit View Insert Format
The following sales figures were compiled from point-of-sale reports taken from the entire chain of U.S. and Canadian distributors. The figures, presented on a region-by-region basis, reflect the retail prices set during the previous fiscal quarter, where consideration was given to the impact of European and Far East import competition. In the gathering of these sales figures, no attempt was made to categorize the customer base with regard to such things as age, income level, education, etc. as was suggested in the commitee meeting last January. While such information would be of great benefit in establishing product emphasis by region, the lack of time and resources prevented the gathering of such data.

	Northeast	Southeast	Mid-West	West	Canada
Gross	1,059,538	347,981	983,944	767,560	954,321
Cost	756,988	157,077	466,933	361,982	403,887
Discounts	125,763	37,740	87,650	72,429	91,872
Net	176,787	153,164	429,361	333,149	458,562

Spreadsheet Object - Not Active

Wordprocessor Program - QTRLYRPT.DOC
File Edit Formula Data Charts Macro Window
Menu Bar Shared With Object Application
The following sales figures were compiled from point-of-sale reports taken from the entire chain of U.S. and Canadian distributors. The figures, presented on a region-by-region basis, reflect the retail prices set during the previous fiscal quarter, where consideration was given to the impact of European and Far East import competition. In the gathering of these sales figures, no attempt was made to categorize the customer base with regard to such things as age, income level, education, etc. as was suggested in the commitee meeting last January. While such information would be of great benefit in establishing product emphasis by region, the lack of time and resources prevented the gathering of such data.

	A	B	C	D	E	F
1		Northeast	Southeast	Mid-West	West	Canada
2	**Gross**	1,059,538	347,981	983,944	77,560	954,321
3	**Cost**	756,988	157,077	466,933	61,982	403,887
4	**Discounts**	125,763	37,740	87,650	72,429	91,872
5	**Net**	176,787	153,164	429,361	333,149	458,562

Spreadsheet Object - Active

Figure 4-14. An in-place active OLE object.

There is only one object activated at any given time and there is no attempt to activate all objects that use the same object application, as a set. For example, if all Paintbrush objects in a document were activated, commands such as Clear All or Delete would be ambiguous. In that case, the user may not know which objects would be affected by such document-scoped commands.

A single click in the container area, or a double click on a new OLE object (which may be nested in the currently active object) deactivates the current object and gives the focus to the new object. An active object may be deactivated by clicking outside its extent in the container document or by pressing ESCAPE. If an in-place object already uses ESCAPE for getting out of its own internal modes, pressing it should return focus to its container, making the object the selection, when the object "escapes" from all its internal modes. If an object uses the ESCAPE key at all times, it is recommended that SHIFT+ESCAPE be used to deactivate the object.

Edits made to an active object immediately and automatically become a part of the container document. Consequently, there is no "Update changes?" prompt when an in-place active object deactivates. Of course, changes to the entire document, embedded or otherwise, can be abandoned by declining to save the file to disk.

Those objects that support resizing while in-place active should include square resize handles within the active hatch pattern as shown in Figure 4-15. The solid black handles should be of the same width as the hatch pattern. To provide optimum clarity to the user, resize handles can have a single white-pixel separation from the diagonal lines of the hatch pattern.

In-place resizing should expose more or less of the object's content (for example, adding or removing rows/columns in the case of a spreadsheet). It should be seen as adjusting the viewport rather than scaling the object's appearance. However, certain objects may default to in-place scaling if cropping is not meaningful.

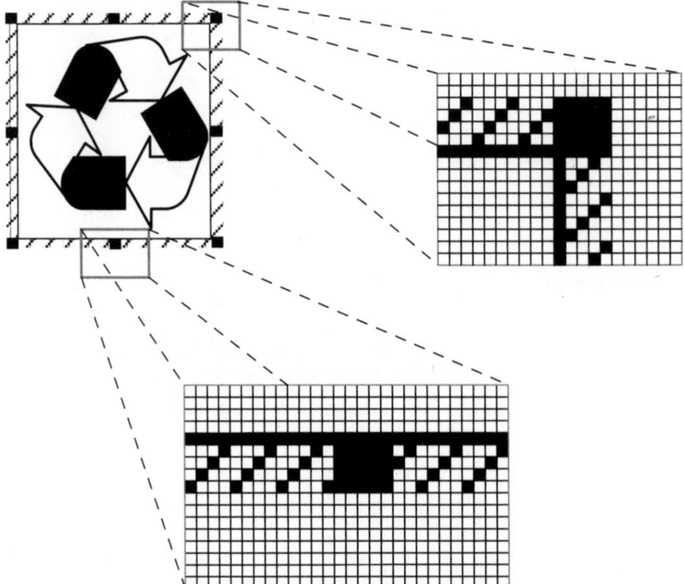

Figure 4-15. The border of an object that supports in-place activation and resizing.

The Open State

The semantics of the open state are similar to that of the open state introduced in OLE 1, with one important distinction. In OLE 1, the open object was seen by the user in a separate open object application that updated changes to the object back to the container document upon exit. In OLE 2, the open object application appears to the user as an alternate viewer onto the same object, under the hatch pattern, still within the container document. Figure 4-16 shows how a selected open object appears to the user. In this example, the container application is a word processor while the object application for the object is a drawing program.

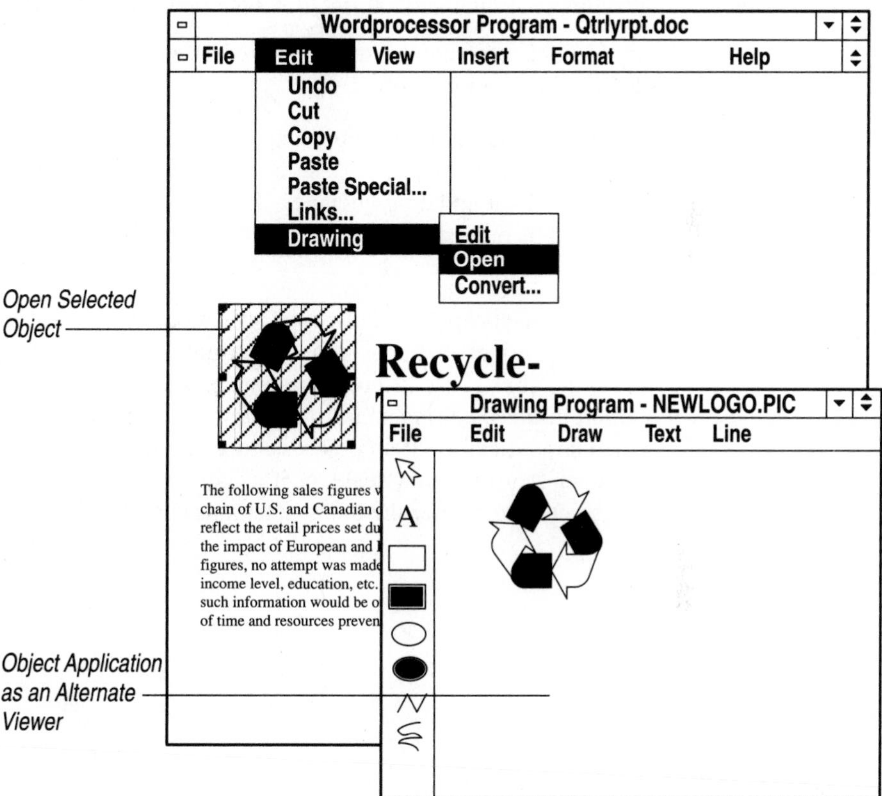

Figure 4-16. An open selected object.

If the user clicks elsewhere in the container document, the object becomes deselected but remains in the open state as indicated in Figure 4-17.

There is no sense of a local version kept within the object application; the opened object in the document and the object within the object application are the same. As a result, changes to the open object made within the object application window are immediately and automatically reflected in the object (beneath the hatch pattern) in the container. There is no longer a need for the Update command or the update confirmation upon exiting the object application.

Nevertheless, open object applications can still include an "Update *<source file>*" command for the user to insist an update at any time. This is useful when the application's "real-time" image updates are not very frequent because they may, generally, be computationally expensive. In any event, an update is always performed automatically at the time the open window is closed.

Import File... commands are still appropriate because they conceptually import a file into the document directly.

This interpretation of open object applications unifies open and in-place activation. In either case, the user is interacting with objects at the document level directly without updating latencies. The only difference is the matter of where the interaction is performed; in-place or in an alternate viewer looking at the same site in the document.

An OLE object capable of in-place activation, should also include the Open verb. The Open verb gives the user the opportunity of seeing more of the object or seeing the object in a different view state. Ideally, an in-place object should support in-place editing at arbitrary view scales because its container might be scaled unpredictably. If an object cannot accommodate in-place editing in its container's current view scale, or if its container does not support in-place editing, the object should enter the open state in a separate window for editing.

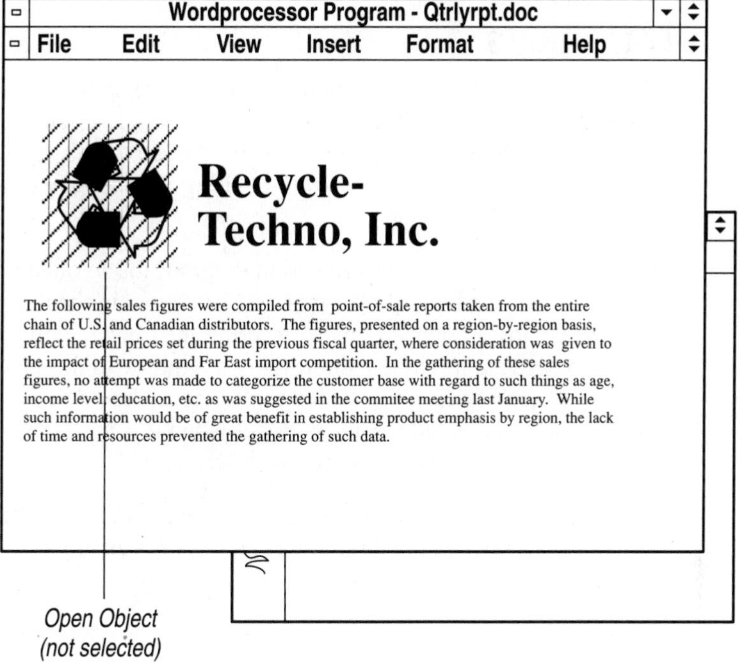

Wordprocessor Program - Qtrlyrpt.doc
File Edit View Insert Format Help
Recycle-
Techno, Inc.
The following sales figures were compiled from point-of-sale reports taken from the entire chain of U.S. and Canadian distributors. The figures, presented on a region-by-region basis, reflect the retail prices set during the previous fiscal quarter, where consideration was given to the impact of European and Far East import competition. In the gathering of these sales figures, no attempt was made to categorize the customer base with regard to such things as age, income level, education, etc. as was suggested in the commitee meeting last January. While such information would be of great benefit in establishing product emphasis by region, the lack of time and resources prevented the gathering of such data.
Open Object
(not selected)

Figure 4-17. An open object, not selected.

When an object is opened, it becomes the selected object of the container document. Also, when the container document is printed, the presentation form of objects should be used. Neither the open nor active hatch patterns should appear in the printed document since these are meta-appearances (like selection indication) and not part of the content.

Any number of objects may be in the opened state. The object is deactivated (closed) by closing the application window that updates the embedded object in the container document. Because object application windows can be modal, the user is free to switch between object application and document windows and edit independently. It follows that the opened object may participate in the container application's selections as usual.

Object State Transitions

The preceding in-place activation examples have shown the OLE 2 *outside-in* rule of activation. This means that any number of single-clicks within or on the border of an object selects but does not activate or open the object . An explicit activation (or open) verb, or double-clicking is necessary to tunnel into the object and work with its contents.

Figure 4-18 shows the state-transition diagram for an outside-in activated object whose primary verb is Edit (in-place). Not shown in the diagram is the effect of double-clicking an opened object to bring the object application window to the front and activate it (similar to bringing a window to the surface by double-clicking its icon again). Container applications should display the northwest arrow pointer above an outside-in OLE object when it is not activated to indicate that it behaves as a single opaque item.

From the user's perspective, outside-in objects can be selected with little or no deliberation. Activating them, however, requires an explicit action, such as double-clicking .

The outside-in rule results from the following considerations:

- Many object applications require several seconds to load, so activating objects indiscriminately on every mouse event would be unmanageable. Instead, the user performs a deliberate action to activate the object.
- Outside-in objects can be selected easily because the user need only click somewhere within the object's extent.

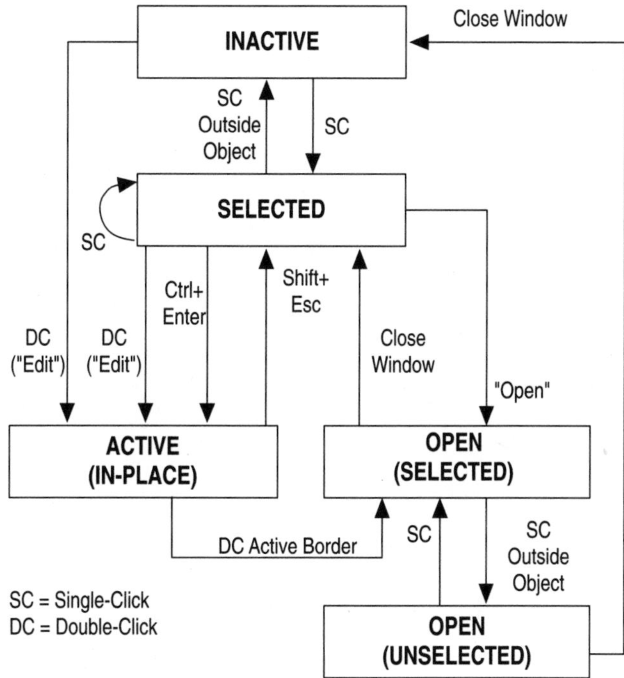

Figure 4-18. Object state transition diagram for outside-in object applications.

To accommodate the broad range of container types and the prospect of new lighter weight, quick-activating objects in the future, OLE also supports an *inside-out* activation model as well as related registry information. This activation model, shown in Figure 4-19, enables a container to ensure uniform activation across its components. The inside-out model also makes it possible to further reduce the editing seam between native and OLE objects by presenting OLE objects to the user as effectively-always-active and ready-to-use elements.

An inside-out object controls the appearance of the pointer as it moves within the object's extent, responds immediately to mouse actions, and is selected as a whole by clicking on its edge (or some other appropriate selection target provided by its container). From the user's perspective, inside-out objects are truly seamless with respect to the container's native data since their behaviors are virtually indistinguishable. The container should clear its current selection when an inside-out object begins its selection (typically on mouse down); otherwise, it appears there are two cooperating selections when only the object's selection is meaningful.

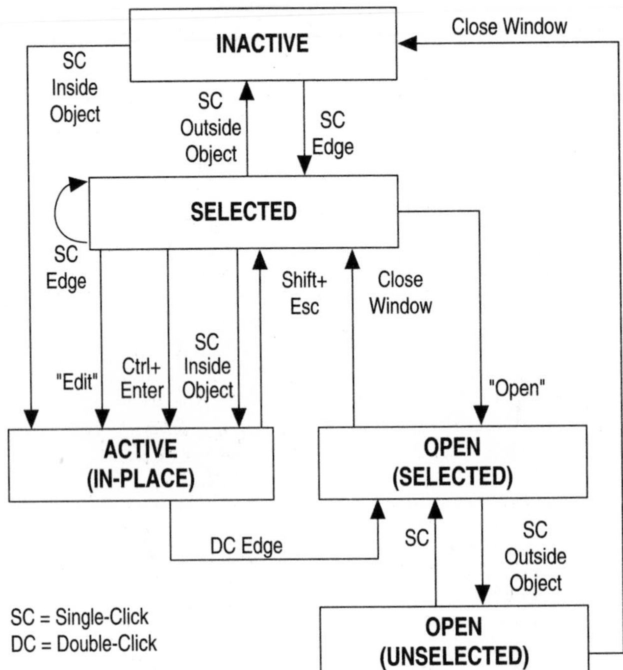

Figure 4-19. Object state transition diagram for inside-out object applications.

There are two class registry bits that express the activation style of an object class to a container. By default an object application is presumed to behave outside-in but, as explained below, the object might also register that it is capable inside-out operation. It might also indicate a preference for inside-out operation. The two class registry bits, OLEMISC_INSIDEOUT and OLEMISC_ACTIVATEWHENVISIBLE, can be obtained by calling the object's **IOleObject::GetMiscStatus** method. These bits are described below.

Bit Name	Meaning
OLEMISC_INSIDEOUT	This object application is capable of running without activating its user interface, thus enabling the application to exhibit inside-out behavior. An instance of this application might affect the mouse pointer and respond immediately to a mouse action (surfacing its user interface after the mouse action is completed).

Bit Name	Meaning
OLEMISC_ACTIVATEWHENVISIBLE	This object application is not only inside-out capable, but actually prefers to be activated inside-out. This preference might stem from the object's user interface, which mandates inside-out (such as with forms control objects whose visual affordances invite immediate interaction), or simply because the object's application costs a container little time or memory to keep activated when in view.

Using the registration information, a container ultimately determines whether it allows the inside-out objects to handle the events directly or whether it intercedes and only activates components on a double click.

Note If an inside-out object's application is unavailable, the appropriate error message in a dialog box should be issued when the user tries to interact with the object, not when the container tries to preload the application. This prevents surfacing error messages to a user whose only intention is to read the document.

The container should choose an activation style that is most appropriate for its specific use and that is in keeping with its own native style of activation so OLE objects can be assimilated most seamlessly. Regardless of which approach the container chooses, it is critical that the container activates the same class of object consistently, either outside-in or inside-out. Any inconsistency in the way a class objects activates hinders its ease of use. Although it is not as critical for objects of different types to activate in the same manner in a given container, it is still recommended that all components of a container uniformly follow either one activation style or the other. Below are four examples of potential container activation strategies:

Outside-In Throughout. This will commonly be the case for compound document editors that often embed large objects and deal with them as whole units. Because compound documents are the popular initial expression of OLE and many of the available objects are not yet inside-out capable, document editors will likely use outside-in throughout to preserve uniformity.

Inside-Out Throughout. Ultimately, the direction of OLE containers is to blend embedded objects with native data seamlessly so that the distinction dissolves. Inside-out throughout containers will become more feasible as increasing numbers of OLE objects support and prefer inside-out activation.

Outside-In Plus Inside-Out for Preferred Objects. Some containers might use an outside-in model for large foreign embeddings but also include some inside-out preferred objects as though they were native objects (by honoring the ACTIVATEWHENVISIBLE preference). For example, a compound document editor might masquerade form control objects as inside-out native data while activating more sluggish spreadsheet and chart objects as outside-in at the same time.

Switch Between Inside-Out Throughout and Outside-In Throughout. Visual programming and forms layout design containers often have the notion of design and run modes. This class of container would typically hold inside-out capable (if not preferable) objects and would alternate between outside-in throughout when designing and inside-out throughout when running.

Separate from the issue of how and when an object activates is the question of how much to distinguish or blend the object and container user interfaces. Again, the ultimate direction is to factor components' and containers' user interfaces into complementary self-contained sets with little or no overlap so that a uniform combination of the two is presented to the user. However, recognizing that many initial in-place components are derived directly from stand-alone applications with fully defined and familiar user interfaces, the initial OLE user interface strategy creates a clear context switch as one interface replaces another. This strategy factors object applications only at the broad level (workspace, active editor, selected object) and exchanges control of the bulk of the interface (active editor menus, control bars, and so on) between the container and object across activations The coarse factoring leaves an object application's original menus intact so that existing users find it familiar to use as an OLE object. This, in combination with the active hatch border, delineates it from the container application.

However, as more refined inside-out objects become available and as containers use OLE Automation to drive components programmatically, objects may choose, or be forced by the container, to surface few if any user interface components. As a result, the delineation between container and component application might become unnecessary or even inappropriate. This use of an object casts it more as a native component of a container rather than as a peer application. As such, neither the menus nor hatch border would be displayed. As a general guideline, if the object's menus appears in menu bar (meaning the object's request was granted by the container), the active hatch border should be displayed to designate the active region. Conversely, if the object's menus do not appear in the menu bar (because the object did not request it or the container refused to do so), the object is being accommodated by the container's user interface and it is not necessary to display the hatch border. Even so, the container can still apply its own focus border style as it would for its own objects.

Undo for Active and Open Objects

Because different applications take control of a window during in-place activation, commands like Undo or Redo require special consideration. How the actions performed within an in-place object are reconciled with actions performed on the native data of the container as it relates to Undo is the main consideration for Undo functionality. The OLE Undo model specifies a single undo stack per open window. Thus, all actions that can be undone, whether generated by an in-place object application or the container's application, conceptually accumulate on the same undo-state sequence. This means that issuing Undo from either the container application's menus or from the in-place object application's menus undoes the last action (that is capable of being undone) performed in that open window, whether it occurred within an in-place object or not.

If the container has the focus and the last action in the window occurred within an embedded object, Undo activates the embedded object, reverse the action, and leave the embedded object active in-place. In the case of open object applications, each open window manages a single stack of states that can be undone. Actions performed in an open object application are local to that application's window and consequently must be undone from there. Actions in the open object application (even if they cause updates in the container) do not contribute to the undo state of the container.

Sending a verb to an object (or double clicking) is not an action that can be undone, so it does not add to a container's undo stack. This includes opening an object into another window for editing: if the user unintentionally opens an object, the object application must be closed normally because that action cannot be undone from the container.

Figure 4-20 shows two windows: container Window A has an in-place active object, and Window B, an open object application. Between the two windows there have been a total of nine actions, all of which can be undonein the order and at the location indicated by the circled numbers. The resulting undo stacks are displayed beneath the windows. The in-place and native actions within Window A have been serialized into the same stack, while the actions in Window B have accumulated on their own separate stack.

The undo actions discussed so far are bound to a single window. When a single action spans multiple windows, it can be undone from the last window involved. In most cases, the user is focused on that window when the mistake is realized. Therefore, if the user had dragged and dropped an item from Window A into Window B of Figure 4-20, the action would be appended to Window B's undo stack. The entire effect of the action can be undone even if multiple windows were affected. Unfortunately, no technical support exists in OLE for this sort of multiwindow undo coordination. As a result, multiwindow actions create, at best, independent actions that cannot be undone in each window participating in the action.

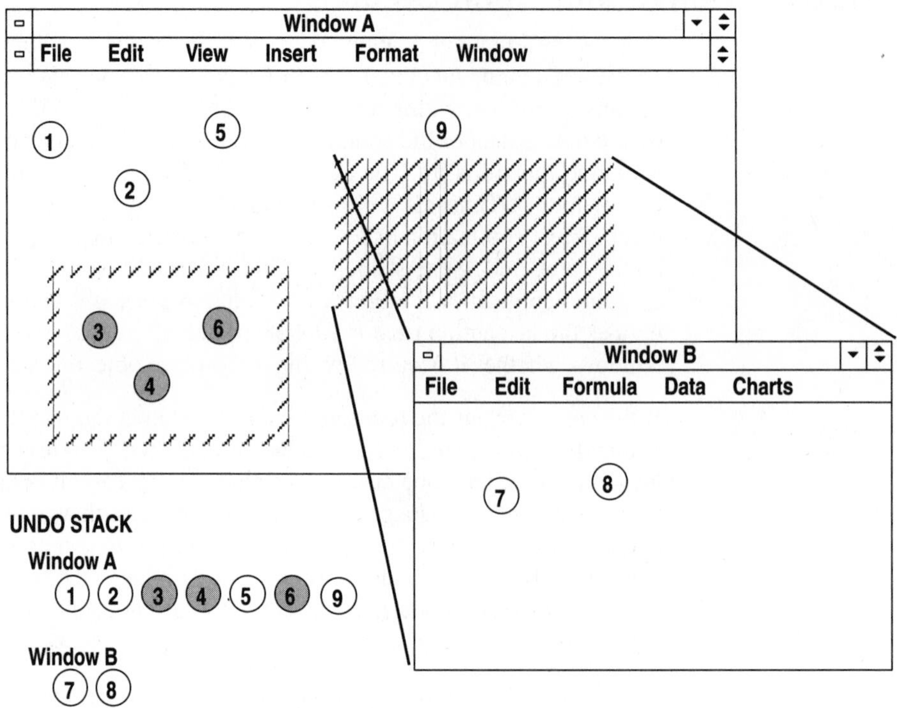

Figure 4-20. Undo stacks of in-place and open objects.

Note The stack of undo states pictured in Figure 4-20 is not meant to imply a specific number of undo levels, but presents a timeline of actions that can be undone at different levels, depending on the degree of undo the container/object supports.

Menu Commands

The addition of in-place activation functionality presents potential problems, as several objects may need to expose their commands in the interface. If no restrictions are imposed on where these commands can appear, users may be faced with an interface that changes unpredictably. In addition, the user will be unable to reliably identify the object to which a given command applies. Developers are faced with the task of accommodating complex negotiations among objects to build menus. To avoid these problems, OLE defines a classification of menus that segregates the interface based on menu groupings.

These include the following categories:

- Workspace menus
- Active Editor menus
- Selected Object submenus

This classification system is designed to enhance the usability of the interface by regularizing and limiting the changes that occur as different objects come and go from the interface. Following are the descriptions of these menu categories.

Workspace Menu(s)

Objects that are the top container in an application control the workspace of that application. This means that, these objects are responsible for the organization of windows in a multiple-document-instance (MDI) application, file-level operations, and how edits are ultimately saved. These objects must supply at least two menus, one of which is a single File menu containing file-level commands such as Open, Close, Save, and Print. If the object is an opened-object object application, the commands in its File menu are modified according to the guidelines shown in Figure 4-21. OLE updates are automatic between the open object application window and the container document, eliminating the need for the Update command or the update confirmation upon closing the open object application.

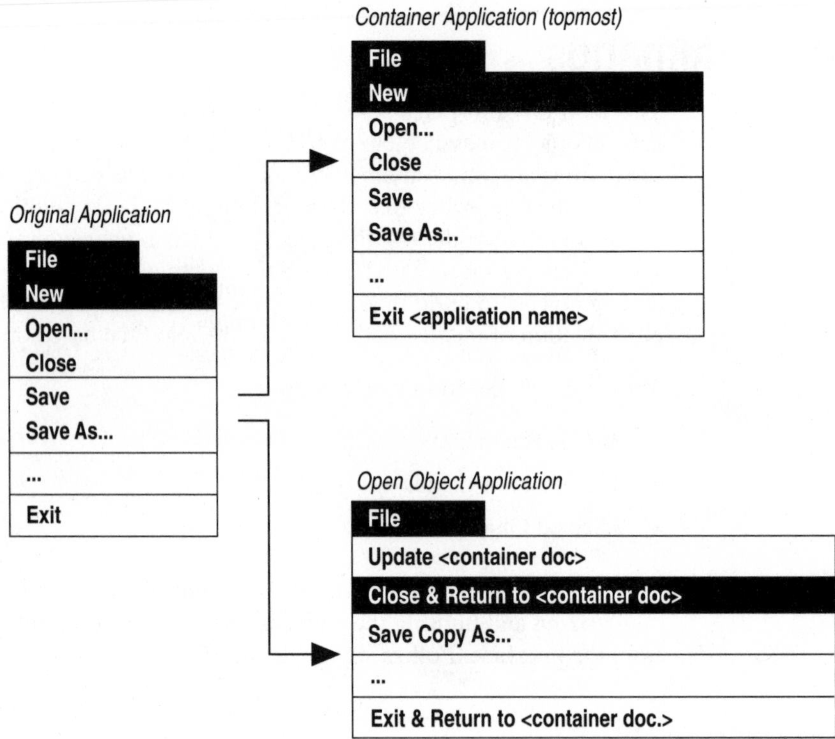

Figure 4-21. The object application and container file menus.

As indicated in Figure 4-22, MDI applications must also supply a Window menu to control the child windows of the application. Workspace menus remain in the menu bar at all times no matter which object is active. It is notable that the View menu is not a workspace menu, but and active editor menu, so any document-level viewing/zooming commands that are to be kept available must be moved to a Workspace menu. If present, the Window menu is the preferable location for them. Also, if the view menu needs to contain a zoom command, this command name should indicate scaling of the object rather than zooming of the entire document.

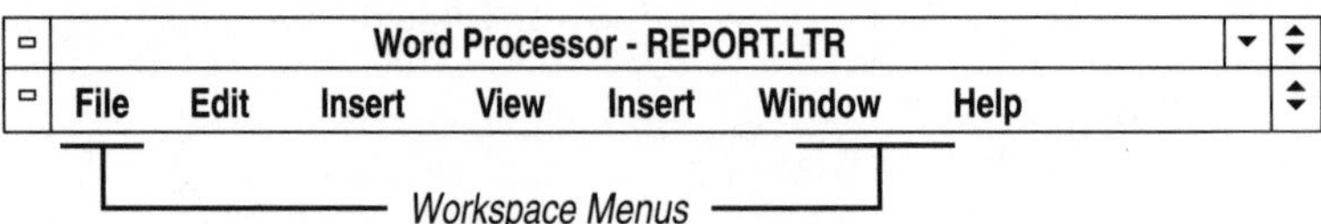

Figure 4-22. Workspace Menus.

Active Editor Menu(s)

Most OLE objects must supply Active Editor menus, similar to those shown in Figure 4-23, that hold the majority of their commands. This includes those commands that actually operate on object content. Commands like moving, deleting, search/replacing, creating new items, applying tools, styles, and help would be located in these menus. Active Editor menus occupy the majority of the menu bar's space and may be slightly different depending on whether the object is activated in-place or opened. As the name suggests, they are executed by the object that is currently active (which might be the top container application). None of these menus are allowed to be named File or Window because those titles are reserved for Workspace menus.

The title bar is not affected by in-place activations; it is always displays the container (workspace) application name followed by the document name. (This is a change from an earlier design which dynamically presented the active object application name followed by <*shortform*> in <*container-document*>.

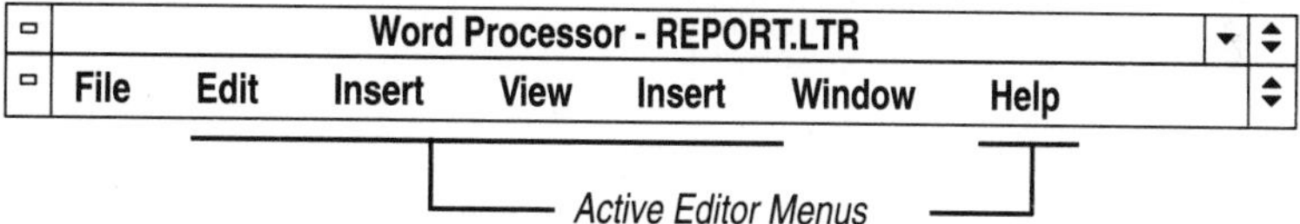

Figure 4-23. Active editor menus.

Objects that use direct manipulation or OLE verbs as their sole user interface do not need to provide active editor menus. Neither do they need to alter the menu bar when activated.

Selected Object Submenu

All container applications must include a menu containing the verbs for any currently selected OLE object in it. This menu is preferably a submenu of an Active Editor menu, such as the Edit menu, or possibly as its own menu on the menu bar. The submenu uses the short form of the object type name. If the object is a link, it must include the word "Linked" preceding the object type name.

The first letter of the appropriately localized word for "Object" should be underscored as the stable mnemonic character for keyboard users. When there is no object selected, the menu command is simply "Object" and it is disabled.

As illustrated in Figure 4-24, the syntax for the submenu of the Active Editor menu is:

[Linked] *<shortform>* Object -> *<verb0>*, ..., *<verbN>*, Convert...

The Convert... command is grayed if there are no other types (classes) registered that are capable of converting or emulating the selected object.

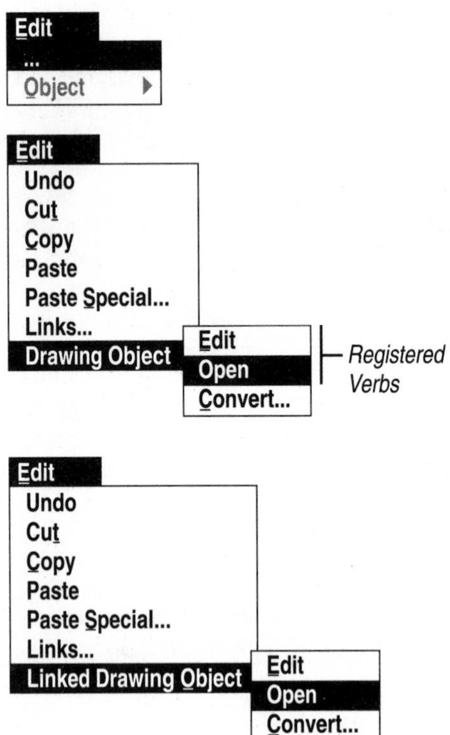

Figure 4-24. Selected object menu.

Menu Summary

To summarize how these menus mesh on the menu bar:

- Workspace menus are present all times in each window whether it is the container application or an opened object application. They include the File and Window menus.
- The File menu commands in an open object application window are modified to point back to the container document and do not include the Update command or the update confirmation found in the OLE 1 user interface.
- The currently active object (possibly the container itself) supplies the Active Editor menu(s) as the bulk of the menu bar.
- If an object is selected, its commands are available through its Selected Object submenu within an active editor menu.

Keyboard Commands

In addition to integrating the groupings of menus already discussed, the keyboard commands associated with them must be blended as well. These keyboard commands include the following categories of key combinations:

- **Mnemonic Keys.** The mnemonic keys are those ALT key sequences that pull down menus and choose commands according to which letters are underscored. The rule is ALT+<*letter*> to pull down the corresponding menu, followed by additional letters to invoke the command.
- **Shortcut Keys.** The shortcut keys are the quick-access key commands that can use any combination of the CTRL, SHIFT, and ALT modifier keys.

The integration strategy is intended to offer all of the mnemonic and shortcut keys used in the previously described Workspace, Active Editor, and Selected Object menus to the user without ambiguity due to duplicate assignment. To do this, the reserved key sequences in each of the three menu categories are not to be reused by the other categories.

Mnemonic Keys

The only chance for the mnemonic keys used in Workspace and Active Editor menus to conflict is between top-level menus, because presumably command mnemonics within each menu have already been uniquely assigned. Applications must be aware of which menu title letters they may use.

- Workspace menus should use File and Window as their mnemonics (or the appropriately localized File and Window words).
- In-place object applications may underscore letters (for mnemonics) in their Active Editor menu titles other than those used for Workspace menus. (If an in-place object application has previously existed as a stand-alone application, its menus probably have avoided these letters already.)
- OLE verbs should be registered with uniquely assigned mnemonics.

If the same mnemonic is used for more than one menu command, pressing ALT+<*letter*> cycles through the mnemonic candidates. To choose a specific menu or command in this manner, press ENTER when the menu or command is highlighted.

Shortcut Keys

The object application is given the first opportunity to intercept a shortcut key event, passing it on to the container application if no match is found. It is important for the object application to avoid using shortcut keys that are likely to be used by a container application. Both container and object applications should use the shortcut key guidelines outlined in "The Windows Interface: An Application Style Guide" for their Workspace menu commands and Active Editor menu commands. Active Editor commands should make use of the standard editing shortcut keys and not the workspace menu shortcut keys.

Note There is no provision for registering shortcut keys for commands on the Selected Object menu shown in Figure 4-24.

In the event the container and object application share a common shortcut key, the active editor intercepts it. This means that if the object application is active, it gets the shortcut key and take appropriate action, with no negotiation or passing to the container application. Similarly, if the container application is the active editor (even if an OLE object is selected), it intercepts and services the key command. In these collision cases, users need to set the focus to the application that is to respond to the shortcut key.

Pop-Up Menus

Just as keyboard commands are shortcuts to the pull-down menu commands, pop-up menus (also called shortcut or context menus) provide quick access to frequently used and contextual commands by means of the mouse. If an application implements pop-up menus, they can be used in the manner described in the following paragraphs.

Pop-up menus are an auxiliary command interface and therefore contain a subset of the pull-down menu commands. This type of menu looks similar to a standard drop-down menu in that it contains a frame, a shadow, and a list of commands with ellipses (where appropriate) and separator lines. However, pop-up menus are popped-up at the pointer's location, as shown in Figure 4-25, eliminating the need for the user to navigate to a menu or button bar. Pop-up menus take up no screen space since they are only displayed upon demand.

By pressing down the right mouse button, a pop-up menu appears, two pixels beneath and to the right of the current pointer position, to display commands that relate to the object beneath the pointer. No items on the pop-up menu should initially be highlighted; it is only after the pointer has entered into the menu that a command should be highlighted. To prevent the user from inadvertently selecting a command, the pointer is not initially positioned on any of the menu commands. The position of the menu allows the user to conveniently move the pointer down into it.

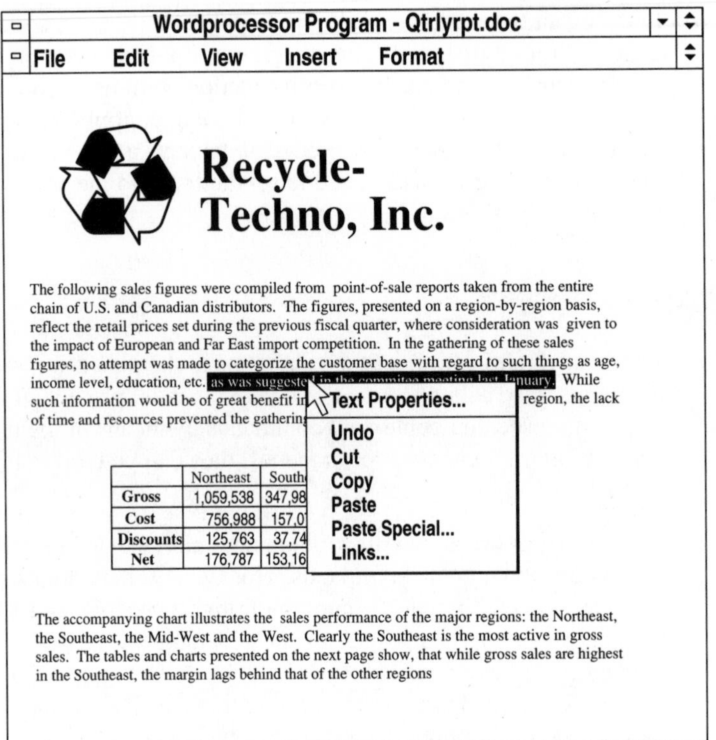

Figure 4-25. Text selection pop-up menu displayed by a word processor.

The pop-up menu is displayed as the right mouse button is pressed down while the pointer is over an object or selection of objects. If the pointer is moved into the menu and the button is released, the command beneath the pointer is executed. If the button is simply released at the button down point (specifically within four pixels of the button down point), the menu remains displayed. However, if the pointer is moved and the button is released outside the menu, then the menu is removed (canceled). This behavior is identical to the that of a drop-down menu when clicked in the menu bar.

Clicking either mouse button within the pop-up menu while the menu is displayed causes that command to be carried out and removes the menu. While the mouse button is held down, selection highlight feedback is provided on the selected command. The action is not executed until the button is released on the command, allowing the user to drag through the menu and highlight other commands or drag off and release to cancel the menu.

While a pop-up menu is displayed, clicking either mouse button outside the menu cancels the menu. This implies that there is at most one pop-up menu displayed at any time. Unlike drop-down menus, the top command of a pop-up menu should not be initially highlighted when the menu first appears. It is only after the mouse pointer is dragged down the menu that any command should be highlighted. As with drop-down menus, the ESC key cancels the menu at any point.

Generally, a pop-up menu is displayed over an explicit selection; such as highlighted text in a word processor document. However, pressing the right button over certain objects both determines the selection and brings up the pop-up menu. For example, pressing the right mouse button over a discrete target such as a spreadsheet cell or an icon could automatically make it the current selection and display its pop-up menu.

The right mouse button may be pressed over items contained outside a normal selection context, such as over interface controls or the screen background. For instance, a pop-up menu over a scroll bar may display useful navigation commands; a pop-up menu over a control bar button may display commands to re-program its function. Invoking pop-up menus on these objects has no effect on the selection within window's content; they are completely separate domains.

If the pointer is positioned so the menu would be appear off the bottom or right side of the screen, the menu position is adjusted so that it is fully visible. Generally, this means that the top-left corner of the menu is slid to the left to avoid the right screen edge or slid up to avoid the bottom screen edge. If the menu would appear both off the bottom and the right edge of the screen, the pop-up menu would be positioned to the left and above the pointer.

The pop-up menu interface provides no mnemonic or shortcut keys because they are defined in terms of the drop-down menus. Pop-up menus are an efficient means of accessing commonly used contextual commands and should contain only frequently used commands and not simply repeat entire drop-down menus. It is recommended that applications arrange commands in pop-up menus from top to bottom in decreasing frequency of use.

Note Including too many commands or multilevel cascade/hierarchical submenus can defeat the purpose of the pop-up menu. While cascade submenus are acceptable, they should be limited to a single level.

The appearance of pop-up menus depends somewhat on their state. When an object is *active*, like the Microsoft Paintbrush Picture below, pop-up menus provided by the object application are in effect. Figure 4-26 shows how a pop-up menu for an active bitmap object might appear.

When an object is *selected*, the pop-up menu is provided by the container application and it should list each of the object's verbs in-line rather than presenting them in a cascade menu. The syntax should be:

<verb> [Linked] <shortform>

It is not necessary to append the word "Object" after the short-form name because mnemonics are not present in pop-up menus and including "Object" would make the menu unreasonably large.

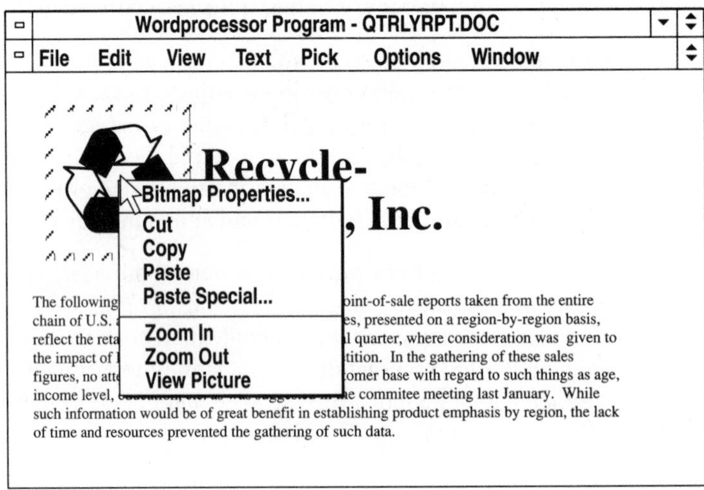

Figure 4-26. Pop-up menu for an active picture object.

Typical pop-up menu commands for verbs could be Edit Picture Link or Play Recording. The Convert... command follows the verb(s) as shown in Figure 4-27.

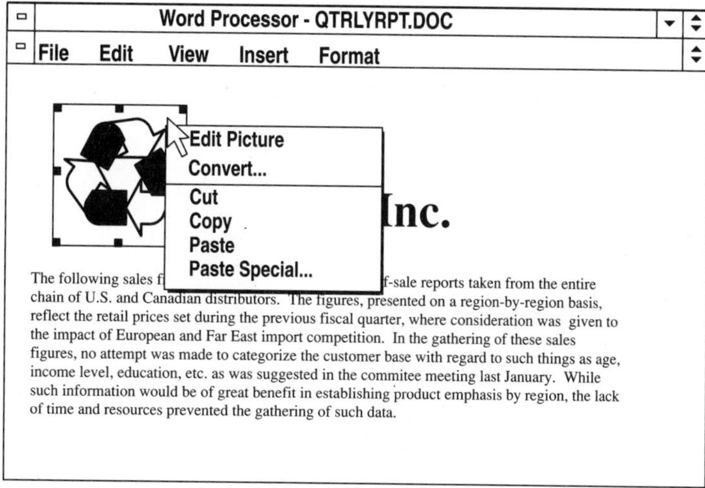
Word Processor - QTRLYRPT.DOC
File
Edit
View
Insert
Format
Edit Picture
Convert...
Cut
Copy
Paste
Paste Special...
Inc.
The following sales f
f-sale reports taken from the entire
chain of U.S. and Canadian distributors. The figures, presented on a region-by-region basis,
reflect the retail prices set during the previous fiscal quarter, where consideration was given to
the impact of European and Far East import competition. In the gathering of these sales
figures, no attempt was made to categorize the customer base with regard to such things as age,
income level, education, etc. as was suggested in the commitee meeting last January. While
such information would be of great benefit in establishing product emphasis by region, the lack
of time and resources prevented the gathering of such data.

Figure 4-27. Pop-up menu for an embedded picture object.

For uniformity, pop-up menus on a selected object should display the object's verbs in order and in line, unlike the cascade verb menu recommendation for the Edit pull-down menu. It is also recommended that a pop-up menu have no more than ten commands. Cascade menus or dialogs are acceptable.

Control Bars, Frame Adornments, Floating Palettes

A object application's commands and interface controls should be presented in their entirety during in-place activation so that users have full access to object application functionality. OLE 2 employs a replacement strategy for arbitrating control bars, frame adornments, floating palettes. Figures 4-28, 4-29, and 4-30, show some examples of these devices.

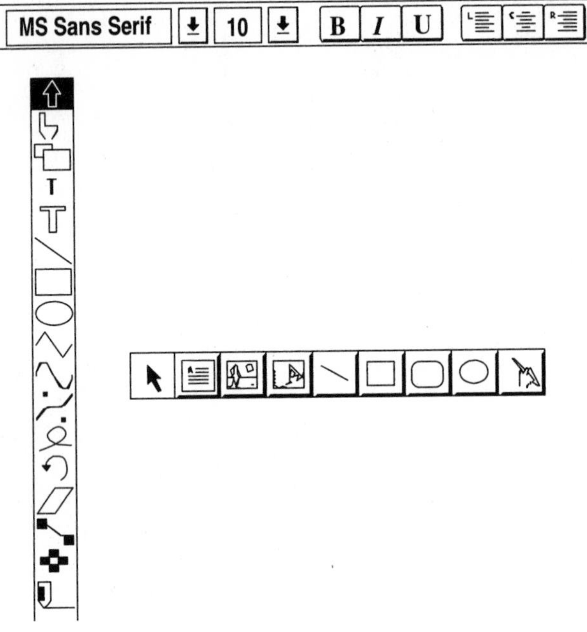

Figure 4-28. Control bar examples.

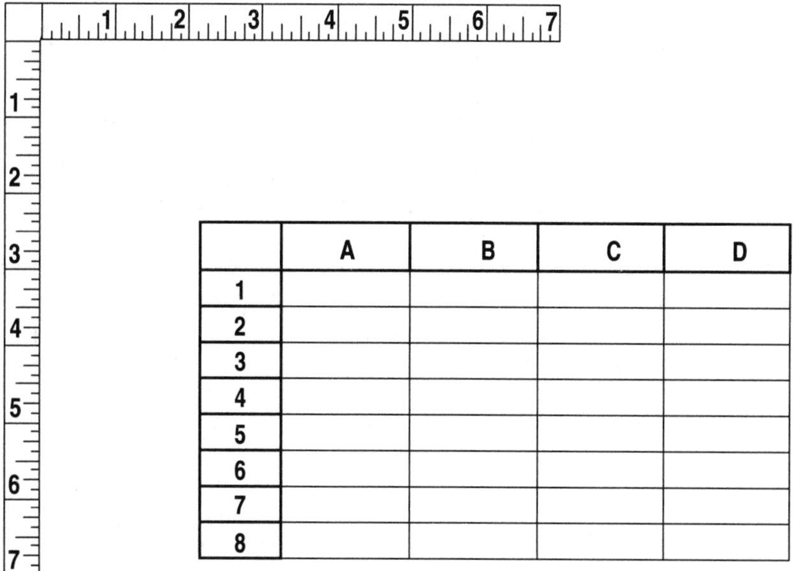
1 2 3 4 5 6 7
1 2 3 4 5 6 7
A
B
C
D
1
2
3
4
5
6
7
8

Figure 4-29. Frame adornment examples.

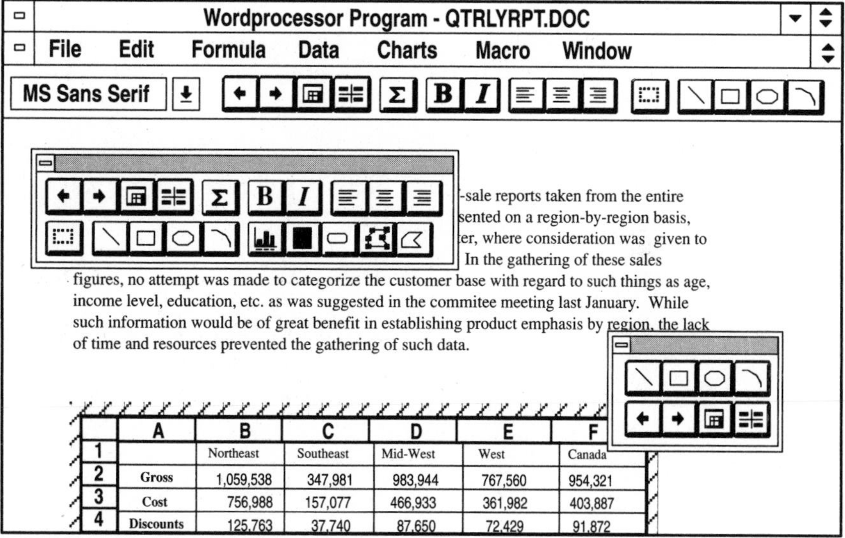
Wordprocessor Program - QTRLYRPT.DOC
File Edit Formula Data Charts Macro Window
MS Sans Serif
Σ
B I
-sale reports taken from the entire
sented on a region-by-region basis,
er, where consideration was given to
In the gathering of these sales
figures, no attempt was made to categorize the customer base with regard to such things as age,
income level, education, etc. as was suggested in the commitee meeting last January. While
such information would be of great benefit in establishing product emphasis by region, the lack
of time and resources prevented the gathering of such data.
A B C D E F
1 Northeast Southeast Mid-West West Canada
2 Gross 1,059,538 347,981 983,944 767,560 954,321
3 Cost 756,988 157,077 466,933 361,982 403,887
4 Discounts 125,763 37,740 87,650 72,429 91,872

Figure 4-30. Floating palette examples.

As with menus on the menu bar, control bars, floating palettes, and frame adornments are displayed and removed in their entirety. The display of floating palettes, which are independent from the container window and are solely under the control of the active object, is relatively simple. Displaying control bars and frame adornments is more complex, because it might require using the same space in the container application window. This could require repainting, relocation, or resizing of some objects.

In keeping with document-centered interaction, swapping active objects' interfaces should keep disturbances of the document's appearance and position to a minimum. Because drop-down and pop-up menus are confined within a particular area and already follow some of the conventions established for Windows applications, their integration into the container is fairly straightforward. However, tool bars and frame adornments are less predictably integrated.

From OLE's perspective control bars, frame adornments, and floating palettes are all basically the same, differing primarily in their location and the degree of shared control between the container and object application. As indicated in Figure 4-31, these types of controls can reside in four locations in the user interface. The choice of location is principally determined by the scope over which the particular control or tool applies.

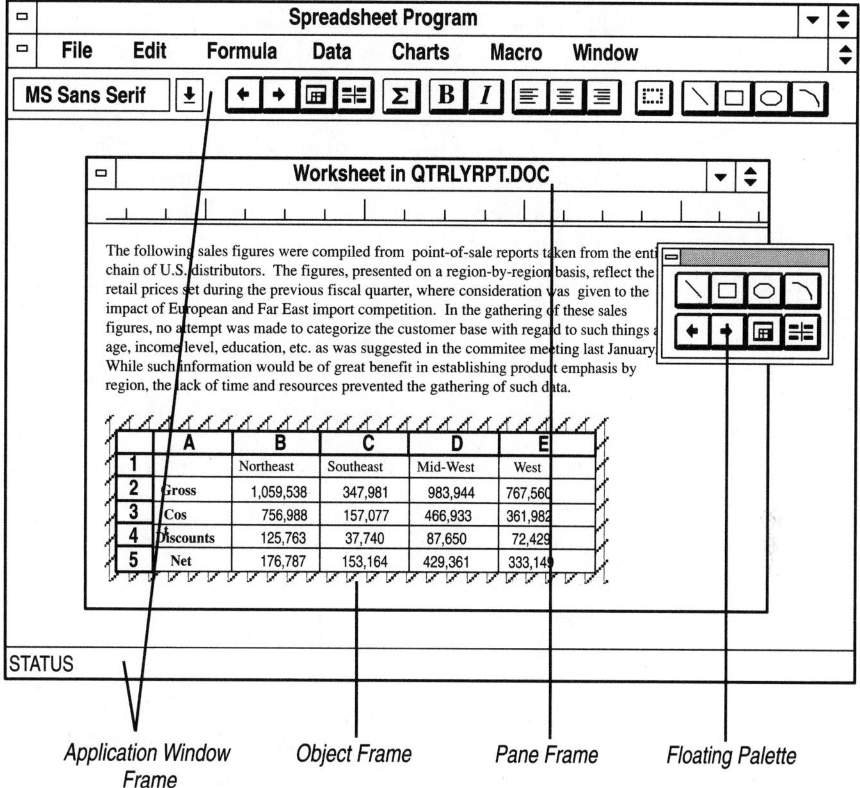

Figure 4-31. Four possible positions for interface controls.

- **Object Frame.** Object-specific controls like a table header or a local coordinate ruler can be placed directly adjacent to the object for tightly coupled interaction between the object and its interface. An object, such as a spreadsheet, may include scroll bars if its content extends beyond the boundaries of its frame.
- **Pane Frame.** Controls and tools that are specific to a view or a single document should be located at the pane level. Rulers and viewing tools are common examples.

- **Application Window Frame.** Tools that apply to the entire document (or documents in the case of an MDI application) may be attached just inside any edge of the application window frame. Popular examples include ribbons, drawing tools, and status lines. Because of Windows' behavior, however, the MDI child windows shift up and down as different-sized toolbars come and go with context switches. This can be disruptive to the user's task, so it is recommended that toolbars either be floated or placed elsewhere when MDI child windows are in the "restored" state.
- **Floating Palette.** Objects can "float" their tools above the document, allowing the user to arrange them as preferred.

As an object becomes active, it requests a specific area from its container in which to post its tools. The container may do one of the following:

- Replace its tool(s) with those of the object if the requested space is already occupied by a container tool.
- Add the object's tool(s) requested space if it is not already occupied by a container tool.
- Refuse to put up the tool(s)at all. (This is the least preferable.)

If container control bars are still visible while an object is active (like the pane ruler in Figure 4-31), they are available for use simply by interacting with them. However, if object-application control bars contain "workspace" commands, such as save, print, or open icons, they must be disabled and should be visually distinguished as unavailable.

As windows are resized and the document is scrolled, the following interface controls are forced to be clipped with respect to their containers.

- An *active object and its frame adornments* are clipped by its immediate window pane just like all document content. Frame adornments can be thought of as handles that lie in the same plane as the object. When the object is clipped, the visible part of the object can be edited in place and the visible frame adornments are operational. Some containers may scroll at certain increments that prevent portions of an embedded object from being edited in place. For example, a large picture embedded in a worksheet cell of a spreadsheet application could exhibit this behavior. The spreadsheet application scrolls vertically in one-row increments so that the top of the pane is always aligned with the top edge of a row. If the embedded picture is too large to fit within the pane at one time, its bottom portion is always clipped and, consequently, never be viewed or edited in place. In cases like this, the user will likely open the picture into its own object application window for editing. Frame adornments of nested embedded objects are also clipped by the immediate window pane, but not by the extent of any parent object.

Objects close to the edge of their container's extent or boundary may potentially surface adornments which will extend beyond the bounds of the container's defined area. In this case, if the container can display items which extend beyond the edge, it should display all the adornments; otherwise, the adornments should be clipped at edge of the container. The container should not temporarily move the object with respect to the content just to accommodate the adornments appearance.

- A *pane-level control* may be potentially clipped by the application window frame (in the case of MDI) and of course an application window-level control may be clipped by other Windows applications.
- A *floating control* floats above all windows.

As indicated in Figure 4-32, alternating between control bars of different sizes in the document pane should have no effect on the content's position as it relates to the pane. In other words, there is no automatic scrolling provision to guarantee the active object remains in view, because in many cases that is not achievable. Consequently pane control bars are thought to lay atop the document's content, requiring the container to repaint parts of the pane as control bars are removed or replaced with smaller ones.

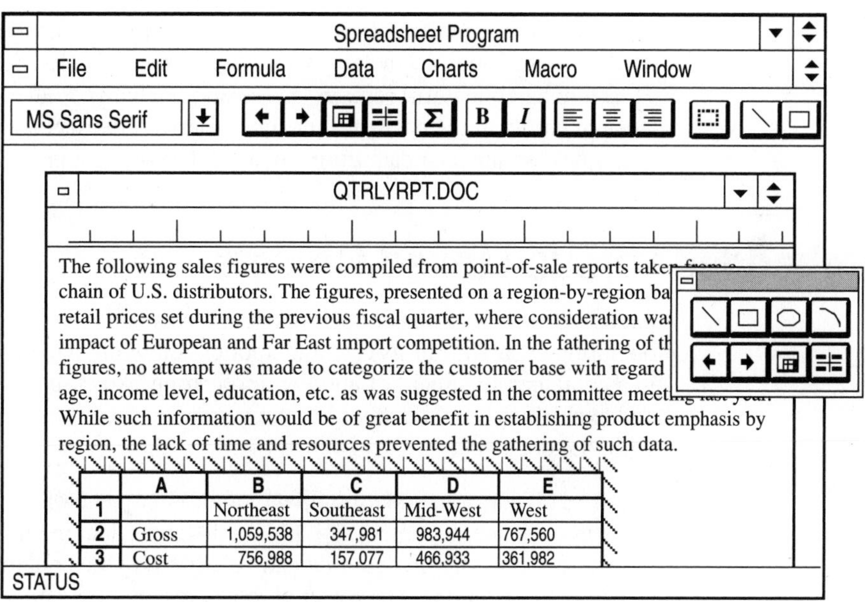
Spreadsheet Program
File
Edit
Formula
Data
Charts
Macro
Window
MS Sans Serif
Σ
B
I
QTRLYRPT.DOC
The following sales figures were compiled from point-of-sale reports take
chain of U.S. distributors. The figures, presented on a region-by-region ba
retail prices set during the previous fiscal quarter, where consideration wa
impact of European and Far East import competition. In the fathering of tl
figures, no attempt was made to categorize the customer base with regard
age, income level, education, etc. as was suggested in the committee meet
While such information would be of great benefit in establishing product emphasis by
region, the lack of time and resources prevented the gathering of such data.
A B C D E
1 Northeast Southeast Mid-West West
2 Gross 1,059,538 347,981 983,944 767,560
3 Cost 756,988 157,077 466,933 361,982
STATUS

Figure 4-32. Interface control clipping.

By preserving the content's position, the user's focus is not disturbed by the active object bumping down to accommodate the new set of control bars, and bumping back up when it is deactivated. This rule is to be followed even if the arriving control bars will clip the object of interest. There is one exception: when the container is to scroll the document as a result of a control bar change. If the document is at its very top or bottom and removing a control bar would expose an undefined area (an area beyond the document's extent), then the document may scroll to take up the space left by the control bar.

When the focus is removed from a window which contains an active object (either because another MDI child window or a different application has taken focus) the following guidelines should be observed for switching the user interface elements.

- With respect to MDI, those user interface elements that the active object puts up in the space *shared* by MDI documents (such as menu bar, frame level toolbars, and the floating palette layer) should be removed as focus is given to another MDI document. The new MDI document will then show the user interface elements of its pending active object (if it has one) in these spaces. This guideline does not apply to workspace-provided tools which equally apply to all MDI documents. Such workspace elements should persist between document focus changes.
- Object user interface elements that are wholly contained within the MDI document window (such as pane rulers, object-frame adornments, and the active hatch pattern) remain visible and unchanged when their document (or application in the case of SDI) loses focus. This scheme preserves the editing context so the user can return focus and easily resume editing.

Embedded versus Linked Objects

An embedded OLE object contains data that retains the original editing and operating capability of its creating application while the embedded object resides in a container document of another application. An embedded object is wholly and exclusively contained within the container document and is saved and moved with that document.

A linked object is an updating image of another piece of data residing at another point in the same document or within a different document altogether. A linked object does not contain data that can be edited by the containing application, but rather an image of the data referred to as presentation data, often a Windows metafile. This image of the source data provides the user with a visual representation of the linked object and provides the user with access to the object's verbs.

Note Based on appearances, the user may interact with a linked object as if the source data of the object were contained in the document. In many instances, users interact with embedded and linked objects and pay little attention to differentiating them.

Automatic and Manual Updating

When a link is created, it is an automatic link by default. Whenever the appearance of its source data changes, the automatically linked object's appearance also changes without any request from the user. The user can specify a link to be manual by means of the Links... dialog box. A manual link means that the linked object is updated only when requested by the user. The update request is issued by choosing the Update Now button within the Links... dialog box and optionally in conjunction with the container's usual "update fields" or "recalc" action.

Verbs and Links

An object responds to the same set of verbs defined for its class whether it is embedded or linked. Issuing verbs like "play" or "rewind" to a linked sound object appears to activate the object in place. However, issuing a verb that is intended to alter the object's content data (such as "open" or "edit") exposes the linked source data by launching the associated object application.

While links may *play* in place, they may not *edit* in place. Editing in place implies that the actual data resides, even if only temporarily, in the document containing the link. It is important to not blur the fact that the link source holds the object's data and that the data does not move to the container of the link for editing. So, in order for link sources to respond to editing verbs, the source object, and any containing objects and documents, are opened to properly respond to the verb.

The most common case of a link responding to an edit verb is when the user double clicks a link whose primary verb is edit. The source document opens to reveal the link source object for editing. This functionality might appear similar to opening an embedded object into a separate window, but this is not the case. Editing a linked object is functionally identical to launching an application on the link source's document, such as through the Program Manager or File Manager. Unlike an opened embedded-object application, which is bound to the container application window and causes the hatch pattern across the object, there is no special association between the link-source and link-destination application windows. The applications operate and close independently.

Note The link source may be on an unmounted network server, so it may require the user to first establish access to the source before OLE can open it. If the user tries to open an available source document, the container should post a message such as "Please connect to \\foo\bar and retry opening the <*object_type*> link."

It is the responsibility of the object application, when implementing the execution of an editing verb, to notify its immediate container that the source needs to be exposed. Below are the three different situations in which an object might notify its container:

- **Embedded**. If the verb is executed by an embedded object, the container document and parent objects are already exposed so there is no need to start the object's container.
- **Already Opened Link Source Document.** If the verb is issued to a link source whose document is already opened, the currently active view of that document (in the case of a multiview or multipane application) scrolls as necessary and unveils the source object ready for interaction.
- **Closed Link Source Document.** The verb notifies its immediate container requesting it to expose the source to the user. All additional containers are opened resulting in the link source being fully exposed and ready for editing.

Types and Links

A link's type is a cached copy of its source's type taken when the last update was issued. Because it is possible to change the type of a link source object, all links derived from a converted object bear the old type and verbs until either an update occurs or the link application is launched. Because out-of-date links might display obsolete verbs to the user, upon issuing a verb from a link to its source, the container should compare the cached link type with that of its sources. If the cached link type has changed, the container should do one of the following:

- If the verb issued from the old link is syntactically identical to one of verbs registered for the source's new type, execute the verb index of that new verb.
- If the issued verb is no longer supported by the link source's new type, issue an error message similar to that shown in Figure 4-33.

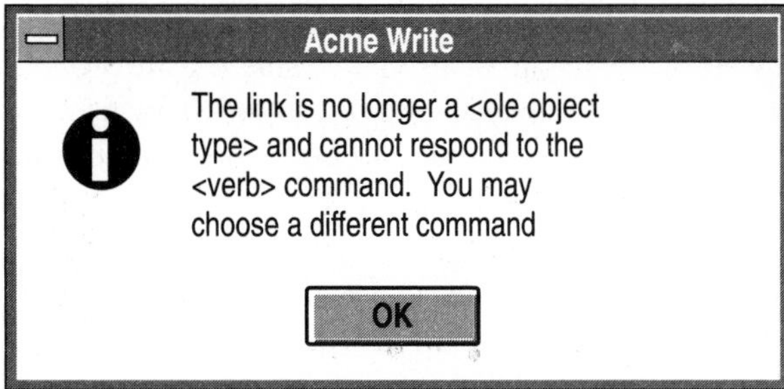

Figure 4-33. Error message for obsolete link verb.

The link should then adopt the source's new type and bear the new verbs in its menu.

Maintaining Links

A link has three properties: the name of its source data, its type (or class as it's known internally), and its updating basis, either automatic (default) or manual. As shown in Figure 4-34, the container application supplies a Links... dialog box that allows the user to change the name of its source data and its updating basis. A link's type is determined by its source's type, and it can be changed by converting it to another type.

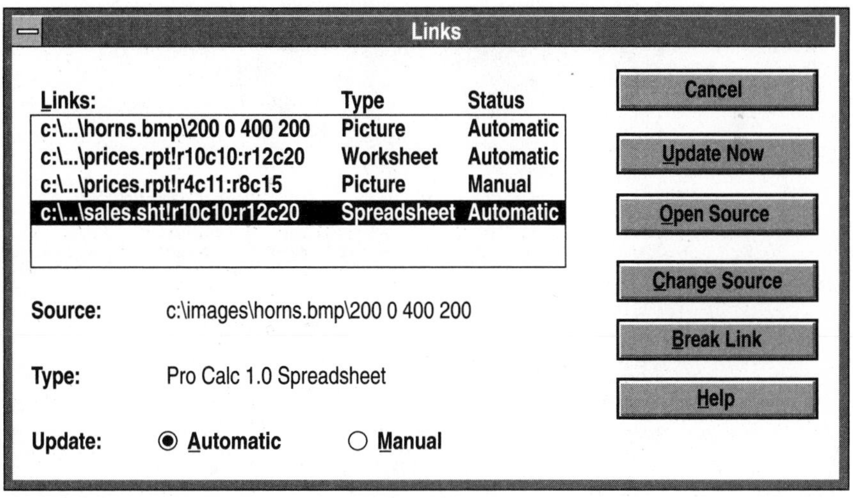

Figure 4-34. The Links dialog box.

If a link's source cannot be found, "Unavailable" should appear in the status column. Multiple link sources from the same file are grouped and indented beneath the common filename. Only the eight-character filename with a three-character extension appears in the list box; the full pathname is exposed in the lower portion of the dialog box.

Allow 15 characters for the Type field, and enough space for "Automatic," "Manual," and "Unavailable" to appear completely. As each link in the list is selected, its type, name, and updating status appear in their entirety in the lower left of the dialog box.

Break Link effectively disconnects the selected link(s). Update Now forces the selected link(s) to connect to their sources and retrieve the latest information..

The Open Source button opens the source document(s) for the selected link(s). The Open Source button should be the default when clicking within the links list, therefore double clicking a list item opens the source of the particular link.

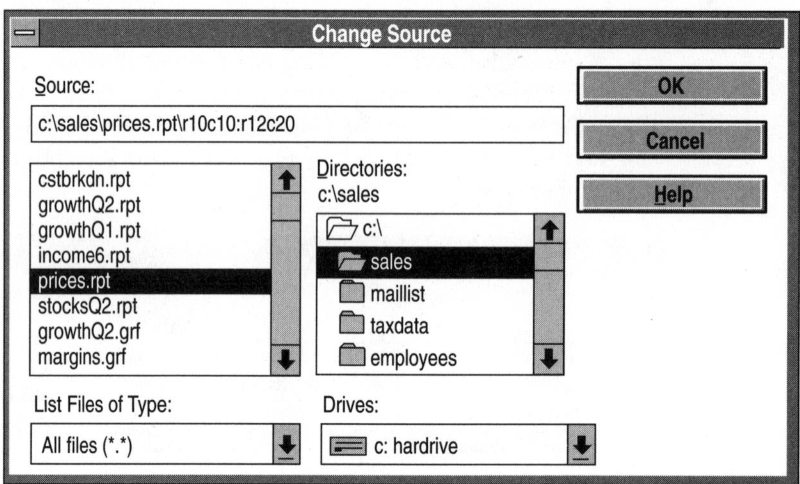

Figure 4-34. The Change Source dialog box.

The Change Source button in the Links... dialog box invokes a Change Source dialog box (shown in Figure 4-35) that is similar to the standard FileOpen dialog box. The Change Source dialog box allows the user to respecify the link source. It edits only the file portion of the link source, so it is up to the user to manually enter the subdocument portion of the string if the source points to a location within the file. The user may key in a source name that does not designate an already existing object. Upon selecting OK, the Change Source dialog box prompts "Invalid Source. Do you wish to correct it? Yes, No."

Answering Yes returns to the Change Source dialog box so the string can be corrected; answering No causes the container to hold onto the unparsed display name of the link source until such time later as the user successfully causes the link to connect to a newly created object that satisfies the dangling reference. Some containers may allow users to connect only to presently valid links.

If multiple links share any portion of their source's names and the user edits that common portion for one link, the user is given the option of making the same change for the other similar links. The dialog box shown in Figure 4-36 is the means by which users redirect links to new locations, such as when directory or file names have been changed.

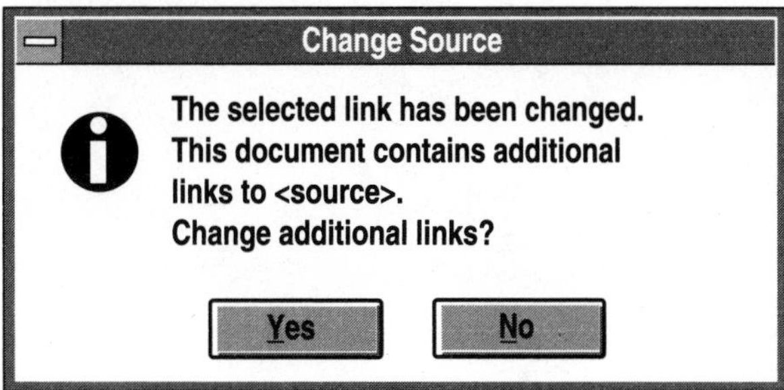

Figure 4-36. Changing additional links with same source message.

Object Transfer Model

This section explains how objects are moved, copied, and linked within and across documents. This is done using:

- The standard clipboard method invoked through commands from either drop-down or pop-up menus.
- The drag and drop method, which enables users to directly drag objects from one location to another.

The clipboard method allows the user to move, copy, and link data and optionally specify data formats. The drag and drop method allows the user to quickly perform moves, copies, and links when little navigation is needed. The two approaches cooperate to give the user both a global and expedient means of arranging information in documents.

Clipboard Method

▶ **Using the clipboard method, a user performs the following steps:**

1. Make a selection in the source document.
2. Choose either Cut (CTRL+X) or Copy (CTRL+V) from the menu (either the Edit pull-down menu or a pop-up menu).
3. Navigate or edit as preferred within the destination document.
4. Choose an insertion point (or a selection if it is to be replaced) within the destination document.
5. Choose Paste [<*shortform*>] (CTRL+V) or Paste Special... to insert the clipboard contents.

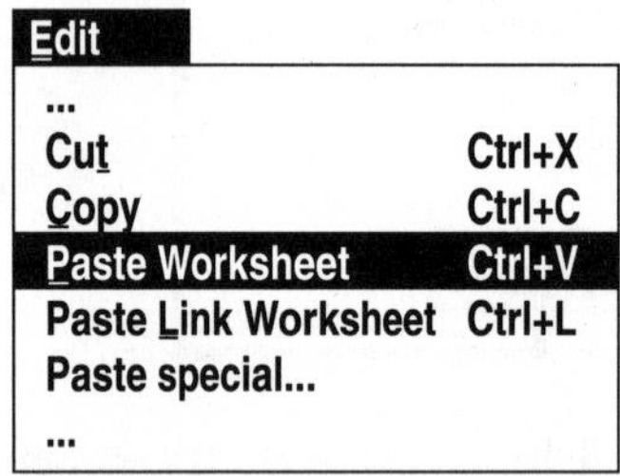

Figure 4-37. The Paste [*shortform*] and Paste Link [*shortform*] menu commands.

The Cut/Paste operation removes the user's selection from the source document and relocates it at the insertion point in the destination document, while the Copy/Paste operation inserts an independent duplicate of the selection, leaving the original unaffected. Choosing Paste Special... displays the dialog box shown in Figure 4-38 to give the user explicit control over how to paste the clipboard's contents. The default Paste operation embeds the object if possible. If the destination document application can edit the clipboard data, the application pastes the data format it is capable of editing. For example, pasting a bitmap object from one bitmap editor to the document of another causes the object to become part of the destination document's data instead of an embedded object.

If the default settings for the Paste operation results in embedding the object, the command should read Paste <*shortform*>; for example, Paste Worksheet and Paste Recording. Similarly, if the container application includes the Paste Link command, the command should read Paste Link Worksheet, Paste Link Recording, and so on. The Paste command appearing on the menu with no item extension simply means the data is going to be pasted as native information without OLE intervention. Note that the short form of the object type is used for <*shortform*>.

The Paste Special dialog box shows the name of the source data (using moniker-type syntax), provides the Paste and Paste Link option buttons, and lists the possible data formats associated with each option button. A section of result text describes the result of the currently chosen function and format. Pictures are displayed with the help text to communicate the end result of the chosen operation. Also note the same Display as Icon option found in the other dialog boxes.

When the Paste option button is selected, the list box shows the full object type name (without the trailing "object") and other native data forms. When the clipboard contains an already linked object, its object type should be preceded by "Linked" in the format list. For example, if the user copied a linked Microsoft Excel 5.0 Worksheet to the clipboard, Paste Special would show "Linked Microsoft Excel 5.0 Worksheet" under the Paste format options since a Paste would insert an exact duplicate of the original linked worksheet.

Native data formats should be expressed in the same terms as the destination application uses in its own menus. When Paste Link is chosen, both the object type (full form) and any native format that supports linking appears. The default formats for the Paste and Paste Link options are the same as what the default Paste [<*shortform*>] and Paste Link [<*shortform*>] would use as formats.

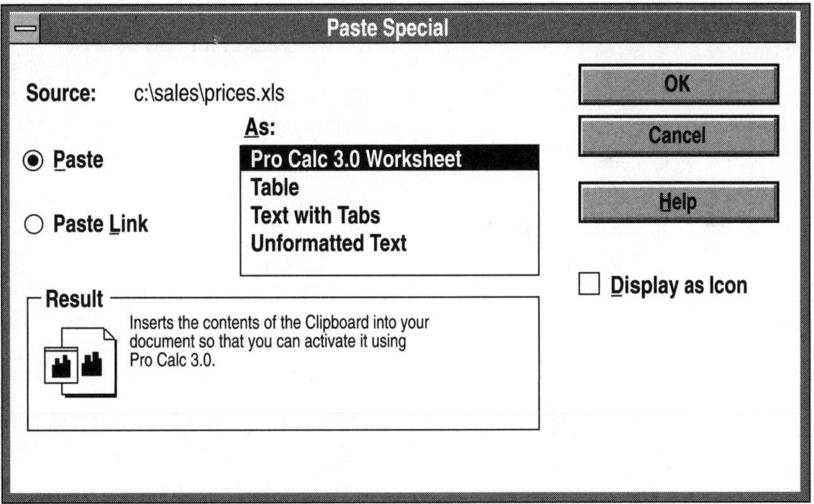

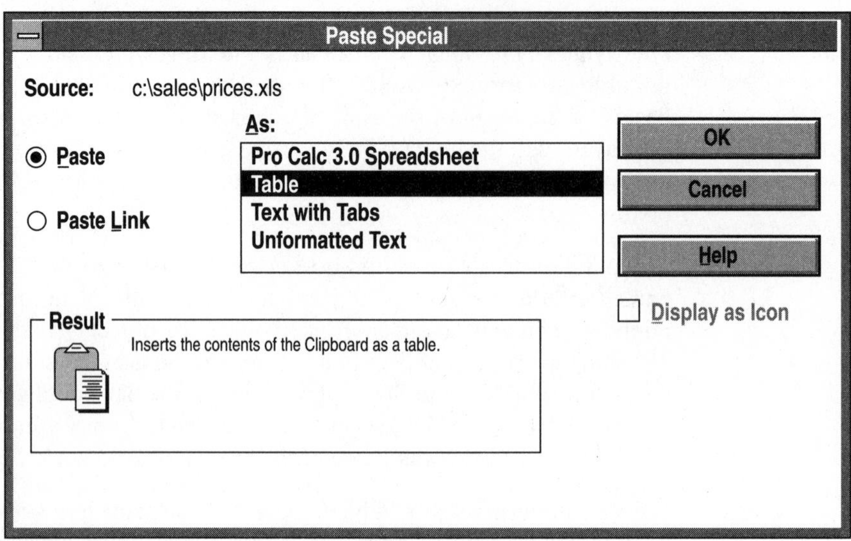
Paste Special
Source: c:\sales\prices.xls
As:
Paste
Paste Link
Pro Calc 3.0 Spreadsheet
Table
Text with Tabs
Unformatted Text
OK
Cancel
Help
Display as Icon
Result
Inserts the contents of the Clipboard as a table.

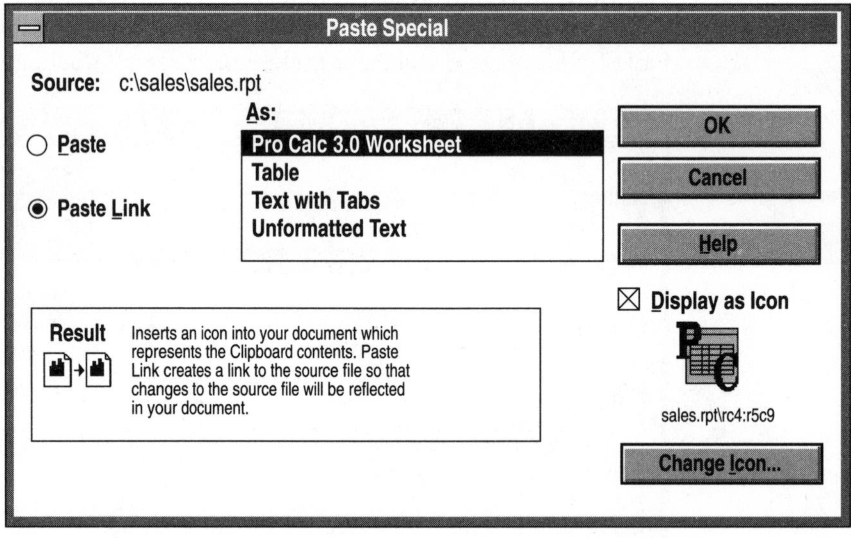
Paste Special
Source: c:\sales\sales.rpt
As:
Paste
Paste Link
Pro Calc 3.0 Worksheet
Table
Text with Tabs
Unformatted Text
OK
Cancel
Help
Display as Icon
Result
Inserts an icon into your document which represents the Clipboard contents. Paste Link creates a link to the source file so that changes to the source file will be reflected in your document.
sales.rpt\rc4:r5c9
Change Icon...

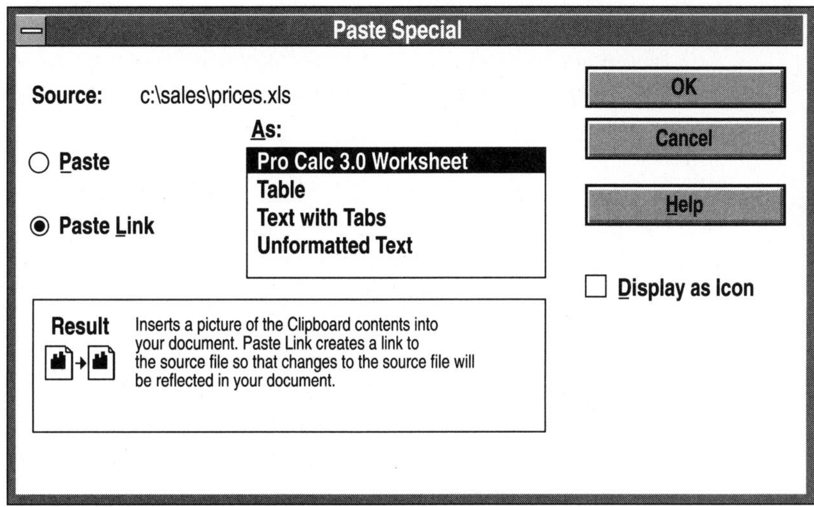

Figure 4-38. The Paste Special dialog box with different selections.

The recommended Result text for the Paste Special dialog box is listed below.

Function	Result Text
Paste.[Linked] Object	Inserts the contents of the Clipboard into your document so you may activate it using *<object app name>*.
Paste.[Linked] Object as Icon	Inserts the contents of the Clipboard into your document so you can activate it using *<object app name>*. It is displayed as an icon.
Paste.Data	Inserts the contents of the Clipboard into your document as *<native type name and optionally an additional help sentence>*.
Paste Link.Object	Inserts a picture of the Clipboard's contents into your document. Paste Link creates a link to the source file so changes to the source file will be reflected in your document.
Paste Link.Object as Icon	Inserts an icon into your document that represents the Clipboard contents. Paste Link creates a link to the source file so that changes to the source file will be reflected in your document.
Paste Link.Data	Inserts the contents of the Clipboard into your document as *<native type name>*. Paste Link creates a link to the source file so that changes to the source file will be reflected in your document.

In implementing the Paste Special (Figure 4-38) and Insert Object dialogs, it is recommended that container applications use monikers to hold the pathnames to link sources. Monikers perform the binding to the object and properly track names across networks.

Drag and Drop Method

Using the drag and drop method for object movement, a user can directly transfer objects from document to document as well as supply objects to system resources such as printers and mailboxes.

▶ **The user's steps for performing a drag and drop are:**

1. Press the left mouse button with the pointer over the object to grab it. For objects such as text or table cells, it may be necessary to first select the correct range. Depending on their visual representation, objects may also be dragged by a move handle or its frame border.
2. Holding the left mouse button, drag the object to the intended target location.
3. Release the left button over the intended insertion point to drop the object.

The pointer should change to the following shape when over invalid drop targets.

Unmodified drag should almost always perform a move operation. Only in exceptional cases (like dragging to a printer) should unmodified drag not perform a move. CTRL-drag should always perform a copy operation. SHIFT-CTRL drag is the suggested modifier for linking, and ALT-drag is suggested for insisting a move operation (mainly for backwards compatibility with existing applications that use it now). In cases where a drop of a particular object or the insisted operation is not permitted (because of improper type or context), the pointer shown above indicates that a drop will not happen. Typically, the pointer's appearance generally suggests which type of transfer is to be performed as feedback to the user.

For example, for a cell selected in a range of embedded worksheet cells, as shown in Figure 4-39, the user would start the drag by grabbing the selection's border with the mouse and pointer.

	A	B	C	D	E	F
1		Northeast	Southeast	Mid-West	West	Canada
2	**Gross**	1,059,538	347,981	983,944	767,560	954,321
3	**Cost**	756,988	157,077	466,933	361,982	403,887
4	**Discounts**	125,[illegible]3	37,740	87,650	72,429	91,872
5	**Net**	176,[illegible]	153,164	429,361	333,149	458,562

Figure 4-39. Select and start drag.

The "move" pointer appears by default and the user has a choice of six different categories of targets. These are enumerated in Figure 4-40. The significance of each of the target categories in this figure is described below.

Drag Scrolling.
: Dragging normally passes over pane borders, but if the user wants to scroll to an out-of-view drop target, the pane can be scrolled while dragging the object. By placing the pointer just 11 pixels inside any one of the pane's four boundaries, the pane scrolls in the direction of that edge (up in the case of Figure 4-40). The corresponding scroll bar arrow immediately depresses when the pointer is within range, but the actual scrolling begins after the pointer is within 11 pixels (on a VGA screen) of the pane edge for an uninterrupted 50 milliseconds and continues until the pointer moves outside the 11-pixel region. The pointer arrow's image is inverted immediately and remains so while it is within the region. After the document has scrolled to the proper point, the user can drop the object at the intended target.

Container Area.
: An object can be dropped in the container of the currently active object.

Active Object.
: This drag is completely internal to the spreadsheet application shown in Figure 4-40 and is handled like a normal dragging in the application.

Other Document.
: In this case, the drag has left the pane (and application window) and is being dropped into another application.

System Resource (Icon).
: Here the object is being dropped on a particular printer that highlights by means of the selection color. Copy is the default operation for the drag and drop operation to a system resource.

Illegal Target.
: When the target cannot accept a drop, such as the screen background in Figure 4-40, the "not allowed" pointer should be displayed.

Inside-out Activated Object (not shown in Figure 4-40).
: Since inside-out activated objects are effectively always active, they can serve as a drop target. They should provide accurate drop target feedback to indicate the result of the dropping item.

Note The "not allowed" pointer should be displayed when dragging over a linked object because OLE does not support dropping on linked targets.

Drag scrolling, *container area*, and *active object* types of targets are possible in any window, not just the active application window. The plus sign near the arrowhead of the *system resource* pointer indicates that the default drag function is copy (not move). The user may insist a move operation by holding down the SHIFT key, insist a copy operation by holding down the CTRL key, or insist a link operation by holding down both the SHIFT and CTRL keys. The drag is qualified by the modifier keys only while they are held down; releasing the modifiers before the drop results in a default drop. The pointer's appearance suggests which type of transfer is to be performed as feedback to the user. (See "The Windows Interface: An Application Design Guide" for these pointer appearances.)

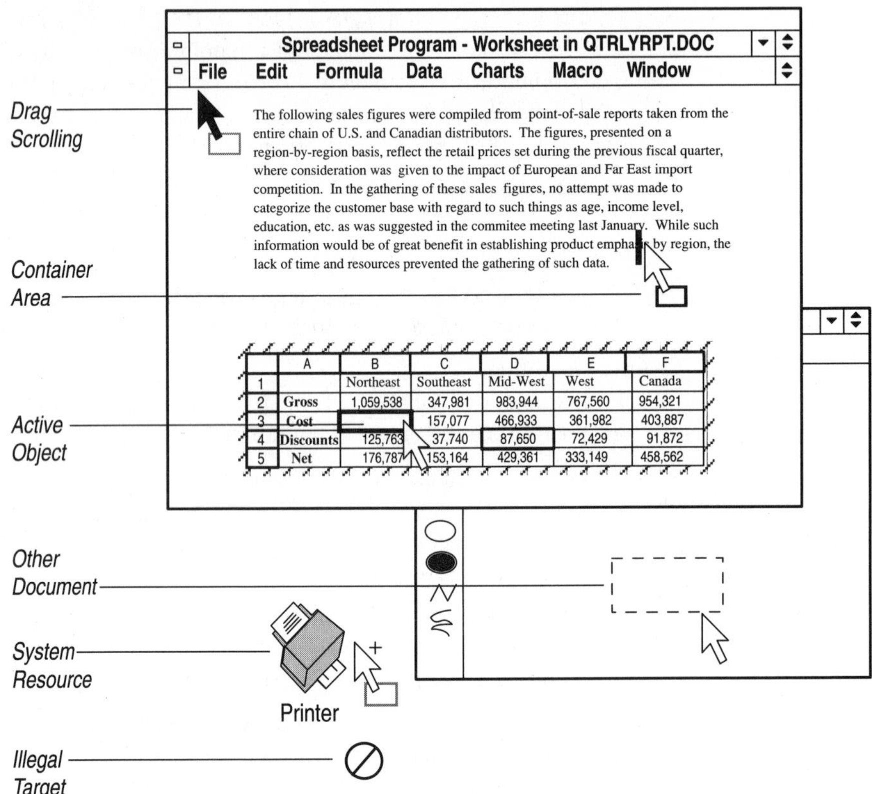
Spreadsheet Program - Worksheet in QTRLYRPT.DOC
File Edit Formula Data Charts Macro Window
Drag Scrolling
The following sales figures were compiled from point-of-sale reports taken from the entire chain of U.S. and Canadian distributors. The figures, presented on a region-by-region basis, reflect the retail prices set during the previous fiscal quarter, where consideration was given to the impact of European and Far East import competition. In the gathering of these sales figures, no attempt was made to categorize the customer base with regard to such things as age, income level, education, etc. as was suggested in the commitee meeting last January. While such information would be of great benefit in establishing product emphasis by region, the lack of time and resources prevented the gathering of such data.
Container Area
A B C D E F
1 Northeast Southeast Mid-West West Canada
2 Gross 1,059,538 347,981 983,944 767,560 954,321
3 Cost 157,077 466,933 361,982 403,887
4 Discounts 125,763 37,740 87,650 72,429 91,872
5 Net 176,787 153,164 429,361 333,149 458,562
Active Object
Other Document
System Resource
Printer
Illegal Target

Figure 4-40. Possible drag and drop targets.

These drag and drop operations produce the same end result as Cut/Paste, Copy/Paste, and Copy/Paste Link, respectively, but there is no implied bearing on the state of the Clipboard because the two transfer methods are completely independent.

(No modifier)	Alt	Ctrl	Shift+Ctrl
		+	=
Determined by destination (recommend move)	Force move	Force copy	Link

When dragging an icon from the Windows File Manager into a document, it should effectively perform an "insert object from file," exposing the content of the object if at all possible. Of course, if the file is not OLE aware, it is embedded and continues to be displayed as a document icon.

An inactive object cannot be used as a drop target because it is unable to give precise feedback on where within itself an item would be dropped.

It is further suggested that the "drop-point" indicator (the checkered I-beam) shown below be displayed with the pointer as target feedback when dragging over text areas. Because text areas are a common drop site, it is particularly necessary for the user to see this consistent feedback.

This is the insertion point
for a drag operation

Dialog Box Messages

If the user attempts to launch an object application that cannot be run as a stand-alone application, the error message of Figure 4-41 should be issued.

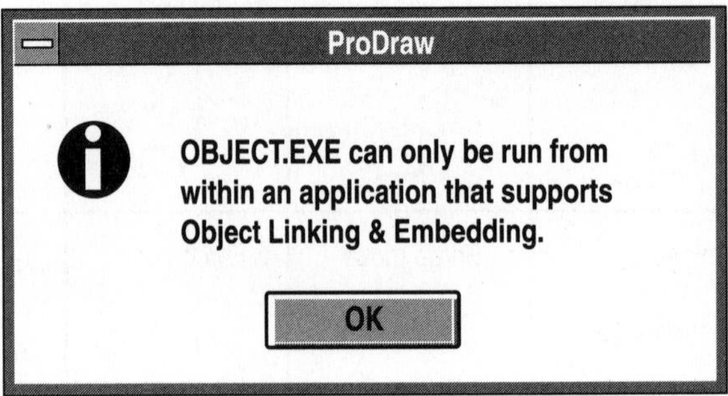

Figure 4-41. Warning Message, object application cannot be run as a stand-alone application.

If the container application fails to locate the requested object application (that is registered in the database) when user selects the entry from the Insert Object dialog, or when the user double clicks on an object, the error message shown in Figure 4-42 should be displayed. Browse... invokes the standard File Open dialog box, and the user-supplied path should be entered in the registration as the new object application pathname.

Note To ensure that the registration database is current, object applications should register themselves, or verify registration, when started.

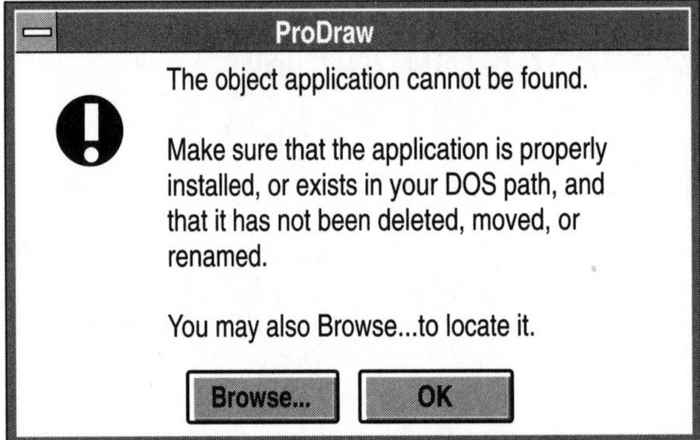

Figure 4-42. Warning Message when object application cannot be found.

An object application can be busy or unavailable for several reasons. For example, it might be busy printing, waiting for user input to a modeless error message, or it could be hung or accidentally deleted. If the object application is not available, the warning message in Figure 4-43 should be displayed.

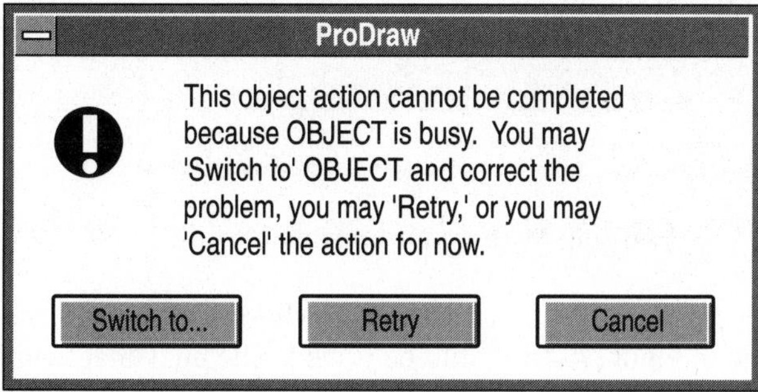

Figure 4-43. Warning Message when object application is busy.

The progress indicator shown in Figure 4-44 should be displayed while the links are being updated (when a document containing automatic links is opened). The Stop button interrupts the update process and prevents any additional links from being updated.

Figure 4-44. Progress Indicator for link updating.

If some of the linked files are unavailable, the warning shown in Figure 4-45 is displayed. This dialog box contains OK and Links... buttons. The OK button closes the dialog box without updating the links. The Links... button displays the Links dialog box (see Figure 4-33) with all the links listed in a list box. Unavailable linked files are marked with the word "Unavailable" in the third column of the list box. The user can attempt to locate the unavailable files by using the Change Source dialog (see Figure 4-35), which is available from the Change Source... command button in the Links dialog.

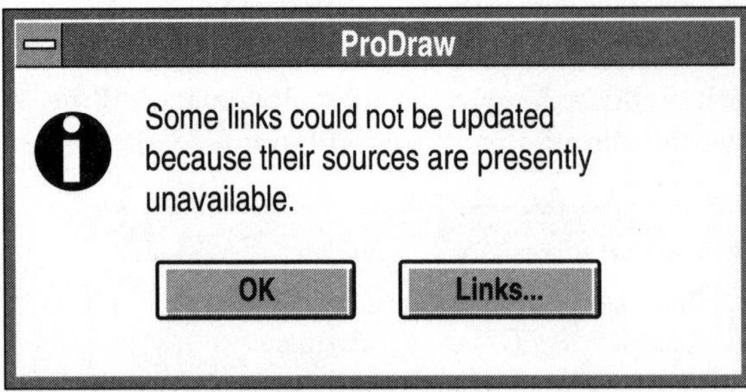

Figure 4-45. Warning Message for unavailable links.

If the user issues a command to a link whose source is unavailable, the warning message in Figure 4-46 should be issued. The unavailable link will be marked as such in the Links dialog.

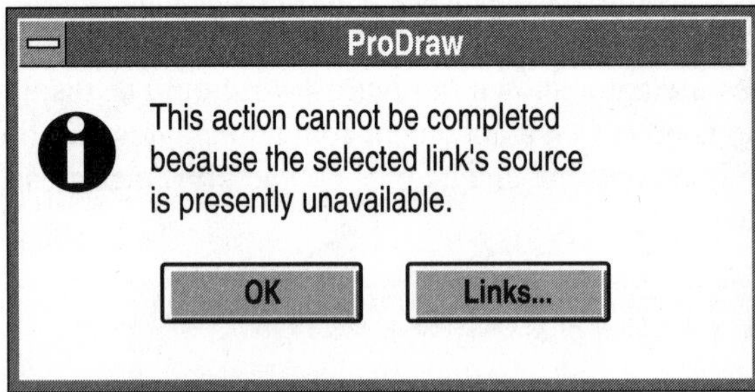

Figure 4-46. Warning Message for issuing a command to an unavailable link.

Status Bar Messages

Menu Commands	Status Bar Message
File Menu	
Update <*container-document*>	Updates the appearance of this <*descriptive type name*> in <*container document*>
Save Copy As...	Save a copy of <*descriptive type name*> in a separate file
File Menu	
Exit & Return to <*container-document*>	Exit <*object application*> and return to <*container-document*>
If the open object is within an MDI application with other open documents, this command should simply be "Exit." There is no way to guarantee a successful "Return to <container document>" after exiting since the container might have been one of the other documents in that MIDI instance.	
Edit Menu	
Paste <*shortform*>	Inserts Clipboard contents as <*descriptive type name*>*
Paste Special...	Inserts Clipboard contents as a linked object, embedded object, or other format
Paste Link <*shortform*>	Inserts a link to <*descriptive class name*> Object from <*source-document*>
Insert Object...	Inserts a new embedded object
<*verb*> [Linked] <*shortform*>**	None
[Linked] <*shortform*> Object ->	Apply the following commands to <*descriptive class name*> Object
[Linked] <*shortform*> Object -> <*verb*>	None
Links...	Allows links to be viewed, updated, opened, or canceled

Menu Commands	Status Bar Message
Options (Preferences) Menu	
Show Objects	Displays the borders around objects (toggle)
Mouse Interface	
When an object is selected	Double click to or press ALT+ENTER to *<primary-verb>****-*<descriptive type name>* Object

*The *<descriptive type name>* is identical to the initially highlighted value in the list box in the Paste Special dialog box. This status bar message indicates the data format used to paste clipboard contents.

**If no verb in the registration database is specified, "Activate" should be used as a default verb.

***The verb that is stored in the registration database will contain "&" (a mnemonic indicator) that needs to be stripped out before the verb is displayed in the status bar.

PART 2

Reference Information

CHAPTER 5

Component Object Interfaces and Functions

IUnknown Interface

The **IUnknown** interface methods enable an application to obtain pointers to other interfaces supported by the same object and to manage the interface pointer(s) obtained on an object. **IUnknown** is used by OLE and all OLE-aware applications. Because **IUnknown** is the interface from which all other OLE interfaces are derived, it *must* be implemented by all applications.

The **IUnknown** interface is implemented and used by both object and container applications. **IUnknown** contains the following methods (see also COMPOBJ.H):

```
DECLARE_INTERFACE(IUnknown)
{
 HRESULT QueryInterface (THIS _ REFIID riid, LPVOID FAR* ppvObj) ;
 ULONG AddRef (THIS ) ;
 ULONG Release (THIS ) ;
};
```

Reference Counting

The **AddRef** and **Release** methods in the **IUnknown** interface keep track of the reference count for an object. When an application obtains access to interface pointer *pInterface*, the application calls *pInterface->AddRef* to increment the reference count. When the application is finished with the pointer, it calls *pInterface->Release*, in much the same way that one might call **GlobalFree** to free a global memory block. When the reference count for a particular interface goes to zero, the interface implementation can be freed. When there are no more interface pointers on an object as a whole, the object can be freed.

The general rules that apply to callers and callees of interface methods are described in the following paragraphs.

- If a local copy of an interface pointer is made from an existing global interface pointer, the local copy must be independently reference-counted. This separate reference count is necessary because the global copy can be destroyed while the local copy is in use.
- If a pointer passed as a parameter is copied into one or more global variables, or as a variable that is not returned to the caller, each copy must be independently reference counted.
- Every instance of an interface pointer returned to a caller must be reference counted. For example, **IUnknown::QueryInterface**, **IOleItemContainer::GetObject**, **IOleContainer::EnumObjects**, and **IClassFactory::CreateInstance** all return interface pointers and must include a call to **AddRef** to increment the reference count on the returned pointer. Every function receiving an interface pointer must call **Release** on that interface.
- Interface pointers that are passed from a caller are temporarily owned. This implies that the methods of that interface can be called and that the object implementing that interface will remain alive during the call(s). If a pointer is returned from one of these interface method calls, the pointer is considered fully owned and its reference count must be incremented. For example, if the temporary pointer is used to call **QueryInterface,** and **QueryInterface** returns a pointer to an interface, the reference count on the returned pointer must be incremented. If this pointer is not returned to the caller, **Release** must be called to decrement its reference count.
- If pointers to two different interfaces are both obtained by calling **QueryInterface** on the same **IUnknown**, **Release** should be called once on each pointer; rather than on **IUnknown** or on one of the pointers twice. This constraint allows future implementations to store reference counts on parts of aggregates rather than on a whole aggregate.

Note When objects are created, their reference count may initially be zero. If a newly created object with a zero reference is passed as a function parameter, it is necessary to ensure the object's stability by incrementing the reference count prior to the function call. This technique is referred to as *artificial reference counting*. After the function returns, the reference count can be decremented. Safeguarding an object through artifical reference counting may also be necessary prior to the object's destruction, which is an unstable time for the object.

Avoiding Reference Counting Cycles

It is possible to create cycles whereby a reference count would never reach zero. This can occur when two objects hold pointers to each other and a third object holds a pointer to one of the other two objects. Two strategies can be implemented to avoid a potential cycle. Depending on the object and its use, it may be possible to avoid reference counting one of the interface pointers. An alternate strategy is to manage separate reference counts, whereby the object is not destroyed until all of the reference counts are zero.

Figure 5-1 illustrates a potential cycle scenario and the two strategies for avoiding that cycle. ObjectX and ObjectY both hold pointers to interfaces in ObjectAB; ObjectAB holds a pointer to InterfaceA in ObjectY. In the first case, ObjectAB avoids a cycle by not counting its reference to ObjectY, as is indicated by the dotted line.

In the second case, ObjectAB avoids a cycle by maintaining separate reference counts, as is indicated by the dotted line.

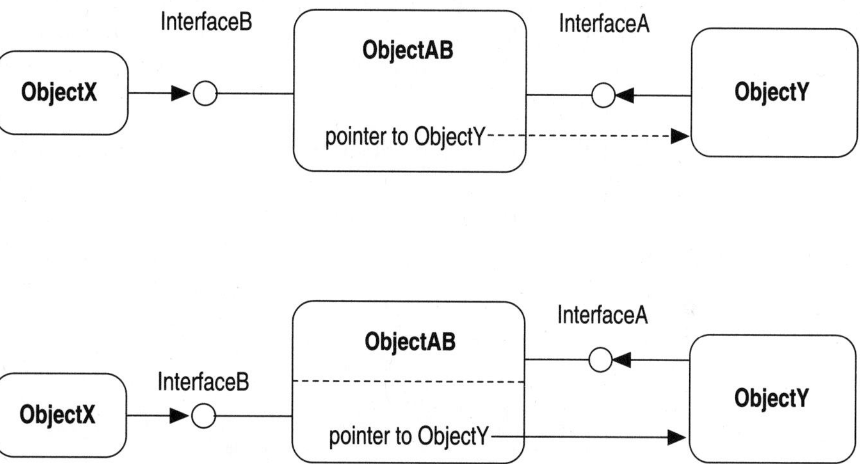

Figure 5-1. Avoiding a reference counting cycle.

Figure 5-2 shows how a reference cycle can occur in an aggregate object. The controlling unknown points to the **IUnknown** implementation in the noncontrol object who in turn points to the controlling unknown. To avoid a cycle, the noncontrol object's pointer to the controlling unknown is not reference counted, as is indicated by the dotted line.

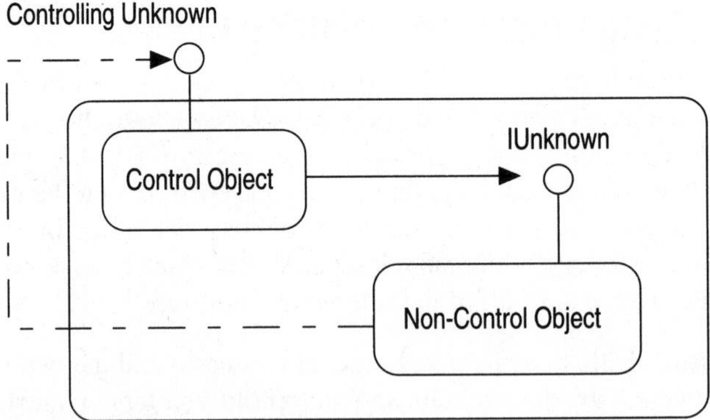

Figure 5-2. Reference counting cycle in an aggregate object.

Optimizing Reference Counting

Reference counting manages the lifetimes of an object so that it is kept alive only if necessary. If it is possible to know the relationships between the lifetimes of two or more copies of an interface pointer, the reference counting process can be streamlined. Most relationships fall into two categories: 1) nested lifetimes and 2) overlapping lifetimes.

Figure 5-3 presents an illustration of the two types of relationships. In a nested lifetime relationship, the first copy of the interface pointer is created followed by the creation of the second copy.

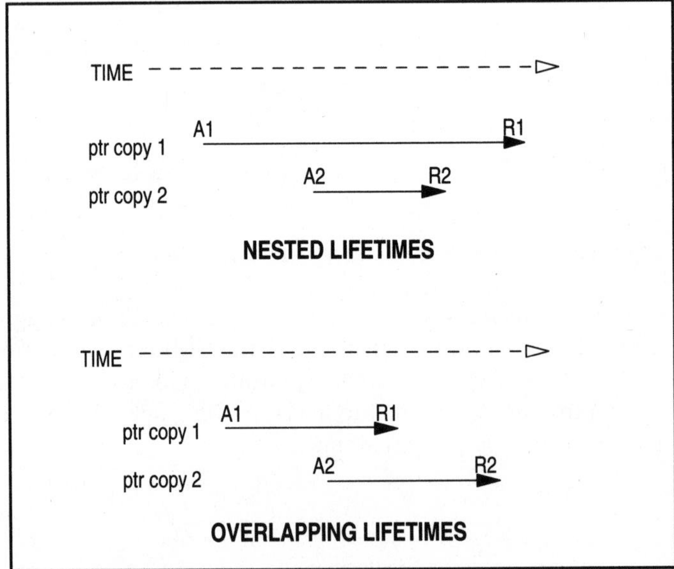

Figure 5-3. Nested versus overlapping lifetimes of an interface pointer.

The second copy is destroyed before the end of the first copy's lifetime. The calls to **AddRef** (A2) and **Release** (R2) can be omitted. The overlapping lifetime relationship begins the same as the nested lifetime relationship with the second interface pointer created after the first. However, with overlapping lifetimes, the first pointer copy is destroyed before the second pointer copy. The **AddRef** (A2) and **Release** (R1) calls can be omitted.

The following general rules are helpful in reference counting optimization:

- ***In* parameters to functions**. An interface pointer passed as a function parameter has a lifetime that is nested in the pointer used to initialize the parameter. Therefore, the function parameter need not be reference counted separately.
- ***Out* parameters from functions**. Parameters returned from function calls (including return values), must have a stable copy of the interface pointer. On exit, the caller must release the pointer. The returned parameter need not be reference counted separately.
- **Local variables**. A function clearly knows the lifetimes of each local pointer variable allocated on the stack frame. It can use this information to omit redundant **AddRef** and **Release** calls.
- **Back pointers**. Data structures often contain two components, A and B, each containing a pointer to the other. If A is known to contain the lifetime of B, then the pointer from B to A need not be reference-counted.

IUnknown::QueryInterface

HRESULT IUnknown::QueryInterface(*riid, ppvObj***)**
REFIID *riid*
LPVOID FAR* *ppvObj*

IUnknown::QueryInterface returns a pointer to a specified interface on a particular object. This function allows a client to query an object to determine what interfaces it supports.

Parameters

riid
Specifies the interface ID of the interface being queried for.

ppvObj
Points to the object (on exit) whose interface is being queried. If the interface specified in *riid* is not supported by the object, E_NOINTERFACE is returned. All errors set **ppvObj* to NULL.

Return Values

Value	Meaning
S_OK	Interface is supported and **ppvObj* is set.
E_NOINTERFACE	Interface is not supported by the object; **ppvObj* is set to NULL.
CO_E_OBJNOTCONNECTED	Handler created but object application is not running. The object application must be running to determine whether it supports interface (much like OLE_E_NOTRUNNING but more general).
REGDB_E_IIDNOTREG	Object application is running, but *riid* cannot be remoted because no information exists in the registration database to indicate how it is to be done.
E_OUTOFMEMORY	Out of memory.
E_INVALIDARG	One or more arguments are invalid.
E_UNEXPECTED	An unexpected error occurred.

Comments

If an object supports multiple interfaces that are each derived from **IUnknown**, calling **IUnknown::QueryInterface**(IID_IUnknown) on any one of the interfaces *must* return the same pointer, regardless of which interface is called. To determine whether two pointers point to the same object, call **IUnknown::QueryInterface**(IID_IUnknown,...) on both and compare the results.

In contrast, queries for interfaces other than **IUnknown** are not required to return the same pointer value each time **QueryInterface** is called to return a pointer to them.

The set of interfaces accessible on an object by using **IUnknown::QueryInterface** must be static, not dynamic. For example, consider the following pointer:

```
ISomeInterface *pSome = (some function returning an ISomeInterface *);
```

where **ISomeInterface** derives from **IUnknown**. Now suppose the following operation is attempted:

```
IOtherInterface * pOther;
HRESULT herr = pSome->QueryInterface(IID_IOtherInterface, &pOther); //line 3
```

Then, based on the assignment made in line 3, the following must be true:

- If *herr*==NOERROR, calling **IUnknown::QueryInterface** a second time from the same *pSome* pointer returns NOERROR again. This action is independent of whether *pOther* was released in the interim.
- If *herr*==E_NOINTERFACE, calling **IUnknown::QueryInterface** a second time from the same *pSome* pointer returns E_NOINTERFACE again.

In lines 1-3, **IUnknown::QueryInterface** must be symmetric, reflexive, and transitive with respect to the set of accessible interfaces as follows:

Symmetric:

```
pOther->QueryInterface(IID_ISomeInterface, ...)
```

must succeed.

Reflexive:: If, in line 3, *pOther* were successfully obtained, then

```
pSome->QueryInterface(IID_ISomeInterface, ...)
```

must succeed.

Transitive: If in line 3, *pOther* were successfully obtained, and the following assignment were then made:

```
IYetAnother * pyet;
HRESULT herr = pother->QueryInterface(IID_IYetAnother, &pyet);  // line 6
```

and `pyet` were successfully obtained in line 6, then

```
pyet->QueryInterface(IID_ISomeInterface, ...)
```

must succeed.

Notice that succes does not mean that two **QueryInterface** calls on the same pointer asking for the same interface must succeed and return exactly the same pointer; all that is required is that **QueryInterface** not indicate that the interface is not available.

Examples

The first example is a simple implementation of **IUnknown::QueryInterface** that returns a pointer to one of two interfaces supported by the application's class object: **IUnknown** or **IClassFactory**. Notice that the *out* parameter, *ppvObj*, is set to NULL initially. If the caller requests another interface, E_NOINTERFACE is returned, indicating that the interface is not supported by the object. Before a pointer is returned, the **IUnknown::AddRef** method for the class object is called to increment the reference count on the object.

```
HRESULT IUnknown_CO_QueryInterface(LPCLASSFACTORY lpThis,
        REFIID riid, LPVOID FAR* ppvObj)
{
    *ppvObj = NULL;
    LPMYCLASSOBJECT lpMyClassObj = (LPMYCLASSOBJECT)lpThis;

    if (IsEqualIID(riid, &IID_IClassFactory) ||
        IsEqualIID(riid, &IID_IUnknown)) {
        IUnknown_CO_AddRef(lpMyClassObj);
        *ppvObj = lpThis;
        return ResultFromScode(S_OK);
```

```
        }
        else
            return ResultFromScode(E_NOINTERFACE);
}
```

The next example is a more complex implementation of **IUnknown::QueryInterface** for a document object. The first check is for **IUnknown**, since the document object supports it in all cases. The next check is whether this object is a data transfer object that has been placed on the clipboard or made available with a drag and drop operation. Data transfer objects support **IDataObject** and **IDropSource** only. If the object is not a data transfer object, **IPersist** and **IPersistFile** are supported. Since **IPersistFile** is derived from **IPersist**, the same pointer is returned when either interface is requested.

```
HRESULT IUnknown_Doc_QueryInterface(
        LPDOC               lpDoc,
        REFIID              riid,
        LPVOID FAR*         ppvObj)
{
    *ppvObj = NULL;
    if (IsEqualIID(riid, &IID_IUnknown)) {
        *ppvObj = (LPVOID) &lpDoc->m_Unknown;
        IUnknown_Doc_AddRef(lpDoc);
        return ResultFromScode(S_OK);
    }
    else if(lpDoc->m_fDataTransferDoc  {
        if (IsEqualIID(riid, &IID_IDataObject)) {
            *ppvObj = (LPVOID) &lpDoc->m_DataObject;
            IUnknown_Doc_AddRef(lpDoc);
            return ResultFromScode(S_OK);
        }
        if ((bDropSource) && IsEqualIID(riid, &IID_IDropSource)) {
            *ppvObj = (LPVOID) &lpDoc->m_DropSource;
            IUnknown_Doc_AddRef(lpDoc);
            return ResultFromScode(S_OK);
        }
    }

    if(IsEqualIID(riid,&IID_IPersist) ||
      IsEqualIID(riid,&IID_IPersistFile)) {
        *ppvObj = (LPVOID) &lpDoc->m_PersistFile;
        IUnknown_Doc_AddRef(lpDoc);
        return ResultFromScode(S_OK);
    }
    return ResultFromScode(E_NOINTERFACE);
}
```

See Also **IUnknown::AddRef**, **IUnknown::Release**

IUnknown::AddRef

ULONG IUnknown::AddRef()

IUnknown::AddRef is used to increment a reference count for every new copy of an interface pointer to a specified interface on a particular object.

Return Values

Value	Meaning
0 to *n*.	The value of the reference count. When fully released, it is zero. This information is used for diagnostics and testing only. It *cannot* be used by shipping code because, in certain situations, it is unstable.

Comments

IUnknown::AddRef is used by container objects to stabilize a copy of an interface pointer. **IUnknown::AddRef** is also used in those instances where the life of the cloned pointer must extend beyond the lifetime of the original pointer. The cloned pointer must be released by calling **IUnknown::Release**.

Objects must be able to maintain (2^{31})-1 outstanding pointer references. Therefore, the internal reference counter that **AddRef** maintains must be a 32-bit unsigned integer.

Example

The following example, **IUnknown_Doc_AddRef**, simply increments the reference count maintained for the document object and then returns it.

```
ULONG IUnknown_Doc_AddRef(LPDOC lpDoc)
{
    ++lpDoc->m_cRef;
    return lpDoc->m_cRef;
}
```

See Also

IUnknown::Release

IUnknown::Release

ULONG IUnknown::Release()

IUnknown::Release decrements the reference count on a specified interface of a particular object. If the object reference count goes to zero as a result of the **Release**, the object is freed from memory.

Return Values

Value	Meaning
0 to *n*.	The value of the reference count on the whole object. When fully released, it is zero. This information can be used for diagnostics and testing only. It *cannot* be used by shipping code because, in certain situations, it is unstable. If a client needs to know that resources have been freed, it must use an interface with higher-level semantics before calling **Release**.

Comments

If **IUnknown::AddRef** has been called on this object's interface *n* times and this is the *n+1th* call to **IUnknown::Release**, the interface pointer will free itself. An object frees itself if the released pointer is the only pointer and if the object supports multiple interfaces through **IUnknown::QueryInterface**.

Note Because of restrictions in the implementation of OLE 2, **IUnknown::Release** must return zero if the identity of the object has been destroyed. This restriction will be removed in future implementations. Therefore, clients *cannot* rely on zero having any special significance other than for debugging purposes.

Note Aggregation of objects restricts the ability to recover interface pointers.

Example

The following example is an implementation of **IUnknown::Release** for a document object. The reference count is decremented and if it has reached zero, **Doc_Destroy** is called to destroy the object.

```
ULONG IUnknown_Doc_Release (LPDOC lpDoc)
{
    ULONG cRef;

    cRef = --lpDoc->m_cRef;
    if (cRef == 0)
        Doc_Destroy((LPDOC)lpDoc);

    return cRef;
}
```

See Also

IUnknown::AddRef, IUnknown::QueryInterface

IClassFactory Interface

The **IClassFactory** interface is used to create instances of an object class in memory. The **IClassFactory** interface is implemented by object applications and is used by OLE. It is optionally implemented by container applications that allow linking to embedded objects.

IClassFactory contains the following methods (see also COMPOBJ.H):

```
DECLARE_INTERFACE_(IClassFactory, IUnknown)
{
  // *** IUnknown methods ***
 HRESULT QueryInterface (THIS _ REFIID riid, LPVOID FAR* ppvObj) ;
 ULONG  AddRef (THIS );
 ULONG  Release (THIS );

  // *** IClassFactory methods ***
 HRESULT CreateInstance (THIS _ LPUNKNOWN pUnkOuter, REFIID riid,  LPVOID FAR* ppvObj) ;
 HRESULT LockServer (THIS _ BOOL fLock) ;

};
```

Object applications and handler implementors implement one class object (that is, one instance of the **IClassFactory** interface) for each object class they support. Object applications register the public availability of their class of objects with **CoRegisterClassObject** so that container applications may connect to them. Object handlers implement and export the **DllGetClassObject** function in order to make available their object class(es).

Creating Instances of an Object Class

▶ **Creating an instance of an object class is done using the appropriate variation of the following steps:**

1. Determine the class of the object to instantiate.

   This step identifies the CLSID (see "Creating New CLSIDs & IIDs") of which an instance is needed. Depending on the task at hand, this differs from situation to situation. Following are some examples:

   - In the Insert Object Dialog, each object type in the list has a unique associated CLSID. If a user wants to insert a given type, an instance of this CLSID is required.
   - When an object is loaded into memory from persistent storage, the class of object that is to manipulate the object data is identified with a unique CLSID that is kept in persistent storage along with the object's data.

2. Obtain the class factory for the specified CLSID.

   This is done by calling **CoGetClassObject**, as shown in the following example (for brevity, this code and the other examples in this section omit error checking):

```
LPCLASSFACTORY lpcf;
CoGetClassObject(clsid, CLSCTX_INPROC, 0, IID_IClassFactory,
    (void**)&lpcf);
```

   The class context (second parameter) is used to specify the type of object application that is to be used. For more information on the class context, see **CoGetClassObject**, later in this chapter.

3. Create an uninitialized instance of the class.

   An uninitialized instance is created using **IClassFactory::CreateInstance**. The interface requested from the object should be the one by which the object is initialized. For OLE embeddings, this interface is **IPersistStorage**, but the particular interface to be used depends on the situation. If the object is being created as part of an aggregate, the controlling unknown is passed.

```
LPPERSISTSTORAGE lpPersistStorage;
lpcf->CreateInstance(NULL, IID_IPersistStorage,
            (LPVOID *)&lpPersistStorage);   // non-aggregate case
lpcf->Release();
```

4. Initialize the newly created instance.

   This involves invoking one or more methods in the requested initialization interface. For OLE embeddings, a reloaded object is initialized with **IPersistStorage::Load**, while a new blank object is initialized with **IPersistStorage::InitNew**.

Until an object is initialized, only the following operations are guaranteed to succeed:

- **QueryInterface** calls to either **IUnknown** or to an initialization interface on the object. Non-initialization interfaces are specifically excluded as the set of these may not be known until the object is initialized. For embedded objects, **IPersistStorage** is the initialization interface.
- **AddRef** and **Release** calls on any obtained interface derived from **IUnknown**.
- Calling initialization methods appropriate for the object. For embedded objects, **IPersistStorage::InitNew** and **IPersistStorage::Load** are the legal methods.

5. Query for some working interface on the instance and clean up.

   Often, when the interface needed on an object has been initialized, it is different than the interface by which initialization is done. In this final step, call **IUnknown::QueryInterface** for the working interface needed and then clean up by releasing the previously obtained pointers:

```
LPOLEOBJECT lpOleObject;
lpPersistStorage->QueryInterface(IID_IOleObject,
    (LPVOID FAR*)&lpOleObject);
lpPersistStorage->Release();
```

Creating New CLSIDs & IIDs

Each class of object must have a unique CLSID so that the particular object can be identified in the presence of any other object(s). CLSIDs are generated with the help of the GUIDGEN.EXE, a Windows utility that is provided with the OLE software development kit. By default, GUIDGEN.EXE puts a DEFINE_GUID macro on the clipboard which you can then paste into your source.

Applications can also call **CoCreateGuid**, which does the same as running GUIDGEN.EXE (GUIDGEN.EXE internally calls **CoCreateGuid**).

GUIDGEN.EXE is both a DOS and a Windows utility, though to use it from DOS requires the WXSERVER.EXE utility to be installed and running. An example of using GUIDGEN.EXE is as follows:

```
[C:\WIN]guidgen /t
80C11F40-7503-1068-8576-00DD01113F11
```

The string representation of a CLSID, as determined by **StringFromCLSID**, is the string generated by GUIDGEN.EXE surrounded by two braces. To create a CLSID from a string, call **CLSIDFromString**, as follows:

```
CLSID clsid;
CLSIDFromString("{80C11F40-7503-1068-8576-00DD01113F11}", &clsid);
```

Interface IDs (IIDs) are allocated in a similar way, except that **IIDFromString** is used in place of **CLSIDFromString**.

OLE also provides the **DEFINE_GUID** macro for declaring and initializing a GUID in hexadecimal. As an example, given the following GUID string, the **DEFINE_GUID** macro can be used to make the number available as an interface ID in a program (*name* is some user defined interface):

```
DEFINE_GUID(name, 0x00000301, 0x0000, 0x0000, 0xc0, 0x00, 0x00, 0x00, 0x00, 0x00, 0x00, 0x46)
```

Using a string returned from GUIDGEN.EXE with **DEFINE_GUID** becomes:

```
DEFINE_GUID(name, 0x414EA760, 0xC1C5, 0x1068, 0xB3, 0x6A, 0x00, 0xDD, 0x01, 0x0F, 0x75, 0x4F)
```

The **DEFINE_GUID** macro also does the initialization of the GUID if `#define INITGUID` was used before `#include <COMPOBJ.H>` or INITGUID.H was included after COMPOBJ.H.

CLSIDs and IIDs can also be obtained by contacting Microsoft directly.

IClassFactory::CreateInstance

HRESULT IClassFactory::CreateInstance(*pUnkOuter, riid, ppvObj*)
LPUNKNOWN *pUnkOuter*
REFIID *riid*
LPVOID FAR * *ppvObj*

IClassFactory::CreateInstance creates an uninitialized instance of an object class. Initialization is subsequently performed using another interface-specific method, such as **IPersistStorage::InitNew**, **IPersistStorage::Load**, **IPersistStream::Load**, or **IPersistFile::Load**.

Parameters

pUnkOuter
Points to the controlling **IUnknown** interface if the object is being created as part of an aggregate. It is NULL if the object is not part of an aggregate.

riid
Identifies the interface by which the caller will communicate with the resulting object and through which it initializes the object.

ppvObj
Points to where the pointer to the object will be returned.

Return Values

Value	Meaning
S_OK	The specified class of the object was created.
CLASS_E_NOAGGREGATION	*pUnkOuter* was non-NULL and the object does not support aggregation.
E_NOINTERFACE	The object pointed to by *ppvObj* does not support the interface identified by *riid*.
E_UNEXPECTED	An unexpected error occurred.
E_OUTOFMEMORY	Out of memory.
E_INVALIDARG	One or more arguments are invalid.

Comments

The *pUnkOuter* parameter indicates whether the object is being created as part of an aggregation. Because object classes must be consciously designed to be aggregate objects, not all classes can participate in aggregation.

The container passes to **IClassFactory::CreateInstance** the interface to be used to communicate with the resulting object instance. The newly created object is usually initialized by using this interface. For OLE compound document objects (embedded and linked), this process is encapsulated by the **OleLoad** helper function.

In general, if an application supports one object class and the class object is registered for single use, only one instance of the object class can be created. The application must refuse to create other instances of the class, returning an error from **IClassFactory::CreateInstance**. The same is true for applications that support multiple object classes, each having a class object registered for single use: a **CreateInstance** for one class followed by a **CreateInstance** for any of the classes should return an error.

To avoid returning an error, applications that support multiple classes with single-use class objects can revoke the registered class object of the first class by calling **CoRevokeClassObject** when a request for instantiating a second class is received. For example, suppose there are two classes, A and B. When **IClassFactory::CreateInstance** is called for class A, revoke the **IClassFactory** for B. When B is created, revoke A. This solution complicates shutdown because one of the **IClassFactory** objects might have already been revoked (and cannot be revoked twice).

Example

The following example shows **IClassFactory::CreateInstance** for a single-use application. Notice that a single-use application does not support the creation of more than one instance of an object at a time; **CreateInstance** guards against this happening. After the new document instance has been created, its reference count is zero. **IUnknown_Doc_QueryInterface** is called to return a pointer to the requested interface. If the requested interface is available, the reference count is incremented to one.

```
HRESULT IClassFactory_CreateInstance (
        LPCLASSFACTORY       lpThis,
        LPUNKNOWN            pUnkOuter,
        REFIID               riid,
        LPVOID FAR*          ppvObj)
{
    LPAPP         lpApp = (LPAPP)g_lpApp;
    LPDOC         lpDoc;
    HRESULT       hrErr;

    *ppvObj = NULL;

    //guard against calling CreateInstance twice for SDI apps
    if (lpApp->m_lpDoc != NULL)
        return ResultFromScode(E_UNEXPECTED);
```

```
    // Create new doc instance and set ref count to 1
    lpApp->m_lpDoc = App_CreateDoc(lpApp, FALSE);
    lpDoc = (LPDOC)lpApp->m_lpDoc;
    if (! lpDoc)
        return ResultFromScode(E_OUTOFMEMORY);

    hrErr = IUnknown_Doc_QueryInterface(lpDoc, riid, ppvObj);
    return hrErr;
}
```

See Also

CoGetClassObject, CoRegisterClassObject, CoRevokeClassObject

IClassFactory::LockServer

HRESULT IClassFactory::LockServer(*fLock***)**
BOOL *fLock*

IClassFactory::LockServer keeps an open object application in memory. Keeping the object application alive in memory allows instances of this class to be created more quickly.

Parameters

fLock
Specifies the lock count. If TRUE, it increments the lock count; if FALSE, it decrements the lock count.

Return Values

Value	Meaning
S_OK	The specified object was either locked (*fLock* = TRUE) or unlocked from memory (*fLock* = FALSE).
E_FAIL	Indicates an unspecified error.
E_OUTOFMEMORY	Out of memory.
E_UNEXPECTED	An unexpected error occurred.

Comments

A container application can call this method to obtain better performance in situations where there is a need to create and release instances frequently.

If the lock count and the class object reference count are both zero, the class object can be freed.

Most clients do not need to call **IClassFactory::LockServer.** It is used primarily by sophisticated clients with special performance needs from certain object classes.

The process that locked the object application is responsible for unlocking it. Once the **IClassFactory** is released, there is no mechanism by which the caller can be guaranteed to later connect to the same class (for example, consider single-use classes). It is an error to call **IClassFactory::LockServer(TRUE)** and then release the **IClassFactory** without first releasing the lock with **IClassFactory::LockServer(FALSE)**.

Most implementations of **IClassFactory::LockServer** do nothing more than call **CoLockObjectExternal**. For more information on locking objects in memory, see "CoLockObjectExternal," later in this chapter.

Example

In the following example, **IClassFactory::LockServer** first checks the value of fLock. If *fLock* is TRUE, the class object reference count is incremented. If *fLock* is FALSE, the reference count is decremented. Then **CoLockObjectExternal** is called to create a strong lock on the application object. The call to **CoLockObjectExternal** is preceeded by an **AddRef** and followed by a **Release,** so that the object remains stable during the call.

```
HRESULT IClassFactory_LockServer (
        LPCLASSFACTORY        lpThis,
        BOOL                  fLock)
{
    LPMYCLASSOBJECT lpMyClassObj = (LPMYCLASSOBJECT)lpThis;
    LPAPP lpApp = (LPAPP)g_lpApp;
    HRESULT hrErr;

    if (fLock)
        ++lpMyClassObj->m_cLock;
    else
        --lpMyClassObj->m_cLock;

    IUnknown_App_AddRef(lpApp);
    hrErr = CoLockObjectExternal((LPUNKNOWN)&lpApp->m_Unknown,
                fLock, TRUE);
    IUnknown_App_Release(lpApp);
    return hrErr;
}
```

IMalloc Interface

The **IMalloc** interface is implemented by OLE and is used by OLE and object handlers to manage memory. To use OLE's implementation of **IMalloc**, an application sets *pMalloc* to NULL in its call to **OleInitialize** and **CoInitialize**. **IMalloc** may also be implemented by applications that manage memory differently than OLE.

IMalloc contains the following methods, the first three of which are similar to the C library functions **malloc**, **realloc**, and **free** (see also COMPOBJ.H):

```
DECLARE_INTERFACE_(IMalloc, IUnknown)
{
  // *** IUnknown methods ***
 HRESULT QueryInterface (THIS _ REFIID riid, LPVOID FAR* ppvObj) ;
 ULONG AddRef (THIS ) ;
 ULONG Release (THIS ) ;

  // *** IMalloc methods ***
 void FAR* Alloc (THIS _ ULONG cb) ;
 void Free (THIS _ void FAR* pv) ;
 void FAR* Realloc (THIS _ void FAR* pv, ULONG cb) ;
 ULONG GetSize (THIS _ void FAR* pv) ;
 int DidAlloc (THIS _ void FAR* pv) ;
 void HeapMinimize (THIS ) ;
};
```

IMalloc::Alloc

void FAR * IMalloc::Alloc(*cb*)
ULONG *cb*

IMalloc::Alloc allocates a block of memory.

Parameters

cb
Specifies the size (in bytes) of the memory block to allocate.

Return Values

Value	Meaning
Allocated memory block	Memory block allocated successfully.
NULL	Insufficient memory available.

Comments

The initial contents of the returned memory block are undefined; there is no guarantee that the block has been initialized. The allocated block may be larger than *cb* bytes because of the space required for alignment and for maintenance information.

If *cb* is 0, **IMalloc::Alloc** allocates a zero-length item and returns a valid pointer to that item. If there is insufficient memory available, **IMalloc::Alloc** returns NULL.

IMalloc::Alloc returns a huge pointer for memory allocations larger than 64K; allocations smaller than 64K return a far pointer.

Applications should always check the return value from this method, even when requesting small amounts of memory, because there is no guarantee the memory will be allocated.

See Also

IMalloc::Free, **IMalloc::Realloc**

IMalloc::Free

void IMalloc::Free(*pv***)**
void FAR * *pv*

IMalloc::Free frees a block of memory previously allocated through a call to **IMalloc::Alloc** or **IMalloc::Realloc**.

Parameters

pv
Points to the memory block to be freed.

Comments

The number of bytes freed equals the number of bytes that were originally allocated or reallocated. After the call, the memory block pointed to by *pv* is invalid and can no longer be used.

Note The *pv* parameter can be NULL, in which case this method is a no-op.

See Also

IMalloc::Alloc, **IMalloc::Realloc**

IMalloc::Realloc

void FAR * IMalloc::Realloc(*pv, cb***)**
void FAR * *pv*
ULONG *cb*

IMalloc::Realloc changes the size of a previously allocated memory block.

Parameters

pv
Points to the memory block to be reallocated. It can be a NULL pointer, as discussed in the following comments.

cb
Specifies the size of the memory block (in bytes) to be reallocated. It can be zero, as discussed in the following comments.

Return Values

Value	Meaning
Reallocated memory block	Memory block successfully reallocated.
NULL	Insufficient memory or *cb* is zero and *pv* is not NULL.

Comments

The *pv* argument points to the beginning of the memory block. If *pv* is NULL, **IMalloc::Realloc** allocates a new memory block in the same way as **IMalloc::Alloc**. If *pv* is not NULL, it should be a pointer returned by a prior call to **IMalloc::Alloc**.

The *cb* argument specifies the size (in bytes) of the new block. The contents of the block are unchanged up to the shorter of the new and old sizes, although the new block can be in a different location. Because the new block can be in a different memory location, the pointer returned by IMalloc::Realloc is not guaranteed to be the pointer passed through the *pv* argument. If *pv* is not NULL and *cb* is zero, then the memory pointed to by *pv* is freed.

For memory allocations larger than 64K; IMalloc::Realloc returns a huge pointer; for allocations smaller than 64K, it returns a far pointer.

IMalloc::Realloc returns a void pointer to the reallocated (and possibly moved) memory block. The return value is NULL if the size is zero and the buffer argument is not NULL, or if there is not enough memory available to expand the block to the given size. In the first case, the original block is freed; in the second, the original block is unchanged.

The storage space pointed to by the return value is guaranteed to be suitably aligned for storage of any type of object. To get a pointer to a type other than void, use a type cast on the return value.

See Also

IMalloc::Alloc, IMalloc::Free

IMalloc::GetSize

ULONG IMalloc::GetSize(*pv*)
void FAR * *pv*

IMalloc::GetSize returns the size (in bytes) of a memory block previously allocated with **IMalloc::Alloc** or **IMalloc::Realloc**.

Parameters

pv
Points to the memory block whose size is requested. If it is a NULL pointer, -1 is returned.

Return Value

Size of allocated memory block in bytes.

See Also

IMalloc::Alloc, IMalloc::Realloc

IMalloc::DidAlloc

int IMalloc::DidAlloc(*pv*)
void FAR * *pv*

IMalloc::DidAlloc determines if this **IMalloc** instance was used to allocate the specified block of memory.

Parameters

pv
Specifies the pointer to the memory block; can be a NULL pointer, in which case, -1 is returned.

Return Values

Value	Meaning
1	The memory block was allocated by this **IMalloc** instance.
0	The memory block was *not* allocated by this **IMalloc** instance.
-1	**DidAlloc** is unable to determine whether or not it allocated the memory block.

Comments

Pointers returned from the shared allocator *cannot* be directly manipulated using the host global memory allocator. Except when a NULL pointer is passed, the shared memory allocator does not return -1 to **IMalloc::DidAlloc**, the allocator always indicates that it either did or did not allocate the passed pointer.

It is permissible that the memory allocator passed to **CoInitialize** always respond with -1 in this function.

See Also **IMalloc::Alloc, IMalloc::HeapMinimize, IMalloc::Realloc**

IMalloc::HeapMinimize

void IMalloc::HeapMinimize()

IMalloc::HeapMinimize minimizes the heap as much as possible by releasing unused memory to the operating system.

Comments Calling **IMalloc::HeapMinimize** is useful when several memory blocks have been freed using **IMalloc::Free** and you want the application to make the freed memory available for other purposes.

See Also **IMalloc::Alloc, IMalloc::Free, IMalloc::Realloc**

IExternalConnection Interface

The **IExternalConnection** interface is optionally implemented by DLL object applications to support the correct shutdown of links to embedded objects. Object handlers never implement this interface.

The stub manager calls **IExternalConnection** methods when external (i.e. linking) connections to an object are made and broken or when **CoLockObjectExternal** is called. Embedded objects should maintain a count of these connections and when the count goes to zero, **IOleObject::Close** should be called.

The **IExternalConnection** interface contains the following methods (see also COMPOBJ.H).

```
DECLARE_INTERFACE_(IExternalConnection, IUnknown)
{
  // *** IUnknown methods ***
  HRESULT QueryInterface (THIS _ REFIID riid, LPVOID FAR* ppvObj) ;
  ULONG AddRef (THIS ) ;
  ULONG Release (THIS ) ;

  // *** IExternalConnection methods ***
  STDMETHOD_(DWORD, AddConnection (THIS _ DWORD extconn, DWORD dwReserved) ;
  STDMETHOD_(DWORD, ReleaseConnection (THIS _ DWORD extconn, DWORD dwReserved,
  BOOL fLastReleaseCloses) ;
};
```

IExternalConnection::AddConnection

DWORD IExternalConnection::AddConnection(*extconn*, *dwReserved*)
DWORD *extconn*
DWORD *dwReserved*

IExternalConnection::AddConnection indicates that another strong external connection has been created on a running object.

extconn
Specifies the type of external connection that exists on the object; see the following comments.

dwReserved
Used by OLE to pass information about the connection; it can be zero, but not necessarily. Therefore, **AddConnection** implementers should not include a check for zero.

Return Values

Value	Meaning
DWORD value	The remaining number of reference counts on the object; used for debugging purposes only.

Comments

An external connection represents strong bindings (by means of a moniker bind) or external locks (by means of **CoLockObjectExternal**). As with all connections (weak or strong), the user can always override them and shutdown the application.

The *extconn* parameter specifies the type of external connection; its value is taken from the enumeration **EXTCONN**, which is defined in COMPOBJ.H as follows:

```
typedef enum tagEXTCONN
{
    EXTCONN_STRONG = 0x0001

}EXTCONN
```

Example

The following is a typical implementation for the **AddConnection** method:

```
DWORD XX::AddConnection(DWORW extconn, DWORD dwReserved)
{
    return extconn&EXTCONN_STRONG ? ++m_cStrong : 0;
}
```

See Also

CoLockObjectExternal, IExternalConnection::ReleaseConnection

IExternalConnection::ReleaseConnection

DWORD IExternalConnection::ReleaseConnection(*extconn, dwReserved, fLastReleaseCloses*)
DWORD *extconn*
DWORD *dwReserved*
BOOL *fLastReleaseCloses*

IExternalConnection::ReleaseConnection indicates the release of an external connection to a running object.

Parameters

extconn
Specifies the type of external connection that exists on the object; the value is obtained from the enumeration **EXTCONN** (see **IExternalConnection::AddConnection**).

dwReserved
Used by OLE used to pass information about the connection; it can be zero, but not necessarily.

fLastReleaseCloses
TRUE specifies that if this is the last external reference to the object, the object should close. FALSE leaves the object in a state in which its closing is controlled by some other means.

Return Values

Value	Meaning
DWORD value	The remaining number of reference counts on the object; used for debugging purposes only.

Comments

Losing the last strong connection (along with *fLastReleaseCloses* == TRUE) causes the object to close. If an object has no closing semantics, then it is not required to count the strong connections. An enumerator object, for example, has no closing semantics.

The following is a typical implementation for **ReleaseConnection**:

```
DWORD XX::ReleaseConnection(DWORD extconn, DWORD dwReserved,
                            BOOL fLastReleaseCloses)
{
    if (extconn & EXTCONN_STRONG)
    {
        if (--m_cStrong == 0 && fLastReleaseCloses)
            save if dirty
            close ...
```

```
            return m_cStrong;
        }
        else
            return 0;
    }
```

See Also **IExternalConnection:AddConnection**

IEnum*X* Interface

A frequent OLE 2 programming task is to iterate through a sequence of items. OLE 2 supports such enumerations through the use of enumerator objects. Enumerators cleanly separate the caller's need to loop over a set of objects from the calling routine's knowledge of how to accomplish that task.

Enumerators are just a concept; there is no interface called IEnumerator or IEnum, because the method signatures in an enumerator interface must be specific to the type of items being enumerated. As a consequence, separate interfaces, such as **IEnumString** and **IEnumUnknown,** are instantiated for each type of item to be enumerated. However, the *only* difference between these interfaces is the type of item being enumerated; all enumerators are used in fundamentally the same way.

All enumerators contain the following methods:

```
template <class ELT_T> interface IEnum : IUnknown {
    virtual    SCODE    Next(ULONG celt, FAR * rgelt, ULONG* pceltFetched)
                                  = 0;
    virtual    SCODE    Skip(ULONG celt) = 0;
    virtual    SCODE    Reset() = 0;
    virtual    SCODE    Clone(IEnum<ELT_T>** ppenum) = 0;
    };
```

The following code example illustrates a typical use of an enumerator. **StringContainer** contains an instance of the **IEnumString** interface that can enumerate a sequence of strings. **SomeFunc** takes a pointer to a **StringContainer** which provides access to the string enumerator. **SomeFunc** loops through each of the strings by calling the enumerator's **Next** method and then releases the enumerator by calling its **Release** method.

```
/* The following is a typical use of an enumerator.*/
interface StringContainer {
    virtual IEnumString* EnumStrings() = 0;
    };
```

```
void SomeFunc(StringContainer * pstringcont) {
    LPSTR lpsz;
    IEnumString* penum;
    penum = pstringcont->EnumStrings();
    while (penum->Next(1, &lpsz, NULL) == S_OK)
        {
        // do something with the string in lpsz
        // free the string in lpsz with the allocator returned by
        // CoGetMalloc(MEMCTX_TASK, ...);
        }
    penum->Release();
    // penum is not valid here
    }
```

Note In general, the actual enumeration interfaces used in OLE are defined and documented with the functions that instantiate the enumerations.

For all enumerators, an application can determine results by keeping track of the total number of elements remaining in the enumeration before the current position.

IEnum*X*::Next

HRESULT IEnum*X*::Next(*celt, rgelt, pceltFetched***)**
ULONG *celt*
<ELT_T> * *rgelt*
ULONG LONG* *pceltFetched*

IEnum*X*::Next retrieves the specified number of items in the enumeration sequence.

Parameters

celt
Specifies the number of elements to return. If the number of elements requested is more than remains in the sequence, only the remaining elements are returned. The number of elements returned is passed through the *pceltFetched* parameter (unless it is NULL).

rgelt
Points to the array in which to return the elements.

pceltFetched
Points to the number of elements actually returned in *rgelt*. The *pceltFetched* parameter cannot be NULL if *celt* is greater than one. If *pceltFetched* is NULL, *celt* must be one.

Return Values

Value	Meaning
S_OK	Returned requested number of elements—**pceltFetched* set if non-NULL. All requested entries are valid.
S_FALSE	Returned fewer elements than requested by *celt*. In this case, unused slots in the enumeration are not set to NULL and **pceltFetched* holds the number of valid entries, even if zero is returned.
E_OUTOFMEMORY	Out of memory.
E_INVALIDARG	Value of *celt* is invalid.
E_UNEXPECTED	An unexpected error occurred.

If an error value is returned, no entries in the *rgelt* array are valid on exit; they are all in an indeterminate state.

Comments

It is illegal to call

```
...Next(celt>1, ...,NULL);
```

Thus, no more than one element can be specified without passing a valid value for *pceltFetched.*

IEnum*X*::Skip

HRESULT IEnum*X*::Skip(*celt***)**
ULONG *celt*

IEnum*X*::Skip skips over a specified number of elements in the enumeration sequence.

Parameters

celt
Specifies the number of elements to be skipped.

Return Values

Value	Meaning
S_OK	The number of elements skipped is equal to *celt.*
S_FALSE	The number of elements skipped is fewer than *celt.*
E_OUTOFMEMORY	Out of memory.
E_INVALIDARG	Value of *celt* is invalid.
E_UNEXPECTED	An unexpected error occurred.

IEnum*X*::Reset

HRESULT IEnum*X*::Reset()

IEnum*X*::Reset resets the enumeration sequence back to the beginning.

Return Values

Value	Meaning
S_OK	The enumeration sequence was reset to the beginning.
S_FALSE	The enumeration sequence was not reset to the beginning.

Comments

There is no guarantee that the same set of objects will be enumerated the second time as was enumerated the first: it depends on the collection being enumerated. It is too expensive for some collections, such as files in a directory, to maintain this condition.

IEnum*X*::Clone

HRESULT IEnum*X*::Clone(*ppenum*)
IEnum*X* FAR *FAR * *ppenum*

IEnum*X*::Clone returns another enumerator containing the same enumeration state as the current one.

Parameters

ppenum
Pointer to the place to return the cloned enumerator. The type of *ppenum* is the same as the enumerator name. For example, if the enumerator name is **IEnumFORMATETC**, *ppenum* is of **IEnumFORMATETC** type.

Return Values

Value	Meaning
E_OUTOFMEMORY	Out of memory.
E_INVALIDARG	Value of *ppenum* is invalid.
E_UNEXPECTED	An unexpected error occurred.

Comments

Using **IEnum*X*::Clone**, it is possible to record a particular point in the enumeration sequence, then return to that point at a later time. The enumerator returned is of the same interface type as the one being cloned.

IMarshal Interface

The **IMarshal** interface is implemented and used by OLE. However, object and container applications can also implement **IMarshal** to provide custom interface marshaling.

The **IMarshal** interface contains the following methods (see also COMPOBJ.H):

```
DECLARE_INTERFACE_(IMarshal, IUnknown)
{
  // *** IUnknown methods ***
 HRESULT QueryInterface (THIS _ REFIID riid, LPVOID FAR* ppvObj) ;
 ULONG  AddRef (THIS );
 ULONG  Release (THIS ) ;

  // *** IMarshal methods ***
 HRESULT GetUnmarshalClass (THIS_ REFIID riid, LPVOID pv, DWORD dwMemctx,
  LPVOID pvMemctx, DWORD mshlflags, LPCLSID pclsid) ;
 HRESULT GetMarshalSizeMax (THIS_ REFIID riid, LPVOID pv,  DWORD dwMemctx,
  LPVOID pvMemctx, DWORD mshlflags, LPDWORD lpdwSize) ;
 HRESULT MarshalInterface (THIS_ LPSTREAM pStm, REFIID riid, LPVOID pv,
  DWORD dwMemctx, LPVOID pvMemctx, DWORD mshlflags) ;
 HRESULT UnmarshalInterface (THIS_ LPSTREAM pStm, REFIID riid, LPVOID FAR* ppvObj) ;
 HRESULT ReleaseMarshalData (THIS_ LPSTREAM pStm) ;
 HRESULT DisconnectObject (THIS_ DWORD dwReserved) ;
};
```

The **IMarshal** interface is used to package and send interface method arguments from one application process to another. In a given call, method arguments are marshaled and unmarshaled in one direction and return values are marshaled and unmarshaled in the other direction. Marshaling allows pointers to interfaces to be passed through remote procedure calls and enables clients in other processes to access and manipulate objects across process boundaries.

Data Structures

This section describes the data structures and enumerations that are used in the **IMarshal** interface methods and related marshaling functions:

MSHCTX Enumeration

The **MSHCTX** enumeration determines the destination context of the marshaling operation and is defined in COMPOBJ.H as follows:

```
typedef enum tagMSHCTX
{
    MSHCTX_LOCAL = 0,
    MSHCTX_NOSHAREDMEM = 1,
} MSHCTX;
```

MSHCTX values have the following meanings:

Marshaling Context Values	Description
MSHCTX_LOCAL	Unmarshaling context is local; it has shared memory access.
MSHCTX_NOSHAREDMEM	Unmarshaling context does not have shared memory access with the marshaling context.

MSHLFLAGS Enumeration

The **MSHLFLAGS** enumeration contains a group of flags that determine how the marshalling is to be done; **MSHFLAGS** is defined in COMPOBJ.H as follows:

```
typedef enum tagMSHLFLAGS
{
    MSHLFLAGS_NORMAL = 0,
    MSHLFLAGS_TABLESTRONG = 1,
    MSHLFLAGS_TABLEWEAK = 2
} MSHLFLAGS;
```

The **MSHLFLAGS** flags have the following meanings:

Marshaling Control Flag Values	Description
MSHLFLAGS_NORMAL	Marshaling is done by passing an interface from one process to another. The marshaled-data-packet that results from the call will be transported to the other process, where it will be unmarshaled (see **CoUnmarshalInterface**). By means of this flag, the marshaled data packet is unmarshaled either one or zero times. If it is unmarshaled successfully, **CoReleaseMarshalData** is not called on the data packet; and any necessary processing is done in the unmarshal itself. If unmarshaling fails, or it is not attempted, only then is **IMarshal::ReleaseMarshalData** called on the data packet.
MSHLFLAGS_TABLESTRONG	Marshaling is happening because the data packet is to be stored in a globally accessible table from which it is to be unmarshaled zero, one, or more times. Further, the presence of the data packet in the table is to count as a reference on the marshaled interface. When removed from the table, it is the responsibility of the table implementor to call **CoReleaseMarshalData** on the data-packet.
MSHLFLAGS_TABLEWEAK	Marshaling is happening because the data packet is to be stored in a globally accessible table from which it is to be unmarshaled zero, one, or more times. However, the presence of the data packet in the table does not count as a reference on the marshaled interface. Destruction of the data packet is done by calling **CoReleaseMarshalData**.

IMarshal::GetUnmarshalClass

HRESULT IMarshal::GetUnmarshalClass(*riid, pv, dwMemctx, pvMemctx, mshlflags, pclsid*)
REFIID *riid*
LPVOID *pv*
DWORD *dwMemctx*
LPVOID *pvMemctx*
DWORD *mshlflags*
LPCLSID *pclsid*

IMarshal::GetUnmarshalClass determines the object class that should be used to create an uninitialized proxy in the unmarshaling process.

Parameters

riid
Specifies the interface ID of the object to be marshaled.

pv
Points to the interface pointer to be marshaled; can be NULL.

dwMemctx
Specifies the destination context relative to the current context in which the unmarshaling is to be done. For a definition of the **MSHCTX** enumeration (on which *dwMemctx* is based), see "Data Structures" at the beginning of the **IMarshal** interface description.

pvMemctx
Reserved for use with future **MSHCTX** values.

mshflags
Specifies why marshaling is taking place. For a definition of the **MSHLFLAGS** enumeration (from which *mshflags* is derived), see "Data Structures"at the beginning of the **IMarshal** interface description.

pclsid
Points to the class to be used in the unmarshaling process.

Return Values

Value	Meaning
S_OK	Object class was successfully obtained.
E_INVALIDARG	An invalid argument was passed as a parameter.
E_UNEXPECTED	An unexpected error occurred.
E_OUTOFMEMORY	Out of memory.
E_FAIL	Object class could not be obtained.

Comments

The *dwMemctx* parameter identifies the destination context, which is relative to the current context in which the unmarshaling is to be done. For example, marshaling might be done differently depending on whether the unmarshaling will happen on the local workstation or on a workstation on the network. An object could do custom marshaling in one case but not the other. The legal values for *dwMemctx* are taken from the enumeration **MSHCTX**.

An implementation of **IMarshal::GetUnmarshalClass** can delegate some destination contexts to the standard marshaling implementation, which is available by calling **CoGetStandardMarshal**. Delegating destination contexts should always be done if the *dwMemctx* parameter contains any flags that the **IMarshal::GetUnmarshalClass** does not understand.

The *mshlflags* parameter indicates the purpose for which the marshal is taking place. The value of *mshlflags* is taken from the enumeration **MSHLFLAGS**.

If the caller already has the *riid* of the interface being marshaled, it should pass the interface pointer through *pv*. If the caller does not have the r*iid*, then it should pass NULL.

The *pv* pointer is sometimes used to determine the appropriate object class. If the **IMarshal** interface needs the class, it can call **QueryInterface** on itself to get the interface pointer. The pointer is passed here only to improve efficiency.

See Also

GetMarshalSizeMax, MarshalInterface, UnmarshalInterface

IMarshal::GetMarshalSizeMax

HRESULT IMarshal::GetMarshalSizeMax(*riid, pv, dwMemctx, pvMemctx, mshlflags, lpdwSize***)**
REFIID *riid*
LPVOID *pv*
DWORD *dwMemctx*
LPVOID *pvMemctx,*
DWORD *mshlflags*
LPDWORD *lpdwSize*

IMarshal::GetMarshalSizeMax returns the upper memory bound needed to write the specified data into an **IMarshal::MarshalInterface** stream.

Parameters

riid
Identifies the interface of the object to be marshaled.

pv
The interface pointer that is to be marshaled; it can be NULL.

dwMemctx
The destination context relative to the current context in which the unmarshaling is to be done. For a definition of the **MSHCTX** enumeration (from which *dwMemctx* is based), see "Data Structures," at the beginning of the **IMarshal** interface description.

pvMemctx
Reserved for use with future **MSHCTX** values.

mshlflags
Specifies why marshaling is taking place. For a definition of the **MSHLFLAGS** enumeration (from which *mshflags* is derived), see the "Data Structures," at the beginning of the **IMarshal** interface description.

lpdwSize
Points to where the maximum marshal size should be returned.

Return Values

Value	Meaning
S_OK	Maximum size needed for marshaling successfully returned.
E_INVALIDARG	An invalid argument was passed as a parameter.
E_UNEXPECTED	An unexpected error occurred.
E_OUTOFMEMORY	Out of memory.
E_FAIL	Object class could not be obtained.

Comments

Calling applications can optionally use the data size returned to preallocate stream buffers for use in the marshaling process.

The *dwMemctx* parameter identifies the destination context, which is relative to the current context in which the unmarshaling is to be done. For example, different marshaling might be done depending on whether the unmarshaling is to happen on the local workstation or on a workstation on the network. An object might do custom marshaling in one case but not the other.

When **IMarshal::MarshalInterface** is called, the **IMarshal** implementation cannot rely on the caller having already called **GetMarshalSizeMax**; it must still be aware of STG_E_MEDIUMFULL errors returned by the stream.

The return value is guaranteed to be valid only as long as the internal state of the object being marshaled does not change. Marshaling should be done immediately after **IMarshal::GetMarshalSizeMax** returns; otherwise, the caller runs the risk that the object might require more memory than was originally indicated for the marshal.

See Also

IMarshal::GetUnmarshalClass, IMarshal::MarshalInterface, IMarshal::UnmarshalInterface

IMarshal::MarshalInterface

HRESULT IMarshal::MarshalInterface(*pStm, riid, pv, dwMemctx, pvMemctx, mshlflags***)**
LPSTREAM *pStm*
REFIID *riid*
LPVOID *pv*
DWORD *dwMemctx*
LPVOID *pvMemctx*
DWORD *mshlflags*

IMarshal::MarshalInterface marshals a reference of the object's interface ID into the specified stream.

Parameters

pStm
Points to the stream in which the object is to be marshaled.

riid
Specifies the interface ID of the object to be marshaled.

pv
Points to the interface to be marshaled; it can be NULL.

dwMemctx
Specifies the destination context relative to the current context in which the unmarshaling will be done. For a definition of the **MSHCTX** enumeration (on which *dwMemctx* is based), see "Data Structures," at the beginning of the **IMarshal** interface description.

pvMemctx
Reserved for use with future **MSHCTX** values.

mshlflags
Specifies why unmarshaling is to be done. For a definition of the **MSHLFLAGS** enumeration (from which *mshflags* is derived), see "Data Structures," at the beginning of the **IMarshal** interface description.

Return Values

Value	Meaning
S_OK	The interface ID reference was marshaled successfully.
E_FAIL	Indicates an unspecified error.
STG_E_MEDIUMFULL.	The medium is full.
E_OUTOFMEMORY	Out of memory.
E_INVALIDARG	One or more arguments are invalid.
E_UNEXPECTED	An unexpected error occurred.

For information on possible stream access errors, see the **IStream** methods.

Comments

Once the contents of the stream are sent to the destination, the interface reference can be restored by using the CLSID used to create the handler and then calling **IMarshal::UnmarshalInterface**. An implementation of **IMarshal::MarshalInterface** writes to the stream any data required for initialization of this proxy.

The *dwMemctx* parameter identifies the destination context, which is relative to the current context in which the unmarshaling is to be done. For example, different marshaling might be done depending on whether the unmarshaling will happen on the local workstation or on a workstation on the network; an object could do custom marshaling in one case but not the other.

An implementation of **IMarshal::MarshalInterface** can delegate some destination contexts to the standard marshaling implementation, which is available by calling the **CoGetStandardMarshal** function. Delegating destination contexts should always be done if the *dwMemctx* parameter contains any flags that the **MarshalInterface** function does not understand.

The data marshaled in a particular **IMarshal::MarshalInterface** call can be unmarshaled zero or more times; marshalers must be able to handle the unmarshaling. If a proxy implementation relies on state information in the object application (such as a stub interface whose functions unmarshal the arguments and then forward the call onto the real receiver), by implication this state must deal with zero or more proxies being created from the same initialization data.

If the caller already has the *riid* of the interface being marshaled, it should pass the interface pointer through *pv*. If the caller does not have the *riid*, it should pass NULL; **IMarshal::MarshalInterface** will call **QueryInterface** on itself to get the interface pointer. On exit from this method, the seek pointer in the data stream must be positioned after the last byte of data written.

See Also

IMarshal::GetUnmarshalClass, IMarshal::GetMarshalSizeMax, IMarshal::UnmarshalInterface

IMarshal::UnmarshalInterface

HRESULT IMarshal::UnmarshalInterface(*pStm, riid, ppvObj*)
LPSTREAM *pStm*
REFIID *riid*
LPVOID FAR * *ppvObj*

IMarshal::UnmarshalInterface initializes a newly created proxy as part of the unmarshaling process.

Parameters

pStm
Points to the stream in which the interface is to be unmarshaled.

riid
Identifies the interface that the caller wants from the object.

ppvObj
Points to where the interface is to be returned.

Return Values

Value	Meaning
S_OK	The proxy was initialized successfully.
E_FAIL	Indicates an unspecified error.
E_OUTOFMEMORY	Out of memory.
E_INVALIDARG	One or more arguments are invalid.
E_UNEXPECTED	An unexpected error occurred.

For information on possible stream access errors, see the **IStream** interface.

Comments

To get the information required to complete the call, **IMarshal::UnmarshalInterface** often calls **QueryInterface**(*riid, ppvObj*) on itself immediately before returning. On exit from this method, the seek pointer in the data stream must be positioned after the last byte of data read.

See Also

IMarshal::GetUnmarshalClass, IMarshal::GetMarshalSizeMax, IMarshal::MarshalInterface

IMarshal::ReleaseMarshalData

HRESULT IMarshal::ReleaseMarshalData(*pStm***)**
LPSTREAM *pStm*

IMarshal::ReleaseMarshalData is called by the unmarshaler (usually **CoReleaseMarshalData** or **CoUnMarshalInterface**) to destroy a marshaled data packet.

Parameters

pStm
Points to a stream that contains the data packet which is to be destroyed.

Return Values

Value	Meaning
S_OK	The data packet was released successfully.
E_FAIL	Indicates an unspecified error.
E_OUTOFMEMORY	Out of memory.
E_INVALIDARG	One or more arguments are invalid.
E_UNEXPECTED	An unexpected error occurred.

See the **IStream** interface for information on possible stream access errors.

See Also

CoUnMarshalInterface, CoReleaseMarshalData

IMarshal::DisconnectObject

HRESULT IMarshal::DisconnectObject(*dwReserved***)**
DWORD *dwReserved*

IMarshal::DisconnectObject is called by **CoDisconnectObject** when the object that is being disconnected supports custom marshaling. This is analogous to how **CoMarshalInterface** defers to **IMarshal::MarshalInterface** if the object supports **IMarshal**.

Parameters

dwReserved
Reserved for future use; must be set to zero by the caller. To ensure compatibility with future use, the callee *must not* check for zero.

Return Values

Value	Meaning
S_OK	The object was disconnected successfully.
E_FAIL	Indicates an unspecified error.
E_OUTOFMEMORY	Out of memory.
E_INVALIDARG	One or more arguments are invalid.
E_UNEXPECTED	An unexpected error occurred.

IStdMarshalInfo Interface

The **IStdMarshalInfo** interface is implemented as part of an object handler to return the CLSID of the object handler that is to marshal data to and from the object. Applications that support activating objects as a different type must use **IStdMarshalInfo** in order to obtain the CLSID of the new object.

IStdMarshalInfo contains the following methods (see also COMPOBJ.H):

```
DECLARE_INTERFACE_(IStdMarshalInfo, IUnknown)
{
  // *** IUnknown methods ***
 HRESULT QueryInterface (THIS _ REFIID riid, LPVOID FAR* ppvObj) ;
 ULONG AddRef (THIS ) ;
 ULONG Release (THIS ) ;

  // *** IStdMarshalInfo method ***
 HRESULT GetClassForHandler (THIS_ DWORD dwMemctx,
  LPVOID pvMemctx, LPCLSID pclsid) ;
};
```

IStdMarshalInfo::GetClassForHandler

HRESULT IStdMarshalInfo::GetClassForHandler(*dwMemctx, pvMemctx, pclsid*)
DWORD *dwMemctx*
LPVOID *pvMemctx*
LPCLSID* *pclsid*

IStdMarshalInfo::GetClassForHandler retrieves the CLSID of the object handler that is used for standard marshaling in the destination process.

Parameters

dwMemctx
Specifies the type of destination context to which this object is being passed. For a definition of the **MSHCTX** enumeration (on which *dwMemctx* is based), see "Data Structures," at the beginning of the **IMarshal** interface description.

pvMemctx
Points to the destination context.

pclsid
Points to where to return the handler's CLSID.

Return Values

Value	Meaning
S_OK	The CLSID was retrieved successfully.
E_OUTOFMEMORY	Out of memory.
E_INVALIDARG	One or more arguments are invalid.
E_UNEXPECTED	An unexpected error occurred.

Comments

Object applications that support class conversion (Activate As in the Convert dialog box) *must* implement the **IStdMarshalInfo** interface so that the correct object handler can be determined in all cases.

Example

In the following example, **IStdMarshalInfo::GetClassForHandler** supports only the MSHCTX_LOCAL context, meaning it supports only the marshaling and unmarshaling of interface parameters local to the workstation, and not over the network. **IStdMarshalInfo::GetClassForHandler** returns the CLSID, which is then used later in object conversion.

For more information on converting and emulating objects, see "Object Class Conversion and Emulation Functions," later in this chapter.

```
HRESULT IStdMarshalInfo_GetClassForHandler(
        LPSTDMARSHALINFO     lpThis,
        DWORD                     dwMemctx,
        LPVOID                    pvMemctx,
        LPCLSID                   pclsid)
{
    // Only handle LOCAL marshal context.
    if (dwMemctx != MSHCTX_LOCAL || pvMemctx != NULL)
        return ResultFromScode(E_INVALIDARG);

    // Return REAL clsid
    *pclsid = CLSID_APP;
    return NOERROR;
}
```

See Also

CoTreatAsClass, CoGetTreatAsClass

Custom Marshaling Functions

The following functions have been created to help in the marshaling and unmarshaling of interface method parameters. These functions are defined as follows (see also COMPOBJ.H):

```
CoGetStandardMarshal(REFIID riid, LPUNKNOWN pUnk, DWORD dwMemctx,
  LPVOID pvMemctx, DWORD mshlflags, LPMARSHAL FAR* ppMarshal);
CoMarshalHresult(LPSTREAM pStm, HRESULT hresult);
CoMarshalInterface(LPSTREAM pStm, REFIID riid, LPUNKNOWN pUnk,
  DWORD dwMemctx, LPVOID pvMemctx, DWORD mshlflags);
CoReleaseMarshalData(LPSTREAM pStm);
CoUmarshalHresult(LPSTREAM pStm, HRESULT FAR* phresult);
CoUnmarshalInterface(LPSTREAM pStm, REFIID riid, LPVOID FAR* ppvObj);
```

OLE relies on shared memory access between the calling application and the called process. Therefore, only communication between processes on one machine is supported. An application is not informed whether a called interface method is local or remote, nor is the method told whether the application that called it is local or remote. OLE achieves this transparency between processes by using what are referred to as *proxy* and *stub* functions.

A *proxy* function is a stand-in for a remote method used in the context of a particular container application. The proxy function packages the in parameters to a interface method in a process known as *marshaling* and sends them across the process boundary to the receiving object application's process space. Here, the parameters are unmarshaled by a corresponding *stub* function. The stub function then calls a method in the object application to do the work. The out parameters and return value are marshaled by the stub function and passed back to the proxy function in the calling application's process space, where they are unmarshaled and returned to the calling application.

The process of marshaling and unmarshaling a method parameter depends on the type of the parameter. The differences usually center around how pointers are followed and when memory allocations are done in order to make a copy of the parameter to pass to the other process.

Conceptually, there are tables in the marshaling and unmarshaling code that describe how to marshal and unmarshal different types of data, including **int**, **long**, **double**, **LPSTR** strings, and various kinds of structures.

If the object being remoted does not support custom marshaling (as indicated by the lack of support for the **IMarshal** interface), then OLE's standard marshaling is used. By using standard marshaling, the actual marshaling and unmarshaling of interface method parameters is handled by OLE.

The object being marshaled can make use of a custom object handler to do some processing locally; however, the majority of requests are sent to the object using the OLE-supplied standard marshaling mechanism. Custom object handlers *must* use standard marshaling, which means that custom handlers must aggregate the OLE 2 default handler, as is described in **OleCreateDefaultHandler**.

Once OLE determines that standard marshaling is to be used, it checks for a custom handler by querying the object for the **IStdMarshalInfo** and the **IPersist** interface. If either of these interfaces is supported, the returned CLSID is used to identify the custom handler to be loaded in the container's process space (see **CoGetClassObject**). The CLSID is obtained by calling the method contained in each of the interfaces.

If a custom handler is not supported, the OLE default remoting handler is used. For components that are not embedded objects, this is the common situation. It corresponds to the classic RPC scenario in which the remote proxy is little more than a forwarder of requests.

Custom Marshaling

Objects can implement their own marshaling and unmarshaling functionality or let OLE do it for them. An OLE object may choose to do custom marshaling for three reasons:

- Objects that are already proxies (or handlers) use custom marshaling to avoid creating proxies to proxies. Instead, new proxies are short circuited back to the original stub. This is an important consideration for both efficiency and robustness.
- An object, whose entire state is kept in shared memory, can often be remoted by creating an object in the container application that communicates directly with the shared memory rather than to the original object. This can improve performance significantly, because access to the remoted object does not result in context switches. The compound file implementations of **IStorage** and **IStream** are examples of this custom marshaling.
- From the time they are created, some objects are not susceptible to changes; that is, their internal state does not change. Monikers are an example of such objects. By using custom marshaling, these kinds of objects can be efficiently remoted by making independent copies of them in their client processes.

Note Because of the way in which an OLE 2 object handler communicates with an object application as an object's running state is entered, it is not possible for embedded objects to use custom marshaling *unless* they are completely implemented in the object handler.

Storing Marshaled Interface Pointers in Global Tables

Usually, marshaled interface pointers are sent across a process boundary from one process to another (container or object) where they are unmarshaled. In this usage, the data packet that results from the marshaling process is unmarshaled just once. However, there are occasions where marshaled interface pointers need to be stored in a globally accessible table. Once in the table, the data packet can be retrieved and unmarshaled zero, one, or more times.

The running object table and the internal table maintained by **CoRegisterClassObject** are examples of this concept . In effect, the marshaled data packet sitting in the table acts much like another pointer to the object. Depending on the semantics of the table in question, the data packet pointer may be either a reference-counted or nonreference-counted pointer to the interface. Thus, depending on the table in which the object is placed, the presence of the object in the table can or might not keep the object alive.

Because of this behavior, the marshaling code must execute at the time these data packets are removed from these tables and destroyed. The packets cannot be simply discarded, because the presence or absence of the internal state they maintain might be important to the object they indicate.

When an interface pointer is marshaled it is told why it is being marshaled. There are three possible reasons for marshaling:

1. This is a typical case of marshal then unmarshal once (this is the responsibility of the unmarshaler).
2. This is a marshal for storing into a global-table case, and the presence of the entry in the table is to count as an additional reference to the interface.
3. This is a marshal for storing into a global-table case; the entry in the table should not count as an additional reference to the interface.

Whenever a marshaled data packet from case 2 or 3 is removed from the table, it is the responsibility of the table implementor to call **CoReleaseMarshalData**.

CoGetStandardMarshal

HRESULT CoGetStandardMarshal(*riid, pUnk, dwMemctx, pvMemctx, mshlflags, ppMarshal*)
REFIID *riid*
LPUNKNOWN *pUnk*
DWORD *dwMemctx*
LPVOID *pvMemctx*
DWORD *mshlflags*
LPMARSHAL FAR **ppMarshal*

CoGetStandardMarshal returns an **IMarshal** instance that performs standard default marshaling and unmarshaling of interface parameters across remote process boundaries.

Parameters

riid
Specifies the interface to be marshaled.

pUnk
Points to the object to be marshaled. This interface does not have to be of type *riid*; it can be any interface on the object which conforms to **IUnknown**. The standard marshaler will internally call **QueryInterface**.

dwMemctx
Specifies the destination context relative to the current context in which the unmarshaling is to be done.

pvMemctx
Points to the associated destination context.

mshlflags
Specifies the destination context relative to the current context in which the unmarshaling is to be done; values are from the enumeration **MSHCTX**. For a definition of **MSHCTX**, see "Data Structures," at the beginning of the **IMarshal** interface description.

ppMarshal
Points to where to return the standard marshaler.

Return Values

Value	Meaning
S_OK	The **IMarshal** instance was returned successfully.
E_OUTOFMEMORY	Out of memory.
E_INVALIDARG	One or more arguments are invalid.
E_UNEXPECTED	An unexpected error occurred.
E_FAIL	Indicates an unspecified error.

Comments

Custom marshaling implementations should delegate any destination contexts they do not understand and those they want the standard marshaler to handle. The standard marshaler is also used when the object being marshaled does not support the **IMarshal** interface.

Note **CoGetStandardMarshal** is not implemented in OLE 2, though a non-functional stub is present. Programmers of custom marshalers should write their code as indicated (see "Custom Marshaling," earlier this chapter) and call this stub for any destination contexts the application does not understand. (With OLE 2, this is guaranteed not to happen because OLE only supports one kind of destination context.) By writing their code this way, programmers of custom marshalers pre-enable themselves for supporting different contexts as they become available (such as when networking support is added).

See Also

IMarshal Interface

CoMarshalHresult

HRESULT CoMarshalHresult(*pStm*, *hresult*)
LPSTREAM *pStm*
HRESULT *hresult*

CoMarshalHresult marshals an **HRESULT** to the specified stream so it can be unmarshaled using **CoUnmarshalHresult**.

Parameters

pStm
Points to the stream used for marshaling.

hresult
Specifies the **HRESULT** in the originating process.

Return Values

Value	Meaning
S_OK	The **HRESULT** was marshaled successfully.
STG_E_INVALIDPOINTER	Bad pointer passed in for *pStm*.
STG_E_MEDIUMFULL	The medium is full.
E_OUTOFMEMORY	Out of memory.
E_INVALIDARG	One or more arguments are invalid.
E_UNEXPECTED	An unexpected error occurred.

Comments

HRESULTs are process-specific; an **HRESULT** valid in one process might not be valid in another. **CoMarshalHresult** is used to marshal an **HRESULT** from one process to another. It is needed only by those developers who are writing custom marshaling code. They are required to use it for marshaling **HRESULT**s, either as parameters or as return codes.

The **HRESULT** returned by **CoMarshalHresult** indicates the success or failure of the marshaling process and is unrelated to the **HRESULT** parameter.

See Also

CoUnmarshalHresult

CoUnmarshalHresult

HRESULT CoUnmarshalHresult(*pStm***,** *phresult***)**
LPSTREAM *pStm*
HRESULT FAR* *phresult*

CoUnmarshalHresult unmarshals an **HRESULT** from the specified stream.

Parameters

pStm
Points to the stream from which the **HRESULT** is marshaled.

phresult
Points to the memory location into which the **HRESULT** is to be put.

Return Values

Value	Meaning
S_OK	The **HRESULT** was unmarshaled successfully.
STG_E_INVALIDPOINTER	Bad pointer passed in for *pStm*.
E_OUTOFMEMORY	Out of memory.
E_INVALIDARG	One or more arguments are invalid.
E_UNEXPECTED	An unexpected error occurred.

Comments

CoUnmarshalHresult is needed only by applications that implement custom marshaling. Custom marshallers must use **CoUnmarshalHresult** to unmarshal all **HRESULT**s.

See Also

CoMarshalHresult

CoMarshalInterface

HRESULT CoMarshalInterface(*pStm, riid, pUnk, dwMemctx, pvMemctx, mshlflags*)
LPSTREAM *pStm*
REFIID *riid*
LPUNKNOWN *pUnk*
DWORD *dwMemctx*
LPVOID *pvMemctx*
DWORD *mshlflags*

CoMarshalInterface marshals the object instance into the specified stream so that it can be unmarshaled in the destination with **CoUnMarshalInterface**. **CoMarshalInterface** only marshals interfaces derived from **IUnknown**.

Parameters

pStm
Specifies the stream into which the object is to be marshaled.

riid
Specifies the interface to which the *pUnk* complies. This interface *must* be derived from **IUnknown**.

pUnk
Points to the interface ID of the object that is to be marshaled. Only objects derived from **IUnknown** can be marshaled.

dwMemctx
Specifies the destination context relative to the current context in which the unmarshaling is to be done; the values are from the enumeration **MSHCTX**. For a definition of **MSHCTX**, see "Data Structures," at the beginning of the **IMarshal** interface description.

pvMemctx
Reserved for future use; must be set to zero by the caller. However, to ensure compatibility with future use, the callee *must not* check for zero.

mshlflags
Specifies the destination context relative to the current context in which the unmarshaling is to be done; the values are from the enumeration **MSHCTX**. For a definition of **MSHCTX**, see "Data Structures," at the beginning of the **IMarshal** interface description.

Return Values

Value	Meaning
S_OK	The object was marshaled successfully.
STG_E_MEDIUMFULL	The medium is full.
STG_E_INVALIDPOINTER	An **IStream** error dealing with the *pStm* parameter.
CO_E_OBJNOTCONNECTED	Similar to OLE_E_NOTRUNNING. The object is loaded but no server is running.

Value	Meaning
E_OUTOFMEMORY	Out of memory.
E_INVALIDARG	One or more arguments are invalid.
E_UNEXPECTED	An unexpected error occurred.
E_FAIL	Indicates an unspecified error.

Comments

The *dwMemctx* parameter identifies the destination context, which is relative to the current context in which the unmarshaling is to be done.

CoMarshalInterface first tries to obtain an **IMarshal** interface from *pUnk* by calling **QueryInterface**. If that fails, the standard marshaler (accessible by **CoGetStandardMarshal** is used. Having obtained an **IMarshal** interface, **CoMarshalInterface** uses the **IMarshal::MarshalInterface** and **IMarshal::GetMarshalSizeMax** methods to marshal the interface. **IMarshal::GetMarshalSizeMax** is not used; the **IStream** interface passed to the **MarshalInterface** function must be able to grow dynamically.

CoMarshalInterface is usually only called by code in interface proxies or stubs that marshal an interface pointer parameter, although it is sometimes used by objects that support custom marshaling.

▶ **To custom marshal an object, the sending application performs the following steps:**

1. Get the CLSID to be used to create an uninitialized proxy in the unmarshaling context by calling **IMarshal::GetUnmarshalClass**.
2. [optional] Get an upper bound on the amount of memory needed to do the marshaling by calling **IMarshal::GetMarshalSizeMax**.
3. Do the marshaling by calling **IMarshal::MarshalInterface**. The CLSID and the data marshaled into the stream are then sent to the destination, where they are unmarshaled.

See Also

CoUnmarshalInterface

CoUnmarshalInterface

HRESULT CoUnmarshalInterface(*pStm, riid, ppvObj***)**
LPSTREAM *pStm*
REFIID *riid*
LPVOID FAR * *ppvObj*

CoUnmarshalInterface unmarshals a previously marshaled object from the specified stream. This function is provided for convenience in unmarshaling previously marshaled objects.

Parameters

pStm
Points to the stream from which the object is to be unmarshaled.

riid
Specifies the interface that is to communicate with the unmarshaled object.

ppvObj
Points to the location where the interface pointer is to be returned.

Return Values

Value	Meaning
S_OK	The interface was unmarshaled successfully.
STG_E_INVALIDPOINTER	An **IStream** error dealing with the *pStm* parameter.
CO_E_OBJNOTCONNECTED	The object application has been disconnected from the remoting system (for example, as a result of **CoDisconnectObject**).
REGDB_E_CLASSNOTREG	An error occurred reading the registration database.
E_OUTOFMEMORY	Out of memory.
E_INVALIDARG	One or more arguments are invalid.
E_UNEXPECTED	An unexpected error occurred.
E_NOINTERFACE	The final **QueryInterface** of this function for the requested interface returned E_NOINTERFACE.
E_FAIL	Indicates an unspecified error.
CoCreateInstance errors	An error occurred when creating the handler (standard or custom marshaling).

Comments

Unmarshaling an object requires the receiving application to perform the following steps:

1. Load the class object corresponding to the CLSID that the object application passed to **IMarshal::GetUnmarshalClass**:

```
LPCLASSFACTORY lpcf;
GetClassObject(cid, CLSCTX_INPROCHANDLER, IID_IClassFactory, &lpcf);
```

2. Instantiate the class, requesting the **IMarshal** interface:

```
LPMARSHAL lpProxy;
lpcf->CreateInstance(NULL, IID_IMarshal, &lpProxy);
```

Note If the proxy is being created as part of an aggregate, the **IUnknown** interface would be requested and the **IMarshal** interface would be queried.

---

3. Initialize the proxy by calling **IMarshal::UnmarshalInterface**. Use a copy of the data originally produced by **IMarshal::MarshalInterface** and request the interface that was originally marshaled:

```
IOriginal * pobj;
lpProxy->UnmarshalInterface(lpstm, IID_Original, &pobj);
lpProxy->Release();
lpcf->Release();
if (MSHLFLAGS_NORMAL){
    reset Stm;
    Release m_data;
}
```

See Also **CoMarshalInterface**

CoReleaseMarshalData

HRESULT CoReleaseMarshalData(*pStm* **)**
LPSTREAM *pStm*

CoReleaseMarshalData destroys a previously marshaled data packet.

Parameters

pStm
Points to a stream containing the data packet to be destroyed.

Return Values

Value	Meaning
S_OK	The data packet was successfully destroyed.
STG_E_INVALIDPOINTER	An **IStream** error dealing with the *pStm* parameter.
E_OUTOFMEMORY	Out of memory.
E_INVALIDARG	*pStm* is invalid.
E_UNEXPECTED	An unexpected error occurred.
E_FAIL	Indicates an unspecified error.

Comments

CoReleaseMarshalData must be called to destroy data packets. Examples of when **CoReleaseMarshalData** should be called include the following situations:

1. An attempt was made to unmarshal the data packet, but failed.
2. A marshaled data packet was removed from a global table.

See Also

IMarshal::ReleaseMarshalData

Component Object Functions

The following functions are used to locate and connect to a class of object, to register a class of object, and to revoke the registration of an object class. These functions are defined as follows (see also COMPOBJ.H):

```
 CoGetClassObject(REFCLSID rclsid, DWORD dwClsContext, LPVOID pvReserved,
   REFIID riid,    LPVOID FAR* ppvObj);
 CoIsHandlerConnected(LPUNKNOWN pUnk);
 CoRegisterClassObject(REFCLSID rclsid, LPUNKNOWN pUnk, DWORD dwClsContext,
   DWORD flags,  LPDWORD lpdwRegister);
 CoRevokeClassObject(DWORD dwRegister);
CoLockObjectExternal(LPUNKNOWN pUnk, BOOL fLock, BOOL fLastUnlockReleases);
CoDisconnectObject(LPUNKNOWN pUnk, DWORD dwReserved);
```

CoGetClassObject

HRESULT CoGetClassObject(*rclsid*, *grfContext*, *pvReserved*, *riid*, *ppvObj*)
REFCLSID *rclsid*
DWORD *dwClsContext*
LPVOID *pvReserved*
REFIID *riid*
LPVOID FAR* *ppvObj*

CoGetClassObject locates and connects to a specified class object.

Parameters

rclsid
Specifies the object class that is to be loaded.

dwClsContext
Specifies the context in which the executable code is to be run.

pvReserved
Reserved for future use; must be NULL.

riid
Specifies the interface to be used to communicate with the class object.

ppvObj
Points to where the interface is to be stored.

Return Values

Value	Meaning
S_OK	The specified object was located and connected to successfully.
REGDB_E_CLASSNOTREG	CLSID is not properly registered.
E_NOINTERFACE	The object pointed to by *ppvObj* does not support the interface identified by *riid.*
REGDB_E_READREGDB	Error reading the registration database.
CO_E_DLLNOTFOUND	In process DLL or handler DLL not found (depends on context).
CO_E_APPNOTFOUND	EXE not found (CLSCTX_LOCAL_SERVER only).
E_ACCESSDENIED	General access failure (returned from **LoadLib/WinExec**).
CO_E_WRONGOSFORAPP	EXE or DLL is written for a different operating system than is currently running.
CO_E_ERRORINAPP	EXE has an error in image.
CO_E_APPSINGLEUSE	EXE can only be launched once.
CO_E_ERRORINDLL	EXE has error in image.
CO_E_APPDIDNTREG	EXE was launched, but it didn't register class object (may or may not have shutdown).
E_OUTOFMEMORY	Out of memory.
E_INVALIDARG	One or more arguments are invalid.
E_UNEXPECTED	An unexpected error occurred.
E_NOINTERFACE	The **QueryInterface** on the class object returned E_NOINTERFACE.

Comments

Given a CLSID, a container can opaquely locate and dynamically load the executable code that manipulates an object by calling **CoGetClassObject**. The container passes to **CoGetClassObject** the CLSID and the interface it wants to use to communicate with the object. Most often, this is the **IClassFactory** interface, through which the container can then make an instance of the object by calling **IClassFactory::CreateInstance.**

If necessary, the object's executable code can be dynamically loaded in order to locate and connect to the class object. The *riid* parameter specifies the interface used by the caller to communicate with the class object; this is usually IID_IClassFactory.

Different pieces of code can be associated with one *rclsid* for use in different execution contexts. The context in which the caller is interested is indicated by the parameter *dwClsContext*, a group of flags taken from the enumeration CLSCTX, which is defined in COMPOBJ.H as follows:

```
typedef enum tagCLSCTX
{
    CLSCTX_INPROC_SERVER = 1
    CLSCTX_INPROC_HANDLER = 2,
    CLSCTX_LOCAL_SERVER = 4
} CLSCTX;
```

The contexts are tried in the order in which they are listed. Multiple values can be OR'd together, indicating that multiple contexts are acceptable to the caller; for example:

```
#define CLSCTX_INPROC (CLSCTX_INPROC_SERVER|CLSCTX_INPROC_HANDLER)
#define CLSCTX_SERVER (CLSCTX_INPROC_SERVER|CLSCTX_LOCAL_SERVER)
```

These contexts are used as follows:

Object Class Context Values	Description
CLSCTX_INPROC_SERVER	The code that creates and manages objects of this class is loaded in the container's process space (runs in same process as caller).
CLSCTX_INPROC_HANDLER	The DLL code that implements container-side structures of this class (when instances of it are accessed remotely) is loaded in the container's process space (runs in same process as caller).
CLSCTX_LOCAL_SERVER	The EXE code that creates and manages objects of this class is loaded in a separate process space (runs on same machine but in a different process).

CoGetClassObject operates by consulting (as appropriate for the context indicated) both the registration database and the existing class objects registered using **CoRegisterClassObject**.

Example uses of particular flag combinations are as follows:

Function Called	Context Flag Used
OleLoad	CLSCTX_INPROC_HANDLER | CLSCTX_INPROC_SERVER Putting an OLE object into the loaded state requires in-process access; however, it doesn't matter if all of the object's functionality is presently available.
IRunnableObject::Run	CLSCTX_INPROC_SERVER | CLSCTX_LOCAL_SERVER Running an OLE object requires connecting to the full code of the object wherever it is located.
CoUnMarshalInterface	CLSCTX_INPROC_HANDLER Unmarshaling needs the form of the class designed for remote access.

See Also **CoRegisterClassObject**, **CoRevokeClassObject**

CoIsHandlerConnected

BOOL CoIsHandlerConnected(*pUnk*)
LPUNKNOWN *pUnk*

CoIsHandlerConnected determines if the specifed handler is connected to its corresponding object.

Parameters

pUnk
Specifies the object in question.

Return Values

Value	Meaning
TRUE	A handler is connected to its object.
FALSE	A handler is not connected to its object.

Comments

If a pointer to the real object is passed in instead of the handler, then TRUE will be returned.

CoRegisterClassObject

HRESULT CoRegisterClassObject(*rclsid, pUnk, dwClsContext, flags, lpdwRegister*)
REFCLSID *rclsid*
LPUNKNOWN *pUnk*
DWORD *dwClsContext*
DWORD *flags*
LPDWORD *lpdwRegister*

CoRegisterClassObject registers a class object with OLE so that other applications can connect to it.

Parameters

rclsid
Specifies the object class being registered.

pUnk
Points to the class object whose availability is being published.

dwClsContext
Specifies the context in which the executable code is to be run: CLSCTX_INPROC_SERVER, CLSCTX_INPROC_HANDLER, or CLSCTX_LOCAL_SERVER. For more information on these context values, see **CoGetClassObject**.

flags
Determines how connections are made to the class object; see the following comments.

lpdwRegister
Points to the value returned by **CoRegisterClassObject** that identifies the class object; later used by **CoRevokeClassObject** to revoke the class registration.

Return Values

Value	Meaning
S_OK	The object was registered successfully.
CO_E_OBJISREG	Object class already registered in the class object table.
E_OUTOFMEMORY	Out of memory.
E_INVALIDARG	One or more arguments are invalid.
E_UNEXPECTED	An unexpected error occurred.

Comments

When an object application starts, it creates an **IClassFactory** instance and calls **CoRegisterClassObject**. Object applications that support several different object classes must allocate a different **IClassFactory** instance for each object class.

Multiple registrations of the same class object is not an error; each registration is independent. Each subsequent registration will yield a unique key in *lpdwRegister*.

CoRegisterClassObject is called by EXE object applications only; it should not be called by object handlers or DLL object applications. These applications must instead implement and export **DllGetClassObject**.

Single-use applications that are being started with the **/Embedding** switch should not register their class of object; multiple-use applications beings started with **/Embedding** must register their class of object.

When the subsequent reference count on the class object reaches zero, the class object can be destroyed, allowing the application to exit.

A sophisticated container can keep an object application running by obtaining its class object and calling **IClassFactory::LockServer**(*TRUE*) on it. However, because some class objects are single use, the container must hold on to the actual class object from which objects are instantiated. This prohibits the container application from using helper functions like **OleLoad.**Instead, the container has to code variants of such functions itself.

The *flags* parameter controls how connections are made to the class object; the values are taken from the enumeration **REGCLS**, which is defined in COMPOBJ.H as follows:

```
typedef enum tagREGCLS {
    REGCLS_SINGLEUSE            = 0,
    REGCLS_MULTIPLEUSE          = 1,
    REGCLS_MULTI_SEPARATE       = 2,
    } REGCLS;
```

Legal values for *flags* are as follows:

Registration Class Flag Values	Description
REGCLS_SINGLEUSE	Once a container has connected to the class object with **CoGetClassObject**, the class object should be removed from public view so that no other container applications can similarly connect to it. This flag is commonly given for single document interface (SDI) applications. Specifying this flag does not affect the responsibility of the object application to call **CoRevokeClassObject**; it must always call **CoRevokeClassObject** when it is done by using an object class.
REGCLS_MULTIPLEUSE	Enables multiple **CoGetClassObject** calls to connect to the same class object.

Registration Class Flag Values	Description
REGCLS_MULTI_SEPARATE	Similar to REGCLS_MULTIPLEUSE, except that REGCLS_MULTI_SEPARATE does not automatically register the class object as CLSCTX_INPROC_SERVER for a local server; instead it provides separate control over each context.

Notice that registering as

```
CLSCTX_LOCAL_SERVER, REGCLS_MULTIPLEUSE
```

is the same as

```
(CLSCTX_INPROC_SERVER|CLSCTX_LOCAL_SERVER), REGCLS_MULTI_SEPARATE
```

but is different than registering as

```
CLSCTX_LOCAL_SERVER, REGCLS_MULTI_SEPARATE.
```

The following table summarizes the allowable flag combinations and the object registrations that are affected by the combinations:

	REGCLS_ SINGLEUSE	**REGCLS_ MULTIPLEUSE**	**REGCLS_ MULTI_ SEPARATE**	**Other**
CLSCTX_ INPROC_ SERVER	Error	Inproc	Inproc	Error
CLSCTX_ LOCAL_ SERVER	Local	Inproc/local	Local	Error
Both of the above	Error	Inproc/local	Inproc/local	Error
Other	Error	Error	Error	Error

The key difference is in the middle columns and the middle rows. In the REGCLS_MULTIPLEUSE column, they are the same (registers multiple use for both inproc and local). In the REGCLS_MULTI_SEPARATE column, CLSCTX_LOCAL_SERVER is local only.

See Also **CoGetClassObject, CoRevokeClassObject, DllGetClassObject**

CoRevokeClassObject

HRESULT CoRevokeClassObject(*dwRegister***)**
DWORD *dwRegister*

CoRevokeClassObject informs OLE that a class object, previously registered with **CoRegisterClassObject**, is no longer available for use.

Parameters

dwRegister
Specifies the token previously returned from **CoRegisterClassObject**.

Return Values

Value	Meaning
S_OK	The class object was successfully revoked.
E_OUTOFMEMORY	Out of memory.
E_INVALIDARG	The *dwRegister* parameter does not map to a registered class object.
E_UNEXPECTED	An unexpected error occurred.

Comments

The object application *must* call **CoRevokeClassObject** on all registered class objects prior to quitting program execution. **CoRevokeClassObject** should be called by class object implementors as part of their release sequence.

Specifying the *flags* value REGCLS_SINGLEUSE in a call to **CoRegisterClassObject** does not affect the responsibility of the object application to revoke registered class objects. This task must always be done prior to quitting.

See Also

CoGetClassObject, CoRegisterClassObject

CoLockObjectExternal

HRESULT CoLockObjectExternal(*pUnk, fLock, fLastUnlockReleases***)**
LPUNKNOWN *pUnk*
BOOL *fLock*
BOOL *fLastUnlockReleases*

CoLockObjectExternal locks an object so its reference count cannot decrement to zero; it is also used to release a lock.

Parameters

pUnk
Points to the object to be locked or unlocked.

fLock

Specifies whether the object is to be locked. TRUE holds a reference to the object, locking it independently of external or internal **AddRef/Release** operations, registrations, or revokes. If *fLock* is TRUE, *fLastLockReleases* is ignored. FALSE releases such locks.

fLastLockReleases

Specifies whether a given lock is the last reference to an object that is supposed to keep it alive. TRUE means release all pointers to the object if this lock is the last reference to the object that is supposed to keep it alive (there may be other references that are not supposed to keep it alive).

Return Values

Value	Meaning
S_OK	The object reference count was locked successfully.
E_OUTOFMEMORY	Out of memory.
E_INVALIDARG	One or more arguments are invalid.
E_UNEXPECTED	An unexpected error occurred.

Comments

CoLockObjectExternal *must* be called in the process in which the object is loaded. From the object's point of view, the lock is implemented by having the system call **IUnknown::AddRef** on the object and then not call **IUnknown::Release** on the object until **CoLockObjectExternal**(...,*FALSE*,...) is later called. Because it acts external to the object, much like the user does, it can be used to maintain a reference count on the object on behalf of the user.

CoLockObjectExternal does not change the typical registration/revoking process for objects. **CoLockObjectExternal** can be used in **IOleContainer::LockContainer**, although the container must still keep a lock count so that it exits when the lock count reaches zero and the container is invisible.

Note During drag and drop operations, the object that exposes the **IDropTarget** interface must have an external lock on it to ensure that a remote connection does not release the object after the drag and drop operation. To lock the object, **CoLockObjectExternal** must be called to lock and **IDropTarget** before calling **RegisterDragDrop**. **CoLockObjectExternal** should be called to free the **IDropTarget** after **RevokeDragDrop** has been called.

OLE uses the concept of *strong* and *weak* locks. Whereas a strong lock on an object will keep it in memory, a weak lock will not. Strong locks are required, for example, when there are links to embedded objects that need to be updated. The embedded object's container must remain in memory until the update process is complete. There must also be a strong lock on an application's class object to ensure the application stays alive until it has finished providing object services to its containers. All external references to an object result in a strong reference lock being placed on the object.

After an application calls **CoRegisterClassObject**, it should call **CoLockObjectExternal** to ask OLE to maintain a strong lock on its class object. **CoLockObjectExternal** locks any object so that its reference count cannot decrement to zero. It can also be used to release such a lock. **CoLockObjectExternal** can *only* be called by the process in which the object is located.

CoLockObjectExternal is typically used in three places:

- Object applications call **CoLockObjectExternal**(*pUnk*, TRUE, TRUE) when they become visible. This call creates a strong lock on behalf of the user. When the application is closing, the lock must be freed with a call to **CoLockObjectExternal** (*pUnk,* FALSE, TRUE).
- The API function, **OleNoteObjectVisible**, can be called instead of **CoLockObjectExternal** in this context. **OleNoteObjectVisible** is simply a wrapper function for **CoLockObjectExternal**.
- A call to **CoLockObjectExternal** can be included in the implementation of **IClassFactory::LockServer**. Containers call **IClassFactory::LockServer** to keep an object application that handles a particular class of object(s) in memory, thereby eliminating startup time and allowing faster throughput during activation.
- A call to **CoLockObjectExternal** can also be in the implementation of **IOleContainer::LockContainer**. **IOleContainer::LockContainer** is called to keep an embedded object's container alive.

Conversely, a container must call **OleSetContainedObject** to weaken its connection to the object so other connections can determine what is to happen to the object while it is visible. **OleSetContainedObject** is similar to calling **CoLockObjectExternal**(*pUnk*, FALSE, FALSE).

If an application manages all aspects of its application and document shutdown completely with calls to **CoLockObjectExternal**, it is not necessary to maintain a private count of calls to **IOleContainer::LockContainer.** Maintaining all aspects of shutdown means that **CoLockObjectExternal** is called whenever one of the following conditions occur:

- A document is created and destroyed or made visible or invisible.
- The application is started and shutdown by the user.
- A pseudo-object is created and destroyed.

For debugging purposes, it may be useful to keep a count of the number of external locks and unlocks made on the application.

Figure 5-4 shows the state of an application after **CoLockObjectExternal** is called. OLE creates a transparent stub manager that keeps track of the type and number of external references counts. As shown, the class object's reference count is two, which reflects the strong lock held by the stub manager and the weak lock held by the application object.

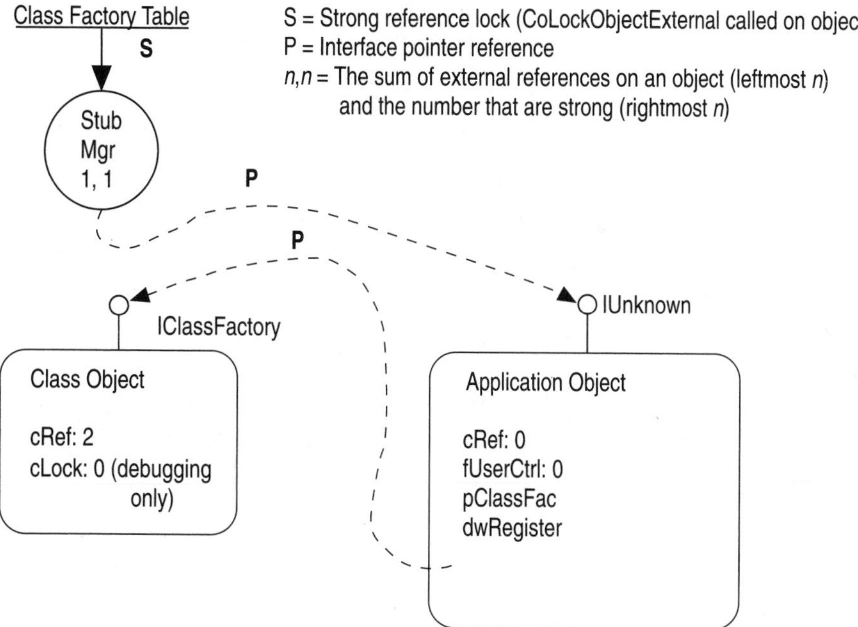

Figure 5-4. Creating a strong reference lock on an object.

Weak locks are created when an object is registered in the running object table or typically when a drop target is registered. When there is a weak lock, the last external release releases the object. The object is still responsible for revoking its drag/drop registration and Running object table registration. This enables a moniker bind and release to shut down the object when it is invisible.

Note A user has explicit control over the lifetime of an application, even if there are external locks on the application. That is, if a user decides to close the application (File, Exit), the application *must* shut down. In the presence of external locks on an object, the application can call **CoDisconnectObject** to force these connections closed prior to shut down.

See Also **IOleContainer::LockContainer**, **OleSetContainedObject**

CoDisconnectObject

HRESULT CoDisconnectObject(*pUnk, dwReserved***)**
LPUNKNOWN *pUnk*
DWORD *dwReserved*

CoDisconnectObject disconnects all remote process connections being maintained on behalf of all the interface pointers on a specified object.

Parameters

pUnk
Points to the object to be disconnected. Can be any interface on the object which is polymorphic with **IUnknown**, not necessarily the exact interface returned by **QueryInterface(IID_IUnknown...)**.

dwReserved
Reserved for future use; must be set to zero by the caller; however, to ensure compatibility with future use, the callee *must not* check for zero.

Return Values

Value	Meaning
S_OK	All remote process connections were deleted successfully.
E_OUTOFMEMORY	Out of memory.
E_INVALIDARG	One or more arguments are invalid.
E_UNEXPECTED	An unexpected error occurred.
E_FAIL	Indicates an unspecified error.

Comments

CoDisconnectObject is not used in the typical course of processing (clients of interfaces should use **IUnknown::Release**). The primary purpose of **CoDisconnectObject** is to give an application process control over remote connections to other processes that might have been made from objects managed by the process. For example, suppose an OLE container loads an embedded object and then links are established between the embedded object and outside containers. If the container application process wanted to exit, it is not useful for these remote connections to keep the object active beyond the lifetime of its container. When the object's container closes, such links should go into a disconnected state. To forcefully close any existing connection(s), the object's container can call **CoDisconnectObject**.

CoDisconnectObject is a privileged operation, to be invoked only by the process in which the object actually is managed.

Before calling **CoDisconnectObject**, the container process should first call **IOleObject::Close** for all OLE objects. The objects will send OnClose notifications to alert all clients of the impending closure.

CoDisconnectObject effectively causes a controlled crash of the remoting connections to the object. This function is a privileged operation, to be invoked only by the process in which the object is actually managed.

DLL Initialization Functions

The following functions can be used to load and unload DLLs. They keep track of reference counts on the loaded DLL, removing them when the libraries are unloaded. The functions are defined as follows (see also COMPOBJ.H):

```
CoLoadLibrary(LPSTR lpszLibName, BOOL bAutoFree);
CoFreeAllLibraries(void);
CoFreeLibrary(HINSTANCE hInst);
CoFreeUnusedLibraries(void);
```

CoLoadLibrary

HINSTANCE CoLoadLibrary(*lpszLibName, bAutoFree*)
LPSTR *lpszLibName*
BOOL *bAutoFree*

CoLoadLibrary loads the DLL of the given name into the caller's process. Usually, this is not called directly by containers, but is called internally by **CoGetClassObject**.

Parameters

lpszLibName
Points to the name of the library to be loaded. The use of this name is the same as in the Windows function **LoadLibrary**.

bAutoFree
Indicates, if TRUE, that this library is freed when it is no longer needed, either through **CoFreeUnusedLibraries** or at uninitialization time through **CoUninitialize**. If it is FALSE, the library should be explicitly freed with **CoFreeLibrary**.

Return Values

Value	Meaning
Module handle	Handle of the now-loaded library.
NULL	Library could not be loaded.

Comments

Internally, the loaded DLL is reference counted, by using **CoLoadLibrary** to increment the count and **CoFreeLibrary** to decrement it.

See Also

CoFreeAllLibraries, CoFreeLibrary, CoFreeUnusedLibraries

CoFreeAllLibraries

void CoFreeAllLibraries()

CoFreeAllLibraries frees all the DLLs that have been loaded with **CoLoadLibrary**, whether or not they are currently in use.

Comments

CoFreeAllLibraries is called internally by **CoUninitialize**; thus containers usually have no need to call this function directly.

See Also

CoLoadLibrary, CoFreeLibrary, CoFreeUnusedLibraries

CoFreeLibrary

void CoFreeLibrary(*hInst*)
HINSTANCE *hInst*

CoFreeLibrary frees a library that was previously loaded with **CoLoadLibrary**(..., FALSE).

Parameters

hInst
Specifies the handle to the library module that is to be freed, as was returned by **CoLoadLibrary**.

Comments

It is illegal to explicitly free a library whose corresponding **CoLoadLibrary** call specified auto-free (**CoLoadLibrary**(...,TRUE)).

See Also

CoFreeAllLibraries, CoFreeUnusedLibraries, CoLoadLibrary

CoFreeUnusedLibraries

void CoFreeUnusedLibraries()

CoFreeUnusedLibraries unloads any DLLs that have been loaded by **CoLoadLibrary**(..., *TRUE*) but are no longer in use.

Comments

Applications should call this function periodically to free resources, either at the top of their message loop or in some idle-time task.

See Also

CoFreeLibrary, CoFreeUnusedLibraries, CoLoadLibrary

Object Creation Function

The following function can be used to create an instance of a specified class of object (see also COMPOBJ.H):

```
CoCreateInstance(REFCLSID rclsid, IUnknown * pUnkOuter, DWORD dwClsContext, REFIID riid,
   LPVOID FAR * ppvObj);
```

CoCreateInstance

HRESULT CoCreateInstance(*rclsid, pUnkOuter, dwClsContext, riid, ppvObj*)
REFCLSID *rclsid*
IUnknown * *pUnkOuter*
DWORD *dwClsContext*
REFIID *riid*
LPVOID FAR * *ppvObj*

CoCreateInstance creates an instance of the specified object class.

Parameters

rclsid
Specifies the CLSID of the object class to create.

pUnkOuter
Specifies the controlling unknown of the aggregate.

dwClsContext
Specifies the context in which the executable is to be run. The values are taken from the enumeration **CLSCTX**. For more information on **CLSCTX**, see the description for **CoGetClassObject**.

riid
Specifies the interface to be used to communicate with the object.

ppvObj
Points to where to return the pointer to the requested interface.

Return Values

Value	Meaning
S_OK	An instance of the specified object class was successfully created.
REGDB_E_CLASSNOTREG	Specified class not registered in registration database.
E_OUTOFMEMORY	Out of memory.
E_INVALIDARG	One or more arguments are invalid.
E_UNEXPECTED	An unexpected error occurred.
CLASS_E_NOAGGREGATION	This class cannot be created as part of an aggregate.

Comments

CoCreateInstance is a helper function that encapsulates the following functionality:

```
CoGetClassObject(rclsid, dwClsContext, NULL, IID_IClassFactory,
     &pCF);
hresult = pCF->CreateInstance(pUnkOuter, riid, ppvObj)
pCF->Release();
```

See Also

CoGetClassObject, IClassFactory::CreateInstance

File Time Conversion Functions

The following functions can be used to convert 16-bit MS-DOS representations of the time and date to 64-bit representations for use on platforms that support the Win32 API. The functions are defined as follows (see also COMPOBJ.H):

```
CoDosDateTimeToFileTime(WORD nDosDate, WORD nDosTime, FILETIME FAR* lpFileTime);
 CoFileTimeNow(FILETIME FAR* lpFileTime);
 CoFileTimeToDosDateTime(FILETIME FAR* lpFileTime, LPWORD lpDosDate, LPWORD, lpDosTime);
```

FILETIME Data Structure

The **FILETIME** data structure is used by the **CoDosDateTimeToFileTime**, **CoFileTimeToDosDateTime**, and **CoFileTimeNow** functions; it is defined in COMPOBJ.H, as follows:

```
typedef struct FARSTRUCT tagFILETIME
{
    DWORD dwLowDateTime;
    DWORD dwHighDateTime;
} FILETIME;
```

CoDosDateTimeToFileTime

BOOL CoDosDateTimeToFileTime (*nDosDate*, *nDosTime*, *lpFileTime*)
WORD *nDosDate*
WORD *nDosTime*
LPFILETIME FAR* *lpFileTime*

CoDosDateTimeToFileTime converts the MS-DOS representation of the time and date to a **FILETIME** structure. This is a 64-bit value representing the number of 100-nanosecond intervals since January 1, 1601.

Parameters

nDosDate
Specifies the 16-bit MS-DOS date.

nDosTime
Specifies the 16-bit MS-DOS time.

lpFileTime
Points to the **FILETIME** structure; for more information, see "**FILETIME** Data Structure," at the beginning of this section.

Return Values

Value	Meaning
TRUE	The **FILETIME** structure was created successfully.
FALSE	The **FILETIME** structure was not created successfully, probably because of invalid arguments.

Comments

The **FILETIME** structure and the **CoDosDateTimeToFileTime** and **CoFileTimeToDosDateTime** functions were originally defined as part of the Win32 API definition. They are provided as part of OLE for use on platforms that do not support Win32 APIs.

MS-DOS records file dates and times as packed 16-bit values. An MS-DOS date has the following format:

Bits	Contents
0-4	Days of the month (1-31).
5-8	Months (1 = January, 2 = February, and so forth.).
9-15	Year offset from 1980 (add 1980 to get actual year).

An MS-DOS time has the following format:

Bits	Contents
0-4	Seconds divided by 2.
5-10	Minutes (0-59).
11-15	Hours (0-23 on a 24-hour clock).

See Also

CoFileTimeToDosDateTime, CoFileTimeNow

CoFileTimeNow

HRESULT CoFileTimeNow(*lpFileTime*)
FILETIME FAR * *lpFileTime*

CoFileTimeNow returns the current time as a **FILETIME** structure.

Parameters

lpFileTime
Points to where to return the **FILETIME** structure; for more information, see "**FILETIME** Data Structure," at the beginning of this section.

Return Values

Value	Meaning
S_OK	The current time was converted to a **FILETIME** structure.
E_OUTOFMEMORY	Out of memory.
E_INVALIDARG	*lpFileTime* is invalid.
E_UNEXPECTED	An unexpected error occurred.
E_FAIL	The current time was not converted to a **FILETIME** structure.

See Also

CoDosDateTimeToFileTime, CoFileTimeToDosDateTime

CoFileTimeToDosDateTime

BOOL CoFileTimeToDosDateTime (*lpFileTime*, *lpDosDate*, *lpDosTime*)
FILETIME FAR * *lpFileTime*
LPWORD *lpDosDate*
LPWORD *lpDosTime*

CoFileTimeToDosDateTime converts a **FILETIME** into MS-DOS date and time values.

Parameter

lpFileTime
Points to the **FILETIME** structure to convert; for more information, see "FILETIME Data Structure" at the beginning of this section.

lpDosDate
Points to the 16-bit MS-DOS date.

lpDosTime
Points to the 16-bit MS-DOS time.

Return Values

Value	Meaning
TRUE	The **FILETIME** structure was converted successfully.
FALSE	The **FILETIME** structure was not converted successfully.

Comments

This is the inverse operation provided by the **CoDosDateTimeToFileTime** function.

See Also

CoDosDateTimeToFileTime, CoFileTimeNow

DLL Object Class Functions

The following functions can be implemented in DLL object handlers to enable containers to access a class of object implemented within an object handler or to indicate whether it is OK to unload a DLL handler from memory. The functions are defined as follows (see also COMPOBJ.H):

```
DllCanUnloadNow(void);
DllGetClassObject(REFCLSID rclsid, REFIID riid, LPVOID FAR* ppvObj);
```

DllCanUnloadNow

HRESULT DllCanUnloadNow()

DllCanUnloadNow indicates whether the DLL is no longer in use and should be unloaded.

Return Values

Value	Meaning
S_OK	DLL can be unloaded now.
S_FALSE	DLL cannot be unloaded now.

Comments

DllCanUnloadNow is not provided with OLE. Rather, it is a function implemented and exported from DLLs supporting the Component Object Model.

DllCanUnloadNow should be exported from DLLs designed to be dynamically loaded in **CoGetClassObject** or **CoLoadLibrary** calls. A DLL is no longer be in use when there are no existing instances of classes it manages; at this point, the DLL can be safely freed by calling **CoFreeUnusedLibraries**.

If the DLL loaded by **CoGetClassObject** fails to export **DllCanUnloadNow**, the DLL will be forcibly unloaded when **CoUninitialize** is called to release the OLE libraries.

See Also

DllGetClassObject

IsValidInterface

BOOL IsValidInterface(*pv***)**
void FAR * *pv*

IsValidInterface determines whether an interface pointer is valid.

Parameters

pv
Specifies the interface pointer to test; points to an instantiation of an interface; must not be NULL.

Return Values

Value	Meaning
TRUE	The interface pointer is valid.
FALSE	The interface pointer is not valid.

See Also **IsValidIid**

IsValidPtrIn

BOOL IsValidPtrIn(*pv,cb***)**
const void FAR* *pv*
UINT *cb*

IsValidPtrIn determines whether a pointer to readable memory is valid.

Parameters

pv
Specifies the pointer to test; points to the beginning of a block of allocated memory; NULL is not acceptable.

cb
Specifies the number of bytes in the block of readable memory to which *pv* points.

Return Values

Value	Meaning
TRUE	The pointer is valid.
FALSE	The pointer is not valid.

See Also **IsValidPtrOut**

IsValidPtrOut

BOOL IsValidPtrOut(*pv*, *cb*)
void FAR * *pv*
UINT *cb*

IsValidPtrOut determines whether a pointer to memory that can be written to is valid.

Parameters

pv
Specifies the pointer to test; points to the beginning of a block of allocated memory. It must not be NULL.

cb
Specifies the number of bytes in the block of writable meory to which *pv* points.

Return Values

Value	Meaning
TRUE	The pointer is valid.
FALSE	The pointer is not valid.

See Also

IsValidPtrIn

OLE Library Functions

The following functions can be used to manage the OLE Component Object Model library. The functions are defined as follows (see also COMPOBJ.H):

```
CoBuildVersion();
CoCreateStandardMalloc(DWORD dwMemctx, LPMALLOC * ppMalloc);
CoGetCurrentProcess();
CoGetMalloc(DWORD dwMemctx, LPMALLOC FAR* ppMalloc);
CoInitialize(LPMALLOC pMalloc);
```

CoBuildVersion

DWORD CoBuildVersion()

CoBuildVersion returns the major and the minor version number of Component Object Model library.

Return Values

Value	Meaning
32-bit integer	The 16 high-order bits are the major build number; the 16 low-order bits are the minor build number.
Eef_OUTOFMEMORY	Out of memory.
E_UNEXPECTED	An unexpected error occurred.

Comments

Applications should call **CoBuildVersion** before using any other Component Object Model library API function or interface method. **CoBuildVersion** returns the major and minor build numbers in a DWORD where the high-order word is the major version number and the low-order word is the minor version number. Applications can run one major version and any minor version. Therefore, the application must check that the returned major version is equal to the expected major version (the version that the application compiled against). If there are differences, **CoInitialize** must not be called.

For any given release of the Component Object Model library, there is a file called OLE*x*VER.H. OLE2VER.H defines the symbol *rmm* as the major version and *rup* as the minor version. It is unlikely that the major build version would change between releases, but applications should still ensure compatibility by calling **CoBuildVersion**.

CoBuildVersion is always the first function an application calls in the Component Object Model library.

```
// excerpt from the current ole2ver.h:
#define rmm     23
#define rup     563

DWORD dwBuildVersion = CoBuildVersion();

// fail if different major version or older minor version.
if (HIWORD(dwBuildVersion) != rmm || LOWORD(dwBuildVersion) < rup)
    //error: don't initialize OLE
else
    CoInitialize (NULL);
```

See Also

CoInitialize, OleBuidVersion

CoGetCurrentProcess

DWORD CoGetCurrentProcess()

CoGetCurrentProcess returns a value that is unique to the current process.

Return Values

Value	Meaning
DWORD value	Unique value for current process that can be used to avoid HTASK reuse problems.

Comments

CoGetCurrentProcess is useful in helping maintain tables that are keyed by processes.

The value returned is not used again until 2^{32} more processes have been created on the current workstation. Because Windows task handles can be reused relatively quickly when a Window's task dies, the value returned by **CoGetCurrentProcess** provides significantly better robustness than the HTASK in cases of abnormal process termination.

CoGetMalloc

HRESULT CoGetMalloc(*dwMemctx, ppMalloc***)**
DWORD *dwMemctx*
LPMALLOC FAR* *ppMalloc*

CoGetMalloc retrieves either the task memory allocator originally passed to **CoInitialize** or the OLE-provided shared memory allocator. Object handlers should use the task allocator returned by **CoGetMalloc** for their local memory management needs.

Parameters

dwMemctx
Specifies a value that indicates whether the memory block is private to a task or shared between processes. See the following comments.

ppMalloc
Points to where the memory allocator is to be returned.

Return Values

Value	Meaning
S_OK	The allocator was retrieved successfully.
E_FAIL	Indicates an unspecified error.
E_INVALIDARG	One or more arguments are invalid.
CO_E_NOTINITIALIZED	Must call **CoInitialize** first.
E_OUTOFMEMORY	Out of memory.

Comments

Legal values for the *dwMemctx* parameter are taken from the enumeration **MEMCTX**, which is defined in COMPOBJ.H as follows:

```
typedef enum tagMEMCTX
{
    MEMCTX_TASK =     1,    // task (private) memory
    MEMCTX_SHARED =   2,    // shared memory (between processes)
} MEMCTX;
```

MEMCTX_TASK returns the task allocator passed to **CoInitialize**. If **CoInitialize** has not yet been called, NULL will be returned through *ppMalloc* and CO_E_NOTINITIALIZED is returned. Specifying MEMCTX_SHARED returns the shared allocator.

The shared allocator returned by **CoGetMalloc** is the OLE-provided implementation of the **IMalloc** interface, which allocates memory so it can be accessed by other applications. Memory allocated by this shared allocator in one application can be freed by the shared allocator in another.

In versions of OLE 2 on platforms other than Windows 16-bit or the Macintosh, the shared memory allocator might not be available. In these cases, **CoGetMalloc**(MEMCTX_SHARED,...) will return E_INVALIDARG. The possible unavailability of the shared memory allocator will not affect custom marshalers; for information on custom marshaling, see the "IMarshal Interface," earlier in this chapter.

CoCreateStandardMalloc

HRESULT CoCreateStandardMalloc(*dwMemctx, ppMalloc*)
DWORD *dwMemctx*
LPMALLOC FAR* *ppMalloc*

CoCreateStandardMalloc creates and returns an OLE-provided memory allocator for the given memory context.

Parameter

dwMemctx
Specifies how the memory block is to be allocated. A value of 1 specifies that the memory block is private to a task (MEMCTX_TASK); 2 specifies that the block is shared between processes (MEMCTX_SHARED). For more information on the MEMCTX values, see **CoGetMalloc**.

ppMalloc
Points to where to return the **IMalloc** memory allocator.

Return Values

Value	Meaning
S_OK	The memory allocator was created successfully.
E_OUTOFMEMORY	Out of memory.
E_INVALIDARG	One or more arguments are invalid.
E_UNEXPECTED	An unexpected error occurred.

Comments

The new allocator creates and maintains its own new heap. All memory allocated in the heap is freed when the last reference to the returned *ppMalloc* is released.

The allocator returned by **CoCreateStandardMalloc** is not the same allocator as that returned by **CoGetMalloc**. This means that the allocator returned here is not the one used for values passed across interface boundaries. Rather, **CoCreateStandardMalloc** provides a handy memory allocator that can be used internally by an object.

See Also

CoGetMalloc

CoInitialize

HRESULT CoInitialize(*pMalloc*)
LPMALLOC *pMalloc*

CoInitialize initializes the Component Object Model library so that it can be used. With the exception of **CoBuildVersion**, this function must be called by applications before any other function in the Component Object Model library.

Parameters

pMalloc
Points to the memory allocator that is to be used for task memory by the library and by object handlers. To access the standard allocator, pass NULL.

Return Values

Value	Meaning
S_OK	The library was initialized successfully.
S_FALSE	Already initialized; didn't use *pMalloc*, if given.
E_OUTOFMEMORY	Out of memory.
E_INVALIDARG	*pMalloc* is invalid.
E_UNEXPECTED	An unexpected error occurred.

Comments

The design of the Component Object Model library allows the application that owns a given process space the opportunity to be in complete control of how memory is allocated and used by components in that space. To be in control, the application should implement the **IMalloc** interface and pass an instance of it (*pMalloc*) to **CoInitialize**; otherwise, it should pass NULL to use the OLE implementation of **IMalloc**.

Calls to **CoInitialize** *must* be balanced by corresponding calls to **CoUninitialize**. Usually, **CoInitialize** is called only once by the process that is to use the Component Object Library. In some instances (for example, two independent pieces of code written as DLLs), there may be competing calls to **CoInitialize**; in these cases, *only* the first successful call to **CoInitialize** initializes the library and only its corresponding balanced call to **CoUninitialize** will uninitialize it. **CoInitialize** returns S_FALSE if the library has already been initialized.

CoInitialize follows the usual reference counting rules described earlier in description of the **IUnknown** interface. Because **CoInitialize** retains the **IMalloc** pointer beyond the duration of the call, it calls *pMalloc*->**AddRef**.

CoInitialize is called internally by **OleInitialize** so most applications do not need to call **CoInitialize**.

See Also

CoUninitialize, OleInitialize

CoUninitialize

void CoUninitialize()

CoUninitialize closes the Component Object Model library, freeing any resources that it maintains and forcing all LRPC connections closed.

Comments

CoInitialize and **CoUninitialize** calls must be balanced; *only* the **CoUninitialize** call corresponding to the **CoInitialize** call that actually initialized the library can uninitialize it.

CoUninitialize should be called on application shutdown, as the last call made to the Component Object Model library and after the application hides its main windows and falls through its main message loop. If there are open conversations remaining, **CoUninitialize** starts a modal message loop and dispatches any pending messages from the containers or server for this OLE application. By dispatching the messages, **CoUninitialize** ensures that the application does not quit before receiving all its pending messages. Non-OLE messages are discarded.

CoUnInitialize is called internally by **OleUnInitialize** most applications do not need to call **CoUnInitialize**.

See Also **CoInitialize, OleUnInitialize**

Object Class Conversion and Emulation Functions

The following functions are used to emulate an object class of one type as a different class; these functions are defined in COMPOBJ.H as follows:

```
CoGetTreatAsClass(REFCLSID clsidOld, LPCLSID pclsidNew);
CoTreatAsClass(REFCLSID clsidOld, LPCLSID pclsidNew);
```

The following functions are defined in OLE2.H and can be used to convert an object of one class to another class:

```
OleDoAutoConvert(LPSTORAGE pStg, LPCLSID pclsidNew);
OleGetAutoConvert(REFCLSID clsidOld, LPCLSID pclsidNew);
OleSetAutoConvert(REFCLSID clsidOld, REFCLSID clsidNew);
GetConvertStg(LPSTORAGE pStg);
SetConvertStg(LPSTORAGE pStg, BOOL fConvert);
```

An object's class determines the verbs and the application the user uses to interact with the object. Usually, an object is activated by the object application corresponding to its CLSID, as registered in the registration database. However, implementing the Convert dialog box in a container application lets users change an object's current type to that of a different object type ("Convert to:"button) or to activate (emulate) objects of one type as if they were objects of another type (Activate as: option button).

Figure 5-5 shows a sample Convert dialog box. When the user selects the Convert to: or "Activate as:" button, the container generates a list of eligible destination object types. Associated with this type list is a list of class names; the corresponding type name for each class is obtained from the registration database entry for that class. In turn, the list of eligible classes is obtained from the main data formats stored by OLE with the object.

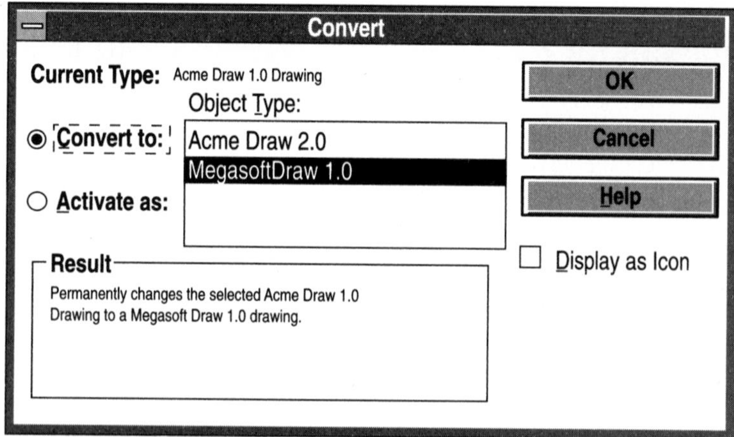

Figure 5-5. The Convert dialog box.

In order to be the destination class of a Convert operation, the object application must register the formats it can read from other objects. These formats are registered under the CLSID\{*clsid*}\Conversion\Readable subkeys in the registration database, as the following database entry template shows:

```
CLSID
    {CLSID} = Main User Type Name
    .
    .
    .
    Conversion
        Readable
            Main = format1, format2,...formatn
        Readwritable
            Main = format1, format2,...formatn
```

To activate an object of a different class as one of its own, the object application registers the formats it can both read and write under the "CLSID\{*clsid*}\Conversion\Readwritable" subkeys.

Note that converting an object to another type can destroy its original data format, while activating an object as a different type preserves the existing object's data format. Selecting an object to be activated as another class of object remains in effect until the user changes the class to a different one using the "Activate As" button.

Tagging Objects for Automatic Conversion and Emulation

Whenever a new version of an object application is being installed and an older version of the application is already present, the setup program should give the user the option of automatically converting the older version of the object class to the newer version the next time an object of that class is activated in the object's container, as shown in Figure 5-6.

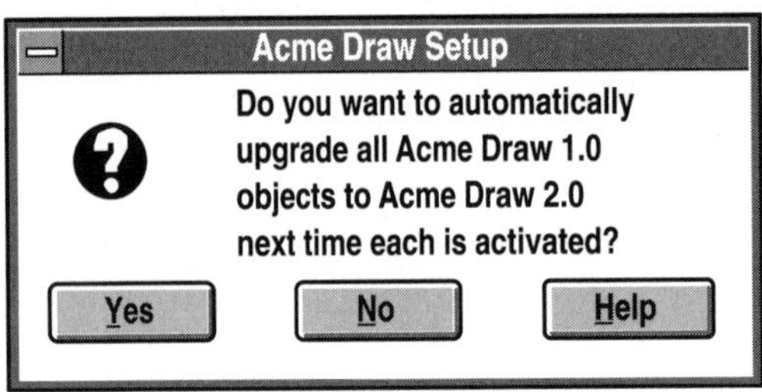
Acme Draw Setup
Do you want to automatically upgrade all Acme Draw 1.0 objects to Acme Draw 2.0 next time each is activated?
Yes
No
Help

Figure 5-6. Automatic conversion prompt during installation.

If the user wants to tag the object class for automatic conversion, the setup program should call the **OleSetAutoConvert** function, passing the object's old and new CLSIDs to **OleSetAutoConvert**. This enables **OleSetAutoConvert** to register the new CLSID in the registration database under the CLSID\{*clsid*}\AutoConvertTo = {*CLSID*} subkey entry. This means the object application of the destination class has to be able to manually convert an object to a different class on a case by case basis, as objects of the tagged class are loaded into memory.

When a container application loads an object that has been tagged for conversion, the container should check whether an automatic conversion is necessary by calling **OleDoAutoConvert**. (If the container calls **OleLoad** to load the object, the call to **OleDoAutoConvert** is done internally by **OleLoad**, and need not be called explicitly.)

Similarly, for automatically converting objects, an object application's setup program can offer to tag an object class for activation as a different class, as shown in Figure 5-7. If the user decides to tag an object class for activation under a different CLSID, the setup program should call **CoTreatAsClass**(*clsidOld*, *clsidNew*) to register the CLSID for the object under the "CLSID\{*clsidOld*}\TreatAs = {*CLSID*}" subkey entry in the registration database.

The AutoTreatAs key is used in conjunction with the TreatAs key. If *clsidOld* has an AutoTreatAs key, then instead of treating *clsidOld* as itself, it is treated as the class indicated by AutoTreatAs.

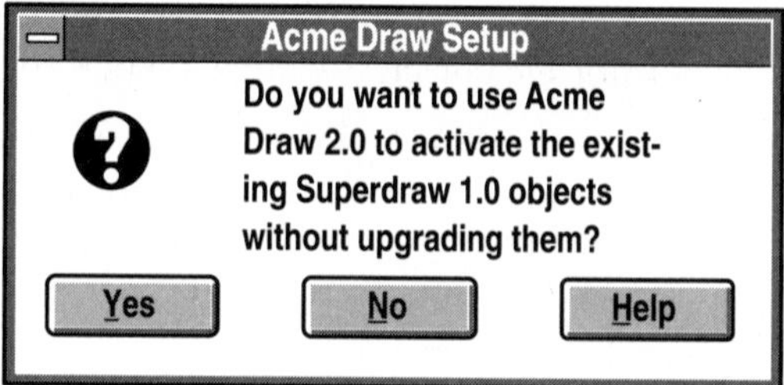

Figure 5-7. Tagging an object for activation as a different class at installation time.

For more information on user interface considerations for installing OLE applications, see the chapter "User Interface Guidelines." For information on the registration database and its subkey entries, see the chapter "Registering Object Applications."

Converting Objects

To convert objects from one type to another, an OLE object application must register (in the registration database) the data formats it can read from objects created by other applications. To activate an object as one of its supported types, the object application registers the data formats it can both read and write (when emulating an object, the object application needs to write the data changes to the object's **IStorage** in the container).

Container Responsibilities

▶ **To convert an object to a different object class as a result of the user selecting the Convert To: option button in the Convert dialog box, OLE containers do the following tasks:**

1. Get the existing user type name and main data format from the object's **IStorage** by calling **ReadFmtUserTypeStg**. (The user type name is used to fill in the "Current Type:" and other strings in the Convert dialog box.)
2. Generate the appropriate list of object destination class types by examining the registration database, looking for all object classes registered as being able to read the object's current main data format. These formats are registered under the "CLSID\{*clsid*}\Conversion\ReadWritable" subkeys. For information on the registration database and the "Conversion/ReadWritable" subkeys in particular, see the chapter "Registering Object Applications."
3. If the object is currently loaded into memory, unload the object. Any objects that are not unloaded will not be used since the conversion takes place at load time, not when the object is put in its running state.
4. Write the object's new CLSID to its **IStorage** by calling **WriteClassStg**.

5. Write the object's new user type name and the existing main clipboard data format to the open **IStorage** object by calling **WriteFmtUserTypeStg**.
6. Set the conversion bit in the object's **IStorage** by calling **SetConvertStg** (*TRUE*). Now when the object is loaded into memory, it is loaded as an object with a new class type and is associated with a new object application.
7. Load the object into memory and call **IOleObject::Update** to achieve the actual conversion of the bits. For more information on loading objects, see "Loading Objects from Storage" in the chapter "Programming Considerations."

Shipped with the OLE 2 SDK is the **ConvertDlg** helper function, which can be used to do steps one and two.

Object Application Responsibilities

Each object application must be able to determine whether to convert an object to a class that it supports. If you do not want your object application to support this concept, do not implement any of the following tasks.

▶ **When the container initializes an object from its open IStorage, the object application must do the following tasks to convert the object:**

1. Read the conversion bit from the object's **IStorage** by calling **GetConvertStg**.
2. If the conversion bit is set in the object's open **IStorage**, then:
   - Read the data from the object's **IStorage** according to its tagged format.
   - When the object is subsequently asked to save itself, write its native format by calling **IPersistStorage::Save** then save the object's new data format and user type by calling **WriteFmtUserTypeStg**.
3. After saving the object, clear the conversion bit by calling **SetConvertStg**(*FALSE*).

Shipped with the OLE SDK is the **ConvertDlg** helper function, which can be used to do steps one and two.

Activating Objects of a Different Class

The Convert dialog box also supports activating an object of one type as a different type. To activate an object as an object of a different class, both container and server applications need to do certain tasks, as described in the following sections.

Container Responsibilities

▶ **To support activating an object as a different class type, containers perform the following tasks:**

1. Get the object's existing user type name and its main data format tag by calling **ReadFmtUserTypeStg**. (The object's type name is used to fill in the blanks in the "Activate as %s:" and other strings in the Convert dialog box.)
2. Generate the list of eligible classes that the object can be activated as by searching the registration database looking for those classes that can both read and write the object's main data format. These entries are listed under the "Conversion\ReadWritable" subkeys for a particular CLSID. For more information on the registration database and the "Conversion/ReadWritable" subkeys in particular, see the chapter "Registering Object Applications."
3. If the object is currently loaded into memory, unload it. Any objects that are not unloaded will not be used since the conversion takes place at load time, not when the object is put in its running state.
4. Ensure that a registration database entry for the existing class of the object is present. If an entry does not currently exist, create one. If the registration database entry for the existing class of the object lacks a main user type entry, then set the main user type string in the database with the object's existing user type obtained from its **IStorage** by calling **ReadFmtUserTypeStg**.
5. Notify OLE that this object is to be treated as a new class of object by calling **CoTreatAsClass**. Note that calling this function causes *all* objects of the old class (other than those that were left in the loaded state) to subsequently be activated as object of the new class.
6. Before loading the object into memory, call **OleDoAutoConvert** to handle any needed object conversion. If the container calls **OleLoad** to load the object, the call to **OleDoAutoConvert** is done internally by **OleLoad**, and need not be called explicitly.
7. Load the object in the typical manner at a later time as needed. For more information on loading objects, see "Loading Objects from Storage" in the chapter "Programming Considerations."

Object Application Responsibilities

Just as it does when converting an object from one class to another, the object application must be able to determine whether to activate an object of a different class as one that it supports. Unless you want your object application to specifically support this, there is no code to implement in the object application.

When activating an object from a different object class as one of its supported class types, an object application only reads the source object's main data format. The conversion bit in the object's **IStorage** must be off.

Although the object is being activated as a different type, its behavior (in response to **IOleObject::EnumVerbs** being called on it) is unchanged from its usual behavior. Any changes made to the object are saved in the object's open **IStorage** object in the container.

▶ **Using the main data format that OLE saved with the object, an object application does the following tasks to activate a different object class as one of its own:**

1. Get the object's current CLSID and user type from its **IStorage** by calling **IStorage::Stat** and **ReadFmtUserTypeStg**, respectively. The current CLSID can be the current class of the object but it might not be. Therefore, treating both cases the same is correct because it allows the former case (class is the same) to be simply a degenerate case of the latter (class not the same).
2. When asked for its CLSID and user type (in calls to **IPersist::GetClassID**,**IOleObject::GetUserClassID**, and **IOleObject::GetUserType**, the object must emulate the object found in the **IStorage**. Note that this will make the old class appear to have the verbs of the new class; however, the object's behavior in response to **IOleObject::EnumVerbs** will remain unchanged from its usual behavior.The class returned in **IStdMarshalInfo::GetClassForHandler** is always the CLSID of the object that is actually running. This is different than **IPersist::GetClassID** only in the Treat As case.
3. Read the data from the object's **IStorage**, which is in the format returned by **ReadFmtUserTypeStg**.

   When the object is subsequently asked to save itself, write the data in the format from which it was originally read.

CoGetTreatAsClass

HRESULT CoGetTreatAsClass(*clsidOld*, *pclsidNew*)
REFCLSID *clsidOld*
LPCLSID *pclsidNew*

CoGetTreatAsClass returns the existing emulation information for a given object class.

Parameter

clsidOld
Specifies the object class for which the emulation information is to be retrieved.

pclsidNew
Points to where to return the CLSID, if any, that emulates the *clsidOld* parameter. CLSID_NULL is returned if there is no such CLSID. The *pclsidNew* parameter cannot be NULL.

Return Values

Value	Meaning
S_OK	Indicates that a value was successfully returned through *pclsidNew*. This means **pclsidNew* is set to a new CLSID.
S_FALSE	Indicates that **pclsidNew* is set to *clsidOld*.
REGDB_E_READREGDB	Error reading the registration database.

See **CLSIDFromString** for other possible errors.

See Also

CoTreatAsClass

CoTreatAsClass

HRESULT CoTreateAsClass(*clsidOld*, *clsidNew*)
REFCLSID *clsidOld*
REFCLSID *clsidNew*

CoTreatAsClass establishes or removes an emulation from one object class to another.

Parameter

clsidOld
Specifies the CLSID of the object class that is to be emulated.

clsidNew
Specifies the CLSID of the object class that should emulate *clsidOld*. This replaces any existing emulation for *clsidOld*. Can be CLSID_NULL, in which case any existing emulation for *clsidOld* is removed.

Return Values

Value	Meaning
S_OK	Emulation connection successfully established or removed.
REGDB_E_CLASSNOTREG	*clsidOld* is not properly registered in the registration database.
REGDB_E_READREGDB	Error reading from registration database.
REGDB_E_WRITEREGDB	Error writing to registration database.

Comments

When *clsidNew* is emulating *clsidOld*, attempts by both **CoGetClassObject** and by object handlers (in particular, the OLE default handler) to consult the registration database for *clsidOld* should be transparently forwarded to the entry for *clsidNew*. For example, launching the object application for *clsidOld* launches the object application for *clsidNew*. The default handler's **IOleObject::EnumVerbs** implementation will enumerate the verbs from *clsidNew*, and so forth.

CoTreatAsClass does no validation on whether an appropriate registration database entry for *clsidNew* currently exists.

During installation, setup programs should use **CoTreatAsClass**(*clsidOld*, NULL) to remove any existing emulation for the classes they install.

See Also

CoGetTreatAsClass

OleDoAutoConvert

HRESULT OleDoAutoConvert(*pStg*, *pclsidNew*)
LPSTORAGE *pStg*
LPCLSID *pclsidNew*

OleDoAutoConvert automatically converts an object to a new class. The object must have been previously tagged for automatic conversion, typically at setup time for the object application.

Parameter

pStg
Points to the persistent representation of the object to be converted.

pclsidNew
Points to the CLSID to which the object was converted; this might be the same as the original class if no auto-conversion was done.

Return Values

Value	Meaning
S_OK	No conversion is needed or a conversion was successfully completed.
REGDB_E_KEYMISSING	Cannot read a key from the registration database.
OleGetAutoConvert errors.	
E_OUTOFMEMORY	Out of memory.
E_INVALIDARG	One or more arguments are invalid.
E_UNEXPECTED	An unexpected error occurred.

See **IStorage::OpenStorage** and **IStorage::OpenStream** for possible errors when accessing storage and stream objects.

IStream errors. Cannot determine existing CLSID or cannot update **IStorage** with new information.

Comments

The object to be converted is found in *pStg*.

OleDoAutoConvert first determines whether any conversion is required by calling **OleGetAutoConvert**. If not, it returns NOERROR. The object's **IStorage** is modified to convert the object.

A container application that supports object conversion should call **OleDoAutoConvert** each time it loads an object. Because it is called internally by **OleLoad**, **OleDoAutoConvert** need not be called explicitly by containers using **OleLoad**. The object must be in the unloaded state when **OleDoAutoConvert** is called.

See Also

OleSetAutoConvert

OleGetAutoConvert

HRESULT OleGetAutoConvert(*clsidOld*, *pclsidNew*)
REFCLSID *clsidOld*
LPCLSID *pclsidNew*

OleGetAutoConvert returns the existing auto-conversion information for a given object class.

Parameter

clsidOld
Specifies the CLSID of the object class for which the auto-conversion information is to be retrieved.

pclsidNew
Points to where to return the class, if any, which auto-converts from *clsidOld*. If there is no such class, CLSID_NULL is returned. *pclsidNew* cannot be NULL.

Return Values

Value	Meaning
S_OK	Indicates that a value was successfully returned through *pclsidNew*.
REGDB_E_CLASSNOTREG	CLSID is not properly registered in the registration database.
REGDB_E_READREGDB	Error reading the registration database.
REGDB_E_KEYMISSING	Auto convert is not active or indicates that there was no registration entry for *clsidOld*.
E_OUTOFMEMORY	Out of memory.
E_INVALIDARG	One or more arguments are invalid.
E_UNEXPECTED	An unexpected error occurred.

Comments

During installation of an object application, the setup program can optionally tag a class of object for automatic conversion to a different class of object. This is done by calling **OleSetAutoConvert**, passing it the CLSIDs of the source and destination object classes. **OleSetAutoConvert** then creates the required "CLSID\{*clsid*}\AutoConvertTo = {CLSID}" entry in the registration database.

On loading an object tagged for conversion, the container calls the **OleGetAutoConvert** function to retrieves the new CLSID from the registration database. To perform the conversion, the container calls **OleDoAutoConvert**.

See Also

OleSetAutoConvert, **OleDoAutoConvert**

OleSetAutoConvert

HRESULT OleSetAutoConvert(*clsidOld*, *clsidNew*)
REFCLSID *clsidOld*
REFCLSID *clsidNew*

OleSetAutoConvert tags an object for automatic conversion to a different class on being loaded.

Parameter

clsidOld
Specifies the CLSID of the object class to be converted.

clsidNew
Specifies the CLSID of the object class that should replace *clsidOld*. This replaces any existing conversion for *clsidOld*. May be CLSID_NULL. If so, any existing conversion for *clsidOld* is removed.

Return Values

Value	Meaning
S_OK	The object was tagged successfully.
REGDB_E_CLASSNOTREG	The CLSID is not properly registered in the registration database.
REGDB_E_READREGDB	Error reading from the registration database.
REGDB_E_WRITEREGDB	Error writing to the registration database.
REGDB_E_KEYMISSING	Cannot read a key from the registration database.
E_OUTOFMEMORY	Out of memory.
E_INVALIDARG	One or more arguments are invalid.
E_UNEXPECTED	An unexpected error occurred.

Comments

OleSetAutoConvert does no validation of whether an appropriate registration database entry for *clsidNew* currently exists. On being called, **OleSetAutoConvert** records the new CLSID for the object under the "CLSID\{*clsidOld*}\AutoConvertTo = CLSID" subkeys in the registration database. For more information on tagging an object class for conversion at the time of setup, see the chapter, "User Interface Guidelines," as well as the section "Converting Objects," earlier in this chapter.

When installing a new CLSID, setup programs may call **OleSetAutoConvert** for various *clsidOld* values for older versions of their applications. They should also call **OleSetAutoConvert**(*clsidNew*, NULL) to remove any existing conversion for the new class.

See Also

OleDoAutoConvert

SetConvertStg

HRESULT SetConvertStg(*pStg*, *fConvert*)
LPSTORAGE *pStg*
BOOL *fConvert*

SetConvertStg sets the conversion bit in an object's **IStorage** so that the setting is retrievable with **GetConvertStg**.

Parameter

pStg
Specifies the **IStorage** in which to set the conversion bit.

fConvert
TRUE tags an object for conversion to another class of object; FALSE clears the conversion bit.

Return Values

Value	Meaning
S_OK	The object's IStorage conversion bit was set successfully.
STG_E_ACCESSDENIED	Access to the **IStorage** not available.
E_OUTOFMEMORY	Out of memory.
E_INVALIDARG	One or more arguments are invalid.
E_UNEXPECTED	An unexpected error occurred.

See IStorage::CreateStream, IStorage::OpenStream, IStream::Read, and IStream::Write for possible storage and stream access errors.

Comments

As part of converting an object from one class to another, container applications call **SetConvertBit** to set the conversion bit in the object's **IStorage**. The bit is set to TRUE, indicating that the object has been tagged for conversion to a new class the next time it is loaded.

The value of the conversion bit is subsequently retrieved by calling **GetConvertStg**. To reset an object's conversion bit, call **SetConvertStg**(*FALSE*).

See Also

GetConvertStg

GetConvertStg

HRESULT GetConvertStorage(*pStg*)
LPSTORAGE *pStg*

GetConvertStorage returns the current value of the conversion bit in an object's **IStorage**, which was previously set with **SetConvertStg**.

Parameter

pStg
Points to the **IStorage** from which to retrieve the conversion bit.

Return Values

Value	Meaning
S_OK	Indicates that the conversion bit is set (TRUE).
S_FALSE	Indicates the conversion bit has been turned off (FALSE) or never been set in this object's storage.
STG_E_ACCESSDENIED	Cannot access the **IStorage.**

See also **IStorage::OpenStream**, **IStorage::OpenStorage**, and **IStream::Read** for storage and stream access errors.

Comments

As part of converting an object from one class to another, object applications call **GetConvertStg** to retrieve the value of the conversion bit in an object's **IStorage**; this bit is usually set by the container application calling **SetConvertStg**(*TRUE*) as part of the user selecting the "Convert To:" option button in the Convert dialog box. After retrieving the bit value, the application should call **SetConvertStg**(*FALSE*) to clear the bit setting.

See Also

SetConvertStg

Error Handling Functions and Macros

The following PropagateResult function and Status Code Macros can be used to handle error and status information returned from OLE interface methods and API functions (see also SCODE.H):

```
PropagateResult(HRESULT hrPrev, SCODE scNew);

#define SCODE_CODE(scode)             ((scode) & 0xFFFF)
#define SCODE_FACILITY(scode)         (((scode)>> 16) & 0x000f)
#define SCODE_SEVERITY(scode)         (((scode) >> 31) & 0x1)
#define SEVERITY_SUCCESS              0
#define SEVERITY_ERROR                1
#define SUCCEEDED(scode)              ((LONG)(scode) >= 0)
#define FAILED(scode)                 ((LONG)(scode)<0)
#define MAKE_SCODE(sev,fac,code)      ((SCODE) (((ULONG)(sev)<<31) |
                                      ((ULONG)(fac)<<16) | ((ULONG)(code))))
#define GetScode(hr)                  ((SCODE)(hr) & 0x800FFFFF)
#define ResultFromScode(sc)           ((HRESULT)((SCODE)(sc) & 0x800FFFFF))
```

Note Throughout the reference portion of this book, specific error codes are described for the individual methods and functions. However, there are three error codes that are common to all methods, even though they may not be specifically noted in all method descriptions.

These common error codes include: E_INVALIDARG, one or more arguments are invalid (only for methods that accept parameters); E_UNEXPECTED, an unexpected error occurred; and E_OUTOFMEMORY, an out of memory condition occurred.

OLE Error Information

OLE interface methods and API functions use a certain stylistic convention in order to pass back to the caller useful return values and/or status or error information. The return value is an opaque "result handle" of type **HRESULT**, and is otherwise passed as the return value in the absence of the need for status information. The return value is passed through a pointer as the last argument.

HRESULT values are defined to be zero for success, and non-zero if error or informational status is being returned. If the result value is non-zero, the application calls the **GetScode** macro to map the **HRESULT** into a known code. **GetScode** is defined to return S_OK for a zero **HRESULT**.

On the implementor's side, an interface method that wants to indicate a result other than simple success must call **ResultFromScode** to generate the corresponding **HRESULT**, and return that to its caller. For convenience, **ResultFromScode** is defined to return zero for a status code of S_OK. The constant NOERROR is defined as an **HRESULT** that corresponds to S_OK.

Sometimes functions will either return a Boolean result or, if the result is not currently available,return an error status. For functions of this type, two special status codes, S_OK and S_FALSE, are used to indicate the return value. This eliminates the need for a separate **BOOL*** parameter for these functions.

HRESULTs do not need to be explicitly freed.

The status codes for the OLE interfaces and APIs are defined in FACILITY_ITF (see the header file SCODE.H for details). By design, none of the OLE-defined status codes have the same value, even if they are returned by different interfaces (although it would have been legal). The following basic interoperability rules and limitations apply to which errors can be returned by which methods or functions:

- Any OLE-defined status code can be returned by any OLE-defined interface method or API function.
- Any error in FACILITY_RPC or FACILITY_DISPATCH, even those not presently defined, can be returned.

The reference portion of this manual lists and describes the most common error codes that are appropriate for each interface method and API function. These are considered to be the legal error codes that can be returned.

Error codes are defined within the context of an inteface implementation. Once defined, success codes cannot be changed or new success codes added. However, new failure codes can be written since they generally only provide hints at what might have gone wrong. Microsoft reserves the right to define new failure codes (but not success codes) for the interfaces described in this book in FACILITY_ITF or new facilities.

Handling Error Information

Keep in mind that it is only legal to return a status code from the implementation of an interface method sanctioned as being legally returnable. Failure to observe this rule invites the possibility of conflict between returned error code values and those sanctioned by the application. In particular, pay attention to this potential problem when propagating error codes from internally called functions.

Applications that call interfaces should guard themselves from imprecise interface implementations by treating any unknown returned error code (in contrast with success code) as synonymous with E_UNEXPECTED. This practice of handling unknown error codes is required by clients of the OLE-defined interfaces and APIs. Because typical programming practice is to handle a few special error codes as special, but to treat the rest generically, this requirement of handling unexpected or unknown error codes is easily met.

The following code sample shows the recommended way of handling unknown errors:

```
HRESULT hrErr;
hrErr = xxMethod();

switch (GetScode(hrErr))  {
    case NOERROR:
        //success
        break;

    case x1:
        .
        .
        break;

    case x2:
        .
        .
        break;

    case E_UNEXPECTED:
    default:
        //general failure
        break;
}
```

The following error check is often used with those routines that don't return anything special (other than S_OK or some unexpected error):

```
if (xxMethod() == NOERROR)
    //success
else
    //general failure;
```

Structure of OLE Error Codes

As shown in Figure 5-8, OLE interface methods and API functions return a 32-bit result handle, which is comprised of a severity code, context information, a facility code, and a status code.

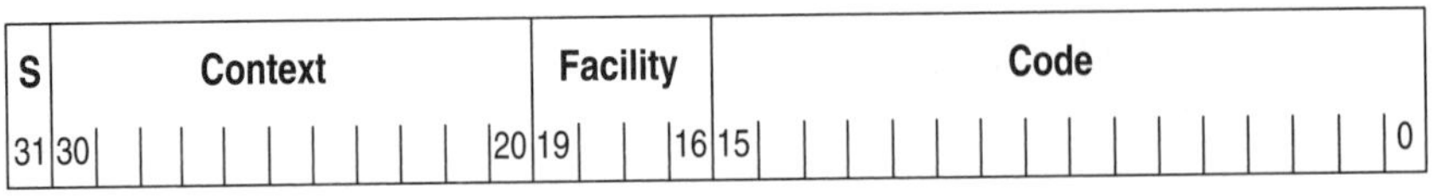

S	Context	Facility	Code
31	30 – 20	19 – 16	15 – 0

S - severity code; 0= success and 1= error
Context - reserved for future use, may or may not be 0
Facility - facility code
Code - facility's status code

Figure 5-8. Order and size of error fields.

Severity Field

Bit 31 is used to indicate success or failure of the given interface or API call. The following values indicate success or failure:

Severity Field Value	Meaning
00	The function completed successfully.
01	The function incurred an error and failed.

Context Field

Bits 20–30 are reserved for future use; applications that generate **SCODEs** must set this field to zero. In general, applications should not examine this field because it might be set to nonzero values in the implementation of **PropagateResult** in future system releases. None of the OLE-defined status codes set these bits.

Facility Field

Bits 16–19 are used to indicate which group of status codes this error belongs to. New facilities are allocated by Microsoft, because they must be unique. However, in nearly all cases FACILITY_ITF will be adequate, as described below:

Facility Field	Description
FACILITY_NULL	This facility is used for common status codes that are applicable to a broad range of functions. S_OK belongs to this facility, for example. This facility code has a value of zero.
FACILITY_RPC	Used for errors that result from an underlying remote procedure call (RPC) implementation. In general, RPC errors are not documented in this manual. This facility has a value of one.
FACILITY_DISPATCH	Used for late binding **IDispatch** interface errors. This facility has a value of two.
FACILITY_STORAGE	Used for persistent-storage-related errors. Status codes whose code (lower 16 bits) value is in the range of DOS error codes (less than 256) have the same meaning as the corresponding DOS error. This facility has a value of three.
FACILITY_ITF	This facility is used for most status codes returned from an interface method. Use of this facility indicates that the meaning of the error code is defined solely by the definition of the particular interface in question. An **SCODE** with exactly the same 32-bit value returned from another interface might have a different meaning. This facility has a value of four.

Code Field

Bits 0–15 are used to describe the error that occurred. The meaning of the code value is related to the facility.

By convention, **SCODEs** generally have names in the following form:

```
<Facility>_<Severity>_<Reason>
```

where *<Facility>* is either the facility name or some other distinguishing identifier, *<Severity>* is a single letter, S or E, that indicates the severity of the error, and *<Reason>* is an identifier that describes the meaning of the code. For example, the status code STG_E_FILENOTFOUND indicates a storage-related error has occurred; specifically, a requested file does not exist. Status codes from FACILITY_NULL omit the *<Facility>*_ prefix.

Codes in FACILITY_ITF

SCODEs with facilities such as FACILITY_NULL and FACILITY_RPC have universal meaning because they are defined at a single source, Microsoft. However, **SCODEs** in FACILITY_ITF are determined by the interface method (or API function) from which they are returned. That is, the same 32-bit value in FACILITY_ITF returned from two different interface methods might have different meanings.

The reason **SCODEs** in FACILITY_ITF can have different meanings in different interfaces is that **SCODEs** are kept to an efficient data type size of 32 bits. Unfortunately 32 bits is not large enough for the development of an allocation system for error codes that avoid conflict between codes allocated by different non-communicating programmers at different times in different places (unlike the handling of interface IDs and CLSIDs). As a result, the 32-bit **SCODE** is structured in a way that allows Microsoft to define some universally defined error codes, while allowing other programmers to define new error codes without fear of conflict. The status code convention is as follows:

1. Status codes in facilities *other than* FACILITY_ITF can only be defined by Microsoft.
2. Status codes in facility FACILITY_ITF are defined solely by the developer of the interface or API that returns the status code. To avoid conflicting error codes, whoever defines the interface is responsible for coordinating and publishing the FACILITY_ITF status codes associated with that interface.

All the OLE-defined FACILITY_ITF codes have a code value in the range of 0x0000–0x01FF. While it is legal to use any codes in FACILITY_ITF, it is recommended that only code values in the range of 0x0200–0xFFFF be used. This recommendation is made as a means of reducing confusion with any OLE-defined errors.

It is also recommended that developers define new functions and interfaces to return error codes as defined by OLE and in facilities other than FACILITY_ITF. In particular, interfaces that have any chance of being remoted using RPC in the future should define the FACILITY_RPC codes as legal. E_UNEXPECTED is a specific error code that most developers will want to make universally legal.

PropagateResult

HRESULT PropagateResult(*hrPrev*, *scNew***)**
HRESULT *hrPrev*
SCODE *scNew*

PropagateResult generates an **HRESULT** to return to a function's caller in cases where the error being returned was caused by an internally called function, which was also returning an **HRESULT** error .

Parameters

hrPrev
Specifies the **HRESULT** returned from the internally called routine.

scNew
Specifies the new **SCODE** to return to *our* caller, wrapped in an **HRESULT**.

Return Values

Value	Meaning
HRESULT	The (new) **HRESULT** that should be returned to the caller.

See Also

GetScode, ResultFromScode

GetScode

SCODE GetScode(*hRes***)**
HRESULT *hRes*

GetScode returns the status code contained in an **HRESULT**.

Parameters

hRes
Specifies the **HRESULT** returned from the internally called routine.

Return Values

Value	Meaning
SCODE	The status code extracted from the specified **HRESULT**.

Comments

GetScode should be used to return the **HRESULT** if an error is being returned as a result of some internal state error. By contrast, it should not be used if the error is being returned as a result of some internally called routine, itself returning an **HRESULT** error. Instead, the calling routine should use **PropagateResult** to return its error.

ResultFromScode

ResultFromScode(*sc*)
SCODE *sc*

ResultFromScode creates a new **HRESULT** that contains the given **SCODE.**

Parameters

sc
Specifies the status code from which the **HRESULT** is to be returned.

Return Values

Value	Meaning
HRESULT	The **HRESULT** created from the specified status code.

Status Code Macros

The following macros can be used to manipulate status code values:

SCODE_CODE

SCODE_CODE(*sc*)
SCODE *sc*

SCODE_CODE returns the error code part from a specified status code.

SCODE_FACILITY

SCODE_FACILITY(*sc*)
SCODE *sc*

SCODE_FACILITY extracts the facility from a specified status code.

SCODE_SEVERITY

SCODE_SEVERITY(*sc*)
SCODE *sc*

SCODE_SEVERITY extracts the severity field from the specified status code.

SUCCEEDED

SUCCEEDED(*sc*)
SCODE *sc*

SUCCEEDED returns TRUE if the severity of the status code is either success or information; otherwise, FALSE is returned. SUCCEEDED works on both **SCODE** and **HRESULT** values.

FAILED

FAILED(*sc*)
SCODE *sc*

FAILED returns TRUE if the severity of the status code is either a warning or error; otherwise, FALSE is returned. FAILED works on both **SCODE** and **HRESULT** values.

MAKE_SCODE

MAKE_SCODE(*sev,fac,sc*)
SEVERITY *sev*
FACILITY *fac*
SCODE *sc*

MAKE_SCODE makes a new status code given a severity, a facility, and a status code.

Debugging Functions

The following functions can be used to display debug information about internal objects (such as monikers, proxies, and stub managers) found in most functional areas of the OLE2 libraries. See also OLE2DBG.H.

DbgDumpObject(IUnknown FAR * pUnk, DWORD dwReserved);
DbgDumpExternalObject(IUnknown FAR * pUnk, DWORD dwReserved);
DbgIsObjectValid(IUnknown FAR * pUnk);
DbgDumpClassName(IUnknown FAR * pUnk);

The functions can be called either in source or in CodeView. CodeView requires a function symbol to be "in scope" before one of the debug functions can be called from the command prompt. For example, if CodeView is stopped within the OLE library, any of the debug APIs can be called, as the code example below for **DbgDumpObject** shows:

```
> ? DbgDumpObject(pFoo, 0)
```

If CodeView is stopped within an application, that application must have a wrapper function that calls the debug API, as shown in the following example:

```
void AppDumpObject( LPUNKNOWN pUnk )
{
    DbgDumpObject(pUnk, 0);
}
```

As shown in the following example, a hexadecimal address may also be used as an argument in Codeview:

```
> ? DbgDumpObject((IUnknown FAR *) 0x43ac120f, 0)
```

Because many objects contain other objects, it is useful to follow a chain or to access an object from out of scope. By default, debug output is sent to the debug terminal (such as DBWIN or CodeView) and to the file, DEBUG.LOG, in the current directory. The following example shows a typical dump obtained by calling **DbgDumpObject** on the an object pointer returned from **OleCreate**:

```
Default Handler @ 5CE74792
    Refcount is 1
    CLSID of app is {00000400-0000-0000-C000-000000000046}

    CLSID of the bits in storage is NULL CLSID

    Unknown delegate object @ 5CE7486A
    Object is running
    Object is an Inproc handler
    Proxy Manager is @ 5CE74866
    Container is locked
    Clientsite object @ 5CE746F8
```

DbgDumpObject

void DbgDumpObject(*pUnk, dwReserved***);**
LPUNKNOWN *pUnk*
DWORD *dwReserved*

DbgDumpObject returns information (such as the type, reference count) about an object.

Parameters

pUnk
Points to the object's **IUnknown** interface implementation.

dwReserved
Reserved for future use; must be set to zero by the caller. However, to ensure compatibility with future use, the callee *must not* check for zero.

See Also

DbgDumpClassName

DbgDumpExternalObject

void DbgDumpExternalObject(*pUnk*, *dwReserved*);
LPUNKNOWN *pUnk*
DWORD *dwReserved*

DbgDumpExternalObject returns information about an object's stub manager.

Parameters

pUnk
Points to the object's **IUnknown** interface implementation.

dwReserved
Reserved for future use; must be set to zero by the caller. However, to ensure compatibility with future use, the callee *must not* check for zero.

DbgIsObjectValid

BOOL DbgIsObjectValid(*pUnk*);
LPUNKNOWN *pUnk*

DbgIsObjectValid does a validation check on the object.

Parameters

pUnk
Points to the object's **IUnknown** interface implementation.

Return Values

Value	Meaning
TRUE	As can best be determined, the object will perform as expected.
FALSE	The object might fail in some operations

Comments

Only objects that support debug dumping will perform the validation, which attempts to verify the integrity of the object. The test includes checking to ensure that the object has a valid reference count and, if there are pointers to other objects, that these objects are valid. There is no guarantee that this object will perform as expected based on calling this function; the information is a best guess at this point in time.

This function is also called by **DbgDumpObject**. If this function fails in **DbgDumpObject**, a message to that effect is displayed on the debug monitor.

See Also

DbgDumpObject

DbgDumpClassName

void DbgDumpClassName(*pUnk***);**
LPUNKNOWN *pUnk*

DbgDumpClassName prints the object's CLSID.

Parameters

pUnk
Points to the object's **IUnknown** interface implementation.

Comments

The CLSID is also displayed as part of the output from **DbgDumpObject**. Once you have the CLSID, you can use RegEdit to search for the string in the registration database to determine which application owns the object.

See Also

DbgDumpObject

String and CLSID Conversion Functions

This section describes the functions that can be used to convert strings, GUIDs, CLSIDs, and ProgIDs from one form to another, using entries listed in the registration database. The functions are defined as follows (see also COMPOBJ.H):

```
CoCreateGUID(GUID FAR* pguid);
IsEqualGUID(REFGUID rguid1, REFGUID rguid2);
IsEqualIID(REFGUID rguid1, REFGUID rguid2);
IsEqualCLSID(REFCLSID clsid1, REFCLSID clsid2);
CLSIDFromProgID(LPCSTR lpszProgID, LPCLSID pclsid);
ProgIDFromCLSID(REFCLSID clsid, LPSTR FAR* lplpszProgID);
CLSIDFromString(LPSTR lpsz, LPCLSID pclsid);
StringFromCLSID(REFCLSID rclsid, LPSTR FAR* lplpsz);
IIDFromString(LPSTR lpsz, LPIID lpiid);
StringFromIID(REFIID rclsid, LPSTR FAR* lplpsz);
StringFromGUID2(REFGUID rguid, LPSTR lpsz, int cbMax);
```

CoCreateGuid

CoCreateGuid(*pguid*)
GUID FAR* *pguid*

CoCreateGuid is used to create a GUID, which is a 128-byte integer used to represent CLSIDs and interface IDs.

Parameters

pguid
Points to where to return the GUID.

Return Values

Value	Meaning/Occurrence
S_OK	The GUID was successfully created.
E_FAIL	The GUID was not created.
REGDB_E_WRITEREGDB	Unable to write necessary state information to registration database.
E_OUTOFMEMORY	Out of memory.
E_INVALIDARG	*pguid* is invalid.
E_UNEXPECTED	An unexpected error occurred.

The implementation of **CoCreateGuid** does not require a network card. If no card is present, a machine identifier is created from varible machine state and stored persistently.

IsEqualGUID

BOOL IsEqualGUID(*rguid1*, *rguid2*)
REFGUID *rguid1*
REFGUID *rguid2*

IsEqualGUID compares two GUIDs to see whether they are equal.

Parameters

rguid1
Specifies the GUID to compare with *rguid2*.

rguid2
Specifies the GUID that is to be compared with *rguid1*.

Return Values

Value	Meaning/Occurrence
TRUE	The GUIDs are equal.
FALSE	The GUIDs are not equal.

Comments **IsEqualGUID** is used by **IsEqualCLSID** and **IsEqualIID**.

See Also **IsEqualCLSID, IsEqualIID**

IsEqualIID

BOOL IsEqualIID(*riid1*, *riid2*)
REFGUID *riid1*
REFGUID *riid2*

IsEqualIID compares two interface IDs to see whether they are equal.

Parameters

rclsid1
Specifies the interface ID to compare with *riid2*.

rclsid2
Specifies the interface IID to be compared with *riid1*.

Return Values

Value	Meaning/Occurrence
TRUE	The interface IDs are equal.
FALSE	The interface IDs are not equal.

See Also **IsEqualGUID, IsEqualCLSID**

IsEqualCLSID

BOOL IsEqualCLSID(*rclsid1*, *rclsid2*)
REFCLSID *rclsid1*
REFCLSID *rclsid2*

IsEqualCLSID compares two CLSIDs to see whether they are equal.

Parameters

rclsid1
Specifies the CLSID to compare with *rclsid2*.

rclsid2
Specifies the CLSID to be compared with *rclsid1*.

Return Values

Value	Meaning/Occurrence
TRUE	The CLSIDs are equal.
FALSE	The CLSIDs are not equal.

See Also **IsEqualGUID, IsEqualIID**

CLSIDFromProgID

HRESULT CLSIDFromProgID(*lpszProgID*, *pclsid*)
LPCSTR *lpszProgID*
LPCLSID *pclsid*

CLSIDFromProgID creates a CLSID from a ProgID, a string that uniquely identifies a given object class.

Parameters

lpszProgID
Points to the ProgID whose CLSID is requested.

pclsid
Points to where to return the CLSID.

Return Values

Value	Meaning
S_OK	The CLSID was created successfully.
CO_E_CLASSSTRING	The registered CLSID for the ProgID is invalid.
REGDB_E_WRITEREGDB	Error writing to the registration database.
E_OUTOFMEMORY	Out of memory.
E_INVALIDARG	One or more arguments are invalid.
E_UNEXPECTED	An unexpected error occurred.

Comments

If the ProgID is the CLSID of an OLE 1 object class, **CLSIDFromProgID** automatically creates a CLSID for it. Because of the restrictions placed on OLE 1 CLSID values, **CLSIDFromProgID** and **CLSIDFromString** are the *only* two functions that can be used to generate a CLSID for an OLE 1 object.

See Also **ProgIDFromCLSID**

ProgIDFromCLSID

HRESULT ProgIDFromCLSID(*clsid, lplpszProgID*)
REFCLSID *clsid*
LPSTR FAR* *lplpszProgID*

ProgIDFromCLSID retrieves the ProgID for a given CLSID.

Parameters

clsid
Specifies the CLSID for which the ProgID is requested.

lplpszProgID
Points to where to return the ProgID.

Return Values

Value	Meaning
S_OK	The ProgID was returned successfully.
REGDB_E_CLASSNOTREG	Class not registered in the registration database.
REGDB_E_READREGDB	Error reading registration database.

Comments

Every OLE 2 object class listed in the Insert Object dialog box must have a *programmatic identifier* (ProgID), a string that uniquely identifies a given object class. In addition to determining the eligibility for the Insert Object dialog box, the ProgID can be used as an identifier in a macro programming language to identify a class. Finally, the ProgID is also the class name used for an OLE 2 class when placed in an OLE 1 container.

ProgIDFromCLSID uses the entries in the registration database (REG.DAT) to do the conversion. OLE 2 application authors are responsible for correctly configuring the registration database at application installation time. For more information on the registration database, see the chapter "Registering Object Applications."

The ProgID string must be different from the class name of any OLE 1 application, including the OLE 1 version of the same application, if there is one. In addition, a ProgID string must not contain more than 39 characters or start with a digit. Except for a single period, it cannot contain any punctuation.

The ProgID must *never* be shown to the user in the user interface. If you need a short human-readable string for an object, call **IOleObject::GetUserType**.

CLSIDFromProgID can be called to create a CLSID from a given ProgID. CLSIDs can be freed with the task allocator (see **CoGetMalloc**).

See Also

CLSIDFromProgID

CLSIDFromString

HRESULT CLSIDFromString(*lpsz, pclsid***)**
LPSTR *lpsz*
LPCLSID *pclsid*

CLSIDFromString converts a string generated by **StringFromCLSID** back into the original CLSID.

Parameters

lpsz
Points to the string representation of the CLSID.

pclsid
Points to where to return the CLSID.

Return Values

Value	Meaning
S_OK	CLSID returned successfully.
E_OUTOFMEMORY	Out of memory.
E_INVALIDARG	One or more arguments are invalid.
E_UNEXPECTED	An unexpected error occurred.

Comments

Because of the restrictions placed on OLE 1 CLSID values, **CLSIDFromProgID** and **CLSIDFromString** are the *only* two functions that can be used to generate a CLSID for an OLE 1 object.

See Also

CLSIDFromProgID, StringFromCLSID

StringFromCLSID

HRESULT StringFromCLSID(*rclsid, lplpsz***)**
REFCLSID *rclsid*
LPSTR FAR* *lplpsz*

StringFromCLSID converts the CLSID into a string of printable characters so that different CLSIDs always convert to different strings.

Parameters

rclsid
Specifies the class identifier of which we want a string representation.

lplpsz
Points to where to return the resulting string.

Return Values

Value	Meaning
S_OK	The character string was successfully converted and returned.
E_OUTOFMEMORY	Out of memory.

Comments

StringFromCLSID is used by OLE to look up CLSIDs as keys in the registration database.

The returned string is freed in the standard way, using the task allocator (see **CoGetMalloc**).

See Also

CLSIDFromString

IIDFromString

HRESULT IIDFromString(*lpsz*, *lpiid***)**
LPSTR *lpsz*
LPIID *lpiid*

IIDFromString converts a string generated by **StringFromIID** back into the original interface ID.

Parameters

lpsz
Points to the string representation of the IID.

lpiid
Points to where to return the IID.

Return Values

Value	Meaning
S_OK	The string was successfully converted.
E_OUTOFMEMORY	Out of memory.
E_INVALIDARG	One or more arguments are invalid.

Comments

The interface ID is converted in a way that guarantees different interface IDs will always convert to different strings. One way this might work, for example, is to print the interface ID in hexadecimal.

See Also

StringFromIID

StringFromIID

HRESULT StringFromIID(*rclsid, lplpsz***)**
REFIID *rclsid*
LPSTR FAR* *lplpsz*

StringFromIID converts an interface ID into a string of printable characters.

Parameters

rclsid
Specifies the interface ID to convert to a string representation.

lplpsz
Points to where to return the resulting string.

Return Values

Value	Meaning
S_OK	The character string was successfully returned.
E_OUTOFMEMORY	Out of memory.

The returned string is freed in the standard way, using the task allocator (see **CoGetMalloc**).

See Also

IIDFromString

StringFromGUID2

int StringFromGUID2(*rguid, lpsz, cbMax***)**
REFGUID *rguid*
LPSTR *lpsz*
int *cbMax*

StringFromGUID2 converts a globally unique interface ID into a string of printable characters.

Parameters

rguid
Specifies the interface ID to convert to a string representation.

lpsz
Points to where to return the resulting string.

cbMax
Specifies the maximum expected size of the returned string.

Return Values

Value	Meaning
0 (zero)	Buffer is too small for returned string.
Non-zero value	The number of characters in the returned string, including the null terminator.

Registration Database Functions

The default handler's implementation of the **GetUserType**, **GetMiscStatus**, and **EnumVerbs** methods of the **IOleObject** interface, and the **EnumFormatEtc** method of the **IDataObject** interface are driven off the registration database when the object is either not running or the running object gives the handler its permission to do so. Refer also to "Registering Object Applications."

The following functions provide direct access to the OLE code which searches the registration database. These functions are primarily used in custom handler or DLL object application. Clients of an object must always ask the object itself for its capabilities, since the object might, for example, be a DLL object application which does not use the registry entries at all.

The registration database functions are defined as follows:

```
OleRegGetUserType (REFCLSID clsid, DWORD dwFormOfType,
    LPSTR FAR* pszUserType);
OleRegGetMiscStatus (REFCLSID clsid, DWORD dwAspect,
    DWORD FAR* pdwStatus);
OleRegEnumFormatEtc (REFCLSID clsid, DWORD dwDirection,
    LPENUMFORMATETC FAR* ppenumFormatetc);
OleRegEnumVerbs (REFCLSID clsid, LPENUMOLEVERB FAR* ppenumOleVerb);
```

OleRegGetUserType

HRESULT OleRegGetUserType (*clsid, dwFormOfType, pszUserType*)
REFCLSID *clsid*
DWORD *dwFormOfType*
LPSTR * *pszUserType*

OleRegGetUserType returns the user type of the indicated class from the registration database.

Parameters

clsid
Specifies the class whose user type is requested.

dwFormOfType
Specifies a value that describes the form of the user-presentable string from the enumeration **USERCLASSTYPE**. For information on **USERCLASSTYPE**, see **IOleObject::GetUserType**.

pszUserType
Points to where to return the user type.

Return Values

Value	Meaning
S_OK	The user type was returned successfully.
E_OUTOFMEMORY	There is insufficient memory to complete the operation.
REGDB_E_CLASSNOTREG	There is no CLSID registed for the class object.
REGDB_E_READREGDB	There was an error reading the registration database.
OLE_E_REGDB_KEY	The *ProgID* = *MainUserTypeName* and *CLSID* = *MainUserTypeName* keys are missing from the registration database.

See Also

IOleObject::GetUserType

OleRegGetMiscStatus

HRESULT OleRegGetMiscStatus (*clsid, dwAspect, pdwStatus*)
REFCLSID *clsid*
DWORD *dwAspect*
DWORD * *pdwStatus*

OleRegGetMiscStatus returns the miscellaneous status information for the given class from the registration database.

Parameters

clsid
Specifies the class whose status information is requested.

dwAspect
Specifies the aspect of the class whose information is requested.

pdwStatus
Points to where to return the status.

Return Values

Value	Meaning
S_OK	The status information was returned successfully.
REGDB_E_CLASSNOTREG	No CLSID is registed for the class object.
REGDB_E_READREGDB	An error occured reading the registration database.
OLE_E_REGDB_KEY	The GetMiscStatus key is missing from the registration database.

See Also

IOleObject::GetMiscStatus

OleRegEnumFormatEtc

HRESULT OleRegEnumFormatEtc (*clsid, dwDirection, ppenumFormatetc*)
REFCLSID *clsid*
DWORD *dwDirection*
LPENUMFORMATETC * *ppenumFormatetc*

OleRegEnumFormatEtc returns an enumerator that enumerates the entries in a FORMATEC data structure containing the supported format information for the indicated class.

Parameters

clsid
Specifies the class whose verbs are requested.

dwDirection
Specifies the set of formats to be enumerated; valid values are taken from the enumeration **DATADIR**:

```
typedef enum tagDATADIR
{
    DATADIR_GET = 1,
    DATADIR_SET = 2,
} DATADIR;
```

DATADIR_GET enumerates those formats that can be passed to **IDataObject::GetData**; DATADIR_SET enumerates those formats that can be passed to **IDataObject::SetData**.

ppenumFormatetc
Points to where to return the enumerator.

Return Values

Value	Meaning
S_OK	The enumerator was returned successfully.
E_OUTOFMEMORY	An out of memory condition occurred.
REGDB_E_CLASSNOTREG	There is no CLSID registed for the class object.
REGDB_E_READREGDB	There was an error reading the registration database.
OLE_E_REGDB_KEY	The DataFormats/GetSet key is missing from the registration database.

See Also **IDataObject::EnumFormatEtc**

OleRegEnumVerbs

HRESULT OleRegEnumVerbs (*clsid, ppenumOleVerb*)
REFCLSID *clsid*
LPENUMOLEVERB * *ppenumOleVerb*

OleRegEnumVerbs returns an enumerator which enumerates the entries in an OLEVERB data structure containing the registered verbs of the indicated class. For information on the OLEVERB structure, refer to For information on the OLEVERB structure, refer to IOleObject::EnumVerbs in the chapter "Compound Document Interfaces and Functions." in the chapter "Compound Document Interfaces and Functions."

Parameters

clsid
Specifies the class whose verbs are requested.

ppenumOleVerb
Points to where to return the enumerator.

Return Values

Value	Meaning
S_OK	The enumerator was returned successfully.
E_OUTOFMEMORY	An out of memory condition occurred.
OLEOBJ_E_NOVERBS	No verbs are registered for the class.
REGDB_E_CLASSNOTREG	No CLSID is registered for the class object.
REGDB_E_READREGDB	An error occurred reading the registration database.
OLE_E_REGDB_KEY	The DataFormats/GetSet key is missing from the registration database.

See Also **IOleObject::EnumVerbs**

CHAPTER 6

Compound Document Interfaces and Functions

The compound document interfaces and supporting functions provide the functionality for the creation and management of compound documents. The use of these interfaces depends on an application's role as a container application, object application, or combination container/object application. Most of the compound document interfaces are implemented by at least one type of OLE application. Therefore, for these interface methods, example implementations are provided to further document what is expected. These examples are based on the Outline series, the sample code provided with the OLE SDK.

IAdviseSink Interface

The **IAdviseSink** interface, implemented by containers and OLE, is used to receive asynchronous notifications. There are three types of asynchronous notifications: compound document (also referred to as OLE notifications), data change, and view change. The compound document notifications are generated when an object closes, is renamed, is saved, or its link source changes.

IAdviseSink implementors register for one or more types of notification and each **IAdviseSink** method is a callback for a specific notification. When an event occurs that applies to a registered notification type, the object application calls the appropriate **IAdviseSink** method. For example, when an embedded object closes, **IAdviseSink::OnClose** is called to notify its container.

IAdviseSink contains the following methods (see also DVOBJ.H):

```
DECLARE_INTERFACE_(IAdviseSink, IUnknown)
{
  // *** IUnknown methods ***
 HRESULT QueryInterface (THIS_ REFIID riid, LPVOID FAR* ppvObj);
 ULONG AddRef (THIS) ;
 ULONG Release (THIS);
```

```
    // *** IAdviseSink methods ***
    void OnDataChange (THIS_ FORMATETC FAR* pFormatetc,
      STGMEDIUM FAR* pmedium);
    void OnViewChange (THIS_ DWORD dwAspect, LONG lindex);
    void OnRename (THIS_ LPMONIKER pmk);
    void OnSave (THIS);
    void OnClose (THIS);
};
```

IAdviseSink::OnDataChange

void IAdviseSink::OnDataChange(*pFormatetc*, *pmedium***)**
LPFORMATETC *pFormatetc*
LPSTGMEDIUM *pmedium*

IAdviseSink::OnDataChange is a notification that data in the calling object has changed.

Parameters

pFormatetc
Points to the data format information on which the data advise was originally set up.

pmedium
Points to the storage medium on which the data is passed.

Comments

Containers and other objects requiring notification when data in the object changes, such as the OLE cache and link objects, call **IDataObject::DAdvise** to set up an advisory connection. Parameters to **IDataObject::DAdvise** include a pointer to a **FORMATETC** structure, a pointer to the **IAdviseSink** interface, and a set of flags.

The **FORMATETC** structure describes the pertinent data in terms of its format, aspect, and storage medium. The set of flags specify one or more values that control the advisory connection. The flag ADVF_NODATA indicates that *pmedium->tymed* might be NULL instead of containing data. The flag ADVF_PRIMEFIRST instructs the object to call **IAdviseSink::OnDataChange** immediately, thereby enabling the advisory sink to receive data right away.

Not all containers register for data change notifications. Those that do not register have an empty implementation of **IAdviseSink::OnDataChange**. An example of a container that would register for data change notifications is one that does not use OLE's caching support. The implementation of **IAdviseSink::OnDataChange** can post an internal message or invalidate the rectangle for the changed data by calling **InvalidateRect** and then wait for a WM_PAINT message.

Making synchronous calls within asynchronous methods is not valid. For example, **IAdviseSink::OnDataChange** cannot contain a call to **IDataObject::GetData**.

When **IAdviseSink::OnDataChange** is called on the cache, the cache is updated; when the method is called on the link object, if the link type is automatic, an update occurs.

The data itself, valid only for the duration of the call, is passed using the storage medium pointed to by *pmedium*. Since the medium is owned by the caller, the sink should not free it. Also, if *pmedium* points to an **IStorage** or **IStream,** the sink must not increment the reference count.

See Also **IDataObject::DAdvise**

IAdviseSink::OnViewChange

void IAdviseSink::OnViewChange(*dwAspect, lindex***)**
DWORD *dwAspect*
LONG *lindex*

IAdviseSink::OnViewChange notifies that an object's view or presentation has changed. These actions typically include redrawing the object.

Parameters

dwAspect
Specifies the aspect, or view, of the object. Contains a value taken from the enumeration, **DVASPECT**:

```
typedef enum tagDVASPECT
{
    DVASPECT_CONTENT        = 1,
    DVASPECT_THUMBNAIL      = 2,
    DVASPECT_ICON           = 4,
    DVASPECT_DOCPRINT       = 8,
    } DVASPECT;
```

lindex
Identifies which piece of the view has changed, currently only -1 is valid.

Comments

Containers register to be notified when an object's view changes by calling **IViewObject::SetAdvise**. Once registered, the object will call the sink's **IAdviseSink::OnViewChange** method when appropriate.

Even though **DVASPECT** values are individual flag bits, *dwAspect* may only represent one value. That is, *dwAspect* cannot contain the result of **DVASPECT** values that have been or'ed together. **DVASPECT** values have the following meaning:

Value	Meaning
DVASPECT_CONTENT	Gives an appropriate representation so that the object can be displayed as an embedded object inside its container; this is the most common value for compound document objects. It is appropriate to use DVASPECT_CONTENT to get a presentation of the embedded object either for rendering on the screen or on a printer; DVASPECT_PRINT, by contrast, indicates the look of the object as if it were printed from the top level.
DVASPECT_THUMBNAIL	Gives an appropriate thumbnail representation so that the object can be displayed in a browsing tool.
DVASPECT_ICON	Gives an iconic representation of the object.
DVASPECT_DOCPRINT	Represents the object as if it were printed using the Print command from the File menu. The described data represents a sequence of pages.

The *lindex* member represents the part of the aspect that is of interest. The value of *lindex* depends on the value of *dwAspect*. If *dwAspect* is either DVASPECT_THUMBNAIL or DVASPECT_ICON, *lindex* is ignored. If *dwAspect* is DVASPECT_CONTENT, *lindex* must be -1, which indicates that the entire view is of interest and is the only value that is currently valid.

To handle changes that affect the extent of the object, containers can set a flag (*fDoGetExtent*) in **OnViewChange** to TRUE and then call **InvalidateRect** to force repainting. In the drawing code, insert the following:

```
if (fDoGetExtent)  {
    fDoGetExtent = FALSE;
    IViewObject2::GetExtent(&newExtents);
    if (newExtents are different)
        relayout the contents.
}
draw the object
```

OnViewChange can be called when the object is in either the loaded or running state.

Example

The implementation of **IAdviseSink::OnViewChange** shown below invalidates the rectangle of the object to force a repaint in the future. The object whose extents may changed is marked (*m_fDoGetExtent* set to TRUE) and a message (WM_U_UPDATEOBJECTEXTENT) is posted to the document indicating that one or more OLE objects may need their extents updated. If drawing is disabled, however, the extent update process is postponed. When this message is processed, the document calls **IOleObject::GetExtent** to determine whether the extents did change. If they did, space is laid out for the object before it is redrawn and the document is marked as dirty.

```
void IAdviseSink_OnViewChange(
        LPADVISESINK        lpThis,
        DWORD               dwAspect,
        LONG                lindex)
{
    LPSITE lpSite;
    LPDOC lpDoc;
    HWND hWndDoc;
    MSG msg;

    lpSite = ((struct CAdviseSinkImpl FAR*)lpThis)->lpSite;
    lpDoc = (LPDOC)lpSite->m_lpDoc;

    lpSite->m_fDoGetExtent = TRUE;
    hWndDoc = GetDocWindow((LPDOC)lpSite->m_lpDoc);

    if (!(lpDoc->m_DisableDraw) &&
         (! PeekMessage(&msg, hWndDoc,  WM_U_UPDATEOBJECTEXTENT,
            WM_U_UPDATEOBJECTEXTENT, PM_NOREMOVE | PM_NOYIELD)) )
                PostMessage(hWndDoc, WM_U_UPDATEOBJECTEXTENT, 0, 0L);

    ForceObjRedraw(lpDoc);
    SetDocModified(lpDoc);
}
```

See Also

IViewObject::SetAdvise

IAdviseSink::OnRename

void IAdviseSink::OnRename(*pmk***)**
LPMONIKER *pmk*

IAdviseSink::OnRename notifies that an object has been renamed.

Parameters

pmk
Points to the new (full) name of the object.

Comments

The **OnRename** notification belongs to a group of notifications that containers register to receive by calling **IOleObject::Advise**. **IAdviseSink::OnRename** is called when the object's name in the container changes or when the container's name changes. Although the container and the OLE link object typically receive this notification, the container can ignore it. The link object, however, must update its moniker. Most containers wil not need to register for OLE advise notifications.

See Also

IAdviseSink2::OnLinkSrcChange

IAdviseSink::OnSave

void IAdviseSink::OnSave()

IAdviseSink::OnSave notifies that an object has been persistently saved.

Comments

Objects call **IAdviseSink::OnSave** to send **OnSave** notifications when the object has been persistently saved, either to the object's original storage or to a new one (i.e. Save or Save As). **OnSave** notifications are usually of interest to object handlers rather than to containers; containers can typically ignore them. When an object handler receives the **OnSave** notification, it updates its cache if the advise flag passed during registration specified ADVFCACHE_ONSAVE.

IOleObject::Advise is called to register for **OnSave** notifications.

See Also

IAdviseSink2::OnLinkSrcChange

IAdviseSink::OnClose

void IAdviseSink::OnClose()

IAdviseSink::OnClose notifies that an object has transitioned from the running into the loaded state and the object application has shut down.

Comments

Containers register to receive **OnClose** notifications by calling **IOleObject::Advise**. **IAdviseSink::OnClose** is called to inform sinks to immediately release pointers to the object because it is shutting down. The OLE link object, in its implementation of **OnClose**, releases its pointer to the bound link source. The container can ignore this notification. It should not revert the object's storage. If necessary, it can unload and reload the object.

IAdviseSink2 Interface

The **IAdviseSink2** interface, an extension of **IAdviseSink**, is optionally implemented by linking container applications. When a linking container stores a representation of the link source outside of the link, it may be desirable to be notified when the link source changes. The **OnLinkSrcChange** notification can be used for this purpose.

IAdviseSink2 , contains one additional method (see also DVOBJ.H).

```
DECLARE_INTERFACE_(IAdviseSink2, IAdviseSink)
{
  // *** IUnknown methods ***
 HRESULT QueryInterface (THIS_ REFIID riid, LPVOID FAR* ppvObj);
 ULONG AddRef (THIS) ;
 ULONG Release (THIS);

  // *** IAdviseSink methods ***
 void OnDataChange (THIS_ FORMATETC FAR* pFormatetc,
  STGMEDIUM FAR* pmedium);
 void OnViewChange (THIS_ DWORD dwAspect, LONG lindex);
 void OnRename (THIS_ LPMONIKER pmk);
 void OnSave (THIS);
 void OnClose (THIS);

  // *** IAdviseSink2 methods ***
 void OnLinkSrcChange (THIS_ LPMONIKER pmk);
};
```

IAdviseSink2::OnLinkSrcChange

void IAdviseSink2::OnLinkSrcChange(*pmk***)**
LPMONIKER *pmk*

IAdviseSink2::OnLinkSrcChange notifies that a link source has changed.

Parameters

pmk
Points to the new link source contained within the link object.

Comments

A container of linked objects implements this method so it is notified of a change in the link source's moniker. A typical container uses the link-source name as part of its application.

IAdviseSink2::OnLinkSrcChange is called by the OLE link object when it receives the **OnRename** notification from the link source (object) application. The link object updates its moniker and sends the **OnLinkSrcChange** notification to containers that have implemented **IAdviseSink2**.

See Also **IAdviseSink::OnRename**

IEnumOLEVERB Interface

The **IEnumOLEVERB** interface is implemented by OLE and by object applications that have a dynamically changing set of verbs. It is used by container applications to enumerate the verbs available for an object.

The **IEnumOLEVERB** interface contains the following methods, as do all enumerators:

```
DECLARE_INTERFACE_(IEnumOLEVERB, IUnknown)
{
  // *** IUnknown methods ***
 HRESULT QueryInterface (THIS_ REFIID riid, LPVOID FAR* ppvObj);
 ULONG AddRef (THIS) ;
 ULONG Release (THIS);

  // *** IEnumOLEVERB methods ***
 HRESULT Next (THIS_ ULONG celt, LPOLEVERB rgelt, ULONG FAR* pceltFetched);
 HRESULT Skip (THIS_ ULONG celt);
 HRESULT Reset (THIS);
 HRESULT Clone (THIS_ IEnumOLEVERB FAR* FAR* ppenumOleVerb);
};
```

IEnumOLEVERB enumerates the entries in an **OLEVERB** structure. The **OLEVERB** structure is defined as follows:

```
typedef struct FARSTRUCT tagOLEVERB
{
    LONG     lVerb;
    LPSTR    lpszVerbName;
    DWORD    fuFlags;
    DWORD    grfAttribs;
} OLEVERB, FAR* LPOLEVERB;
```

Refer to the discussion of the **IEnum*X* Interface** in the "Component Object Interfaces and Functions" chapter for more information.

IOleAdviseHolder Interface

The **IOleAdviseHolder** interface, implemented by OLE, is used by object applications to manage OLE notification registration and deregistration. It also sends notifications to registered sinks when appropriate. Use of the **IOleAdviseHolder** methods is optional because object applications can provide their own notification management if preferred. **IOleAdviseHolder** is provided solely for the convenience of object application implementors.

IOleAdviseHolder contains the following methods (see also OLE2.H).

```
DECLARE_INTERFACE_(IOleAdviseHolder, IUnknown)
{
  // *** IUnknown methods ***
  HRESULT QueryInterface (THIS_ REFIID riid, LPVOID FAR* ppvObj);
  ULONG AddRef (THIS) ;
  ULONG Release (THIS);

  // *** IOleAdviseHolder methods ***
  HRESULT Advise (THIS_ LPADVISESINK pAdvise, DWORD FAR* pdwConnection);
  HRESULT Unadvise (THIS_ DWORD dwConnection);
  HRESULT EnumAdvise (THIS_ LPENUMSTATDATA FAR* ppenumAdvise);
  HRESULT SendOnRename (THIS_ LPMONIKER pmk);
  HRESULT SendOnSave (THIS);
  HRESULT SendOnClose (THIS);
};
```

IOleAdviseHolder::Advise

HRESULT IOleAdviseHolder::Advise(*pAdvise, pdwConnection*)
LPADVISESINK *pAdvise*
DWORD FAR* *pdwConnection*

IOleAdviseHolder::Advise sets up an advisory connection between the object and an advisory sink through which the sink can be informed of events that occur in the object.

Parameters

pAdvise
Points to the advisory sink that should be informed of changes.

pdwConnection
Points to a token that can be passed to **IOleAdviseHolder::Unadvise** to delete the advisory connection.

Return Values

Value	Meaning
S_OK	Advisory connections set up successfully.
E_INVALIDARG	*pAdvise* is NULL.

Comments

Sinks that need to receive compound document (OLE) notifications for an object call **IOleObject::Advise** to register. Compound document notifications include **OnSave**, **OnRename**, **OnLinkSrcChange**, and **OnClose**. The implementation of **IOleObject::Advise** generally calls **CreateOleAdviseHolder** to instantiate an **IOleAdviseHolder** interface instance and then delegates the call to **IOleAdviseHolder::Advise**.

If an advisory connection is successfully set up, the callee returns a nonzero value through *pdwConnection* . If a connection fails to be established, zero is returned. The connection can be deleted by passing this nonzero token back to the object in a call to **IOleAdviseHolder::Unadvise**.

See Also

IOleAdviseHolder::UnAdvise, IOleAdviseHolder::EnumAdvise, IOleObject::Advise

IOleAdviseHolder::Unadvise

HRESULT IOleAdviseHolder::Unadvise(*dwConnection***)**
DWORD *dwConnection*

IOleAdviseHolder::Unadvise deletes an advisory connection previously established with **IOleAdviseHolder::Advise**.

Parameters

dwConnection
Contains a nonzero value previously returned from **IOleAdviseHolder::Advise** in *pdwConnection.*

Return Values

Value	Meaning
S_OK	Advisory connection deleted successfully.
OLE_E_NOCONNECTION	*dwConnection* does not represent a valid advisory connection.

See Also

IOleAdviseHolder::Advise, IOleAdviseHolder::EnumAdvise, IOleObject::Unadvise

IOleAdviseHolder::EnumAdvise

HRESULT IOleAdviseHolder::EnumAdvise(*ppenumAdvise*)
LPENUMSTATDATA FAR* *ppenumAdvise*

IOleAdviseHolder::EnumAdvise enumerates the advisory connections currently established on the object.

Parameters

ppenumAdvise
Points to where the new enumerator should be returned. NULL is a legal return value; indicating that there are presently no advisory connections on the object.

Return Values

Value	Meaning
S_OK	Enumerator returned successfully.
E_FAIL	Enumerator could not be returned.

Comments

While an enumeration is in progress, the effect of registering or revoking advisory connections on what is to be enumerated is undefined. The returned enumerator is of type **IEnumSTATDATA.** It enumerates items of type **STATDATA**, which are defined as follows:

```
typedef struct tagSTATDATA {
    FORMATETC          Formatetc;
    DWORD              grfAdvf;
    IAdviseSink FAR*   pAdvise;
    DWORD              dwConnection;
    }STATDATA;
```

See Also

IOleAdviseHolder::Advise, IOleAdviseHolder::UnAdvise, IOleObject::EnumAdvise

IOleAdviseHolder::SendOnRename

HRESULT IOleAdviseHolder::SendOnRename(*pmk*)
LPMONIKER *pmk*

IOleAdviseHolder::SendOnRename calls **IAdviseSink::OnRename** on all of the advisory sinks currently registered in the advise holder.

Parameters

pmk
Points to the new full moniker of the object.

Return Values

Value	Meaning
S_OK	Appropriate sinks were sent OnRename notifications.

IOleAdviseHolder::SendOnSave

HRESULT IOleAdviseHolder::SendOnSave()

IOleAdviseHolder::SendOnSave calls **IAdviseSink::OnSave** on all of the sinks currently registered in the advise holder.

Return Values

Value	Meaning
S_OK	Appropriate sinks were sent OnSave notifications.

See Also

IAdviseSink::OnSave

IOleAdviseHolder::SendOnClose

HRESULT IOleAdviseHolder::SendOnClose()

IOleAdviseHolder::SendOnClose calls **IAdviseSink::OnClose** on all of the sinks currently registered in the advise holder.

Return Values

Value	Meaning
S_OK	Appropriate sinks were sent OnClose notifications.

See Also

IAdviseSink::OnClose

IOleClientSite Interface

The **IOleClientSite** interface, implemented by containers, is the object's view of its context: where it is anchored in the document, where it gets its storage, user interface, and other resources. **IOleClientSite** interface is used by object applications to request services from its container. A container must provide one instance of **IOleClientSite** for every compound document object it contains.

IOleClientSite contains the following methods (see also OLE2.H):

```
DECLARE_INTERFACE_(IOleClientSite, IUnknown)
{
  // *** IUnknown methods ***
```

```
    HRESULT QueryInterface (THIS_ REFIID riid, LPVOID FAR* ppvObj);
    ULONG AddRef (THIS) ;
    ULONG Release (THIS);

    // *** IOleClientSite methods ***
    HRESULT GetContainer (THIS_ LPOLECONTAINER FAR* ppContainer);
    HRESULT OnShowWindow (THIS_ BOOL fShow);
    HRESULT GetMoniker (THIS_ DWORD dwAssign, DWORD dwWhichMoniker,
     LPMONIKER FAR* ppmk);
    HRESULT RequestNewObjectLayout (THIS);
    HRESULT SaveObject (THIS);
    HRESULT ShowObject (THIS);


};
```

IOleClientSite::GetContainer

HRESULT IOleClientSite::GetContainer(*ppContainer*)
LPOLECONTAINER FAR* *ppContainer*

IOleClientSite::GetContainer returns a pointer to the embedding container's **IOleContainer** interface.

Parameters

ppContainer
Points to where the object's **IOleContainer** interface pointer is to be returned.

Return Values

Value	Meaning
S_OK	**IOleContainer** interface pointer successfully returned.
OLE_E_NOT_SUPPORTED	Client site is in OLE 1 container.
E_NOINTERFACE	**IOleContainer** is not implemented by container.

Comments

IOleClientSite::GetContainer can be used to traverse up a hierarchy of compound document objects. A successful call to **IOleClientSite::GetContainer** can be followed by **IOleContainer::QueryInterface**, asking for **IOleObject** and **IOleObject::GetClientSite** to get the client site for the next object. The sequence of three calls can be repeated for each object.

Simple containers that do not support linking to embedded objects may not need to implement this method. This containers should return E_NOINTERFACE and set **ppContainer* to NULL.

Example

The following example, a typical implementation of **IOleClientSite::GetContainer**, calls **QueryInterface** on the document object to get a pointer to **IOleContainer**.

```
HRESULT IOleClientSite_GetContainer
    (LPOLECLIENTSITE lpThis, LPOLECONTAINER FAR* ppContainer)
{
    HRESULT hrErr;
    lpSite = ((struct COleClientSiteImpl FAR*)lpThis)->lpSite;
    hrErr = IUnknown_Doc_QueryInterface(
            (LPDOC)lpSite->m_lpDoc,
            &IID_IOleContainer,
            (LPVOID FAR*)ppContainer);

    return hrErr;
}
```

See Also

IOleClientSite::SaveObject, IOleClientSite::GetMoniker, IOleClientSite::RequestNewObjectLayout

IOleClientSite::OnShowWindow

HRESULT IOleClientSite::OnShowWindow(*fShow*)
BOOL *fShow*

IOleClientSite::OnShowWindow notifies a container when an object's windows become visible or invisible. This method is called when an object is open in its own window as opposed to being in-place active.

Parameters

fShow
Indicates whether or not an object window is becoming visible.

Return Values

Value	Meaning
S_OK	Shading/hatching has been successfully removed or added.

Comments

An object calls **IOleClientSite::OnShowWindow** if an **IOleObject::DoVerb** call causes it to show its window. **IOleClientSite::OnShowWindow** adds or removes object shading. If *fShow* is TRUE, the object is open in a window elsewhere and shading/hatching should be added. If *fShow* is FALSE, the window is not open elsewhere and shading/hatching should be removed.

Example

The implementation of **IOleClientSite::OnShowWindow** shown below checks the value of *fShow* and if it is TRUE, a flag in the site object is also set to TRUE, and **ForceDataRedraw** is called to redraw the data. If *fShow* is FALSE, the flag is reset, **ForceDataRedraw** is called, and the container document window is then brought to the top with focus restored.

```
HRESULT IOleClientSite_OnShowWindow(LPOLECLIENTSITE lpThis, BOOL fShow)
{
    RECT   rect;
    BOOL   fErase;

    LPSITE lpSite = ((struct COleClientSiteImpl FAR*)lpThis)->lpSite;
    LPDOC  lpDoc = (LPDOC)lpSite->m_lpDoc;
    LPDATA lpData = GetDocData(lpDoc);

    if (fShow) {
        lpSite->m_fObjWinOpen = TRUE;
        ForceDataRedraw(lpData, FALSE);
    }
    else {
        lpSite->m_fObjWinOpen = FALSE;
        ForceLineRedraw(lpData, TRUE);
        BringWindowToTop(lpDoc->m_hWndDoc);
        SetFocus(lpDoc->m_hWndDoc);
    }
    return ResultFromScode(S_OK);
}
```

IOleClientSite::GetMoniker

HRESULT IOleClientSite::GetMoniker(*dwAssign, dwWhichMoniker, ppmk*)
DWORD *dwAssign*
DWORD *dwWhichMoniker*
LPMONIKER FAR**ppmk*

IOleClientSite::GetMoniker returns the container's moniker, the object's moniker relative to the container, or the object's full moniker.

Parameters

dwAssign

Specifies the type of moniker to be returned in *ppmk*. Valid values are contained in the enumeration **OLEGETMONIKER**:

```
typedef enum tagOLEGETMONIKER
{
    OLEGETMONIKER_ONLYIFTHERE      = 1,
    OLEGETMONIKER_FORCEASSIGN      = 2,
```

```
    OLEGETMONIKER_UNASSIGN          = 3,
    OLEGETMONIKER_TEMPFORUSER       = 4
} OLEGETMONIKER;
```

OLEGETMONIKER_ONLYIFTHERE returns a moniker only if one has previously been assigned.

OLEGETMONIKER_FORCEASSIGN returns an assigned moniker.

OLEGETMONIKER_UNASSIGN removes moniker assignment and returns NULL.

OLEGETMONIKER_TEMPFORUSER returns a temporary, unassigned moniker. This flag is used when a moniker is needed, for example, to represent data being copied to the clipboard at the time of the copy. Forced moniker assignment should be postponed until such time that a Paste Link actually occurs.

dwWhichMoniker

Specifies which moniker to return in *ppmk*; the value is taken from the enumeration **OLEWHICHMK**:

```
typedef enum tagOLEWHICHMK
{
    OLEWHICHMK_CONTAINER    = 1,
    OLEWHICHMK_OBJREL       = 2,
    OLEWHICHMK_OBJFULL      = 3
}OLEWHICHMK;
```

OLEWHICHMK_CONTAINER indicates that the moniker belonging to the object's container, typically a file moniker, should be returned.

OLEWHICHMK_OBJREL returns the object's moniker relative to the client site, typically an item moniker. OLEWHICHMK_OBJFULL returns the object's full moniker, typically a Composite Moniker.

ppmk

Points to where to return the moniker.

Return Values

Value	Meaning
S_OK	Requested moniker returned successfully.
E_FAIL	An unspecified error occurred.
E_UNEXPECTED	A relatively catastrophic failure has occurred.
E_NOTIMPL	This container cannot assign monikers to objects.

Comments

Every container that may contain links should support **IOleClientSite::GetMoniker** to give out OLEWHICHMK_CONTAINER, thus enabling link tracking when the link client and link source files move, but maintain the same relative position.

An object must not persistently store its full moniker or its container's moniker, because these can change while the object is not loaded.

When a link is made to an entire embedded object or to pieces of it, the embedded object needs a moniker to use in constructing a composite moniker indicating the source of the link. If the embedded object does not already have a moniker, it can call **IOleClientSite::GetMoniker** to request one.

In some cases, an object may no longer need the moniker previously assigned to it; such as high-frequency links used for object connections in a programming language. In such circumstances, the object can call **IOleClientSite::GetMoniker** with OLEGETMONIKER_UNASSIGN to inform its container that it no longer needs the moniker; the container can unassign the moniker as an optimization.

Example

The implementation of **IOleClientSite::GetMoniker** shown below calls three other functions to return the requested moniker. Depending on the value of *dwWhichMoniker*, IOleClientSite_GetMoniker calls either GetFullDocMoniker to get the full moniker of the document, CGetFullMoniker to get the full moniker of the container, or CGetRelMoniker to get the moniker of the object relative to the container. If a valid moniker is returned, **IOleClientSite::GetMoniker** returns S_OK (or NOERROR). Otherwise, E_FAIL is returned.

```
HRESULT IOleClientSite_GetMoniker(
        LPOLECLIENTSITE     lpThis,
        DWORD               dwAssign,
        DWORD               dwWhichMoniker,
        LPMONIKER FAR*      ppmk)
{
    LPSITE lpSite;
    lpSite = ((struct COleClientSiteImpl FAR*)lpThis)->lpSite;
    *ppmk = NULL;

    switch (dwWhichMoniker)
    {
        case OLEWHICHMK_CONTAINER:
            *ppmk = GetFullDocMoniker
                ((LPDOC)lpThis->m_lpDoc, dwAssign);
            break;

        case OLEWHICHMK_OBJREL:
            *ppmk = CGetRelMoniker(lpSite, dwAssign);
            break;

        case OLEWHICHMK_OBJFULL:
            *ppmk = CGetFullMoniker(lpSite, dwAssign);
            break;
    }
    if (*ppmk != NULL)
        return ResultFromScode(S_OK);
```

```
    else
        return ResultFromScode(E_FAIL);
}
```

GetFullDocMoniker returns a moniker for the following three types of documents:

- Data transfer document: a document that is copied to the clipboard or is participating in a drag operation.
- Document under user control (new or reopened).
- Document that is an embedded object. In this case the document belongs to an application that can serve as both a container and a creator of objects.

In the first case, the moniker that represents the source document of the copied data is returned. GetFullDocMoniker is called recursively with the source of the copy passed as the first parameter. In the second case, GetFullDocMoniker returns the file moniker stored with the document after calling **AddRef** to increase its reference count. In the last case where the document is itself an embedded object, **IOleClientSite::GetMoniker** is called on the container to return the moniker.

```
LPMONIKER GetFullDocMoniker(LPDOC lpDoc, DWORD dwAssign)
{
    LPMONIKER pmk = NULL;

    if (lpDoc->m_lpSrcDocOfCopy) {
        if (! lpDoc->m_fLinkSourceAvail)
            return NULL;
        pmk = GetFullDocMoniker(lpDoc->m_lpSrcDocOfCopy, dwAssign);
    }
    else if (lpDoc->m_lpFileMoniker) {
        lpDoc->m_lpFileMoniker->lpVtbl->AddRef(lpDoc->m_lpFileMoniker);
        pmk = lpDoc->m_lpFileMoniker;
    }
    else if (((LPDOC)lpDoc)->m_lpClientSite) {
        ((LPDOC)lpDoc)->m_lpClientSite->lpVtbl->GetMoniker(
                ((LPDOC)lpDoc)->m_lpClientSite,
                dwAssign,
                OLEWHICHMK_OBJFULL,
                &pmk
        );
    }
    return pmk;
}
```

CGetRelMoniker returns an item moniker with the name of the object's storage according to the value of *dwAssign*. If *dwAssign* is GETMONIKER_FORCEASSIGN, **CreateItemMoniker** is called to create the item moniker if it is being assigned for the first time. **IOleObject::SetMoniker** is then called to instruct the object to register it in the running object table.. If *dwAssign* is GETMONIKER_ONLYIFTHERE, the *m_fMonikerAssigned* flag in the container site is checked to determine if a moniker is currently assigned before **CreateItemMoniker** is called. If *dwAssign* is GETMONIKER_TEMPFORUSER, the item moniker is generated without checking whether the moniker is currently assigned. In the last case, where *dwAssign* is GETMONIKER_UNASSIGN, the *m_fMonikerAssigned* flag is set to FALSE.

```
LPMONIKER CGetRelMoniker(LPSITE lpSite, DWORD dwAssign)
{
    LPMONIKER pmk = NULL;

    switch (dwAssign)
    {
    case GETMONIKER_FORCEASSIGN:
            CreateItemMoniker("\\", lpSite->m_szStgName, &pmk);
            if (! lpSite->m_fMonikerAssigned) {
                lpSite->m_fMonikerAssigned = TRUE;
                SetDocModified(lpSite->m_lpDoc);
                if (lpSite->m_lpOleObj) {
                    lpSite->m_lpOleObj->lpVtbl->SetMoniker(
                     lpSite->m_lpOleObj, OLEWHICHMK_OBJREL, pmk);
                }
            }
            break;

        case GETMONIKER_ONLYIFTHERE:
            if (lpSite->m_fMonikerAssigned)
                CreateItemMoniker("\\", lpSite->m_szStgName, &pmk);
            break;

        case GETMONIKER_TEMPFORUSER:
            CreateItemMoniker("\\", lpSite->m_szStgName, &pmk);
            break;

        case GETMONIKER_UNASSIGN:
            lpSite->m_fMonikerAssigned = FALSE;
            break;
    }
    return pmk;
}
```

CGetFullMoniker returns a composite moniker. First, GetFullDocMoniker is called to get the file moniker of the document. Next, CGetRelMoniker is called to get the item moniker for the container site. If both of these monikers are returned successfully, **CreateGenericComposite** is called to generate the composite moniker and **Release** is called to decrement the reference count on the file and item monikers.

```
LPMONIKER CGetFullMoniker(LPSITE lpSite, DWORD dwAssign)
{
    LPMONIKER pmkDoc = NULL;
    LPMONIKER pmkItem = NULL;
    LPMONIKER pmkFull = NULL;

    pmkDoc = GetFullDocMoniker((LPDOC)lpSite->m_lpDoc, dwAssign);
    if (! pmkDoc) return NULL;

    pmkItem = CGetRelMoniker(lpSite, dwAssign);
    if (pmkItem) {
        CreateGenericComposite(pmkDoc, pmkItem,
            (LPMONIKER FAR*)&pmkFull);
        (LPUNKNOWN)pmkItem->lpVtbl->Release((LPUNKNOWN)pmkItem);
    }
    if (pmkDoc)
        (LPUNKNOWN)pmkDoc->lpVtbl-Release((LPUNKNOWN)pmkDoc);
    return pmkFull;
}
```

See Also

IOleClientSite::SaveObject, IOleClientSite::GetContainer, IOleClientSite::RequestNewObjectLayout

IOleClientSite::RequestNewObjectLayout

HRESULT IOleClientSite::RequestNewObjectLayout()

IOleClientsite::RequestNewObjectLayout is called when a compound document object is going to request more or less room.

Return Values

Value	Meaning
S_OK	Request for new layout succeeded.
E_NOTIMPL	Client site does not support requests for new layout.

Comments

Currently, there is no standard mechanism by which a container would engage in a negotiation process to determine *how much* room the object would like. When such a mechanism is defined, responding to it will be optional on containers' part.

See Also **IOleClientSite::SaveObject, IOleClientSite::GetMoniker, IOleClientSite::GetContainer**

IOleClientSite::SaveObject

HRESULT IOleClientSite::SaveObject()

IOleClientSite::SaveObject requests that the object attached to this client site be saved.

Return Values

Value	Meaning
S_OK	Object was saved successfully.
E_FAIL	Object was not loaded.
Values returned from **IPersistStorage::Save**, **IPersistStorage::SaveCompleted**, or **IOleObject::Update**	Refer to description of methods.

Comments

IOleClientSite::SaveObject is synchronous; by the time it returns, the save will be completed. **IOleClientSite::SaveObject** is called by objects when the user chooses the File Update or Exit commands.

Example

This example checks that the object is loaded before starting the save operation by examining the **IPersistStorage** pointer. If the object is loaded, the object is told to save itself with a call to the helper function **OleSave**. It is not sufficient to only call **IPersistStorage::Save**. **WriteClassStg**, the API function that writes the class of an object to storage, must also be called. **OleSave** makes the call to **WriteClassStg** automatically. Regardless of whether **OleSave** succeeds or fails, **IPersistStorage::SaveCompleted** must be called.

```
HRESULT IOleClientSite_SaveObject(LPOLECLIENTSITE lpThis)
{
    SCODE       sc = S_OK;
    HRESULT     hrErr;
    BOOL        fSameAsLoad = TRUE;
    LPPERSISTSTORAGE lpPStg = lpSite->m_lpPStg;
    LPSITE  lpSite = ((struct COleClientSiteImpl FAR*)lpThis)->lpSite;

    if (! lpPStg)
        return ResultFromScode(E_FAIL);

    SetDocDirty (lpDoc);
    hrErr = OleSave (lpPStg,lpSite->m_lpStg, fSameAsLoad);
    if (hrErr != NOERROR)
        sc = GetScode(hrErr);
```

```
    hrErr = lpPStg->lpVtbl->SaveCompleted (lpPStg, NULL);
    if (hrErr != NOERROR) {
        if (sc == S_OK)
            sc = GetScode(hrErr);
    }
    return ResultFromScode(sc);
}
```

See Also **IOleClientSite::GetMoniker, IOleClientSite::GetContainer, IOleClientSite::RequestNewObjectLayout**

IOleClientSite::ShowObject

HRESULT IOleClientSite::ShowObject()

IOleClientSite::ShowObject tells the container to position the object so it is visible to the user. This method ensures that the container itself is visible and not minimized.

Return Values

Value	Meaning
S_OK	Container has tried to make the object visible.
OLE_E_NOT_SUPPORTED	Client site is in OLE 1 container.

Comments **IOleClientSite::ShowObject** is typically part of an object's implementation of **IOleObject::DoVerb**. If this container is itself an embedded object, it will recursively invoke **IOleClientSite::ShowObject** on its container.

It is possible that the container is not able to position the object so it is either partially or completely visible at the present time. Therefore, when **ShowObject** returns, the object cannot rely on its degree of visibility. The intent of **ShowObject** is to respond to the request for visibility whenever possible.

After an object being edited in place scrolls into view, it is necessary to ask it to update its rectangle for the new clip RECT coordinates.

IOleContainer Interface

The **IOleContainer** interface, implemented by containers and object applications, is used to enumerate objects in a container. **IOleContainer** is typically implemented by applications that support standard linking and linking to embeddings, however, it is useful for other applications as well. An extension of **IOleContainer**, **IOleItemContainer**, is used by item monikers in their bind process. The **IOleContainer** interface inherits from **IParseDisplayName**.

IOleContainer is generic to many kinds of containers. It provides name parsing and enumeration of objects, that is, an outside-in view of the composite set of objects managed by a container. OLE 2 applications will normally use **IOleItemContainer** to expose the contents of a container.

Simple, non-linking containers need not implement **IOleContainer**. The default object handler provides default behavior when a pointer to **IOleContainer** is not available.

IOleContainer contains the following methods (see also OLE2.H):

```
DECLARE_INTERFACE_(IOleContainer, IParseDisplayName)
{
  // *** IUnknown methods ***
 HRESULT QueryInterface (THIS_ REFIID riid, LPVOID FAR* ppvObj);
 ULONG AddRef (THIS) ;
 ULONG Release (THIS);

  // *** IParseDisplayName method ***
 HRESULT ParseDisplayName (THIS_ LPBC pbc, LPSTR lpszDisplayName,
  ULONG FAR* pchEaten, LPMONIKER FAR* ppmkOut);

  // *** IOleContainer methods ***
 HRESULT EnumObjects) ( DWORD grfFlags,
  LPENUMUNKNOWN FAR* ppenumUnknown);
 HRESULT LockContainer (THIS_ BOOL fLock);
};
```

IOleContainer::EnumObjects

HRESULT IOleContainer::EnumObjects(*grfFlags*, *ppenumUnknown*)
DWORD *grfFlags*
LPENUMUNKNOWN FAR* *ppenumUnknown*

IOleContainer::EnumObjects enumerates the objects in the current container.

Parameters

grfFlags
Controls the enumeration. Valid values are taken from the enumeration **OLECONTF**:

```
typedef enum tagOLECONTF
{
    OLECONTF_EMBEDDINGS     =  1,
    OLECONTF_LINKS          =  2,
    OLECONTF_OTHERS         =  4,
    OLECONTF_ONLYUSER       =  8,
```

```
    OLECONTF_ONLYIFRUNNING  = 16
} OLECONTF;
```

The values have following meanings:

Value	Meaning
OLECONTF_EMBEDDINGS	Enumerates the embedded objects in the container.
OLECONTF_LINKS	Enumerate the linked objects in the container.
OLECONTF_OTHER	Enumerates all objects in the container other than OLE compound document objects. If this flag is not given, pseudo objects in the container will be omitted.
OLECONTF_ONLYUSER	Enumerates only those objects the user is aware of. For example, hidden named-ranges in Microsoft Excel would not be enumerated using this value.
OLECONTF_ONLYIFRUNNING	Enumerates only the objects that are currently running inside this container.

ppenumUnknown
Points to where the enumerator, of type **IEnumUnknown**, should be returned. For more information, see the discussion of enumerators in the "IEnumX Interface" section of the "Component Object Interfaces and Functions" chapter.

Return Values

Value	Meaning
S_OK	Enumerator successfully returned.
E_FAIL	An unspecified error occurred.
E_NOTIMPL	Object enumeration not supported.

Comments

EnumObjects should be implemented to allow programmatic clients the ability to find out what elements the container holds. It is not called in standard linking scenarios.

See Also

IOleItemContainer Interface

IOleContainer::LockContainer

HRESULT IOleContainer::LockContainer(*fLock***)**
BOOL *fLock*

IOleContainer::LockContainer is used by an embedded object to manually control the running of its container.

Parameters

fLock
Specifies whether to lock (TRUE) or unlock (FALSE) a container.

Return Values

Value	Meaning
S_OK	Container was locked successfully.
E_FAIL	An unspecified error occurred.
E_OUTOFMEMORY	Container could not be locked due to lack of memory.

Comments

An embedded object calls **IOleContainer::LockContainer** to ensure that its container remains alive when other containers are linked to it and require an update. **IOleContainer::LockContainer** calls **CoLockObjectExternal** which keeps the embedding container alive after all external references are released.

IOleContainer::LockContainer with the *fLock* parameter set to TRUE is called when an embedded object transitions to the running state. When the embedded object shuts down (transitions from running to loaded), it calls **IOleContainer::LockContainer** with the *fLock* parameter set to FALSE . However, if the user selects File Close from the menu, all outstanding **LockContainer** locks are ignored and the document will shut down.

The container must keep track of whether and how many calls to **LockContainer**(TRUE) have been made. Each call to **LockContainer** with *fLock* set to TRUE must be balanced by a call to **LockContainer** with *fLock* set to FALSE. Object applications typically need not call **LockContainer**; the default handler makes these calls automatically for object applications implemented as .EXEs as the object transitions to and from the running state. Object applications not using the default handler, such as DLL object applications, must make the calls directly.

Example

The following example illustrates the use of artificial reference counting to protect the stability of an object during an important operation. **AddRef** is called before the call to **CoLockObjectExternal**; **Release** is called after the call. For more information about artificial reference counting, see "Reference Counting Rules" in the "Component Object Interfaces and Functions" chapter.

```
HRESULT IOleContainer_LockContainer(LPOLECONTAINER lpThis, BOOL fLock)
{
    HRESULT hrErr;
    LPDOC lpDoc = ((struct CDocOleItemContainerImpl FAR*)lpThis)->lpDoc;

    IUnknown_Doc_AddRef(lpDoc);
    hrErr = CoLockObjectExternal((LPUNKNOWN)&lpDoc->m_Unknown,
              fLock, TRUE);
    IUnknown_Doc_Release(lpDoc);
```

```
    return hrErr;
}
```

IOleItemContainer Interface

The **IOleItemContainer** interface, an extension to **IOleContainer,** is used to bind item monikers. Containers that use item monikers to identify contained objects must implement **IOleItemContainer**. **IOleItemContainer** contains the following methods (see also OLE2.H):

```
DECLARE_INTERFACE_(IOleItemContainer, IOleContainer)
{
  // *** IUnknown methods ***
  HRESULT QueryInterface (THIS_ REFIID riid, LPVOID FAR* ppvObj);
  ULONG AddRef (THIS) ;
  ULONG Release (THIS);

  // *** IParseDisplayName method ***
  HRESULT ParseDisplayName (THIS_ LPBC pbc, LPSTR lpszDisplayName,
   ULONG FAR* pchEaten, LPMONIKER FAR* ppmkOut);

  // *** IOleContainer methods ***
  HRESULT EnumObjects (THIS_ DWORD grfFlags,
   LPENUMUNKNOWN FAR*ppenumUnknown);
  HRESULT LockContainer (THIS_ BOOL fLock);

  // *** IOleItemContainer methods ***
  HRESULT GetObject (THIS_ LPSTR lpszItem, DWORD dwSpeedNeeded,
   LPBINDCTX pbc, REFIID riid, LPVOID FAR* ppvObj);
  HRESULT GetObjectStorage (THIS_ LPSTR lpszItem, LPBINDCTX pbc,
   REFIID riid, LPVOID FAR* ppvStorage);
  HRESULT IsRunning (THIS_ LPSTR lpszItem);
};
```

IOleItemContainer::GetObject

HRESULT IOleItemContainer::GetObject(*lpszItem, dwSpeedNeeded, pbc, riid, ppvObj***)**
LPSTR *lpszItem*
DWORD *dwSpeedNeeded*
LPBINDCTX *pbc*
REFIID *riid*
LPVOID FAR* *ppvObj*

IOleItemContainer::GetObject is called as part of the item moniker binding process. It returns the object represented by *lpszItem.*

Parameters

lpszItem
Points to the item in this container to which the item moniker should be bound.

dwSpeedNeeded
Indicates how long the caller is willing to wait to get to the object. Valid values are from the enumeration **BINDSPEED**:

```
typedef enum tagBINDSPEED
{
    BINDSPEED_INDEFINITE  = 1,
    BINDSPEED_MODERATE    = 2,
    BINDSPEED_IMMEDIATE   = 3
} BINDSPEED;
```

These values have the following semantics:

Value	Meaning
BINDSPEED_INDEFINITE	Caller will wait indefinitely.
BINDSPEED_MODERATE	Caller will wait a moderate amount of time.
BINDSPEED_IMMEDIATE	Caller will wait only a short time.

If BINDSPEED_IMMEDIATE is specified, the object should be returned only if it is already running or if it is a pseudo-object. This is an object internal to the item container, such as a cell range in a spreadsheet or a character range in a word processor. Otherwise, MK_E_EXCEEEDEDDEADLINE should be returned.

BINDSPEED_MODERATE is specified if the speed needed in the bind context is greater than 2500 milliseconds. BINDSPEED_MODERATE includes those objects indicated by BINDSPEED_IMMEDIATE, plus those objects that are always running when loaded. In this case, the designated object should be loaded, checked to see whether it is running and if so, it should be returned. . Otherwise, MK_E_EXCEEEDEDDEADLINE should be returned.

BINDSPEED_INDEFINITE indicates that time is of no concern to the caller. BINDSPEED_INDEFINITE is specified if the speed needed in the bind context is 0.

pbc
Points to the actual bind context.

riid
Specifies the interface with which a connection to that object should be made.

ppvObj
: Points to where the bound-to object is returned. If an object cannot be returned, NULL is returned.

Return Values

Value	Meaning
S_OK	Object returned successfully.
MK_E_EXCEEEDEDDEADLINE	Deadline was exceeded.
MK_E_SYNTAX	Error in parsing a display name or creating a file moniker.
MK_E_NOOBJECT	Intermediate object could not be found.
MK_E_INTERMEDIATEINTERFACENOTSUPPORTED	Intermediate object needed did not support a required interface.
E_NOINTERFACE	The object cannot be returned because it does not support the interface identified by *riid*.
E_OUTOFMEMORY	Object cannot be returned due to lack of memory.

Comments

If MK_E_EXCEEEDEDDEADLINE was returned, the caller can retrieve the moniker of the object for which the deadline was exceeded by calling the method *pbc*->**GetObjectParam** with the keys ExceededDeadline, ExceededDeadline1, ExceededDeadline2, and so on.

IOleItemContainer::GetObject first checks to see if the given item designates an embedded object. If the item is an embedded object, **IOleItemContainer::GetObject** loads and runs the object, and then returns it. If the item is not an embedded object, **IOleItemContainer::GetObject** checks to see if it designates a local object within the container. (This latter case is similar to **OLESERVERDOC::GetObject** in OLE 1.)

dwSpeedNeeded contains shorthand information found in the bind context. The value contained in *dwSpeedNeeded* is derived from the *dwTickCountDeadline* member in the bind context structure (receive via *pbc*). Instead of using *dwSpeedNeeded*, sophisticated containers can call *pbc*->**GetBindOptions** to get more specific information about the time limit.

Example

The container implementation of **IOleItemContainer::GetObject** shown below loops through its list of document objects, looking for a match for *lpszItem*. If a match is found, the item name is valid and the value of *dwSpeedNeeded* is checked. If *dwSpeedNeeded* is BINDSPEED_IMMEDIATE and the object is not yet loaded, MK_E_EXCEEDEDDEADLINE is returned.

When the object is loaded, **IOleItemContainer::GetObject** calls **IOleObject::GetMiscStatus** to determine whether the object can be linked to from the inside. Objects that can be linked to from the inside can generate a moniker that binds to the running OLE object. Only OLE 2 embedded objects are of this type; OLE linked objects and OLE 1 embedded objects cannot be linked to from the inside. If the object is one of the latter two types, MK_E_NOOBJECT is returned.

OleIsRunning is called next to determine whether the object is running. The object must be running before **IOleItemContainer::GetObject** can query for the requested interface. If it is not yet running and *dwSpeedNeeded* is BINDSPEED_MODERATE, MK_E_EXCEEDEDDEADLINE is returned.

```
HRESULT IOleItemContainer_GetObject(
        LPDOC           lpDoc,
        LPSTR           lpszItem,
        DWORD           dwSpeedNeeded,
        REFIID          riid,
        LPVOID FAR*     ppvObj)
{
    LPLIST      lpList = &((LPDOC)lpDoc)->m_List;
    int         i;
    LPITEM      lpItem;
    BOOL        fMatchFound = FALSE;
    DWORD       dwStatus;
    HRESULT     hrErr;

    *ppvObj = NULL;
    for (i = 0; i < lpList->m_nNumObjs; i++) {
        lpItem=GetItem(lpItem, i);
        // is item OLE object?
        if (lpItem && (GetItemType(lpItem)==OLEOBJTYPE)) {
            LPSITE lpSite = (LPSITE)lpItem;
            // is item the one we're looking for?
            if (lstrcmp(lpSite->m_szStgName, lpszItem) == 0) {
                fMatchFound = TRUE;
                if (lpSite->m_lpOleObj == NULL) {
                    if (dwSpeedNeeded == BINDSPEED_IMMEDIATE)
                        return ResultFromScode(MK_E_EXCEEDEDDEADLINE);

                    LoadOleObject(lpSite);
                    if (! lpSite->m_lpOleObj)
                        return ResultFromScode(E_OUTOFMEMORY);
                }
                lpSite->m_lpOleObj->lpVtbl->GetMiscStatus(
                                lpSite->m_lpOleObj,
                                DVASPECT_CONTENT,
                                (LPDWORD)&dwStatus);
                if (dwStatus & OLEMISC_CANTLINKINSIDE)
```

```
                        return ResultFromScode(MK_E_NOOBJECT);

                    if (! OleIsRunning(lpSite->m_lpOleObj)) {
                        if (dwSpeedNeeded == BINDSPEED_MODERATE)
                            return ResultFromScode(MK_E_EXCEEDEDDEADLINE);

                        hrErr = RunOleObject(lpSite);
                        if (hrErr != NOERROR)
                            return hrErr;
                    }

                    lpSite->m_lpOleObj->lpVtbl->QueryInterface(
                                (LPUNKNOWN)lpSite->m_lpOleObj,
                                riid,
                                (LPVOID FAR*)ppvObj);
                    break;
                }
            }
        }

        if (*ppvObj != NULL) {
            return NOERROR;
        } else
            return (fMatchFound ? ResultFromScode(E_NOINTERFACE)
                                : ResultFromScode(MK_E_NOOBJECT));
}
```

The following object application implementation of **IOleItemContainer::GetObject** returns a pseudo object that corresponds to *lpszItem*. If *lpszItem* does not represent a valid pseudo object, MK_E_NOOBJECT is returned.

```
HRESULT IOleItemContainer_GetObject(
        LPDOC               lpDoc,
        LPSTR               lpszItem,
        REFIID              riid,
        LPVOID FAR*         ppvObj
)
{
    LPPSEUDOOBJ lpPseudoObj;
    LPPSOBJLIST lpPSObjList = (LPPSOBJLIST)((LPDOC)lpDoc)->m_lpPSObjList;
    *ppvObj = NULL;

    lpPseudoObj = GetPseudoObj(lpPSObjList, lpszItem, lpDoc);
    if (! lpPseudoObj) {
        *ppvObj = NULL;
        return ResultFromScode(MK_E_NOOBJECT);
    }
```

```
return PseudoObj_QueryInterface(lpPseudoObj, riid, ppvObj);
}
```

IOleItemContainer::GetObjectStorage

HRESULT IOleItemContainer::GetObjectStorage(*lpszItem, pbc, riid, ppvStorage***)**
LPSTR *lpszItem*
LPBINDCTX *pbc*
REFIID *riid*
LPVOID FAR* *ppvStorage*

IOleItemContainer::GetObjectStorage returns access to the object's storage using the indicated interface.

Parameters

lpszItem
Points to the item name for the object to whose storage access is being requested.

pbc
Points to the bind context. Can be ignored for most containers.

riid
Identifies the interface by which the caller wishes to access that storage. Often either IID_IStorage or IID_IStream is used.

ppvStorage
Place at which to return the requested interface.

Return Values

Value	Meaning
S_OK	Object's storage returned successfully.
E_FAIL	Cannot return object's storage.
MK_E_NOOBJECT	Object could not be found.
MK_E_NOSTORAGE	An attempt was made to access or bind to the storage of an object which does not have one.

In order for **IOleItemContainer::GetObjectStorage** to succeed, the object represented by *lpszItem* must have an independently identifiable piece of storage, as is the case of an embedded object. If no such storage exists, NULL is returned in *ppvStorage* and MK_E_NOSTORAGE is the return value.

Example

The example below is implemented in a container that supports linking to its embeddings. **IOleItemContainer::GetObjectStorage** first checks to make sure that the requested interface is the **IStorage** interface because for this container, only **IStorage** is used. If **IStorage** is being requested, **IOleItemContainer::GetObjectStorage** cycles through the list of objects for the specified document, looking for a compound document object with a storage name that matches *lpszItem*. If a match is found, a pointer to the storage is returned. If no match is found, MK_E_NOOBJECT is returned.

```
HRESULT IOleItemContainer_GetObjectStorage(
            LPOLEITEMCONTAINER  lpThis,
            LPSTR               lpszItem,
            LPBINDCTX           pbc,
            REFIID              riid,
            LPVOID FAR*         lplpStg
)
{
    LPDOC lpDoc = ((struct CDocOleItemContainerImpl FAR*)lpThis)->lpDoc;
    LPLIST              lpList = &((LPDOC)lpDoc)->m_List;
    int                 i;
    LPITEM              lpItem;

    *lplpStg = NULL;
    if (! IsEqualIID(riid, &IID_IStorage))
        return ResultFromScode(E_FAIL);

    for (i = 0; i < lpList->m_nNumObjs; i++) {
        lpItem=GetItem(lpItem, i);
        if (lpItem && (GetItemType(lpItem)==OLEOBJTYPE)) {
            LPSITE lpSite = (LPSITE)lpItem;
            if (lstrcmp(lpSite->m_szStgName, lpszItem) == 0) {
                (LPSTORAGE FAR *)*lplpStg = lpSite->m_lpStg;
                lpSite->m_lpStg->lpVtbl->AddRef(lpSite->m_lpStg);
                break;
            }
        }
    }
    if (*lplpStg != NULL)
        return ResultFromScode(S_OK);
    else
        return ResultFromScode(MK_E_NOSTORAGE);
}
```

IOleItemContainer::IsRunning

HRESULT IOleItemContainer::IsRunning(*lpszItem*)
LPSTR *lpszItem*

IOleItemContainer::IsRunning indicates whether the specified item in this item container is running.

Parameters

lpszItem
Points to the item name for the object whose status is being queried.

Return Values

Value	Meaning
S_OK	Object is running.
S_FALSE	Object is not running.
MK_E_NOOBJECT	Object does not allow linking inside.
E_OUTOFMEMORY	Ran out of memory while running the object.

Examples

The first example below is from a container application. **IOleItemContainer::IsRunning** first locates the object represented by *lpszItem* by looping through the document's list of objects. If the object is found and is not yet loaded, it is not considered running and S_FALSE is returned. When the object is loaded, **IOleObject::GetMiscStatus** is called to determine whether this object can be linked to from the inside. If it cannot, MK_E_NOOBJECT is returned. The last call is to **OleIsRunning** to check if the object is, in fact, running.

```
HRESULT IOleItemContainer_IsRunning(LPDOC lpDoc, LPSTR lpszItem)
{
    LPLIST      lpList = &((LPDOC)lpDoc)->m_List;
    int         i;
    LPITEM      lpItem;
    DWORD       dwStatus;

    for (i = 0; i < lpList->m_nNumObjs; i++) {
        lpItem=GetItem(lpItem, i);
        if (lpItem && (GetItemType(lpItem)==OLEOBJTYPE)) {
            LPSITE lpSite = (LPSITE)lpItem;
            if (lstrcmp(lpSite->m_szStgName, lpszItem) == 0) {
                if (! lpSite->m_lpOleObj) {
                    return ResultFromScode(S_FALSE);
                }
                lpSite->m_lpOleObj->lpVtbl->GetMiscStatus (
                                lpSite->m_lpOleObj,
                                DVASPECT_CONTENT,
                                (LPDWORD)&dwStatus   );
                if (dwStatus & OLEMISC_CANTLINKINSIDE)
                    return ResultFromScode(MK_E_NOOBJECT);
```

```
                if (OleIsRunning(lpSite->m_lpOleObj))
                    return NOERROR;
                else
                    return ResultFromScode(S_FALSE);
            }
        }
    }
    return ResultFromScode(MK_E_NOOBJECT);
}
```

The following version of **IOleItemContainer::IsRunning,** taken from an object application, looks in a table of pseudo-object names for a match for *lpszItem.* If a match is found, NOERROR is returned; otherwise MK_E_NOOBJECT is returned.

```
HRESULT IOleItemContainer_IsRunning(LPDOC lpDoc, LPSTR lpszItem)
{
    LPPSNAME lpPSName;
    LPPSOBJLIST lpPSObjList = (LPPSOBJLIST)((LPDOC)lpDoc)->m_lpPSObjList;

    lpPSName = (LPPSNAME)FindName(lpPSObjList, lpszItem);
    if (lpPSName)
        return NOERROR;
    else
        return ResultFromScode(MK_E_NOOBJECT);
}
```

IOleObject Interface

IOleObject, implemented by object applications and by OLE, contains methods for compound document object management. It is the primary interface by which a linked or embedded object provides functionality to its container.

IOleObject contains the following methods, as defined in OLE2.H:

```
DECLARE_INTERFACE_(IOleObject, IUnknown)
{
  // *** IUnknown methods ***
 HRESULT QueryInterface (THIS_ REFIID riid, LPVOID FAR* ppvObj);
 ULONG AddRef (THIS) ;
 ULONG Release (THIS);

  // *** IOleObject methods ***
 HRESULT SetClientSite (THIS_ LPOLECLIENTSITE pClientSite);
 HRESULT GetClientSite (THIS_ LPOLECLIENTSITE FAR* ppClientSite);
 HRESULT SetHostNames (THIS_ LPCSTR szContainerApp, LPCSTR szContainerObj);
 HRESULT Close (THIS_ DWORD dwSaveOption);
 HRESULT SetMoniker (THIS_ DWORD dwWhichMoniker, LPMONIKER pmk);
 HRESULT GetMoniker (THIS_ DWORD dwAssign, DWORD dwWhichMoniker,
```

```
    LPMONIKER FAR* ppmk);
   HRESULT InitFromData (THIS_ LPDATAOBJECT pDataObject,
    BOOL fCreation, DWORD dwReserved);
   HRESULT GetClipboardData (THIS_ DWORD dwReserved, LPDATAOBJECT FAR* ppDataObject);
   HRESULT DoVerb (THIS_ LONG iVerb, LPMSG lpmsg, LPOLECLIENTSITE pClientSite,
    LONG lindex, HWND hwndParent LPCRECT lprcPosRect);
   HRESULT EnumVerbs (THIS_ LPENUMOLEVERB FAR* ppenumOleVerb);
   HRESULT Update (THIS);
   HRESULT IsUpToDate (THIS);
   HRESULT GetUserClassID (THIS_ CLSID FAR* pclsid);
   HRESULT GetUserType (THIS_ DWORD dwFormOfType, LPSTR FAR* lpszUserType);
   HRESULT SetExtent (THIS_ DWORD dwAspect, LPSIZEL lpsizel);
   HRESULT GetExtent (THIS_ DWORD dwAspect, LPSIZEL lpsizel);
   HRESULT Advise (THIS_ LPADVISESINK pAdvise, DWORD FAR* lpdwConnection);
   HRESULT Unadvise (THIS_ DWORD dwConnection);
   HRESULT EnumAdvise (THIS_ LPENUMSTATDATA FAR* ppenumStatData);
   HRESULT GetMiscStatus (THIS_ DWORD dwAspect, DWORD FAR* pdwStatus);
   HRESULT SetColorScheme (THIS_ LPLOGPALETTE lpLogpal);
};
```

IOleObject::SetClientSite

HRESULT IOleObject::SetClientSite(*pClientSite*)
LPOLECLIENTSITE *pClientSite*

IOleObject::SetClientSite informs a newly created or loaded embedded object of its client site within the container.

Parameters

pClientSite
Points to the object's client-site interface.

Return Values

Value	Meaning
S_OK	Client site successfully set.
E_UNEXPECTED	Object is not embedded in a container.

Comments

Each embedded object has an associated client site through which the object communicates with its container. **IOleObject::SetClientSite** must be called whenever an embedded object is created or loaded.

Example

The following code sample first checks that the target of the call is an embedded object. Next, if the object already has a non-NULL client site pointer, the pointer is released before a new one is set. To enable the object to hold on to the new client site pointer, **AddRef** is called to increment the reference count.

```
HRESULT IOleObject_SetClientSite
    (LPOLEOBJECT pThis, LOLECLIENTSITE pClientSite)
{
    LPDOC lpDoc = ((struct CDocOleObjectImpl FAR*)lpThis)->lpDoc;
    if (lpDoc->m_docInitType != DOCTYPE_EMBEDDED)
        return ResultFromScode(E_UNEXPECTED);

    if (lpDoc->m_lpClientSite)
        lpDoc->m_lpClientSite->lpVtbl->Release(lpDoc->m_lpClientSite);

    lpDoc->m_lpClientSite = (LPOLECLIENTSITE) pClientSite;
    if (pClientSite)
        pClientSite->lpVtbl->AddRef(pClientSite);

    return ResultFromScode(S_OK);
}
```

IOleObject::GetClientSite

HRESULT IOleObject::GetClientSite(*ppClientSite***)**
LPOLECLIENTSITE FAR* *ppClientSite*

IOleObject::GetClientSite queries an object for the pointer to its current client site within its container.

Parameters

ppClientSite
Points to the location at which to return the client site.

Return Values

Value	Meaning
S_OK	Client site pointer returned successfully.

Comments

The returned client site pointer will be NULL if the embedded object's client site has not yet been initialized.

Example

The implementation of **IOleObject_GetClientSite** shown below increments the reference count on the client site before returning a pointer to it.

```
HRESULT IOleObject_GetClientSite(
        LPOLEOBJECT             lpThis,
        LPOLECLIENTSITE FAR*    ppClientSite)
{
    LPDOC lpDoc = ((struct CDocOleObjectImpl FAR*)lpThis)->lpDoc;
    if (lpDoc->m_lpClientSite != NULL)  {
        lpDoc->m_lpClientSite->lpVtbl->AddRef
                (lpDoc->m_lpClientSite);
        *ppClientSite = lpDoc->m_lpClientSite;
```

```
    return NOERROR;
}
```

IOleObject::SetHostNames

HRESULT IOleObject::SetHostNames(*lpszContainerApp*, *lpszContainerObj*)
LPCSTR *lpszContainerApp*
LPCSTR *lpszContainerObj*

IOleObject::SetHostNames specifies window title information to be used when an object is open for editing.

Parameters

lpszContainerApp
Points to the user-presentable name of the container application.

lpszContainerObj
Points to the name of the container document that contains this object. Can be NULL.

Return Values

Value	Meaning
S_OK	Window title information set successfully.

Comments

Since these identifying strings are not stored as part of the persistent state of the object, **IOleObject::SetHostNames** must be called each time the object is loaded or run.

Example

The example of **IOleObject::SetHostNames** first copies *lpszContainerObj* to the document object's local structure. The OLE 2 user model conventions do not require the use of *lpszContainerApp*. The second half of the window title is constructed and then concatenated to the end of *lpszContainerApp* to form the complete window title. The complete window title for an embedded object in an SDI container application or a MDI application with a maximized child should appear as follows:

<object app name> - *<object short type>* in *<container document>*

Otherwise, the title should be:

<object app name> - *<container document>*

UpdateMenu is then called to make the following changes to the File menu:

- Remove File/New and File/Open (SDI ONLY)
- Change File/Save As.. to File/Save Copy As..

- Change File menu so it contains "Update" instead of "Save"
- Change File/Exit to File/Exit & Return to <*container document*>"

```
HRESULT IOleObject_SetHostNames(
        LPOLEOBJECT             lpThis,
        LPCSTR                  szContainerApp,
        LPCSTR                  szContainerObj)
{
    LPDOC lpDoc = ((struct CDocOleObjectImpl FAR*)lpThis)->lpDoc;

    lstrcpyn((LPSTR)lpDoc->m_szContainerApp, szContainerApp,
        sizeof(lpDoc->m_szContainerApp);
    lstrcpyn((LPSTR)lpDoc->m_szContainerObj, szContainerObj,
        sizeof(lpDoc->m_szContainerObj);

    wsprintf(lpDoc->m_szFileName, "%s in %s",
            (LPSTR)SHORTUSERTYPENAME, (LPSTR)lpDoc->m_szContainerObj);

    lpDoc->m_lpszDocTitle = lpDoc->m_szFileName;
    SetTitle(lpDoc);
    UpdateMenu(lpDoc);
    return NOERROR;
}
```

See Also **IOleObject::GetUserType**

IOleObject::Close

HRESULT IOleObject::Close(*dwSaveOption***)**
DWORD *dwSaveOption*

IOleObject::Close transitions an embedded object back to the loaded state, shutting down the object application.

Parameters

dwSaveOption
Determines if the object is saved as part of the transition to the loaded state. Valid values are taken from the enumeration **OLECLOSE**:

```
typedef enum tagOLECLOSE
{
    OLECLOSE_SAVEIFDIRTY = 0,
    OLECLOSE_NOSAVE      = 1,
    OLECLOSE_PROMPTSAVE  = 2
} OLECLOSE;
```

OLECLOSE_SAVEIFDIRTY indicates that the object is always to be saved if it is dirty.

OLECLOSE_NOSAVE indicates that a save is not to occur whether the object is dirty or not.

OLECLOSE_PROMPTSAVE indicates that the user should determine whether the save should occur by being prompted with a message.

Note The OLE 2 user model dictates that embedded objects always be saved when closed *without* any prompting to the user. This is the recommendation regardless of whether the object is activated in place or open in its own window. This is a change from the OLE 1 user model in which object applications always prompt to save changes.

Return Values

Value	Meaning
S_OK	Object closed successfully.
OLE_E_PROMPTSAVECAN CELLED	The user was prompted to save but chose the Cancel button from the prompt message box.

Comments

IOleObject::Close is called by the object's embedding container. This is one way that an object may be closed; the release of the object's last remaining interface pointer is another way. Calling **IOleObject::Close** when the object is not running has no effect.

If **IOleObject::Close** is called on an open embedded object and there are no other visible documents, the application window should be hidden. If there are no other document/objects running, the application should also shut down. However, if there are other invisible documents/objects being used programmatically, such as in the silent update scenario, the application must only hide, postponing a shut down until the other documents are released by their clients.

The following pseudo code shows the recommended way of handling *dwSaveOption*:

```
switch (dwSaveOption)  {
    case OLECLOSE_SAVEIFDIRTY:
        If dirty, save. Then close.

    case OLECLOSE_NOSAVE:
        Close

    case OLECLOSE_PROMPTSAVE:
        If object visible, but not in-place active:
            If not dirty, close.
            Otherwise, switch(prompt)   {
                case IDYES:
                    Save and close
```

```
            case IDNO:
                Close
            case IDCANCEL:
                return OLE_E_PROMPTSAVECANCELLED

    If object invisible (includes UI deactivated object)
        If dirty, save and close
        NOTE: No prompt - not appropriate to prompt if object
              is not visible.

    If object is in-place active:
        If dirty, save and close
        NOTE: No prompt - not appropriate to prompt if object
              is active in-place.
```

Example

The following implementation of **IOleObject::Close** is for an SDI object application that supports in-place activation, drag and drop, and linking to pseudo objects. IOleObject_Close starts by checking for the following conditions and returns if either of them are true:

- the document is already closed
- the document is in the process of closing.

The value of *dwSaveOption* is examined in DoSaveIfRequired. If dwSaveOption is set to OLECLOSE_PROMPTSAVE, the user is prompted for a decision on saving. A save occurs to a dirty object without prompting if *dwSaveOption* is OLECLOSE_SAVEIFDIRTY. If *dwSaveOption* is OLECLOSE_NOSAVE, no save occurs. **IOleObject::Close** calls **IOleClientSite::SaveObject** to ask the container to save the object if appropriate.

After the optional save has finished, if the object is currently in-place active, it is deactivated. **OleFlushClipboard**is called if the object is the source for clipboard data. **OleFlushClipboard** flushes the clipboard, leaving all hGlobal-based data directly on the clipboard. If the object is registered in the running object table, its registration is revoked.

Next the container document hidden and **CoLockObjectExternal** is called to release the external lock made when the document was made visible. Since the application is being shut down (*fShutdown* is TRUE), OLE is instructed to release its reference count on the document if there are no more strong locks.

All pseudo objects or other compound document objects that exist within the documented are closed (CloseAllPseudoObjs and CloseAllOleObjs).

If there are outstanding data advise connections established with the ADVF_DATAONSTOP flag, data change notifications are sent (**IAdviseSink::OnDataChange**) to these connections and the **IDataAdviseHolder** interface pointer is released.

If there are outstanding OLE advise connections, **IAdviseSink::OnClose** is called to notify these registered sinks and the **IOleAdviseHolder** interface pointer is released.

The last steps involve releasing pointers to the client site in the container, calling **CoDisconnectObject** to forcibly disconnect any remoting clients, and decrementing the reference count on both the document and the application level objects. Calling **CoDisconnectObject** breaks any remaining strong locks, guaranteeing that the object will get its final releases to make the reference count decrement to zero.

```
HRESULT IOleObject_Close (LPOLEOBJECT lpThis, DWORD   dwSaveOption)
{
    LPDOC    lpDoc = ((struct CDocOleObjectImpl FAR*)lpThis)->lpDoc;
    BOOL     fStatus;
    LPAPP    lpApp = (LPAPP)g_lpApp;
    LPDOC    lpClipboardDoc;
    LPLIST   lpList = (LPLIST)&((LPDOC)lpDoc)->m_List;
    LPRUNNINGOBJECTTABLE prot;
    HRESULT hrErr;

    if (! lpDoc)         return NOERROR;

    if (lpDoc->m_fObjIsClosing)          return NOERROR;

    if (! DoSaveIfRequired((LPDOC)lpDoc, dwSaveOption))
        return ResultFromScode(E_FAIL);

    lpDoc->m_fObjIsClosing = TRUE;   // guard against recursive call
    IUnknown_App_AddRef(lpApp);
    IUnknown_Doc_AddRef(lpDoc);

    DoInPlaceDeactivate((LPDOC)lpDoc);
    lpClipboardDoc = (LPDOC)lpApp->m_lpClipboardDoc;
    if (lpClipboardDoc &&   lpClipboardDoc->m_lpSrcDocOfCopy == lpDoc)
        FlushClipboard(lpApp);

    if (*lpDoc->m_dwRegROT != NULL) {
        hrErr = GetRunningObjectTable(0,(LPRUNNINGOBJECTTABLE FAR*)&prot);
        if (hrErr == NOERROR) {
            prot->lpVtbl->Revoke(prot, *lpdwRegister);
            *lpDoc->m_dwRegROT = NULL;
            prot->lpVtbl->Release(prot);
        }
    }

    if (IsWindowVisible(lpDoc->m_hWndDoc))   {
        CoLockObjectExternal((LPUNKNOWN)&lpDoc->m_Unknown, FALSE, TRUE);
        ShowWindow(((LPDOC)lpDoc)->m_hWndDoc, SW_HIDE);
    }
```

```
    if (lpDoc->m_lpClientSite && !lpDoc->m_fInPlaceVisible) {
        lpDoc->m_lpClientSite->lpVtbl->OnShowWindow(
            lpDoc->m_lpClientSite,
            FALSE);
    }

    CloseAllPseudoObjs(lpDoc);
    CloseAllOleObjs(lpDoc);

    if (lpDoc->m_fSendDataOnStop && lpDoc->m_lpDataAdviseHldr) {
        lpDoc->m_lpDataAdviseHldr->lpVtbl->SendOnDataChange(
                    lpDoc->m_lpDataAdviseHldr,
                    (LPDATAOBJECT)&lpDoc->m_DataObject,
                    0,
                    ADVF_DATAONSTOP);
        lpDoc->m_lpDataAdviseHldr->lpVtbl->Release
                        (lpDoc->m_lpDataAdviseHldr);
        lpDoc->m_lpDataAdviseHldr = NULL;
    }

    if (lpDoc->m_lpOleAdviseHldr) {
        lpDoc->m_lpOleAdviseHldr->lpVtbl->SendOnClose(
                    lpDoc->m_lpOleAdviseHldr);
        lpDoc->m_lpOleAdviseHldr->lpVtbl->Release
            (lpDoc->m_lpOleAdviseHldr);
        lpDoc->m_lpOleAdviseHldr = NULL;
    }

    if(lpDoc->m_lpClientSite) {
        lpDoc->m_lpClientSite->lpVtbl->Release
            (lpDoc->m_lpClientSite);
        lpDoc->m_lpClientSite = NULL;
    }

    CoDisconnectObject((LPUNKNOWN)&lpDoc->m_Unknown, TRUE);
    IUnknown_Doc_Release(lpDoc);
    IUnknown_App_Release(lpApp);
    return NOERROR;
}
```

IOleObject::SetMoniker

HRESULT IOleObject::SetMoniker(*dwWhichMoniker, pmk*)
DWORD *dwWhichMoniker*
LPMONIKER *pmk*

IOleObject::SetMoniker notifies the object of either its own moniker or its container's moniker, depending on the value for *dwWhichMoniker*.

Parameters

dwWhichMoniker
Specifies which moniker is passed in *pmk*.

pmk
Points to where to return the moniker.

Return Values

Value	Meaning
S_OK	Moniker successfully set.
E_FAIL	No client site for object.

Comments

IOleObject::SetMoniker is usually called only by the object's container, since the container is responsible for maintaining the object's identity.

If *dwWhichMoniker* is set to **OLEWHICHMK_OBJREL**, the moniker passed in *pmk* is the moniker of the object in the container's document. That is, if this moniker is composed onto the moniker of the object's container and the resulting moniker is bound, then the object itself will be connected to.

If *dwWhichMoniker* is **OLEWHICHMK_CONTAINER**, then the object is being notified that the name of its container has changed. If the object has registered itself as running and either of these monikers changes, then the object will need to change the name under which it is registered. Also, any of the object's presently loaded subobjects may need to be informed that the name of *their* container has changed. Refer to the description of **IRunningObjectTable::Register** for more information.

The moniker of an object relative to its container is stored by the object handler as part of the object's persistent state. The moniker of the object's container must not be persistently stored inside the object, because the container can be renamed at any time.

Example

The following implementation of **IOleObject::SetMoniker** first checks that the document object has a valid client site pointer and if it doesn't, **SetMoniker** fails. Next, a call is made to **IOleClientSite::GetMoniker** to get the full, absolute moniker from the container. The document is registered as running with the full moniker in the running object table and an OnRename notification is sent with a call to **IAdviseSink::OnRename**.

```
/* if the passed moniker was NOT a full moniker then we must call
```

```
    **    back to our ClientSite to get our full moniker. this is
    **    needed in order to register in the RunningObjectTable. if we
    **    don't have a ClientSite then this is an error.
    */
DOCTYPE_EMBEDDED -              /* OLE2NOTE: if this is a FILE-based or
untitled document
            **    then we should accept this new moniker as our
document's
            **    moniker. we will remember this moniker instead of the
            **    FileMoniker that we have by default. this allows
            **    systems that use special monikers to track the
            **    location of documents to inform a document that is a
            **    link source of its special moniker. this enables the
            **    document to use this special moniker when building
            **    composite monikers to identify contained objects and
            **    pseudo objects (ranges).
not full moniker:

    /* if the passed moniker was NOT a full moniker then we must call
    **    back to our ClientSite to get our full moniker. this is
    **    needed in order to register in the RunningObjectTable. if we
    **    don't have a ClientSite then this is an error.
    */


            */
after GetRunningObjectTable call:
        /* register as running if a valid moniker is passed
        **
        ** OLE2NOTE: we deliberately register the new moniker BEFORE
        **    revoking the old moniker just in case the object
        **    currently has no external locks. if the object has no
        **    locks then revoking it from the running object table will
        **    cause the object's StubManager to initiate shutdown of
        **    the object.
        */


HRESULT IOleObject_SetMoniker(
        LPOLEOBJECT             lpThis,
        DWORD                   dwWhichMoniker,
        LPMONIKER               pmk)
{
    LPRUNNINGOBJECTTABLE prot;
    LPDOC lpDoc = ((struct CDocOleObjectImpl FAR*)lpThis)->lpDoc;
    LPMONIKER    pmkFull = NULL;
    HRESULT      hrErr;

    if (lpDoc->m_lpClientSite == NULL)
        return ResultFromScode(E_FAIL);
```

```
if (dwWhichMoniker == OLEWHICHMK_OBJFULL) {
    IUnknown_Doc_AddRef(lpDoc);
    hrErr = GetRunningObjectTable
        (0,(LPRUNNINGOBJECTTABLE FAR*)&prot);
    if (hrErr == NOERROR) {
        if (pmk) {
            prot->lpVtbl->Register (prot, 0, lpDoc->m_Unknown,
                pmk,&lpDoc->m_dwRegROT);
            if (lpDoc->m_dwRegROT != 0)
                prot->lpVtbl->Revoke(prot, dwOldRegister);
            (LPUNKNOWN)prot->lpVtbl->Release((LPUNKNOWN)prot);
        }
    }
    // Send OnRename notification to linking clients
    if (pmk && lpDoc->m_lpOleAdviseHldr) {
        lpDoc->m_lpOleAdviseHldr->lpVtbl->SendOnRename(
                    lpDoc->m_lpOleAdviseHldr, pmk);
    }

    // Send OnRename notification to all pseudo objects
    PseudoObjectsSendOnRename(
        (LPNAMETABLE)lpDoc->m_lpNameTable, pmk);
    IUnknown_Doc_Release(lpDoc);

    // if file-based, use new moniker instead of our file moniker
    if (lpDoc->m_docInitType != DOCTYPE_EMBEDDED) {
        if (lpDoc->m_lpFileMoniker) {
            lpDoc->m_lpFileMoniker->lpVtbl->Release(
                    lpDoc->m_lpFileMoniker);
        }
        lpDoc->m_lpFileMoniker = pmk;
        pmkFull->lpVtbl->AddRef(pmk);
    }
    return NOERROR;
}

// not OLEWHICHMK_FULL
if (lpDoc->m_lpClientSite == NULL)
    return ResultFromScode(E_FAIL);

hrErr = lpDoc->m_lpClientSite->lpVtbl->GetMoniker(
        lpDoc->m_lpClientSite,
        OLEGETMONIKER_ONLYIFTHERE,
        OLEWHICHMK_OBJFULL,
        &pmkFull
);
if (hrErr != NOERROR)
    return hrErr;

IUnknown_Doc_AddRef(lpDoc);
```

```
    hrErr = GetRunningObjectTable
            (0,(LPRUNNINGOBJECTTABLE FAR*)&prot);

    if (hrErr == NOERROR) {
        if (pmkFull) {
            prot->lpVtbl->Register (prot, 0, lpDoc->m_Unknown,
                pmkFull,&lpDoc->m_dwRegROT);
            if (lpDoc->m_dwRegROT != 0)
                prot->lpVtbl->Revoke(prot, dwOldRegister);
            (LPUNKNOWN)prot->lpVtbl->Release((LPUNKNOWN)prot);
        }
    }
    if (pmkFull && lpDoc->m_lpOleAdviseHldr) {
        lpDoc->m_lpOleAdviseHldr->lpVtbl->SendOnRename(
                    lpDoc->m_lpOleAdviseHldr, pmkFull);
    }

    // Send OnRename notification to all pseudo objects
    PseudoObjectsSendOnRename(
            (LPNAMETABLE)lpDoc->m_lpNameTable, pmkFull);
    IUnknown_Doc_Release(lpDoc);

    if (pmkFull)
        (LPUNKNOWN)pmkFull->lpVtbl->Release((LPUNKNOWN)pmkFull);

    return NOERROR;
}
```

See Also **IAdviseSink::OnRename, IRunningObjectTable::Register**

IOleObject::GetMoniker

HRESULT IOleObject::GetMoniker(*dwAssign*, *dwWhichMoniker*, *ppmk***)**
DWORD *dwAssign*
DWORD *dwWhichMoniker*
LPMONIKER FAR**ppmk*

IOleObject::GetMoniker returns a moniker that can be used to connect to the object.

Parameters

dwAssign
Determines how the moniker is assigned to the object. Depending on the value of *dwAssign*, **IOleObject::GetMoniker** returns either an assigned or unassigned moniker. The valid values for *dwAssign* are taken from the enumeration **OLEGETMONIKER**, with the exception of **OLEGETMONIKER_UNASSIGN**:

```
typedef enum tagOLEGETMONIKER
{
    OLEGETMONIKER_ONLYIFTHERE = 1,
    OLEGETMONIKER_FORCEASSIGN = 2,
    OLEGETMONIKER_UNASSIGN    = 3,
    OLEGETMONIKER_TEMPFORUSER = 4
} OLEGETMONIKER;
```

OLEGETMONIKER_ONLYIFTHERE returns a moniker only if one has already been assigned to the object.

In the event that the object does not already have a moniker, **OLEGETMONIKER_FORCEASSIGN** forces moniker assignment.

OLEGETMONIKER_TEMPFORUSER returns a temporary, unassigned moniker.

dwWhichMoniker
Specifies the form of the moniker being requested; valid values are taken from the enumeration **OLEWHICHMK**:

```
typedef enum tagOLEWHICHMK
{
    OLEWHICHMK_CONTAINER = 1,
    OLEWHICHMK_OBJREL    = 2,
    OLEWHICHMK_OBJFULL   = 3
} OLEWHICHMK;
```

OLEWHICHMK_CONTAINER is the moniker of the object's container.

OLEWHICHMK_OBJREL is the moniker of the object relative to the container.

OLEWHICHMK_OBJFULL is the composition of the first two values.

ppmk
Place at which to return the object's moniker.

Return Values

Value	Meaning
S_OK	Requested moniker returned successfully.
E_FAIL	Object cannot return a moniker.
MK_E_SYNTAX	Syntax error in **CreateFileMoniker**.
E_OUTOFMEMORY	**CreateFileMoniker** failed due to lack of memory.

Comments

It is not legal to pass **OLEGETMONIKER_UNASSIGN** to **IOleObject::GetMoniker**; see **IOleClientSite::GetMoniker** for information on when to use **OLEGETMONIKER_UNASSIGN**.

Example

The following implementation of **IOleObject::GetMoniker** retrieves the moniker from the container if the current document is an embedded object or calls **CreateFileMoniker** to generate a file moniker if the document is file-based. If the document is new or not yet fully initialized, a moniker is not available and E_FAIL is returned.

```
HRESULT IOleObject_GetMoniker(
        LPOLEOBJECT             lpThis,
        DWORD                   dwAssign,
        DWORD                   dwWhichMoniker,
        LPMONIKER FAR*          ppmk)
{
    LPDOC       lpDoc = ((struct CDocOleObjectImpl FAR*)lpThis)->lpDoc;
    HRESULT     hrErr;
    SCODE       sc;

    *ppmk = NULL;

    // Doc is an embedded object; retrieve moniker from container
    if (lpDoc->m_lpClientSite) {
        sc = GetScode( lpDoc->m_lpClientSite->lpVtbl->GetMoniker(
                lpDoc->m_lpClientSite,
                dwAssign,
                dwWhichMoniker,
                ppmk) );

    // Doc is user document; return file moniker stored with doc
    } else if (lpDoc->m_lpFileMoniker) {
        if (dwWhichMoniker == OLEWHICHMK_CONTAINER)
            sc = E_INVALIDARG;  // no CONTAINER moniker
        else {
            *ppmk = lpDoc->m_lpFileMoniker;
            (*ppmk)->lpVtbl->AddRef(*ppmk);
            sc = S_OK;
        }

        // Doc is not yet fully initialized => no moniker
    } else
        sc = E_FAIL;

    return ResultFromScode(sc);
}
```

See Also

IOleClientSite::GetMoniker

IOleObject::InitFromData

HRESULT IOleObject::InitFromData(*pDataObject, fCreation, dwReserved*)
LPDATAOBJECT *pDataObject*
BOOL *fCreation*
DWORD *dwReserved*

IOleObject::InitFromData initializes the contents of an object with data available from *pDataObject*.

Parameters

pDataObject
Points to the data transfer object from which the initialization data is obtained; can be NULL, indicating that the caller wants to know if it is worthwhile trying to send data.

fCreation
TRUE indicates the initial creation of the object; FALSE indicates a more general programmatic data transfer.

dwReserved
Reserved for future use; must be zero.

Return Values

Value	Meaning
S_OK	Object successfully attempted to initialize if *pDataObject* is not NULL; object can attempt a successful initialization if *pDataObject* is NULL.
S_FALSE	Object made no attempt to initialize if *pDataObject* is not NULL; object can not attempt to initialize if *pDataObject* is NULL.
E_NOTIMPL	Object does not support **InitFromData**.
OLE_E_NOTRUNNING	Object must be running to perform the operation.

Comments

It is the container's responsibility to decide if it is desirable to have a new object based on the current selection. The object returns S_OK if an attempt at initialization is made. The container should call **IOleObject::GetMiscStatus** to check the value of the **OLEMISC_INSERTNOTREPLACE** bit. If the bit is on, the new object is inserted after the selected data. If the bit is off, the new object replaces the selected data.

The object returns S_FALSE if it can never initialize itself from caller-provided data or cannot initialize itself with the data provided in this case. No return value is specified to indicate whether or not the call to **IOleObject::InitFromData** really did anything; the subsequent *pDataObject* method calls to actually transfer the data will serve this purpose.

If *fCreation* is TRUE, the object is being initialized with data from its container as part of the creation sequence. The *pDataObject* provided by the container has the same contents as it would have for a copy operation. That is, if the container were to call **OleSetClipboard** rather than **IOleObject::InitFromData**, the contents of *pDataObject* would be identical.

If *fCreation* is FALSE, the caller is attempting to do a more general programmatic paste operation. The object should replace its current contents with the data pointed to by *pDataObject*, just as it would for a Paste operation. The normal constraints that an object applies when pasting should be applied here. For example, if the shape of the data provided is unacceptable, the object should fail to initialize and return S_FALSE.

See Also

IOleObject::GetMiscStatus, IDataObject::SetData

IOleObject::GetClipboardData

HRESULT IOleObject::GetClipboardData(*dwReserved, ppDataObject*)
DWORD *dwReserved*
LPDATAOBJECT FAR **ppDataObject*

IOleObject::GetClipboardData returns a data transfer object that contains exactly what would have been passed to **OleSetClipboard** in a copy operation.

Parameters

dwReserved
Reserved for future use; must be zero.

ppDataObject
Points to the location where the data transfer object is to be returned.

Return Values

Value	Meaning
S_OK	Data transfer object successfully returned.
E_NOTIMPL	**GetClipboardData** not supported.
OLE_E_NOTRUNNING	Object is not running.

Comments

The difference between the *pDataObject* returned from **IOleObject::GetClipboardData** and **IOleObject::QueryInterface** (*IID_IDataObject,...*) is that the former data transfer object is a snapshot copy; it does not change as the object changes. The data object retrieved through the **QueryInterface** call may change as the object changes.

See Also

IOleObject::InitFromData

IOleObject::DoVerb

HRESULT IOleObject::DoVerb(*iVerb, lpmsg, pClientSite, lindex , hwndParent, lprcPosRect***)**
LONG *iVerb*
LPMSG *lpmsg*
LPOLECLIENTSITE *pClientSite*
LONG *lindex*
HWND *hwndParent*
LPCRECT *lprcPosRect*

IOleObject::DoVerb requests an object to perform one of its verbs.

Parameters

iVerb
The number assigned to the verb specifying the action to take.

lpmsg
Points to the message that caused the verb to be invoked.

pClientSite
Points to the client site of the embedding or linking container in which the verb was invoked.

lindex
Reserved for future use; should always be zero.

hwndParent
Handle of the document window containing the object.

lprcPosRect
Points to the rectangle containing the coordinates of the bounding rectangle in which the destination document displays the object. This position is in container window pixel coordinates with respect to *hwndParent*.

Return Values

Value	Meaning
S_OK	Object successfully invoked specified verb.
OLE_E_NOT_INPLACEACTIVE	*iVerb* set to OLEIVERB_UIACTIVATE or OLEIVERB_INPLACEACTIVATE and object is not currently open.
OLE_E_CANTBINDTOSOURCE	The object handler or link object cannot connect to the link source.
DV_E_LINDEX	Invalid *lindex*.
OLEOBJ_S_CANNOT_DOVERB_NOW	The verb is valid, but object cannot do it now.
OLEOBJ_S_INVALIDHWND	DOVERB was successful but *hwnd* is invalid.
OLEOBJ_E_NOVERBS	The object does not support any verbs.

Value	Meaning
OLEOBJ_S_INVALIDVERB	Object does not recognize a positive verb number. Verb is treated as OLEIVERB_PRIMARY.
MK_CONNECTMANUALLY	Link source is across a network that is not connected to a drive on this machine.
OLE_E_CLASSDIFF	Class for source of link has undergone a conversion.
E_NOTIMPL	Object does not support in-place activation or object does not recognize a negative verb number.

Comments

Verbs are available on an object while it is selected in its container. **DoVerb** can be invoked from either an object's container or one of its currently-connected link clients.

A container can determine the set of verbs available to an object by calling **IOleObject::EnumVerbs**. **EnumVerbs** returns an **OLEVERB** structure; **DoVerb** matches the value of *iVerb* against the *iVerb* member of the structure to determine which the verb to perform.

Except for a set of verbs predefined by OLE, the meaning of a particular verb is determined by the object's application. The following table describes the predefined verbs:

Verb	Description
OLEIVERB_PRIMARY (0L)	Verb that is invoked when the user double-clicks the object in its container. Object defines the semantics of the verb. If the object supports in-place activation, the primary verb usually activates the object in-place.
OLEIVERB_SHOW (-1L)	Indicates that the object is to be shown to the user for editing or viewing. Used to show a newly-inserted object to the user for initial editing.
OLEIVERB_OPEN (-2L)	Causes the object to be open edited in a separate window. If the object does not support open editing, this verb has the same semantics as OLEIVERB_SHOW.
OLEIVERB_HIDE (-3L)	Causes the object to remove its user interface from the user's view.
OLEIVERB_UIACTIVATE (-4L)	Used to activate the object in-place and show any user interface tools that it needs, such as menus or toolbars. If the object does not support in-place activation, it should return E_NOTIMPL.

Verb	Description
OLEIVERB_INPLACEACTIVATE	Used to run the object and install its window, but not attempt to install user interface tools. In this state an inside-out style of object can take focus and then negotiate for menus and other tools. An outside-in style object returns E_NOTIMPL.
OLEIVERB_DISCARDUNDOSTATE	Used to tell objects to discard any undo state that they may be maintaining without deactivating the object.

Any *positive* verb number that is not understood by the object should be treated as synonymous with the primary verb and OLE_S_INVALIDVERB returned. Negative verbs that are not understood should be ignored and E_NOTIMPL returned.

If the verb was invoked by some means other than a menu selection, the caller passes the Windows message that caused the verb to be invoked through *lpmsg*. On a double-click, a MSG structure containing WM_LBUTTONDBLCLK, WM_MBUTTONDBLCLK, or WM_RBUTTONDBLCLK should be passed. If there is no message, *lpmsg* should be NULL. The object should not examine the *hwnd* member of the passed MSG structure. All of the other MSG members, however, can be used.

Like the **OleActivate** function in OLE 1, **IOleObject::DoVerb** automatically runs the object's server. If an error occurs during verb execution, the server is shut down.

There are two cases when **DoVerb** is called:

- the embedding container makes the call
- a link delegates its **DoVerb** call

In the first case, the client site pointer passed to **DoVerb** is the same as the embedding site, the pointer passed with **IOleObject::SetClientSite**. In the second case, the passed client site is not the same as the embedding site.

When **IOleObject::DoVerb** is invoked on an OLE link, it may return OLE_E_CLASSDIFF or MK_CONNECTMANUALLY. The former error is returned when a link has been made to an object that has been subjected to some sort of conversion while the link was passive. The latter error is returned when the link source is located on a network drive that is not currently connected to the caller's machine. The only way to connect a link under these conditions is to first call **QueryInterface**, asking for **IOleLink**, allocate a bind context, and run the link source by calling **IOleLink::BindToSource**.

Container applications that do not support in-place activation can still play multimedia players in-place using the *hwndParent* and *lprcPosRect* parameters. Containers must pass valid *hwndParent* and *lprcPosRect* parameters to **IOleObject::DoVerb**.

Example

Typical implementations of **IOleObject::DoVerb** contain a switch statement that tests the valid values for *iVerb*. The table below summarizes the cases covered in the switch statement implemented in the **IOleObject::DoVerb** example that follows. Notice that OLEIVERB_DISCARDUNDOSTATE is not a supported verb; it is treated as invalid.

Value of iVerb	Action Taken
Unknown negative value	Do nothing and return E_NOTIMPL.
Unknown positive value	Treat as primary verb and return OLEOBJ_S_INVALIDVERB.
OLEIVERB_SHOW	If object is already open in a window, make the window visible. If object is not yet open and in-place activation is supported, initiate in-place activation. If object is not yet open and in-place activation is not supported, show object for in a window.
OLEIVERB_OPEN	Start an open editing session and, if necessary, in-place deactivate.
OLEIVERB_HIDE	If the object is active in-place, remove the object's user interface. If the object is active in an open window, hide the window.
OLEIVERB_UIACTIVATE OLEIVERG_INPLACEACTIVATE	If the window is not yet open, start an in-place activation session. If the window is already open, return OLE_E_NOT_INPLACEACTIVE.

```
HRESULT IOleObject_DoVerb(
        LPOLEOBJECT             lpThis,
        LONG                lVerb,
        LPMSG                   lpmsg,
        LPOLECLIENTSITE         lpActiveSite,
        LONG                lindex,
        HWND                hwndParent,
        LPCRECT                 lprcPosRect
)
{
    LPDOC lpDoc = ((struct CDocOleObjectImpl FAR*)lpThis)->lpDoc;
    SCODE sc = S_OK;
    switch (lVerb) {

        default:
            if (lVerb < 0) {
```

```
                return ResultFromScode(E_NOTIMPL);
            } else {
                sc = OLEOBJ_S_INVALIDVERB;
            }

            // deliberately fall through to Primary Verb

        case 0:
        case OLEIVERB_SHOW:
            if ( lpDoc->m_lpClientSite
              && ! (IsWindowVisible(lpDoc->m_hWndDoc)
              && ! lpDoc->m_fInPlaceActive) )
                DoInPlaceActivate(lpDoc, lVerb, lpmsg, lpActiveSite);
            ShowWindow(lpDoc);
            break;

        case 1:
        case OLEIVERB_OPEN:
            DoInPlaceDeactivate(lpDoc);
            ShowWindow(lpDoc);
            break;

        case OLEIVERB_HIDE:
            if (lpDoc->m_fInPlaceActive) {
                lpDoc->m_OleInPlaceObject->lpVtbl->UIDeactivate
                    ((LPOLEINPLACEOBJECT)&lpDoc->m_OleInPlaceObject);
                HideWindow(lpDoc, FALSE /*fShutdown*/);
            }
            break;

        case OLEIVERB_UIACTIVATE:
             OLEIVERB_INPLACEACTIVATE:

            //outside-in style of object
            if (IsWindowVisible(lpDoc->m_hWndDoc) &&
                        ! lpDoc->m_fInPlaceActive ) {
                sc = OLE_E_NOT_INPLACEACTIVE;
            } else {
                    sc = GetScode(DoInPlaceActivate(
                        lpDoc, lVerb, lpmsg, lpActiveSite) );
                    if (SUCCEEDED(sc))
                    ShowWindow(lpDoc);
            }
            break;
    }
    return ResultFromScode(sc);
}
```

See Also **IOleObject::EnumVerbs, OleRun, IOleLink::BindToSource**

IOleObject::EnumVerbs

HRESULT IOleObject::EnumVerbs(*ppenumOleVerb*)
LPENUMOLEVERB FAR * *ppenumOleVerb*

IOleObject::EnumVerbs enumerates the verbs available for an object in increasing order by verb number.

Parameters

ppenumOleVerb
Points to where the new enumerator should be returned.

Return Values

Value	Meaning
S_OK	Verb(s) enumerated successfully.
OLE_S_USEREG	Delegate to the default handler to use the entries in the registration database to provide the enumeration.
OLEOBJ_E_NOVERBS	Object does not support any verbs.

Comments

The default handler's implementation of **IOleObject::EnumVerbs** uses the registration database to enumerate an object's verbs. If an object application wants to use the default handler's implementation, it should return OLE_S_USEREG.

The enumeration returned is of type **IEnumOLEVERB**:

```
typedef Enum < OLEVERB > IEnumOLEVERB;
```

where **OLEVERB** is defined as:

```
typedef struct tagOLEVERB
{
    LONG    iVerb;
    LPSTR   lpszVerbName;
    DWORD   fuFlags;
    DWORD   grfAttribs;
} OLEVERB;
```

The following table describes the members of the **OLEVERB** structure:

OLEVERB Member	Description
iVerb	Verb number being enumerated. If the object supports OLEIVERB_OPEN, OLEIVERB_SHOW and/or OLEIVERB_HIDE (or other predefined verb), these will be the first verbs enumerated, since they have the lowest verb numbers.
lpszVerbName	Name of the verb. On Windows, this value is suitable for passing to **AppendMenu** (may have embedded amperand characters that indicate accelerator keys). On the Macintosh, the following metacharacters may be included: ▪ ! which marks the menu item with the subsequent character ▪ < which sets the character style of the item ▪ (which disables the item. The meta-characters / and ^ are not permitted.
fuFlags	On Windows, a group of flags taken from the flag constants beginning with MF_ defined in **AppendMenu**. Container should use these flags in building the object's verb menu. All flags defined in **AppendMenu** are supported except for: ▪ MF_BITMAP ▪ MF_OWNERDRAW ▪ MF_POPUP
grfAttribs	Group of flag bits taken from the enumeration OLEVERBATTRIB. OLEVERBATTRIB_NEVERDIRTIES indicates that the execution of this verb can never cause the object to become dirty and require saving to persistent storage. OLEVERBATTRIB_ONCONTAINERMENU indicates that this verb should be placed on the container's menu of object verbs when the object is selected. OLEIVERB_HIDE, OLEIVERB_SHOW, and OLEIVERB_OPEN never have this value set.

Note For more information on the Windows **AppendMenu** function, see the Microsoft Windows 3.1 Software Development Kit.

See Also **IOleObject::DoVerb**

IOleObject::Update

HRESULT IOleObject::Update()

IOleObject::Update ensures that any data or view caches maintained within the object are up-to-date.

Return Values

Value	Meaning
S_OK	All caches are up-to-date.
E_FAIL	An unspecified error occurred.
OLE_E_CANT_BINDTOSOURCE	Cannot run object to get updated data.
CACHE_E_NOCACHE_UPDATED	No caches were updated.
CACHE_S_SOMECACHES_NOTUPDATED	Some caches were not updated.

Comments

When applied to an OLE link object, **IOleObject::Update** first finds the link source and gets a new presentation from it. This process may involve running one or more object applications, which could be time consuming.

With an embedded object, **IOleObject::Update** works recursively, calling **IOleObject::Update** on each of its linked and embedded objects and running the object if needed.

See Also

IOleObject::IsUpToDate

IOleObject::IsUpToDate

HRESULT IOleObject::IsUpToDate()

IOleObject::IsUpToDate recursively checks whether or not an object is up-to-date.

Return Values

Value	Meaning
S_OK	Object is up-to-date.
S_FALSE	Object is not up-to-date.
OLE_E_UNAVAILABLE	Status of object cannot be determined in a timely manner.

Comments

A linked object can become out-of-date if the link source has been updated. An embedded object that contains links to other objects can also become out-of-date. In general, determining whether an object is out-of-date can be as expensive as actually updating the object. In these cases, **IOleObject::IsUpToDate** should return OLE_E_UNAVAILABLE rather than do a lengthy query. In those cases where the answer may be learned efficiently, the function can return either S_OK or S_FALSE.

See Also

IOleObject::UpDate

IOleObject::GetUserClassID

HRESULT IOleObject::GetUserClassID(*pclsid***)**
LPCLSID *pclsid*

IOleObject::GetUserClassID returns the class identifier of the object that corresponds to the type returned in **IOleObject::GetUserType**.

Parameters

pclsid
Points to the class identifier (CLSID) to be returned.

Return Values

Value	Meaning
S_OK	CLSID returned successfully.
E_FAIL	An unspecified error occurred.

Comments

GetUserClassID returns the CLSID as the user knows it. For embedded objects, this is always the CLSID that is persistently stored and is returned by **IPersist::GetClassID**. For linked objects, this is the CLSID of the last bound link source. If a Treat As operation is taking place, this is the CLSID of the application being emulated (also the CLSID that will be written into storage).

Example

The example below of **IOleObject::GetUserClassID** sets *pclsid* to a different value depending on whether or not the object is being treated as an object of a different class. If a Treat As operation is in progress, the CLSID written in the storage of the object is returned. Otherwise, **IOleObject::GetUserClassID** returns the CLSID of the application.

```
HRESULT IOleObject_GetUserClassID(LPOLEOBJECT lpThis, LPCLSID pclsid)
{
    LPDOC lpDoc = ((struct CDocOleObjectImpl FAR*)lpThis)->lpDoc;
    if (! IsEqualCLSID(&lpDoc->m_clsidTreatAs, &CLSID_NULL))
        *pclsid = lpDoc->m_clsidTreatAs;
    else
        *pclsid = CLSID_APP;
```

```
    return ResultFromScode(S_OK);
}
```

See Also **IOleObject::GetUserType, IPersist::GetClassID**

IOleObject::GetUserType

HRESULT IOleObject::GetUserType(*dwFormOfType, lpszUserType***)**
DWORD *dwFormOfType*
LPSTR FAR* *lpszUserType*

IOleObject::GetUserType determines the user-presentable identification (human-readable) string for an object's type, such as "Word Document." The information returned is the same as for **IOleObject::GetUserClassID**; **GetUserClassID** returns the information in binary form while **GetUserType** returns it in printable form.

Parameters

dwFormOfType
A value that describes the form of the user-presentable string. Valid values are obtained from the **USERCLASSTYPE** enumeration:

```
typedef enum tagUSERCLASSTYPE {
    USERCLASSTYPE_FULL = 1,
    USERCLASSTYPE_SHORT = 2,
    USERCLASSTYPE_APPNAME = 3
} USERCLASSTYPE;
```

USERCLASSTYPE_FULL is the full type name of the class.

USERCLASSTYPE_SHORT is a short name (maximum of 15 characters) that is used for popup menus and the Links dialog box.

USERCLASSTYPE_APPNAME is the name of the application servicing the class and is used in the Result text in dialogs.

lpszUserType
Points to the place where the address of type string will be placed. The caller must free *lpszUserType* using the current **IMalloc** instance.

Return Values

Value	Meaning
S_OK	User type successfully returned.
OLE_S_USEREG	Delegate to the default handler's implementation using the registration database to provide the requested information.

Comments

The default handler's implementation of **IOleObject::GetUserType** uses the object's class identifier (*pclsid* returned by **IOleObject::GetUserClassID**) and *dwFormOfType* as a key into the registration database. If an entry is found which matches the whole key, then the entry is returned. If only the CLSID part of the key is found, the lowest-numbered entry available (usually USERCLASSTYPE_FULL) is used. If the CLSID is not found, or there are no user types registered for the class, the user type currently found in the object's storage is used.

An object application can delegate to the default handler by returning OLE_S_USEREG. If the user type name is an empty string, "Unknown Object" is returned.

Example

The following implementation of **IOleObject::GetUserType** calls the OLE helper function **OleRegGetUserType** to return the appropriate user type. If a the object is being treated as an object of a different class, the user type for the class stored in *lpDoc->m_clsidTreatAs* is returned. Otherwise, **OleRegGetUserType** returns the application's CLSID.

```
HRESULT IOleObject_GetUserType(
        LPOLEOBJECT             lpThis,
        DWORD                   dwFormOfType,
        LPSTR FAR*              lpszUserType
)
{
    LPDOC lpDoc = ((struct CDocOleObjectImpl FAR*)lpThis)->lpDoc;
    *lpszUserType = NULL;

    if ( (TreatAs) &&
         (! IsEqualCLSID  (&lpDoc->m_clsidTreatAs, &CLSID_NULL)) )
    return OleRegGetUserType ((REFCLSID)&lpDoc->m_clsidTreatAs,
            dwFormOfType, lpszUserType);
    else
        return OleRegGetUserType ((REFCLSID)&CLSID_APP, dwFormOfType,
            lpszUserType);
}
```

See Also

IOleObject::SetHostNames, IOleObject::GetUserClassID, ReadFmtUserTypeStg

IOleObject::SetExtent

HRESULT IOleObject::SetExtent(*dwAspect, lpsizel)*
DWORD *dwAspect*
LPSIZEL *lpsizel*

IOleObject::SetExtent sets the rectangular limits (logical size) that an object has available in the container.

Parameters

dwAspect
Describes the aspect of the object whose limit is to be set; the value is obtained from the enumeration **DVASPECT** (see "FORMATETC Data Structure"). Different aspects of the object may have different extents. The most common value is DVASPECT_CONTENT.

lpsizel
Specifies the size limit for the object.

Return Values

Value	Meaning
S_OK	Object has resized successfully.
E_FAIL	Object's size is fixed.
OLE_E_NOTRUNNING	Object is not running.

Comments

Containers call **IOleObject::SetExtent** to inform objects how much space is available to them. If possible, the object should compose itself accordingly. The units device are in HIMETRIC.

SetExtent may only be called when the object is running. Therefore, if a container resizes while the object is not running, the container must remember to inform the object by calling **SetExtent** at a later time when the object is running. If the OLEMISC_RECOMPOSEONRESIZE bit is set, the container should force the object to run before calling **SetExtent**.

If the object's size is fixed (that is, cannot be set by its container), **SetExtent** should return E_FAIL.

See Also

IOleObject::GetExtent, IViewObject2::GetExtent

IOleObject::GetExtent

HRESULT IOleObject::GetExtent(*dwAspect, lpsizel***)**
DWORD *dwAspect*
LPSIZEL *lpsizel*

IOleObject::GetExtent gets an object's current extent, the extent that the object will actually use. This call is made to the running object; to get the extent from the cache, **IViewObject2::GetExtent** is called.

Parameters

dwAspect
Describes the aspect of the object whose limit is to be retrieved; the value is obtained from the enumeration **DVASPECT**.

lpsizel
Points to where the object's extent is to be returned.

Return Values

Value	Meaning
S_OK	Extent information successfully returned.
E_INVALIDARG	Invalid value for *dwAspect*.

The extent returned from **IOleObject::GetExtent** may differ from the one last set by **IOleObject::SetExtent**. To the object, **IOleObject::SetExtent** offers advice on what rectangle to use.

Example

The following implementation of **IOleObject::GetExtent** checks the value of *dwAspect*. If *dwAspect* is DVASPECT_CONTENT, the width and height of the entire document in himetric units is calculated and returned in *lpsizel*.

```
HRESULT IOleObject_GetExtent(
        LPOLEOBJECT             lpThis,
        DWORD                   dwAspect,
        LPSIZEL                 lpsizel)
{
    LPDOC lpDoc = (LPDOC)((struct CDocOleObjectImpl FAR*)lpThis)->lpDoc;
    if (dwAspect == DVASPECT_CONTENT    {
            CalcExtentInHimetric (lpDoc, lpsizel);
            return ResultFromScode(S_OK);
    }
    else
        return ResultFromScode(E_INVALIDARG);
}
```

See Also

IOleObject::SetExtentIViewObject2::GetExtent

IOleObject::Advise

HRESULT IOleObject::Advise(*pAdvise, pdwConnection***)**
LPADVISESINK *pAdvise*
DWORD FAR* *pdwConnection*

IOleObject::Advise sets up an advisory connection between the object and an advisory sink through which the sink can be informed of close, save, rename, and link source change events that happen in the object.

Parameters

pAdvise
Points to the advisory sink that should be informed of changes.

pdwConnection
Points to a token that can be passed to **IOleObject::Unadvise** to delete the advisory connection.

Return Values

Value	Meaning
S_OK	Advisory connection set up successfully.
E_OUTOFMEMORY	Cannot set up the connection due to lack of memory.

Comments

When an advisory sink registers for notifications using this call, the advisory sink will receive compound document (OLE) notifications via a call to the appropriate method in the sink's implementation of the **IAdviseSink** and/or **IAdviseSink2** interfaces.

Objects can take advantage of the functionality provided by **IOleAdviseHolder** interface, implemented by OLE, in their implementation of **IOleObject::Advise**, **Unadvise**, and **EnumAdvise**.

If an advisory connection is successfully set up, the callee returns a non-zero value through *pdwConnection* (if a connection fails to be established, zero is returned). The connection can be deleted by passing this non-zero token back to the object in a call to **IOleObject::Unadvise**.

Example

The following example is a typical implementation of **IOleObject::Advise**. **IOleObject::Advise** calls **CreateOleAdviseHolder** to create an instance of the advise holder, and if the creation is successful, calls **IOleAdviseHolder::Advise** to do the actual work.

```
HRESULT IOleObject_Advise(
        LPOLEOBJECT             lpThis,
        LPADVISESINK            pAdvise,
        LPDWORD                 lpdwConnection)
{
    LPDOC lpDoc = ((struct CDocOleObjectImpl FAR*)lpThis)->lpDoc;

    if (lpDoc->m_lpOleAdviseHldr == NULL &&
        CreateOleAdviseHolder(&lpDoc->m_lpOleAdviseHldr) != NOERROR)
            return ResultFromScode(E_OUTOFMEMORY);

    return (lpDoc->m_lpOleAdviseHldr->lpVtbl->Advise
                (lpDoc->m_lpOleAdviseHldr, pAdvise, lpdwConnection));
}
```

See Also

IOleObject::UnAdvise, IOleObject::EnumAdvise, IOleAdviseHolder::Advise

IOleObject::Unadvise

HRESULT IOleObject::Unadvise(*dwConnection*)
DWORD *dwConnection*

IOleObject::Unadvise deletes an advisory connection previously established with **IOleObject::Advise.**

Parameters

dwConnection
Contains a non-zero value previously returned from **IOleObject::Advise** through its *pdwConnection* parameter.

Return Values

Value	Meaning
S_OK	Connection removed successfully.
E_FAIL	**IOleAdviseHolder** instance no longer available.
OLE_E_NOCONNECTION	*dwConnection* is not a valid connection ID.

Example

The implementation of **IOleObject_Unadvise** shown below delegates to its advise holder, calling **IOleAdviseHolder::Unadvise** to delete the connection.

```
HRESULT IOleObject_Unadvise(LPOLEOBJECT lpThis, DWORD dwConnection)
{
    LPDOC lpDoc = ((struct CDocOleObjectImpl FAR*)lpThis)->lpDoc;

    if (lpDoc->m_lpOleAdviseHldr == NULL)
        ReturnFromScode(E_FAIL);

    return (lpDoc->m_lpOleAdviseHldr->lpVtbl->Unadvise
              (lpDoc->m_lpOleAdviseHldr, dwConnection));
}
```

See Also

IOleObject::Advise, IOleObject::EnumAdvise

IOleObject::EnumAdvise

HRESULT IOleObject::EnumAdvise(*ppenumStatData*)
LPENUMSTATDATA FAR * *ppenumStatData*

IOleObject::EnumAdvise enumerates the advisory connections registered for an object.

Parameters

ppenumStatData
Points to where the new enumerator should be returned. NULL is a legal return value; it indicates that the object does not have any advisory connections.

Return Values

Value	Meaning
S_OK	Enumerator returned successfully.
E_FAIL	**IOleAdviseHolder** instance no longer available.

Comments

IOleObject::EnumAdvise enumerates items of type **STATDATA**:

```
typedef struct STRUCT tagSTATDATA
{
    FORMATETC FormatEtc;
    DWORD advf;
    LPADVISESINK pAdvise;
    DWORD dwConnection;
} STATDATA;
```

Only the *pAdvise* and *dwConnection* members of **STATDATA** are relevant for **IOleObject::EnumAdvise**.

While an enumeration is in progress, the effect of registering or revoking advisory connections on what is to be enumerated is undefined.

Example

The following example uses the advise holder to enumerate the object's connections. If the **IOleAdviseHolder** instance cannot be found, E_FAIL is returned; otherwise, the result of the call to **IOleAdviseHolder::EnumAdvise** is returned.

```
HRESULT IOleObject_EnumAdvise(
        LPOLEOBJECT             lpThis,
        LPENUMSTATDATA FAR*     ppenumAdvise)
{
    LPDOC lpDoc = ((struct CDocOleObjectImpl FAR*)lpThis)->lpDoc;

    *ppenumAdvise = NULL;
    if (lpDoc->m_lpOleAdviseHldr == NULL)
        return ResultFromScode(E_FAIL);

    return (lpDoc->m_lpOleAdviseHldr->lpVtbl->EnumAdvise
            (lpDoc->m_lpOleAdviseHldr, ppenumAdvise));
}
```

See Also

IOleObject::Advise, IOleObject::UnAdvise

IOleObject::GetMiscStatus

HRESULT IOleObject::GetMiscStatus(*dwAspect, pdwStatus*)
DWORD *dwAspect*
DWORD FAR* *pdwStatus*

IOleObject::GetMiscStatus returns object status information.

Parameters

dwAspect
The aspect of the object against which status information is being requested. The value is obtained from the enumeration **DVASPECT** (see **IViewObject::Draw**).

pdwStatus
Points to where the status information is returned. May not be NULL.

Return Values

Value	Meaning
S_OK	Information returned successfully.
OLE_S_USEREG	Delegate to the default handler implementation to retrieve the MiscStatus information from the registration database.
CO_E_CLASSNOTREG	There is no CLSID registered for the object.
CO_E_READREGDB	Error accessing the registration database.

Comments

Objects store status information in the registration database; the default handler's implementation of **IOleObject::GetMiscStatus** retrieves this information if the object is not running. If the object is running, the default handler invokes **IOleObject::GetMiscStatus** on the running object.

The information stored varies depending on the object; the status values that can be returned are taken from the enumeration **OLEMISC**:

```
typedef enum tagOLEMISC
{
    OLEMISC_RECOMPOSEONRESIZE             = 1,
    OLEMISC_ONLYICONIC                    = 2,
    OLEMISC_INSERTNOTREPLACE              = 4,
    OLEMISC_STATIC                        = 8,
    OLEMISC_CANTLINKINSIDE                = 16,
    OLEMISC_CANLINKBYOLE1                 = 32,
    OLEMISC_ISLINKOBJECT                  = 64,
    OLEMISC_INSIDEOUT                     = 128,
    OLEMISC_ACTIVATEWHENVISABLE           = 256,
    OLEMISC_RENDERINGISDEVICEINDEPENDENT  = 512,
} OLEMISC;
```

These values have the following meanings:

OLEMISC Value	Description
OLEMISC_RECOMPOSEONRESIZE	If true, signifies that when the size that the container allocates to the object changes, the object would like the opportunity to recompose its picture. When resize occurs, the object is likely to do something other than scale its picture. The container should force the object to run so it can call **IOleObject::GetExtent.**
OLEMISC_ONLYICONIC	This object has no useful content view other than its icon. From the user's perspective, the Display As Icon checkbox (in the Paste Special dialog box) for this object should always be checked. Note that such an object should still have a drawable content aspect; it will look the same as its icon view.
OLEMISC_INSERTNOTREPLACE	Indicates that this is the kind of object that when inserted into a document should be inserted beside the selection instead of replacing it. An object which linked itself to the selection with which it was initialized would set this bit. Containers should examine this bit after they have initialized the object with the selection. See **IOleObject::InitFromData**.
OLEMISC_STATIC	Indicates that this object is a static object. See **OleCreateStaticFromData**.
OLEMISC_CANTLINKINSIDE	Indicates that this is the kind of object that should not be the link source that when bound to runs the object. That is, if when the object is selected, its container wishes to offer the Link Source format in a data transfer, then the link, when bound, must connect to the outside of the object. The user would see the object selected in its container, not open for editing. Some objects that do not want to implement being the source of a link when they are embedded may want to set this bit.

OLEMISC Value	Description
OLEMISC_CANLINKBYOLE1	Indicates that this object can be linked to by OLE 1 containers. This bit is used in the *dwStatus* field of the OBJECTDESCRIPTOR structure transferred with the Object and Link Source Descriptor formats. An object can be linked by OLE 1 if it is not an embedded object or pseudo object contained within an embedded object.
OLEMISC_ISLINKOBJECT	This object is a link object. This bit is significant to OLE and is set by the OLE 2 link object; object applications have no need to set this bit.
OLEMISC_INSIDEOUT	This object is capable of activating in-place, without requiring installation of menus and toolbars to run. Several such objects can be active concurrently. Some containers, such as forms, may choose to activate such objects automatically.
OLEMISC_ACTIVATEWHEN VISIBLE	This bit is set only when OLEMISC_INSIDEOUT is set, and indicates that this object prefers to be activated whenever it is visible. Some containers may always ignore this hint.
OLEMISC_RENDERINGIS DEVICEINDEPENDENT	This object does not pay any attention to target devices. Its presention data will be the same in all cases.

Example

Two different implementations of **IOleObject::GetMiscStatus** are provided below. The first implementation is from an object application. It returns information about whether the object can be linked to by an OLE 1 container and the type of in-place activation the object prefers. An object can be linked to by OLE 1 containers if it is an untitled document, a file, or a selection of data within a file.

```
HRESULT IOleObject_GetMiscStatus(
        LPOLEOBJECT             lpThis,
        DWORD                   dwAspect,
        DWORD FAR*              lpdwStatus)
{
    LPDOC lpDoc = ((struct CDocOleObjectImpl FAR*)lpThis)->lpDoc;
    *lpdwStatus = 0;

    if (lpDoc->m_docInitType == DOCTYPE_NEW ||
        lpDoc->m_docInitType == DOCTYPE_FROMFILE)
        *lpdwStatus |= OLEMISC_CANLINKBYOLE1;

    if (dwAspect == DVASPECT_CONTENT)
```

```
        *lpdwStatus |= (OLEMISC_INSIDEOUT | OLEMISC_ACTIVATEWHENVISIBLE);
    return NOERROR;
}
```

The second implementation is also from an object application and illustrates how to delegate to the default handler's implementation.

```
HRESULT IOleObject_GetMiscStatus(
        LPOLEOBJECT             lpThis,
        DWORD                   dwAspect,
        DWORD FAR*              lpdwStatus)
{
    LPDOC lpDoc = ((struct CDocOleObjectImpl FAR*)lpThis)->lpDoc;
    *lpdwStatus = 0;

    // Tell OLE to get information from registration database
    return ResultFromScode(OLE_S_USEREG);
}
```

IOleObject::SetColorScheme

HRESULT IOleObject::SetColorScheme(*lpLogPal***)**
LOGPALETTE FAR* *lpLogPal*

IOleObject::SetColorScheme specifies the color palette that the object application should use when it edits the specified object.

Parameters

lpLogPal
Points to a LOGPALETTE structure that specifies the recommended palette.

Return Values

Value	Meaning
S_OK	Color palette received successfully.
E_NOTIMPL	Object does not support setting palettes.
OLE_E_PALETTE	Invalid LOGPALETTE structure pointed to by *lpLogPal*.
OLE_E_NOTRUNNING	Object must be running to perform this operation.

Comments

IOleObject::SetColorScheme sends the object's application the color palette recommended by the container, although object applications are not required to use the recommended palette.The object application should:

1. Allocate and fill in it own LOGPALETTE structure that contains the colors passed via *lpLogPal*.
2. Create a palette from the application-defined LOGPALETTE structure using **CreatePalette**. This palette can be used to render objects and color menus as the user edits objects in the document.

The first palette entry in the LOGPALETTE structure specifies the foreground color recommended by the container. The second palette entry specifies the background color. The first half of the remaining palette entries are fill colors and the second half are colors for the lines and text.

Container applications typically specify an even number of palette entries. When there is an uneven number of entries, the server should round up to the fill colors; that is, if there are five entries, the first three should be interpreted as fill colors and the last two as line and text colors.

IRunnableObject Interface

The **IRunnableObject** interface, implemented by object handlers and DLL object applications, is one way that handlers and DLL object applications find out when to transition into the running state and when to become a contained object. The **IRunnableObject** interface supports the handling of silent updates.

In the running state, the DLL object application must keep a lock on the container (by calling **IOleContainer::LockContainer**), just as the default object handler does. This is necessary to make linking to embedded objects work correctly.

The **IRunnableObject** interface contains the following methods (see also OLE2.H):

```
DECLARE_INTERFACE_(IRunnableObject, IUnknown)
{
HRESULT (GetRunningClass) (LPCLSID pclsid);
HRESULT (Run) (LPBC lpbc);
BOOL (IsRunning) ();
HRESULT (LockRunning) (BOOL flock, BOOL fLastUnlockCloses);
HRESULT (SetContainedObject) (BOOL fContained);
}
```

IRunnableObject::GetRunningClass

HRESULT IRunnableObject::GetRunningClass(*pclsid***)**
LPCLSID *pclsid*;

IRunnableObject::GetRunningClass returns the CLSID of the embedded object.

Parameters

pclsid
Points to where to return the CLSID of the object.

Return Values

Value	Meaning
S_OK	CLSID was returned successfully.
E_INVALIDARG	One or more arguments are invalid.
E_UNEXPECTED	An unexpected error occurred.

Comments

In cases where the object is being emulated as a different object class (through a call to **CoTreatAsClass**), the CLSID returned is that of the object that is actually running. For example, suppose that ABC is emulating an XYZ object; calling **IRunnableObject::GetRunningClass** on XYZ returns the CLSID of ABC.

See Also

CoTreatAsClass

IRunnableObject::Run

HRESULT IRunnableObject::Run(*lpbc***)**
LPBC *lpbc*

IRunnableObject::Run puts an object in its running state.

Parameters

lpbc
Points to the bind context for the run operation; may be NULL.

Return Values

Value	Meaning
S_OK	The object was successfully put into its running state.
E_OUTOFMEMORY	Out of memory.
E_UNEXPECTED	An unexpected error occurred.

Comments

If the object is not already running, calling **IRunnableObject::Run** can be an expensive operation, on the order of many seconds. If the object is already running, then this method has no effect on the object.

The object should register in the running object table if it has a moniker assigned. The object should not hold any strong locks on itself; instead, it should remain in the unstable, unlocked state. The object should be locked when the first external connection is made to the object. As part of their **Run** implementation, handlers and DLL object applications should call **IOleContainer::LockContainer**(TRUE) to lock the object.

When called on a linked object, **IRunnableObject::Run** may return OLE_E_CLASSDIFF in cases when the link has been made to an object that has been converted to a new class of object since the link was last activated. In this case, if the client want to continue, it should call **IOleLink::BindToSource** before proceeding.

OleRun is a helper function that wraps the functionality offered by this method. Its implementation is to call **QueryInterface**, asking for **IRunnableObject**, followed by a call to **IRunnableObject::Run**.

See Also **OleRun**

IRunnableObject::IsRunning

BOOL IRunnableObject::IsRunning()

IRunnableObject::IsRunning detemines whether or not an object is currently in the running state.

Return Values

Value	Meaning
TRUE	The object is in its running state.
FALSE	The object is not in its running state.

Comments **OleIsRunning** is a helper function that wraps the functionality offered by this method. Its implementation is to call **QueryInterface**, asking for **IRunnableObject**, followed by a call to **IRunnableObject::IsRunning**.

See Also **OleIsRunning**

IRunnableObject::LockRunning

HRESULT IRunnableObject::LockRunning(*fLock*, *fLastUnlockCloses*)
BOOL *fLock*
BOOL *fLastUnlockCloses*

IRunnableObject::LockRunning locks an already-running object into its running state or unlocks it from its running state.

Parameters

fLock
TRUE locks the object into its running state, FALSE unlocks the object from its running state.

fLastUnlockCloses
Specifies how the object should be closed. TRUE closes the object if this is the last unlock on the object; FALSE leaves the object in its locked state.

Return Values

Value	Meaning
S_OK	The object was either locked or unlocked, depending on the value of *fLock*.
E_FAIL	The object was not running.
E_OUTOFMEMORY	Out of memory.
E_INVALIDARG	One or more arguments are invalid.
E_UNEXPECTED	An unexpected error occurred.

Comments

Most implementations of **IRunnableObject::LockRunning** will call **CoLockObjectExternal**.

See Also

CoLockObjectExternal

IRunnableObject::SetContainedObject

HRESULT IRunnableObject::SetContainedObject(*fContained***)**
BOOL *fContained*

IRunnableObject::SetContainedObject indicates that the object is contained as an embedding in an OLE container.

Parameters

fContained
TRUE specifes that the object is contained in an OLE container; FALSE that it is not.

Return Values

Value	Meaning
S_OK	Object has been marked as a contained embedding.
E_OUTOFMEMORY	Out of memory.
E_INVALIDARG	One or more arguments are invalid.
E_UNEXPECTED	An unexpected error occurred.

Comments

This method indicates that the object is contained as an embedded object. The method is called with *fContained* set to TRUE by embedding containers after calling **OleLoad**, or **OleCreate**. Normally, embedding containers call **IRunnableObject::SetContainedObject** with *fContained* set to TRUE once and never call it again, even before they close. consequently, the use of this method wtih *fContained* set to FALSE is rare.

By default, all external connections to an object are strong reference locks in that the external connection controls the lifetime of the object. Calling **IRunnableObject::SetContainedObject** on a strong external connection transitions the strong lock to a weak lock, allowing other connections to determine the fate of the object while it is invisible. When an object is visible, it is controlled by **OleNoteObjectVisible**(*pUnk*, TRUE) or **CoLockObjectExternal**.

OleSetContainedObject is a helper function that wraps the functionality offered by this method.

See Also

OleSetContainedObject, OleNoteObjectVisible
CoLockObjectExternal

Compound Document Functions

The functions described in this section are used by container and object applications to manage and send OLE notifications and to control the state of a compound document object. These functions are defines as follows (see also OLE2.H):

```
HRESULT CreateOleAdviseHolder(LPOLEADVISEHOLDER FAR* ppOAHolder);
BOOL OleIsRunning(LPOLEOBJECT pOleObject);
HRESULT OleRun(LPUNKNOWN pUnk);
HRESULT OleLockRunning(LPUNKNOWN pUnk, BOOL fLock, BOOL fLastUnlockCloses);
HRESULT OleNoteObjectVisible(LPUNKNOWN pUnk, BOOL fVisible);
HRESULT OleSetContainedObject(LPUNKNOWN pUnk, BOOL fContained);
```

CreateOleAdviseHolder

HRESULT CreateOleAdviseHolder(*ppOAHolder*)
LPOLEADVISEHOLDER FAR * *ppOAHolder*

CreateOleAdviseHolder returns an instance of an OLE-provided implementation of the **IOleAdviseHolder** interface.

Parameters

ppOAHolder
Points to where to return the new **IOleAdviseHolder** instance.

Return Values

Value	Meaning
S_OK	**IOleAdviseHolder** instance returned successfully.
E_OUTOFMEMORY	Cannot return the **IOleAdviseHolder** instance because there is not enough memory.

Example

The following example illustrates a typical use of **CreateOleAdviseHolder**. In an object application's implementation of **IOleObject::Advise**, **CreateOleAdviseHolder** is called to return an **IOleAdviseHolder** instance. If the call fails, E_OUTOFMEMORY is returned. If the all succeeds, S_OK is returned.

```
hrErr = CreateOleAdviseHolder(&lpObj->m_lpOleAdviseHldr);
if (hrErr != NOERROR)
    return ResultFromScode(E_OUTOFMEMORY);
else
    return ResultFromScode(S_OK);
```

OleIsRunning

BOOL OleIsRunning(*pOleObject*)
LPOLEOBJECT *pOleObject*

OleIsRunning determines whether an object is running.

Parameters

pOleObject
Points to the object in question.

Return Values

Value	Meaning
TRUE	Object is running.
FALSE	Object is not running.

Comments

OleIsRunning is a helper function that wraps the functionality offered by **IRunnableObject::IsRunning** and can be called in place of that method.

See Also

IRunnableObject::IsRunning

OleRun

HRESULT OleRun(*pUnk*)
LPUNKNOWN *pUnk*

OleRun places an object into the running state if it is not already running.

Parameters

pUnk
Points to the object that should be made running.

Return Values

Value	Meaning
S_OK	The object was successfully placed in the running state.
OLE_E_CLASSDIFF	Source of an OLE link has been converted.

Comments

Calling **OleRun** can be expensive if the object is not running, because an object application must be launched. If the object is already running, a call to **OleRun** has no effect.

When invoked on an OLE link object, **OleRun** may return OLE_E_CLASSDIFF, which indicates that the link source has been converted while the link has been passive. The caller can invoke **IOleLink::BindToSource** to proceed in this case.

OleRun is a helper function that wraps the functionality offered by **IRunnableObject::Run** and can be called in place of that method.

See Also

IRunnableObject::Run

OleLockRunning

HRESULT OleLockRunning(*pUnk, fLock, fLastUnlockCloses*)
LPUNKNOWN *pUnk*
BOOL *fLock*
BOOL *fLastUnlockCloses*

OleLockRunning locks an object into its running state or unlocks it from its running state.

Parameters

pUnk
Points to the object that is to be locked or unlocked.

fLock
TRUE locks the object into its running state, FALSE unlocks the object from its running state.

fLastUnlockCloses
Specifies how the object should be closed. TRUE closes the object if this is the last unlock on the object; FALSE leaves the object in its locked state.

Return Values

Value	Meaning
S_OK	The object was either locked or unlocked, depending on the value of *fLock*.
E_OUTOFMEMORY	Out of memory.
E_INVALIDARG	One or more arguments are invalid.
E_UNEXPECTED	An unexpected error occurred.

Comments

OleLockRunning is a helper function that wraps the functionality offered by **IRunnableObject::LockRunning** and can be called in place of that method.

See Also

IRunnableObject::LockRunning

OleNoteObjectVisible

HRESULT OleNoteObjectVisible(*pUnk, fVisible***)**
LPUNKNOWN *pUnk*
BOOL *fVisible*

OleNoteObjectVisible locks a visible object such that its reference count cannot decrement to zero; and releases such a lock.

Parameters

pUnk
Points to the object that is to be locked or unlocked.

fVisible
Indicates whether the object is visible. If TRUE, OLE holds the object visible and alive regardless of external or internal **AddRef** and **Release** operations, registrations, or revokes. If FALSE, OLE releases its hold and the object can lose visibility.

Return Values

Value	Meaning
S_OK	Object locked or unlocked successfully.
E_OUTOFMEMORY	Lock/unlock operation could not be completed due to lack of memory.
E_INVALIDARG	One or more arguments are invalid.
E_UNEXPECTED	Lock/unlock operation could not be completed for reasons other than lack of memory or invalid arguments.

Comments

OleNoteObjectVisible is a wrapper for a call to **CoLockObjectExternal** (*pUnk, fVisible, TRUE*). It is provided as a separate API to reinforce the need to lock an object when it becomes visible to the user and to release the object when it becomes invisible. Sophisticated objects may opt to call **CoLockObjectExternal** directly.

See Also

CoLockObjectExternal

OleSetContainedObject

HRESULT OleSetContainedObject(*pUnk, fContained*)
LPUNKNOWN *pUnk*
BOOL *fContained*

OleSetContainedObject indicates that the object is contained as an embedding.

Parameters

pUnk
Points to the object that is a contained embedding.

fContained
TRUE if the object is an embedded object; FALSE otherwise.

Return Values

Value	Meaning
S_OK	Object has been marked as a contained embedding.
E_OUTOFMEMORY	Object could not be marked as a contained embedding due to lack of memory.
E_INVALIDARG	One or more arguments are invalid.
E_UNEXPECTED	An unexpected error happened.

Comments

Normally containers call **OleSetContainedObject** with *fContained* set to TRUE one time, either after creating the object initially or after loading it, and never call it again, even before they close. Consequently, the use of **OleSetContainedObject** with *fContained* set to FALSE is rare.

Because all external connection(s) to an object start out strong, becoming a contained object weakens (unlocks) the connection(s), enabling other connections to determine the object's fate.

OleSetContainedObject is a helper function that wraps the functionality offered by **IRunnableObject::SetContainedObject** and can be called in place of that method.

See Also

IRunnableObject::SetContainedObject

Object Creation Functions

OLE provides several functions that create or aid in the creation of compound document object of different types. These functions are defined as follows (see also OLE2.H):

```
HRESULT OleCreate(REFCLSID rclsid, REFIID riid, DWORD renderopt, LPFORMATETC pFormatetc,
   LPOLECLIENTSITE pClientSite, LPSTORAGE pStg, LPVOID FAR* ppvObj);
HRESULT OleCreateDefaultHandler(REFCLSID rclsid, LPUNKNOWN pUnkOuter, REFIID riid,
   LPVOID FAR* ppvObj);
HRESULT OleCreateEmbeddingHelper(REFCLSID rclsid, LPUNKNOWN pUnkOuter, DWORD flags,
   LPCLASSFACTORY pCF, REFIID riid, LPVOID FAR* ppvObj);
HRESULT OleCreateFromData(LPDATAOBJECT pDataObject, REFIID riid, DWORD renderopt,
   LPFORMATETC pFormatetc, LPOLECLIENTSITE pClientSite, LPSTORAGE pStg, LPVOID FAR* ppvObj);
HRESULT OleCreateFromFile(REFCLSID rclsid, LPCSTR lpszFileName, REFIID riid, DWORD renderopt,
   LPFORMATETC lpFormatetc, LPOLECLIENTSITE pClientSite, LPSTORAGE pStg, LPVOID FAR* ppvObj);
HRESULT OleCreateLink(LPMONIKER pmk, REFIID riid, DWORD renderopt, LPFORMATETC lpFormatetc,
   LPOLECLIENTSITE pClientSite, LPSTORAGE pStg, LPVOID FAR* ppvObj);
HRESULT OleCreateLinkFromData(LPDATAOBJECT pDataObject, REFIID riid, DWORD renderopt,
   LPFORMATETC pFormatetc, LPOLECLIENTSITE pClientSite, LPSTORAGE pStg, LPVOID FAR* ppvObj);
HRESULT OleCreateLinkToFile(LPCSTR lpszFileName, REFIID riid, DWORD renderopt,
   LPFORMATETC lpFormatetc, LPOLECLIENTSITE pClientSite, LPSTORAGE pStg, LPVOID FAR* ppvObj);
HRESULT OleCreateStaticFromData(LPDATAOBJECT pDataObject, REFIID iid, DWORD renderopt,
   LPFORMATETC pFormatetc, LPOLECLIENTSITE pClientSite, LPSTORAGE pStg, LPVOID FAR* ppvObj);
HRESULT OleQueryLinkFromData(LPDATAOBJECT pDataObject);
HRESULT OleQueryCreateFromData(LPDATAOBJECT pDataObject);
```

Object Creation Parameters

Many of the object creation functions have parameters in common. The following table defines these parameters as they are used in the majority of the functions. For each function where the usage is different, additional comments are included with the description of the function.

Parameter	Description
renderopt	Indicates the caching that the container wants in the newly created object.
pDataObject	Points to the data transfer object from which a compound document object is to be created.
pFormatetc	Points to the data formats and medium information that control the caching to be done in the newly created object.
riid	Contains the interface to be used to communicate with the new object. The most common value is IID_IOleObject.

Parameter	Description
pClientSite	Points to the client site. May be NULL. If NULL, the caller must call **IOleObject::SetClientSite** before attempting any operations. If non-NULL, OleCreate calls **IOleObject::SetClientSite** before returning.
ppvObj	Points to the place at which the newly created instance of *riid* should be returned.
pStg	Points to the storage that will be used for the object. May not be NULL.

Valid values for the *renderopt* parameter are taken from the enumeration **OLERENDER**:

```
typedef enum tagOLERENDER
{
    OLERENDER_NONE   = 0,
    OLERENDER_DRAW   = 1,
    OLERENDER_FORMAT = 2,
    OLERENDER_ASIS   = 3
} OLERENDER;
```

For most of the creation functions, these values have the following semantics:

Value	Meaning
OLERENDER_NONE	The container is not requesting any locally cache drawing or data retrieval capabilities in the object. *pFormatetc* is ignored for this option.
OLERENDER_DRAW	The container will draw the content of the object on the screen (a NULL target device) using **IViewObject::Draw**. The object determines the data formats that need to be cached. Only the *ptd* and *dwAspect* members of *pFormatetc* are significant, since the object may cache things differently depending on the parameter values. However, *pFormatetc* can legally be NULL here, in which case the object is to assume the display target device and the DVASPECT_CONTENT aspect.
OLERENDER_FORMAT	The container will pull one format from the object using **IDataObject::GetData**. The format of the data to be cached is passed in *pFormatetc*, which may not in this case be NULL.

Value	Meaning
OLERENDER_ASIS	The container is not requesting any locally cache drawing or data retrieval capabilities in the object. *pFormatetc* is ignored for this option. The difference between this and OLERENDER_NONE is important in other helper functions such as **OleCreateFromData** and **OleCreateLinkFromData**.

Some of the API functions have different or additional semantics for these values. Appropriate comments are included with each function description.

OleCreate

HRESULT OleCreate(*rclsid, riid, renderopt, pFormatetc, pClientSite, lpStg, ppvObj*)
REFCLSID *rclsid*
REFIID *riid*
DWORD *renderopt*
LPFORMATETC *pFormatetc*
LPOLECLIENTSITE *pClientSite*
LPSTORAGE *lpStg*
LPVOID FAR* *ppvObj*

OleCreate creates an embedded object of a specified class. This method is typically used in implementing the Insert New Object scenario.

Parameters

rclsid
Identifies the class of the embedded object to be created.

The *riid, renderopt, pFormatetc, pClientSite,lpStg,* and *ppvObj* parameters are described above in the Object Creation Parameters section.

Return Values

Value	Meaning
S_OK	Embedded object created successfully.
E_OUTOFMEMORY	Embedded object cannot be created due to lack of memory.

Comments

When **OleCreate** returns, the object is blank and in the loaded state. Containers typically then call **OleRun** or **IOleObject::DoVerb** to show the object for initial editing.

The cache is not necessarily filled by the time that **OleCreate** returns. Instead, the cache is filled as appropriate for the passed *renderopt* and *pFormatetc* the first time the object enters the running state. Between the return of **OleCreate** and a subsequent running of the object, the caller may add additional caching control with a call to **IOleCache::Cache**.

OleCreateDefaultHandler

HRESULT OleCreateDefaultHandler(*rclsid, pUnkOuter, riid, ppvObj*)
REFCLSID *rclsid*
LPUNKNOWN *pUnkOuter*
REFIID *riid*
LPVOID FAR * *ppvObj*

OleCreateDefaultHandler creates a new instance of the default handler to service the specified *rclsid.*

Parameters

rclsid
ID of object class to be loaded.

pUnkOuter
Points to the controlling **IUnknown** if the handler is to be aggregated; NULL if it is not to be aggregated.

The *riid* and *ppvObj* parameters are described above in the Object Creation Parameters section.

Return Values

Value	Meaning
S_OK	Default handler created successfully.
E_OUTOFMEMORY	Default handler cannot be created due to lack of memory.

Comments

OleCreateDefaultHandler initializes the new default handler instance in such a way that when the running state needs to be entered, a local server of class *rclsid* will be created.

Calling **OleCreateDefaultHandler** is the same as calling **CoCreateInstance**(*rclsid, pUnkOuter, CLSCTX_INPROC_HANDLER, riid, ppvObj*) if the given class does not have a special object class handler.

OleCreateDefaultHandler is used internally when the *rclsid* is not registered and by handler writers that want to use the services of the default handler.

OleCreateEmbeddingHelper

HRESULT OleCreateEmbeddingHelper(*rclsid, pUnkOuter, flags, pCF, riid, ppvObj*)
REFCLSID *rclsid*
LPUNKNOWN *pUnkOuter*
DWORD *flags*
LPCLASSFACTORY *pCF*
REFIID *riid*
LPVOID FAR * *ppvObj*

OleCreateEmbeddingHelper creates an embedding helper object using application supplied code aggregated with pieces of the OLE default object handler; this helper object can be created and used in a specific context and role, as determined by the caller.

Parameters

rclsid
Specifies the CLSID of the object class that is to be helped.

pUnkOuter
Points to the controlling **IUnknown** if the handler is to be aggregated; NULL if it is not to be aggregated.

flags
Specifies the role and creation context for the embedding helper; see the following comments for legal values.

pCF
Points to the application's **IClassFactory** instance; can be NULL.

riid
Specifies the interface ID of the desired by the caller.

ppvObj
Points to where to return the newly created embedding helper.

Return Values

Value	Meaning
S_OK	Embedding helper was created successfully.
E_NOINTERFACE	Interface not supported by the object.
E_OUTOFMEMORY	Out of memory.
E_INVALIDARG	One or more arguments are invalid.
E_UNEXPECTED	An unexpected error occurred.

Comments

OleCreateEmbeddingHelper is used to create a new instance of the OLE default handler that can be used to support objects in various roles. The caller passes to **OleCreateEmbeddingHelper** a pointer to its **IClassFactory** implementation; this object and the default handler are then aggregated to create the new embedding helper object.

OleCreateEmbeddingHelper is usually used to support one of the following implementations:

- An object application is being used as both a container and a server, and the application supports inserting objects into itself, either directly or indirectly. In this case, the application will register its CLSID for different contexts (**CoRegisterClassObject** (*Clsid*, *lpUnk*, CLSCTX_LOCAL_SERVER | CLSCTX_INPROC_SERVER, REGCLS_MULTI_SEPARATE, *lpdwRegister*)). The local class is used to create the object and the in-process class creates the embedding helper, passing in the pointer to the first object's class factory in *pCF*.
- An in-process object handler. In this case, the DLL creates the embedding helper by passing in a private class factory in *pCF*.

The *flags* parameter indicates how the embedding helper is to be used and how and when the embedding helper is initialized. The values for *flags* are obtained by or'ing together values from the following table:

Values for *flags* Parameter	Purpose
EMBDHLP_INPROC_HANDLER	EMBDHLP_INPROC_HANDLER creates an embedding helper that is used with an EXE object application; specifiying this flag is the same as calling **OleCreateDefaultHandler**.
EMBDHLP_INPROC_SERVER	EMBDHLP_INPROC_SERVER creates an embedding helper that can be used with DLL object applications; specifically the helper exposes the caching features of the default object handler.
EMBDHLP_CREATENOW	EMBDHLP_CREATENOW creates the application-supplied piece immediately.
EMBDHLP_DELAYCREATE	EMBDHLP_DELAYCREATE delays creating the application-supplied piece until the object is put into its running state.

Calling

```
OleCreateEmbeddingHelper
    (rclsid, pUnkOuter, EMBDHLP_INPROC_HANDLER | EMBDHLP_CREATENOW,
    NULL, riid, ppvObj)
```

is the same as calling

```
OleCreateDefaultHandler(rclsid, pUnkOuter, riid, ppvObj)
```

See Also **OleCreateDefaultHandler**

OleCreateFromData

HRESULT OleCreateFromData(*pDataObject, riid, renderopt, pFormatetc, pClientSite, pStg, ppvObj*)
LPDATAOBJECT *pDataObject*
REFIID *riid*
DWORD *renderopt*
LPFORMATETC *pFormatetc*
LPOLECLIENTSITE *pClientSite*
LPSTORAGE *pStg*
LPVOID FAR* *ppvObj*

OleCreateFromData creates an embedded object from a data transfer object retrieved either from the clipboard or as part of a drag and drop operation.

Parameters

pDataObject
Points to the data transfer object that holds the data from which the object will be created.

riid
Identifies the interface that the caller is to use to communicate with the new object.

renderopt
Indicates the type of caching desired for the newly created object. The use of renderopt is as defined in the Object Creation Parameters section, with the following additional comments that relate to how the new object's cache is initialized:

Value	Meaning
OLERENDER_DRAW and OLERENDER_FORMAT	If the format to be cached is currently present in the appropriate cache initialization pool (the old object for the Embedded Object format, the other formats in *pDataObject* for Embed Source), then it is used. If the format is not present, then the cache is initially empty, but will be filled the first time the object is run. No other formats are cached in the newly created object.
OLERENDER_NONE	The newly created object has nothing cached. In the Embedded Object case, any copied existing cached data is removed.

Value	Meaning
OLERENDER_ASIS	In the Embedded Object case, the new object has exactly those things cached within itself that the original old source object had cached within itself. In the Embed Source case, the newly created object has nothing cached. The idea is that this option is to be used by more sophisticated containers. After this call, such containers will call **IOleCache::Cache** and **IOleCache::Uncache** calls to set up exactly what they want cached. In the Embed Source case, they will then also call **IOleCache::InitCache**.

The *riid, pClientSite, pStg, pFormatetc,* and *ppvObj* parameters are described above in the Object Creation Parameters section.

Return Values

Value	Meaning
S_OK	Embedded object created successfully.
OLE_E_STATIC	OLE can only create a static object.
DV_E_FORMATETC	No acceptable formats are available for object creation.

Comments

The *renderopt* and *pFormatetc* parameters can be used by the caller to control the caching that is done in the newly created object. The interaction between *renderopt* and *pFormatetc* in determining what is to be cached is described in the **OleCreate** function. **OleCreateFromData** makes use of either the Embedded Object or the Embed Source data formats in *pDataObject* to create the object. (For more information on these Clipboard formats, refer to the "Data Transfer/Caching Interfaces and Functions" chapter.)

The main difference between these two formats is where the appropriate cache-initialization data lies. In the Embedded Object case, the source is an existing embedded object; the cache inside the object itself has the appropriate data. In the Embed Source case, it is the formats available in *pDataObject* other than Embed Source which should initialize the cache.

If the "FileName" clipboard format is present in the data transfer object, **OleCreateFromData** creates a package containing the indicated file. This format is placed on the clipboard by the Microsoft Windows 3.1 File Manager when the user selects the File Copy To menu command. If a package is not made, **OleCreateFromData** tries to create an object using the Embedded Object format if it is available and ithe Embed Source format if it is not available. If neither of these formats are available and the data transfer object supports the **IPersistStorage** interface, **OleCreateFromData** calls **IPersistStorage::Save** to ask the object to save itself.

OleCreateFromFile

HRESULT OleCreateFromFile(*rclsid, lpszFileName, riid, renderopt, pFormatetc, pClientSite, pStg, ppvObj*)
REFCLSID *rclsid*
LPCSTR *lpszFileName*
REFIID *riid*
DWORD *renderopt*
LPFORMATETC *pFormatetc*
LPOLECLIENTSITE *pClientSite*
LPSTORAGE *pStg*
LPVOID FAR* *ppvObj*

OleCreateFromFile creates an embedded object of the indicated class from the contents of a named file. The newly created object is not shown to the user for editing.

Parameters

rclsid
Reserved for future use. Must be CLSID_NULL.

lpszFile
Specifies the full path name of the file from which the object should be initialized.

The *riid, renderopt, pFormatetc, pClientSite, pStg,* and *ppvObj* parameters are described above in the Object Creation Parameters section.

Return Values

Value	Meaning
S_OK	Embedded object successfully created.
STG_E_FILENOTFOUND	File not bound.
OLE_E_CANT_BINDTOSOURCE	Not able to bind to source.
STG_E_MEDIUMFULL	The medium is full.
DV_E_TYMED	Invalid TYMED.
DV_E_LINDEX	Invalid LINDEX.
DV_E_FORMATETC	Invalid FORMATETC structure.
E_OUTOFMEMORY	OLE libraries have not been properly initialized.

Comments

OleCreateFromFile is used in the Insert File operation of the Insert Object dialog box. It creates either a package if the ProgID in the registration database contains the PackageOnFileDrop key or an OLE 2 embedded object as appropriate for the class of the file (see **GetClassFile**). If an embedded object is created, **OleCreateFromFile** creates a file moniker for the file.

Unless it can manage with no conversion of representation, this function uses **IPersistFile::Load** on a new instance of the class *rclsid* object to open the file. It then calls **QueryInterface** to access f**IPersistStorage** and calls **IPersistStorage::Save**(..., false, true) to indicate to the object that it should convert representations.

OleCreateLink

HRESULT OleCreateLink(*pmk, riid, render opt, pFormatetc, pClientSite, pStg, ppvObj*)
LPMONIKER *pmk*
REFIID *riid*
DWORD *renderopt*
LPFORMATETC *pFormatetc*
LPOLECLIENTSITE *pClientSite*
LPSTORAGE *pStg*
LPVOID FAR* *ppvObj*

OleCreateLink creates an OLE compound-document link object. The source of the link is initialized with *pmk*.

Parameters

pmk
Points to an **IMoniker** interface instance indicating the linked object's source.

The *riid, renderopt, pFormatetc, pClientSite, pStg,* and *ppvObj* parameters are described above in the Object Creation Parameters section.

Return Values

Value	Meaning
S_OK	The compound-document link object was created successfully.
OLE_E_CANT_BINDTOSOURC E	Not able to bind to source. Binding is necessary to get cache's initialization data.

Comments

When a container creates a linked object, it should assign a moniker to the newly-created link and inform the link object of the moniker using **IOleObject::SetMoniker** (OLEWHICHMK_OBJREL, ...). If the container doesn't already have a moniker, it should also obtain one by requesting its client site with **IOleClientSite::GetMoniker** (OLEGETMONIKER_FORCEASSIGN, ...). Once obtained, the container should inform the link of this moniker with **IOleObject::SetMoniker** (OLEWHICHMK_CONTAINER, ...).

In the event that the client site fails to give a moniker to the link's container, the container should assign a moniker to the link object that is relative to the link's container. This moniker is needed for link tracking to work: all link objects need to have monikers assigned to generate relative moniker paths.

OleCreateLinkFromData

HRESULT OleCreateLinkFromData(*pDataObject, riid, renderopt, pFormatetc, pClientSite, pStg, ppvObj***)**
LPDATAOBJECT *pDataObject*
REFIID *riid*
DWORD *renderopt*
LPFORMATETC *pFormatetc*
LPOLECLIENTSITE *pClientSite*
LPSTORAGE *pStg*
LPVOID FAR* *ppvObj*

OleCreateLinkFromData creates a linked object from a data transfer object retrieved either from the clipboard or as part of a drag and drop operation.

Parameters

pDataObject
Points to the data transfer object from which the linked object is to be created.

The *riid, renderopt, pFormatetc, pClientSite, pStg,* and *ppvObj* parameters are described above in the Object Creation Parameters section.

Return Values

Value	Meaning
S_OK	The linked object was created successfully.
CLIPBRD_E_CANT_OPEN	Not able to open the clipboard.
OLE_E_CANT_GETMONIKER	Not able to extract object's moniker.
OLE_E_CANT_BINDTOSOURCE	Not able to bind to source. Binding is necessary to get cache's initialization data.

Comments

OleCreateLinkFromData is similar in function to **OleCreateFromData** in that it creates a compound document object from a data transfer object. However, where **OleCreateFromData** uses the Embedded Object or Embed Source formats from the data transfer object, **OleCreateLinkFromData** uses the Link Source format. From the perspective of cache initialization, the Link Source format behaves like Embed Source.

If the FileName format is available, **OleCreateLinkFromData** creates a package containing a link to the indicated file. If a package cannot be made, **OleCreateLinkFromData** looks for the Link Source format with which to create a linked object.

See Also

OleCreateLink

OleCreateLinkToFile

HRESULT OleCreateLinkToFile(*lpszFileName, riid, renderopt, pFormatetc, pClientSite, pStg, ppvObj***)**
LPCSTR *lpszFileName*
REFIID *riid*
DWORD *renderopt*
LPFORMATETC *pFormatetc*
LPOLECLIENTSITE *pClientSite*
LPSTORAGE *pStg*
LPVOID FAR* *ppvObj*

OleCreateLinkToFile creates an object that is linked to a file.

Parameters

lpszFileName
Points to the source file to be linked to.

The *riid, renderopt, pFormatetc, pClientSite, pStg,* and *ppvObj* parameters are described above in the Object Creation Parameters section.

Return Values

Value	Meaning
S_OK	The object was created successfully.
STG_E_FILENOTFOUND	File name is invalid.
OLE_E_CANT_BINDTOSOURCE	Not able to bind to source.

Comments

OleCreateLinkToFile can create links to non-OLE aware files, using the Windows Packager.

OleCreateStaticFromData

HRESULT OleCreateStaticFromData(*pDataObject, riid, renderopt, pFormatetc, pClientSite, pStg, ppvObj***)**
LPDATAOBJECT *pDataObject*
REFIID *riid*
DWORD *renderopt*
LPFORMATETC *pFormatetc*
LPOLECLIENTSITE *pClientSite*
LPSTORAGE *pStg*
LPVOID FAR* *ppvObj*

OleCreateStaticFromData creates a static object from a data transfer object.

Parameters

pDataObject

Points to the data transfer object from which the object is to be created.

The *riid, renderopt, pFormatetc, pClientSite, pStg,* and *ppvObj* parameters are described above in the Object Creation Parameters section. However, it is an error to pass OLERENDER_NONE and OLERENDER_ASIS in *renderopt.*

Return Values

Value	Meaning
S_OK	The static object was created successfully.

Comments

Any object that provides an **IDataObject** interface can be converted to a static object using **OleCreateStaticFromData**. **OleCreateStaticFromData** is useful in implementing the Convert To Picture option for a link.

Static objects can be created only if the source supports one of the OLE rendered formats (METAFILEPICT / DIB / BITMAP).

Static objects can be pasted from the clipboard using **OleCreateStaticFromData**. **OleQueryCreateFromData** will return OLE_S_STATIC if either CF_METAFILEPICT, CF_DIB, or CF_BITMAP is present and an OLE format is not present. But **OleCreateFromData** will not automatically create the static object in this case, if the container wants to paste a static object it should call **OleCreateStaticFromData**.

The new static object is of class CLSID_StaticMetafile (in the case of CF_METAFILEPICT) and CLSID_StaticDib (in the case of CF_DIB or CF_BITMAP). The static object will set the OLEMISC_STATIC and OLE_CANTLINKINSIDE bits returned from **IOleObject::GetMiscStatus**. The static object will have the aspect DVASPECT_CONTENT and an *lindex* of -1.

The *pDataObject* will still be valid after **OleCreateStaticFromData** returns. It is the caller's reponsibility to free *pDataObject*; OLE does not release it.

There cannot be more than one presentation stream in a static object.

Note The OLESTREAM<->IStorage conversion API functions also convert static objects.

See Also

OleCreateFromData

OleQueryCreateFromData

HRESULT OleQueryCreateFromData(*pDataObject*)
LPDATAOBJECT *pDataObject*

OleQueryCreateFromData checks whether a container application can create an embedded object from the given data transfer object.

OleQueryCreateFromData tests for the presence of the following formats in the data object:

Embedded Object
Embed Source
cfFileName
CF_METAFILEPICT
CF_DIB
CF_BITMAP

Parameters

pDataObject
Points to the data transfer object that will be queried.

Return Values

Value	Meaning
S_OK	Formats that support embedded object creation are present.
S_FALSE	No formats are present that support either embedded or static object creation.
OLE_S_STATIC	Formats that support static object creation are present.

Comments

Containers should use **OleQueryCreateFromData** with the data transfer object retrieved with **OleGetClipboard** as part of the process of deciding to enable or disable their Edit/Paste or Edit/Paste Special... commands. **OleCreateFromData** or **OleCreateStaticFromData** is used to actually create the object.

OleQueryCreateFromData returns OLE_S_STATIC when either CF_METAFILEPICT, CF_BITMAP, or CF_DIB are available and none of the other OLE formats are offered.

OleQueryCreateFromData does not test for the presence of these formats on the clipboard; it looks for the specified formats in the data transfer object. A successful return from **OleQueryCreateFromData** does not guarantee a subsequent successful return from **OleCreateFromData** or **OleCreateStaticFromData**.

OleQueryLinkFromData

HRESULT OleQueryLinkFromData(*pDataObject***)**
LPDATAOBJECT *pDataObject*

OleQueryLinkFromData operates in a manner similar to **OleQueryCreateFromData**, but determines whether a linked object (rather than an embedded object) can be created from the data transfer object.

Parameters

pDataObject
Points to the data transfer object that is to be created.

Return Values

Value	Meaning
S_OK	Formats that support linked object creation are present.
S_FALSE	Formats that support embedded object creation are not present.

OLE Initialization Functions

The following functions are used to manage the OLE2.DLL (see also OLE2.H):

```
DWORD OleBuildVersion();
HRESULT OleInitialize(LPMALLOC pMalloc);
void OleUninitialize(void);
```

OleBuildVersion

DWORD OleBuildVersion()

OleBuildVersion returns the major and the minor version number of the OLE library, OLE2.DLL.

Return Values

Value	Meaning
32-bit integer	The 16 high-order bits are the major build number; the 16 low-order bits are the minor build number.

Comments

Applications can be compiled to run against only one released major build version of the OLE library while they are using any of the incremental minor build versions. For example, an application that was compiled against build version 17.0 of the library would safely run against 17.0 and any of the minor build version releases—provided the minor build versions are greater than or equal to the minor version that the application was compiled against. However, if the library was updated to major build version 18.0 or later and the application had not been compiled against that build version, then the application should fail to initialize the library.

For any given release of the OLE library there is a file called OLE*x*VER.H, which contains the major and minor build versions, defined as *rmm* and *rup*. To get the build versions, applications call **OleBuildVersion**, which returns the major and minor build version numbers from this file. It is unlikely that the major build version would change between releases, but applications should still ensure compatibility by calling **OleBuildVersion**. If the major version number is different than that expected by the application, the application must not call **OleInitialize**.

OleBuildVersion will always be the very first function that an application calls in the OLE2.DLL library.

```
#define rmm     21
#define rup     373

DWORD dwBuildVersion = OleBuildVersion();

// fail if different major version or older minor version.
if (HIWORD(dwBuildVersion) != rmm || LOWORD(dwBuildVersion) < rup)
    return ResultFromScode(E_FAIL);         //Do not initialize OLE
else
    OleInitialize(NULL);
```

See Also

OleInitialize, CoBuildVersion

OleInitialize

HRESULT OleInitialize(*pMalloc***)**
LPMALLOC *pMalloc*

OleInitialize initializes the OLE library so that it can be used.

Parameters

pMalloc
Points to the memory allocator that is to be used for task memory by the OLE library and by object handlers. To use the OLE implementation of **IMalloc**, pass NULL as this parameter.

Return Values

Value	Meaning
S_OK	The library was initialized successfully.
S_FALSE	OLE library is already initialized; *pMalloc* not used.
OLE_E_WRONGCOMPOBJ	COMPOBJ.DLL is the wrong version for OLE2.DLL.
E_OUTOFMEMORY	Out of memory.
E_UNEXPECTED	An unexpected error occurred.

Comments

With the exception of **OleBuildVersion**, **OleInitialize** *must* be called by applications before any other function in the OLE library.

Calls to **OleInitialize** *must* be balanced by corresponding calls to **OleUninitialize**. Normally, **OleInitialize** is called only once by the process that wants to use the OLE library. In some instances (for example, two independent pieces of code written as DLLs) there may be competing calls to **OleInitialize**; in these cases, *only* the first successful call to **OleInitialize** will initialize the library and only its corresponding balanced call to **OleUninitialize** will uninitialize the library.

OleInitialize will return S_FALSE if the library has already been initialized. An application must not call **OleUninitialize** if the corresponding call to **OleInitialize** did not return S_OK; therefore, applications should set a flag after a successful initialization and test the value of the flag before closing or reinitializing the libraries. Only the application that initialized the libraries can unitialize them.

OleInitialize follows the normal reference counting rules described earlier in the description of the **IUnknown** interface. Since **OleInitialize** retains the *pMalloc* pointer beyond the duration of the call, it calls *pMalloc*->**AddRef**. Applications can release this pointer by calling *pMalloc*->**Release**.

See Also

OleUninitialize, CoInitialize

OleUninitialize

void OleUninitialize()

OleUninitialize uninitializes the OLE library, freeing any resources that it maintains.

Comments

OleUninitialize should be called on application shutdown, as the last call made to the OLE library. **OleUninitialize** internally calls **CoUninitialize** to uninitialize the Component Object Library.

Calls to **OleUninitialize** must be balanced with a previous corresponding call to **OleInitialize**; *only* the **OleUninitialize** call that corresponds to the **OleInitialize** call that actually did the initialization will unitialize the library.

See Also

OleInitialize, CoUninitialize

CHAPTER 7

Data Transfer/Caching Interfaces and Functions

Overview of Data and Presentation Transfer

OLE provides a generalized data and presentation transfer mechanism usable in a wide range of situations, including those related to compound documents. Data can be copied to the clipboard or dragged and then pasted or dropped into the same document, a different document, or a different application. Delayed rendering, a technique whereby data is not actually transferred until it is needed for rendering, is an integral part of data transfer. Only information about the impending transfer, such as data formats and mediums, is initially made available at copy or cut time. A Source application creates a *data transfer object* that holds a copy of the selected data and exposes methods for retrieving the data and receiving change notifications.

When a paste occurs, the receiving application makes a call to get the actual data from the source application. The receiving application can request both the data format and the medium across which the data should be transferred. The ability to select formats and mediums at run time allows objects to be transferred in the most efficient manner. A large object can be transferred using a storage object or a file, for example, while a smaller object can be transferred as a GDI object by using the clipboard.

OLE supports the caching of presentation data in the container's storage so that a compound document object can be shown in its container without running the object's application. Multiple presentations can also be cached; the container can choose to maintain presentations for multiple target devices, such as the screen and the printer.

Data and Presentation Transfer Structures and Enumerations

This section discusses the data structures and enumerations that play a central role in the transfer and caching of data and presentation information.

The **FORMATETC** structure is a generalized clipboard format, enhanced to encompass a target device, the *aspect,* or view of the data, and a storage medium. Where one might expect to find a clipboard format, a **FORMATETC** data structure is used instead.

The **STGMEDIUM** structure is a generalized global memory handle commonly used to pass one body of code to another. Where one would expect to find a global memory handle involved in a data transfer, OLE uses a **STGMEDIUM** structure in its place.

The **DVTARGETDEVICE** structure contains enough information about a Windows target device so that a handle to a device context (hDC) can be created using the Windows **CreateDC** function.

The **ADVF** enumeration is a set of advisory flags that specifies values for controlling advisory connections and caching.

FORMATETC Data Structure

The **FORMATETC** structure is used by the data and presentation interfaces as the means for passing information. For example, in **IDataObject::GetData** a **FORMATETC** structure is used to indicate exactly what kind of data the caller is requesting. For more information on the **IDataObject** interface, see "IDataObject Interface," later in this chapter.

The **FORMATETC** data structure is defined as follows:

```
typedef struct FARSTRUCT tagFORMATETC
{
    CLIPFORMAT          cfFormat;
    DVTARGETDEVICE FAR* ptd;
    DWORD               dwAspect;
    LONG                lindex;
    DWORD               tymed;
} FORMATETC, FAR* LPFORMATETC;
```

The *cfFormat* member indicates the particular clipboard format of interest. There are three types of formats recognized by OLE:

- standard interchange formats, such as CF_TEXT,
- private application formats understood only by the application offering the format, or by
- other applications similar in functionality, or OLE formats.

The OLE formats are used to create linked or embedded objects and are described in the following sections. The concept of clipboard formats should already be familiar to windows programmers. For more information on clipboard formats and related functions, such as **RegisterClipboardFormat**, see the *Microsoft Windows Software Development Kit.*

The *ptd* member points to a **DVTARGETDEVICE** data structure containing information about the target device for which the data is being composed. A NULL value is used whenever the data format is insensitive to the target device or when the caller doesn't care what device is used. In the latter case, if the data requires a target device, the object should pick an appropriate default device (often the display for visual objects). Data obtained from an object with a NULL target device (especially when the data format is insensitive to the device) can be thought of as an alternate form of the native representation of the object: a representation that can be used for data interchange. The resulting data is usually the same as it would be if the user chose the Save As command from the File menu and selected an interchange format.

The *dwAspect* member enables the caller to request multiple aspects, roles, or views of the object using a single clipboard format. Most data and presentation transfer and caching methods pass aspect information. For example, a caller might request an object's iconic picture, using the metafile clipboard format to retrieve it.

Values for *dwAspect* are taken from the enumeration **DVASPECT**:

```
typedef enum tagDVASPECT
{
    DVASPECT_CONTENT      = 1,
    DVASPECT_THUMBNAIL    = 2,
    DVASPECT_ICON         = 4,
    DVASPECT_DOCPRINT     = 8,
} DVASPECT;
```

Even though **DVASPECT** values are individual flag bits, *dwAspect* can only represent one value. That is, *dwAspect* cannot contain the result of **DVASPECT** values that have been or-ed together. **DVASPECT** values have the following meaning:

Value	Meaning
DVASPECT_CONTENT	Provides a representation so the object can be displayed as an embedded object inside its container; this is the most common value for compound document objects. It is appropriate to use DVASPECT_CONTENT to get a presentation of the embedded object for rendering either on the screen or on a printer; DVASPECT_DOCPRINT, by contrast, indicates the look of the object as though it were printed.
DVASPECT_THUMBNAIL	Provides a thumbnail representation so that the object can be displayed in a browsing tool. The thumbnail is approximately a 120 by 120 pixel 6-color device-independent bitmap wrapped in a metafile.
DVASPECT_ICON	Provides an iconic representation of the object.
DVASPECT_DOCPRINT	Represents the object as though it were printed using the Print command from the File menu. The described data represents a sequence of pages.

The *lindex* member represents the part of the aspect that is of interest. The value of *lindex* depends on the value of *dwAspect***.** If *dwAspect* is either DVASPECT_THUMBNAIL or DVASPECT_ICON, *lindex* is ignored. If *dwAspect* is DVASPECT_CONTENT or DVASPECT_DOCPRINT, *lindex* must be -1 which indicates that the entire view is of interest and is the only value that is currently valid.

The *tymed* member indicates the means by which data is conveyed in a particular data transfer operation. In addition to being passed through global memory, data can be passed either through a disk file or an instance of one of the OLE storage-related interfaces.

Each clipboard format has a natural expression as either a *flat* format or a *structured*, hierarchical format. All standard formats, such as CF_TEXT, are expressed as flat formats. The OLE embedded object formats, Embedded Object and Embed Source, transfer data using the structured format. There are three types of medium that are used to transfer those formats designated as flat formats: hglobal, stream, and file; and a single type of structured media: storage.

It is always appropriate to ask for a particular format on either a flat or a structured medium, as appropriate for the natural expression of the format. Additionally, it is plausible to ask that a format whose natural expression is a structured format be provided on a flat format: the structured-to-flat mapping is provided by the compound file implementation of the structured storage model.

However, it is not appropriate to ask for a flat format on a structured medium. For example, CF_TEXT cannot be passed on TYMED_ISTORAGE.

Valid values for *tymed* are taken from the following enumeration **TYMED**. These values may be or-ed together to represent a composite value.

```
typedef enum tagTYMED
{
    TYMED_HGLOBAL    = 1,
    TYMED_FILE       = 2,
    TYMED_ISTREAM    = 4,
    TYMED_ISTORAGE   = 8,
    TYMED_GDI        = 16,
    TYMED_MFPICT     = 32,
    TYMED_NULL       = 0
} TYMED;
```

The **TYMED** values have specific meanings and required release behavior. However, for any of the TYMED values, if *pUnkForRelease* is non-NULL, *pUnkForRelease*->**Release** is always called. The following table describes each of the **TYMED** values and their mechanisms for release:

Value	Meaning	Release Mechanism
TYMED_HGLOBAL	Pass the data in a global memory handle, much as data is passed using DDE. All global handles must be allocated with the GMEM_SHARE flag.	GlobalFree(*hGlobal*)
TYMED_FILE	Pass the data in the contents of a file on the disk.	OpenFile(*lpszFile*, *&of*, OF_DELETE)
TYMED_ISTREAM	Pass the data using an instance of the **IStream** interface. The passed data is available through calls to the **IStream::Read**.	*pStm*->Release()
TYMED_ISTORAGE	Pass the data using an instance of the **IStorage** interface; the passed data are the streams and storage objects nested beneath the **IStorage**.	*pStg*->Release()
TYMED_GDI	Pass the data as a GDI object (bitmap).	DeleteObject ((HGDI)*hGlobal*)

Value	Meaning	Release Mechanism
TYMED_MFPICT	Passes the data as a CF_METAFILEPICT, which contains a nested global handle.	LPMETAFILEPICT *pMF*; *pMF*=GlobalLock(*hGlobal*); DeleteMetaFile(*pMF*->hMF); GlobalUnlock(*hGlobal*); GlobalFree(*hGlobal*);
TYMED_NULL	This is not actually a medium; it indicates that no data is being passed.	

STGMEDIUM Data Structure

The **STGMEDIUM** structure describes a medium of transfer and is defined as follows:

```
typedef struct tagSTGMEDIUM
{
    DWORD           tymed;

    union {
    HANDLE          hGlobal;
    LPSTR           lpszFileName;
    LPSTREAM        pstm;
    LPSTORAGE       pstg;
};
   LPUNKNOWN pUnkForRelease;
} STGMEDIUM;
```

A **STGMEDIUM** structure is a tagged union whose *tymed* member corresponds to the **TYMED** enumeration. Each type of medium specified in **FORMATETC**::*tymed* has a matching **STGMEDIUM** *tymed* member through which occurrences of that medium are passed.

STGMEDIUM can be set to NULL by setting the *tymed* member to TYMED_NULL.

The *pUnkForRelease* member is used to provide flexibility of medium ownership. It is helpful to have the following ownership scenario choices:

- The callee owns the medium, freeing all resources when finished.
- The callee does not own the medium and informs the caller when finished so that resources can then be freed.

The provider of the medium indicates its choice of ownership scenarios in the value it provides in *pUnkForRelease*. A NULL value indicates that the receiving body of code owns and can free the medium. A non-NULL pointer specifies that **ReleaseStgMedium**can always be called to free the medium. For a detailed explanation of how storage mediums are freed and *pUnkForRelease* is used, see the description of **ReleaseStgMedium** in this chapter.

DVTARGETDEVICE Data Structure

The **DVTARGETDEVICE** data structure, used to describe a target device, is defined as follows:

```
typedef struct tagDVTARGETDEVICE
{
    DWORD tdSize;
    WORD  tdDriverNameOffset;
    WORD  tdDeviceNameOffset;
    WORD  tdPortNameOffset;
    WORD  tdExtDevmodeOffset;
    BYTE  tdData[1];
} DVTARGETDEVICE;
```

The *tdSize* member specifies the size of **DVTARGETDEVICE** structure in bytes. The initial size is included so that the structure can be copied more easily.

The next four members specify the offset from the beginning of the **DVTARGETDEVICE** structure to the device driver name, the device name, the port name, and the **DEVMODE** structure retrieved by the calling **ExtDeviceMode**. The strings indirectly indicated by *tdDeviceNameOffset*, *tdDriverNameOffset*, and *tdPortNameOffset* should be NULL-terminated. A NULL device or port name can be specified by setting the appropriate offset fields to zero.

The *tdData* member specifies an array of bytes containing data for the target device. It is not necessary to include empty strings in *tdData*.

Some OLE 1 client applications incorrectly construct target devices by allocating only DEVMODE.*dmSize* number of bytes in their OLETARGETDEVICE for the DEVMODE structure. The number of bytes to be allocated should be the sum of DEVMODE.*dmSize* + DEVMODE.*dmDriverExtra*. When a call is made to **CreateDC** with an incorrect target device, the printer driver tries to access the additional bytes and unpredictable results can occur. To protect against a crash and make the additional bytes available, OLE pads the size of OLE 2 target devices created from OLE 1 target devices.

The following code example, from the sample user library function OleStdCreateTargetDevice, illustrates how to correctly construct a target device structure. Applications can call OleStdCreateTargetDevice to completely handle the target device construction.

```
DVTARGETDEVICE FAR* OleStdCreateTargetDevice(LPPRINTDLG lpPrintDlg)
{
    DVTARGETDEVICE FAR* ptd=NULL;
    LPDEVNAMES lpDevNames, pDN;
    LPDEVMODE lpDevMode, pDM;
    UINT nMaxOffset;
    LPSTR pszName;
    DWORD dwDevNamesSize, dwDevModeSize, dwPtdSize;

    if ((pDN = (LPDEVNAMES)GlobalLock(lpPrintDlg->hDevNames)) == NULL) {
        GlobalUnlock(lpPrintDlg->hDevNames);
        GlobalUnlock(lpPrintDlg->hDevMode);
        return ptd;
    }

    if ((pDM = (LPDEVMODE)GlobalLock(lpPrintDlg->hDevMode)) == NULL) {
        GlobalUnlock(lpPrintDlg->hDevNames);
        GlobalUnlock(lpPrintDlg->hDevMode);
        return ptd;
    }

    nMaxOffset =  (pDN->wDriverOffset > pDN->wDeviceOffset) ?
        pDN->wDriverOffset : pDN->wDeviceOffset ;

    nMaxOffset =  (pDN->wOutputOffset > nMaxOffset) ?
        pDN->wOutputOffset : nMaxOffset ;

    pszName = (LPSTR)pDN + nMaxOffset;

    dwDevNamesSize = (DWORD)(nMaxOffset+lstrlen(pszName) + 1;
    dwDevModeSize = (DWORD) (pDM->dmSize + pDM->dmDriverExtra);

    dwPtdSize = sizeof(DWORD) + dwDevNamesSize + dwDevModeSize;

    if ((ptd = (DVTARGETDEVICE FAR*)OleStdMalloc(dwPtdSize)) != NULL) {

        // copy in the info
        ptd->tdSize = (UINT)dwPtdSize;

        lpDevNames = (LPDEVNAMES) &ptd->tdDriverNameOffset;
        _fmemcpy(lpDevNames, pDN, (size_t)dwDevNamesSize);
        lpDevMode=(LPDEVMODE)
            ((LPSTR)&ptd->tdDriverNameOffset+dwDevNamesSize);
         _fmemcpy(lpDevMode, pDM, (size_t)dwDevModeSize);
```

```
        ptd->tdDriverNameOffset += 4 ;
        ptd->tdDeviceNameOffset += 4 ;
        ptd->tdPortNameOffset   += 4 ;
        ptd->tdExtDevmodeOffset = (UINT)dwDevNamesSize + 4 ;
    }

    return ptd;
}
```

ADVF Enumeration

The values defined in the **ADVF** enumeration are used to specify information about connections of the types shown below:

- data advisories
- view advisories
- cache connections.

The valid values for **ADVF**, which can be or-ed together to form a composite value, are defined as follows:

```
typedef enum tagADVF
{
    ADVF_NODATA              = 1,
    ADVF_PRIMEFIRST          = 2,
    ADVF_ONLYONCE            = 4,
    ADVF_DATAONSTOP          = 64,
    ADVFCACHE_NOHANDLER      = 8,
    ADVFCACHE_FORCEBUILTIN   = 16,
    ADVFCACHE_ONSAVE         = 32
} ADVF;
```

Depending on the method in which the **ADVF** value is being used, the values may have different meanings. Some of the methods use only a subset of the values; other methods use all of them.

ADVF_NODATA, when passed to **IDataObject::DAdvise** is a request to avoid sending data with subsequent **IAdviseSink::OnDataChange** calls. TYMED_NULL is passed as the storage medium. The recipient of the data change notification can later retrieve the latest data by calling **IDataObject::GetData.** ADVF_NODATA however, is just a request. The data object may choose to provide the data anyway, especially when more than one advisory connection has been made specifying the same FORMATETC data structure.

When ADVF_NODATA is passed to **IViewObject::SetAdvise**, it returns E_INVALIDARG.

When ADVF_NODATA is passed to **IOleCache::Cache**, it is an indication that the cache should not be updated by changes made to the running object. Instead, the container will update the cache by explicitly calling **IOleCache::SetData**. This situation typically occurs when the iconic aspect of an object is being cached.

ADVF_PRIMEFIRST requests that a data or view change notification be sent or the cache updated immediately without waiting for a change in the current data or view.

ADVF_ONLYONCE automatically deletes the advisory connection after sending one data or view notification. The advisory sink receives only one **IAdviseSink** call. A nonzero connection ID is returned if the connection is established so the caller can use it to delete the connection. For data change notifications, the combination of ADVF_ONLYONCE | ADVF_PRIMEFIRST provides, in effect, an asynchronous **IDataObject::GetData** call.

When used with caching, ADVF_ONLYONCE updates the cache one time only, on receipt of the first OnDataChange notification. After the update is complete, the advisory connection between the object and the cache is disconnected.

ADVF_DATAONSTOP is meaningful for data change notifications only when ADVF_NODATA is also given. This value indicates that just before the advisory connection shuts down, a call to **IAdviseSink::OnDataChange** should be made that provides the data with it. Without this value, by the time an **OnDataChange** call without data reaches the sink, the source might have completed its shut down and the data might not be accessible. Sinks that specify this value should, in **OnDataChange**, accept data if it is being passed because they may not get another chance to retrieve it.

For cache connections, ADVF_DATAONSTOP updates the cache as part of object closure. ADVF_DATAONSTOP is not applicable to view change notifications.

ADVFCACHE_NOHANDLER, ADVFCACHE_FORCEBUILTIN, and ADVFCACHE_ONSAVE are applicable only to the caching methods. The ADVFCACHE_NOHANDLER value is reserved for future use.

ADVFCACHE_FORCEBUILTIN forcefully caches data that requires only code shipped with OLE or the underlying operating system to be present in order to produce it with **IDataObject::GetData** or **IViewObject ::Draw**, as appropriate. By specifying this value, the container can ensure that the data can be retrieved even when the object or handler code is not available. This value is used by DLL object applications and object handlers that perform the drawing of their objects. ADVFCACHE_FORCEBUILTIN instructs OLE to cache presentation data to ensure that there is a presentation in the cache.

ADVFCACHE_ONSAVE updates the cached representation only when the object containing the cache is saved. The cache is also updated when the OLE object transitions from the running state back to the loaded state (because a subsequent save operation would require rerunning the object).

OLE Clipboard Formats

There are three types of formats that are made available by using the **FORMATETC** structure when an application copies to the clipboard. They include the following:

- Standard Windows formats, such as CF_TEXT
- Private application formats understood only by the application offering the format or by other applications that are similar in functionality
- OLE-defined formats

Of interest here are the OLE-defined formats. They are used to describe data that can become an embedded or linked compound document object. The formats are made available in order of their fidelity of description of the data. In other words, the format that best represents the data selection is made available first. This intentional ordering encourages a receiving application to use the first format if possible.

There are six OLE-defined formats. The formats with the term "Source" in their name are used to create embedded or linked objects; the Embedded Object format can be used to create either object type. The "Descriptor" formats are used to describe the data selection on the clipboard and are made available in conjunction with the other formats. These formats are summarized below and described in detail in subsequent sections:

OLE Format	Usage
Embed Source (CF_EMBEDSOURCE)	Creates an embedded object from an object application's native data.
Link Source (CF_LINKSOURCE)	Creates a standard new linked object.
Custom Link Source (CF_CUSTOMLINKSOURCE)	Creates a custom new linked object
Embedded Object (CF_EMBEDDEDOBJECT)	Creates an embedded or linked object from a container's existing embedded object.
Object Descriptor (CF_OBJECTDESCRIPTOR)	Describes the data being transferred and is made available with all transfers.

OLE Format	Usage
Link Source Descriptor (CF_LINKSOURCEDESCRIPTOR)	Describes the link being transferred in the link source.

OLE provides helper functions to render and query for each of the OLE formats in its sample code library. The following table describes the available helper functions:

Sample Library Helper Function	Description
OleStdGetOleObjectData	Renders Embedded Object and Embed Source data.
OleStdGetLinkSourceData	Renders Link Source data
OleStdGetObjectDescriptor	Renders Object Descriptor and Link Source Descriptor data.
OleStdQueryOleObjectData	Queries for Embedded Object and Embed Source data.
OleStdQueryLinkSourceData	Queries for Link Source data.
OleStdQueryObjectDescriptorData	Queries for Object Descriptor and Link Source Descriptor data.

Embed Source Format

The Embed Source format is offered when the data selection can be the source of a new embedded object in a container. Embed source data is arranged exactly like it is in the normal persistent representation of an embedded object. Only the normal native data of the object is placed inside the transferred **IStorage**; presentations of the object are not be passed.

When an embedded object is created for the first time, as is the case with Embed Source, the formats available with the data transfer object can be used to initialize the cache for the newly created embedded object. When the transfer operation is done using the clipboard, **OleSetClipboard** can also offer these other formats to non-OLE-aware applications.

Link Source Format

The Link Source format is offered when the data selection can be the source of a new linked object in a container. Link Source data contains a class identifier (CLSID) and a moniker intended to represent the link source.

Data in Link Source format is always passed on a flat storage medium. This means that a medium of type TYMED_ISTORAGE is never appropriate. The contents of the medium are a serialized CLSID immediately followed by the serialized data of the moniker.

The CLSID is retrievable with **ReadClassStm**, and the moniker can be deserialized with **IPersistStream::Load**. A link can be created from the resulting moniker using **OleCreateLink**.

The cache in the new linked object is initialized with the formats available only from the data transfer object.

Custom Link Source Format

Custom Link Source is offered by applications that implement a custom link object to fully or partially replace the default link object provided by OLE. Applications may want to use a custom link object for their objects that have special rendering needs.

The custom link object is a DLL object and is registered as an INPROC_SERVER in the registration database. The custom link object implements the following interfaces:

Interface	Usage
IPersistStorage	Compound document storage
IDataObject	Data transfer
IOleCache2	Compound document cache support
IViewObject2	Compound document view support
IRunnableObject	Required by all in-process servers.
IExternalConnection	Required by all in-process servers.
IOleLink	Compound document link management
IOleObject	Compound document object support

The typical custom link object used for special rendering will implement **IPersistStorage**, **IDataObject**, **IOleCache2**, and **IViewObject2** and then aggregate OLE's standard link object implementation for the remaining interfaces.

To use a custom link object, objects must register a special key in the registration database:

```
HKEY_CLASSES_ROOT\CLSID\{...}\UseCustomLink
```

When the Link Source format is available and a user initiates a paste link, the link source application is asked whether or not it supports Custom Link Source. If Custom Link Source is supported, the link source application writes the CLSID of the custom link object into a specified **IStorage**. When the linked object is instantiated, the CLSID is read from the storage and passed to **CoCreateInstance**, which uses it to create the custom link object.

The moniker passed with the Link Source data is given to the custom link object so it can bind the newly created linked object when necessary.

Embedded Object Format

The Embedded Object format is offered when the data selection is an embedded object and indicates that either a linked or embedded object can be created. Embedded Object should be first in the list of formats that are made available.

The Embedded Object data is arranged exactly like the Embed Source data. To create an embedded object from the Embedded Object format, a receiving application copies the contents of the data selection's storage object into a new storage object. Before a copy can be safely done, it is necessary to check whether the object has changed since it was last saved. If it has, the object can be saved directly into the new storage. If no change has been made, the method **IStorage::CopyTo** can be called to copy the contents from the original storage to the new storage. The following code illustrates this logic:

```
lpObject->QueryInterface(IID_IPersistStorage, &lpPersistStorage);
if (lpPersistStorage->IsDirty() == NOERROR)  {
    OleSave(lpPersistStorage, lpNewStorage, FALSE);
    lpPersistStorage->SaveCompleted(lpNewStorage);
}
else  {
    lpPersistStorage->CopyTo(lpNewStorage);
}
```

The main difference between Embed Source and Embedded Object lies in the way that the cache for the new compound document object is initialized. When an embedded object is created for the first time, as is the case with Embed Source, only the formats available with the data transfer object can be used to initialize the cache for the newly created embedded object. With the Embedded Object format, the presentations in the cache of the embedded object itself are available as well.

Object Descriptor Format

The Object Descriptor format is offered whenever data is copied. Object Descriptor data is made available in an instance of an **OBJECTDESCRIPTOR** data structure. The **OBJECTDESCRIPTOR** structure consists of the following elements:

```
ULONG           cbSize
CLSID           clsid
DWORD           dwDrawAspect
SIZEL           sizel
POINTL          pointl
DWORD           dwStatus
DWORD           dwFullUserTypeName
DWORD           dwSrcOfCopy
```

The *cbSize* is the size of the **OBJECTDESCRIPTOR** structure in bytes.

The *clsid* is used to obtain the icon for the 'DisplayAsIcon' option in the Paste Special dialog and is applicable only if the Embed Source or Embedded Object formats are offered. If neither of these formats are offered, the value of *clsid* should be CLSID_NULL.

The value of the *dwDrawAspect* field is typically DVASPECT_CONTENT or DVASPECT_ICON. If the source application did not draw the object originally, the *dwDrawAspect* field contains a zero value (which is not the same as DVASPECT_CONTENT).

The *sizel* field contains the true extents from the object, available through a call to **IOleObject::GetExtent**. Setting the *sizel* field is optional; its value can be (0, 0) for applications that do not draw the object being transferred.

The *pointl* field is the offset in HIMETRIC units from the upper-left corner of the object where a drag operation was initiated. This field is only meaningful for a drag and drop transfer operation. The value is (0,0) for other transfer situations, such as a clipboard copy and paste.

The *dwStatus* field contains miscellaneous status flags for the object. These flags are defined by the OLEMISC enumeration and are returned by calling **IOleObject::GetMiscStatus**.

The *dwFullUserTypeName* field is the offset from the beginning of the data structure to the null-terminated string that specifies the full user type name of the object. The value is zero if the string is not present.

The *dwSrcOfCopy* field is the offset from the beginning of the data structure to the null-terminated string that specifies the source of the transfer. The *dwSrcOfCopy* field is typically implemented as the display name of the temporary moniker that identifies the data source. The value for *dwSrcOfCopy* is displayed in the Source line of the Paste Special dialog. A zero value indicates that the string is not present. If *dwSrcOfCopy* is zero, the string 'Unknown Source' is displayed in the Paste Special dialog.

Link Source Descriptor Format

The Link Source Descriptor format, like Object Descriptor, contains information about the source of a compound document object. Link Source Descriptor is always offered when Link Source is offered. The same data is included for both formats. However, with Link Source Descriptor, the value of *dwSrcOfCopy* can represent either a pseudo object in the source application, referred to as an *outside link*, or the running embedded object, referred to as an *inside link*. For example, consider the case in which a word processor links to a drawing that is a linked object within a spreadsheet program.

If the new link is an *inside link*, the draw program is launched to edit the drawing when a word processor user double-clicks. The link source is the original object application used to create the drawing. If the new link is an *outside link*, the spreadsheet program becomes the link source and is used for editing.

When a link is copied, the source field will show the display name of the link source and the list box in the Paste dialog will show "Linked <object full type>. The result text and image will not be changed since they typically apply to both linking or embedding. It is the responsibility of the copying application to add the "Linked" to the full user type name given in the Link Source Descriptor data.

Copying to the Clipboard

Applications that support clipboard copy typically have a standard set of formats they always offer and another set to offer selectively, depending on the data being copied. This standard set of formats is application-specific. For example, a pure container that does not support linking to its embedded objects would offer a different set of formats than an object application that supports linking to pseudo objects. Applications that are to maintain compatibility with OLE 1 must offer CF_METAFILEPICT.

The following table suggests possible format offerings by application type. In all cases except for the container copying native data or multiple compound document objects, it is assumed that the data selection can be the source of a linked object. The placement of Picture relative to the other formats in the table is somewhat arbitrary. It is up to the application to determine where Picture belongs. Otherwise, the ordering is intentional. Containers that do not draw their objects (use them pictorially) do not need to offer a picture format.

Type of Application	**Data Selection**
Container application	single compound document object
Container application	native data or multiple compound document objects
Object application	native data
Container/object application	single compound document object
Container/object application	native data or multiple compound document objects

A consideration when offering Link Source for an embedded object in an unsaved container document is whether the object is running or merely loaded. If the object is not running, and a link is created before the container document is saved, no OnRename notification will be sent when the document is saved. Thus, the link will be broken. To ensure that links are valid whenever possible, containers should only permit linking to data in saved documents.

A few conditions can change the set of offered formats. Link Source and Link Source Descriptor should be removed from the data transfer object if either a moniker cannot be provided to represent the data selection, or, in the case of a copy, the data has changed since the copy was initiated. If the data selection is a single embedded object in a container, Embedded Object, Object Descriptor, and the formats provided by the loaded object are dynamically added to the list of offered formats.

Pasting From the Clipboard

An application implementing paste operations retrieves the data transfer object from the clipboard and looks for an acceptable format among the list of formats that are available. If the first acceptable format is one that the application can edit, the selection is typically treated as data that is native to the application and a linked or embedded object is not created, thus avoiding the extra overhead involved in compound document object creation. For example, if the data selection is a paragraph from a word processor application that offers CF_TEXT as its first available format and the receiving application is also a word processor, the receiving application can integrate the paragraph directly into its document. A user will be able to edit the pasted data in the same way as the rest of the document.

If only CF_METAFILEPICT, CF_DIB, or CF_BITMAP is available, a static object can be created from the data by calling **OleCreateStaticFromData**. Static objects are pictures for which OLE provides a compound document object wrapping, making it possible for containers to treat them as though they were linked or embedded objects. A static object has the class ID, CLSID_StaticMetafile and the aspect DVASPECT_CONTENT. Static objects cannot be edited.

Special consideration are involved if the selected format is a private one that transfers with a storage object. The receiving container cannot copy the data directly from the source storage object into the destination document because substorage and stream objects used to hold private data cannot be opened twice. However, if the selected data is local to the receiving container, it can simply be copied directly from the source document into the destination document. It is only the nonlocal case that requires an alternate method of transfer.

In order for the container to take advantage of the direct copy optimization in the local case, the container must have a way to determine whether it placed the original data on the clipboard. If a data transfer object exists (assuming the application creates one as part of its copy operation), its **IDataObject** interface pointer can be compared with the **IDataObject** interface pointer retrieved with **OleGetClipboard** or **IDropTarget::DragEnter**. If these pointers are the same, it is safe to assume that the copied data and the new embedded object are from the same container.

To copy data from one storage object into another storage object in the nonlocal case, a container application can create a temporary document. The data is loaded from the source storage object and copied into the temporary document. The contents of the temporary document are then copied into the real container document and the temporary document is destroyed.

IDataObject Interface

The **IDataObject** interface plays a central role in the transferring and caching of data and presentations. **IDataObject** contains methods that retrieve, store, and enumerate data, and handle data change notifications. All applications that transfer data implement **IDataObject** regardless of whether they are containers or object applications. All applications that receive data use **IDataObject**. **IDataObject** contains the following methods (see also DVOBJ.H):

```
DECLARE_INTERFACE_(IDataObject, IUnknown)
{
  // *** IUnknown methods ***
 HRESULT QueryInterface (THIS_ REFIID riid, LPVOID FAR* ppvObj);
 ULONG AddRef (THIS) ;
 ULONG  Release (THIS);

  // *** IDataObject methods ***
 HRESULT GetData (THIS_ LPFORMATETC pFormatetc,
  LPSTGMEDIUM pmedium);
 HRESULT GetDataHere (THIS_ LPFORMATETC pFormatetc,
  LPSTGMEDIUM pmedium);
 HRESULT QueryGetData (THIS_ LPFORMATETC pFormatetc );
 HRESULT GetCanonicalFormatEtc (THIS_ LPFORMATETC pFormatetc,
  LPFORMATETC pFormatetcOut);
 HRESULT SetData (THIS_ LPFORMATETC pFormatetc, STGMEDIUM FAR * pmedium,
  BOOL fRelease);
 HRESULT EnumFormatEtc (THIS_ DWORD dwDirection,
  LPENUMFORMATETC FAR* ppenumFormatetc );
 HRESULT DAdvise (THIS_ FORMATETC FAR* pFormatetc, DWORD advf,
  LPADVISESINK pAdvise, DWORD FAR* pdwConnection);
 HRESULT DUnadvise (THIS_ DWORD dwConnection);
 HRESULT EnumDAdvise (THIS_ LPENUMSTATDATA FAR* ppenumAdvise );
};
```

IDataObject::GetData

HRESULT IDataObject::GetData(*pFormatetc*, *pmedium*)
LPFORMATETC *pFormatetc*
LPSTGMEDIUM *pmedium*

IDataObject::GetData retrieves data in a specified format using a specified storage medium.

Parameters

pFormatetc
Points to the format to use for returning the data.

pmedium
Points to the storage medium to use for returning the data. This is the storage medium provided by the callee.

Return Values

Value	Meaning
S_OK	Data was successfully retrieved and placed in the storage medium provided.
E_INVALIDARG	One or more arguments are invalid.
E_OUTOFMEMORY	Ran out of memory.
E_UNEXPECTED	A relatively catastrophic failure.
DV_E_LINDEX	Invalid value for *lindex*; currently, only -1 is supported.
DV_E_FORMATETC	Invalid value for *pFormatetc*.
DV_E_TYMED	Invalid *tymed* value.
DV_E_DVASPECT	Invalid *dwAspect* value.
OLE_E_NOTRUNNING	Object application is not running.
DATA_E_FORMATETC	Cannot support the requested media.

Comments

It is valid to ask **GetData** to return data in a specified format on one of a specified group of mediums. Multiple mediums can be specified by or-ing together the *tymed* values in the **FORMATETC** structure passed to **GetData**. The callee allocates the medium and decides how the resources associated with that medium are to be released. **GetData** determines the best medium, given its selection, and attempts to transfer the data. Only one medium can be returned. If this initial transfer fails, **GetData** might try one of the other mediums specified before returning an error.

Conceptually, the *pmedium* parameter is an *out* parameter, implying that the caller allocates the **STGMEDIUM** structure and the callee fills it in. The callee determines who is responsible for releasing the medium's resources and sets *pmedium->pUnkForRelease* to the appropriate value.

Supporting transfer of data with the **IStorage** medium requires special handling. Because it is not possible to transfer ownership of a root **IStorage** object from one process to another, the callee must retain ownership of the data by setting the *pUnkForRelease* field in the **STGMEDIUM** structure passed in by the caller. Alternatively, callers should consider using **IDataObject::GetDataHere** because it is more efficient.

Data transferred across a stream extends from position zero of the stream pointer through to the position immediately before the current stream pointer (the stream pointer position upon exit).

Example

The following implementation of **IDataObject::GetData** is from an object application that supports the standard metafile format and the Embed Source, Link Source, and Object Descriptor OLE formats. IDataObject_GetData first checks for CF_METAFILEPICT with a *tymed* value of TYMED_MFPICT and the content and print aspects. Any other aspects or mediums are not supported for CF_METAFILEPICT. If the CF_METAFILEPICT format is requested and memory can be allocated for the medium, the data is returned. Otherwise, the value of *m_fDataTransferDoc* is examined to determine whether this document is being used for data transfer. If the document is not a data transfer object, the only supported format is metafile. If the document is a data transfer object, IDataObject_GetData renders Object and Link Source Descriptor, Embed Source, and Link Source. For each format, the medium is checked to ensure it is appropriate and one of the sample helper functions is called to render the data.

```
HRESULT IDataObject_GetData (
        LPDATAOBJECT        lpThis,
        LPFORMATETC         pFormatetc,
        LPSTGMEDIUM         pmedium
)
{
    LPAPP lpApp = (LPAPP)g_lpApp;
    LPDOC lpDoc = ((struct CDocDataObjectImpl FAR*)lpThis)->lpDoc;
    HRESULT         hrErr;
    SCODE           sc;
    SIZEL           sizel;
    POINTL          pointl;
    LPSTR           lpszSrcOfCopy = NULL;
    IBindCtx   FAR *pbc = NULL;
    HGLOBAL         hObjDesc;
    DWORD           dwStatus = 0;
    LPDOC           lpSrcDocOfCopy=(LPDOC)lpDoc->m_lpSrcDocOfCopy;
```

```
LPMONIKER lpSrcMonikerOfCopy = GetFullMoniker(
            lpDoc->m_lpSrcDocOfCopy,
            &lpDoc->m_lrSrcSelOfCopy,
            GETMONIKER_TEMPFORUSER);

pmedium->pUnkForRelease = NULL;
pmedium->tymed = NULL;
pmedium->u.hGlobal = NULL;

if (pFormatetc->cfFormat == CF_METAFILEPICT &&
   (pFormatetc->dwAspect & (DVASPECT_CONTENT |
    DVASPECT_DOCPRINT))){
    if (!(pFormatetc->tymed & TYMED_MFPICT))
        return ResultFromScode(DATA_E_FORMATETC);

    pmedium->u.hGlobal = GetMetafilePictData(lpDoc, NULL);
    if (! pmedium->u.hGlobal)
        return ResultFromScode (E_OUTOFMEMORY);

    pmedium->tymed = TYMED_MFPICT;
    return NOERROR;
}

if (! lpDoc->m_fDataTransferDoc)
    return ResultFromScode(DATA_E_FORMATETC);

if (pFormatetc->cfFormat == lpApp->m_cfObjectDescriptor ||
    (pFormatetc->cfFormat == lpApp->m_cfLinkSrcDescriptor &&
            lpDoc->m_fLinkSourceAvail)) {
    // Verify caller asked for correct medium
    if (!(pFormatetc->tymed & TYMED_HGLOBAL))
        return ResultFromScode(DATA_E_FORMATETC);

    // Get dwStatus value
    IOleObject_GetMiscStatus(
            (LPOLEOBJECT)&lpDoc->m_OleObject,
            DVASPECT_CONTENT,
            &dwStatus
    );

    // Get extent of document in HIMETRIC
    GetExtent(lpDoc, &sizel);
    pointl.x = pointl.y = 0;

    if (lpSrcMonikerOfCopy) {
        CreateBindCtx(0, (LPBC FAR*)&pbc);
        lpSrcMonikerOfCopy->lpVtbl->GetDisplayName(
            lpSrcMonikerOfCopy, pbc, NULL, &lpszSrcOfCopy);
        pbc->lpVtbl->Release(pbc);
        lpSrcMonikerOfCopy->lpVtbl->Release(lpSrcMonikerOfCopy);
```

```
        } else {
            // this document has no moniker; use FullUserTypeName
            lpszSrcOfCopy = FULLUSERTYPENAME;
        }

        pmedium->u_hGlobal =  OleStdGetObjectDescriptorData
            (CLSID_APP, DVASPECT_CONTENT, sizel, pointl, dwStatus,
             FULLUSERTYPENAME, lpszSrcOfCopy);

        if (lpSrcMonikerOfCopy && lpszSrcOfCopy)
            OleStdFreeString(lpszSrcOfCopy, NULL);

        if (! pmedium->u.hGlobal)
            return ResultFromScode(E_OUTOFMEMORY);

        pmedium->tymed = TYMED_HGLOBAL;
        return NOERROR;

    } else if (pFormatetc->cfFormat == lpApp->m_cfEmbedSource) {
        return ( OleStdGetOleObjectData
                ((LPPERSISTSTORAGE)&lpDoc->m_PersistStorage,
                  pFormatetc, pmedium, FALSE) );
    } else if (pFormatetc->cfFormat == lpApp->m_cfLinkSource) {
        if (lpDoc->m_fLinkSourceAvail) {
            LPMONIKER lpmk;
            lpmk = GetFullMoniker((LPDOC)lpDoc->m_lpSrcDocOfCopy,
                      &lpDoc->m_lrSrcSelOfCopy, GETMONIKER_FORCEASSIGN);
            if (lpmk)  {
                hrErr = OleStdGetLinkSourceData(lpmk,
                          (LPCLSID)&CLSID_APP, pFormatetc, pmedium);
                lpmk->lpVtbl->Release(lpmk);
                return hrErr;
            } else
                return ResultFromScode(E_FAIL);
        } else
                return ResultFromScode(DATA_E_FORMATETC);
    } else
        return ResultFromSCode(DATA_E_FORMATETC);

    return NOERROR;
}
```

See Also **IDataObject::SetData, IDataObject::GetDataHere, IEnumFORMATETC, ReleaseStgMedium**

IDataObject::GetDataHere

HRESULT IDataObject::GetDataHere(*pFormatetc*, *pmedium*)
LPFORMATETC *pFormatetc*
LPSTGMEDIUM *pmedium*

IDataObject::GetDataHere retrieves data in a specified format using a storage medium provided by the caller.

Parameters

pFormatetc
Points to the format to use for returning the data.

pmedium
Points to the storage medium to use for returning the data. This is the storage medium provided by the caller.

Return Values

Value	Meaning
S_OK	Data was successfully retrieved and placed in the storage medium provided.
E_INVALIDARG	One or more arguments are invalid.
E_OUTOFMEMORY	Ran out of memory.
E_UNEXPECTED	A relatively catastrophic failure.
DV_E_LINDEX	Invalid value for *lindex*; currently only -1 is supported.
DV_E_FORMATETC	Invalid FORMATETC structure pointed to by *pFormatetc*.
DV_E_TYMED	Invalid *tymed* value.
DV_E_DVASPECT	Invalid *dwAspect* value.
OLE_E_NOTRUNNING	Object application is not running.
DATA_E_FORMATETC	Cannot support the requested media.
STG_E_MEDIUMFULL	The caller-provided medium is not large enough.

Comments

GetDataHere is like **GetData** except that the caller allocates the medium across which the data is to be transferred. **GetDataHere** is called when the clipboard selection or data being dragged is an embedded object.

When the transfer medium is a stream, assumptions are made about where the data is being returned and the position of the stream's seek pointer. In a **GetData** call, the data returned is from stream position zero through just before the current seek pointer of the stream (the position on exit). For **GetDataHere**, the data returned is from the stream position on entry through just before the position on exit.

The callee must fill in the actual medium provided by the caller in the hGlobal case. That is, the callee cannot allocate a new hGlobal; it must put the data in the medium provided by the caller. The caller always sets the field *pmedium->tymed* to the value of *pFormatetc->tymed* because *pFormatetc->tymed* can only indicate one medium.

Example

The following example of IDataObject_GetDataHere is from an object application. After checking that the current document is a data transfer object, OleStdGetOleObjectData is called to transfer Embed Source data with the medium supplied by the caller, a storage object.

```
HRESULT IDataObject_GetDataHere (
        LPDATAOBJECT      lpThis,
        LPFORMATETC       pFormatetc,
        LPSTGMEDIUM       pmedium
)
{
    LPAPP           lpApp = (LPAPP)g_lpApp;
    LPDOC lpDoc = ((struct CDocDataObjectImpl FAR*)lpThis)->lpDoc;
    HRESULT         hrErr;
    SCODE           sc;

    // Must be a data transfer document
    pmedium->pUnkForRelease = NULL;
    if (! lpDoc->m_fDataTransferDoc)
        return ResultFromScode(DATA_E_FORMATETC);

    if (pFormatetc->cfFormat == lpApp->m_cfEmbedSource) {
        hrErr = OleStdGetOleObjectData(
                (LPPERSISTSTORAGE)&lpDoc->m_PersistStorage,
                pFormatetc,
                pmedium,
                FALSE   /* fUseMemory -- (use file-base stg) */
        );
        return hrErr;

    } else
        return ResultFromScode(DATA_E_FORMATETC);
}
```

See Also

IDataObject::GetData

IDataObject::QueryGetData

HRESULT IDataObject::QueryGetData(*pFormatetc***)**
LPFORMATETC *pFormatetc*

IDataObject::QueryGetData determines whether a call to **IDataObject::GetData** would succeed if it were passed *pFormatetc*.

Parameters

pFormatetc
Points to the format to use for transferring data.

Return Values

Value	Meaning
S_OK	Data in the specified format would be successfully returned.
DATA_E_FORMATETC	Data in the specified format would not be successfully returned.
E_INVALIDARG	One or more arguments are invalid.
E_OUTOFMEMORY	Ran out of memory.
E_UNEXPECTED	A relatively catastrophic failure.
DV_E_LINDEX	Invalid value for *lindex*; currently only -1 is supported.
DV_E_FORMATETC	Invalid FORMATETC structure.
DV_E_TYMED	Invalid *tymed* value.
DV_E_DVASPECT	Invalid *dwAspect* value.
OLE_E_NOTRUNNING	Object application is not running.

Example

IDataObject_QueryGetData is a container's implementation; several formats and mediums are supported. For the private formats, the helper function OleStdQueryFormatMedium is called to determine whether the specified FORMATETC structure includes TYMED_HGLOBAL because this format can only be rendered using global memory. For Embedded Object, the set of formats offered must include the formats available from the object itself. Therefore, the call is delegated to the object's IDataObject_QueryGetData implementation. For all other formats, the appropriate sample library helper function is called.

```
HRESULT IDataObject_QueryGetData (
        LPDATAOBJECT   lpThis,
        LPFORMATETC    pFormatetc
)
{
    LPAPP lpApp = (LPAPP)g_lpApp;
    LPDATAOBJECT  lpDataObj = NULL;
    LPDOC lpDoc = ((struct CDocDataObjectImpl FAR*)lpThis)->lpDoc;
    LPCLISITE lpCliSite;
    SCODE sc;
    HRESULT hrErr;
```

```
    if (lpDoc->m_fEmbeddedObjectAvail) {
        lpDataObj = (LPDATAOBJECT)GetSingleOleObject(lpDoc,
                    &IID_IDataObject, (LPCLISITE FAR*)&lpCliSite);
    }

    if (pFormatetc->cfFormat == lpApp->m_cfEmbeddedObject &&
              lpDoc->m_fEmbeddedObjectAvail ) {
        sc = GetScode( OleStdQueryOleObjectData(pFormatetc) );

    } else if (pFormatetc->cfFormat == lpApp->m_cfLinkSource &&
          lpDoc->m_fLinkSourceAvail) {
        sc = GetScode( OleStdQueryLinkSourceData(pFormatetc) );

    } else if((pFormatetc->cfFormat == (lpApp)->m_cfPrivate ||
          pFormatetc->cfFormat == CF_TEXT) ) {
        sc = GetScode( OleStdQueryFormatMedium(pFormatetc,
                          TYMED_HGLOBAL) );

    } else if (pFormatetc->cfFormat == lpApp->m_cfEmbeddedObject &&
          lpDoc->m_fEmbeddedObjectAvail ) {
        sc = GetScode( OleStdQueryOleObjectData(pFormatetc) );

    } else if (pFormatetc->cfFormat == lpApp->m_cfLinkSource &&
              lpDoc->m_fLinkSourceAvail) {
        sc = GetScode( OleStdQueryLinkSourceData(pFormatetc) );

    } else if ( pFormatetc->cfFormat == lpApp->m_cfObjectDescriptor ||
        (pFormatetc->cfFormat == lpApp->m_cfLinkSrcDescriptor &&
         lpDoc->m_fLinkSourceAvail) ) {
        sc = GetScode( OleStdQueryObjectDescriptorData(pFormatetc) );

    } else if (pFormatetc->cfFormat == CF_METAFILEPICT &&
        lpDoc->m_fEmbeddedObjectAvail && lpCliSite &&
        (pFormatetc->dwAspect & lpCliSite->m_dwDrawAspect)) {
        sc = GetScode( OleStdQueryFormatMedium(pFormatetc,
                           TYMED_MFPICT) );

    } else if (lpDataObj) {
        hrErr = lpDataObj->lpVtbl->QueryGetData(lpDataObj, pFormatetc);
        sc = GetScode(hrErr);

    } else {
        sc = DATA_E_FORMATETC;
    }

    if (lpDataObj)
        (LPUNKNOWN)lpDataObj->lpVtbl->Release ((LPUNKNOWN)lpDataObj);
    return ResultFromScode(sc);
}
```

See Also **IDataObject::GetData, FORMATETC**

IDataObject::GetCanonicalFormatEtc

HRESULT IDataObject::GetCanonicalFormatEtc(*pFormatetc*, *pFormatetcOut*)
LPFORMATETC *pFormatetc*
LPFORMATETC *pFormatetcOut*

IDataObject::GetCanonicalFormatEtc communicates to the caller which **FORMATETC** data structures produce the same output data.

Parameters

pFormatetc
Points to the format and medium in which the caller wants to obtain the returned data.

pFormatetcOut
Points to where to return the canonical equivalent of *pFormatetc*.

Return Values

Value	Meaning
S_OK	The returned FORMATETC structure is different than the one that was passed.
E_INVALIDARG	One or more arguments are invalid.
E_OUTOFMEMORY	Ran out of memory.
E_UNEXPECTED	A relatively catastrophic failure.
DATA_S_SAMEFORMATETC	The FORMATETC structures are the same and no value needs to be put in *pFormatetcOut*.
DV_E_LINDEX	Invalid value for *lindex*; currently, only -1 is supported.
DV_E_FORMATETC	Invalid FORMATETC structure.
OLE_E_NOTRUNNING	Object application is not running.

Comments

Often, a given data object returns the same data for more than one requested FORMATETC structure. This is especially true for target devices. The returned data is often insensitive to the particular target device in question. To enable callers to prevent caching duplicate sets of data, **IDataObject::GetCanonicalFormatEtc** provides the means by which objects can indicate to the caller which FORMATETC structures produce the same results.

The callee should pick a canonical representative of the set of FORMATETC structures equivalent to the one passed by the caller in *pFormatetc* and return that through *pFormatetcOut*. *pFormatetcOut* is allocated by the caller and filled in by the callee. The *tymed* member of both FORMATETC structure pointers (*pFormatetc->tymed* and *pFormatecOut->tymed*) is not significant and should be ignored.

The simplest implementation of **IDataObject::GetCanonicalFormatEtc** returns DATA_S_SAMEFORMATETC and sets *pFormatetcOut->ptd* to NULL. This type of implementation implies that the callee, usually a more sophisticated application, **is** sensitive to target devices.

Examples

The following implementation of **IDataObject::GetCanonicalFormatEtc** checks that the outgoing **FORMATETC** pointer is valid before initializing its *ptd* member to NULL. If either of the **FORMATETC** pointers are invalid, E_INVALIDARG is returned. A call to **IDataObject::QueryGetData**determines if the format information supplied in *pFormatetc* is supported. If the information is supported, the contents of *pFormatetcOut* is set to the contents of *pFormatetc*. When *pFormatetc->ptd* is NULL, an indication that the caller does not care about target devices, DATA_S_SAMEFORMATETC is returned. When *pFormatetc->ptd* is not NULL, **GetCanonicalFormatEtc** sets it to NULL and returns NOERROR.

```
HRESULT IDataObject_GetCanonicalFormatEtc(LPDATAOBJECT lpThis,
            LPFORMATETC pFormatetc, LPFORMATETC pFormatetcOut);
{
    HRESULT hrErr;

    if (!pFormatetcOut)
        return ResultFromScode(E_INVALIDARG);

    pFormatetcOut->ptd = NULL;

    if (!pFormatetc)
        return ResultFromScode(E_INVALIDARG);

    hrErr = lpThis->lpVtbl->QueryGetData(lpThis,pFormatetc);
    if (hrErr != NOERROR)        return hrErr;

    *pFormatetcOut = *pFormatetc;
    if (pFormatetc->ptd == NULL)
        return ResultFromScode(DATA_S_SAMEFORMATETC);
    else {
        pFormatetcOut->ptd = NULL;
        return NOERROR;
    }
}
```

The next example shows how sophisticated applications that are sensitive to target devices would implement **IDataObject::GetCanonicalFormatEtc**:

```
HRESULT IDataObject_GetCanonicalFormatEtc(LPDATAOBJECT lpThis,
    LPFORMATETC pFormatetc, LPFORMATETC pFormatetcOut)
{
    HRESULT hrErr;

    if (!pFormatetcOut)
        return ResultFromScode(E_INVALIDARG);

    pFormatetcOut->ptd = NULL;

    if (!pFormatetc)
        return ResultFromScode(E_INVALIDARG);

    hrErr = lpThis->lpVtbl->QueryGetData(lpThis,pFormatetc);
    if (hrErr != NOERROR)        return hrErr;

    *pFormatetcOut = *pFormatetc;
    return ResultFromScode(DATA_S_SAMEFORMATETC);
```

See Also **FORMATETC**

IDataObject::SetData

HRESULT IDataObject::SetData(*pFormatetc*, *pmedium*, *fRelease***)**
LPFORMATETC *pFormatetc*
LPSTGMEDIUM *pmedium*
BOOL *fRelease*

IDataObject::SetData sends data in a specified format.

Parameters

pFormatetc
Points to the format to use when interpreting the data contained in the storage medium.

pmedium
Points to the storage medium (an *in* parameter only) containing the actual data.

fRelease
Indicates who has ownership of the storage medium after completing the method. If *fRelease* returns TRUE, the callee takes ownership, freeing the medium after it has been used. If *fRelease* returns FALSE, the caller retains ownership and the callee uses the storage medium for the duration of the call only.

Return Values

Value	Meaning
S_OK	Data was successfully used.
E_INVALIDARG	One or more arguments are invalid.
E_OUTOFMEMORY	Ran out of memory.
E_UNEXPECTED	A relatively catastrophic failure.
DV_E_LINDEX	Currently only *lindex* -1 is supported. Passing any other lindex results in an error.
DV_E_FORMATETC	Invalid FORMATETC structure.
DV_E_TYMED	Invalid *tymed* value.
DV_E_DVASPECT	Invalid *dwAspect* value.
OLE_E_NOTRUNNING	Object application is not running.

Comments

The callee does not take ownership of the data until it has successfully used it. That is, DATA_E_FORMATETC or another error code is not returned. If the callee does take ownership, it must free the medium by calling **ReleaseStgMedium**.

Example

Data transfer objects do not support **IDataObject::SetData** so an initial check for document type is made. If the check succeeds and the requested format is supported, the data is pasted and S_OK is returned. Otherwise, either E_FAIL or DATA_E_FORMATETC is returned. E_FAIL indicates the document represents a data transfer object; DATA_E_FORMATETC indicates an unsupported format was specified.

```
HRESULT IDataObject_SetData (
        LPDATAOBJECT    lpThis,
        LPFORMATETC     pFormatetc,
        LPSTGMEDIUM     pmedium,
        BOOL            fRelease
)
{
    LPDOC lpDoc = ((struct CDocDataObjectImpl FAR*)lpThis)->lpDoc;
    LPAPP lpApp = (LPAPP)g_lpApp;

    // Data transfer objects cannot accept data
    if (lpDoc->m_fDataTransferDoc)
        return ResultFromScode(E_FAIL);

    if (pFormatetc->cfFormat == lpApp->m_cfPrivate) {
        SetRedraw ( lpDoc, FALSE );
        ClearAllLines(lpDoc);
        PastePrivateData(lpDoc,pmedium->u.hGlobal,-1);
        SetRedraw ( lpDoc, TRUE );

    } else if (pFormatetc->cfFormat == CF_TEXT) {
        SetRedraw ( lpDoc, FALSE );
```

```
            ClearAllLines(lpDoc);
            PasteTextData(lpDoc,pmedium->u.hGlobal,-1);
            SetRedraw ( lpDoc, TRUE );

        } else
            return ResultFromScode (DATA_E_FORMATETC);

        return ResultFromScode (S_OK);
    }
```

See Also **IDataObject::GetData, ReleaseStgMedium**

IDataObject::EnumFormatEtc

HRESULT IDataObject::EnumFormatEtc(*dwDirection, ppenumFormatetc*)
DWORD *dwDirection*
LPENUMFORMATETC FAR * *ppenumFormatetc*

IDataObject::EnumFormatEtc enumerates the formats that can be used to store data obtained with **IDataObject::GetData** or sent with **IDataObject::SetData**.

Parameters

dwDirection
Indicates the set of formats to be enumerated; valid values are taken from the enumeration **DATADIR**:

```
typedef enum tagDATADIR
{
    DATADIR_GET = 1,
    DATADIR_SET = 2,
} DATADIR;
```

DATADIR_GET enumerates formats that can be passed to **IDataObject::GetData.** DATADIR_SET enumerates formats that can be passed to **IDataObject::SetData**.

ppenumFormatetc
Points to where to return the instantiated enumerator.

Return Values

Value	Meaning
S_OK	Enumerator returned successfully.
E_INVALIDARG	One or more arguments are invalid.
E_OUTOFMEMORY	Ran out of memory.
E_NOTIMPL	The direction indicated by *dwDirection* is not supported.
OLE_S_USEREG	Request that OLE enumerate the formats from the registration database.

Comments

The enumeration returned by **IDataObject::EnumFormatEtc** is not a guarantee of support because the formats can change over time. Accordingly, applications should treat the enumeration as a hint to the format types that can be passed.

EnumFormatEtc is called when one of the following actions occurs:

- An application calls **OleSetClipboard.** OLE must determine whether it is necessary to put OLE 1 compatibility formats on the clipboard.
- Data is being pasted from the clipboard or dropped. An application uses the first acceptable format.
- The Paste Special dialog box is displayed. The target application builds the list of formats from the **FORMATETC** entries.

Formats can be registered statically in the registration database or dynamically during application initialization. If an application has an unchanging list of formats and these formats are registered in the registration database, it can ask OLE to perform the enumeration using the registration database by calling **OleRegEnumFormatEtc** or by returning OLE_S_USEREG. OLE_S_USEREG instructs the default handler to call **OleRegEnumFormatEtc**. Object applications that are implemented as DLL object applications cannot return OLE_S_USEREG; they must call **OleRegEnumFormatEtc** directly.

Private formats can be enumerated for OLE 1 objects, if they are registered with the RequestDataFormats or SetDataFormats keys in the registration database. Also, private formats can be enumerated for OLE 2 objects, if they are registered with the GetDataFormats or SetDataFormats keys.

For OLE 1 objects whose servers do not have RequestDataFormats or SetDataFormats information registered in the registration database, calling **EnumFormatEtc** with DATADIR_GET only enumerates the Native, Metafile, DIB, Bitmap, and Text formats, regardless of whether they support these formats or others. Calling **EnumFormatEtc** with DATADIR_SET on such objects only enumerates Native, regardless of whether the object supports being set with other formats.

The **FORMATETC** structure returned by the enumeration usually indicates a NULL target device (*ptd*). This is appropriate because, unlike the other members of **FORMATETC**, the target device does not participate in the object's decision as to whether it can accept or provide the data in an **IDataObject::SetData** or **IDataObject::GetData** call, respectively.

FORMATETC::*tymed* often indicates that more than one kind of storage medium is acceptable.

Example

The following object application implementation of **IDataObject::EnumFormatEtc** enumerates the static list of formats that are registered in the registration data if this document represents a user document. It is not required that a user document (such as a nondata transfer object) enumerate the OLE formats.

If the document is a data transfer object, the offered formats might or might not include Link Source and Link Source Descriptor depending on whether a moniker is available. If a moniker is not available, the number of formats is decremented by 2 and Link Source and Link Source Descriptor are removed from the list. The sample code library provides an implementation of **IEnumFormatEtc** that is used in **IDataObject::EnumFormatEtc**. By calling OleStdEnumFmtEtc_Create, an instance of the enumerator is returned. Notice that *dwDirection* must be DATADIR_GET; no other options are supported.

```
HRESULT IDataObject_EnumFormatEtc(
        LPDATAOBJECT            lpThis,
        DWORD                   dwDirection,
        LPENUMFORMATETC FAR*    lplpenumFormatEtc
)
{
    LPDOC lpDoc=((struct CDocDataObjectImpl FAR*)lpThis)->lpDoc;
    HRESULT hrErr;
    LPAPP  lpApp = (LPAPP)g_lpApp;
    int nActualFormats;
    SCODE sc = S_OK;

    *lplpenumFormatEtc = NULL;

    if (! ((LPDOC)lpDoc)->m_fDataTransferDoc)
        return OleRegEnumFormatEtc(
            (REFCLSID)&CLSID_APP, dwDirection, lplpenumFormatEtc);

    if (dwDirection == DATADIR_GET) {
        nActualFormats = lpApp->m_nDocGetFmts;

        // Moniker not available - exclude CF_LINKSOURCE and
        // CF_LINKSRCDESCRIPTOR. These formats deliberately listed
        // last in the array of possible "Get" formats.
        if (! lpDoc->m_fLinkSourceAvail)
            nActualFormats -= 2;
```

```
        // Call sample library enumerator method
        *lplpenumFormatEtc = OleStdEnumFmtEtc_Create(
            nActualFmts, lpApp->m_arrDocGetFmts);
        if (*lplpenumFormatEtc == NULL)
            sc = E_OUTOFMEMORY;
    } else if (dwDirection == DATADIR_SET) {
        return ResultFromScode (E_NOTIMPL);
    } else {
        return ResultFromScode (E_INVALIDARG);
    }
```

See Also **IDataObject::SetData, IDataObject::GetData OleRegEnumFormatEtc**

IDataObject::DAdvise

HRESULT IDataObject::DAdvise(*pFormatetc, advf, pAdvise, pdwConnection***)**
FORMATETC FAR * *pFormatetc*
DWORD *advf*
LPADVISESINK *pAdvise*
DWORD FAR * *pdwConnection*

IDataObject::DAdvise creates a connection between the data transfer object and an advisory sink through which the sink can be informed when the object's data changes.

Parameters

pFormatetc
Points to the format to use when reporting changes to the specified sink.

advf
Contains a group of flags from the enumeration ADVF that specify information about the advisory connection.

pAdvise
Points to the advisory sink that should be informed of changes.

pdwConnection
Points to where to return the token that can later be passed to **IDataObject::DUnadvise** to remove an advisory connection.

Return Values

Value	Meaning
S_OK	The connection was successfully created.
E_INVALIDARG	One or more arguments are invalid.
E_OUTOFMEMORY	Ran out of memory.
E_UNEXPECTED	A relatively catastrophic failure.
DV_E_LINDEX	Invalid value for *lindex*; currently only -1 is supported.
DATA_E_FORMATETC	Cannot support the requested media.
OLE_E_ADVISENOTSUPPORTED	Advisory notifications are not supported.

Comments

Data transfer object implementations of **IDataObject** typically do not support advisory notifications and return OLE_E_ADVISENOTSUPPORTED from **IDataObject::DAdvise.**

Callers register through this method to be notified when data in the format and medium specified in *pFormatetc* changes. When a change occurs, a call is made to *pAdvise->OnDataChange*. Those who implement **IDataObject::DAdvise** can use the functionality provided in the **IDataAdviseHolder** interface. OLE supplies an **IDataAdviseHolder** implementation, accessible by calling **CreateDataAdviseHolder**.

If an advisory connection is successfully established, the object returns a nonzero value through *pdwConnection*; if a connection fails to be established, it returns zero. The caller can remove the established connection by passing the nonzero value of *pdwConnection* back to the object in a call to **IDataObject::DUnadvise**.

Containers of linked objects can set up advisory connections directly with the bound link source or indirectly via the standard OLE link object who manages the connection. Connection that are set up through the OLE link object are destroyed when the link object is deleted. Connections that are set up with the bound link source are not automatically deleted; the container must explicitly call **IDataObject::UnDAdvise** on the bound link source to delete it.

Example

The following example of **IDataObject::DAdvise** illustrates how to establish a wildcard advise and how to use the default implementation of **IDataAdviseHolder**. After initializing the *out* parameter, *lpdwConnection,* and checking that this implementation is not being exposed by a data transfer object that does not support data change notification, IDataObject_DAdvise determines whether the caller is setting up an advise for a format and medium that is supported. If so, **CreateDataAdviseHolder** is called to return an **IDataAdviseHolder** interface pointer so that **IDataAdviseHolder::Advise** can be called.

```
HRESULT IDataObject_DAdvise(
        LPDATAOBJECT         lpThis,
        FORMATETC FAR*       pFormatetc,
        DWORD                advf,
        LPADVISESINK         pAdvise,
        DWORD FAR*           lpdwConnection
)
{
    LPDOC lpDoc=((struct CDocDataObjectImpl FAR*)lpThis)->lpDoc;
    SCODE sc;
    HRESULT hrErr;

    *lpdwConnection = 0;

    if (lpDoc->m_fDataTransferDoc) {
        return ResultFromScode (OLE_E_ADVISENOTSUPPORTED);
    }

    if ( !( pFormatetc->cfFormat == NULL && pFormatetc->ptd == NULL
        && pFormatetc->dwAspect == -1L && pFormatetc->lindex == -1L
        && pFormatetc->tymed == -1L)
        && (hrErr = IDataObject_QueryGetData
            (lpThis, pFormatetc)) != NOERROR) {
            return hrErr;
    }

    if (lpDoc->m_lpDataAdviseHldr == NULL &&
        CreateDataAdviseHolder(&lpDoc->m_lpDataAdviseHldr) != NOERROR) {
            return ResultFromScode (E_OUTOFMEMORY);
    }

    return ( lpDoc->m_lpDataAdviseHldr->lpVtbl->Advise(
                lpDoc->m_lpDataAdviseHldr,
                (LPDATAOBJECT)&lpDoc->m_DataObject,
                pFormatetc,
                advf,
                pAdvise,
                lpdwConnection ));
}
```

See Also **IDataAdviseHolder** interface, **IAdviseSink::OnDataChange**, **IDataObject::DUnadvise**

IDataObject::DUnadvise

HRESULT IDataObject::DUnadvise(*dwConnection*)
DWORD *dwConnection*

IDataObject::DUnadvise deletes an advisory connection previously established by **IDataObject::DAdvise**.

Parameters

dwConnection
Specifies a nonzero value previously returned from **IDataObject::DAdvise**.

Return Values

Value	Meaning
S_OK	The connection was successfully deleted.
E_FAIL	The *pdwConnection* value does not indicate a valid connection.
E_OUTOFMEMORY	Ran out of memory.
OLE_E_ADVISENOTSUPPORTED	This **IDataObject** implementation does not support data advises.
OLE_E_NOCONNECTION	There is no connection for this connection identifier.

Comments The *dwConnection* parameter is a nonzero value returned through *pdwConnection* in **IDataObject::DAdvise**. If this value does not actually indicate a valid connection, E_FAIL is returned. If the advisory connection being deleted was initially set up using **IDataAdviseHolder::Advise**, **IDataAdviseHolder::Unadvise** should be called to delete it.

Example After determining that this method is not part of a data transfer object implementation and that the interface pointer to **IDataAdviseHolder** is still valid, IDataObject_DUnadvise deletes the connection specified by *dwConnection* by calling **IDataAdviseHolder::Unadvise**.

```
HRESULT IDataObject_DUnadvise(LPDATAOBJECT lpThis, DWORD dwConnection)
{
    LPDOC lpDoc=((struct CDocDataObjectImpl FAR*)lpThis)->lpDoc;
    SCODE sc;
    HRESULT hrErr;

    if (lpDoc->m_fDataTransferDoc)
        return ResultFromScode (OLE_E_ADVISENOTSUPPORTED);
```

```
    if (lpDoc->m_lpDataAdviseHldr == NULL)
            return ResultFromScode (E_FAIL);

    return (lpDoc->m_lpDataAdviseHldr->lpVtbl->Unadvise
                (lpDoc->m_lpDataAdviseHldr, dwConnection));
}
```

See Also **IDataObject::DAdvise**

IDataObject::EnumDAdvise

HRESULT IDataObject::EnumDAdvise(*ppenumAdvise***)**
LPENUMSTATDATA FAR * *ppenumAdvise*

IDataObject::EnumDAdvise enumerates the advisory connections currently established on an object.

Parameters

ppenumAdvise
Points to where the new enumerator should be returned. NULL indicates there are no connections.

Return Values

Value	Meaning
S_OK	Enumerator returned successfully.
E_FAIL	Enumerator cannot be returned.
E_OUTOFMEMORY	Ran out of memory.
OLE_E_ADVISENOTSUPPORTED	Advisory notifications not supported.

Comments

The returned enumerator enumerates data stored in **STATDATA** structure format. The **STATDATA** structure is defined as follows:

```
typedef struct tagSTATDATA
{
    FORMATETC formatetc;
    DWORD advf;
    LPADVISESINK pAdvSink;
    DWORD dwConnection;
} STATDATA;
```

While an enumeration is in progress, registering or revoking advisory connections on what is later enumerated is undefined. If there are no connections on the object, NULL is returned through *ppenumAdvise*.

Example

IDataObject::EnumDAdvise below is implemented much like **IDataObject::Unadvise**. Checks are made for an implementation that supports data change notifications and a valid **IDataAdviseHolder** interface pointer after which the corresponding **IDataAdviseHolder** method is called to return the enumerator.

```
HRESULT IDataObject_EnumDAdvise(
        LPDATAOBJECT        lpThis,
        LPENUMSTATDATA FAR* lplpenumAdvise
)
{
    LPDOC lpDoc=((struct CDocDataObjectImpl FAR*)lpThis)->lpDoc;
    HRESULT hrErr;
    SCODE sc;

    *lplpenumAdvise = NULL;

    if (lpDoc->m_fDataTransferDoc)
        return ResultFromScode (OLE_E_ADVISENOTSUPPORTED);

    if (lpDoc->m_lpDataAdviseHldr == NULL)
        return ResultFromScode (E_FAIL);

    return (lpDoc->m_lpDataAdviseHldr->lpVtbl->EnumAdvise(
                lpDoc->m_lpDataAdviseHldr,
                lplpenumAdvise));
}
```

CreateDataAdviseHolder

HRESULT CreateDataAdviseHolder(*ppDAHolder***)**
LPDATAADVISEHOLDER FAR * *ppDAHolder*

CreateDataAdviseHolder returns an instance of the **IDataAdviseHolder** interface. The **IDataAdviseHolder** methods are used by objects that support data advisory connections to manage registration and notification; **IDataAdviseHolder** is described in the next section.

Parameters

ppDAHolder
Points to where to return the new interface instance.

Return Values

Value	Meaning
S_OK	**IDataAdviseHolder** instance successfully returned.
E_OUTOFMEMORY	**IDataAdviseHolder** instance could not be returned due to lack of memory.

IDataAdviseHolder Interface

The **IDataAdviseHolder** interface keeps track of the set of **IDataObject::DAdvise** calls and sends data change notifications when appropriate.

Object applications and handlers implementing **IDataObject::DAdvise**, **DUnadvise**, and **EnumDAdvise** can forward these calls to the corresponding methods in **IDataAdviseHolder**. The examples shown in the discussion of these **IDataObject** methods illustrates how to do this.

The **IDataAdviseHolder** interface is implemented by OLE and is used by object applications. It contains the following methods (see also DVOBJ.H):

```
DECLARE_INTERFACE_(IDataAdviseHolder, IUnknown)
{
  // *** IUnknown methods ***
  HRESULT QueryInterface (THIS_ REFIID riid, LPVOID FAR* ppv);
  ULONG AddRef (THIS) ;
  ULONG Release (THIS);

  // *** IDataAdviseHolder methods ***
  HRESULT Advise (THIS_ LPDATAOBJECT pDataObject, FORMATETC FAR* pFetc,
    DWORD advf, LPADVISESINK pAdvise, DWORD FAR* pdwConnection);
  HRESULT Unadvise (THIS_ DWORD dwConnection);
  HRESULT EnumAdvise (THIS_ LPENUMSTATDATA FAR* ppenumAdvise);
  HRESULT SendOnDataChange (THIS_ LPDATAOBJECT pDataObject, DWORD dwReserved,
    DWORD advf);
};
```

IDataAdviseHolder::Advise

HRESULT IDataAdviseHolder::Advise(*lpDataObject*, *pFormatetc*, *advf*, *pAdvise*, *pdwConnection***)**
LPDATAOBJECT *lpDataObject*
LPFORMATETC * *pFormatetc*
DWORD *advf*
LPADVISESINK *pAdvise*
DWORD FAR * *pdwConnection*

IDataAdviseHolder::Advise creates a connection between the data object and an advisory sink through which the sink can be informed when the object's data changes.

Parameters

lpDataObject
Points to the source of the data.

pFormatetc
Points to the format to use when reporting changes to the specified sink.

advf
Contains a group of flags from the enumeration ADVF that specify information about the advisory connection. For more information, see the description of the **ADVF** enumeration earlier in this chapter.

pAdvise
Points to the advisory sink that should be informed of changes.

pdwConnection
Points to where to return the token that can later be used to delete an advisory connection by passing it to **IDataAdviseHolder::Unadvise**.

Return Values

Value	Meaning
S_OK	The advisory connection was created.
E_INVALIDARG	One or more arguments are invalid.
DV_E_LINDEX	Invalid value for *lindex*; currently only -1 is supported.

Comments

Callers register to be notified when data in the format and medium specified in *pFormatetc* changes. A call is made to *pAdvise*->**OnDataChange** when a change occurs.

If an advisory connection is successfully established, the object returns a nonzero value through *pdwConnection.* If a connection fails to be established, it returns zero. The caller can delete the established connection by passing the nonzero value of *pdwConnection* back to the object in a call to **IDataAdviseHolder::Unadvise**.

See Also

IDataObject::DUnadvise, CreateDataAdviseHolder

IDataAdviseHolder::Unadvise

HRESULT IDataAdviseHolder::Unadvise(*dwConnection***)**
DWORD *dwConnection*

IDataAdviseHolder::Unadvise deletes an advisory connection previously established by **IDataAdviseHolder::Advise**.

The *dwConnection* parameter here is a nonzero value returned through the *pdwConnection* parameter in **IDataAdviseHolder::Advise**. If this value does not actually indicate a valid connection, E_FAIL is returned.

Parameters

dwConnection
Specifies a nonzero value previously returned from **IDataAdviseHolder::Advise**.

Return Values

Value	Meaning
S_OK	The previously established advisory connection was successfully deleted.
OLE_E_NOCONNECTION	The *dwConnection* parameter does not represent a valid connection.

IDataAdviseHolder::EnumAdvise

HRESULT IDataAdviseHolder::EnumAdvise(*ppenumAdvise*)
LPENUMSTATDATA FAR * *ppenumAdvise*

IDataAdviseHolder::EnumAdvise enumerates the advisory connections currently established on an object.

Parameters

ppenumAdvise
Points to where the new enumerator should be returned. NULL indicates there are presently no connections.

Return Values

Value	Meaning
S_OK	Enumerator successfully returned.
E_OUTOFMEMORY	Enumerator could not be returned due to lack of memory.

Comments

While an enumeration is in progress, the effect of registering or revoking advisory connections on what is later enumerated is undefined. If there are presently no connections on the object, NULL is returned through *ppenumAdvise*.

IDataAdviseHolder::SendOnDataChange

HRESULT IDataAdviseHolder::SendOnDataChange(*lpDataObject, dwReserved, advf*)
LPDATAOBJECT *lpDataObject*

DWORD *dwReserved*
DWORD *advf*

IDataAdviseHolder::SendOnDataChange calls **IAdviseSink::OnDataChange** for all advisory sinks currently registered with the data-advise holder whenever changes of interest to the object referred to by *lpDataObject* occur.

Parameters

lpDataObject
Points to the source of the data to be passed in the **IAdviseSink::OnDataChange** call(s). This is the object in which the data change has just occurred.

dwReserved
Reserved, must be zero.

advf
Contains a group of flags from the enumeration **ADVF** that specify information about the notification to be sent.

Return Values

Value	Meaning
S_OK	Data change notification successfully sent.
E_OUTOFMEMORY	Notification could not be sent due to lack of memory.

Comments

If the ADVF_NODATA flag is not specified when the advisory connection is initially set up, data is passed with the **IAdviseSink::OnDataChange** call. This data is obtained by calling *lpDataObject*->**GetData**.

The value for *advf* is typically NULL. The only exception occurs when the object is shutting down and is sending the last data change notification for one or more clients that request only one data notification when the object shuts down. In this case, the value ADVF_DATAONSTOP should be passed for *advf*. None of the other **ADVF** flags are meaningful for **SendOnDataChange**. For more information, see the discussion of the **ADVF** enumeration earlier in this chapter.

IEnumFORMATETC Interface

The **IEnumFORMATETC** interface enumerates arrays of **FORMATETC** data structures. **IEnumFORMATETC** is one of the standard enumerator interfaces described in the "Component Object Interfaces and Functions" chapter. Applications can implement the **IEnumFORMATETC** interface to use in **IDataObject::EnumFormatEtc** to enumerate the entries in a data transfer object's **FORMATETC** structure.

The following data structure is the sample code **IEnumFORMATETC** object. The first member is a pointer to the **IEnumFORMATETC** virtual function table. The other members keep track of the reference count on the interface, the current position within the enumeration, the total number of items available, and a **FORMATETC** structure pointer.

```
typedef struct tagOleStdEnumFmtEtc
{
    IEnumFORMATETCVtbl FAR* lpVtbl;
    ULONG m_dwRefs;        /* reference count */
    ULONG m_nIndex;        /* current index in list */
    ULONG m_nCount;        /* how many items in list */
    LPFORMATETC m_lpEtc;  /* list of formatetc */
} OLESTDENUMFMTETC, FAR* LPOLESTDENUMFMTETC;
```

The OleStdEnumFmtEtc_Create function in the sample code returns an **IEnumFORMATETC** interface pointer that can be used to enumerate through an object's array of format information. For an illustration of how this is done, see the code example under the description of **IDataObject::EnumFormatEtc**.

IEnumSTATDATA Interface

The **IEnumSTATDATA** interface enumerates through a set of data change notifications. **IEnumSTATDATA** is one of the standard enumerator interfaces described in the "Component Object Interfaces and Functions" chapter. Applications can implement **IEnumSTATDATA** to use in **IDataObject::EnumAdvise** or take advantage of the implementation provided in **IDataAdviseHolder::EnumAdvise.**

IViewObject Interface

The **IViewObject** interface is similar to the **IDataObject** interface but operates in the context of drawing pictures instead of getting data. **IViewObject** supports the display and printing of data and the registration of view change notifications.

The **IViewObject** interface enables an object to be drawn on a caller-provided device context. The caller can ask the object to compose a picture for a target device that is independent of the drawing device context. As a result, the picture can be composed for one target device and drawn on another device context. Different object representations can also be selected. For example, a caller can ask for an embedded object's content or iconic representation.

Unlike most interfaces, **IViewObject** is never accessed remotely. Architectural considerations prohibit the remote access of an instance of the **IViewObject** interface between processes within the Windows operating system.

The **IViewObject** interface contains the following methods (see also DVOBJ.H):

```
DECLARE_INTERFACE_(IViewObject, IUnknown)
{
  // *** IUnknown methods ***
 HRESULT QueryInterface (THIS_ REFIID riid, LPVOID FAR* ppvObj);
 ULONG AddRef (THIS) ;
 ULONG Release (THIS);

  // *** IViewObject methods ***
 HRESULT Draw (THIS_ DWORD dwAspect, LONG lindex,
  void FAR* pvAspect, DVTARGETDEVICE FAR * ptd, HDC hicTargetDev,
  HDC hdcDraw, LPCRECTL lprcBounds, LPCRECTL lprcWBounds,
  BOOL (CALLBACK * pfnContinue) (DWORD), DWORD dwContinue);
 HRESULT GetColorSet (THIS_ DWORD dwAspect, LONG lindex,
  void FAR* pvAspect, DVTARGETDEVICE FAR * ptd, HDC hicTargetDev,
  LPLOGPALETTE FAR* ppColorSet);
 HRESULT Freeze (THIS_ DWORD dwAspect, LONG lindex,
  void FAR* pvAspect, DWORD FAR* pdwFreeze);
 HRESULT Unfreeze (THIS_ DWORD dwFreeze);
 HRESULT SetAdvise (THIS_ DWORD dwAspect, DWORD advf,
  LPADVISESINK pAdvise);
 HRESULT GetAdvise (THIS_ DWORD FAR* pAspect, DWORD FAR* padvf,
  LPADVISESINK FAR* ppAdvise);
};
```

IViewObject::Draw

HRESULT IViewObject::Draw(*dwAspect, lindex, pvAspect, ptd, hicTargetDev, hdcDraw, lprcBounds, lprcWBounds, pfnContinue, dwContinue***)**
DWORD *dwAspect*
LONG *lindex*
void * *pvAspect*
DVTARGETDEVICE * *ptd*
HDC *hicTargetDev*
HDC *hdcDraw*
LPCRECTL *lprcBounds*
LPCRECTL *lprcWBounds*
BOOL (CALLBACK * *pfnContinue*) **(DWORD)**
DWORD *dwContinue*

IViewObject::Draw draws a pictorial representation of an object on a device context.

Parameters

dwAspect
Specifies the requested view of the object. This parameter contains only one value taken from the enumeration **DVASPECT**. For more information, see the description of **FORMATETC::dwAspect**.

lindex
Indicates the piece of the object that is of interest. Currently, only -1 is supported. Any other value results in an error.

pvAspect
Currently, this pointer must be NULL.

ptd
Points to the target device for which the picture should be rendered. If this value is NULL, the picture should be rendered for a default target device, usually a display device.

hicTargetDev
Specifies the information context on the target device indicated by *ptd*. This can be a device context, but is not necessarily. If *ptd* is NULL, *hicTargetDev* must be also.

hdcDraw
Specifies the device context onto which the drawing should actually be done.

lprcBounds
Points to a **RECT** structure that indicates the rectangle on which the object should be drawn. This parameter controls the positioning and stretching of the object.

lprcWBounds
A NULL pointer unless *hdcDraw* is a metafile device context. If it is non-NULL, *lprcWBounds* is used in the enumeration of the metafile records to adjust the records' coordinates. This parameter points to a **RECT** structure defining the bounding rectangle of the metafile underneath *hdcDraw*. The rectangle indicated by *lprcBounds* is nested inside this rectangle and they are in the same coordinate space. The left and top members of the **RECT** structure specify the window origin, but the right and bottom members specify the window extents (not the bottom right corner point as in a true **RECT** structure).

pfnContinue
Points to a callback function that the view object should call periodically during a lengthy drawing operation to determine whether the operation should be canceled. The callback function should be exported; otherwise, a GP fault occurs if it attempts to access a global variable.

FALSE terminates the drawing and alerts **IViewObject::Draw** to return DRAW_E_ABORT.

dwContinue
Contains a value that should be passed back as the argument to the function in *pfnContinue*.

Return Values

Value	Meaning
S_OK	Object successfully drawn.
E_INVALIDARG	One or more arguments are invalid.
E_OUTOFMEMORY	Ran out of memory.
OLE_E_BLANK	No data to draw from.
E_ABORT	Draw operation aborted.
VIEW_E_DRAW	Error in drawing.
DV_E_LINDEX	Invalid value for *lindex*; currently only -1 is supported.
DV_E_DVASPECT	Invalid value for *dwAspect*.
OLE_E_INVALIDRECT	Invalid rectangle.

Comments

The *hicTargetDev* parameter is typically an information context on the *ptd* target device. Objects almost always need an information context for the target device. However, callers must be aware that it might be a full device context instead. Because callers usually have a device context available, the *hicTargetDev* parameter is passed by the caller for the convenience of the object.

For **IViewObject::Draw**, there is a relationship between the *dwAspect* value and the *lindex* and *lprcbounds* values. The *lprcbounds* value specifies the rectangle on *hdcDraw* into which the drawing is to be mapped. For DVASPECT_THUMBNAIL, the object draws whatever it wants to draw, and it maps it into the space given in the best way. The client has no compositional control. Some objects might scale to fit while some might scale to fit but preserve aspect ratio. In addition, some might scale full width, but crop the bottom. For DVASPECT_ICON, the container can control the compositional size of the icon by using **IOleObject::Set/GetExtent**, if the object supports **IOleObject**, or with **IViewObject2::GetExtent**. Otherwise, the compositional size of the icon is implicitly determined by the object itself and the container has no control over it. With DVASPECT_DOCPRINT, the Windows API functions **StartPage** and **EndPage** should be used and the compositional size and other characteristics of the page should be taken from *hicTargetDev*.

Note Object handlers (such as the default handler) that implement **IViewObject:Draw** by playing a metafile have to treat **SetPaletteEntries** metafile records in a special way because of Microsoft Windows 3.1's behavior. The Microsoft Windows 3.1 function **PlayMetaFile** sets these palette entries to the foreground--they need to be set to the background palette. Use **EnumMetaFile** to do this.

IViewObject::GetColorSet

HRESULT IViewObject::GetColorSet(*dwAspect, lindex, pvAspect, ptd, hicTargetDev, ppColorSet***)**
DWORD *dwAspect*
LONG *lindex*
void FAR * *pvAspect*
DVTARGETDEVICE FAR * *ptd*
HDC *hicTargetDev*
LPLOGPALLETTE FAR * *ppColorSet*

IViewObject::GetColorSet returns the set of colors that would be used by a call to **IViewObject::Draw** with the corresponding parameters.

Parameters

dwAspect
Specifies the requested view of the object. This parameter contains only one value taken from the enumeration **DVASPECT**. For more information, see the description of **FORMATETC::dwAspect.**

lindex
Indicates the piece of the object that is of interest. Currently only -1 is supported. Any other value results in an error.

pvAspect
Currently, this pointer must be NULL.

ptd
Points to the target device for which the picture should be rendered. If this value is NULL, the picture should be rendered for a default target device, usually a display device.

hicTargetDev
Specifies the information context on the target device indicated by *ptd*. This parameter can be a device context, but is not necessarily. If *ptd* is NULL, *hicTargetDev* must be also.

ppColorSet
Points to where to return the set of colors that would be used. If the object does not return the color set, NULL is returned.

Return Values

Value	Meaning
S_OK	Set of colors successfully returned.
S_FALSE	Set of colors is empty or the object does not care to give the information out.
E_INVALIDARG	One or more arguments are invalid.
E_OUTOFMEMORY	Ran out of memory.

Value	Meaning
E_UNEXPECTED	A relatively catastrophic failure.
DV_E_LINDEX	Invalid value for *lindex*; currently only -1 is supported.
DV_E_DVASPECT	Invalid value for *dwAspect*.

Comments

IViewObject::GetColorSet recursively queries any nested objects and returns a color set that represents the union of all colors requested. The color set eventually percolates to the top-level container that owns the window frame. This container can call **IViewObject::GetColorSet** on each of its embedded objects to obtain all the colors needed to draw the embedded objects. The container can use the color sets obtained in conjunction with the colors it needs to set the overall color palette.

The default handler implements **IViewObject::GetColorSet** by looking at the data it has on hand to draw the picture. If the drawing format is a DIB, the palette found in the DIB is used. For a regular bitmap, no color information is returned. If the drawing format is a metafile, the handler enumerates the metafile, looking for a CreatePalette metafile record. If one is found, the handler uses it as the color set.

Object applications that rely on the default handler for drawing and that use metafiles for doing so should provide a SetPaletteEntries record when they generate their metafiles. If a SetPaletteEntries record is not found, the handler returns S_FALSE.

IViewObject::Freeze

HRESULT IViewObject::Freeze(*dwAspect*, *lindex*, *pvAspect*, *pdwFreeze*)
DWORD *dwAspect*
LONG *lindex*
void FAR * *pvAspect*
DWORD FAR * *pdwFreeze*

IViewObject::Freeze informs an object that it should not change its drawn representation until a subsequent **IViewObject::Unfreeze** is called.

Parameters

dwAspect
Specifies the requested view of the object. This parameter contains only one value taken from the enumeration **DVASPECT**.

lindex
Indicates the piece of the object that is of interest. Currently only -1 is supported. Any other value results in an error.

pvAspect
Currently, this pointer must be NULL.

pdwFreeze
Points to where to return the key that is later passed to **IViewObject::Unfreeze**. This key is an index that the default cache uses to keep track of which object is frozen.

Return Values

Value	Meaning
S_OK	Presentation successfully frozen.
VIEW_S_ALREADYFROZEN	Presentation has already been frozen.
OLE_E_BLANK	Nothing in the cache.
DV_E_LINDEX	Invalid value for *lindex*; currently, only -1 is supported.
DV_E_DVASPECT	Invalid value for *dwAspect.*

Comments

After calling **IViewObject::Freeze**, successive calls to **IViewObject::Draw** (using the same parameters) produce the same picture, until **IViewObject::Unfreeze** is called. The most common use of this method is for banded printing.

While in a frozen state, view notifications are not sent. Pending view notifications are deferred to the subsequent call to **IViewObject::Unfreeze**.

See Also

IViewObject::Unfreeze

IViewObject::Unfreeze

HRESULT IViewObject::Unfreeze(*dwFreeze***)**
DWORD*dwFreeze*

IViewObject::Unfreeze unfreezes a previously frozen drawing by calling **IViewObject::Freeze**.

Parameters

dwFreeze
Contains a key previously returned from **IViewObject::Freeze**. This key determines which object to unfreeze.

Return Values

Value	Meaning
S_OK	Drawing was successfully unfrozen.
OLE_E_NOCONNECTION	Error in the unfreezing process or the object is currently not frozen

See Also

IViewObject::Freeze

IViewObject::SetAdvise

HRESULT IViewObject::SetAdvise(*dwAspect, advf, pAdvise*)
DWORD *dwAspect*
DWORD *advf*
LPADVISESINK *pAdvise*

IViewObject::SetAdvise sets up an advisory connection between the view object and an advisory sink through which the sink can be informed of changes made to an object's drawings.

Parameters

dwAspect
Specifies the view of the object for which the advisory connection is to be established. This parameter contains only one value taken from the enumeration **DVASPECT**.

advf
Contains a group of flags from the enumeration **ADVF** that specify information about the advisory connection.

pAdvise
Points to the advisory sink that is to be informed of changes. A NULL value deletes any existing advisory connection.

Return Values

Value	Meaning
S_OK	The advisory connection was successfully established.
E_INVALIDARG	One or more arguments are invalid.
E_OUTOFMEMORY	Ran out of memory.
OLE_E_ADVISENOTSUPPORTED	Advisory notifications are not supported.
DV_E_DVASPECT	Invalid value for *dwAspect*.

Comments

Callers register with this method to be notified when an object's view changes. When a change does occur, a call is made to *pAdvise*->**OnViewChange**. At any time, a given **IViewObject** instance can support only one advisory connection. An existing advisory connection can be deleted by calling **IViewObject::SetAdvise** with *pAdvise* set to NULL.

See Also

IViewObject::GetAdvise, IAdviseSink::OnDataChange

IViewObject::GetAdvise

HRESULT IViewObject::GetAdvise(*pAspect, padvf, ppAdvise*)
DWORD FAR * *pAspect*
DWORD FAR * *padvf*
LPADVISESINK FAR * *ppAdvise*

IViewObject::GetAdvise retrieves the existing advisory connection, if any, on the object.

Parameters

pAspect
Points to where to return the most recent **SetAdvise**(*dwAspect*, ...) parameter. It can be NULL, indicating that the caller does not want this value returned.

padvf
Analogous to *pAspect*, but with respect to the *advf* parameter to **SetAdvise**. Can be NULL.

ppAdvise
Analogous to *pdwAspect*, but with respect to the *pAdvise* parameter to **SetAdvise**. Can be NULL.

Return Values

Value	Meaning
S_OK	The existing advisory connection was retrieved.
E_INVALIDARG	One or more arguments are invalid.
E_OUTOFMEMORY	Ran out of memory.

Comments

IViewObject::GetAdvise returns the values passed in the most recent call to **IViewObject::SetAdvise**.

See Also

IViewObject::SetAdvise

IViewObject2 Interface

The **IViewObject2** interface is an extension to **IViewObject** implemented by DLL object applications and object handlers. A default implementation is provided with the OLE libraries. The interface is used by containers and object handlers to get the view extents of an object. **IViewObject2** contains the following methods (see also DVOBJ.H):

```
DECLARE_INTERFACE_(IViewObject2, IViewObject)
{
  // *** IUnknown methods ***
  HRESULT QueryInterface (THIS_ REFIID riid, LPVOID FAR* ppvObj);
```

```
    ULONG AddRef (THIS) ;
    ULONG Release (THIS);

    // *** IViewObject methods ***
   HRESULT Draw (THIS_ DWORD dwAspect, LONG lindex,
    void FAR* pvAspect, DVTARGETDEVICE FAR * ptd, HDC hicTargetDev,
    HDC hdcDraw, RECTL lprcBounds, RECTL lprcWBounds,
    BOOL (CALLBACK * pfnContinue) (DWORD), DWORD dwContinue);
   HRESULT GetColorSet (THIS_ DWORD dwAspect, LONG lindex,
    void FAR* pvAspect, DVTARGETDEVICE FAR * ptd, HDC hicTargetDev,
    LPLOGPALETTE FAR* ppColorSet);
   HRESULT Freeze (THIS_ DWORD dwAspect, LONG lindex,
    void FAR* pvAspect, DWORD FAR* pdwFreeze);
   HRESULT Unfreeze (THIS_ DWORD dwFreeze);
   HRESULT SetAdvise (THIS_ DWORD dwAspect, DWORD advf,
    LPADVISESINK pAdvise);
   HRESULT GetAdvise (THIS_ DWORD FAR* pAspect, DWORD FAR* padvf,
    LPADVISESINK FAR* ppAdvise);

    // *** IViewObject2 methods ***
    HRESULT GetExtent (THIS_ DWORD dwAspect, LONG lindex,
            DVTARGETDEVICE FAR * ptd, LPSIZEL lpsizel);
};
```

IViewObject2::GetExtent

IViewObject2::GetExtent(*dwAspect, lindex, ptd, lpsizel*)
DWORD *dwAspect*
DWORD *lindex*
DVTARGETDEVICE *ptd*
LPSIZEL *lpsizel*

IViewObject2::GetExtent retrieves the view extent of an object, returning the size of the object in the cache.

Parameters

dwAspect
Specifies the requested view of the object. This parameter contains only one value taken from the enumeration **DVASPECT**. See the description of **FORMATETC::dwAspect** for details.

lindex
Indicates the piece of the object that is of interest. Currently, only -1 is supported. Any other value results in an error.

ptd
Points to the target device for which the object's extent should be returned.

lpsizel
Points to where the object's extent is to be returned.

Return Values

Value	Meaning
S_OK	The object's extent was successfully returned.
OLE_E_BLANK	Appropriate cache is not available.
E_OUTOFMEMORY	Insufficient memory.

Comments

OLE provides a default implementation of **IViewObject2::GetExtent** that searches only the cache for the extent. This method is never remoted to the object application. To prevent the object from being run if it isn't already running, containers call **IViewObject2::GetExtent** rather than **IOleObject::GetExtent** to determine the extents of the presentation to be drawn.

See Also

IOleObject::GetExtent

IOleCache Interface

The **IOleCache** interface enables objects to control what data gets cached inside an embedded object and to determine the data that will be available to the container when the object is not running or is unavailable.

The **IOleCache** interface is implemented by OLE and is used by container applications. **IOleCache** contains the following methods (see also DVOBJ.H):

```
DECLARE_INTERFACE_(IOleCache, IUnknown)
{
  // *** IUnknown methods ***
 HRESULT QueryInterface (THIS_ REFIID riid, LPVOID FAR* ppvObj);
 ULONG AddRef (THIS) ;
 ULONG Release (THIS);

  // *** IOleCache methods ***
 HRESULT Cache (THIS_ LPFORMATETC pFormatetc, DWORD advf,
  LPDWORD lpdwConnection);
 HRESULT Uncache (THIS_ DWORD dwConnection);
 HRESULT EnumCache (THIS_ LPENUMSTATDATA FAR* ppenumStatData);
 HRESULT InitCache (THIS_ LPDATAOBJECT pDataObject);
 HRESULT SetData (THIS_ LPFORMATETC pFormatetc, STGMEDIUM FAR * pmedium,
  BOOL fRelease);
};
```

IOleCache::Cache

HRESULT IOleCache::Cache(*pFormatetc*, *advf*, *lpdwConnection*)
LPFORMATETC *pFormatetc*
DWORD *advf*
LPDWORD * *lpdwConnection*

IOleCache::Cache specifies the formats and other data to be cached inside an embedded object.

Parameters

pFormatetc
Points to the data formats that are to be cached.

advf
Contains a group of flags from the enumeration **ADVF** that specify information about the cache connection. The values that are valid for **IOleCache::Cache** are:

ADVF_NODATA

ADVF_ONLYONCE

ADVF_PRIMEFIRST

ADVFCACHE_NOHANDLER

ADVFCACHE_FORCEBUILTIN

ADVFCACHE_ONSAVE

More detailled information about the **ADVF** enumeration can be found at the beginning of this chapter.

lpdwConnection
Points to a returned token value that can later be used to turn caching off. The OLE implementation of caching always uses nonzero numbers for connection identifiers and does not return a value greater than or equal to 0x8000.

Return Values

Value	Meaning
S_OK	Requested data or view successfully cached.
E_INVALIDARG	One or more arguments are invalid.
E_OUTOFMEMORY	Ran out of memory.
E_UNEXPECTED	A relatively catastrophic failure.
CACHE_S_FORMATETC_ NOTSUPPORTED	Indicates the cache was created, but the object application does not support the specified format. Cache creation will succeed even if the format is not supported, allowing the caller to fill the cache. If the caller does not need to keep the cache, **IOleCache::UnCache** should be called.

Value	Meaning
CACHE_S_SAMECACHE	Indicates a cache already exists for the FORMATETC passed to **IOleCache::Cache.** In this case, the new advise flags are assigned to the cache, and the previously assigned connection identifier is returned. The new advise flags are assigned to the cache, and the previously assigned connection identifier are to be returned.
DV_E_LINDEX	Invalid value for *lindex*; currently only -1 is supported.
DV_E_TYMED	The value is not valid for *pFormatetc->tymed.*
DV_E_DVASPECT	The value is not valid for *pFormatetc->dwAspect.*
DV_E_CLIPFORMAT	The value is not valid for *pFormatetc->cfFormat.*
CO_E_NOTINITIALIZED	The cache's storage is not initialized.
DV_E_DVTARGETDEVICE	The value is not valid for *pFormatetc->ptd.*
OLE_E_STATIC	The cache is for static object and it already has a cache node.

Comments **IOleCache::Cache** can specify either data caching by passing a valid data format in *pFormatetc* or view (presentation) caching by passing a zero data format in *pFormatetc* as follows:

```
pFormatetc->cfFormat == 0
```

With view caching, the object itself decides on the format to cache.

A custom object handler can choose not to store data in a given format. Instead, it can synthesize it on demand when requested.

The *advf* value of ADVFCACHE_FORCEBUILTIN ensures that presentation data can be retrieved after the container document has been moved where the object application or object handler is not available.

When **IOleCache::Cache** is called with *pFormatetc->dwAspect* set to DVASPECT_CONTENT, *pFormatetc->lindex* set to -1, and *pFormatetc->ptd* set to NULL for static objects, no cache is created and *lpdwConnection* will be NULL. S_OK is returned, however, because the caching code is able to draw from the native data.

See Also **IOleCache::Uncache**

IOleCache::Uncache

HRESULT IOleCache::Uncache(*dwConnection*)
DWORD *dwConnection*

IOleCache::Uncache deletes a cache connection created with **IOleCache::Cache**.

Parameters

dwConnection
Contains the nonzero value previously returned through the *pdwConnection* parameter in a call to **IOleCache::Cache**.

Return Values

Value	Meaning
S_OK	The cache connection was deleted.
OLE_E_NOCONNECTION	No cache connection exists for *dwConnection*.

See Also **IOleCache::Cache**

IOleCache::EnumCache

HRESULT IOleCache::EnumCache(*ppenumStatData*)
LPENUMSTATDATA FAR * *ppenumStatData*

IOleCache::EnumCache enumerates presently established cache connections.

Parameters

ppenumStatData
Points to where to return the new enumerator. NULL is a legal value and indicates that there are currently no connections.

Return Values

Value	Meaning
S_OK	The cache enumerator successfully returned.
E_OUTOFMEMORY	The cache enumerator could not be returned due to lack of memory.

See Also **IOleCache::Cache**

IOleCache::InitCache

HRESULT IOleCache::InitCache(*pDataObject*)
LPDATAOBJECT *pDataObject*

IOleCache::InitCache fills the cache using the data provided by using the passed data transfer object from the clipboard or a drag and drop operation.

Parameters

pDataObject
Points to the data transfer object from which the cache is to be initialized.

Return Values

Value	Meaning
S_OK	The cache was filled using the data provided.
E_INVALIDARG	The value is not valid for *pDataObject*.
E_OUTOFMEMORY	The cache could not be initialized due to lack of memory.
OLE_E_NOTRUNNING	The cache is not running.
CACHE_E_NOCACHE_UPDATED	Indicates none of the caches were updated.
CACHE_S_SOMECACHES_NOTUPDATED	Indicates only some of the existing caches were updated.

Comments

IOleCache::InitCache is usually called when an object is created with Embed Source or Link Source data, either by **OleCreateFromData**, **OleCreateLinkFromData** or containers that do not use either of these helper functions. Containers that do not use helper functions to create objects will usually want to use **IOleCache::Cache** to set up the cache entries which are then filled by **InitCache**.

See Also

IOleCache::Cache

IOleCache::SetData

HRESULT IOleCache::SetData(*pFormatetc*, *pmedium*, *fRelease*)
LPFORMATETC *pFormatetc*
STGMEDIUM FAR * *pmedium*
BOOL *fRelease*

IOleCache::SetData fills the cache using the data contained in the storage medium.

Parameters

pFormatetc
Points to the format of the data being set.

pmedium
Points to the storage medium (an *in* parameter only) that contains the data.

fRelease
Indicates ownership of the storage medium after completion of the method. If *fRelease* is TRUE, the callee takes ownership, freeing the medium when it is finished using it. When *fRelease* is FALSE, the caller retains ownership and is responsible for freeing the medium. The callee can only use the storage medium for the duration of the call.

Return Values

Value	Meaning
S_OK	The cache was filled.
E_OUTOFMEMORY	Ran out of memory.
DV_E_LINDEX	The value is not valid for *pFormatetc->lindex*. Currently, only -1 is supported.
DV_E_FORMATETC	The FORMATETC structure is invalid.
DV_E_TYMED	The value is not valid for *pFormatetc->tymed*.
DV_E_DVASPECT	The value is not valid for *pFormatetc->dwAspect*.
OLE_E_BLANK	Uninitialized object.
DV_E_TARGETDEVICE	The object is static and *pFormatetc->ptd* is non-NULL.
STG_E_MEDIUMFULL	Medium is full.

Comments

IOleCache::SetData is usually called when an object is created from the clipboard or through a drag and drop operation and Embed Source data is used to create the object. **SetData** is similiar to **InitCache**; the difference is that **SetData** initializes the cache using a single format and **InitCache** uses multiple formats.

See Also

IOleCache::Cache, IOleCache::InitCache

IOleCache2 Interface

The **IOleCache2** interface is an extension of the **IOleCache** interface that adds the ability for a client of an object to update each of the maintained caches. **IOleCache2** is implemented by OLE and used by containers and DLL object applications to update one or more caches created with **IOleCache::Cache**. **IOleCache2** contains the following methods (see also DVOBJ.H):

```
DECLARE_INTERFACE_(IOleCache2, IOleCache)
{
   // *** IUnknown methods ***
   HRESULT QueryInterface (THIS_ REFIID riid, LPVOID FAR* ppvObj);
   ULONG AddRef (THIS) ;
```

```
    ULONG Release (THIS);

    // *** IOleCache methods ***
    HRESULT Cache (THIS_ LPFORMATETC pFormatetc, DWORD advf, LPDWORD lpdwConnection);
    HRESULT Uncache (THIS_ DWORD dwConnection);
    HRESULT EnumCache (THIS_ LPENUMSTATDATA FAR* ppenumStatData);
    HRESULT InitCache (THIS_ LPDATAOBJECT pDataObject);
    HRESULT SetData (THIS_ LPFORMATETC pformatetc, STGMEDIUM FAR * pmedium, BOOL fRelease);

    // *** IOleCache2 methods ***
    HRESULT UpdateCache (THIS_ LPDATAOBJECT pDataObject, DWORD grfUpdf,
                            LPVOID pReserved);
    HRESULT DiscardCache (THIS_ DWORD dwDiscardOptions);

};
```

Even though a default implementation is provided with OLE, a DLL object application might need to provide its own implementation, depending on how it caches data.

IOleCache2::UpdateCache

HRESULT IOleCache2::UpdateCache(*pDataObject, dwgrfUpdf, lpReserved***)**
LPDATAOBJECT *pDataObject*
DWORD *grfUpdt*
LPVOID *pReserved*

IOleCache2::UpdateCache updates the cache(s) according to the value of the *grfUpdt* parameter.

Parameters

pDataObject
Points to the object that is the source for updating the cache; can be NULL.

grfUpdt
Specifies the type of cache to update. See the Comments section below.

pReserved
Reserved parameter; must be NULL.

Return Values

Value	Meaning
S_OK	The cache(s) were updated according to the value specified in *grfUpdt.*
E_OUTOFMEMORY	Out of memory.
E_INVALIDARG	One or more arguments are invalid.
E_UNEXPECTED	An unexpected error occurred.

Value	Meaning
OLE_E_NOTRUNNING	The specified *pDataObject* is not running.
CACHE_E_NOCACHE_UPDATED	None of the caches were updated.
CACHE_S_SOMECACHES_NOTUPDATED	Some of the caches were updated.

Comments

IOleCache2::UpdateCache can be called by containers or DLL object applications requiring more control over caching. This method is used when the caches need to be updated without updating the object.

The *pDataObject* points to the source for updating the cache(s). Typically, non-NULL values are passed by handlers and DLL object applications. Containers most often pass a NULL *pDataObject*, in which case, the source is obtained from the running object.

The *grfUpdt* parameter controls the caches that get updated. The value is obtained by combining values from the following table:

Cache Control Values	Description
UPDFCACHE_NODATACACHE	Updates caches created by using ADVF_NODATA in the call to **IOleCache::Cache**.
UPDFCACHE_ONSAVECACHE	Updates caches created by using ADVFCACHE_ONSAVE in the call to **IOleCache::Cache**.
UPDFCACHE_ONSTOPCACHE	Updates caches created by using ADVFCACHE_ONSTOP in the call to **IOleCache::Cache**.
UPDFCACHE_NORMALCACHE	Dynamically updates the caches (as is normally done when the object sends out OnDataChange notices).
UPDFCACHE_IFBLANK	Updates the cache if blank, regardless of any other flag specified.
UPDFCACHE_ONLYIFBLANK	Updates only caches that are blank.
UPDFCACHE_ IFBLANKORONSAVECACHE	The equivalent of UPDFCACHE_IFBLANK | UPDFCACHE_ONSAVECACHE.
UPDFCACHE_ALL	Updates all caches.
UPDFCACHE_ ALLBUTNODATACACHE	Updates all caches except those created with ADVF_NODATA in the call to **IOleCache::Cache**.

IOleCache2::DiscardCache

HRESULT IOleCache2::DiscardCache(*dwDiscardOptions***)**
DWORD *dwDiscardOptions*

IOleCache2::DiscardCache flushes the cache(s) that are in memory. The cache will satisfy subsequent **IDataObject::GetData** calls by reverting to disk-based data.

Parameters

dwDiscardOptions
Indicates whether data is to be saved prior to the discard. Valid values are from the enumeration DISCARDCACHE:

```
typedef enum tagDISCARDCACHE {
    DISCARDCACHE_SAVEIFDIRTY        = 0
    DISCARDCACHE_NOSAVE             = 1
    } DISCARDCACHE;
```

DISCARDCACHE_SAVEIFDIRTY indicates that all of the dirty data in the cache(s) should be saved before the discard occurs. Containers that have drawn a large object and need to free up memory may want to specify DISCARDCACHE_SAVEIFDIRTY so that the newest presentation is saved for the next time the object must be drawn.

DISCARDCACHE_NOSAVE indicates that no save is necessary. Containers that have activated an embedded object, made some changes, and then called **IOleObject::Close**(OLECLOSE_NOSAVE) to rollback the changes may want to specify this option to ensure that the native and presentation data are not out of sync.

Return Values

Value	Meaning
S_OK	The cache(s) were discarded according to the value specified in *dwDiscardOptions*.
OLE_E_NOSTORAGE	There is no storage available for saving the dirty data in the cache.

Comments

IOleCache2::DiscardCache is useful for low memory conditions.

See Also

IOleCache, IOleCacheControl

IOleCacheControl Interface

The **IOleCacheControl** interface is used almost exclusively by object handlers or DLL object applications as the means by which the cache part of the handler is connected to the running object's **IDataObject** implementation. This allows the cache to receive notifications from the running object. Containers have no need for this interface; they should use **IRunnableObject** or **OleRun** instead.

IOleCacheControl contains the following methods (see also DVOBJ.H):

```
DECLARE_INTERFACE_(IOleCacheControl, IUnknown)
{
  // *** IUnknown methods ***
  HRESULT QueryInterface (THIS_ REFIID riid, LPVOID FAR* ppvObj);
  ULONG AddRef (THIS) ;
  ULONG  Release (THIS);

  // *** IOleCacheControl methods ***
  HRESULT OnRun (THIS_ LPDATAOBJECT pDataObject);
  HRESULT OnStop (THIS);
};
```

IOleCacheControl::OnRun

HRESULT IOleCacheControl::OnRun(*pDataObject*)
LPDATAOBJECT *pDataObject*

IOleCacheControl::OnRun notifies the cache that the compound document object that is its data source has entered its running state.

Parameters

pDataObject
Points to the object that is entering the running state.

Return Values

Value	Meaning
S_OK	The cache was notified and *pDataObject* is valid.
E_OUTOFMEMORY	Out of memory.
E_INVALIDARG	One or more invalid arguments.
E_UNEXPECTED	An unexpected error occurred.

Comments

When **OnRun** is called, the cache sets up advisory notifications as necessary. If the cache is already running, **OnRun** returns S_OK.

Some DLL object applications might use the cache in a passive manner and not call **IOleCacheControl::OnRun**. These applications will need to call **IOleCache2::UpdateCache, IOleCache::InitCache,** or **IOleCache::SetData** to fill the cache when necessary to ensure that the cache gets updated.

IOleCacheControl::OnRun does not create a reference count on *pDataObject*. It is the responsibility of the caller of **OleRun** to ensure that the lifetime of *pDataObject* lasts until **OnStop** is called.

Calling **IOleCacheControl::OnRun** creates a data advisory sink between the running object and the cache. The sink is destroyed when **IOleCacheControl::OnStop** is called.

See Also **IOleCacheControl::OnStop, IOleCache2::UpdateCache**

IOleCacheControl::OnStop

HRESULT IOleCacheControl::OnStop()

IOleCacheControl::OnStop notifies the cache it should terminate any existing connection previously given to it by using **IOleCacheControl::OnRun**. No indication is given as to whether a connection existed or not.

Return Values

Value	Meaning
S_OK	The cache was notified and the advise sink was successfully removed.
E_OUTOFMEMORY	Out of memory.
E_UNEXPECTED	An unexpected error occurred.

Comments The data advisory sink between the running object and the cache is destroyed as part of calling **IOleCacheControl::OnStop**.

See Also **IOleCacheControl::OnRun**

Clipboard Functions

The following functions are used in conjunction with clipboard and other data transfer operations (see also OLE2.H).

```
OleSetClipboard(LPDATAOBJECT pDataObject);
OleGetClipboard(LPDATAOBJECT FAR* pDataObject);
OleFlushClipboard(void);
OleIsCurrentClipboard(LPDATAOBJECT pDataObject);
```

OleSetClipboard

HRESULT OleSetClipboard(*pDataObject*)
LPDATAOBJECT *pDataObject*

OleSetClipboard puts the indicated **IDataObject** instance on the clipboard.

Parameters

pDataObject
Points to an **IDataObject** instance from which the data to be presented to the clipboard can be obtained. This parameter can be NULL, in which case the clipboard is emptied.

Return Values

Value	Meaning
S_OK	*pDataObject* was placed on the clipboard.
CLIPBRD_E_CANT_OPEN	**OpenClipboard** failed.
CLIPBRD_E_CANT_EMPTY	**EmptyClipboard** failed.
CLIPBRD_E_CANT_CLOSE	**CloseClipboard** failed.

Comments

Any **IDataObject** formats that are offered on a global handle medium (TYMED_HGLOBAL, TYMED_MFPICT, or TYMED_GDI) and formatted with a NULL target device are offered on the clipboard using delayed rendering. The formats necessary for OLE 1 compatibility are synthesized from the OLE 2 formats that are present and put on the clipboard.

OleSetClipboard assigns ownership of the clipboard to an internal OLE window handle. This is done so that delayed rendering can be used with the synthesized OLE 1 compatibility formats. The clipboard is emptied before any data is made available. If the clipboard is currently open by another window, **OleSetClipboard** fails. The internal OLE window handle satisfies WM_RENDERFORMAT messages by delegating to **IDataObject** instance.

Passing NULL for *pDataObject* is legal and it empties the clipboard. If the contents of the clipboard are the result of a previous **OleSetClipboard** call and the clipboard is released, the *pDataObject* that was passed to the previous call is released. The clipboard owner should use this as a signal that the data it previously offered is no longer on the clipboard.

Note If an application needs to leave data on the clipboard after shutting down, it can call **OleSetClipboard** (NULL) and then use the normal Windows clipboard mechanisms for putting data on the clipboard. Calling **OleFlushClipboard** is another option; see the following description of **OleFlushClipboard** for more information.

See Also

OleGetClipboard

OleGetClipboard

HRESULT OleGetClipboard(*pDataObject*)
LPDATAOBJECT FAR * *pDataObject*

OleGetClipboard retrieves the instance of the **IDataObject** from the clipboard that was placed there by using **OleSetClipboard**.

Parameters

pDataObject
Points to where to return the **IDataObject** instance. NULL is only returned in *pDataObject* if **OleGetClipboard** returns S_FALSE.

Return Values

Value	Meaning
S_OK	The **IDataObject** instance was successfully retrieved.
S_FALSE	Another object owns the clipboard.
E_OUTOFMEMORY	Ran out of memory.
CLIPBRD_E_BAD_DATA	Cannot get the contents of *pDataObject* from clipboard. The data on the clipboard is invalid.
CLIPBRD_E_CANT_CLOSE	**CloseClipboard** failed.

Comments

If no instance of **IDataObject** exists on the clipboard, **OleGetClipboard** returns an OLE-provided instance of **IDataObject** that wraps the contents of the clipboard.

OleGetClipboard also transforms OLE 1 clipboard format data into the representation expected by an OLE 2 caller. When the FILENAME format is on the clipboard, **OleGetClipboard** also offers Embed Source.

The original **IDataObject** instance is not actually returned. Instead, **OleGetClipboard** returns an OLE-provided **IDataObject** implementation that forwards everything to the original except release and accords it special treatment. This allows **OleGetClipboard** to know when its caller is done with the **IDataObject** instance it returns through *pDataObject*.

OleGetClipboard allows only one client at a time to access the clipboard. No other client can access it until the first client has released it. To call either **OleSetClipboard** or **OleFlushClipboard**, access to the clipboard must first be obtained with a call to **OleGetClipboard**. Callers of **OleGetClipboard** should only hold on to the returned **IDataObject** for a very short time. It consumes resources in the application that offered it.

See Also

OleSetClipboard, OleFlushClipboard

OleFlushClipboard

HRESULT OleFlushClipboard()

OleFlushClipboard carries out the clipboard shutdown sequence, removing the **IDataObject** instance.

Return Values

Value	Meaning
S_OK	The clipboard has been flushed.
CLIPBRD_E_CANT_OPEN	**OpenClipboard** failed.
CLIPBRD_E_CANT_CLOSE	**CloseClipboard** failed.

Comments

OleFlushClipboard empties the clipboard as does **OleSetClipboard**(NULL). The difference is that **OleFlushClipboard** leaves all hGlobal-based formats offered by the data transfer object, including the OLE 1 compatibility formats, on the clipboard so that they are available after application shutdown.

Applications should call **OleSetClipboard**(NULL) if there is either no need to leave data on the clipboard after shutdown or if data will be placed on the clipboard using the standard Windows clipboard API functions. Applications should call **OleFlushClipboard** to enable pasting and paste-linking of OLE objects after shutdown.

To invoke **OleFlushClipboard**, the caller must first have obtained access to the clipboard by calling **OleGetClipboard**. After the flush, the **IDataObject** returned from **OleGetClipboard** is invalid for anything but a release operation (**IUnknown::Release**).

See Also

OleGetClipboard

OleIsCurrentClipboard

HRESULT OleIsCurrentClipboard(*pDataObject*)
LPDATAOBJECT *pDataObject*

OleIsCurrentClipboard determines whether the *pDataObject* put on the clipboard by the caller using **OleSetClipboard**(*pDataObject*) is *still* on the clipboard.

Parameters

pDataObject
Points to an **IDataObject** instance.

Return Values

Value	Meaning
S_OK	Indicates that *pDataObject* is currently on the clipboard and the caller is the owner of the clipboard.
S_FALSE	Indicates that *pDataObject* is not on the clipboard.

See Also **OleSetClipboard**, **OleGetClipboard**

Data Transfer, Caching, and Drawing Functions

The following functions are used in conjunction with drawing and caching operations.

```
OleDraw (LPUNKNOWN pUnk, DWORD dwAspect, HDC hdcDraw,
   LPCRECT lprcBounds);
OleDuplicateData (HANDLE hSrc, CLIPFORMAT cfFormat, UINT uiFlags);
CreateDataCache (LPUNKNOWN pUnk, REFCLSID rclsid, REFIID iid,
   LPVOID FAR * ppvObj);
ReleaseStgMedium (STGMEDIUM pmedium);
```

OleDraw

HRESULT OleDraw(*pUnk*, *dwAspect*, *hdcDraw*, *lprcBounds*)
LPUNKNOWN *pUnk*
DWORD *dwAspect*
HDC *hdcDraw*
LPCRECT *lprcBounds*

OleDraw is a helper function that can be used to draw objects.

Parameters

pUnk
Points to the object that is to be drawn.

dwAspect
Contains a value taken from the enumeration **DVASPECT**, described earlier in this chapter.

hdcDraw
Specifies the device context onto which the drawing should actually be done. Cannot be a metafile device context.

lprcBounds
Points to a **RECT** structure that indicates the rectangle on which the object should be drawn. This parameter controls the positioning and stretching of the object.

Return Values

Value	Meaning
S_OK	Object was successfully drawn.
E_INVALIDARG	One or more arguments are invalid.
E_OUTOFMEMORY	Ran out of memory.
OLE_E_BLANK	There is no data to draw from.
E_ABORT	The draw operation was aborted.
VIEW_E_DRAW	An error occurred in drawing.
OLE_E_INVALIDRECT	The rectangle is invalid.
DV_E_NOIVIEWOBJECT	The object doesn't support the **IViewObject** interface.

Comments

OleDraw calls *pUnk*->**QueryInterface**, asking for **IViewObject**, converts the **RECT** structure to a **RECTL** structure, and then calls **IViewObject::Draw** as follows:

```
lpViewObj->Draw(dwAspect,-1,0,0,0,hdcDraw,&rectl,0,0,0);
```

OleDraw should not be used to draw into a metafile because it does not specify the *lprcWBounds* parameter. This value is required for drawing into metafiles.

See Also

IViewObject::Draw

OleDuplicateData

HANDLE OleDuplicateData(*hSrc*, *cfFormat*, *uiFlags*)
HANDLE *hSrc*
CLIPFORMAT *cfFormat*
UNIT *uiFlags*

OleDuplicateData is a helper function that duplicates metafiles, bitmaps, and global memory and returns a new handle of the same type.

Parameters

hSrc
Specifies the handle of the source data.

cfFormat
Specifies the clipboard format of the source data.

uiFlags
Specifies the flags to be used in global memory allocation. If the value of *uiFlags* is NULL, GMEM_MOVEABLE is used as a default.

Return Values

Value	Meaning
Handle to the duplicated data.	Data was successfully duplicated.
NULL	Error duplicating data.

Comments

The CF_METAFILEPICT, CF_PALETTE, or CF_BITMAP formats receive special handling; all other formats are duplicated byte-wise. For the formats that are duplicated byte-wise, *hSrc* must be a global memory handle.

CreateDataCache

HRESULT CreateDataCache(*pUnk,rclsid, riid, ppvObj)*
LPUNKNOWN *pUnk*
REFCLSID *rclsid*
REFIID *riid*
LPVOID FAR * *ppvObj*

CreateDataCache creates a cache object and returns a pointer to the interface identified by *riid*. The returned object supports **IOleCache**, **IOleCache2**, and **IOleCacheControl** for controlling the cache, **IPersistStorage** for reading and writing to persistent storage, **IDataObject** without advise support, **IViewObject**, and **IViewObject2**. **CreateDataCache** can be used with DLL object applications and handlers that do not use the OLE default handler as an aggregate object.

Parameters

pUnk
Specifies the controlling unknown if this cache object is to be instantiated as part of an aggregate. Can be NULL, indicating that no aggregation will occur.

rclsid
Specifies the CLSID that is used *only* to generate default icon labels; most often, this will be CLSID_NULL.

riid
The interface that the caller is to use to communicate with the newly created cache, typically, this is IID_IOleCache. Callers can also request IID_IDataObject, IID_IViewObject, and IID_IPersistStorage.

ppvObj
Pointer to where to return the cache object.

Return Values

Value	Meaning
S_OK	A new instance of the OLE provided cache implementation was returned.
E_INVALIDARG	One or more arguments are invalid.
E_OUTOFMEMORY	Ran out of memory.

Value	Meaning
E_NOINTERFACE	The interface represented by *iid* is not supported by the object; *ppvObj* is set to NULL.

Comments

The returned object supports **IOleCache** for controlling the cache, **IPersistStorage** for reading and writing to persistent storage, and **IDataObject** for handling data transfers (the **IDataObject** object *does not* offer support for data advises).

Typically, **CreateDataCache** is called only by DLL object applications to obtain a default cache implementation.

See Also

IOleCache, IDataObject, IPersistStorage

ReleaseStgMedium

void ReleaseStgMedium(*pmedium*)
LPSTGMEDIUM *pmedium*

ReleaseStgMedium frees the specified storage medium.

Parameters

pmedium
Points to the storage medium that is to be freed.

Comments

After this call, the storage medium is invalid and can no longer be used.

Sometimes the original provider of the medium wishes to maintain control of the freeing of the medium. If this is the case and the medium is TYMED_HGLOBAL, TYMED_MFPICT, or TYMED_GDI, **ReleaseStgMedium** does nothing. If the medium is TYMED_FILE, **ReleaseStgMedium** does nothing to the actual disk file. The file name string, however, is freed using the standard memory management mechanism. For TYMED_ISTREAM, **ReleaseStgMedium** calls **IStream::Release**; for TYMED_ISTORAGE, **IStorage::Release** is called. Following all these actions, *pmedium->pUnkForRelease->***Release** is invoked.

If the receiving of the medium is to free it, as is indicated by *pUnkForRelease* being set to NULL, **ReleaseStgMedium** does the following:

Medium	ReleaseStgMedium Action
TYMED_HGLOBAL	Calls **GlobalFree** on the handle.
TYMED_GDI	Calls **DeleteObject** on the handle.
TYMED_MFPICT	The *hMF* that it contains is deleted with **DeleteMetaFile**, then the handle itself is passed to **GlobalFree**.
TYMED_FILE	Frees the disk file by deleting it. Frees the file name string by using the standard memory management paradigm.
TYMED_ISTREAM	**Calls IStream::Release**.
TYMED_ISTORAGE	**Calls IStorage::Release**.

Icon Extraction Helper Functions

OleGetIconOfFile

HGLOBAL OleGetIconOfFile(*lpszPath, fUseFileAsLabel*)
LPSTR *lpszPath*
BOOL *fUseFileAsLabel*

OleGetIconOfFile returns a handle to a metafile (hMetaPict) containing an icon and label (filename) for the specified filename.

Parameters

lpszPath
Points to the path, including the filename, to use to locate the file.

fUseFileAsLabel
Determines whether the icon's label is to be the filename (TRUE) or if there is no filename (FALSE).

Return Values

Value	Meaning
HGLOBAL	hMetaPict containing the icon and label. If there's no CLSID in the registration database for the file in *lpszPath*, then "Document" is used. If *lpszPath* is NULL, NULL is returned.

OleGetIconOfClass

HGLOBAL OleGetIconOfClass(*rclsid, lpszLabel, fUseTypeAsLabel***)**
REFCLSID *rclsid*
LPSTR *lpszLabel*
BOOL *fUseTypeAsLabel*

OleGetIconOfClass returns a hMetaPict containing an icon and human-readable label for the specified class.

Parameters

rclsid
Points to the CLSID to use.

lpszLabel
Points to the label to use for the icon.

fUseTypeAsLabel
Indicates whether to use the CLSID's user type name as the label for the icon (TRUE) or not (FALSE).

Return Values

Value	Meaning
HGLOBAL	hMetaPict containing the icon and label. If the CLSID is not found in the registration database, NULL is returned.

OleMetafilePictFromIconAndLabel

HGLOBAL OleMetafilePictFromIconAndLabel(*hIcon, lpszLabel, lpszSourceFile, iIconIndex***)**
HICON *hIcon*
LPSTR *lpszLabel*
LPSTR *lpszSourceFile*
UINT *iIconIndex*

OleMetafilePictFromIconAndLabel creates a METAFILEPICT structure (defined in windows.h) that contains a metafile in which the icon and label are drawn.

Parameters

hIcon
The handle to the icon that is to be drawn into the metafile.

lpszLabel
Points to the string that is to be used as the label for the icon.

lpszSourceFile
Points to the string, as it is obtained from the user or the registration database, that contains the local pathname of the icon.

iIconIndex
Provides the index into *lpszSourceFile* from where the icon was obtained.

Return Values

Value	Meaning
HGLOBAL	Global memory handle containing a METAFILEPICT structure, where the metafile uses the MM_ANISOTROPIC mapping mode. The extents reflect both the icon and the label.

CHAPTER 8

Linking Interfaces and Functions

OLE 2 uses a mechanism known as a moniker to for linking and naming. A moniker is a conceptual handle to a link at its source which can be stored with the linked object's consumer. A moniker's main operation is to bind, or connect, to the object to which it points. The binding process invokes whatever algorithms are necessary to locate and run the link source object.

Two types of monikers are stored for each linked object: one that represents the absolute path to the link source and one that provides a relative path. When a linked object is activated, the relative moniker is used first to bind to the link source, using the absolute moniker only if the relative one fails. Using a relative moniker in addition to the absolute moniker supports the following link tracking situations:

- The link source and the link consumer (the linked object) have been copied or moved but retain the same relative structure, such as two documents in the same directory. Another case is a link between two objects, both embedded in a third document. In these situations, the relative moniker succeeds in binding.
- The link source does not move, but the link consumer does move, and in such a way that the relative structure is not maintained. In this case, the relative moniker fails to bind, but the absolute moniker does bind.

This chapter describes the interfaces and functions that enable linking to occur. All of these interfaces are implemented by OLE; applications typically use those implementations.

The following table provides a brief summary of the interfaces that support linking.

Interface Name	Inplemented By	Used By
IMoniker	OLE and some object applications	Used by OLE to manage the binding of monikers to their sources.
IEnumMoniker	OLE	Used by OLE, certain containers, and object applications to enumerate items that are monikers.
IOleLink	OLE	Used by containers to manage monikers inside of links and to manage the link's update options.
IBindCtx	OLE	Used by OLE to accumulate the set of objects that are bound during an operation and that should be released when the operation is completed.
IRunningObjectTable	OLE	Used by OLE and object applications to access the running object table.
IParseDisplayName	Containers and object applications	Used by OLE to transform the display name of an object into a moniker.

IMoniker Interface

The **IMoniker** interface is typically implemented and used by OLE. However, some advanced applications that do not organize thier data in files, such as database-oriented applications, may need to implement a new moniker type. **IMoniker** contains the following methods (see also MONIKER.H):

```
DECLARE_INTERFACE_(IMoniker, IPersistStream)
{
   // *** IUnknown methods ***
  HRESULT QueryInterface (THIS_ REFIID riid, LPVOID FAR* ppvObj);
  ULONG AddRef (THIS);
  ULONG Release (THIS);

   // *** IPersist methods ***
  HRESULT GetClassID)(THIS_ LPCLSID lpClassID);

   // *** IPersistStream methods ***
  HRESULT IsDirty (THIS);
  HRESULT Load (THIS_ LPSTREAM pStm);
  HRESULT Save (THIS_ LPSTREAM pStm, BOOL fClearDirty);
  HRESULT GetSizeMax (THIS_ ULARGE_INTEGER FAR * pcbSize);
```

```
    // *** IMoniker methods ***
    HRESULT BindToObject (THIS_ LPBC pbc, LPMONIKER pmkToLeft, REFIID riidResult,
     LPVOID FAR* ppvResult);
    HRESULT BindToStorage (THIS_ LPBC pbc, LPMONIKER pmkToLeft, REFIID riid, LPVOID FAR* ppvObj);
    HRESULT Reduce (THIS_ LPBC pbc, DWORD dwReduceHowFar, LPMONIKER FAR* ppmkToLeft,
     LPMONIKER FAR * ppmkReduced);
    HRESULT ComposeWith (THIS_ LPMONIKER pmkRight, BOOL fOnlyIfNotGeneric,
     LPMONIKER FAR* ppmkComposite);
    HRESULT Enum (THIS_ BOOL fForward, LPENUMMONIKER FAR* ppenumMoniker);
    HRESULT IsEqual (THIS_ LPMONIKER pmkOtherMoniker);
    HRESULT Hash (THIS_ LPDWORD pdwHash);
    HRESULT IsRunning (THIS_ LPBC pbc, LPMONIKER pmkToLeft, LPMONIKER pmkNewlyRunning);
    HRESULT GetTimeOfLastChange (THIS_ LPBC pbc, LPMONIKER pmkToLeft, FILETIME FAR* pfiletime);
    HRESULT Inverse (THIS_ LPMONIKER FAR* ppmk);
    HRESULT CommonPrefixWith (THIS_ LPMONIKER pmkOther, LPMONIKER FAR* ppmkPrefix);
    HRESULT RelativePathTo (THIS_ LPMONIKER pmkOther, LPMONIKER FAR*
    HRESULT GetDisplayName (THIS_ LPBC pbc, LPMONIKER pmkToLeft, ppmkRelPath);
     LPSTR FAR* lplpszDisplayName);
    HRESULT ParseDisplayName (THIS_ LPBC pbc, LPMONIKER pmkToLeft,
     LPSTR lpszDisplayName, ULONG FAR* pchEaten, LPMONIKER FAR* ppmkOut);
    HRESULT IsSystemMoniker (THIS_ LPDWORD pdwMksys);
};
```

The **IMoniker** interface contains methods to control and access monikers. Different classes of monikers can exist; currently OLE supports these classes: *generic composite, file, item, pointer, and anti-* monikers. Supporting a moniker class means providing a unique implementation of the **IMoniker** interface for that class.

Generic composite (or simply composite) monikers are a sequenced collection of other monikers. In general, each type of moniker is designed to be part of a composite moniker that specifies the complete path to an object. The composition here is generic in that it has no knowledge of the pieces involved other than that they are monikers.

Each moniker class can store arbitrary data in its persistent representation and can run arbitrary code at binding time. If there is an identifiable piece of persistent storage in which the object is stored, **IMoniker::BindToStorage** can be used to gain access to it. Many objects (all OLE embedded objects, for example) have such identifiable storage. Others, such as the objects that are the ranges on a spreadsheet, do not.

The most basic operation in the **IMoniker** interface is **IMoniker::BindToObject**, which binds a moniker to the object to which it points. **IMoniker::BindToObject** runs whatever algorithm is necessary to locate the object and returns a pointer to a specified interface type to the caller.

Most monikers have a textual representation that is meaningful to the user and can be retrieved with **IMoniker::GetDisplayName**. The API function **MkParseDisplayName** turns a textual display name into the appropriate moniker. Using this function is usually as expensive as actually binding to the object.

Monikers can compare themselves to other monikers using **IMoniker::IsEqual**. A hash value useful for storing monikers in lookup tables is available through **IMoniker::Hash**. The earliest time after which the object that the moniker points to is known not to have changed can be obtained with **IMoniker::GetTimeOfLastChange**.

A moniker can be requested to rewrite itself into an equivalent moniker by calling **IMoniker::Reduce**. This function returns a new moniker that binds to the same object, but does so in a more efficient way.

Pointers to instances of the **IMoniker** interface can be marshaled to other processes, just as with any other interface pointer. Many monikers cannot be changed once they have been created; nor do they maintain an object state outside themselves. Item monikers are an example of a class of such monikers. These monikers, which can be replicated any time, usually support custom marshaling (see **IMarshal** interface) so they can serialize and deserialize themselves in the destination context (see "IPersistStream" regarding serialization).

IMoniker::BindToObject

HRESULT IMoniker::BindToObject(*pbc*, *pmkToLeft*, *riid*, *ppvObj***)**
LPBC *pbc*
LPMONIKER *pmkToLeft*
REFIID *riid*
LPVOID FAR * *ppvObj*

IMoniker::BindToObject locates and loads the object referenced by a given moniker.

Parameters

pbc
Points to the bind context, an instance of the **IBindCtx** interface, to be used for this binding operation.

pmkToLeft
Points to the moniker of the object to the left of this moniker.

riid
Identifies the interface by which the caller wants to connect to the object.

ppvObj
On a successful return, points to the instantiated object, unless BINDFLAGS_JUSTTESTEXISTENCE was specified in the binding options. If BINDFLAGS_JUSTTESTEXISTENCE was specified, NULL can be returned instead.

Return Values

Value	Meaning
S_OK	The binding operation was successful.
MK_E_NOOBJECT	Some, possibly intermediate, object could not be found during an operation such as binding or parsing a display name.
MK_E_EXCEEDEDDEADLINE	The process was not completed within the time limit specified by the bind context.
MK_E_CONNECTMANUALLY	During some process (binding, parsing a display name, and so on) OLE was unable to connect to a network device. The application receiving this error should call **IBindCtx::GetObjectParam** with the key "ConnectManually" to retrieve the moniker of the network device, get the display name, and put up a dialog box asking the user for a password, and so on.
MK_E_INTERMEDIATE INTERFACENOTSUPPORTED	An object was found but did not support an interface required for an operation. (During binding, for example, a container is expected to support the **IOleItemContainer** interface, and during parsing of display names a container is expected to support the **IParseDisplayName** interface.)
E_UNEXPECTED	An unexpected error occurred.
E_OUTOFMEMORY	Ran out of memory.
STG_E_ACCESSDENIED	Unable to access the storage object.
IOleItemContainer::GetObject errors.	Binding to a moniker containing an item moniker can return any of the errors associated with this function.

Comments

Because each type of OLE moniker is designed to be part of a composite moniker, any given piece has a prefix of the composite to its left, and a suffix of the composite to its right. If **IMoniker::BindToObject** is called on a given piece, most often the **IMoniker::BindToObject** function requires the services of the object indicated by the prefix to its left. An item moniker, for example, requires the **IOleItemContainer** interface of the object to its left.

The bind context contains a time limit in which the caller wants the binding process to be completed. If the process is not completed within the specified time, it fails and returns MK_E_EXCEEDEDDEADLINE. The moniker of the object for which the deadline was exceeded can be retrieved by calling **IBindCtx::GetObjectParam** with the keys ExceededDeadline, ExceededDeadline1, ExceededDeadline2, and so on. (This capability is not often used with **IMoniker::BindToObject**; it is more often used with other **IMoniker** methods such as **IMoniker::GetTimeOfLastChange**.)

The running object table is accessible from the bind context using the **IBindCtx::GetRunningObjectTable** method.

Note Binding to the right of the present piece of a composite moniker may involve binding to other objects. Consequently, binding a moniker can be an expensive operation since the composite moniker often needs to start object applications and open files. To avoid loading the object and releasing it, then loading it again later, **IMoniker::BindToObject** can use the bind context passed through the *pbc* parameter until the binding process is complete. For more information on bind contexts, see the section, "IBindCtx Interface."

See Also **IBindCtx::GetBindOptions, IBindCtx::GetRunningObjectTable, IBindCtx::RegisterObjectBound, IMoniker::GetTimeOfLastChange**

IMoniker::BindToStorage

HRESULT IMoniker::BindToStorage(*pbc, pmkToLeft, riid, ppvObj*)
LPBC *pbc*
LPMONIKER *pmkToLeft*
REFIID *riid*
LPVOID FAR* *ppvObj*

IMoniker::BindToStorage returns access to the persistent storage of the receiver (that is, the location that contains the presentation of the information) by using the specified interface, rather than access to the object itself.

Parameters

pbc
Points to the bind context to be used during this binding operation.

pmkToLeft
Points to the moniker of the object to the left of this moniker.

riid
Identifies the interface to bind to the persistent storage. Common interfaces passed here include **IStorage**, **IStream**, and **ILockBytes**.

ppvObj
Points to where the instantiated storage is placed. NULL can be returned if BINDFLAGS_JUSTTESTEXISTENCE was specified in the binding options.

Return Values

Value	Meaning
S_OK	The binding operation was successful.
MK_E_NOSTORAGE	An attempt was made to access or bind to the storage of an object that does not have storage.
MK_E_EXCEEDEDDEADLINE	The process was not completed within the time specified by the bind context.
MK_E_CONNECTMANUALLY	During some process (binding, parsing a display name, and so on), OLE was unable to connect to a network device. For more information, see **IMoniker::BindToObject**.
MK_E_INTERMEDIATE INTERFACENOTSUPPORTED	An object was found but did not support an interface required for an operation. (For example, during binding, a container is expected to support the **IOleItemContainer** interface, and during parsing of display names a container is expected to support the **IParseDisplayName** interface.)
E_OUTOFMEMORY	Ran out of memory.
STG_E_ACCESSDENIED	Unable to access the storage object.
IOleItemContainer::GetObject errors.	Binding to a moniker containing an item moniker can return any of the errors associated with this function.

Comments

For example, a composite moniker that refers to a spreadsheet embedded in a word processing document, such as:

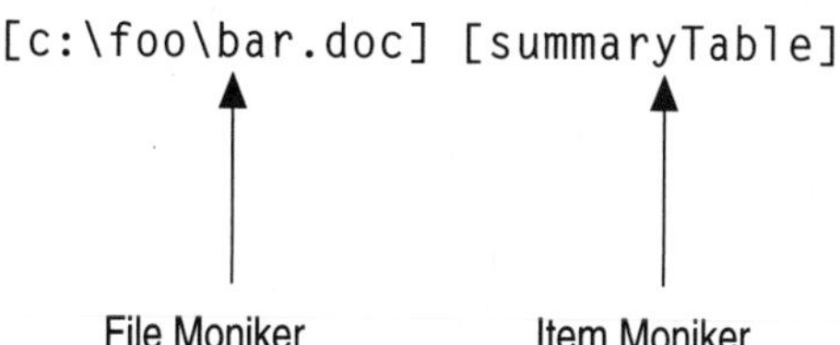

Calling **IMoniker::BindToObject** on this composite lets the caller communicate with the spreadsheet; calling **IMoniker::BindToStorage** lets the caller communicate with the **IStorage** instance in which it resides.

IMoniker::BindToStorage is usually called during the right-to-left recursion process of **IMoniker::BindToObject** when it has been invoked on a generic composite moniker. Sometimes, monikers at the tail of the composite don't require access to the object on their left; they merely require access to its persistent storage. These monikers can be bound more efficiently by not binding to the objects of the monikers to their left.

Some objects do not have an identifiable piece of storage. Attempting to call **IMoniker::BindToStorage** on a moniker with this type of object(s) fails with the error MK_E_NOSTORAGE.

Using the bind context in **IMoniker::BindToStorage** is the same as in **IMoniker::BindToObject**.

See Also **IMoniker::BindToObject**

IMoniker::Reduce

HRESULT IMoniker::Reduce(*pbc, dwReduceHowFar, ppmkToLeft, ppmkReduced***)**
LPBC *pbc*
DWORD *dwReduceHowFar*
LPMONIKER FAR * *ppmkToLeft*
LPMONIKER FAR * *ppmkReduced*

IMoniker::Reduce returns a more efficient or equally efficient moniker that refers to the same object.

Parameters

pbc
Points to the bind context to use.

dwReduceHowFar
Specifies how this moniker should be reduced.

ppmkToLeft
On entry, *ppmkToLeft* points to the moniker that prefixes this one within the composite, that is, the moniker to the left of the current moniker. On exit, the pointer will be NULL or non-NULL. Non-NULL indicates that the previous prefix should be disregarded and the moniker returned through *ppmkToLeft* used as the prefix in its place (this is not usual). NULL indicates that the prefix should not be replaced. Most monikers will NULL out this parameter before returning. *ppmkToLeft* is an in/out parameter. It must be released before NULLING out. For more information on in/out parameters, see the discussion of parameter types in the section on "Memory Management" in the "Overview" chapter.

ppmkReduced
Points (on exit) to the reduced form of the moniker; it can be NULL.

Return Values

Value	Meaning
S_OK	The reduction of the moniker was successful.
MK_S_REDUCED_TO_SELF	The **IMoniker::Reduce** operation output is the same as the input, and further calls to **Reduce** will have no effect.
MK_E_EXCEEDEDDEADLINE	The process was not completed within the time specified by the bind context.
E_UNEXPECTED	An unexpected error occurred.
E_OUTOFMEMORY	Insufficient memory.

Comments

Most monikers simply reduce to themselves (because they cannot be reduced any further). A moniker that reduces to itself passes itself through *ppmkReduced* and then returns MK_S_REDUCED_TO_SELF. A moniker that reduces to nothing should pass NULL through *ppmkReduced* and return S_OK.

Reducing a moniker that is a composite of other monikers returns the composite of the reduced pieces.

The *dwReduceHowFar* parameter controls the reduction process and it has the following values:

```
typedef enum tagMKRREDUCE {
    MKRREDUCE_ONE         = 3<<16,
    MKRREDUCE_TOUSER      = 2<<16,
    MKRREDUCE_THROUGUSER  = 1<<16,
    MKRREDUCE_ALL         = 0
    } MKRREDUCE;
```

These values have the following meanings:

Value	Meaning
MKRREDUCE_ONE	Performs only one reduction step on the moniker. In general, the caller must have specific knowledge about the particular kind of moniker to be able to take advantage of this option.
MKRREDUCE_TOUSER	Reduce the moniker to a form that the user identifies as a persistent object. If no such point exists, this option should be treated as MKRREDUCE_ALL.
MKRREDUCE_THROUGHUSER	Reduce the moniker to where any further reduction would prevent the user from identifying it as a persistent object. Often, this is the same stage as MKRREDUCE_TOUSER.
MKRREDUCE_ALL	Reduce the moniker until it is reduced to itself.

Being able to programmatically reduce a moniker to a display name recognizable to the user is an important of moniker reduction. Paths in the file system, bookmarks in word-processing documents, and range names in spreadsheets are all examples of user identities. In contrast, a macro or an alias encapsulated in a moniker is not a user identity.

The bind context parameter is used as it is in **IMoniker::BindToObject**. Implementations of **IMoniker::Reduce** should note the time limit imposed by the caller and the reporting of the object moniker which, had it been running, would have allowed the reduction to progress further. For more information, see the "IBindCtx Interface" in this chapter.

See Also **IBindCtx Interface, IMoniker::BindToObject**

IMoniker::ComposeWith

HRESULT IMoniker::ComposeWith(*pmkRight, fOnlyIfNotGeneric, ppmkComposite***)**
LPMONIKER *pmkRight*
BOOL *fOnlyIfNotGeneric*
LPMONIKER FAR * *ppmkComposite*

IMoniker::ComposeWith returns a new composite moniker formed from the moniker on the left and the moniker pointed to by *pmkRight*. This operation uses the pieces of the path to an object to form the full path.

Parameters

pmkRight
Points to the moniker to compose onto the end of the *pmkComposite*.

fOnlyIfNotGeneric
Controls what should be done in the case where using a generic composite is the way to form a composite.

ppmkComposite
Points (on exit) to the resulting composite moniker, which may be NULL.

Return Values

Value	Meaning
S_OK	The composite moniker was returned successfully.
MK_E_NEEDGENERIC	This error is returned when **IMoniker::ComposeWith** is called with *fOnlyIfNotGeneric* equal to TRUE, but the moniker only supports generic composition.
E_OUTOFMEMORY	Ran out of memory.
E_UNEXPECTED	An unexpected error occurred.

Comments

There are two kinds of composite monikers: those that know nothing about their pieces other than that they are monikers, and those that know more. The former is often referred to as a *generic composite moniker*. A generic composite moniker is a moniker made up of other simpler monikers stored in a left-to-right order. An example of the second type of moniker might be the result of composing a file moniker containing a relative path onto the end of another file moniker. The result could be a new file moniker containing the complete path.

Applications can call the API function, **CreateGenericComposite**, to create a generic composite moniker. Non-generic composite monikers can collapse a path within a storage domain to a more efficient representation in a subsequent **IMoniker::Reduce** operation. However, none of the monikers provided by OLE are capable of this.

In general, each moniker class should have a set of special monikers (possibly empty) that can be composed onto the end of a moniker of a given class in a nongeneric way. The moniker class understands enough of the semantics of these special monikers to realize they are more than just that they are monikers. Each **IMoniker::ComposeWith** implementation examines *pmkRight* to see whether it is such a special moniker for this implementation. Often, *pmkRight* is asked for its class, but other possibilities exist, such as using **QueryInterface**. A common case of such special monikers are anti monikers.

If *pmkRight* is special, the **IMoniker::ComposeWith** implementation does whatever is appropriate for that special case. If not, *fOnlyIfNotGeneric* controls what should occur. If *fOnlyIfNotGeneric* is true, NULL should be passed back through *ppmkComposite* and the status, MK_E_NEEDGENERIC, returned. If *fOnlyIfNotGeneric* is FALSE, a generic composite should be returned using **CreateGenericComposite**. Most callers of **ComposeWith** should set *fOnlyIfNotGeneric* to FALSE.

In any situation where *pmkRight* completely negates the receiver (that is, irrespective of *fOnlyIfNotGeneric*), and the resulting composite is empty, NULL should be passed back through *ppmkComposite* and the status S_OK returned.

The pieces of a moniker that have been composed together can be enumerated using **IMoniker::Enum**. On a generic composite, this enumerates the monikers contained within it. On other monikers, the particular pieces returned are implementation specific.

Composition of monikers is an associative operation. That is, if A, B, and C are monikers, then

$(A \circ B) \circ C$

is always equal to

$A \circ (B \circ C)$

where $\circ$ represents the composition operation. Each implementation of **IMoniker::ComposeWith** must maintain this invariant.

IMoniker::Enum

HRESULT IMoniker::Enum(*fForward, ppenumMoniker***)**
BOOL *fForward*
LPENUMMONIKER FAR * *ppenumMoniker*

IMoniker::Enum enumerates the composite pieces of a generic composite moniker.

Parameters

fForward
Specifies the enumeration order. TRUE enumerates the monikers in the normal order; FALSE causes a reverse enumeration order.

ppenumMoniker
Points (on exit) to the returned enumerator. Can be NULL to indicate there is nothing to enumerate.

Return Values

Value	Meaning
S_OK	The enumerator was returned successfully.
E_OUTOFMEMORY	Ran out of memory.
E_UNEXPECTED	An unexpected error occurred.

Comments

IMoniker::Enum operates differently with different moniker classes. For example, enumerating a file moniker might enumerate the internally stored path into its components, even though they are not stored internally as separate monikers. If the moniker has no discernible internal structure, it simply passes back NULL through *ppenumMoniker* instead of an enumerator.

The returned enumeration is of the type **IEnumMoniker**, defined as:

```
typedef Enum<IMoniker*> IEnumMoniker;
```

This is shorthand for:

```
interface IEnumMoniker : IUnknown
{
  virtual SCODE Next(ULONG celt, IMoniker* rgelt,
    ULONG* pceltFetched) = 0;
  virtual SCODE Skip(ULONG celt) = 0;
  virtual SCODE Reset() = 0;
  virtual SCODE Clone(IEnumMoniker** ppenumMoniker) = 0;
};
```

See Also **IEnumUnknown Interface, IEnumString Interface**

IMoniker::IsEqual

HRESULT IMoniker::IsEqual(*pmkOther*)
LPMONIKER FAR * *pmkOther*

IMoniker::IsEqual compares two monikers and indicates whether they are equal.

Parameters

pmkOther
Points to the moniker to use for comparison.

Return Values

Value	Meaning
S_OK	The two monikers are alike.
S_FALSE	The two monikers are not alike.

Comments

IMoniker::IsEqual is used to implement the running object table.

The moniker entries in the running object table indicate which objects are running, providing a way for link consumers to connect to the appropriate running object.

Two monikers that can compare as equal in either order must also hash to the same value.

See Also **IMoniker::Hash**

IMoniker::Hash

HRESULT IMoniker::Hash(*pdwHash*)
LPDWORD *pdwHash*

IMoniker::Hash returns a 32-bit integer associated with this moniker. The returned integer can be used to maintain tables of monikers. The moniker can be hashed to determine a hash bucket in the table, then compared against all the monikers in the hash bucket by calling **IMoniker::IsEqual**.

Parameters

pdwHash
Points to where to return the hash value.

Return Values

Value	Meaning
S_OK	The integer was returned successfully.

Comments

Two monikers that compare as equal in either order hash to the same value. Implementations of **IsEqual** and **Hash** are closely related and must always be written together.

The value returned by **IMoniker::Hash** is invariant under marshaling: if a moniker is marshaled to a new context, **Hash** invoked on the unmarshaled moniker in the new context returns the same value as **Hash** invoked on the original moniker. This is the only way that a global table of monikers such as the running object table can be maintained in shared space, yet accessed from many processes. Thus, implementations of **IMoniker::Hash** should not rely on the memory address of the moniker, but only its internal state.

See Also

IMoniker::IsEqual

IMoniker::IsRunning

HRESULT IMoniker::IsRunning(*pbc, pmkToLeft, pmkNewlyRunning*)
LPBC FAR * *pbc*
LPMONIKER FAR * *pmkToLeft*
LPMONIKER FAR * *pmkNewlyRunning*

IMoniker::IsRunning determines whether the specified moniker is running.

Parameters

pbc
Points to the usual bind context.

pmkToLeft
Points to the moniker to the left of this one in the composite in which it is found.

pmkNewlyRunning
If non-NULL, this is the moniker most recently added to the running object table and **IMoniker::IsRunning** can assume that without this moniker in the running object table, **IsRunning** would return S_FALSE. Can be NULL.

Return Values

Value	Meaning
S_OK	The moniker is running.
S_FALSE	The moniker is not running.
E_UNEXPECTED	An unexpected error occurred.

Comments

This moniker gains access to the running object table, which is used to determine if the object is running, by calling **IBindCtx::GetRunningObjectTable**. *pmkToLeft* is the moniker to the left of this object in the generic composite in which it is found, if any. *pmkNewlyRunning*, if non-NULL, is the moniker that has most recently been added to the running object table. **IsRunning** can assume that without *pmkNewlyRunning* in the running object table, **IsRunning** would have returned S_FALSE. Thus, the only way this moniker can now be running is if the newly running moniker is itself running. This allows for some n^2 to n reductions in algorithms that use monikers. Implementations of this method in various kinds of moniker classes are roughly as follows:

Generic composite moniker implementation:

```
if (pmkToLeft != NULL)
    return (pmkToLeft->ComposeWith(this))->IsRunning(pbc, NULL,
            pmkNewlyRunning);
if (pmkNewlyRunning != NULL) {
    if (pmkNewlyRunning->IsEqual(this) == NOERROR)
        return NOERROR;
}
else if (pRunningObjectTable -> IsRunning(this) == NOERROR)
    return NOERROR;

// otherwise, forward it on to my last element.
return this->Last()->IsRunning(pbc, this->AllButLast(),
    pmkNewlyRunning);
```

For moniker classes that do not support wildcard matching:

```
if (pmkToLeft == NULL) {
    if (pmkNewlyRunning != NULL)
        return pmkNewlyRunning->IsEqual(this);
    else
        return pRunningObjectTable->IsRunning(this);
else
    return ResultFromScode(S_FALSE);
```

For moniker classes that support a wild card entry that always matches any instance of the moniker class (all instances of the moniker class with the same moniker to their left are deemed to be running if the wild card is present):

```
if (pmkToLeft == NULL) {
    if (pmkNewlyRunning != NULL)
        return pmkNewlyRunning->IsEqual(this) == NOERROR ||
        pmkNewlyRunning->IsEqual(my wild card moniker) == NOERROR
    if (pRunningObjectTable->IsRunning(this) == NOERROR)
        return NOERROR;
    return pRunningObjectTable->IsRunning(my wild card moniker);
}
else
    return pmkToLeft->ComposeWith(my wild card moniker)->IsRunning
        (pbc, NULL, pmkNewlyRunning);
```

Some moniker classes have a wild card entry that matches only those object that are currently running: This is specifically the behavior of item monikers.

```
if (pmkToLeft == NULL) {
    if (pmkNewlyRunning != NULL) {
        if (pmkNewlyRunning->IsEqual(this) == NOERROR)
            return NOERROR;
        if (pmkNewlyRunning->IsEqual(wild card moniker) !=
            NOERROR)
            return ResultFromScode(S_FALSE);
        goto TestBind:
        return pRunningObjetTable -> IsRunning;
    }
}
if (pmkToLeft->ComposeWith(my wild card moniker)->IsRunning
        (pbc, NULL, pmkNewlyRunning) != NOERROR)
    return ResultFromScode(S_FALSE);

TestBind:
    // In general, connect to the container and ask if object
    // is running. The use of IOleItemContainer is specific to
    // item monikers, but the theme is a general one.
    IOleItemContainer *pcont;
    pmkToLeft->BindToObject(pbc, NULL, IID_IOleItemContainer,
        &pcont);
    return pcont->IsRunning(szItemString);
```

IMoniker::GetTimeOfLastChange

HRESULT IMoniker::GetTimeOfLastChange(*pbc, pmkToLeft, pFileTime***)**
LPBC *pbc*
LPMONIKER *pmkToLeft*
FILETIME FAR * *pFileTime*

IMoniker::GetTimeOfLastChange provides date and time information needed to determine if a linked or embedded object containing linked objects, is up to date.

pbc
Points to the bind context to be used for this operation.

pmkToLeft
Points to the moniker to the left of this one in the composite in which it is found.

pFileTime
Points to where to return the time of the last change.

Return Values

Value	Meaning
S_OK	The date/time information was returned successfully.
MK_E_EXCEEDEDDEADLINE	The process was not completed within the time specified by the bind context.
MK_E_CONNECTMANUALLY	During some process (binding, parsing a display name, and so on.) OLE was unable to connect to a network device. For more information, see **IMoniker::BindToObject**.
MK_E_UNAVAILABLE	The time of the change is unavailable, and will not be available no matter what deadline is used.
E_UNEXPECTED	An unexpected error occurred.

Comments

If all the objects in a document are not up-to-date, the user should be prompted to update them. Updating out-of-date objects causes them to be bound and to retrieve a new presentation. **IMoniker::GetTimeOfLastChange** does not bind to the object to determine whether it is out of date. Instead, it returns the best available answer based on the time-of-last-change information for objects already running. Many monikers point to an object contained in the object denoted by the moniker to the left. Implementations of **IMoniker::GetTimeOfLastChange** can often take advantage of the fact that objects cannot have changed at a date later than the object in which they are contained. That is, these monikers can simply forward the call onto the moniker to their left.

The returned time of change is reported using a **FILETIME** structure, defined in COMPOBJ.H as:

```
typedef struct FARSTRUCT tagFILETIME
{
    DWORD dwLowDateTime;
    DWORD dwHighDateTime;
} FILETIME;
```

Time is indicated in units of 100 nanoseconds allowing the times of fast-changing data to be recorded with precision. For information about converting between DOS date and time structures and OLE's **FILETIME** structure, see the descriptions of the **CoDosDateTimeToFileTime** and **CoFileTimeToDosDateTime** functions.

If the time of last change is unavailable, for example, because the deadline was exceeded, then a time of FILETIME_MAX should be passed back. If the deadline was exceeded, then the status MK_E_EXCEEDEDDEADLINE should be returned. If the time of change is unavailable, and would not be available no matter what deadline were used, then MK_E_UNAVAILABLE should be returned; otherwise, S_OK should be returned.

If *pmkToLeft* is NULL, **IMoniker::GetTimeOfLastChange** should first check for a recorded change-time in the running object table with **IRunningObjectTable::GetTimeOfLastChange** before proceeding with other strategies. Moniker classes that support wild cards must consider exactly what gets put in the running object table and look for the appropriate item because generic composite monikers know nothing of wild cards, they may even need to do that in the non-NULL *pmkToLeft* case.

See Also **IMoniker::IsRunning**, **IRunningObjectTable** Interface

IMoniker::Inverse

HRESULT IMoniker::Inverse(*ppmk***)**
LPMONIKER FAR * *ppmk*

IMoniker::Inverse returns a moniker that destroys this moniker when it is composed to the end of this moniker.

Parameters

ppmk
Points to where to return the inverse moniker.

Return Values

Value	Meaning
S_OK	The inverse moniker has been returned successfully.
MK_E_NOINVERSE	A moniker class that does not have inverses was asked for one.
E_OUTOFMEMORY	Ran out of memory.

Comments

IMoniker::Inverse is needed in implementations of the **IMoniker::RelativePathTo** member function, which is important for supporting monikers that track object movement.

IMoniker::Inverse is an abstract generalization of the ".." operation in MS-DOS file systems. For example, a file moniker representing the path "a\b\c\d" would have as its inverse a moniker containing the path "..\..\..\..", because "a\b\c\d" composed with "..\..\..\.." yields nothing.

The inverse of a moniker does not destroy just that particular moniker, but all monikers with a similar structure. Thus, the inverse of a generic composite moniker is the reverse composite, or the inverse of its pieces. Nongeneric composite monikers (such as the preceding file moniker example) also have nontrivial inverses. However, there are many kinds of monikers whose inverse is trivial. As the moniker adds one more piece to an existing structure; its inverse is a moniker with the last piece of the existing structure removed. A moniker that removes the last piece of a generic moniker when it is composed onto the end of that generic moniker is called an anti moniker. An OLE-provided implementation of an anti moniker can be created by calling the **CreateAntiMoniker** helper function. A moniker with no internal structure can return an anti moniker as its inverse.

Not all monikers have inverses. The inverse of an anti moniker, for example, does not exist. Neither do the inverses of most monikers that are themselves inverses. Monikers that have no inverse cannot have relative paths formed from other objects inside the objects they denote to other objects outside.

See Also

CreateAntiMoniker, IMoniker::RelativePathTo

IMoniker::CommonPrefixWith

HRESULT IMoniker::CommonPrefixWith(*pmkOther*, *ppmkPrefix*)
LPMONIKER *pmkOther*
LPMONIKER FAR * *ppmkPrefix*

IMoniker::CommonPrefixWith returns the longest common prefix that the receiver shares with the moniker pointed to by *pmkOther*.

pmkOther
Points to the (other) moniker whose common prefix is to be returned.

ppmkPrefix
Points to where to return the common prefix moniker. If the common prefix does not exist, NULL is returned.

Return Values

Value	Meaning
S_OK	The common prefix exists but is neither the receiver nor *pmkOther*.
MK_S_NOPREFIX	No common prefix exists.
MK_S_HIM	The other moniker is the prefix of the receiver moniker.
MK_S_US	The two monikers (the receiver and the other moniker) are equal.
MK_S_ME	The receiver moniker (the moniker whose **CommonPrefixWith** method is called) is a prefix of the other moniker.
MK_E_NOTBINDABLE	**IMoniker::CommonPrefixWith** was called on a relative moniker. The moniker cannot be bound to something until it is composed with a container moniker.
E_OUTOFMEMORY	Ran out of memory.

This functionality is useful in constructing relative paths and in performing some of the calculations on monikers needed by the Edit/Links... dialog box.

IMoniker::CommonPrefixWith should only be called on absolute monikers; for example, a file moniker that starts with a share or drive name, followed by items. It should not be called on relative monikers.

IMoniker::RelativePathTo

HRESULT IMoniker::RelativePathTo(*pmkOther, ppmkRelPath***)**
LPMONIKER *pmkOther*
LPMONIKER FAR **ppmkRelPath*

IMoniker::RelativePathTo returns the relative path to a moniker that will yield *pmkOther* when composed onto the end of this moniker, or a moniker with a similar structure.

Parameters

pmkOther
Points to the moniker to which a relative path should be taken.

ppmkRelPath
Points to where to return the relative path; cannot be NULL.

Return Values

Value	Meaning
S_OK	A meaningful relative path has been returned.
MK_S_HIM	The only form of the relative path is the other moniker.
MK_E_NOTBINDABLE	**IMoniker::RelativePathTo** was called on a relative moniker. The moniker cannot be bound to something until it is composed with a container moniker.
E_OUTOFMEMORY	Ran out of memory.
E_UNEXPECTED	An unexpected error occurred.

Comments

Conceptually, implementations of this function determine the longest prefix that the receiver and *pmkOther* have in common. This breaks the receiver and *pmkOther* into two parts each, say (P,T_{me}) and (P,T_{him}) respectively, where P is the maximal common prefix. The correct relative path result is then:

$$T_{me}^{-1} \circ T_{him}$$

That is, inverse $(T_{me}) \circ T_{him}$.

For any given implementation of **IMoniker::RelativePathTo**, the same *pmkOther* monikers are usually treated in a special manner, as they would be with **IMoniker::ComposeWith**. For example, file monikers might treat other file monikers in a special manner in both cases.

IMoniker::RelativePathTo should be called only on absolute monikers; for example, a file moniker that starts with a share or drive name, followed by items. It should not be called on relative monikers.

See Also

IMoniker::GetDisplayName

IMoniker::GetDisplayName

HRESULT IMoniker::GetDisplayName(*pbc, pmkToLeft, lplpszDisplayName***)**
LPBC *pbc*
LPMONIKER *pmkToLeft*
LPSTR FAR * *lplpszDisplayName*

IMoniker::GetDisplayName returns the current display name for this moniker. If none exists, it is NULL.

Parameters

pbc
Points to the bind context for this operation.

pmkToLeft
Points to the moniker to the left of this one in the composite in which it is found. Most monikers do not require this when calling **IMoniker::GetDisplayName**.

lplpszDisplayName
Points (on exit) to the current display name for this moniker. It is NULL if the moniker does not have a display name or if the time limit was exceeded.

Return Values

Value	Meaning
S_OK	The display name was returned successfully.
MK_E_EXCEEDEDDEADLINE	The process was not completed within the time specified by the bind context. The moniker of the object of which the deadline was exceeded can be retrieved
E_OUTOFMEMORY	Ran out of memory.
E_NOTIMPL	There is no display name.

Comments

To obtain the current display name of a moniker, **IMoniker::GetDisplayName** may have to access the storage of the object to which it refers, if not the object itself, which can be an expensive operation. As with other **IMoniker** functions, the *pbc* parameter specifies, as part of the overall bind context, a time limit within which the operation should be completed or fail, returning MK_E_EXCEEDEDDEADLINE if it is unable to do so.

Callers have the tendency to cache and use the last successful result obtained when they do not have quick access to the display name of a moniker (the standard implementation of OLE link does this).

Display names should be thought of as an annotation on the moniker that helps distinguish one moniker from another. Although rare, there might be more than one moniker with the same display name.

There is no guarantee that a display name obtained from a moniker will parse back into that moniker when calling **MkParseDisplayName** with it, though failure to do so also is rare.

A moniker that is a prefix of another has a display name that is a (string) prefix of the display name of the second moniker.

Monikers that are designed to be part of a generic composite must include any preceding delimiter as part of their display name. Many monikers take a parameter for this delimiter in their instance creation functions.

See Also **MkParseDisplayName**

IMoniker::ParseDisplayName

HRESULT IMoniker::ParseDisplayName(*pbc, pmkToLeft, lpszDisplayName, pchEaten, ppmkOut***)**
LPBC *pbc*
LPMONIKER *pmkToLeft*
LPSTR *lpszDisplayName*
ULONG FAR* *pchEaten*
LPMONIKER FAR * *ppmkOut*

IMoniker::ParseDisplayName parses the composite moniker's remaining display name. The *lpszDisplayName* parameter is the yet-to-be-parsed tail of the display name. The **IMoniker::ParseDisplayName** function parses as much of the remaining tail as is appropriate for a display name within the object identified by `(pmkToLeft ° (the receiver))` and returns the corresponding moniker.

Parameters

pbc
Points to the bind context that is to be used to accumulate bound objects.

pmkToLeft
Points to the moniker to the left of this one in the so-far-parsed display name.

lpszDisplayName
Points to the display name to be parsed.

pchEaten
Points to the number of characters of the input name this parse consumed.

ppmkOut
Points to the resulting moniker.

Return Values

Value	Meaning
S_OK	The parse operation was completed successfully.
MK_E_SYNTAX	An error in the syntax of a filename was encountered while parsing a display name or while creating a file moniker.
E_OUTOFMEMORY	Ran out of memory.
E_UNEXPECTED	An unexpected error occurred.
IMoniker::BindToObject errors.	Parsing display names may cause binding. Thus, any error associated with this function may be returned.

Comments

The main loop of **MkParseDisplayName** finds the next moniker piece by calling **IMoniker::ParseDisplayName** and passing NULL through *pmkToLeft*. If the moniker that has been parsed to this point is a generic composite, the composite forwards this information onto its last piece, passing the prefix of the composite to the left of the piece in *pmkToLeft*.

Some moniker classes are able to parse their display names themselves because they are designed to designate only certain kinds of objects. Other monikers will need to bind to the object that they designate to do the parsing. These objects should not be released by **IMoniker::ParseDisplayName**, but instead should be transferred to the bind context for later release.

If a syntax error occurs, NULL is returned through *ppmkOut*. The number of characters that were successfully parsed in the display name is returned through *pchEaten*.

See Also

MkParseDisplayName

IMoniker::IsSystemMoniker

HRESULT IMoniker::IsSystemMoniker(*pdwMksys***)**
LPDWORD *pdwMksys*

IMoniker::IsSystemMoniker determines whether this moniker is a type of moniker whose implementation semantics are conceptually important to the binding process.

pdwMksys
Points to where to return the enumerated moniker type; may not be NULL.

Return Values

Value	Meaning
S_OK	The moniker is a system moniker.
S_FALSE	The moniker is not a system moniker.

Comments

The values returned through *pdwMksys* are taken from the following enumeration:

```
typedef enum tagMKSYS {
    MKSYS_NONE              = 0,
    MKSYS_GENERICCOMPOSITE = 1,
    MKSYS_FILEMONIKER       = 2,
    MKSYS_ANTIMONIKER       = 3,
    MKSYS_ITEMMONIKER       = 4,
    MKSYS_POINTMONIKER      = 5,
    } MKSYS;
```

All user implementations of this function should simply return MKSYS_NONE through the *pdwMksys* parameter.

Note New values to the **MKSYS** enumeration may be defined in the future; therefore, callers of **IMoniker::IsSystemMoniker** should explicitly test against the return values that they care about and not assume that the returned value is one of the values listed here.

IParseDisplayName Interface

The **IParseDisplayName** interface is used to transform the display name of an object into a moniker. **IParseDisplayName** is implemented by container and object applications and is used by OLE. It contains the following method (see also OLE2.H):

```
DECLARE_INTERFACE_(IParseDisplayName, IUnknown)
{
   // *** IUnknown methods ***
  HRESULT QueryInterface (THIS_ REFIID riid, LPVOID FAR* ppvObj);
  ULONG AddRef (THIS);
  ULONG Release (THIS);

   // *** IParseDisplayName method ***
  HRESULT ParseDisplayName (THIS_ LPBC pbc, LPSTR lpszDisplayName,
    ULONG FAR* pchEaten, LPMONIKER FAR* ppmkOut);
};
```

IParseDisplayName::ParseDisplayName

HRESULT IParseDisplayName::ParseDisplayName(*pbc, lpszDisplayName, pchEaten, ppmkOut***)**
LPBC *pbc*
LPSTR *lpszDisplayName*
ULONG FAR * *pchEaten*
LPMONIKER FAR * *ppmkOut*

IParseDisplayName::ParseDisplayName parses an object's display name into a moniker to the object.

Parameters

pbc
Points to the bind context to be used to accumulate bound objects.

lpszDisplayName
Points to the display name to be parsed.

pchEaten
Points to the number of characters parsed from the display name.

ppmkOut
Points to the resulting moniker; NULL on error.

Return Values

Value	Meaning
S_OK	The parse operation was successful.
MK_E_SYNTAX	An error in the syntax of a filename was encountered while parsing a display name or while creating a moniker.
MK_E_NOOBJECT	Some, possibly intermediate, object could not be found during some operation, such as binding or parsing a display name.
MK_E_INTERMEDIATEINTERFACE NOTSUPPORTED	An object was found but did not support an interface required for an operation. For example, during binding, a container is expected to support the **IOleItemContainer** interface, and during parsing of display names a container is expected to support the **IParseDisplayName** interface.
E_UNEXPECTED	Failure of unknown cause.
E_OUTOFMEMORY	Ran out of memory.
IMoniker::BindToObject errors.	MK_E_EXCEEDEDDEADLINE and MK_E_CONNECTMANUALLY.

Comments

The *lpszDisplayName* parameter is the yet-to-be-parsed tail of the display name.

If a syntax error occurs, NULL should be returned through *ppmkOut*. The number of characters that were successfully parsed should be returned through *pchEaten*.

See Also

MkParseDisplayName

IBindCtx Interface

The **IBindCtx** interface, typically implemented and used by OLE, is passed to many of the moniker management operations. The primary purpose of the **IBindCtx** instance is to accumulate the set of objects that get bound during an operation, but that should be released when the operation is complete. This is particularly useful in binding generic composite monikers because using the bind context in this way avoids binding an object and releasing it, only to have it bound again when the operation moves to another piece of the composite.

Additionally, the bind context passes a group of parameters that do not change as an operation moves from one piece of a generic composite to another. Some of the binding options have a related return value in certain error conditions; the bind context provides the means by which they can be returned. The bind context is also the only means through which moniker operations should access contextual information about their environment.

All calls that query or set the state of the environment are funneled through the bind context. (Doing this allows for future enhancements that can dynamically modify binding behavior.) In OLE 2, the most important piece of contextual information that moniker operations need to access is the running object table. Monikers should always access this table indirectly through **IBindCtx::GetRunningObjectTable**, rather than using the API function **GetRunningObjectTable**.

The **IBindCtx** interface allows for future extensions to the passed-in contextual information in the form of the ability to maintain a string-keyed table of objects. For more information, see **IBindCtx::RegisterObjectParam** and related functions.

The **IBindCtx** interface contains the following methods (see also MONIKER.H):

```
DECLARE_INTERFACE_(IBindCtx, IUnknown)
{
  // *** IUnknown methods ***
 HRESULT QueryInterface (THIS_ REFIID riid, LPVOID FAR* ppvObj);
 ULONG AddRef (THIS);
 ULONG Release (THIS);
```

```
    // *** IBindCtx methods ***
    HRESULT RegisterObjectBound (THIS_ LPUNKNOWN pUnk);
    HRESULT RevokeObjectBound (THIS_ LPUNKNOWN pUnk);
    HRESULT ReleaseBoundObjects (THIS);

    HRESULT SetBindOptions (THIS_ LPBIND_OPTS pbindopts);
    HRESULT GetBindOptions (THIS_ LPBIND_OPTS pbindopts);
    HRESULT GetRunningObjectTable (THIS_ LPRUNNINGOBJECTTABLE FAR* pprot);
    HRESULT RegisterObjectParam (THIS_ LPSTR lpszKey, LPUNKNOWN pUnk);
    HRESULT GetObjectParam (THIS_ LPSTR lpszKey, LPUNKNOWN FAR* ppUnk);
    HRESULT EnumObjectParam (THIS_ LPENUMSTRING FAR* ppenumString);
    HRESULT RevokeObjectParam (THIS_ LPSTR lpszKey);
};
```

IBindCtx::RegisterObjectBound

HRESULT IBindCtx::RegisterObjectBound(*pUnk***)**
LPUNKNOWN *pUnk*

IBindCtx::RegisterObjectBound registers an object as needing to be released when the moniker binding operation has been completed.

pUnk
Points to the object being registered as needing to be released.

Return Values

Value	Meaning
S_OK	The object was registered successfully.
E_INVALIDARG	One or more arguments are invalid.
E_UNEXPECTED	An unexpected error occurred.

Comments

A call to **IBindCtx::RegisterObjectBound** causes the bind context to create an additional reference to the passed-in object (with **IUnknown::AddRef**). The caller must still release its own copy of the pointer.

Calling **IBindCtx::RegisterObjectBound** twice with the same object requires two calls to **IBindCtx::RevokeObjectBound** to completely remove the registration of the object within the bind context.

See Also

IBindCtx::RevokeObjectBound

IBindCtx::RevokeObjectBound

HRESULT RevokeObjectBound(*pUnk*)
LPUNKNOWN *pUnk*

IBindCtx::RevokeObjectBound removes an object previously registered in the bind context.

pUnk
Points to the object that is to be removed from the bind context.

Return Values

Value	Meaning
S_OK	The object was removed successfully.
MK_E_NOTBOUND	**IBindCtx::RevokeObjectBound** was called for an object that was not registered by **IBindCtx::RegisterObjectBound**.
E_OUTOFMEMORY	Ran out of memory.
E_INVALIDARG	One or more arguments are invalid.

Comments

The **IBindCtx::RevokeObjectBound** function undoes the effect of **IBindCtx::RegisterObjectBound** by removing one occurrence of the object from the registered set in the bind context.

Applications usually release objects as a set by calling **IBindCtx::ReleaseBoundObjects** and do not typically call **IBindCtx::RevokeObjectBound**.

See Also

IBindCtx::RegisterObjectBound, IBindCtx::ReleaseBoundObjects

IBindCtx::ReleaseBoundObjects

HRESULT IBindCtx::ReleaseBoundObjects()

IBindCtx::ReleaseBoundObjects releases all objects currently registered in the bind context.

Return Values

Value	Meaning
S_OK	The objects were released successfully.

Holding a bind context without calling **IBindCtx::ReleaseBoundObjects** prevents the reference count form going to zero for all objects bound during the binding process. This includes OLE item containers and the link sources themselves.

IBindCtx::SetBindOptions

HRESULT IBindCtx::SetBindOptions(*pbindopts*)
LPBIND_OPTS *pbindopts*

IBindCtx::SetBindOptions stores a block of bind options in the bind context so they can be used in **IMoniker** operations using the same bind context.

pbindopts
Points to the block of bind options to store in the bind context. These can be retrieved later with **IBindCtx::GetBindOptions**.

Return Values

Value	Meaning
S_OK	The parameters were stored successfully.
E_OUTOFMEMORY	Ran out of memory.

Using **IBindCtx::SetBindOptions** to store a block of data is an alternative to passing parameters to a function. Because bind options are common to most **IMoniker** methods and the bind options do not change as the binding progresses, it is more efficient to store the block of bind options with **IBindCtx::SetBindOptions** than to pass the options to each **IMoniker** method.

BIND_OPTS is defined as follows:

```
typedef struct tagBIND_OPTS {
    DWORD   cbStruct;       // size in bytes of BIND_OPTS.
    DWORD   grfFlags;
    DWORD   grfMode;
    DWORD   dwTickCountDeadline;
} BIND_OPTS;
```

The *grfFlags* member is a group of Boolean flags. Legal values that can be or-ed together are taken from the enumeration **BINDFLAGS** (see below). Moniker implementations should ignore any bits in this field that they do not understand.

The *grfMode* member is a group of flags that indicates the caller's intended use for the object received from the associated moniker binding operation. Constants for this member are taken from the **STGM** enumeration. For more information, see "Storage Access Modes" described in the chapter "Persistent Storage Interfaces and Functions."

When applied to a **IMoniker::BindToObject** operation, the most significant flag values are: STGM_READ, STGM_WRITE, and STGM_READWRITE. Some binding operations may make use of other flags, particularly STGM_DELETEONRELEASE or STGM_CREATE, but such cases would be quite esoteric.

When applied to the **IMoniker::BindToStorage** operation, most STGM values are potentially useful.

The default value for *grfMode* is STGM_READWRITE | STGM_SHARE_EXCLUSIVE.

The *dwTickCountDeadline* member indicates when the caller wants the operation to be completed. This parameter lets the caller limit the execution time of an operation when it is more important that the operation perform quickly rather than accurately. This capability is most often used with **IMoniker::GetTimeOfLastChange**, though it can be usefully applied to other operations as well.

This 32-bit unsigned value is a time in milliseconds on the local clock maintained by the **GetTickCount** function. A value of zero indicates "no deadline"; however, because zero is also a valid return value from **GetTickCount**, callers should handle this case. Callers should also handle clock wrapping cases; if the value in this variable is less than the current time by more than 231 milliseconds, it should be interpreted as indicating a time in the future of its indicated value plus 232 milliseconds.

Typical deadlines will allow for a few hundred milliseconds of execution. Each function should try to complete its operation by this time on the clock, or fail with the error MK_E_EXCEEDEDDEADLINE if it cannot. Functions are not required to be absolutely accurate in this regard, since it is almost impossible to predict how long execution might take (thus, callers cannot rely on the operation being completed by the deadline), but operations that exceed their deadline excessively will usually cause intolerable user delays in the operation of their callers. In practice, the use of deadlines is a heuristic that callers can impose on the execution of moniker operations.

If a moniker operation exceeds its deadline because one or more objects it uses are not running, and, if one of these had been running, the operation would have completed more of its execution, the monikers of these objects should be recorded in the bind context. This is done by using **IBindCtx::RegisterObjectParam** under the parameter names "ExceededDeadline," "ExceededDeadline1," "ExceededDeadline2," and so on. Use the first name in this series that is currently unused because it gives the caller some knowledge of when to try the operation again.

The enumeration **BINDFLAGS**, which contains the legal values for the bit field **BIND_OPTS**::*grfFlags*, is defined as follows:

```
typedef enum tagBINDFLAGS {
    BIND_MAYBOTHERUSER      =  1,
    BIND_JUSTTESTEXISTENCE  =  2,
} BINDFLAGS;
```

These flags have the following meanings.

BINDFLAGS Value	Description
BINDFLAGS_MAYBOTHERUSER	If present, this sort of interaction is permitted. If not present, the operation to which the bind context containing this parameter is applied should not interact with the user in any way, such as by asking for a password for a network volume that needs mounting. If prohibited from interacting with the user when it otherwise would, an operation can elect to use a different algorithm that does not require user interaction, or it can fail with the error MK_MUSTBOTHERUSER.
BINDFLAGS_JUSTTESTEXISTENCE	If present, this value indicates that the caller of the moniker operation to which this flag is being applied is not actually interested in having the operation carried out, but only in learning whether the operation could have been carried out had this flag not been specified. For example, this flag lets the caller indicate only an interest in finding out whether an object actually exists by using this flag in a **IMoniker::BindToObject** call. Moniker implementations can, however, ignore this possible optimization and carry out the operation in full. Callers must be able to deal with both cases. See individual routine descriptions for details of exactly what status is returned.

IBindCtx::GetBindOptions

HRESULT IBindCtx::GetBindOptions(*pbindopts*)
LPBIND_OPTS * *pbindopts*

IBindCtx::GetBindOptions returns the current binding options stored in this bind context.

pbindopts
Points to the structure of binding options to be filled in (the caller-supplied **BIND_OPTS** structure).

Return Values

Value	Meaning
S_OK	The binding options were returned successfully.
E_INVALIDARG	One or more arguments are invalid. For example, the size is not correct or parameter not readable.

Comments

The caller must correctly set the *cbStruct* member in the **BIND_OPTS** structure before calling **IBindCtx::GetBindOptions**.

The stored parameters can be retrieved with **IBindCtx::GetBindOptions**. Using a block of parameters is an alternative way to pass parameters that are common to **IMoniker** operations and that do not change as the operation moves from one piece of a generic composite to another.

The *pbindopts* parameter is of type **BIND_OPTS**, which is defined as:

```
typedef struct tagBIND_OPTS
{
    DWORD   cbStruct;
    DWORD   grfFlags;
    DWORD   grfMode;
    DWORD   dwTickCountDeadline;
} BIND_OPTS;
```

See Also

IBindCtx::SetBindOptions

IBindCtx::GetRunningObjectTable

HRESULT IBindCtx::GetRunningObjectTable(*pprot***)**
LPRUNNINGOBJECTTABLE FAR * *pprot*

IBindCtx::GetRunningObjectTable returns access to the running object table relevant to this binding process.

pprot
Points to where to return the running object table.

Return Values

Value	Meaning
S_OK	The pointer was returned successfully.
E_UNEXPECTED	An unexpected error occurred.

Comments

Moniker implementations should get access to the running object table by using **IBindCtx::GetRunningObjectTable**, rather than the global API **GetRunningObjectTable**. The appropriate running object table is determined implicitly when the bind context is created.

See Also

GetRunningObjectTable

IBindCtx::RegisterObjectParam

HRESULT IBindCtx::RegisterObjectParam(*lpszKey, pUnk***)**
LPSTR *lpszKey*
LPUNKNOWN *pUnk*

IBindCtx::RegisterObjectParam registers an object pointer in an internally maintained table of object pointers.

lpszKey
Points to the name under which the object is being registered.

pUnk
Points to the object to be registered.

Return Values

Value	Meaning
S_OK	The object was registered successfully.
E_OUTOFMEMORY	Ran out of memory.

Comments

IBindCtx::RegisterObjectParam registers the object under the name specified in the *lpszKey* parameter. The table of pointers is used to pass contextual information to the binding process. String keys are compared on a case-sensitive basis.

Like **IBindCtx::RegisterObjectBound**, **IBindCtx::RegisterObjectParam** creates an additional reference to the passed-in object using **IUnknown::AddRef**. Calling **IBindCtx::RegisterObjectParam** a second time with a different object (using the same *lpszKey*), replaces the object stored in the first call to the method.

See Also

IBindCtx::RegisterObjectBound, IUnknown::AddRef

IBindCtx::GetObjectParam

HRESULT IBindCtx::GetObjectParam(*lpszKey, ppUnk***)**
LPSTR *lpszKey*
LPUNKNOWN FAR * *ppUnk*

IBindCtx::GetObjectParam finds the specified object pointer in the internally maintained table of contextual object pointers and returns the corresponding object, if one exists.

Parameters

lpszKey
Points to the key under which to look for an object.

ppUnk
Points to where to return the object's interface pointer. NULL is returned on failure.

Return Values

Value	Meaning
S_OK	The object was returned successfully.
E_OUTOFMEMORY	Ran out of memory.

See Also

IBindCtx::EnumObjectParam

IBindCtx::EnumObjectParam

HRESULT IBindCtx::EnumObjectParam(*ppenumString*)
LPENMSTRING FAR * *ppenumString*

IBindCtx::EnumObjectParam returns an enumeration of the internally maintained table of contextual object pointers.

ppenumString
Points to where to return the string enumerator.

Return Values

Value	Meaning
S_OK	The enumerator was returned successfully.
E_OUTOFMEMORY	Ran out of memory.

See Also **IEnumString Interface**

IBindCtx::RevokeObjectParam

HRESULT IBindCtx::RevokeObjectParam(*lpszKey*)
LPSTR *lpszKey*

IBindCtx::RevokeObjectParam revokes the registration of the object currently found under this key in the internally maintained table of contextual object pointers, if any such key is currently registered.

lpszKey
Points to the key whose registration is to be revoked.

Return Values

Value	Meaning
S_OK	The object registration was revoked successfully.
E_FAIL	Key not present.

See Also **IBindCtx::RegisterObjectParam**

IEnumMoniker Interface

The **IEnumMoniker** interface is implemented by OLE and used by OLE, object applications, and certain containers to enumerate through items that are monikers. It is used specifically in the implementation of **IRunningObjectTable::EnumRunning**.

The **IEnumMoniker** interface contains the following methods, as do all enumerators:

```
DECLARE_INTERFACE_(IEnumMoniker, IUnknown)
{
  // *** IUnknown methods ***
  HRESULT QueryInterface (THIS_ REFIID riid, LPVOID FAR* ppvObj);
  ULONG AddRef (THIS);
  ULONG Release (THIS);

  // *** IEnumMoniker methods ***
  HRESULT Next (THIS_ ULONG celt, LPMONIKER FAR* rgelt, ULONG FAR* pceltFetched);
  HRESULT Skip (THIS_ ULONG celt);
  HRESULT Reset (THIS);
  HRESULT Clone (THIS_ IEnumMoniker FAR* FAR* ppenum);
};
```

For more information, see the discussion of enumerators in the "IEnum*X* Interface" in the "Component Object Interfaces and Functions" chapter.

There are two architecturally distinct types of compound document objects: linked and embedded. The distinction between them is where the native representation of the object is persistently stored. An embedded object's native data is stored inside the container document, which also contains the presentation of the object. A linked object's native data is not kept with the linked object itself, but is kept with the source of the data, also known as the link source.

Compound document applications can support different levels of linking. Object applications can support linking to file-based documents, as well as linking to ranges of items (*pseudo objects*) in the document.

Applications that support linking must create and register a file moniker for their documents. Existing documents typically use the filename for the file moniker; new documents create a unique, temporary name that is replaced when the document is saved. Applications call **CreateFileMoniker** to create the file moniker, passing it the moniker name and where to return the pointer to the **IMoniker** instance.

File monikers for existing documents are registered in the running object table, a global table that stores information about running link sources. Registering a document's file moniker ensures that the document can be accessed by its linking container(s). When a container attempts to bind to the linked object, the moniker within the linked object first checks the running object table to see whether the object is already running. If the moniker for the object is registered, the container is connected to the running instance of the object; otherwise, the object handler is loaded and the object is placed in the running state.

Applications that support linking to documents that have not yet been saved will register the new document's temporary moniker. Applications must be aware that linking to unsaved documents can cause broken links if the container closes before the new document is saved and a permanent file moniker registered.

Note Registering a file moniker in the running object table results in a weak reference lock being put on the document object. Although this lock is not strong enough to hold the document alive should the user decide to close the document, the document object should still revoke the moniker's registration as part of its close routine.

IOleLink Interface

The main architectural difference, from a container's perspective, between an embedded object and a linked object is that the linked object supports the **IOleLink** interface. **IOleLink** contains functionality by which the moniker inside the linked object and the linked object's update options are manipulated. OLE provides an implementation of **IOleLink** that is used by containers.

The **IOleLink** interface contains the following methods (see also OLE2.H):

```
DECLARE_INTERFACE_(IOleLink, IUnknown)
{
   // *** IUnknown methods ***
  HRESULT QueryInterface (THIS_ REFIID riid, LPVOID FAR* ppvObj);
  ULONG AddRef (THIS);
  ULONG Release (THIS);

   // *** IOleLink methods ***
  HRESULT SetUpdateOptions (THIS_ DWORD dwUpdateOpt);
  HRESULT GetUpdateOptions (THIS_ LPDWORD pdwUpdateOpt);
  HRESULT SetSourceMoniker (THIS_ LPMONIKER pmk, REFCLSID rclsid);
  HRESULT GetSourceMoniker (THIS_ LPMONIKER FAR* ppmk);
  HRESULT SetSourceDisplayName (THIS_ LPCSTR lpszDisplayName);
```

```
    HRESULT GetSourceDisplayName (THIS_ LPSTR FAR* lplpszDisplayName);
    HRESULT BindToSource (THIS_ DWORD bindflags, LPBINDCTX pbc);
    HRESULT BindIfRunning (THIS);
    HRESULT GetBoundSource (THIS_ LPUNKNOWN FAR* ppUnk);
    HRESULT UnbindSource (THIS);
    HRESULT Update (THIS_ LPBINDCTX pbc);
};
```

IOleLink::SetUpdateOptions

HRESULT IOleLink::SetUpdateOptions(*dwUpdateOpt*)
DWORD *dwUpdateOpt*

IOleLink::SetUpdateOptions sets the link update options for the linked object.

dwUpdateOpt
Specifies when the data and presentation cache on the link consumer is updated.

Return Values

Value	Meaning
S_OK	The operation was completed successfully.
E_INVALIDARG	One or more arguments are invalid.

Comments

The *dwUpdateOpt* parameter controls when the data and/or presentation cache on the link consumer is updated. *dwUpdateOpt* is taken from the enumeration **OLEUPDATE**, defined as follows:

```
typedef enum tagOLEUPDATE {
    OLEUPDATE_ALWAYS = 1,
    OLEUPDATE_ONCALL = 3,
    } OLEUPDATE;
```

The values in **OLEUPDATE** are used as follows:

Value	Purpose
OLEUDPATE_ALWAYS	Update the link object whenever possible. This option supports the Automatic link-update option in the Links dialog box.
OLEUPDATE_ONCALL	Update the link object only when the **IOleObject::Update** member function is called. This option supports the Manual link-update option in the Links dialog box.

IOleLink::GetUpdateOptions

HRESULT IOleLink::GetUpdateOptions(*pdwUpdateOpt*)
LPDWORD *pdwUpdateOpt*

IOleLink::GetUpdateOptions retrieves link update options previously set with **IOleLink::SetUpdateOptions**.

pdwUpdateOpt
Points to where to return the flags taken from the **OLEUPDATE** enumeration.

Return Values

Value	Meaning
S_OK	The operation was completed successfully.

Comments

OLEUPDATE is defined in **IOleLink::SetUpdateOptions**.

See Also

IOleLink::SetUpdateOptions

IOleLink::SetSourceMoniker

HRESULT IOleLink::SetSourceMoniker(*pmk, rclsid*)
LPMONIKER *pmk*
REFCLSID *rclsid*

IOleLink::SetSourceMoniker stores a moniker that indicates the source of the link inside of the linked object.

Parameters

pmk
Points to the new moniker; may be NULL.

rclsid
Specifies the CLSID of the moniker.

Return Values

Value	Meaning
S_OK	The operation was completed successfully.

Comments

The stored moniker becomes part of the persistent state of the object. Setting the source moniker also allows an application to set the expected class of the object without binding to it. In order to support link source tracking, linked objects also store a relative moniker, which is computed as

```
pmkContainer->RelativePathTo(pmkLinkSource)
```

When a linked object is in the running state (the source moniker has been bound and connected), it registers to receive rename notifications from its link source. When a notification is received, the linked object updates its source moniker to the new name. It registers itself for notifications to handle situations in which a link is made to a newly created document that has never been saved. For example, newly created Excel spreadsheets are named "SHEET1," "SHEET2," and so on. Only when they are saved for the first time do they acquire a persistent identity that is appropriate to store in the links to them. As long as the source document is saved before its link consumer is closed, the linked object will be able to track the source of the link.

The NULL option is used for the Cancel Link option of the Edit Links dialog box to indicate a static link. A static link continues to load and draw out of its cache, but cannot implement other verbs because the connection to its link source has been broken.

IOleLink::GetSourceMoniker

HRESULT IOleLink::GetSourceMoniker(*ppmk***)**
LPMONIKER FAR * *ppmk*

IOleLink::GetSourceMoniker retrieves the moniker for the current link source.

ppmk
Points to the address where the moniker currently in the link should be placed.

Return Values

Value	Meaning
S_OK	The operation was completed successfully.
MK_E_UNAVAILABLE	The moniker is unavailable, and would not be available no matter what deadlines were used.

IOleLink::SetSourceDisplayName

HRESULT IOleLink::SetSourceDisplayName(*lpszDisplayName***)**
LPCSTR *lpszDisplayName*

IOleLink::SetSourceDisplayName parses a linked object's display name into a moniker, and stores the moniker in the linked object.

lpszDisplayName
The display name of the new link source; may not be NULL.

Return Values

Value	Meaning
S_OK	The operation completed successfully.
MK_E_SYNTAX	An error in the syntax of a filename was encountered while parsing a display name or creating a file moniker.
E_OUTOFMEMORY	Ran out of memory.

Comments

Monikers used to indicate the source of linked objects have a display name that can be shown to the user in dialog boxes. Display names can be parsed into monikers using the **MkParseDisplayName** function. Most often, the location of a link source is provided directly in a moniker, such as the moniker passed through the clipboard in a Copy/Paste Link operation. Less frequently, the moniker originates in a textual form, such as in the text box in the Edit Links dialog, provided with the OLE user interface library.

Monikers originating in textual form need to be parsed into monikers before they can be stored as the source of a linked object. If the caller is to do the parsing, it calls **MkParseUserName** and then passes the returned moniker to **IOleLink::SetSourceMoniker**. To let the linked object do the parsing, the caller should call **IOleLink::SetSourceDisplayName**. In this case, the display name is parsed and the resulting moniker stored in its place before the linked object needs to be bound for the first time.

See Also

MkParseDisplayName

IOleLink::GetSourceDisplayName

HRESULT IOleLink::GetSourceDisplayName(*lplpszDisplayName*)
LPSTR FAR * *lplpszDisplayName*

IOleLink::GetSourceDisplayName retrieves the display name of the linked object's source.

lplpszDisplayName
Points to where to return the name of the link source; cannot be NULL.

Return Values

Value	Meaning
S_OK	The operation completed successfully.
MK_E_EXCEEDEDDEADLINE	During some process (binding, parsing a display name, etc.) a deadline was exceeded.
E_OUTOFMEMORY	Ran out of memory.
E_UNEXPECTED	An unexpected error occurred.

Comments

The display name of a linked object's moniker can be obtained from its source moniker using **IMoniker::GetDisplayName**. However, the display name might either be unavailable or might not be obtained quickly enough to suit the caller because it could require that object applications be run. So that a reasonable representation of the link source is always available to the callers, linked objects keep a cache of their source's display name, which is updated each time the linked object connects to its source.

See Also

IMoniker::GetDisplayName

IOleLink::BindToSource

HRESULT IOleLink::BindToSource(*bindflags, pbc*)
DWORD *bindflags*
LPBINDCTX *pbc*

IOleLink::BindToSource binds the moniker contained within the linked object.

Parameters

bindflags
The *bindflags* parameter controls the behavior of the binding operation; it contains values taken from the enumeration **OLELINKBIND**, described in the Comments section.

pbc
Points to the bind context.

Return Values

Value	Meaning
S_OK	The binding operation was successful.
MK_E_NOOBJECT	Some, possibly intermediate, object could not be found during an operation such as binding or parsing a display name.
MK_E_EXCEEDEDDEADLINE	The process was not completed within the time specified by the bind context.
MK_E_CONNECTMANUALLY	During some process (binding, parsing a display name, and so on.) OLE was unable to connect to a network device. The application receiving this error should call **IBindCtx::GetObjectParam** with the key "ConnectManually" to retrieve the moniker of the network device, get the display name, and put up a dialog box asking the user for a password, and so on.
MK_E_INTERMEDIATE INTERFACENOTSUPPORTED	An object was found but it did not support an interface required for an operation. During binding, for example, a container is expected to support the **IOleItemContainer** interface, and during parsing of display names a container is expected to support the **IParseDisplayName** interface.)
E_NOINTERFACE	Interface not supported.
E_OUTOFMEMORY	Ran out of memory.
OLE_E_CLASSDIFF	The bind operation failed because the class is different than the last time the object was successfully bound.
STG_E_ACCESSDENIED	Incorrect permission for accessing this storage object.
E_UNEXPECTED	Failure of unknown cause.
IMoniker::BindToObject errors.	All **IMoniker::BindToObject** errors.

Comments

When a user activates a linked object and the object application must be located, **IOleLink::BindToSource** is invoked to connect the object to the object application. If the object cannot be found, MK_E_NOOBJECT is returned.

The time limit specified in the bind context identifies the amount of time within which the binding operation must be completed. A value of zero specifies an infinite time. For more information, see the **BIND_OPTS** structure in the description for **IBindCtx::SetBindOptions**.

When binding a linked object, the current class of the link source might not be the same as it was when the linked object tried to connect. For example, the class of a link to a Lotus spreadsheet object that the user subsequently converted (using the Convert dialog) to an Excel sheet would now be different.

The *bindflags* parameter contains values taken from the enumeration **OLELINKBIND**:

```
typedef enum tagOLELINKBIND {
    OLELINKBIND_EVENIFCLASSDIFF = 1,
    } OLELINKBIND:
```

If **OLELINKBIND_EVENIFCLASSDIFF** is not provided, **IOleLink::BindToSource** returns **OLE_E_CLASSDIFF** when the class is different than when the linked object was last successfully bound. If **OLELINKBIND_EVENIFCLASSDIFF** is given, the bind process proceeds even if the class has changed.

See Also **IBindCtx::SetBindOptions**

IOleLink::BindIfRunning

HRESULT IOleLink::BindIfRunning()

IOleLink::BindIfRunning binds the link to the link source, using **IOleLink::BindToSource**(NULL, NULL), if the source is currently running.

Return Values

Value	Meaning
S_OK	The link was bound to the link source.

Comments **IOleLink::BindIfRunning** tries only the relative moniker in the running object table, when both a relative and absolute moniker are present. It tries the absolute moniker only if no relative moniker is present, otherwise it fails.

See Also **IOleLink::BindToSource**

IOleLink::GetBoundSource

HRESULT IOleLink::GetBoundSource(*ppUnk***)**
LPUNKNOWN FAR* *ppUnk*

IOleLink::GetBoundSource retrieves the object to which this link source is currently connected, if any source is present.

ppUnk
Points to where to return the currently-connected source of this object. It cannot be NULL. If no source is currently connected, NULL is returned.

Return Values

Value	Meaning
S_OK	The object was retrieved successfully.
E_FAIL	No link source is currently connected.
E_UNEXPECTED	Failure of unknown cause.

Comments

If there is no source currently connected, then **IOleLink::GetBoundSource** returns E_FAIL and NULL is returned through **ppUnk*.

IOleLink::UnbindSource

HRESULT IOleLink::UnbindSource()

IOleLink::UnbindSource unbinds a currently linked object from the link source.

Return Value

Value	Meaning
S_OK	The unbind operation was completed successfully.

IOleObject::Close calls **IOleLink::UnbindSource** for linked objects.

See Also

IOleObject::Close, IOleLink::BindToSource

IOleLink::Update

IOleLink::Update(*pbc*)
LPBINDCTX *pbc*

IOleLink::Update updates a linked object with the latest data from the link source. This function finds the link source if necessary and gets a new presentation from the source. This process may require the running of one or more object applications.

pbc
Points to the bind context to be used for the update.

Return Values

Value	Meaning
S_OK	All caches updated successfully.
CACHE_E_NOCACHE_UPDATED	The bind operation worked but no caches were updated.
CACHE_S_SOMECACHES_NOTUPDATED	The bind operation worked but not all caches were updated.
MK_E_NOOBJECT	The bind operation failed. Some, possibly intermediate, object could not be found during an operation such as binding or parsing a display name.
MK_E_EXCEEDEDDEADLINE	The bind operation failed so the process was not completed within the time specified by the bind context.
MK_E_CONNECTMANUALLY	The bind operation failed. OLE was unable to connect to a network device. The application receiving this error should call **IBindCtx::GetObjectParam** with the key "ConnectManually" to retrieve the moniker of the network device, get the display name, and put up a dialog box asking the user for a password, and so on.
MK_E_INTERMEDIATEINTERFACE NOTSUPPORTED	The bind operation failed. An object was found but did not support an interface required for binding. (A container is expected to support the **IOleItemContainer** interface, and during parsing of display names a container is expected to support the **IParseDisplayName** interface.)

Value	Meaning
E_NOINTERFACE	Interface not supported. The bind operation failed.
E_OUTOFMEMORY	Ran out of memory. The bind operation failed.
OLE_E_CLASSDIFF	The bind operation failed because the class is different from the last time the object was successfully bound.
STG_E_ACCESSDENIED	Incorrect permissions for accessing this storage object.
OLE_E_CANT_BINDTOSOURCE	Unable to bind to the source.
E_UNEXPECTED	Failure of unknown cause. The bind operation failed.

Comments

IOleLink::Update ensures that the linked object has the latest data from the link source. This function is useful for automatic links, when the link is not bound, and for all cases involving manual links.

The *pbc* parameter is used when the linked object has to bind to the link source. The link source is locked for the duration of the update. This function does not call **IOleObject::Update** on the link source; it just gets the necessary data by using **IDataObject::GetData**.

See Also

IOleObject Interface

IRunningObjectTable Interface

The **IRunningObjectTable** interface provides access to the running object table, a globally accessible lookup table that keeps track of the objects that are currently running on the workstation. When a container tries to bind to a running object, it can look in the running object table to determine whether an instance is currently running and if it is, bind to that instance instead of loading the object a second time. The table contains a series of data pairs, of the form:

```
(pmk, pUnk)
```

The *pmk* element points to the moniker that, if successfully bound, connects to the running object. The *pUnk* element points to the available running object's implementation of **IUnknown**. During the binding process, monikers consult the *pmk* entries in the running object table to see whether an object is already running.

Clients of objects access the running object table by calling **GetRunningObjectTable** or **IBindCtx::GetRunningObjectTable,** which return an instance of the **IRunningObjectTable** interface.

The **IRunningObjectTable** interface, implemented by OLE and used by OLE and object applications, contains the following methods (see also MONIKER.H):

```
DECLARE_INTERFACE_(IRunningObjectTable, IUnknown)
{
  // *** IUnknown methods ***
 HRESULT QueryInterface (THIS_ REFIID riid, LPVOID FAR* ppvObj);
 ULONG AddRef (THIS);
 ULONG Release (THIS);

  // *** IRunningObjectTable methods ***
 HRESULT Register (THIS_ DWORD grfFlags, LPUNKNOWN pUnk,
  LPMONIKER pmk, LPDWORD FAR * pdwRegister);
 HRESULT Revoke (THIS_ DWORD dwRegister);
 HRESULT IsRunning (THIS_ LPMONIKER pmk);
 HRESULT GetObject (THIS_ LPMONIKER pmk,
  LPUNKNOWN FAR* ppUnk);
 HRESULT NoteChangeTime (THIS_ DWORD dwRegister, FILETIME FAR * pFiletime);
 HRESULT GetTimeOfLastChange (THIS_ LPMONIKER pmk, FILETIME FAR * pFileTime);
 HRESULT EnumRunning (THIS_ LPENUMMONIKER FAR * ppenumMoniker );
};
```

IRunningObjectTable::Register

HRESULT IRunningObjectTable(*grfFlags, pUnk, pmk, pdwRegister*)
DWORD *grfFlags*
LPUNKNOWN *pUnk*
LPMONIKER *pmk*
LPDWORD *pdwRegister*

IRunningObjectTable::Register registers a running object in the running object table.

Parameters

grfFlags
Specifies the strength or weakness of the registration. Zero specifies weak registration and one specifies strong registration. Weak registration enables objects to be connected to and released only once. Strong registration enables multiple clients connect to and release an active object multiple times. Strong registration can be specified using the constant ROTFLAGS_REGISTRATIONKEEPSALIVE = 1

pUnk
Points to the object that has just entered the running state.

pmk
Points to the moniker that is to bind to the newly running object.

pdwRegister
Points to where to return a value that can later be used to revoke the registration. It cannot be NULL. Zero is never returned as a valid registration value, so, unless **IRunningObjectTable::Register** fails, **pdwRegister* is never NULL on exit.

Return Values

Value	Meaning
S_OK	The object was registered successfully.
MK_S_MONIKERALREADY REGISTERED	An attempt was made to register a given *pmk* a second time.
E_OUTOFMEMORY	Ran out of memory.
E_INVALIDARG	One or more arguments are invalid.
E_UNEXPECTED	Failure of an unknown cause.

Comments

If the moniker pointed to by *pmk* is bound to during registration, the object pointed to by *pUnk* should be used as the result of the bind operation (with an appropriate **QueryInterface**).

The moniker *pmk* should be fully reduced before registration. For information on reducing monikers, see **IMoniker::Reduce** described earlier. If an object is known by more than one fully reduced moniker, it should register itself under all such monikers.

OLE compound document objects should call **IRunningObjectTable::Register** as soon as the following conditions are all true simultaneously:

1. The object is in the running state.
2. The object knows its full moniker (see the **IOleObject::SetMoniker** member function description.)
   A. A moniker has been assigned to the object that is relative to the object's container (this is part of the persistent state of the object).
   B. The object knows the current moniker of its container, almost always obtained by the object's container calling **IOleObject::SetMoniker**.
3. A link is made to the object or something it contains.

OLE objects register themselves as running by using their full moniker (see also **IOleObject::GetMoniker**). Generally, if a link has ever been made to an object, the object must assume that the link might still exist. For example, the consumer of the link might be on a floppy disk somewhere and later reappear. (The exceptions are rare situations where a link is created but almost immediately destroyed before the link source is saved.)

Attempting to register an object under the same moniker returns MK_S_MONIKERALREADYREGISTERED. In most cases, the application revokes the pending registration (in some rare cases, multiple objects may want to register under the same moniker).

With weak registration only, the registration entry becomes invalid as soon as the last external connection to the object is released. Presumably the object will release itself as a result of the loss of connections. In the process of doing so, it revokes its registration. An object that registers itself should always revoke itself from the running object table by calling **IRunningObjectTable::Revoke**.

See Also **IRunningObjectTable::Revoke, IOleObject::SetMoniker**

IRunningObjectTable::Revoke

HRESULT IRunningObjectTable::Revoke(*dwRegister*)
DWORD *dwRegister*

IRunningObjectTable::Revoke revokes an object's registration from the running object table.

dwRegister
Specifies a value previously returned from the **IRunningObjectTable::Register** member function.

Return Values

Value	Meaning
S_OK	The object registration has been successfully undone.
E_INVALIDARG	The object is not registered as running.
E_UNEXPECTED	Failure of unknown cause.

Comments **IRunningObjectTable::Revoke** revokes a registration made previously through **IRunningObjectTable::Register**, presumably because the object is about to quit running.

Whenever any of the conditions that put an object in the running state cease to be true, the object should revoke its registration(s).

See Also **IRunningObjectTable::Register**

IRunningObjectTable::IsRunning

HRESULT IRunningObjectTable::IsRunning(*pmk*)
LPMONIKER *pmk*

IRunningObjectTable::IsRunning determines whether an object with this moniker is currently registered as running.

pmk
Points to the moniker to compare against entries in the running object table to determine whether the object is running.

Return Values

Value	Meaning
S_OK	The object is registered as running.
S_FALSE	The object is not registered as running.

Comments

In general, this function should only be called by implementations of **IMoniker::IsRunning**. Clients of monikers should invoke this on their monikers rather than asking the running object table directly.

The running object table compares monikers by sending **IMoniker::IsEqual** to the monikers already in the table with *pmkOjbectName* on the right as an argument.

See Also

IMoniker::IsEqual

IRunningObjectTable::GetObject

HRESULT IRunningObjectTable::GetObject(*pmk*, *ppUnk*)
LPMONIKER *pmk*
LPUNKNOWN FAR * *ppUnk*

IRunningObjectTable::GetObject returns the running object designated by *pmk*.

Parameters

pmk
Points to the moniker of the object to return.

ppUnk
Points to where to return the pointer to the object. A NULL value indicates the object is not registered.

Return Values

Value	Meaning
S_OK	The object has been successfully returned.
MK_E_UNAVAILABLE	The object is not registered as running.

Comments

Moniker implementations use **IRunningObjectTable::GetObject** to determine whether an object is already running, and, if so, to get the pointer to the object.

The running object table compares monikers by sending **IMoniker::IsEqual** to the monikers already in the table with *pmk* on the right as an argument.

See Also

IRunningObjectTable::IsRunning

IRunningObjectTable::NoteChangeTime

HRESULT IRunningObjectTable::NoteChangeTime(*dwRegister, pFiletime***)**
DWORD *dwRegister*
FILETIME FAR * *pFiletime*

IRunningObjectTable::NoteChangeTime makes a note of the time that a particular object changed so that **IMoniker::GetTimeOfLastChange** can report an appropriate time-of-last-change.

Parameters

dwRegister
Identifies which object has changed. This is the value returned by the **IRunningObjectTable::Register** call. When an object is registered in the running object table (using **IRunningObjectTable::Register**), a *dwRegister* value is returned that is used to identify that object in other running object table methods. Here it is used to denote which object has changed.

pFiletime
Points (on entry) to the time at which the object changed.

Return Values

Value	Meaning
S_OK	The object has been successfully returned.
E_INVALIDARG	No such connection exists.

Comments

For each object, OLE needs to know a time past which the object has not changed. This is used, for example, to determine whether links are up to date. While an object is on disk, this time comes from the file time stamp, but when the object is in the running state, the change times are recorded in the running object table. When an object application changes an object, it should call this method with the file time corresponding to the current instant, which can be retrieved by calling **CoFileTimeNow**.

See Also **CoFileTimeNow, IRunningObjectTable::Register**

IRunningObjectTable::GetTimeOfLastChange

HRESULT IRunningObjectTable::GetTimeOfLastChange(*pmk, pFiletime***)**
LPMONIKER *pmk*
FILETIME FAR * *pFiletime*

IRunningObjectTable::GetTimeOfLastChange reports the time of change recorded for the given moniker.

Parameters

pmk
Points to the moniker whose time of last change is being checked.

pFiletime
On exit, points to the time at which the object last changed.

Return Values

Value	Meaning
S_OK	The time of change has been successfully reported.
MK_E_UNAVAILABLE	Either no time has been recorded for the moniker, or the object is not registered as running.

Comments

When invoked with *pmkToLeft* = NULL, **IMoniker::GetTimeOfLastChange** calls **IRunningObjectTable::GetTimeOfLastChange** as its first task.

The running object table compares monikers by sending **IsEqual** to the monikers already in the table with *pmk* on the right as an argument.

IRunningObjectTable::GetTimeOfLastChange is not typically used by applications. Applications instead call **IMoniker::GetTimeOfLastChange**. In most cases, if the object is registered in the running object table, the answer is the same, but in some cases, such as when the moniker contains wild card items, **IMoniker::GetTimeOfLastChange** returns the correct result while **IRunningObjectTable::GetTimeOfLastChange** might fail to find the moniker in the running object table. **IMoniker::GetTimeOfLastChange** also returns the correct result when the object is passive (on disk).

See Also **IMoniker::GetTimeOfLastChange; IRunningObjectTable::NoteChangeTime**

IRunningObjectTable::EnumRunning

HRESULT IRunningObjectTable::EnumRunning(*ppenumMoniker*)
LPENUMMONIKER FAR * *ppenumMoniker*

IRunningObjectTable::EnumRunning allows applications to enumerate the monikers of all the objects registered as running in the running object table.

ppenumMoniker
Points to the location that is to receive the pointer to the returned moniker enumerator.

Return Values

Value	Meaning
S_OK	Enumerator successfully returned.
E_OUTOFMEMORY	Ran out of memory.

Comments

The monikers that have been passed to **IRunningObjectTable::Register** are enumerated. The returned enumerator is of type **IEnumMoniker**. For more information, see the description of "IEnumMoniker Interface" in this chapter.

Linking Functions

```
BindMoniker(LPMONIKER pmk, DWORD grfOpt, REFIID riid, LPVOID FAR* ppvObj);
CreateAntiMoniker(LPMONIKER FAR* ppmk);
CreateBindCtx(DWORD dwReserved, LPBC FAR* ppbc);
CreateFileMoniker(LPSTR lpszPathName, LPMONIKER FAR* ppmk);
CreateItemMoniker(LPSTR lpszDelim, LPSTR lpszItem,
  LPMONIKER FAR* ppmk);
CreatePointerMoniker(LPUNKNOWN pUnk, LPMONIKER FAR* ppmk);
CreateGenericComposite(LPMONIKER pmkFirst, LPMONIKER pmkRest, LPMONIKER FAR* ppmkComposite);
GetRunningObjectTable( DWORD dwReserved, LPRUNNINGOBJECTTABLE FAR* pprot);
MkParseDisplayName(LPBC pbc, LPSTR szUserName, ULONG FAR * pchEaten, LPMONIKER FAR * ppmk);
MonikerRelativePathTo(LPMONIKER pmkSrc, LPMONIKER pmkDest,
  LPMONIKER FAR* ppmkRelPath, BOOL fCalledFromMethod);
MonikerCommonPrefixWith(LPMONIKER pmkThis, LPMONIKER pmkOther,
  LPMONIKER FAR* ppmkCommon);
```

BindMoniker

HRESULT BindMoniker(*pmk, grfOpt, riid, ppvObj*)
LPMONIKER *pmk*
DWORD *grfOpt*
REFIID *riid*
LPVOID FAR * *ppvObj*

BindMoniker binds a moniker with the specified interface and returns the result.

Parameters

pmk
Points to the moniker that is to be bound.

grfOpt
Reserved for future use; must be zero.

riid
Identifies the interface to connect to the object.

ppvObj
Points to the address to place the resulting object.

Return Values

Value	Meaning
S_OK	The bind operation was successful.
MK_E_NOOBJECT	Some, possibly intermediate, object could not be found during some operation, such as binding or parsing a display name.
E_OUTOFMEMORY	Ran out of memory.
IMoniker::BindToObject errors.	All **IMoniker::BindToObject** errors.

BindMoniker is a helper function that packages the following functionality:

```
IBindCtx pbc;
CreateBindCtx(0, &pbc);
pmk->BindToObject(pbc, NULL, riid, ppvObj);
pbc->Release();
```

See Also

IMoniker::BindToObject

CreateAntiMoniker

HRESULT CreateAntiMoniker(*ppmk*)
LPMONIKER FAR * *ppmk*

CreateAntiMoniker creates and returns a new anti moniker.

ppmk
Pointer to where to return the new anti moniker.

Return Values

Value	Meaning
S_OK	The anti moniker was created successfully.
E_OUTOFMEMORY	Ran out of memory.

Comments

An anti moniker is a moniker that when composed onto the end of a generic moniker removes the last piece. Anti monikers provide no functional use; they exist solely to support implementations of the **IMoniker::Inverse** member function.

See Also

IMoniker::Inverse

CreateBindCtx

HRESULT CreateBindCtx(*dwReserved, ppbc*)
DWORD*dwReserved*
LPPBC FAR * *ppbc*

CreateBindCtx allocates and initializes a new bind context using an OLE-supplied implementation.

Parameters

dwReserved
Reserved for future use; must be zero.

ppbc
Points to where to store the new bind context.

Return Values

Value	Meaning
S_OK	The bind context was allocated and initialized successfully.
E_OUTOFMEMORY	Ran out of memory.

Comments

The default values for the following members of the **BIND_OPTS** structure in the newly created bind context are:

```
grfFlags = 0
grfMode = STGM_READWRITE
dwTickCountDeadline = 0
```

See Also

IBindCtx::SetBindOptions

CreateFileMoniker

HRESULT CreateFileMoniker(*lpszPathName*, *ppmk***)**
LPSTR *lpszPathName*
LPMONIKER FAR * *ppmk*

CreateFileMoniker creates a moniker from a path name.

Parameters

lpszPathName
Points to the path of the needed file.

ppmk
Points to the newly created moniker.

Return Values

Value	Meaning
S_OK	The moniker was created successfully.
MK_E_SYNTAX	An error in the syntax of a path was encountered while creating a moniker.
E_OUTOFMEMORY	Ran out of memory.

Comments

The path can be absolute or relative. In the latter case, the resulting moniker will need to be composed onto another file moniker before it can be bound. In either case, it is often necessary that other monikers are composed onto the end of this moniker to access the subpieces of the document stored in the file.

CreateItemMoniker

HRESULT CreateItemMoniker(*lpszDelim*, *lpszItem*, *ppmk*)
LPSTR *lpszDelim*
LPSTR *lpszItem*
LPMONIKER FAR * *ppmk*

CreateItemMoniker allocates and returns a new item moniker.

Parameters

lpszDelim
Points to a string that will prefix *lpszItem* in the display name of this moniker. Often an exclamation mark: "!".

lpszItem
Points to the item name to pass to **IOleItemContainer::GetObject.**

ppmk
Points to where to put the new item moniker.

Return Values

Value	Meaning
S_OK	The moniker was created successfully.
E_OUTOFMEMORY	Ran out of memory.

Comments

The resulting moniker will be composed onto the end of a second moniker that binds to an object supporting the **IOleItemContainer** interface. When bound, the resulting composite moniker extracts the object of the indicated name from within the object container.

The *lpszItem* parameter is the item name that will later be passed to **IOleItemContainer::GetObject**. The *lpszDelim* parameter is simply another string that can prefix *lpszItem* in the display name of the item moniker.

See Also

IOleItemContainer::GetObject

CreatePointerMoniker

HRESULT CreatePointerMoniker(*pUnk*, *ppmk***)**
LPUNKNOWN *pUnk*
LPMONIKER FAR * *ppmk*

CreatePointerMoniker creates a pointer moniker from the specified interface pointer.

Parameters

pUnk
Points to the **IUnknown** interface pointer from which the pointer moniker will be created.

ppmk
Points to the location that will contain a pointer to the new pointer moniker.

Return Values

Value	Meaning
S_OK	The pointer moniker was created successfully.
E_UNEXPECTED	An unexpected error occurred.
E_OUTOFMEMORY	Ran out of memory.

Comments

A pointer moniker is essentially a wrapping of a pointer so that it can be passed to those interfaces that require monikers. The result of binding a pointer moniker is the pointer itself. Pointer monikers cannot be loaded and saved.

Think of pointers as a referencing mechanism into the "active space," that is, a process's memory. Most moniker implementations are by contrast references into "passive space," that is, the representation of an object on disk. Pointer monikers provide a means by which a given use of a moniker can transparently reference either active or passive space. **IMoniker** methods treat pointer monikers slightly differently, as described in the following table.

Method	Treatment
BindToObject	Turns into a **QueryInterface** on the pointer.
BindToStorage	Returns MK_E_NOSTORAGE.
Reduce	Reduces the moniker to itself.
ComposeWith	Always does a generic composition.
Enum	Returns NULL.
IsSystemMoniker	Returns MKSYS_POINTERMONIKER.
IsEqual	Uses the identity test paradigm on pointers after first checking the other moniker for the right class.
Hash	Returns a constant.
GetTimeOfLastChange	Returns MK_E_UNAVAILABLE.

Method	Treatment
Inverse	Returns an anti moniker.
RelativePathTo	Returns the other moniker.
GetDisplayName	Returns NULL.
ParseDisplayName	Binds to the *punk* pointer using the **IParseDisplayName** interface and works from there.

Instances of pointer monikers refuse to be serialized; that is, **IPersistStream::Save** will return an error. These monikers can, however, be marshaled to a different process in an RPC call; internally, OLE marshals and unmarshals the pointer using the standard paradigm for marshaling interface pointers.

CreateGenericComposite

HRESULT CreateGenericComposite(*pmkFirst, pmkRest, ppmkComposite*)
LPMONIKER *pmkFirst*
LPMONIKER *pmkRest*
LPMONIKER FAR * *ppmkComposite*

CreateGenericComposite allocates and returns a new composite moniker.

Parameters

pmkFirst
Points to the first element(s) in the new composite; cannot be NULL. *pmkFirst* can point to any type of moniker, including a generic composite.

pmkRest
Points to the last element(s) in the new composite; cannot be NULL. *pmkRest* can point to any type of moniker, including a generic composite.

ppmkComposite
Points to where to return the new composite.

Return Values

Value	Meaning
S_OK	The composite moniker was allocated successfully.
E_OUTOFMEMORY	Ran out of memory.

Comments

Most monikers are a composite, that is, made up of other moniker pieces, and referred to as a *generic composite moniker*. All generic composite monikers are instances of the **GenericCompositeMoniker** class, whose implementation is provided with OLE—there is no need for two generic composite moniker classes.

The OLE-provided implementations of the **IMoniker::Reduce** and **IMoniker::BindToObject** functions for the **GenericCompositeMoniker** class are particularly important, as they manage the interactions between the various elements of the composite and, as a consequence, define the semantics of binding to the moniker.

Generic composite monikers of size zero or of size one are never exposed outside of OLE's internal **GenericCompositeMoniker** method implementations. From a client perspective, a generic composite moniker always contains at least two elements.

Generic composites get flattened into their component pieces before being put into the new composite. **CreateGenericComposite** will be called by implementations of **IMoniker::ComposeWith** when they need to do a generic compose operation.

See Also **IMoniker::ComposeWith**

GetRunningObjectTable

HRESULT GetRunningObjectTable(*dwReserved***,** *pprot***)**
LPRUNNINGOBJECTTABLE FAR * *pprot*

GetRunningObjectTable returns a pointer to the running object table for the caller's context.

pprot
Points to where to return the running object table pointer.

Return Values

Value	Meaning
S_OK	The operation completed successfully.

MkParseDisplayName

HRESULT MkParseDisplayName(*pbc, szUserName, pchEaten, ppmk***)**
LPBC *pbc*
LPSTR *szUserName,*
ULONG FAR * *pchEaten*
LPMONIKER FAR * *ppmk*

Given a string, **MkParseDisplayName** returns a moniker of the object that *szUserName* refers to. This operation is known as parsing.

Parameters

pbc
Points to the bind context in which to accumulate bound objects.

szUserName,
Points to the display name to be parsed.

pchEaten
Points, on exit, to the number of characters of the display name that were successfully parsed.

ppmk
Points to the resulting moniker.

Return Values

Value	Meaning
S_OK	The parse operation was successful and the moniker was created.
MK_E_SYNTAX	An error in the syntax of a filename was encountered while parsing a display name or while creating a moniker.
E_OUTOFMEMORY	Ran out of memory.
IParseDisplayName errors.	Any **IParseDisplayName** errors.

Comments

When a display name is parsed into a moniker, it is resolved into its component moniker pieces.

If a syntax error occurs, the number of successfully parsed characters is returned in *pchEaten* and NULL is returned through *ppmk*. Otherwise, the value returned through *pchEaten* indicates the size of the display name.

In general, parsing a display name is as expensive as binding to the object that it refers to because various name space managers need to be connected to by the parsing mechanism. Objects are not released by the parsing operation itself, but are instead handed over to the passed-in bind context. Thus, if the moniker resulting from the parse is immediately bound using this bind context, the redundant loading of objects is minimized.

Most compound document links are created by a user doing Copy followed by Paste Link rather than by typing in the name of the link source. This link is created programmatically with no need for an intermediate form that is a human-readable textual representation. The primary use of **MkParseDisplayName** lies instead in textual programming languages that permit remote references as syntactic elements. The expression language of a spreadsheet is a good example of such a language. **MkParseDisplayName** is also used in the implementation of the standard Edit Links dialog. The parsing process is an inductive one, an initial step gets the process going, then an inductive step is repeatedly applied. At any point after the beginning of the parse, a certain prefix of *szUserName* has been parsed into a moniker, and a suffix of the display name remains not understood. This is illustrated in Figure 8-1.

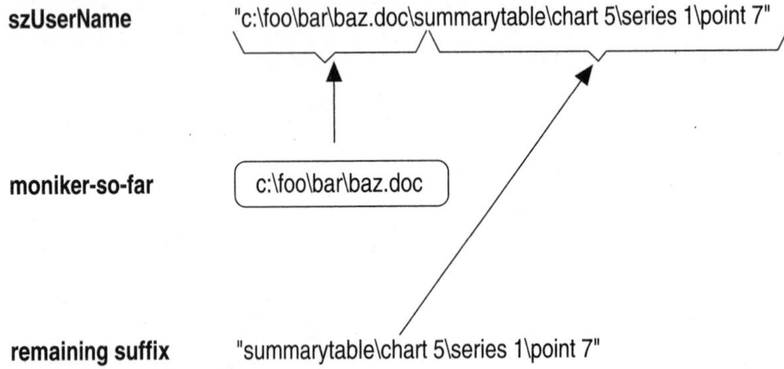

Figure 8-1. Intermediate stage in parsing a display name into a moniker.

The inductive step, using **IMoniker::ParseDisplayName**, asks the moniker-so-far to use as much as it needs of the remaining suffix and then return the corresponding moniker and new suffix. The moniker is composed onto the end of the existing moniker-so-far, and the process repeats. Implementations of **IMoniker::ParseDisplayName** vary in exactly where the knowledge of how to carry out the parsing is kept. Some monikers are only used in particular kinds of containers. It is likely that these monikers know the legal display name syntax within the objects that they denote, and can carry out the processes completely within **IMoniker::ParseDisplayName**.

Typically, however, the moniker-so-far is generic, meaning that it is not specific to one kind of container, and thus cannot know the legal syntax for the elements within the container, as is the case with file monikers and item monikers.

Generic monikers employ the following strategy to carry out parsing. First, the moniker connects to the class of object that it currently denotes, asking for **IParseDisplayName** interface (see the **CoGetClassObject** function). If that succeeds, it then uses the obtained interface pointer to attempt to carry out the parse. If the class refuses to handle the parse, then the moniker binds to the object it denotes, asking again for **IParseDisplayName**. If this fails, the parse is aborted. The effect is that ultimately an object gets to be in control of the syntax of the elements it contains.

Certain objects can carry out parsing more efficiently by having a moniker or their class do the parsing on their behalf. Notice that the OLE 2 parsing machinery knows nothing of the legal syntax of display names (with the exception of the initial parsing step. (See the following code sample). It will help the user if display names in different contexts do not have unnecessarily different syntax. While some rare circumstances call for special purpose syntax, it is recommended that the syntax for display names be the same as that of the native file system syntax. Most importantly, the delimiters used to separate one part of the display name from the next should be the same ones used by the native file system. It is less important that the piece of the path between the delimiters conform to the syntax of the file system; this is recommended unless there are clear reasons to do otherwise. Specifically, the recommended syntax for display names on MS-DOS is:

```
displayName     ::=     initialPart [path]
initialPart     ::=     drive ':'  |  '\\' server '\' share
path        ::=     delim pathPiece
delim           ::=     '\' | '/' | ! | '['
pathPiece       ::=     identifier
drive           ::=     identifier
server          ::=     identifier
share           ::=     identifier
identifier      ::=     (any character but a delim)*
```

To accommodate existing practice, the parsing process should treat an exclamation mark as a delimiter. However, in **IMoniker::GetDisplayName**, such exclamation marks should be converted to the normal '\' delimiter. Unless there is a good reason for doing so, applications should use only the characters listed above for delimiters.

Monikers and objects that have implementations on more than one platform, such as file monikers, should always parse according to the syntax of the platform on which they are currently running. When asked for their display name, monikers should also show delimiters appropriate to the platform on which they are currently running, even if they were originally created on a different platform. Users should always see delimiters appropriate for the host platform.

In order to accommodate monikers that are not file monikers or composite monikers that begin with a file moniker, the moniker must begin with an '@' sign followed by a ProgID. Following the ProgID can be anything that would normally follow a filename.

For example, to parse a string such as "@Realtime\MSFT", where "Realtime" is a ProgID registered in the registration database, the parsing process first looks for a file named "@Realtime" in the current directory. (Note that '@'is a legal filename character.) IF that fails, the parsing process looks for the ProgID "Realtime" in the registration database. If found, it looks up the CLSID and then tries the **IParseDisplayName** interface first from the class factory, if that fails , it creates an instance of the class and tries to get the **IParseDisplayName** interface. If one of these succeeds, the full string, "@Realtime\MSFT" is passed to the **ParseDisplayName** method and a moniker is returned.

The initial step of the parsing process needs to determine the initial moniker-so-far. **MkParseDisplayName** knows the syntax that the display name of a moniker can legally begin with, and it uses this knowledge to choose the initial moniker. In OLE 2, this syntax is fixed because a legal display name must begin with a filename. However, that filename can be drive absolute, drive relative, working-directory relative, or begin with an explicit network share name.

The initial moniker is determined by trying the following strategies, in order, using the first to succeed.

1. All prefixes of *szDisplayName* that consist solely of valid filename characters are consulted as file monikers in the running object table. This is attempted in order to support documents that are as yet unsaved.
2. The maximal prefix of *szDisplayName*, which consists solely of valid filename characters, is checked to see if an OLE1 document is registered by that name (this is a DDE broadcast or two). In this case, the returned moniker is an internal moniker provided by the OLE1 compatibility layer of OLE2.
3. The file system is consulted to check whether a prefix of *szDisplayName* matches an existing file. If so, the filename may be drive absolute, drive relative, working-directory relative, or begin with an explicit network share name. This is the common case.
4. If the initial character of *szDisplayName* is an '@', the longest string immediately following it that conforms to the legal ProgID syntax is determined. This is converted to a CLSID with **CLSIDFromProgID**. If this is an OLE2 class, the class object is so designated and an instance of it is asked in turn for the **IParseDisplayName** interface. The resulting **IParseDisplayName** interface is then given the whole string to parse, starting with the '@'. If the CLSID is an OLE1 class, then the string following the ProgID is considered as an OLE1 / DDE filename!item syntax link designator.

See Also **IMoniker::ParseDisplayName, GetDisplayName**

MonikerRelativePathTo

HRESULT MonikerRelativePathTo(*pmkSrc*, *pmkDest*, *ppmkRelPath*, *dwReserved*)
LPIMONIKER *pmkSrc*
LPIMONIKER *pmkDest*
LPIMONIKER *ppmkRelPath*
BOOL *dwReserved*

MonikerRelativePathTo creates a moniker specifying the relative path from *pmkSrc* to *pmkDest*.

Parameters

pmkSrc
The moniker pointing to the start of the relative path.

pmkDest
The moniker to be expressed relative to *pmkSrc*.

ppmkRelPath
The location to be filled with the relative moniker.

dwReserved
Reserved for future use, must be nonzero.

Return Values

Value	Meaning
S_OK	The parse operation was completed successfully.
MK_S_HIM	The other moniker is the prefix of the receiver moniker.
MK_E_NOTBINDABLE	**MonikerRelativePathTo** was called on a relative moniker. The moniker cannot be bound to something until it is composed with a container moniker.
E_UNEXPECTED	An unexpected error occurred.
E_OUTOFMEMORY	Ran out of memory.

Comments

MonikerRelativePathTo is not called by any code except implementations of moniker classes and can be ignored unless you are implementing a new class of monikers.

If you are implementing a class of monikers, you should implement **IMoniker::RelativePathTo** as indicated by the following pseudo code:

```
HRESULT CMyMoniker::RelativePathTo (
            IMoniker * pmkOther,
            IMoniker **ppmkRelPath  )
{
    Does pmkOther point to a moniker of a type treated as special
        by this class?
    If so, execute special case code.
    Otherwise,
        return MonikerRelativePathTo( this, pmkOther, ppmkRelPath,
            0);
}
```

This function is necessary to handle those cases where *pmkOther* points to a generic composite moniker.

MonikerRelativePathTo should only be called on absolute monikers, meaning that a file moniker that starts with a share or drive name and followed by items. It should not be called on relative monikers.

See Also **IMoniker::RelativePathTo**

MonikerCommonPrefixWith

HRESULT MonikerCommonPrefixWith(*pmkThis*, *pmkOther*, *ppmkPrefix*)
LPMONIKER *pmkThis*
LPMONIKER *pmkOther*
LPMONIKER FAR * *ppmkPrefix*

MonikerCommonPrefixWith returns the longest common prefix that the moniker pointed to by *pmkThis* shares with the moniker pointed to by *pmkOther*.

Parameters

pmkThis
The starting moniker for computing the longest common prefix.

pmkOther
The other moniker to use for computing the longest common prefix.

ppmkPrefix
The place at which the moniker of the longest common prefix common to *pmkThis* and *pmkOther* is to be returned. Cannot be NULL

Return Values

Value	Meaning
S_OK	The prefix operation was completed successfully.
MK_S_HIM	The other moniker is the prefix of the receiver moniker.
MK_S_ME	The receiver moniker, the moniker whose **CommonPrefixWith** method is called, is a prefix of the other moniker.
MK_S_US	The receiver and the other moniker are equal.
MK_E_NOPREFIX	The monikers have no common prefix.
MK_E_NOTBINDABLE	**MonikerCommonPrefixWith** was called on a relative moniker. The moniker cannot be bound to something until it is composed with a container moniker.
E_UNEXPECTED	An unexpected error occurred.
E_OUTOFMEMORY	Ran out of memory.

MonikerCommonPrefixWith is solely for the use of moniker implementors. Clients should instead compute the common prefix between two monikers using *pmkSrc*->**CommonPrefixWith**(*pmkOther, ppmkPrefix*).

Implementations of **IMoniker::CommonPrefixWith** call **MonikerCommonPrefixWith** as part of their internal processing. Such a method should first check whether the other moniker is a type it recognizes and handles in a special way. If not, it should call **MonikerCommonPrefixWith**, passing itself as *pmkSrc* and the other moniker as *pmkDest*. **MonikerCommonPrefixWith** will handle the generic composite cases correctly.

MonikerCommonPrefixWith should only be called on absolute monikers, that is, a file moniker that starts with a share or drive name, followed by items. It should not be called on relative monikers.

See Also

IMoniker::CommonPrefixWith

CHAPTER 9

Persistent Storage Interfaces and Functions

This chapter describes the interfaces, API functions, and helper functions that support the OLE structured storage model, the implementation of which is commonly referred to as *compound files*.

The following table provides a brief summary of the interfaces that support OLE's storage model.

Interface	Implemented By	Used By
IStorage	Implemented by OLE.	Used by containers to instantiate a directory-like collection of storage and stream objects in which an embedded object's native data is saved. Object applications are given a valid *pStg* for embedded objects while an object is in the running state.
IStream	Implemented by OLE.	Used by container and object applications to read and write the underlying bytes of data that comprise an **IStorage** object. **IStream** instances are analogous to files.
IRootStorage	Implemented by OLE.	Used by containers to switch the underlying disk file that **IStorage** objects are being saved to.
ILockBytes	Implemented by OLE.	Generally, used only by OLE to manipulate the byte array that underlies a compound file.
IEnumSTATSTG	Implemented by OLE.	Used to enumerate **IStorage** objects. An instance of the enumeration is available by calling **IStorage::EnumElements**.

Interface	Implemented By	Used By
IPersist	Implemented by object handlers and object applications.	Used to obtain an object's CLSID. The base interface from which the three other persistence-related interfaces derive: **IPersistStorage**, **IPersistStream**, and **IPersistFile**.
IPersistStorage	Implemented by object handlers and object applications.	Used by containers to read and write a compound document object's native data to and from its **IStorage**.
IPersistStream	Implemented by OLE.	Used by containers to save and reload objects stored in a simple serial stream rather than in an **IStorage** object (such as a moniker).
IPersistFile	Implemented by object applications and optionally by container applications to support linking to embedded objects and to file-based objects.	Used by OLE to load an outer-level document object residing in a file, as opposed to one that is embedded inside a compound document.

Structured Storage Overview

Objects are saved to their containing documents using the **IStorage** instance passed to the object by its container. Usually, the container opens a child **IStorage** object within its own **IStorage** instance. Each **IStorage** instance can contain many levels of nested storage objects—objects contained within objects. Having obtained an **IStorage** object for itself by calling **IStorage::CreateStorage**, an object has the streams and substorages available for saving its data.

An object can use as many streams as needed to save its native data. In addition to the native data stream, OLE uses one or more streams to store information about the object, including the object's cached presentation, identifying information about the object application, and link connectivity information. (This information is later used to load an object into memory using the **OleLoad** function and to convert objects from one type to another.)

To better understand the concept of storing objects, consider the word processing document shown in Figure 9-1. The document contains an embedded worksheet object, which in turn has a chart embedded in it.

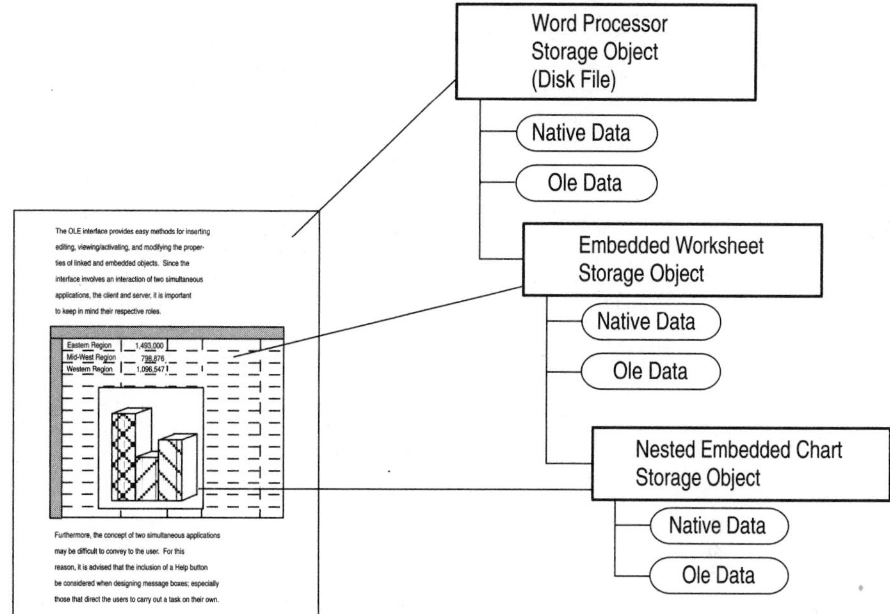

Figure 9-1. Word processing document with nested levels of objects.

The word processing document is saved and opened as the outermost root **IStorage** object. The embedded worksheet and chart objects are saved as child storage objects. Inside these storage objects, IStream objects are created in which the object's actual native data is saved (streams are also created for saving OLE information about each object). Once an application has obtained a valid **IStorage** instance (by calling the **StgCreateDocfile** or **StgOpenStorage** functions), the needed data streams are created by calling **IStorage::CreateStream**. From this root **IStorage** object, child **IStorage** objects can be created to save the document's contained objects. These child **IStorage** elements are created by calling **IStorage::CreateStorage** To open an existing **IStorage** object, applications call the **IStorage::OpenStorage** function. Child **IStorage** objects and their collective **IStreams** can be arbitrarily nested to any level in an open root **IStorage** object.

Note Child storage objects and streams *must* always be opened in STG_SHARE_EXCLUSIVE access mode.

It is the container application's responsibility to open the **IStorage** instances for its embedded objects in the appropriate access mode. Most often, this is transacted read-write/deny-write mode, but the exact choice depends on how the container is allocating the **IStorage** object. The object and OLE must be free to read from and write to the **IStream** objects inside the **IStorage** object.

The following access modes are available when opening **IStorage** objects:

Access Mode	Purpose
STGM_TRANSACTED | STGM_READWRITE	Using this mode, an object can freely write to its **IStorage** instance. OLE takes care of the transaction, freeing the container from the task. This is the most common mode.
STGM_TRANSACTED | STGM_READ | STGM_SHARE_DENY_ WRITE	In transacted mode, write permissions are enforced at the time of the commit operation, not as changes are being made. Thus, this mode does not prevent the object from being able to write freely to its **IStorage** instance.
STGM_DIRECT | STGM_READWRITE	From the object's view, this mode behaves like transacted read and write. However, in this mode the container is responsible for keeping the changes to the object separate from the original version of the object when the container was loaded (and to which the object should revert if the container is closed without saving).

Although an embedded object can freely write to its own **IStorage** object, it cannot commit changes. Because of this, the container is responsible for committing changes to its root **IStorage** object. This is done by calling **IStorage:Commit** on the open **IStorage** object.

An OLE object's **IStorage** instance can be put into one of three states: normal, no scribble, and hands off, as described in the following table:

Storage State	Description
Normal	Upon being created or loaded into memory, all OLE 2 embedded objects are given an **IStorage** instance they hold while they are either loaded or running. While in the running state, objects are free to write or "scribble" into their open **IStorage** instance. Unless **IPersistStorage::Save** or **IPersistStorage::HandsOffStorage** is called on the object, this is the normal, default state for an object.
No Scribble	The state of an object between the time **IPersistStorage::Save** finishes and **IPersistStorage::SaveCompleted** is called. In no-scribble mode, the object can read from its storage, but it cannot write to it until **IPersistStorage:: SaveCompleted** is called, which puts the object back in normal state.

Storage State	Description
Hands Off	The state of an object when **IPersistStorage::HandsOffStorage** is called on the object. The object is unable to read or write to its storage until **IPersistStorage::SaveCompleted** is called, which puts the object and any of its child storages back in the normal state. There are two variations to the hands off state, hands off from normal and hands off after save, as described in the following sections.

The following diagram shows the storage state transitions. Unmarked transitions are illegal.

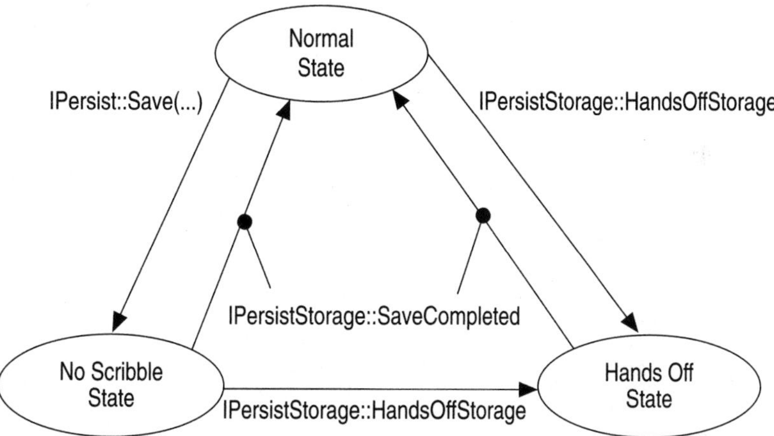

Figure 9-2. Transitions between the OLE storage states.

The object should not clear its dirty bit if **IPersistStorage::HandsOffStorage** is called prior to **IPersistStorage::Save** and **IPersistStorage::SaveCompleted** being called. To ensure that the object is saved correctly, the following recommendation should be followed. For more information, see the example for **IPersistStorage::SaveCompleted**, later in this chapter.

1. In the application's initialization code, create the following variables:

```
m_fSaveWithSameAsLoad = FALSE
m_fNoScribbleMode = FALSE;
```

2. In the **IPersistStorage::Save** code, set the variables to the following values:

```
m_fSaveWithSameAsLoad = fSameAsLoad
m_fNoScribbleMode = TRUE;
```

3. In the **IPersistStorage::SaveCompleted** code, compare the object's **IStorage** pointer to *m_fSaveWithSameAsLoad* and then clear the dirty bit as appropriate:

```
if (pStg != NULL || m_fSaveWithSameAsLoad)
{
    if (m_fNoScribbleMode) {
        clear dirty bit
        send on save
    }
    m_fSaveWithSameAsLoad = FALSE;
}
m_fNoScribbleMode = FALSE;
```

The following tables describe the storage states and the transitions as various **IPersistStorage** methods are called. The state is not changed if an error occurs. Notice the relationship between clearing the dirty flag and calling **IAdviseSink::OnSave** to send notifications to connected advise sinks: the object calls **OnSave** precisely at the moment when it transitions from dirty to non-dirty.

Uninitialized State

In the uninitialized state, the object has been created, but not yet initialized.

IPersistStorage Method Called	Action to Take	State Entered
InitNew (*pStg*)	Create a new object containing default data as defined by the object application.	Normal
Load (*pStg*)	Initialize the object from the data found in *pStg*.	Normal
GetClassID	Error: E_UNEXPECTED.	Uninitialized
Other **IPersistStorage** methods	Error: E_UNEXPECTED.	Uninitialized

Normal State

In the normal state, the object has been initialized and has a valid pointer to its **IStorage**. In this state, the object can freely read from and write to its storage. This is the default state for an embedded object, and is the state in which the object is found except when it is uninitialized or is undergoing a save operation.

IPersistStorage Method Called	Action to Take	State Entered
Save(*pStgSave*, TRUE)	Recursively save any dirty embeddings. Write data as appropriate into *pStgSave*. This call is used in the low memory save sequence and must not fail for lack of memory.	No scribble
Save(*pStgNew*, FALSE)	Recursively save any dirty embeddings. Write data as appropriate into *pStgNew*.	No scribble
HandsOffStorage	Recursively invoke **HandsOffStorage** on any loaded embeddings. Release *pStgCur* and any storage elements opened from there.	Hands off from normal
SaveCompleted	Error: E_UNEXPECTED. No other change of state.	Normal
InitNew or **Load**	Error: E_UNEXPECTED. No other change of state.	Normal
Other **IPersistStorage** methods	Error: E_UNEXPECTED.	Uninitialized

No Scribble State

In the no scribble state, the object has a valid **IStorage** and can read from it, but is not allowed to write to it. The primary reason for the existence of this state is to give the object's container a chance to save the object's data. Most containers just call **IStorage::Commit**, but some, such as databases, use other techniques for saving.

This state is parameterized by a Boolean value, *fSavedToCurrentStorage*, that indicates whether the object was saved into *pStgCur* or a separate **IStorage**. This is used to control the clearing of the dirty flag on error.

IPersistStorage Method Called	Action to Take	State Entered
SaveCompleted(NULL)	If *fSavedToCurrentStorage* is TRUE, then if the dirty flag is set, clear it and call **IAdviseSink::OnSave** to notify connected advise sinks.	Normal

IPersistStorage Method Called	Action to Take	State Entered
SaveCompleted(*pStgNew*)	Do the equivalent of **HandsOffStorage** followed by **SaveCompleted**(*pStgNew*).	Normal or hands off after save; see below.
HandsOffStorage	Recurse on any loaded embeddings. Release *pStgCur* and any subelements opened.	Hands off after save
Save	This transition indicates a bug on the container's part: it has erroneously omitted an intervening call to **SaveCompleted**. The object can either fail (E_UNEXPECTED) or carry out the save a second time and succeed.	No scribble
InitNew or **Load**	Error: E_UNEXPECTED.	No scribble
Other **IPersistStorage** methods	Error: E_UNEXPECTED.	Uninitialized

Hands-Off

In the hands off state, the object just saved its internal state into a storage, and was then told not to access its internal storage (this happens in the low memory save sequence). When the object eventually gets back a new storage, it is guaranteed to get back a storage containing exactly the bits that were just saved.

IPersistStorage Method Called	Action to Take	State Entered
SaveCompleted(*pStgNew*)	(Re)open the streams and storages needed. The bits in *pStgNew* are guaranteed to be the same as those last saved. Notice that if Save(*pStgSave*, false), were used, bits in *pStgNew* are different than those in the *pStgCur* being held and that was revoked in **HandsOffStorage**. If this function is successful, then if the dirty flag is set, clear it and call **IAdviseSink::OnSave** to notify connected advise sinks.	Normal, if able to reconnect to the new storage. Otherwise, if unsuccessful , fail with E_OUTOFMEMORY and remain in hands off after save.
SaveCompleted(NULL)	Error: E_INVALIDARG or E_UNEXPECTED.	Hands off after save
HandsOffStorage	Error: E_UNEXPECTED.	Hands off after save
Save	Error: E_UNEXPECTED.	Hands off after save
InitNew or **Load**	Error: E_UNEXPECTED.	Hands off after save
Other **IPersistStorage** methods	Error: E_UNEXPECTED.	Uninitialized

Hands Off From Normal

In the hands off from normal state, the container temporarily prevents the object from accessing its storage until the container is done with it. When the container releases the storage back to the object, it returns a storage with exactly the same bits as were there when the object was in the hands off mode. Thus, the object does not need to completely reinitialize its internal state. Instead, the object can simply reconnect to the new storage by opening the appropriate streams and/or storages.

IPersistStorage Method Called	Action to Take	State Entered
SaveCompleted(*pStgNew*)	*pStgNew* is the new replacement **IStorage** for the one revoked by **HandsOffStorage**. The bits in the storage are guaranteed to be the same as those that were in the revoked storage. (Re)open the streams and storages needed. Do not clear the dirty flag even if this function is successful. Do not call **IAdviseSink::OnSave**.	If able to reconnect to new storage, enter normal(*pStgNew*). If unsuccessful, (for example, unable to reopen data streams) fail (E_OUTOFMEMORY, and so on) and remain in hands off from normal.
SaveCompleted(NULL)	Error: E_INVALIDARG or E_UNEXPECTED.	Hands off from normal
HandsOffStorage	Error: E_UNEXPECTED.	Hands off from normal
Save	Error: E_UNEXPECTED.	Hands off from normal
InitNew or **Load**	Error: E_UNEXPECTED.	Hands off after save
Other **IPersistStorage** methods	Error: E_UNEXPECTED.	Uninitialized

Saving Objects to Storage

To save its contained embeddings, an object's top-level container performs the following tasks:

1. Call **OleSave** on the **IStorage** object of each immediate embedded object, passing the **IStorage** object a pointer to where the object is to be saved. The object then recursively calls **OleSave** on any of its nested embeddings.

   The **OleSave** function first calls the **WriteClassStg** function to save the object's CLSID before calling the object handler's **IPersistStorage::Save** method. (Usually, the object handler is the OLE-provided default handler.) The default handler's implementation of the **IPersistStorage::Save** first saves the object's presentation cache and then calls the object application's **IPersistStorage::Save** method to save the object's native data.

   Finally, **OleSave** calls **IStorage::Commit** on the **IStorage** object to commit the changes back one level to the transaction state of the root **IStorage** object.

2. After **OleSave** returns, the top-level container must call **IPersistStorage::SaveCompleted** on the immediate embedded objects to return them and any of their nested embeddings to the normal storage mode. Unless this is done, the object is left in the no-scribble mode it entered when **OleSave** called **IPersistStorage::Save**.

Note **IPersistStorage::SaveCompleted** is always called on the **IStorage** object containing the object. It is a call that recurses to all currently loaded or running embedded objects. Should **IPersistStorage::SaveCompleted** fail, the object(s) does not return to normal storage mode. In this case, the container should back out any changes that have been committed and try instead to save the object following the recommendations for saving an object in low-memory situations. For more information, see "Saving Objects in Low Memory," in the "Programming Considerations" chapter.

Saving a linked object is not different from saving an embedded object. To save a linked object that is not loaded or running, the **IStorage::CopyTo** method can be used. When an object is in the loaded or running state, **OleSave** should be called because it saves all changes.

Note Static objects are saved into a stream called CONTENTS. Static metafile data gets saved in "placeable metafile format" and static DIB data gets saved in "DIB file format." These formats are defined to be the OLE standards for metafile and DIB. All data transferred using an **IStream** or a file (that is, via **IOleObject::GetDataHere**) must be in these formats. Also, all objects whose default file format is a metafile or DIB must write their data into a CONTENTS stream using these standard formats.

The **OleSave** and **IPersistStorage::Save** functions use the *fSameAsLoad* flag to determine whether the storage object that the object is being saved to is the same one from which the object was loaded. The value of *fSameAsLoad* can be combined with the value of the *pStg* passed to these functions to determine the routine being used to save the compound document, as shown in the following table:

Value of *fSameAsLoad*	**Value of *pStg* passed to IPersistStorage:: SaveCompleted**	**Save Routine to call**
TRUE	NULL	File Save
FALSE	*pStg*	File Save As
FALSE	NULL	File Save Copy As

A container should save both the document's native data stream and any information on behalf of the compound document object, including the following data:

Data Saved on Behalf of a Compound Document Object	Description
szStgName	Stores the name of object's persistent **IStorage** element.
fMonikerAssigned	Keeps track of whether or not a moniker was assigned to the compound document object.
dwDrawAspect	Determines how to display the object when it is later loaded into memory: as an embedded object, a thumbnail representation (appropriate for browsing tools), an iconic representation, or as a sequence of pages (as if the object had been printed).

Opening Storage Objects

IStorage objects are handled differently, depending on whether the application is an object application or a container and whether the File New or File Open command was selected. The following sections discuss the different approaches.

Note In order to work properly, OLE compound files require that file range-locking be enabled. This is done through the MS-DOS SHARE.EXE command (on Windows for Workgroups, range locking is part of the system and need not be installed). For more information on the recommended value settings for SHARE.EXE, see the appendix, "Creating Distribution Disks."

File New

When opening a new untitled document, a container create a temporary root **IStorage** object in which to create child **IStorage** objects for saving compound document objects. This outermost root **IStorage** object forms the base from which all object storage elements are created in the container.

A temporary root **IStorage** object is created with a call to the **StgCreateDocfile** function, specifying NULL for the document filename (*pwcsName*) and STG_DELETEONRELEASE as one of the values to the *grfMode* parameter. Additional values for the *grfMode* parameter determine the access mode (transacted or directin which to open the **IStorage** object.

In *transacted mode*, the changes to an object are buffered in temporary files until the application commits (saves) or reverts (destroys) the changes. In *direct mode*, the changes are immediately saved to the open **IStorage** object with no chance of undoing the changes. By default, if no mode value is specified, the **IStorage** object is opened in direct mode.

Containers must provide scribble-enabled storage to the objects they contain. However, sometimes there is a need to instantiate an object in read-only mode. If the object's storage is read only, it *must* also be opened in transacted mode, since transacted mode is the only scribble-enabled read only mode. An object can call **IStorage::Stat** to determine is storage mode.

A root **IStorage** object opened in direct mode and that can be written to must always specify STGM_SHARE_EXCLUSIVE for its access mode.

File Open

When opening a file-based document, an application needs to be able to open the document as an **IStorage** object and read the document's data. Object applications typically read in the data and then close the **IStorage** object until it is time to save the document. Containers, on the other hand, must keep their root **IStorage** object open at all times to ensure compound document objects have access to their storage.

To open an existing **IStorage** object, an application calls **StgOpenStorage**, passing it the **IStorage** filename and the access mode to use.

Loading Objects from Storage

An application that saves its application data to **IStorage** objects — after opening an existing **IStorage** — proceeds to initialize the document object with the contents of the **IStream** object(s). To read the contents of an **IStorage** object, an application calls **IStorage::OpenStream**, which opens an existing named **IStream** instance using the access mode specified by the *grfMode* parameter. To read the contents of an open data stream into memory, an application calls **IStream::Read**.

An **IStorage** object can have nested child **IStorage** objects, which are accessed through **IStorage::OpenStorage**.

As part of opening and reading **IStorage** objects, applications should test the compatibility of the document with the current version of the application. If the document is incompatible, the application should display an error message and open an untitled document instead. Testing for compatibility can be done easily by storing the version number of the application as part of its native data.

Storage Access Mode Flags

Storage Creation Flags

STGM_CREATE, STGM_CONVERT, and STGM_FAILIFTHERE specify the action taken when trying to create a new **IStorage** or **IStream** object when an object by the specified name already exists. Only one of these flags can be used in a given creation call. STGM_FAILIFTHERE is the default.

None of the flags should be passed to calls that open existing **IStorage** or **IStream** objects.

STGM_CREATE

STGM_CREATE indicates an existing **IStorage** or **IStream** object should be removed before the new one replaces it. A new object is always created when this flag is specified.

STGM_CONVERT

This flag is applicable only to the creation of **IStorage** objects. The STGM_CONVERT flag is used in three situations:

- When an application is trying to create a **IStorage** object on a disk where a file of that name already exists.
- Inside another **IStorage** object where one of the data streams already has the specified name.
- Inside an **ILockBytes** instance.

STGM_CONVERT allows the creation to proceed while preserving existing data. The old data is saved to a stream named **CONTENTS** containing the same data that was in the old **IStorage**, **IStream**, or **ILockBytes** instance. In the **IStorage** and **ILockBytes** cases, the data flattening to a stream is done regardless of whether the existing file or **ILockBytes** currently contains a layered storage object.

STGM_FAILIFTHERE

STGM_FAILIFTHERE causes the create operation to fail if an existing object with the specified name exists. In this case, STG_E_FILEALREADYEXISTS is returned.

STGM_FAILIFTHERE applies to both **IStorage** and **IStream** objects.

Temporary Storage Creation Flag

The STGM_DELETEONRELEASE flag indicates that the underlying file is to be automatically destroyed when the root **IStorage** object is released. This capability is most useful for creating temporary files.

Transaction Flags

OLE's structured storage model supports both transacted and direct mode. In *transacted mode*, all changes are buffered and the buffered changes are written to disk or discarded only when an explicit commit or revert request occurs. A snapshot copy of the compound file is made so the original version of the file can be maintained.

In *direct mode*, no such buffering occurs and every change is followed by an automatic commit. Direct mode STGM_DIRECT is the default access mode, and is implied by the absence of STGM_TRANSACTED

STGM_DIRECT

STGM_DIRECT is always specified for **IStream** objects. STGM_TRANSACTED is not supported by OLE for stream objects.

For root **IStorage** objects, direct mode is only supported in three combinations of permissions flags, as is illustrated below:

- STGM_READ | STGM_SHARE_EXCLUSIVE | STGM_READWRITE | STGM_SHARE_DENY_WRITE
- STGM_PRIORITY | STGM_READ
- STGM_READ | STGM_SHARE_DENY_WRITE |

  STGM_READWRITE | STGM_SHARE_EXCLUSIVE |

  STGM_READ | STGM_PRIORITY | STGM_SHARE_DENY_NONE

STGM_TRANSACTED

The transaction for each open object is nested in the transaction for its parent storage object. Therefore, committing changes at the child level is dependent on committing changes in the parent and a commit of the root storage object (top-level parent) is necessary before changes to an object are actually written to disk. The changes percolate upward: inner objects publish changes to the transaction of the next object outwards. Outermost objects publish changes permanently into the file system.

Transacted mode is not required on the parent storage object in order to use transacted on a contained object.

The scope of changes that are buffered in transacted mode is very broad. A storage or stream object can be opened, have arbitrary changes made to it, and then have the changes reverted, preserving the object as it was when it was first opened. The creation and destruction of elements within a storage object is scoped by its transaction.

Priority Flag

The STGM_PRIORITY flag allows an **IStorage** object to be opened so that a subsequent copy operation can be done at reduced cost. STGM_PRIORITY allows an application to read certain streams from storage before opening the storage object in a mode that would require a snapshot copy to be made.

Priority mode has exclusive access to the committed version of the **IStorage** object. While a compound file is open in priority mode, no other opening of the compound file can commit changes—even one that was opened before the priority mode opening. Therefore, applications should keep **IStorage** objects open in priority mode for as short a time as possible.

Calling **StgOpenStorage** with a non-NULL *ppStgOpen* parameter takes a storage object currently open in priority mode to normal operating mode, without the possibility of losing access to the file to another process during an otherwise-necessary close and reopen operation.

When using STGM_PRIORITY, the following rules apply:

- STGM_DIRECT and STGM_READ must be specified with STGM_PRIORITY.
- STGM_WRITE and STGM_READWRITE must not be specified.

Access Permission Flags

The permission flags specify the degree of access applications have to an object as well as the access others have. The following are general rules regarding permissions:

- Children of storage objects opened in direct mode must have permissions at least as restrictive as those of the parent.
- Children of storage objects opened in transacted mode can have any permissions.
- Storage objects opened in transacted, read-only (STGM_READ) mode are modifiable but the changes cannot be committed.
- Either write permissions or transacted mode is needed on a parent storage in order to open a child storage or stream with write permission.

STGM_READ

When applied to an **IStream**, STGM_READ enables applications to successfully call **IStream::Read**. If STGM_READ is omitted, **IStream::Read** will return an error.

When applied to an **IStorage**, STGM_READ allows the enumeration of the storage object's elements and enables applications to open these elements in read mode. Parents of storage objects to be opened in read mode must also have been opened in read mode; otherwise, an error is returned.

STGM_WRITE

STGM_WRITE enables an object to commit changes to the storage. Specifically, unless this flag has been given, **IStorage::Commit** and **IStream::Commit** will fail. An open object whose changes cannot be committed can save its changes by copying the storage or stream with **IStorage::CopyTo** or **IStream::CopyTo**.

In direct mode, changes are committed after every change operation. Thus, write permissions are needed to call any function that causes a change. On streams, this includes **IStream::Write** and **IStream::SetSize**.

If an **IStorage** is opened in direct mode without write permission and an **IStream** within it is opened in direct mode but without write permission, writing to the stream fails because it causes an implicit commit to be made on the **IStorage**. Similarly, trying to create or destroy a contained element in this storage object also causes an implicit commit, resulting in an error.

STGM_READWRITE

STGM_READWRITE is the logical combination of the STGM_READ and STGM_WRITE. However, the defined value of STGM_READWRITE is not equal to (STGM_READ | STGM_WRITE).

STGM_SHARE_DENY_READ

When successfully applied to a root **IStorage**, the STGM_SHARE_DENY_READ flag prevents others from opening the object in read mode. The open call fails and returns an error if the object is presently open in deny-read mode.

STGM_SHARE_DENY_READ is most useful when opening root storage objects. Deny modes on inner elements are still useful if some component is coordinating the opening of these inner elements, such as might happen in a Copy/Paste operation.

Opening a parent storage object with STGM_SHARE_DENY_READ applies only to that opening, not the entire global network-wide set of openings of the parent.

Deny modes are most useful when applied to the opening of a root **IStorage** object. Deny modes on inner elements are still useful if some component is coordinating the opening of these inner elements, such as might happen in the implementation of Copy/Paste. STGM_SHARE_DENY_WRITE is also important in avoiding snapshot copy operations.

STGM_SHARE_DENY_WRITE

When successfully applied to either an **IStorage** or an **IStream**, the STGM_SHARE_DENY_WRITE flag prevents subsequent openings of the **IStorage** or **IStream** from specifying write mode. The open call fails and returns an error if the **IStorage** or **IStream** is presently open in write mode. For information about the interaction of this flag with nested openings, see the earlier discussion about STGM_SHARE_DENY_READ.

STGM_SHARE_DENY_WRITE can be used to avoid unnecessary snapshot copy operations. Attempting to open a compound file storage object without specifying STGM_SHARE_DENY_WRITE is expensive because a snapshot copy of the storage object must be created.

For applications that have an "all in memory" model of dealing with persistent storage, the expense of the snapshot copy can be reduced by specifying STGM_PRIORITY. STGM_PRIORITY allows applications to read some of the elements before use and excluding them from the snapshot copy.

STGM_SHARE_EXCLUSIVE

STGM_SHARE_EXCLUSIVE is the logical combination of the STGM_SHARE_DENY_READ and STGM_SHARE_DENY_WRITE. All child **IStorage** and **IStream** objects must be opened with STGM_SHARE_EXCLUSIVE.

Writable child **IStorage** objects, **IStream** objects, and root **IStorage** objects can only be opened using STGM_SHARE_EXCLUSIVE.

STGM_SHARE_DENY_NONE

STGM_SHARE_DENY_NONE indicates that neither read access nor write access should be denied to subsequent openings. This is the default sharing mode and if no STGM_SHARE_* flag is explicitly given, STGM_SHARE_DENY_NONE is implied. This differs from the Windows **OpenFile** function in which the default is a "compatibility mode" indicated by OF_SHARE_COMPAT. OLE does not support compatibility mode.

Storage Naming Conventions

Many storage-related functions take a string name as a parameter to specify a particular element of interest within some container. Depending on which component actually stores these names, different conventions and restrictions apply. The two components of relevant interest are the underlying file system and implementations of storage objects.

Names of root **IStorage** objects are actual names of files in the underlying file system. Thus, they obey the conventions and restrictions the file system imposes. Filename strings passed to storage-related functions are passed on uninterpreted and unchanged to the file system.

Names of elements contained within storage objects are managed by the implementation of the particular storage object. All implementations of storage objects must support element names 32 characters in length (including the NULL terminator). Some implementations might choose to support longer names. Whether the storage object does any case conversion is implementation defined. As a result, applications that define element names must choose names that are acceptable in either situation. OLE compound files support names up to 32 characters in length. Notably, they do not do case conversion.

The following naming conventions apply to elements inside an **IStorage** instance:

- The characters "." and ".." are reserved.
- Element names cannot contain the characters "\", "/", ":", or "!".

In addition, the name space in an **IStorage** instance is partitioned into different areas of ownership. Different pieces of code can create elements in each area of the name space.

- Element names beginning with characters other than \0x01 through \0x1F (decimal 1 through decimal 31) are for use by the embedded object stored in the **IStorage** instance. Conversely, the embedded object must not use element names beginning with these characters.
- Element names beginning with a \0x01 and \0x02 are for the exclusive use of the OLE libraries.
- Element names beginning with a \0x03 are for the exclusive use of the container in which the object is embedded. The container can use this space to persistently store information associated with the object.
- Element names beginning with a \0x04 are for the exclusive use of the structured storage implementation. For example, they are useful if the implementation supports interfaces besides **IStorage** that need persistent state.
- All other names beginning with \0x05 through \0x1F are reserved for future use by the system.

String Name Block (SNB)

A string name block (SNB) is a pointer to an array of pointers to strings, that ends in a NULL pointer. SNB is defined as:

```
typedef LPSTR *SNB;
```

String name blocks are used to exclude particular contained storages or streams in storage object open calls.

STATSTG Structure

The **STATSTG** structure is used in **IEnumSTATSTG::Next**, and the **Stat** methods in **IStorage**, **IStream**, and **ILockBytes**.

The **STATSTG** structure is defined as follows in STORAGE.H:

```
typedef struct tagSTATSTG{
    char FAR * pwcsName;
    DWORD type;
    ULARGE_INTEGER cbSize;
    FILETIME mtime;
    FILETIME ctime;
    FILETIME atime;
    DWORD grfMode;
    DWORD grfLocksSupported;
    CLSID clsid;
    DWORD grfStateBits;
    DWORD Reserved;
} STATSTG;
```

The *pwcsName* member is the name of the storage element. *pwcsName* is allocated and filled in by the callee and later freed by the caller. The following code illustrates how to free *pwcsName* using the standard allocator:

```
LPMALLOC pMalloc;
CoGetMalloc(MEMCTX_TASK, &pMalloc);
pMalloc->Free(statstg.pwcsName);
pMalloc->Release();
```

In some cases, such as when a name does not exist for a byte array, NULL is returned in *pwcsName*.

The *type* member identifies the type of the element. Legal values are found in the enumeration **STGTY**:

```
typedef enum tagSTGTY
```

```
{
    STGTY_STORAGE   = 1,      //Storage object
    STGTY_STREAM    = 2,      //Stream object
    STGTY_LOCKBYTES = 3,      //Byte array object
} STGTY;
```

The *cbSize* member is the size of the element. It is the byte count for stream objects and byte arrays, and it is undefined for storage objects.

The next three members provide the date and time information. The modification date and time is returned in *mtime,* the creation date and time is returned in *ctime,* and the closest approximation of the time of last access is returned in *atime.*

The modification time differs depending on whether the storage element uses transacted or direct mode. Transacted mode elements return the time of the last commit operation invoked on the element. Direct mode elements return the later of the following:

- The time of the last explicit commit operation invoked on the element (using **IStorage::Commit** or **IStream::Commit**). In direct mode, committing changes has the effect of flushing the buffer.
- The time of the last release operation (using **IStorage::Release** or **IStream::Release**) in a situation where changes have been made because the stream or storage was opened or the last set of changes were committed. In this case, the release operation internally does a flush of the buffers.

In the compound file implementation, the time returned in *atime* is the same as *mtime* for internal elements. Whatever is supported in the underlying file system or exposed by **ILockBytes::Stat** for root elements (on MS-DOS FAT, is the same as *mtime*).

All **FILETIME** values here are in UTC time (Greenwich time). For more information on the **FILETIME** structure and the APIs with which to set the file time on a storage object, see the section "File Time Conversion Functions" in the chapter "Component Object Interfaces and Functions."

The *grfMode* member is the mode in which the element was opened. It is valid only on **Stat** method calls.

The *grfLocksSupported* member is a group of Boolean flags relevant only for stream objects and byte arrays. Legal values are combinations of values from the enumeration **LOCKTYPE**. For each lock type, *grfLocksSupported* indicates whether a call to **IStream::LockRegion** or **ILockBytes::LockRegion** will ever be worthwhile.

```
typedef enum tagLOCKTYPE
{
    LOCK_WRITE      = 1,
    LOCK_EXCLUSIVE  = 2,
```

```
    LOCK_ONLYONCE   = 4
} LOCKTYPE;
```

For each flag, a FALSE (zero) value indicates that the specified type of write locking is not supported. A TRUE value indicates write locking can be supported, but there is no guarantee. Any other value returns the error STG_E_INVALIDFUNCTION.

The *clsid* member is relevant only for storage objects and represents the CLSID associated with the storage, if any. The *clsid* is CLSID_NULL for newly created storages.

The *grfStateBits* member is relevant only for storage objects and is the value most recently set with **IStorage::SetStateBits**.

The *Reserved* member is reserved for future use.

IEnumSTATSTG Interface

The **IEnumSTATSTG** interface enumerates items of type **STATSTG**. An instance of the **IEnumSTATSTG** interface is returned by calling **IStorage::EnumElements**.

The **IEnumSTATSTG** interface contains the following methods, as do all enumerators (see also STORAGE.H):

```
DECLARE_INTERFACE_(IEnumSTATSTG, IUnknown)
{
...
 HRESULT Next (ULONG celt, STATSTG FAR * rgelt[], ULONG *pceltFetched);
 HRESULT Skip (ULONG celt);
 HRESULT Reset ();
 HRESULT Clone (LPENUMSTATSTG FAR * ppenumStatStg);
};
```

For more information on enumerator objects, see **IEnum*X*** in the chapter called "Component Object Interfaces and Functions."

IStorage Interface

The **IStorage** interface is implemented by OLE and is used by containers to instantiate a directory-like collection of storage and stream objects in which an embedded object's native data is saved. An application can also save its native data to **IStorage**. For an overview of saving application documents, see the chapter "Programming Considerations."

The **IStorage** interface contains methods for managing root **IStorage** objects, child **IStorage** objects, and **IStream** objects. **IStorage** instance pointers can be marshaled to other processes, just as any other interface pointer can. When an **IStorage** interface pointer is remoted to a process that has shared memory access with the original process, the custom marshaling facilities of OLE are used to create a remote version of the original object. This remote version does not need to communicate with the original process to carry out its functions.

An OLE application must release any owned **IStorage** instance pointers regardless of whether a higher-level **IStorage** has caused the pointers to become invalid. This is necessary to deallocate memory. When a parent **IStorage** releases its last reference or reverts, all child **IStorages** are invalidated.

IStorage::Release is used to close an open **IStorage** object, making the **IStorage** invalid. In addition, **Release** reverts any logical uncommitted changes to the **IStorage**.

Notice that **IStorage::Release** does not return any error status that might arise from the cleanup. Applications that care about errors during cleanup should explicitly call **IStorage::Revert** or **IStorage::Commit** as appropriate before calling **Release**. This is similar to closing file handles in traditional file systems because once the file close has been attempted, no reasonable error handling is possible.

See **IUnknown::Release** for possible return values.

IStorage contains the following methods (see also STORAGE.H).

```
DECLARE_INTERFACE_(IStorage, IUnknown)
{
  // *** IUnknown methods ***
 HRESULT QueryInterface (THIS_ REFIID riid, LPVOID FAR* ppvObj);
 ULONG AddRef (THIS);
 ULONG Release (THIS);

  // *** IStorage methods ***
 HRESULT CreateStream (THIS_ const char FAR* pwcsName, DWORD grfMode,
   DWORD dwReserved1, DWORD dwReserved2, LPSTREAM FAR* ppStm);
 HRESULT OpenStream (THIS_ const char FAR* pwcsName, void FAR *pReserved1,
   DWORD grfMode, DWORD dwReserved2, LPSTREAM FAR* ppStm);
 HRESULT CreateStorage (THIS_ const char FAR* pwcsName, DWORD grfMode,
   DWORD dwReserved1, DWORD dwReserved2, LPSTORAGE FAR* ppStg);
 HRESULT OpenStorage (THIS_ const char FAR* pwcsName, LPSTORAGE FAR *pstgPriority,
   DWORD grfMode, SNB snbExclude, DWORD dwReserved, LPSTORAGE FAR* ppStg);
 HRESULT CopyTo (THIS_ DWORD dwCiidExclude, IID const FAR *rgiidExclude,
   SNB snbExclude, LPSTORAGE FAR* pStgDest);
 HRESULT MoveElementTo (THIS_ const char FAR* lpszName, LPSTORAGE FAR *pStgDest,
   char const FAR* lpszNewName, DWORD grfFlags);
 HRESULT Commit (THIS_ DWORD grfCommitFlags);
 HRESULT Revert (THIS);
```

```
    HRESULT EnumElements (THIS_ DWORD dwReserved1, void FAR *pReserved2,
      DWORD dwReserved3, LPENUMSTATSTG FAR* ppenumStatStg);
    HRESULT DestroyElement (THIS_ const char FAR* pwcsName);
    HRESULT RenameElement (THIS_ const char FAR* pwcsOldName,
      const char FAR* pwcsNewName);
    HRESULT SetElementTimes (THIS_ const char FAR *lpszName, FILETIME const FAR *pctime,
      FILETIME const FAR *patime, FILETIME const FAR *pmtime);
    HRESULT SetClass (THIS_ REFCLSID rclsid);
    HRESULT SetStateBits (THIS_ DWORD grfStateBits, DWORD grfMask);
    HRESULT Stat (THIS_ STATSTG FAR *pStatStg, DWORD grfStatFlag);
};
```

IStorage::CreateStream

HRESULT IStorage::CreateStream (*pwcsName*, *grfMode*, *dwReserved1*, *dwReserved2*, *ppStm*)
const char FAR * *pwcsName*
DWORD *grfMode*
DWORD *dwReserved1*
DWORD *dwReserved2*
LPSTREAM FAR* *ppStm*

IStorage::CreateStream creates and immediately opens a new **IStream** object contained in this storage object.

Parameters

pwcsName
Points to the name by which the newly created stream can later be reopened.

grfMode
Defines the access mode to use when opening the newly created stream. For more information, see the following comments.

dwReserved1
Reserved for future use; must be set to zero by the caller. However, to ensure future compatibility, the callee must not explicitly test for zero.

dwReserved2
Reserved for future use; must be set to zero by the caller. However, to ensure future compatibility, the callee must not explicitly test for zero.

ppStm
Points to where the opened **IStream** interface is returned (**ppStm*). Valid only if the operation is successful. This parameter is NULL if there is an error.

Return Values

Value	Meaning
S_OK	The stream was created successfully.
STG_E_ACCESSDENIED	Insufficient permissions to create stream.

Value	Meaning
STG_E_FILEALREADYEXISTS	The stream with the specified name already exists and *grfMode* is set to STGM_FAILIFTHERE.
STG_TOOMANYOPENFILES	There are too many open files.
STG_E_INSUFFICIENTMEMORY	Out of memory.
STG_E_INVALIDFLAG	Unsupported value(s) specified in *grfMode*.
STG_E_INVALIDPOINTER	A bad pointer was passed in.
STG_E_INVALIDPARAMETER	Invalid parameter.
STG_E_REVERTED	The object has been invalidated by a revert operation above it in the transaction tree.
STG_E_INVALIDNAME	Invalid value for *pwcsName*.

Comments

If *pwcsName* specifies a stream that does not exist, **IStorage::CreateStream** creates a new stream. If a stream already exists with the name specified in *pwcsName*, the STGM_CREATE or STGM_FAILIFTHERE access modes (defined by the *grfMode* parameter) indicate how to create the stream. If STGM_CREATE is specified, any existing stream is destroyed and then replaced with a newly created stream. If STGM_FAILIFTHERE is specified, the function fails and returns the error STG_E_FILEALREADYEXISTS. Any destruction and creation of the stream is subject to the transaction mode of the parent storage.

All elements within a storage object—including both streams and other storage objects—are kept in the same name space.

See Also

IStorage::OpenStream

IStorage::OpenStream

HRESULT IStorage::OpenStream(*pwcsName*, *pReserved1*, *grfMode*, *dwReserved2*, *ppStm***)**
const char FAR* *pwcsName*
void FAR* *pReserved1*
DWORD *grfMode*
DWORD *dwReserved2*
LPSTREAM FAR* *ppStm*

IStorage::OpenStream opens an existing named stream according to the access mode *grfMode*.

Parameters

pwcsName
Points to the name of the stream to open.

pReserved1
Reserved for future use; must be set to NULL by the caller. However, the callee should ignore the value.

grfMode
Defines the access mode to use when opening the stream. For more information, see the following comments.

dwReserved2
Reserved for future use; must be set to zero by the caller. However, the callee should ignore the value.

ppStm
Points to where the opened **IStream** is returned (**ppStm*).Valid only if the operation is successful. *ppStm* is NULL if there is an error.

Return Values

Value	Meaning
S_OK	The stream was opened successfully.
STG_E_ACCESSDENIED	Insufficient permissions to open the stream.
STG_E_FILENOTFOUND	The stream with specified name does not exist.
STG_E_INSUFFICIENTMEMORY	Out of memory.
STG_E_INVALIDFLAG	Unsupported value(s) specified in *grfMode*.
STG_E_INVALIDNAME	Invalid name.
STG_E_INVALIDPOINTER	Invalid pointer.
STG_E_REVERTED	The object has been invalidated by a revert operation above it in the transaction tree.
STG_E_INVALIDPARAMETER	Invalid parameter.

Comments

The permissions on this storage object impose some restrictions on the permissions that can be given in *grfMode*. For more information about permissions, see "Storage Access Modes," earlier in this chapter.

Opening streams in transacted mode is not supported by OLE. Opening the same stream more than once from the same open **IStorage** instance is also not supported. This behavior is enforced by requiring the caller of **IStorage::OpenStream** to specify STGM_SHARE_EXCLUSIVE in *grfMode*. The call fails with STG_E_INVALIDFUNCTION if these flags are not specified.

OLE's compound file implementation does not support passing STG_DELETEONRELEASE to **IStorage::OpenStream**, although other implementations of **IStorage** might have this capability.

See Also

IStorage::CreateStream

IStorage::CreateStorage

HRESULT IStorage::CreateStorage(*pwcsName, grfMode, dwReserved1, dwReserved2, ppStg*)
const char FAR* *pwcsName*
DWORD *grfMode*
DWORD *dwReserved1*
DWORD *dwReserved2*
LPSTORAGE FAR* *ppStg*

IStorage::CreateStorage creates and opens a new **IStorage** object within this storage object.

Parameters

pwcsName
Points to the name by which the newly created storage can later be (re)opened.

grfMode
Defines the access mode to use when opening the newly created storage object.

dwReserved1
Reserved for future use; must be set to zero by the caller. However, to ensure future compatibility, the callee must not explicitly test for zero.

dwReserved2
Reserved for future use; must be set to zero by the caller. However, to ensure future compatibility, the callee must not explicitly test for zero.

ppStg
Points to where the opened storage is returned (**ppStg*). Valid only if the operation is successful. This parameter is NULL if there is an error.

Return Values

Value	Meaning
S_OK	The storage object was created successfully.
STG_E_ACCESSDENIED	Insufficient permissions to create storage object.
STG_E_FILEALREADYEXISTS	The specified file already exists.
STG_E_TOOMANYOPENFILES	Too many files are open.
STG_S_CONVERTED	The existing stream with the specified name was replaced with a new storage object containing a single stream called CONTENTS.
STG_E_INSUFFICIENTMEMORY	Out of memory.
STG_E_REVERTED	The object has been invalidated by a revert operation above it in the transaction tree.
STG_E_INVALIDFLAG	Invalid flag value(s) were specified in *grfMode*.
STG_E_INVALIDNAME	Invalid name.
STG_E_INVALIDPOINTER	Invalid pointer.
STG_E_INVALIDPARAMETER	Invalid parameter.

Comments

If a storage object does not exist with the name specified by *pwcsName*, it is created. If a storage object already exists with the name specified by *pwcsName*, the following values for *grfMode* indicate how to proceed:

Storage Access Flag	Meaning
STGM_CREATE	If a storage object with the specified name already exists, remove it and replace it with a new storage object.
STGM_CONVERT	If such an element exists, and is an **IStream**, the stream is to be replaced with a new storage object that contains one stream named "**CONTENTS**". This stream contains exactly the data that was in the old stream before the conversion.
STGM_FAILIFTHERE	Do not create a new storage object if one already exists; return STG_E_FILEALREADYEXISTS.
STGM_DELETEONRELEASE	Delete the root **IStorage** object when it receives it final release.

See Also

IStorage::OpenStorage

IStorage::OpenStorage

HRESULT IStorage::OpenStorage(*pwcsName*, *pstgPriority*, *grfMode*, *snbExclude*, *dwReserved*, *ppStg***)**
const char FAR* *pwcsName*
LPSTORAGE *pstgPriority*
DWORD *grfMode*
SNB *snbExclude*
DWORD *dwReserved*
LPSTORAGE FAR* *ppStg*

IStorage::OpenStorage opens an existing **IStorage** object contained within this storage object according to the access mode *grfMode*.

Parameters

pwcsName
Points to the name of the storage element to open. The *pwcsName* parameter is ignored if *pstgPriority* is non-NULL. I this case, the name of the element is taken from *pstgPriority*.

pstgPriority
Typically NULL. A non-NULL value points to a previous opening of the storage object, usually one that was opened in priority-mode. When *pstgPriority* is non-NULL, the container should close and reopen the storage object without admitting the possibility that some concurrent process could steal away access permissions already obtained.

grfMode
Defines the access mode to use when opening the storage object; see the following comments.

snbExclude
Specifies a non-NULL value that points to a block of stream names in this **IStorage** instance which are to be emptied as the **IStorage** is opened. This exclusion happens independently of a snapshot copy. Can be NULL.

For more information on *snbExclude* and the *pstgPriority* parameters, see the **StgOpenStorage** function.

dwReserved
Reserved for future use; must be zero.

ppStg
Points to where the opened **IStorage** instance is returned. Valid only if the operation is successful. This parameter is NULL if there is an error.

Return Values

Value	Meaning
S_OK	The storage object was opened successfully.
STG_E_ACCESSDENIED	Insufficient permissions to open **IStorage** object.
STG_E_FILENOTFOUND	The storage object with the specified *pwcsName* does not exist.
STG_E_INSUFFICIENTMEMORY	Out of memory.
STG_E_REVERTED	The object has been invalidated by a revert operation above it in the transaction tree.
STG_E_INVALIDFLAG	Invalid flag value(s) specified in *grfMode*.
STG_E_INVALIDNAME	Invalid name.
STG_E_INVALIDPOINTER	Invalid pointer.
STG_E_INVALIDPARAMETER	Invalid parameter.

Comments

After the function returns, the **IStorage** instance contained in *pstgPriority* is invalid, and can no longer be used. Use the one in *ppStg* instead.

The compound file implementation of storage objects does not support including STGM_PRIORITY in *grfMode*; that is, it does not support opening non-root storage objects in priority mode. For more information on access permissions, see the warning in the description of DENY_WRITE related to opening a storage object read and/or write mode without specifying DENY_WRITE.

Root **IStorage** objects can be opened with STGM_DELETEONRELEASE, in which case the object is destroyed when it receives its final release. This is useful for creating temporary **IStorage** objects.

The compound file implementation does not support simultaneous openings of a storage object from the same open **IStorage** instance. This behavior is enforced by requiring the caller to specify STGM_SHARE_EXCLUSIVE in *grfMode*. **IStorage::OpenStorage** fails with the error STG_E_INVALIDFUNCTION if this flag is not specified.

See Also **StgOpenStorage**

IStorage::CopyTo

HRESULT IStorage::CopyTo(*ciidExclude*, *rgiidExclude*, *snbExclude*, *pStgDest*)
DWORD *ciidExclude*
IID const FAR* *rgiidExclude*
SNB *snbExclude*
LPSTORAGE *pStgDest*

IStorage::CopyTo copies the entire contents of an open **IStorage** object into the storage object *pStgDest*.

Parameters

ciidExclude
Specifies the number of elements in the array pointed to by *rgiidExclude*. If *rgiidExclude* is NULL, *ciidExclude* is ignored.

rgiidExclude
Specifies an array of interface identifiers the caller takes responsibility for copying from the source to the destination. It can be NULL, indicating that all other objects are to be copied. If non-NULL, an array length of zero indicates that no other objects are to be copied, only the state exposed by the **IStorage** object.

snbExclude
Points to a block of named elements in this **IStorage** that are not to be copied to the destination. It can be NULL. If IID_IStorage is the *rgiidExclude* array, this parameter is ignored.

pStgDest
Points to the open storage object where this open storage object is to be copied.

Return Values

Value	Meaning
S_OK	The storage object was successfully copied.
STG_S_DESTLACKSINTERFACE	The destination lacks an interface of the source object requested to be copied.
STG_E_ACCESSDENIED	The destination storage object is a child of the source storage object.
STG_E_MEDIUMFULL	The storage medium is full; cannot create new storage object.
STG_E_TOOMANYOPENFILES	Too many open files.
STG_E_INSUFFICIENTMEMORY	Out of memory.
STG_E_INVALIDPOINTER	Invalid pointer.
STG_E_INVALIDPARAMETER	Invalid parameter.

Comments

The *pStgDest* parameter can be a different implementation of the **IStorage** interface than the source. Thus, **IStorage::CopyTo** can only use the publicly available functionality of *pStgDest*.

If *pStgDest* is transacted, it can be reverted by calling **IStorage::Revert**.

The copy operation merges elements contained in the source **IStorage** with those already present in the destination. The copy process is recursive, invoking **IStorage::CopyTo** and **IStream::CopyTo** on the elements nested inside the source. If an attempt is made to copy a stream on top of an existing stream with the same name, the existing destination stream is first removed and then replaced with the source stream. Attempting to copy an **IStorage** on top of an existing destination **IStorage** does not remove the existing storage. Thus, after the copy operation, the **IStorage** contains older elements if they were not replaced by newer ones.

If the destination **IStorage** is a (transitive) child of the source, **IStorage::CopyTo** fails and returns STG_E_ACCESSDENIED.

The *rgiidExclude* parameter specifies an array of interface identifiers the caller knows about and does *not* want copied from source to destination. Presumably, the caller takes care of copying the state behind these interfaces. It is not an error for this array to include an interface this **IStorage** does not support; such interfaces are simply ignored. The **IStorage** interface *is* explicitly allowed to be in this array. In the event the destination lacks an interface of the source that was requested to be copied, this does *not* affect the other interfaces copied and STG_S_DESTLACKSINTERFACE is returned.

The *snbExclude* parameter specifies a block of named elements of the **IStorage** the caller wants excluded from the copy operation. Elements of these names are not created or otherwise touched in the destination.

A consequence of these rules is that:

```
pStg->CopyTo(0, 0, 0, pStgDest)
```

copies everything possible from the source to the destination. This is the most commonly used form of this operation.

See Also

IStorage::MoveElementTo, IStorage::Revert

IStorage::MoveElementTo

HRESULT IStorage::MoveElementTo(*lpszName*, *pStgDest*, *lpszNewName*, *grfFlags***)**
const char FAR* *lpszName*
LPSTORAGE *pStgDest*
const char FAR* *lpszNewName*
DWORD *grfFlags*

IStorage::MoveElementTo moves an **IStorage** element to the indicated new destination container.

Parameters

lpszName
Points to the name of the element of this **IStorage** to be moved.

pStgDest
Points to the destination container into which the element is to be placed.

lpszNewName
Points to the new name to give to the element in its new container.

grfFlags
Specifies how the move is to happen. For more information, see the following comments.

Return Values

Value	Meaning
S_OK	The storage element was moved successfully.
STG_E_ACCESSDENIED	Insufficient permissions.
STG_E_FILENOTFOUND	The element could not be found.
STG_E_FILEALREADYEXISTS	The specified file already exists.
STG_E_INSUFFICIENTMEMORY	Out of memory.
STG_E_TOOMANYOPENFILES	Too many open files.
STG_E_REVERTED	The object has been invalidated by a revert operation above it in the transaction tree.
STG_E_INVALIDFLAG	Invalid flag.
STG_E_INVALIDNAME	Invalid name.

Value	Meaning
STG_E_INVALIDPOINTER	Invalid pointer.
STG_E_INVALIDPARAMETER	Invalid parameter.

Comments

Unless both this **IStorage** and the destination **IStorage** have some special knowledge about each other's implementation (for example, they could be different instances of the *same* implementation), then **IStorage::MoveElementTo** is similar to an **IStorage::CopyTo** on the indicated element, followed by a removal of the original element.

The *grfFlags* parameter controls how the move is to happen. Its values are taken from the enumeration **STGMOVE**:

```
typedef enum tagSTGMOVE {
STGMOVE_MOVE = 0,
STGMOVE_COPY = 1,
} STGMOVE;
```

These flags have the following meanings:

Values for *grfFlags*	Meaning
STGMOVE_MOVE	Carry out the move operation, as expected.
STGMOVE_COPY	Carry out the first part of the move operation but do not remove the original element. With this flag, the behavior resulting from copying an element on top of itself (that is, *pStgDest* is the same as the source **IStorage,** and *lpszNewName* = *lpszName*) is undefined.

See Also

IStorage::CopyTo

IStorage::Commit

HRESULT IStorage::Commit(*grfCommitFlags*)
DWORD *grfCommitFlags*

IStorage::Commit commits any changes made to an **IStorage** object since it was opened or last committed to persistent storage.

Parameters

grfCommitFlags
Controls how the object is to be committed to **IStorage**. For more information, see the following comments.

Return Values

Value	Meaning
S_OK	The Commit operation was successful.
STG_E_NOTCURRENT	Another opening of the storage object has committed changes. Indicates the possibility of overwriting changes.
STG_E_MEDIUMFULL	No space left on device to commit.
STG_E_TOOMANYOPENFILES	Too many open files.
STG_E_REVERTED	The object has been invalidated by a revert operation above it in the transaction tree.
STG_E_INVALIDFLAG	Invalid flag.
STG_E_INVALIDPARAMETER	Invalid parameter.

Comments

Calling **IStorage::Commit** has no effect if the storage object was opened in direct mode, except when invoked on a direct mode root storage object, it ensures that any internal memory buffers have been written out to disk (or to the underlying **ILockBytes**, as appropriate).

In transacted mode, **IStorage::Commit** causes the changes that have been made since the storage object was opened or since the last commit was done to be permanently reflected in the object's persistent image. The commit is subject to the transaction of the object's parent storage. If the parent reverts at a later time, the changes currently being committed are rolled back.Calling **IStorage::Commit** has no effect on currently-opened storages or streams in this object. Changes to these nested storages and streams are not automatically committed but they are still valid and can be used. Committing involves informing the parent storage of the changes the object is currently informed about. Thus, this object has to be informed of changes from inner transactions before it can publish changes to its parent.

The *grfCommitFlags* parameter consists of the or-ing of elements from the enumeration **STGC**:

```
typedef enum tagSTGC
{
    STGC_DEFAULT = 0,
    STGC_OVERWRITE  = 1,
    STGC_ONLYIFCURRENT  = 2,
    STGC_DANGEROUSLYCOMMITMERELYTODISKCACHE = 4
} STGC;
```

The caller can specify STGC_DEFAULT or any combination of the other elements.

STGC_OVERWRITE allows new data to overwrite the old data, reducing space requirements. STGC_OVERWRITE is not recommended for normal operation, but it could be useful in the following situations:

- A commit was tried and STG_E_MEDIUMFULL was returned.
- The user has somehow specified a willingness to risk overwriting the old data.
- A low memory save sequence is being used to end up with a smaller file.

The commit operation obtains all the disk space it needs before attempting to store the new data, whether or not STGC_OVERWRITE is specified. If space requirements prohibit the save, the old data will be intact, including all uncommitted changes.

However, if the commit fails due to reasons other than lack of disk space and STGC_OVERWRITE was specified, it is possible that neither the old nor the new version of the data will be intact.

STGC_ONLYIFCURRENT prevents multiple users of an **IStorage** from overwriting the other's changes. STGC_ONLYIFCURRENT commits changes only if no one else has made changes since the last time this user opened the **IStorage** or committed. If other changes have been made, STG_E_NOTCURRENT is returned. If the caller chooses to overwrite the changes, **IStorage::Commit** can be called with *grfCommitFlags* set to STGC_DEFAULT.

STGC_DANGEROUSLYCOMMITMERELYTODISKCACHE commits the changes, but does not save them to the disk cache.

When committing root storage objects, care must be taken to ensure that the operation is successfully completed or that, when failing, the old committed contents of the **IStorage** are still intact. In the OLE compound file implementation, unless *grfCommitFlags* is set to STGC_OVERWRITE, a two-phase commit process is used. First, all new data is written to unused space in the underlying file, growing it as necessary. Once this has been successfully completed, a table in the file is updated using a single sector write to indicate the new data is to be used in place of the old. The old data becomes free space, to be used at the next commit.

If the storage object was opened with some of its elements excluded, the caller is responsible for rewriting them before calling **Commit**. The storage must have been opened in write mode in order for the commit to succeed.

Unless multiple simultaneous writers on the same storage object are prohibited, applications usually specify at least STGC_ONLYIFCURRENT in *grfCommitFlags* to prevent the changes made by one writer from inadvertently overwriting the changes made by another.

See Also **IStorage::Revert, IStream::Commit**

IStorage::Revert

HRESULT IStorage::Revert()

IStorage::Revert discards all changes made in or made visible to this storage object by nested commits since the storage object was opened or last committed.

Return Values

Value	Meaning
S_OK	The revert operation was successful.
STG_E_INSUFFICIENTMEMORY	The revert operation failed due to lack of memory.
STG_E_TOOMANYOPENFILES	Too many open files.
STG_E_REVERTED	The object has been invalidated by a revert operation above it in the transaction tree.

Comments

After **IStorage::Revert** finishes, any existing elements that were opened from the reverted **IStorage** object are invalid and can no longer be used. The error STG_E_REVERTED is returned on all calls except **IStorage::Release** using these openings.

Because commits happen implicitly and immediately, calling **IStorage::Revert** on a storage opened in direct mode only invalidates any child openings.

IStorage::EnumElements

HRESULT IStorage::EnumElements(*dwReserved1*, *pReserved2*, *dwReserved3*, *ppenumStatStg*)
DWORD *dwReserved1*
void FAR* *pReserved2*
DWORD *dwReserved3*
LPENUMSTATSTG FAR* *ppenumStatStg*

IStorage::EnumElements enumerates the elements immediately contained within this storage object.

Parameters

dwReserved1
Reserved for future use; must be zero.

pReserved2
Reserved for future use; must be NULL.

dwReserved3
Reserved for future use; must be zero.

ppenumStatStg
Points to where to return the enumerator from which the elements of this storage can be obtained; NULL if there is an error. See the description of **IEnumSTATSTG** in this chapter.

Return Values

Value	Meaning
S_OK	The enumeration was successful.
STG_E_INSUFFICIENTMEMORY	The enumeration failed due to lack of memory.
E_OUTOFMEMORY	The enumeration failed due to lack of memory.
STG_E_REVERTED	The object has been invalidated by a revert operation above it in the transaction tree.
STG_E_INVALIDPOINTER	Invalid pointer.
STG_E_INVALIDPARAMETER	Invalid parameter.

Comments

The storage object must be open in read mode to allow the enumeration of its elements.

The order in which the elements are enumerated and whether the enumerator is a snapshot or always reflects the current state of the storage on which it was opened (not necessarily the state at which the enumerator was initialized), depends on the **IStorage** implementation. The OLE compound file implementation makes a snapshot.

See Also

IEnumSTATSTG

IStorage::DestroyElement

HRESULT IStorage::DestroyElement(*pwcsName*)
const char FAR* *pwcsName*

IStorage::DestroyElement removes an element from this storage, subject to the transaction mode in which the storage object was opened.

Parameters

pwcsName
Points to the element to remove.

Return Values

Value	Meaning
S_OK	The element was successfully removed.
STG_E_ACCESSDENIED	Insufficient permissions.
STG_E_FILENOTFOUND	The element could not be found.

Value	Meaning
STG_E_TOOMANYOPENFILES	Too many open files.
STG_E_INSUFFICIENTMEMORY	Out of memory.
STG_E_REVERTED	The object has been invalidated by a revert operation above it in the transaction tree.
STG_E_INVALIDPOINTER	Invalid pointer.
STG_E_INVALIDNAME	Invalid name.
STG_E_INVALIDPARAMETER	Invalid parameter.

Comments

The existing open instance of this element from this parent instance becomes invalid after **IStorage::DestroyElement** is called.

IStorage::RenameElement

HRESULT IStorage::RenameElement(*pwcsOldName*, *pwcsNewName*)
const char FAR* *pwcsOldName*
const char FAR* *pwcsNewName*

IStorage::RenameElement renames an element contained in storage, subject to the transaction state of the **IStorage** object.

Parameters

pwcsOldName
Points to the old name of the element.

pwcsNewName
Points to the new name of the element.

Return Values

Value	Meaning
S_OK	The element was successfully renamed.
STG_E_ACCESSDENIED	The element named *pwcsNewName* already exists.
STG_E_FILENOTFOUND	The element could not be found.
STG_E_FILEALREADYEXISTS	The specified file already exists.
STG_E_TOOMANYOPENFILES	Too many open files.
STG_E_INSUFFICIENTMEMORY	Not enough memory to rename the element.
STG_E_REVERTED	The object has been invalidated by a revert operation above it in the transaction tree.
STG_E_INVALIDPOINTER	Invalid pointer.
STG_E_INVALIDNAME	Invalid name.
STG_E_INVALIDPARAMETER	Invalid parameter.

Comments

An **IStorage** element *cannot* be renamed while it is open.
IStorage::RenameElement is *not* guaranteed to work in low memory conditions.

IStorage::SetElementTimes

HRESULT IStorage::SetElementTimes(*lpszName*, *pctime*, *patime*, *pmtime*)
const char FAR* *lpszName*
FILETIME const FAR* *pctime*
FILETIME const FAR* *patime*
FILETIME const FAR* *pmtime*

IStorage::SetElementTimes sets the modification, access, and creation times of the indicated element of this storage object.

Parameters

lpszName
Points to the name of the element to change.

pctime
Points to the new creation time.

patime
Points to the new access time.

pmtime
Points to the new modification time.

Return Values

Value	**Meaning**
S_OK	The time values were successfully set.
STG_E_ACCESSDENIED	The element named *pwcsNewName* already exists.
STG_E_FILENOTFOUND	The element could not be found.
STG_E_FILEALREADYEXISTS	The specified file already exists.
STG_E_TOOMANYOPENFILES	Too many open files.
STG_E_INSUFFICIENTMEMORY	Not enough memory to rename the element.
STG_E_REVERTED	The object has been invalidated by a revert operation above it in the transaction tree.
STG_E_INVALIDPOINTER	Invalid pointer.
STG_E_INVALIDNAME	Invalid name.
STG_E_INVALIDPARAMETER	Invalid parameter.

Comments

Each of the time value parameters can be NULL, indicating that no modification should occur.

It is possible that one or more of these time values are not supported by the underlying file system. **IStorage::SetElementTimes** sets the times that can be set and ignores the rest.

The compound file implementation maintains modification and change times for internal storage objects. For root storage objects, whatever is supported by the underlying file system (or **ILockBytes**) is used. The compound file implementation does not maintain any time stamps for internal streams. Unsupported time stamps are reported as zero, enabling the caller to test for support.

IStorage::SetClass

HRESULT IStorage::SetClass(*rclsid***)**
REFCLSID *rclsid*

IStorage::SetClass persistently stores the object's CLSID.

Parameter

rclsid
Specifies the CLSID to be associated with this **IStorage**.

Return Values

Value	Meaning
S_OK	The CLSID was successfully stored.
STG_E_ACCESSDENIED	Unable to access the storage object.
STG_E_REVERTED	The object has been invalidated by a revert operation above it in the transaction tree.
STG_E_MEDIUMFULL	Not enough space was left on device to complete the operation.

Comments

The current CLSID for an **IStorage** can be retrieved with **IStorage::Stat**. When initially created, **IStorage** instances have an associated CLSID of CLSID_NULL.

See Also

IStorage::Stat

IStorage::SetStateBits

HRESULT IStorage::SetStateBits(*grfStateBits*, *grfMask***)**
DWORD *grfStateBits*
DWORD *grfMask*

IStorage::SetStateBits stores up to 32 bits of state information in this **IStorage**.

Parameters

dwgrfStateBits
Specifies the new values of the bits to set. No legal values are defined for these bits; they are all reserved for future use and must not be used by applications.

dwgrfMask
Specifies a binary mask indicating which bits in *dwgrfStateBits* are significant in this call.

Return Values

Value	Meaning
S_OK	The state was successfully set.
STG_E_ACCESSDENIED	The caller cannot change state information.
STG_E_INVALIDFLAG	Invalid flag specified in *dwgrfStateBits* or *dwgrfMask*.
STG_E_INVALIDPARAMETER	Invalid parameter.

Comments

The current value of this state is retrievable with **IStorage::Stat**. When a storage object is initially created, this state value is zero.

See Also

IStorage::Stat

IStorage::Stat

HRESULT IStorage::Stat(*pStatStg, grfStatFlag*)
LPSTATSTG *pStatStg*
DWORD *grfStatFlag*

IStorage::Stat returns statistics about this open storage object.

Parameters

pStatStg
Points to a **STATSTG** structure filled by the callee with the statistics of this storage object.

grfStatFlag
Controls the level of statistics returned about the storage object. For more information, see the following comments.

Return Values

Value	Meaning
S_OK	The statistics were successfully returned.
STG_E_ACCESSDENIED	The storage object cannot be accessed.
STG_E_INSUFFICIENTMEMORY	Not enough memory to rename the element.
STG_E_REVERTED	The object has been invalidated by a revert operation above it in the transaction tree.
STG_E_INVALIDFLAG	Invalid flag specified in *dwgrfStatflag*.

Value	Meaning
STG_E_INVALIDPOINTER	Invalid pointer.

Comments

With *grfStatFlag* set to STATFLAG_NONAME, *pStatStg->pwcsName* is not returned (that is, it is returned as NULL), thus saving an alloc/free operation.

The *grfStatFlag* values are taken from the enumeration **STATFLAG**, which is defined as follows:

```
typedef enum tagSTATFLAG
{
        STATFLAG_DEFAULT = 0,
        STATFLAG_NONAME  = 1
} STATFLAG;
```

See Also

ReadClassStg, **IEnumSTATSTG**

IStream Interface

The **IStream** interface is mplemented by OLE and used by containers to read and write the underlying bytes of data comprising an **IStorage** object. **IStream** instances are analogous to files. **IStream** is the interface to which the stream elements of a **IStorage** object conform. By design, instances of this interface present almost exactly the same semantics as that of MS-DOS FAT file handles, except that range locking is not supported by the compound file implementation.

The **IStream** interface supports streams up to 2^{64} bytes in length and it requires a 64-bit value to represent their seek pointers. OLE compound files can only support streams up to 2^{32} bytes in length and, therefore, read and write operations (using **IStream::Read** and **IStream::Write**, respectively) are always limited to 2^{32} bytes at a time.

Pointers to instances of the **IStream** interface can be marshaled to other processes, just as any other interface pointer can. When the destination is another process that has shared memory access with the original process, the compound file implementation of **IStream** uses OLE's custom marshaling facilities to create a remote version of the original stream. This stream does not need to communicate with the original process to carry out its functions. The remote version of a stream shares the same seek pointer as the original stream. However, if this functionality is not needed, **IStream::Clone** can be called to create a clone of the stream, which is then passed to the remote process.

Releasing an **IStream** invalidates the stream and, as a result, the stream can no longer be used for any operations.

The **IStream** interface contains the following methods (see also STORAGE.H):

```
DECLARE_INTERFACE_(IStream, IUnknown)
{
  // *** IUnknown methods ***
 HRESULT QueryInterface (THIS_ REFIID riid, LPVOID FAR* ppvObj);
 ULONG AddRef (THIS) ;
 ULONG Release (THIS);

  // *** IStream methods ***
 HRESULT Read (THIS_ VOID HUGEP *pv, ULONG cb, ULONG FAR *pcbRead);
 HRESULT Write (THIS_ VOID const HUGEP *pv, ULONG cb, ULONG FAR *pcbWritten);
 HRESULT Seek (THIS_ LARGE_INTEGER dlibMove, DWORD dwOrigin,
  ULARGE_INTEGER FAR *plibNewPosition);
 HRESULT SetSize (THIS_ ULARGE_INTEGER libNewSize);
 HRESULT CopyTo (THIS_ LPSTREAM pStm, ULARGE_INTEGER cb,
  ULARGE_INTEGER FAR *pcbRead, ULARGE_INTEGER FAR *pcbWritten);
 HRESULT Commit (THIS_ DWORD dwCommitFlags);
 HRESULT Revert (THIS);
 HRESULT LockRegion (THIS_ ULARGE_INTEGER libOffset, ULARGE_INTEGER cb,
  DWORD dwLockType);
 HRESULT UnlockRegion (THIS_ ULARGE_INTEGER libOffset, ULARGE_INTEGER cb,
  DWORD dwLockType);
 HRESULT Stat (THIS_ STATSTG FAR *pStatStg, DWORD grfStatFlag);
 HRESULT Clone)(THIS_ LPSTREAM FAR* ppStm);
};
```

IStream::Read

HRESULT IStream::Read(*pv*, *cb*, *pcbRead*)
VOID HUGEP * *pv*
ULONG *cb*
ULONG FAR* *pcbRead*

IStream::Read reads data from the stream starting at the current seek pointer.

Parameters

pv
: Points to the buffer into which the stream data should be stored.

cb
: Specifies the number of bytes of data to read from the stream.

pcbRead
: Points (after the call) to the number of bytes actually read from the stream. It can be NULL, indicating the caller is not interested in this value.

Return Values

Value	Meaning
S_OK	The data was successfully read from the stream.
S_FALSE	The data could not be read from the stream.
STG_E_ACCESSDENIED	Insufficient access.
STG_E_INVALIDPOINTER	A bad pointer was passed in for *pv* or *pcbRead*.
STG_E_REVERTED	The object has been invalidated by a revert operation above it in the transaction tree.
STG_E_WRITEFAULT	Disk error during a write operation.
Other errors.	Any **ILockBytes** or system errors.

Comments

To read from the stream, STGM_READ mode is required on the stream. The number of bytes actually read is returned in *pcbRead*, even if an error is returned. The seek pointer is adjusted for the number of bytes actually read.

If the end of the stream was reached during the read, the number of bytes read might be fewer than requested. In this case, an error is not returned and the number of bytes actually read is merely returned through *pcbRead*. This is the same end of file behavior presently found in MS-DOS FAT file systems.

Some implementations might choose to return S_FALSE instead of S_OK when fewer than the requested number of bytes are returned. Callers must be prepared to deal with this (typically, by comparing **pcbRead* on exit against the number of bytes requested for the read.)

See Also

IStream::Write

IStream::Write

HRESULT IStream::Write(*pv*, *cb*, *pcbWritten***)**
VOID const HUGEP * *pv*
ULONG *cb*
ULONG FAR* *pcbWritten*

IStream::Write attempts to write *cb* bytes from the buffer pointed to by *pv* into the stream starting at the current seek pointer.

Parameters

pv
: Points to the buffer containing the data to be written to the stream.

cb
: Defines the number of bytes of data to write into the stream.

pcbWritten
After the call, points to the number of bytes actually written into the stream. It can be NULL, indicating the caller is not interested in this value.

Return Values

Value	Meaning
S_OK	The data was successfully written into the stream.
STG_E_MEDIUMFULL	No space left on device.
STG_E_ACCESSDENIED	Insufficient access.
STG_E_CANTSAVE	Data cannot be written for reasons other than no access or space.
STG_E_INVALIDPOINTER	A bad pointer was passed in for *pv* or *pcbWritten*.
STG_E_REVERTED	The object has been invalidated by a revert operation above it in the transaction tree.
STG_E_WRITEFAULT	Disk error during a write operation.
Other errors.	Any **ILockBytes** or system errors.

Comments

Writing a count of zero bytes is always a no-op. For a non-zero byte-count, if the seek pointer is currently past the end of the stream, the size of the stream is increased so the seek pointer can be reached. The fill bytes written to the stream are not initialized to any particular value. Except for writing a count of zero bytes past the end-of-file (for which **IStream::SetSize** can be used), this is the same end-of-file behavior as in the MS-DOS FAT file system.

In the compound file implementation, **IStreams** are not sparse. Any fill bytes are eventually allocated on the disk and assigned to the stream.

The number of bytes actually written is always returned in *pcbWritten*, even if an error is returned. The seek pointer is adjusted for the number of bytes actually written.

See Also

IStream::Read

IStream::Seek

HRESULT IStream::Seek(*dlibMove, dwOrigin, plibNewPosition***)**
LARGE_INTEGER *dlibMove*
DWORD *dwOrigin*
ULARGE_INTEGER FAR* *plibNewPosition*

IStream::Seek adjusts the location of the seek pointer on the stream.

Parameters

dlibMove
Specifies the displacement to be added to the location indicated by *dwOrigin*. If *dwOrigin* is STREAM_SEEK_SET, this is interpreted as an unsigned value rather than a signed value.

dwOrigin
Specifies the seek mode; the origin with respect to which *dlibMove* should be interpreted; see the following comments.

plibNewPosition
Points (after this call is completed) to the beginning of the stream. It can be NULL, indicating the caller is not interested in this value.

Return Value

Value	Meaning
S_OK	The seek pointer has been successfully adjusted.
STG_E_INVALIDPOINTER	A bad pointer was passed in for *plibNewPosition*.
STG_E_INVALIDFUNCTION	*dwOrigin* contains invalid value.
STG_E_REVERTED	The object has been invalidated by a revert operation above it in the transaction tree.
STG_E_WRITEFAULT	Disk error during a write operation.
Other errors.	Any **ILockBytes** or system errors.

Comments

It is an error to seek before the beginning of the stream, but it is not an error to seek past the end of the stream. Seeking past the end of the stream is useful for subsequent writes, because the stream will be extended at that time to the seek position immediately before the write is done.

The *dwOrigin* parameter can have one of the following values:

```
typedef enum tagSTREAM_SEEK
{
    STREAM_SEEK_SET = 0,
    STREAM_SEEK_CUR = 1,
    STREAM_SEEK_END = 2
} STREAM_SEEK;
```

These values have the following effects:

Values for *dwOrigin*	Meaning
STREAM_SEEK_SET	Sets the seek position relative to the beginning of the stream; *dlibMove* is the new seek position.
STREAM_SEEK_CUR	Sets the seek position relative to the current position of the stream; *dlibMove* is the (signed) displacement to be made.
STREAM_SEEK_END	Sets the seek position relative to the current end of the stream; *dlibMove* is the (signed) displacement to be made.

Calling **Seek** with *dlibMove* set to zero and *dwOrigin* set to STREAM_SEEK CUR returns the current seek position through *plibNewPosition*.

IStream::SetSize

HRESULT IStream::SetSize(*libNewSize***)**
ULARGE_INTEGER *libNewSize*

IStream::SetSize changes the size of the stream.

Parameters

libNewSize
Specifies the new size of the stream.

Return Value

Value	Meaning
S_OK	The stream size was successfully changed.
STG_E_MEDIUMFULL	Lack of space prohibited change of stream size.
STG_E_INVALIDFUNCTION	High DWORD of *libNewSize* != 0.
STG_E_REVERTED	The object has been invalidated by a revert operation above it in the transaction tree.
STG_E_WRITEFAULT	Disk error during a write operation.
Other errors.	Any **ILockBytes** or system errors.

Comments

The seek pointer is not affected by the change in stream size. If *libNewSize* is larger than the current stream size, the stream is extended with fill bytes of undefined value, much as is done in an **IStream::Write** call if the seek pointer is past the current end-of-stream. If *libNewSize* is smaller than the current stream, the stream is truncated to the indicated size.

In most stream implementations, calling **IStream::SetSize** is an effective way of trying to obtain a large chunk of contiguous space. However, no guarantee is made that the space will be contiguous.

See Also

IStream::Write

IStream::CopyTo

HRESULT IStream::CopyTo(*pStm*, *cb*, *pcbRead*, *pcbWritten***)**
LPSTREAM *pStm*
ULARGE_INTEGER *cb*

ULARGE_INTEGER FAR* *pcbRead*
ULARGE_INTEGER FAR* *pcbWritten*

IStream::CopyTo copies data from one stream to another stream, starting at the current seek pointer in each stream.

Parameters

pStm
Points to the stream into which the data should be copied (*lpstm* can be a clone of the source stream).

cb
Specifies the number of bytes to read from the source stream.

pcbRead
Contains the number of bytes actually read from the source stream. It can be NULL, indicating the caller is not interested in this value.

pcbWritten
Contains the number of bytes actually written into the destination stream. It can be NULL, indicating the caller is not interested in this value.

Return Value

Value	Meaning
S_OK	The stream was successfully copied.
STG_E_MEDIUMFULL	Lack of space prohibited copy.
STG_E_INSUFFICIENTMEMORY	Out of memory.
STG_E_INVALIDPOINTER	A bad pointer for *pstm*, *pcbRead*, or *pcbWritten*.
STG_E_READFAULT	Disk error during read.
	Can also return any error codes from **IStream::Read**, **IStream::Write**, and **IStream::Seek**.
STG_E_REVERTED	The object has been invalidated by a revert operation above it in the transaction tree.
STG_E_WRITEFAULT	Disk error during a write operation.
Other errors.	Any **ILockBytes** or system errors.

Comments

IStream::CopyTo is equivalent to reading *cb* bytes into memory using **IStream::Read** and then immediately writing them to the destination stream using **IStream::Write**. Copying a stream onto a clone of itself can always be done in a safe manner.

Setting *cb* to its maximum large-integer value causes the remainder of the source stream to be copied.

The number of bytes actually read or written is always returned in *pcbRead* and *pcbWritten* respectively. The seek pointer in each stream instance is adjusted for the number of bytes read or written.

If **IStream::CopyTo** returns an error, no assumptions can be made about the seek positions of either the source or destination streams and the values in *pcbRead* and *pcbWritten is* not meaningful. One result of this is that if **IStream::CopyTo** returns successfully, *pcbRead* and *pcbWritten* are equal.

See Also **IStream::Read, IStream::Write**

IStream::Commit

HRESULT IStream::Commit(*grfCommitFlags*)
DWORD *grfCommitFlags*

IStream::Commit commits any changes made to the **IStorage** object containing the stream.

Parameters

grfCommitFlags
Controls how the object is to be committed to storage. The *grfCommitFlags* parameter consists of the OR-ing of elements from the enumeration **STGC**. For more information about *grfCommitFlags* , see "**IStorage::Commit**" earlier in this chapter.

Return Values

Value	Meaning
S_OK	The stream was successfully committed.
STG_E_MEDIUMFULL	The commit failed due to lack of space on device.
STG_E_REVERTED	The object has been invalidated by a revert operation above it in the transaction tree.
STG_E_WRITEFAULT	Disk error during a write operation.
Other errors.	Any **ILockBytes** or system errors.

Comments

OLE does not support **IStream** objects being opened in transacted mode. Therefore, calling **IStream::Commit** in transacted mode is a no-op.

However, for other implementations, **IStream::Commit** causes the changes made to this stream since it was opened or last committed to be permanently reflected in the persistent image of the stream. This is subject to any transaction of the parent storage object of the stream. That parent can still cancel changes by calling **IStream::Revert** at a later time.

In direct mode, **IStream::Commit** ensures that any memory buffers have been flushed out to the stream's underlying open **IStorage** instance. This is much like a "flush" call in traditional file systems. In compound files, **IStream** instances are only available inside **IStorage** instances. Thus, the open parent **IStorage** also needs to be flushed and committed.

See Also **IStorage::Commit**

IStream::Revert

HRESULT IStream::Revert()

IStream::Revert discards all changes made to the stream since it was opened or last committed in transacted mode. In direct mode, **IStream::Revert** is a no-op.

Return Values

Value	Meaning
S_OK	The stream was successfully reverted.
STG_E_REVERTED	The object has been invalidated by a revert operation above it in the transaction tree.
STG_E_WRITEFAULT	Disk error during a write operation.
Other errors.	Any **ILockBytes** or system errors.

Comment OLE does not support **IStream** objects being opened in transacted mode. Accordingly, most applications have no need to call this function.

IStream::LockRegion

HRESULT IStream::LockRegion(*libOffset*, *cb*, *dwLockType***)**
ULARGE_INTEGER *libOffset*
ULARGE_INTEGER *cb*
DWORD *dwLockType*

IStream::LockRegion locks a range of bytes in the stream. This method is *not* supported in the current release of OLE.

Parameters

libOffset
Specifies the beginning of the region to lock.

cb
Specifies the length of the region to be locked, in bytes.

dwLockType
Specifies the kind of lock being requested.

Return Values

Value	Meaning
S_OK	The range of bytes was successfully locked
STG_E_INVALIDFUNCTION	The function is not supported in this release.
STG_E_LOCKVIOLATION	Requested lock is supported, but cannot be presently granted because of an existing lock.

Comments

Range locking is not supported by compound files so calling **IStream::LockRegion** is a no-op. It might or might not be supported by other implementations.

The range of bytes begins with the byte at the offset *libOffset*, and extends for *cb* bytes toward the end of the stream. The specified range of bytes can extend past the current end of the stream.

Three types of locking can be supported: locking to exclude other writers, locking to exclude other readers or writers, and locking that allows only one requestor to obtain a lock on the given range, which is usually an alias for one of the other two lock types. A given stream instance might support either of the first two types, or both. The lock type is specified by *dwLockType*; using one of the following values:

```
typedef enum tagLOCKTYPE
{
    LOCK_WRITE      = 1,
    LOCK_EXCLUSIVE  = 2,
    LOCK_ONLYONCE   = 4
}   LOCKTYPE;
```

These values mean the following:

Values for *dwLockType*	Purpose
LOCK_WRITE	If the lock is granted, reading the specified region of the stream can be done by calling **IStream::Read** from any opening of this stream. Attempts to write to this region from any opening of this stream other than the one to which the lock was granted returns the error STG_E_ACCESSDENIED.
LOCK_EXCLUSIVE	Attempts to read or write this stream by other stream openings return the error STG_E_ACCESSDENIED.
LOCK_ONLYONCE	If the lock is granted, no other lock can be obtained on the bytes in the given region. Usually this lock type is an alias for some other lock type and other semantics can occur as a side effect. The underlying implementation can use the appropriate file system primitive to accomplish the lock.

For information on how a caller can determine whether locking is supported; see the discussion of **IStream::Stat** and its parameter block, **STATSTG**.

Any region locked with **IStream::LockRegion** must later be explicitly unlocked by calling **IStream::UnlockRegion** with exactly the same values for *libOffset*, *cb*, and *dwLockType*. Two adjacent regions cannot be locked separately and then unlocked with a single unlock call.

All locks on a stream must be explicitly unlocked before the stream is released.

See Also **IStream::Stat, IStream::UnlockRegion**

IStream::UnlockRegion

HRESULT IStream::UnlockRegion(*libOffset, cb, dwLockType***)**
ULARGE_INTEGER *libOffset*
ULARGE_INTEGER *cb*
DWORD *dwLockType*

IStream::UnlockRegion unlocks a region of the stream previously locked with **IStream::LockRegion**. This method is *not* supported in the current release of OLE.

Parameter

libOffset
Specifies the beginning of the region to unlock.

cb
Specifies the length of the region to be locked, in bytes.

dwLockType
Specifies the kind of lock being released.

Return Value

Value	**Meaning**
S_OK	The requested unlock was granted.
STG_E_LOCKVIOLATION	The requested unlock cannot be granted.
STG_E_INVALIDFUNCTION	The function is not supported in this release.

Comments Any locked region must be explicitly unlocked using **IStream::UnlockRegion**, with exactly the same *libOffset*, *cb*, and *dwLockType* parameters specified as in the original **IStream::LockRegion** call. Two adjacent regions cannot be locked separately and then unlocked with a single unlock call.

See Also **IStream::LockRegion**

IStream::Stat

HRESULT IStream::Stat(*pStatStg, grfStatFlag*)
LPSTATSTG *pStatStg*
DWORD *grfStatFlag*

IStream::Stat returns relevant statistics concerning this open stream.

Parameters

pStatStg
Points to a **STATSTG** structure filled with the statistics of this open stream.

grfStatFlag
Controls the level of statistics returned about this open stream object; see the following comments.

Return Values

Value	Meaning
S_OK	The statistics were successfully returned.
STG_E_INSUFFICIENTMEMORY	The stream could not be accessed due to lack of memory.
STG_E_INVALIDFLAG	A bad flag was passed into *grfStatFlag*.
STG_E_INVALIDPOINTER	A bad pointer was passed in for *pStatStg*.
STG_E_REVERTED	The object has been invalidated by a revert operation above it in the transaction tree.
STG_E_WRITEFAULT	Disk error during a write operation.
Other errors.	Any **ILockBytes** or system errors.

Comments

The values for *grfStatFlag* are taken from the enumeration **STATFLAG**, which is defined as follows:

```
typedef enum tagSTATFLAG
{
        STATFLAG_DEFAULT = 0,
        STATFLAG_NONAME  = 1
} STATFLAG;
```

See Also

IStorage::Stat, IEnumSTATSTG

IStream::Clone

HRESULT IStream::Clone(*ppStm*)
LPSTREAM FAR* *ppStm*

IStream::Clone returns a new **IStream** object that is a clone of this stream.

Parameters

ppStm
Points to where the new stream should be returned.

Return Values

Value	Meaning
S_OK	The stream was successfully copied.
STG_E_INSUFFICIENT-MEMORY	The stream could not be copied due to lack of memory.
STG_E_INVALIDPOINTER	A bad pointer was passed in for *ppStm*.
STG_E_REVERTED	The object has been invalidated by a revert operation above it in the transaction tree.
STG_E_WRITEFAULT	Disk error during a write operation.
E_OUTOFMEMORY	The stream could not be copied due to lack of memory.
Other errors.	Any **ILockBytes** or system errors.

Comments

The new **IStream** sees the same underlying stream data as does the original stream. Writes made through one instance are immediately visible through the other. Byte range locking is shared between the streams and a clone is not treated as "foreign" with respect to byte range locking. However, the cloned stream *does* have a seek pointer that is independent of the original. The initial setting of the seek pointer in the cloned stream is the same as the current setting of the seek pointer in the original at the time of the clone operation.

IRootStorage Interface

The **IRootStorage** interface is implemented by OLE and is used by containers to switch the underlying disk file that **IStorage** objects are being saved to. The interface contains the following method (see also STORAGE.H):

```
DECLARE_INTERFACE_(IRootStorage, IUnknown)
{
  // *** IUnknown methods ***
  HRESULT QueryInterface (THIS_ REFIID riid, LPVOID FAR* ppvObj);
  ULONG AddRef (THIS);
  ULONG Release (THIS);

  // *** IRootStorage methods ***
  HRESULT SwitchToFile (THIS_ LPSTR lpstrFile);
};
```

IRootStorage::SwitchToFile

HRESULT IRootStorage::SwitchToFile(*lpstrFile*)
LPSTR *lpstrFile*

IRootStorage::SwitchToFile makes a copy of the file underlying this **IStorage** in the file indicated by *lpstrFile*. Associates the **IStorage** object with this new file rather than with its current file, including uncommitted changes.

Parameters

lpstrFile
Specifies the filename of the new base file.

Return Values

Value	Meaning
S_OK	The file was successfully copied.
STG_E_INVALIDPARAMETER	One or more invalid arguments.
STG_E_MEDIUMFULL	The storage medium is full.
STG_E_ACCESSDENIED	Insufficient permissions to access the storage.
STG_E_REVERTED.	The object has been invalidated by a revert operation above it in the transaction tree.
STG_E_INVALIDPOINTER	A bad pointer was passed in for *lpstrFile*.
STG_E_FILEALREADYEXISTS.	The file specified by *lpstrFile* already exists.
System errors.	As in **ILockBytes**, a file can return any system error. Most notably, STG_* error codes from 0x001 to 0x057.

Comments

It is illegal to call **IRootStorage::SwitchToFile** if this **IStorage** or anything contained within it has been marshaled to another process. As a consequence, any embedded objects contained within the object owning this **IStorage** must be put in the hands off storage mode before calling this function.

IRootStorage::SwitchToFile operates without consuming any additional memory or file handles.

See Also

IPersistStorage::HandsOffStorage

ILockBytes Interface

The **ILockBytes** interface is implemented and used by OLE to manipulate the actual byte array underlying a root compound file. OLE provides an implementation of **ILockBytes** that can be used when the byte array is a real disk file, as is often the case.Some OLE containers are "database-like," meaning they store objects in places other than disk files. These containers can write their own **ILockBytes** implementation to direct data into their file system, or data store.

ILockBytes differs from **IStream** in that it has no seek pointer. Offsets are provided as part of the method call, rather than by an explicit seek pointer. However, some of the **ILockBytes** methods behave the same as in their **IStream** counterpart, such as **SetSize**, **LockRegion**, and **UnlockRegion**.

Compound files use region locking to negotiate permissions when several copies of OLE on remote systems contend for the same storage object. When the compound file implementation of either **IStorage** or **IStream** is being marshaled to another process, the underlying **ILockBytes** interface pointer is marshaled to the same destination process. This marshaling is typically done by the default remoting mechanism. At the destination, a proxy **ILockBytes** instance is created whose function implementations call back to the original **ILockBytes** instance. To make remote access more efficient, **ILockBytes** implementors should consider implementing custom marshaling using OLE's marshaling support. For more information, see the **IMarshal** interface.

The **ILockBytes** interface contains the following methods (see also STORAGE.H):

```
DECLARE_INTERFACE_(ILockBytes, IUnknown)
{
  // *** IUnknown methods ***
 HRESULT QueryInterface (THIS_ REFIID riid, LPVOID FAR* ppvObj);
 ULONG AddRef (THIS);
 ULONG Release (THIS);

  // *** ILockBytes methods ***
 HRESULT ReadAt (THIS_ ULARGE_INTEGER ulOffset, VOID HUGEP *pv, ULONG cb,
  ULONG FAR *pcbRead);
 HRESULT WriteAt (THIS_ ULARGE_INTEGER ulOffset, VOID const HUGEP *pv, ULONG cb,
  ULONG FAR *pcbWritten);
 HRESULT Flush (THIS);
 HRESULT SetSize (THIS_ ULARGE_INTEGER cb);
 HRESULT LockRegion (THIS_ ULARGE_INTEGER libOffset, ULARGE_INTEGER cb,
  DWORD dwLockType);
 HRESULT UnlockRegion (THIS_ ULARGE_INTEGER libOffset, ULARGE_INTEGER cb,
  DWORD dwLockType);
 HRESULT Stat (THIS_ STATSTG FAR *pStatStg, DWORD grfStatFlag);
};
```

ILockBytes::ReadAt

HRESULT ILockBytes::ReadAt(*ulOffset*, *pv*, *cb*, *pcbRead*)
ULARGE_INTEGER *ulOffset*
void HUGEP * *pv*
ULONG *cb*
ULONG FAR* *pcbRead*

ILockBytes::ReadAt reads a specified number of bytes from the **ILockBytes** byte array starting at a specified position.

Parameters

ulOffset
Specifies the offset in the byte array at which to begin reading.

pv
Points to the buffer into which the data should be read.

cb
Specifies the number of bytes to read.

pcbRead
Specifies (after the call) the number of bytes actually read. The caller can set *pcbRead* to NULL, indicating this value is not of interest. The *pcbRead* parameter is zero if there is an error.

Return Values

Value	Meaning
S_OK	Some or all of the data requested was read.
STG_E_ACCESSDENIED	The data could not be read due to insufficient access to the byte array.
E_FAIL	The data could not be read for reasons other than insufficient access.
STG_E_INVALIDHANDLE	An invalid floppy change has been made.
System errors.	The document file's **ILockBytes** on a file can return any system error. Most notably, STG_* error codes from 0x001 to 0x057.

Comments

The number of bytes actually read is always returned in *pcbRead*, even if an error is returned.

The number of bytes actually read might be less than requested if the end of the byte array is reached during the read operation. This is the same "end of file" behavior as presently found in MS-DOS FAT file system files.

See Also

ILockBytes::WriteAt

ILockBytes::WriteAt

HRESULT ILockBytes::WriteAt(*ulOffset*, *pv*, *cb*, *pcbWritten*)
ULARGE_INTEGER *ulOffset*
VOID const HUGEP * *pv*
ULONG *cb*
ULONG FAR* *pcbWritten*

ILockBytes::WriteAt writes data to the byte array.

Parameters

ulOffset
Specifies the offset in the byte array at which to begin writing the data.

pv
Points to the buffer containing the data to be written.

cb
Specifies the number of bytes to write.

pcbWritten
Specifies (after the call) the number of bytes actually read. The caller can set *pcbWritten* to NULL, indicating this value is not of interest. The *pcbWritten* parameter is zero if there is an error.

Return Values

Value	Meaning
S_OK	Some or all of the data requested was written.
STG_E_ACCESSDENIED	The data could not be written due to insufficient access to the byte array.
E_FAIL	The data could not be written for reasons other than insufficient access.
STG_E_MEDIUMFULL	**ILockBytes::WriteAt** return STG_E_MEDIUMFULL for disk-full rather than a partly-successful write as MS-DOS does.
STG_E_INVALIDHANDLE	An invalid floppy change has been made.
System errors.	The document file's **ILockBytes** on a file can return any system error. Most notably, STG_* error codes from 0x001 to 0x057.

Comments

If the offset specified by *ulOffset* is past the end of the byte array, **LockBytes::WriteAt** first increases the size of the byte array, filling it with bytes of an undefined value. This is not done if *cb* is zero, because writing a count of zero bytes is always a no-op.

The number of bytes actually written is returned in *pcbWritten*, even if an error is returned.

See Also

ILockBytes::ReadAt

ILockBytes::Flush

HRESULT ILockBytes::Flush()

ILockBytes::Flush ensures that any internal buffers maintained by the **ILockBytes** implementation are written out to the backing store.

Return Value

Value	Meaning
S_OK	The flush operation was successful.
STG_E_ACCESSDENIED	The data could not be written due to insufficient access to the backing store.
STG_E_MEDIUMFULL	The data could not be written due to insufficient space on the medium.
E_FAIL	The data could not be written for reasons other than insufficient access or no space left.
STG_E_TOOMANYFILESOPEN	Under certain circumstances, **Flush** does a dump-and-close to flush. This can lead to STG_E_TOOMANYFILESOPEN if there are no file handles available.
STG_E_INVALIDHANDLE	An invalid floppy change has been made.
System errors.	OLE's **ILockBytes** implementation on a file can return any system error. Most notably, STG_* error codes from 0x001 to 0x057.

Comments

ILockBytes::Flush is used by the OLE compound file implementation during a transacted commit operation to protect against loss of data.

See Also

IStorage::Commit

ILockBytes::SetSize

HRESULT ILockBytes::SetSize(*cb***)**
ULARGE_INTEGER *cb*

ILockBytes::SetSize changes the size of the byte array.

Parameters

cb
Specifies the new size of the byte array.

Return Value

Value	Meaning
S_OK	The size of the byte array was successfully changed.
STG_E_MEDIUMFULL	Data could not be written due to insufficient space on the storage medium.
STG_E_ACCESSDENIED	Insufficient permissions to byte array.
E_FAIL	The size of the byte array could not be changed due to miscellaneous errors.
STG_E_INVALIDHANDLE	An invalid floppy change has been made.
System errors.	OLE's **ILockBytes** implementation on a file can return any system error. Most notably, STG_* error codes from 0x001 to 0x057.

Comments

If the new size is larger than the current size of the byte array, **ILockBytes::SetSize** first extends the size of the byte array, filling it with bytes of an undefined value. If *cb* is smaller than the current size of the byte array, the array is truncated to the indicated size.

Note Callers cannot rely on STG_E_MEDIUMFULL being returned at the appropriate time because the MS-DOS FAT does not support this correctly. However, some **ILockBytes** implementations do support it so callers must be able to deal with this return code.

ILockBytes::LockRegion

HRESULT ILockBytes::LockRegion(*libOffset*, *cb*, *dwLockType*)
ULARGE_INTEGER *libOffset*
ULARGE_INTEGER *cb*
DWORD *dwLockType*

ILockBytes::LockRegion locks a range of bytes in the byte array.

Parameters

libOffset
Specifies the beginning of the region to lock.

cb
Specifies the number of bytes to lock.

dwLockType
Specifies the type of lock access; see the following comments.

Return Values

Value	Meaning
S_OK	The requested lock was granted.
STG_E_LOCKVIOLATION	The requested lock is supported, but cannot be presently granted because of an existing lock.
STG_E_INVALIDFUNCTION	Invalid value for *dwLockType*.
STG_E_SHAREREQUIRED	The 16-bit file implementation can return STG_E_SHAREREQUIRED if it is unable to lock because no sharing support is loaded.
STG_E_INVALIDHANDLE	An invalid floppy change has been made.
System errors.	The document file's **ILockBytes** on a file can return any system error. Most notably, STG_* error codes from 0x001 to 0x057.

Comments

The *libOffset* parameter specifies the beginning of the lock range, extending *cb* bytes towards the end of the array. The range of bytes can extend past the current end of the array.

Region locking is optional for **ILockBytes** implementors. Whether region locking is supported depends on how the storage objects constructed on top of the byte array are used. If it can be known that, at any one time, only one storage object is to be opened on the storage behind the byte array, region locking can be ignored. However, if the **ILockBytes** is built on top of a disk file, multiple simultaneous openings of a storage object are possible and region locking is needed to coordinate these accesses.

The lock type is specified by *dwLockType*, using one of the following values from the **LOCKTYPE** enumeration, defined in Storage.H as follows:

```
typedef enum tagLOCKTYPE{
    LOCK_WRITE      = 1,
    LOCK_EXCLUSIVE  = 2,
    LOCK_ONLYONCE   = 4,
}LOCKTYPE;
```

A given **ILockBytes** instance might support one or all types. OLE's compound file implementation onlysupports LOCK_ONLYONCE. These values have the following meaning:

Types of Locks	Purpose
LOCK_WRITE	If the lock is granted, reading the specified region of the stream can be done by calling **IStream::Read** from any opening of this stream. Attempts to write to this region from any opening of this stream other than the one to which the lock was granted returns the error STG_E_ACCESSDENIED.

Types of Locks	Purpose
LOCK_EXCLUSIVE	Attempts to read or write this stream by other stream openings return the error STG_E_ACCESSDENIED.
LOCK_ONLYONCE	If the lock is granted, no other LOCK_ONLYONCE lock can be obtained on the bytes in the given region. Usually this lock type is an alias for some other lock type and other semantics might occur as a side effect.

For information on how a caller can determine whether locking is supported; see **ILockBytes::Stat** and its parameter block **STATSTG**.

See Also **IStream::LockRegion, ILockBytes::UnlockRegion**

ILockBytes::UnlockRegion

HRESULT ILockBytes::UnlockRegion(*libOffset, cb, dwLockType***)**
ULARGE_INTEGER *libOffset*
ULARGE_INTEGER *cb*
DWORD *dwLockType*

ILockBytes::UnlockRegion unlocks a region previously locked with **ILockBytes::LockRegion**.

Parameters

libOffset
Specifies the beginning of the region to unlock.

cb
Specifies the number of bytes to unlock.

dwLockType
Specifies the type of lock access.

Return Values

Value	Meaning
S_OK	The requested unlock was granted.
STG_E_LOCKVIOLATION	The requested unlock cannot be granted.
STG_E_INVALIDFUNCTION	Invalid value for *dwLockType*.
STG_E_INVALIDHANDLE	An invalid floppy change has been made.
System errors.	OLE's **ILockBytes** implementation on a file can return any system error. Most notably, STG_* error codes from 0x001 to 0x057.

Comments

Any locked region must be explicitly unlocked using **ILockBytes::UnlockRegion**, using exactly the same *libOffset*, *cb*, and *dwLockType* parameters that were specified in the original **ILockBytes::LockRegion** call. Two adjacent regions cannot be locked separately and then unlocked with a single unlock call.

See Also

ILockBytes::LockRegion

ILockBytes::Stat

HRESULT ILockBytes::Stat(*pStatStg*, *grfStatFlag*)
LPSTATSTG *pStatStg*
DWORD *grfStatFlag*

ILockBytes::Stat returns relevant statistics about this byte array.

Parameters

pStatStg
Points to a **STATSTG** structure filled with statistics about this byte array; will be zero if an error occurs. For more information, see the **STATSTG** structure at the beginning of this chapter.

grfStatFlag
Specifies the level of statistics to return for this object. For more information, see the following comments.

Return Values

Value	Meaning
S_OK	Stat operation was successful.
STG_E_ACCESSDENIED	Statistics cannot be returned because access to the byte array cannot be granted.
E_OUTOFMEMORY	Memory not available for stat operation.
E_FAIL	Stat operation did not succeed due to errors other than lack of access or available memory.
STG_E_INSUFFICIENTMEMORY	The name cannot be allocated.
STG_E_UNKNOWN	The file time can't be converted to FILETIME format.
STG_E_INVALIDHANDLE	An invalid floppy change has been made.
System errors.	The document file's **ILockBytes** on a file can return any system error. Most notably, STG_* error codes from 0x001 to 0x057.

Comments

The **ILockBytes::Stat** call is used by the compound file implementation to respond to an **IStorage::Stat** call invoked on a root storage object.

If no reasonably interpretable name for the **ILockBytes** exists, this function should return NULL in *pStatStg->pwcsName*.

The values for *grfStatFlag* are taken from the enumeration of **STATFLAG**, which is defined as follows:

```
typedef enum tagSTATFLAG
{
    STATFLAG_DEFAULT = 0,
    STATFLAG_NONAME  = 1
} STATFLAG;
```

See Also **IEnumSTATSTG** Interface

IPersist Interface

The **IPersist** interface is the base interface from which the **IPersistStorage**, **IPersistStream**, and **IPersistFile** interfaces are derived. **IPersist** is implemented by object applications and used by container applications to get the CLSID associated with an object.

IPersist consists of the following methods (see also OLE2.H):

```
DECLARE_INTERFACE_(IPersistStorage, IPersist)
{
  // *** IUnknown methods ***
 HRESULT QueryInterface (THIS_ REFIID riid, LPVOID FAR* ppvObj);
 ULONG AddRef (THIS);
 ULONG Release (THIS);

  // *** IPersist methods ***
 HRESULT GetClassID (THIS_ LPCLSID pclsid);
};
```

IPersist::GetClassID

HRESULT IPersist::GetClassID(*pclsid***)**
pclsid

IPersist::GetClassID returns a document object's CLSID.

Parameter *pclsid*
Points to where to return the CLSID.

Return Values

Value	Meaning
S_OK	The CLSID was successfully returned.
E_FAIL	The CLSID could not be returned.

Comments

The returned CLSID can be used to locate and dynamically load object-specific code into the caller's context.

When an object is being treated as an object of a different class (that is, an object that is normally edited by class A is currently being edited as class B), the CLSID returned from **IPersistStorage::GetClassID** is different that the CLSID of the current editor. The current editor may want to change the object's CLSID in the file so that the original editor (or a different one altogether) would no longer be able to edit theobject. For example, it might be desirable to change the CLSID of an object from an old version of an application that is being treated as an object from a new version after the addition of a feature that is unintelligible to the old version. The object would change what it returns from **IPersistStorage::GetClassID**.

To change the persistent representation of an object's CLSID, an application must initiate a save and directly (if the object is a file-level link source) or indirectly (if the object is an embedding) cause the new CLSID to be written to the storage. The OnSave notification should be sent to all of the object's clients, informing them of the need to update their notion of the CLSID.

Example

The following example shows the **GetClassID** method for an object application that supports emulating objects of different types. In the example, the application checks to see whether it is currently performing a "Treat As" operation, in which case it would return the CLSID of the object it is emulating. A simple application would just return its own CLSID.

For more information on converting and emulating objects of different classes, see the chapter "Component Object Interfaces and Functions."

```
HRESULT IPersist_GetClassID(
        LPPERSISTSTORAGE        lpThis,
        LPCLSID                 pclsid)
{
    LPDOC lpDoc =
        ((struct CDocPersistStorageImpl FAR*)lpThis)->lpDoc;
    if (bTreatAs)  {
        if (! IsEqualCLSID(&lpDoc->m_clsidTreatAs, &CLSID_NULL))
            *pclsid = lpDoc->m_clsidTreatAs;
        else
            *pclsid = CLSID_APP;
    }
    else
        *pclsid = CLSID_APP;
    return NOERROR;
}
```

IPersistFile Interface

The **IPersistFile** interface is implemented by object applications and optionally by container applications.

IPersistFile permits applications to load and save documents stored in disk files (as opposed to objects stored in **IStorage** instances). Because the information needed to open a file varies from one application to another, the application is responsible for opening the file. Generally, **IPersistFile** is used to bind a linked object. In the container's case, this would be a link to an embedded object).

IPersistFile contains the following methods (see also OLE2.H):

```
DECLARE_INTERFACE_(IPersistFile, IPersist)
{
  // *** IUnknown methods ***
 HRESULT QueryInterface (THIS_ REFIID riid, LPVOID FAR* ppvObj);
 ULONG AddRef (THIS);
 ULONG Release (THIS);

  // *** IPersist methods ***
 HRESULT GetClassID (THIS_ LPCLSID pclsid);

  // *** IPersistFile methods ***
 HRESULT IsDirty (THIS);
 HRESULT Load (THIS_ LPCSTR lpszFileName, DWORD grfMode);
 HRESULT Save (THIS_ LPCSTR lpszFileName, BOOL fRemember);
 HRESULT SaveCompleted (THIS_ LPCSTR lpszFileName);
 HRESULT GetCurFile (THIS_ LPSTR FAR * lplpszFileName);
};
```

IPersistFile::IsDirty

HRESULT IPersistFile::IsDirty()

IPersistFile::IsDirty checks a document object for changes since it was last saved.

Return Value

Value	Meaning
S_OK	The object has changed.
S_FALSE	The object has not changed.

Comments

The dirty flag is conditionally cleared in **IPersistFile::Save**. A simple object with no contained objects simply checks its dirty flag. A container with one or more contained objects need to maintain an internal dirty flag that reflects any one object being dirty. In practice, recursive polling isn't needed in the **IsDirty** method; rather, a container can keep its internal dirty flag up to date by the appropriate use of **IAdviseSink::OnDataChange** notifications.

Example

In the following example, **IsDirty** returns NOERROR if the object is dirty; otherwise it returns S_FALSE.

```
HRESULT IPersistFile_IsDirty(LPPERSISTFILE lpThis)
{
    LPDOC lpDoc = ((struct IPersistFileImpl FAR*)lpThis)->lpDoc;

    if (lpDoc->m_cfModified)
        return ResultFromScode(S_OK);
    else
        return ResultFromScode(S_FALSE);
}
```

See Also

IPersistFile::Save

IPersistFile::Load

HRESULT IPersistFile::Load(*lpszFileName*, *grfMode***)**
LPCSTR *lpszFileName*
DWORD *grfMode*

IPersistFile::Load loads the document object contained in the given filename.

Parameters

lpszFileName
Points to the absolute path of the file to open.

grfMode
Specifies the access mode with which the caller intends to use the file. The values for this parameter are described under "Storage Access Mode Flags" earlier in this chapter.

Return Values

IPersistFile::Load can return any of the error codes that begin with STG_E, in addition to the following codes.

Value	Meaning
S_OK	The document was successfully loaded.
E_FAIL	The document could not be loaded.
E_OUTOFMEMORY	There is not enough memory to load the document.

Comments

The filename must be an absolute path. **IPersistFile::Load** is an initialization function only and it does not show the loaded document to the user.

The *grfMode* values express only the intent that the caller has in opening the file. The application can add more restrictive permissions as necessary. Zero is a valid value; the object should interpret the request as though the user opened the file using default values.

IPersistFile::Load is called by the File Moniker implementation of **IMoniker::BindToObject**.

Example

In the following example for an object application, **IPersistFile::Load** loads the object into memory with read-write permission. Because the object loads all information into memory at load time, it closes the file after loading.

```
HRESULT IPersistFile_Load (LPPERSISTFILE lpThis,
                LPCSTR lpszFileName, DWORD grfMode)
{
    LPDOC lpDoc = ((struct IPersistFileImpl FAR*)lpThis)->lpDoc;
    SCODE sc;
    HRESULT         hrErr;
    LPSTORAGE       lpSrcStg;
    BOOL            fStatus;

    hrErr = StgOpenStorage(lpszFileName,
            NULL,
            STGM_READ | STGM_SHARE_DENY_WRITE,
            NULL,
            0,
            &lpSrcStg);

    sc = GetScode(hrErr);
    if ( (sc == STG_E_FILENOTFOUND) ||
         (sc == STG_E_FILEALREADYEXISTS) ||(sc != S_OK) )
            return ResultFromScode(E_FAIL);

    //Load the object
    if(! LoadDocFromStg(lpDoc, lpSrcStg))
        return ResultFromScode(E_FAIL);

    //Register the object in the running object table
    fStatus = SetDocFileName(lpDoc, lpszFileName, lpSrcStg);
    if (! fStatus)
        return ResultFromScode(E_FAIL);

    //Release the storage
    (LPUNKNOWN)lpSrcStg->lpVtbl->Release(LPUNKNOWN(lpSrcStg);
    return ResultFromScode(S_OK);
}
```

See Also **IMoniker::BindToObject**

IPersistFile::Save

HRESULT IPersistFile::Save(*lpszFileName, fRemember***)**
LPCSTR *lpszFileName*
BOOL *fRemember*

IPersistFile::Save saves a copy of the object to the indicated filename.

Parameters

lpszFileName
Points to the file in which the document should be saved.

fRemember
Determines which disk file the document is to be logically associated with after the call is completed. Valid only if *lpszFileName* is non-NULL.

Return Values

IPersistFile::Save can return any of the error codes beginning with STG_E in addition to the following codes.

Value	Meaning
S_OK	The file was successfully saved.
E_FAIL	The file could not be saved.

Comments

The *lpszFileName* parameter can be NULL, indicating that a simple "File Save" operation is requested to the now-current filename. A non-NULL value indicates either a "File Save As" or a "File Save Copy As" operation. In this case, the full path of the destination file is specified in the *lpszFileName* parameter.

The *fRemember* parameter determines whether a "Save As" or a "Save Copy As" operation is requested by the user. If *fRemember* is TRUE, the file pointed to by *lpszFileName* should become the current working copy of the document ("Save As"). FALSE indicates that after completing the **IPersistFile::Save** call, the working copy should be whatever it was before **IPersistFile::Save** was called ("Save Copy As").

If, upon exiting, the saved file is the current working copy, the internal dirty flag maintained by the object should be cleared and the container must call **IPersistFile::SaveCompleted** at some later time when it is done with the data in the file.

Whenever a file is saved with a new name, the object should send a rename notification (call **IAdviseSink::OnRename**) to its existing advisory connections.

Some clients of objects might find calling **IPersistFile::Save** useful for programmatically manipulating documents. **IPersistFile::Save** is not called by OLE.

Example

In the following example, **Save** checks *fRemember* and *lpszFileName* to see which type of save operation is needed to save the object.

```
HRESULT IPersistFile_Save (LPPERSISTFILE lpThis,
                          LPCSTR lpszFileName,BOOL fRemember)
{
    LPDOC lpDoc =((struct CDocPersistFileImpl FAR*)lpThis)->lpDoc;
    SCODE sc;
    LPSTORAGE lpDestStg = NULL;
    HRESULT hrErr;
    BOOL fStatus;

    // Can only save file-based documents
    if ( (lpszFileName==NULL ||
         (lpszFileName != NULL && fRemember)) &&
         ((lpDoc->m_docInitType != DOCTYPE_FROMFILE &&
           lpDoc->m_docInitType != DOCTYPE_NEW)) ) {
        return ResultFromScode(E_INVALIDARG);
    }

    if (fRemember) {
        if (lpszFileName) {
            fStatus = SetDocFileName(lpDoc,
                    (LPSTR)lpszFileName, NULL);
            if (! fStatus) goto error;
        } else
            // use current filename
            lpszFileName = lpDoc->m_szFileName;
    } else if (! lpszFileName)
        return ResultFromScode(E_FAIL);

    hrErr = StgCreateDocfile(lpszFileName,
      STGM_READWRITE|STGM_DIRECT|STGM_SHARE_EXCLUSIVE|STGM_CREATE,
      0, &lpDestStg);
    if (hrErr != NOERROR)
        return ResultFromScode(E_FAIL);

    if(WriteClassStg(lpDestStg, &CLSID_APP) != NOERROR)
        return ResultFromScode(E_FAIL);

    fStatus = SaveDocSelToStg(lpDoc, NULL, uFormat, lpDestStg,
                FALSE, fRemember);
    if (! fStatus)
        return ResultFromScode(E_FAIL);

    (LPUNKNOWN)lpDestStg->lpVtbl->Release((LPUNKNOWN)lpDestStg);
```

```
        if (fRemember)
            SetDocModified(lpDoc, FALSE, FALSE, FALSE);

        SendAdvise ((LPDOC)lpDoc,  OLE_ONSAVE,  NULL, 0);
        return ResultFromScode(S_OK);
}
```

See Also **IPersistFile::SaveCompleted**

IPersistFile::SaveCompleted

HRESULT IPersistFile::SaveCompleted(*lpszFileName*)
LPCSTR *lpszFileName*

IPersistFile::SaveCompleted indicates the caller has saved the file with a call to **IPersistFile::Save** and is finished working with it.

Parameters

lpszFileName
Points to the filename in which the document was saved.

Return Value

Value	Meaning
S_OK	S_OK is returned in all cases.

Example

The following **IPersistFile::SaveCompleted** sample does nothing more than return NOERROR. This is because the object application never allows scribbling to its file after an object has been saved. Had the object been allowed to scribble to its storage, it would have needed to clear the no scribble bit set in the call to **IPersistFile::Save**.

```
HRESULT IPersistFile_SaveCompleted (LPPERSISTFILE lpThis,
                                    LPCSTR lpszFileName)
{
    return NOERROR;
}
```

See Also **IAdviseSink::OnSave, IPersistFile::Save**

IPersistFile::GetCurFile

HRESULT IPersistFile::GetCurFile(*lplpszFileName*)
LPSTR FAR * *lplpszFileName*

IPersistFile::GetCurFile returns either the absolute path of the document's currently-associated file, or the default filename prompt, if there is no currently-associated file.

Parameters

lplpszFileName
Points to where to return the current path or the default save prompt of the document, as appropriate.

Return Values

Value	Meaning
S_OK	The return value is a pathname.
S_FALSE	The return value is the save prompt.
E_OUTOFMEMORY	Not enough memory to successfully return a value.
E_FAIL	Failure due to reasons other than insufficient memory.

Example

In the following example, **GetCurFile** ensures that memory for the *lpszFileName* has been properly allocated using a registered instance of the **IMalloc** interface. **GetCurFile** then checks to see whether there is a valid filename (DOCTYPE_FROMFILE TRUE) passed in. **GetCurFile** releases the **IMalloc** instance just before returning.

```
HRESULT IPersistFile_GetCurFile (LPPERSISTFILE lpThis,
                         LPSTR FAR* lplpszFileName)
{
    LPDOC lpDoc = ((struct CDocPersistFileImpl FAR*)lpThis)->lpDoc;
    LPMALLOC lpMalloc;
    LPSTR lpsz;
    SCODE sc;

    *lplpszFileName = NULL;

/*********************************************************************
    ** OLE2NOTE: Memory returned for the lplpszFileName must be
    **    allocated appropriately using the currently registered IMalloc
    **    interface. This allows ownership of the memory to be
    **    passed to the caller, even if in another process.

*********************************************************************/
    CoGetMalloc(MEMCTX_TASK, &lpMalloc);
    if (! lpMalloc) {
        return ResultFromScode(E_FAIL);
    }

    if (lpDoc->m_docInitType == DOCTYPE_FROMFILE) {
        /* valid filename associated; return filename */
        lpsz = (LPSTR)lpMalloc->lpVtbl->Alloc(
                lpMalloc,
```

```
                lstrlen((LPSTR)lpDoc->m_szFileName)+1);
        if (!lpsz){
            sc = E_OUTOFMEMORY;
            goto error;
        {
        lstrcpy(lpsz, (LPSTR)lpDoc->m_szFileName);
        sc = S_OK;
    } else {
        /* no file associated; return default file save prompt */
        lpsz=(LPSTR)lpMalloc->lpVtbl->Alloc(lpMalloc, sizeof(DEFEXTENSION)+3);
        wsprintf(lpsz, "*.%s", DEFEXTENSION);
        sc = S_FALSE;
    }

error:
    (LPUNKNOWN)lpMalloc->lpVtbl->Release((LPUNKNOWN)lpMalloc);
    *lplpszFileName = lpsz;
    return ResultFromScode(sc);
}
```

IPersistStorage Interface

The **IPersistStorage** interface is implemented by object applications and/or object handlers. The interface's methods are used by OLE and container applications to manipulate an object's **IStorage**.

IPersistStorage consists of the following methods (see also OLE2.H):

```
DECLARE_INTERFACE_(IPersistStorage, IPersist)
{
  // *** IUnknown methods ***
  HRESULT QueryInterface (THIS_ REFIID riid, LPVOID FAR* ppvObj);
  ULONG AddRef (THIS);
  ULONG Release (THIS);

  // *** IPersist methods ***
  HRESULT GetClassID (THIS_ LPCLSID pclsid);

  // *** IPersistStorage methods ***
  HRESULT IsDirty (THIS);
  HRESULT InitNew (THIS_ LPSTORAGE pStg);
  HRESULT Load (THIS_ LPSTORAGE pStg);
  HRESULT Save (THIS_ LPSTORAGE pStgSave, BOOL fSameAsLoad);
  HRESULT SaveCompleted (THIS_ LPSTORAGE pStgNew);
  HRESULT HandsOffStorage (THIS);
};
```

IPersistStorage::IsDirty

HRESULT IPersistStorage::IsDirty()

IPersistStorage::IsDirty checks an object for changes since it was last saved.

Return Values

Value	Meaning
S_OK	The object has changed since the last save.
S_FALSE	The object has not changed since the last save.
E_OUTOFMEMORY	Memory constraints prohibit the successful determination of whether the object has changed.
E_FAIL	It is not possible to determine whether or not the object has changed due to errors other than lack of memory.

Comments

Logically, the same sort of recursive calls to currently loaded objects must be done as in **IPersistStorage::Save**. Thus, an object is dirty if it or any of its contained objects are dirty. In practice, recursive polling is not needed in the **IsDirty** method. Rather, a container can keep its internal dirty flag up to date by the appropriate use of **IAdviseSink::OnDataChange** notifications.

The dirty flag must be conditionally cleared in the subsequent call to **IPersistStorage::Save**.

Example

In the following example, **IsDirty** returns NOERROR if the document or any contained objects have changed; otherwise, it returns S_FALSE.

```
HRESULT  IPersistStg_IsDirty(LPPERSISTSTORAGE  lpThis)
{
    LPDOC lpDoc = ((struct IPersistStorageImpl FAR*)lpThis)->lpDoc;

    if (lpDoc->m_cfModified)
        return NOERROR;
    else
        return ResultFromScode(S_FALSE);
}
```

See Also

IAdviseSink::OnDataChange, IPersistStorage::Save

IPersistStorage::InitNew

HRESULT IPersistStorage::InitNew(*pStg*)
LPSTORAGE *pStg*

IPersistStorage::InitNew initializes the specified **IStorage** object.

Parameters

pStg
Points to the **IStorage** instance to initialize.

Return Values

Value	Meaning
S_OK	The new **IStorage** instance successfully returned.
CO_E_ALREADYINITIALIZED	This **IStorage** instance has already been initialized.
E_OUTOFMEMORY	Memory constraints prohibit the successful initialization of the **IStorage** instance.
E_FAIL	The **IStorage** instance could not be initialized due to errors other than lack of memory.

Comments

An object that uses **IPersistStorage** must have access to a valid **IStorage** instance at all times while it is running. This includes the time just after the object has been created but before it has been made persistent. The object's container must provide the object with access to an **IStorage** instance during this time by calling **IPersistStorage::InitNew**. Depending on the container's state, a temporary file might need to be created for this purpose.

If the object wants to retain the **IStorage** instance, it must call **AddRef** to increment its reference count.

Example

The following **IPersistStorage::InitNew** example calls **WriteFmtUserTypeStg** to save the object's data format to storage before initializing the document as one that contains an embedded object. Because an object should not open any storage or streams during an **IPersistStorage::Save** call (to preserve existing memory in case of low-memory saves), this **InitNew** example opens necessary streams ahead of time.

```
HRESULT IPersistStg_InitNew(LPPERSISTSTORAGE lpThis,
                            LPSTORAGE pStg)
{
    LPDOC lpDoc = ((struct IPersistStorageImpl FAR*)lpThis)->lpDoc;
    LPAPP lpApp = (LPAPP)g_lpApp;
    LPSTR lpszUserType = (LPSTR)FULLUSERTYPENAME;
    HRESULT hrErr;
    SCODE sc;
```

```
    WriteFmtUserTypeStg(pStg,lpApp->m_cfPrivate,lpszUserType);

    // set the document to a new embedded object.
    if (! InitDocNewEmbed(lpDoc)) {
        sc = E_FAIL;
        goto error;
    }

    lpDoc->m_dwStorageMode = STGMODE_NORMAL;

    /*   An object application CANNOT open or create any streams or
    **   storages when IPersistStorage::Save(fSameAsLoad==TRUE) is
    **   called. Thus, an embedded object should hold onto its storage
    **   and pre-open and hold open any streams it might need later
    **   to guarantee that it can save in low memory situations.
    */
    hrErr = pStg->lpVtbl->CreateStream(
            pStg,
            "LineList",
            STGM_WRITE | STGM_SHARE_EXCLUSIVE | STGM_CREATE,
            0,
            0,
            &lpDoc->m_lpLLStm);

    if (hrErr != NOERROR) {
        sc = GetScode(hrErr);
        goto error;
    }

    if (hrErr != NOERROR) {
        sc = GetScode(hrErr);
        goto error;
    }

    lpOleDoc->m_pStg = pStg;

    // OLE2NOTE: Hold onto IStorage* pointer, by calling AddRef on it
    pStg->lpVtbl->AddRef(pStg);
    return NOERROR;

error:
    return ResultFromScode(sc);
}
```

See Also **IUnknown::AddRef**

IPersistStorage::Load

HRESULT IPersistStorage::Load(*pStg*)
LPSTORAGE *pStg*

IPersistStorage::Load loads an object into memory or in the running state, depending on whether the container or object handler calls the method.

Parameters

pStg
Points to the **IStorage** instance from which to load or run the object.

Return Values

Value	Meaning
S_OK	The object was loaded successfully.
CO_E_ALREADYINITIALIZED	The object was already loaded.
E_OUTOFMEMORY	Memory constraints prohibit the object from loading.
E_FAIL	The object could not be loaded due to errors other than lack of memory.
IStorage errors	Can also return any of the error codes from **IStorage** methods.

Comments

When **IPersistStorage::Load** is called by the container on the object handler, **Load** places the object in the loaded state. When **IPersistStorage::Load** is called by the object handler, **Load** places the object in the running state.

The **IStorage** instance passed in *pStg* contains the persistent representation of the object created when **IPersistStorage::Save** was called. The object should load whatever state information it needs. The object handler and/or object can hold onto the open **IStorage** instance while it is in the loaded or running state.

Example

In the following example, **IPersistStorage::Load** checks to see whether the object is being converted to another class of object. If it is, **Load** sets the dirty flag on the document (to force a save of the object to its new **IStorage** when the document is closed). To ensure that it can save in low memory situations, **Load** pre-opens its needed data streams before calling **AddRef** on the object's **IStorage**.

For more information on converting objects of one class type to another, see the chapter, "Component Object Interfaces and Functions."

```
HRESULT IPersistStg_Load(LPPERSISTSTORAGE lpThis,
                                  LPSTORAGE pStg)
{
    LPDOC lpDoc = ((struct IPersistStorageImpl FAR*)lpThis)->lpDoc;
    SCODE sc;
    HRESULT hrErr;
```

```
if (LoadDocFromStg((LPDOC)lpDoc, pStg)) {
    ((LPDOC)lpDoc)->m_docInitType = DOCTYPE_EMBEDDED;

    lpDoc->m_dwStorageMode = STGMODE_NORMAL;

    /* Check if the ConvertStg bit is on. If
    ** so, clear the ConvertStg bit and mark the
    ** document as dirty so as to force a save when the document
    ** is closed. The actual conversion of the bits should be
    ** performed when the data is loaded from the IStorage*.
    ** Any conversion of data formats would be done in
    ** ServerDoc_LoadFromStg function.
    */
    if (GetConvertStg(pStg) == NOERROR) {
        SetConvertStg(pStg, FALSE);

        //set dirty flag to document
        ServerDoc_m_cfModified = TRUE;
    }

} else {
    sc = E_FAIL;
    goto error;
}

/* Pre-open and hold open any streams needed to guarantee saves
   during low memory conditions.
*/
if (lpDoc->m_lpLLStm)
    OleStdRelease((LPUNKNOWN)lpDoc->m_lpLLStm);
hrErr = pStg->lpVtbl->OpenStream(
        pStg,
        "LineList",
        NULL,
        STGM_READWRITE | STGM_SHARE_EXCLUSIVE,
        0,
        &lpDoc->m_lpLLStm);

if (hrErr != NOERROR) {
    sc = GetScode(hrErr);
    goto error;
}

if (lpDoc->m_lpNTStm)
    OleStdRelease((LPUNKNOWN)lpDoc->m_lpNTStm);
hrErr = pStg->lpVtbl->OpenStream(
        pStg,
        "NameTable",
        NULL,
        STGM_READWRITE | STGM_SHARE_EXCLUSIVE,
```

```
                0,
                &lpDoc->m_lpNTStm);

    if (hrErr != NOERROR) {
        sc = GetScode(hrErr);
        goto error;
    }

    lpDoc->m_pStg = pStg;

    // Hold onto IStorage* pointer, by calling AddRef on it
    pStg->lpVtbl->AddRef(pStg);

    return NOERROR;

error:
    return ResultFromScode(sc);
}
```

See Also **IPersistStorage::Save**

IPersistStorage::Save

HRESULT IPersistStorage::Save(*pStgSave*, *fSameAsLoad***)**
LPSTORAGE *pStgSave*
BOOL *fSameAsLoad*

IPersistStorage::Save saves an object to storage, including any nested objects.

Parameters

pStgSave
Points to the **IStorage** instance in which the object is to be saved.

fSameAsLoad
Indicates whether *pStgSave* is the same **IStorage** instance from which the object was loaded or just created.

Return Values

Value	Meaning
S_OK	The object was loaded successfully.
STG_E_MEDIUMFULL	The object could not be saved due to lack of disk space.
E_FAIL	The object could not be saved due to errors other than lack of memory.

Comments

If *fSameAsLoad* is TRUE, the object writes incremental changes to *pStgSave*. If *fSameAsLoad* is FALSE, the caller is either cloning the object or responding to a Save As request and the object must copy all of its state to the new storage. Any state information from the object's old storage (the storage from which the object was loaded) must also be saved.

IPersistStorage::Save saves any currently-loaded nested objects within the object by recursively calling **IPersistStorage::Save**, **OleSave**, or **IStorage::CopyTo**. Nonloaded nested objects do not need to have anything done to them (*fSameAsLoad* is TRUE) or they can be handled by copying their storage objects (*fSameAsLoad* is FALSE).

The object should not call **IStorage::Commit** on *pStgSave*. It is the responsibility of the caller to deal with the newly-saved changes. Often, the caller is using the transaction support, so it is appropriate to commit the changes with **IPersistStorage::Commit**. The object should *not* write its CLSID to *pStgSave* because this too is to be done by the caller.

After the save, it is the callee's responsibility to put the object in the no scribble state. This temporarily revokes the object's right to write to its **IStorage** until **IPersistStorage::SaveCompleted** is called—a call that *must* be made after **IPersistStorage::Save** is called. When **SaveCompleted** is called, the object should, if necessary, clear the dirty flag reported by **IPersistStorage::IsDirty**. Because the storage is off limits between the time **Save** is completed and **SaveCompleted** is called, the caller of **Save** should call **SaveCompleted** as quickly as possible.

If *pStgSave* is not the current storage for the object (*fSameAsLoad* is FALSE) when the function exits, *pStgSave* can no longer be used.

Implementations of **IPersistStorage::Save** generally call **WriteFmtUserTypeStg** internally.

Example

In the following example, **Save** saves the dirty object(s) to storage and then puts the storage in the no scribble state, where it remains until **SaveCompleted** is called.

```
HRESULT IPersistStg_SaveCompleted(
        LPPERSISTSTORAGE        lpThis,
        LPSTORAGE               pStgNew)
{
    LPDOC lpDoc =
            ((struct CDocPersistStorageImpl FAR*)lpThis)->lpDoc;
    HRESULT hrErr;

    /* OLE2NOTE: This sample application is a pure object application.
    **    a container/object application would have to call
    **    SaveCompleted for each of its contained compound document
    **    objects. if a new storage was given, then the container/object
```

```
**    would have to open the corresponding new sub-storage for each
**    compound document object and pass as an argument in the
**    SaveCompleted call.
*/

/* OLE2NOTE: it is only legal to perform a Save or SaveAs operation
**    on an embedded object. if the document is a file-based
**    documentthen we can not be changed to a IStorage-base object.
**
**      fSameAsLoad   pStgNew     Type of Save     Send OnSave
**    ---------------------------------------------------------
**         TRUE        NULL        SAVE              YES
**         TRUE        ! NULL      SAVE *            YES
**         FALSE       ! NULL      SAVE AS           YES
**         FALSE       NULL        SAVE COPY AS      NO
**
**    * This is a strange case that is possible. It is inefficient
**    for the caller; it would be better to pass pStgNew==NULL for
**    the Save operation.
*/
if ( ((lpDoc->m_fSaveWithSameAsLoad && pStgNew==NULL) || pStgNew)
      && (lpOutlineDoc->m_docInitType != DOCTYPE_EMBEDDED) ) {
    return ResultFromScode(E_INVALIDARG);
}
/* OLE2NOTE: Inform any linking clients that the document has been
**    saved. In addition, any currently active pseudo objects
**    should also inform their clients. Object should only broadcast
**    an OnSave notification if a Save or SaveAs operation was
**    performed. Object should NOT want to send the notification if
**    a SaveCopyAs operation was performed.
*/
if (pStgNew || lpDoc->m_fSaveWithSameAsLoad) {

    /* OLE2NOTE: If IPersistStorage::Save has been called, then
    **    object needs to clear the dirty bit and send OnSave
    **    notification. If HandsOffStorage is called directly
    **    without first calling Save, then object does NOT clear
    **    the dirty bit and send OnSave when SaveCompleted is
    **    called.
    */
    if (lpDoc->m_fNoScribbleMode) {
        OutlineDoc_SetModified(lpOutlineDoc, FALSE, FALSE, FALSE);
        ServerDoc_SendAdvise (
                lpDoc,
                OLE_ONSAVE,
                NULL,    /* lpmkDoc -- not relevant here */
                0);      /* advf -- not relevant here */
    }
    lpDoc->m_fSaveWithSameAsLoad = FALSE;
}
```

```
    lpDoc->m_fNoScribbleMode = FALSE;

    /* OLE2NOTE: An embedded object must guarantee that it can save
    **    even in low memory situations. it must be able to
    **    successfully save itself without consuming any additional
    **    memory. this means that an object app is NOT supposed to open
    **    or create any streams or storages when
    **    IPersistStorage::Save(fSameAsLoad==TRUE) is called. thus an
    **    embedded object should hold onto its storage and pre-open and
    **    hold open any streams that it will need later when it is time
    **    to save. if this is a SaveAs situtation, then we want to
    **    pre-open and hold open our streams to guarantee that a
    **    subsequent save will be successful in low-memory. if we fail
    **    to open these streams then we want to force ourself to close
    **    to make sure the can't make editing changes that can't be
    **    later saved.
    */
    if ( pStgNew && !lpDoc->m_fSaveWithSameAsLoad ) {

        // release previous streams
        if (lpOleDoc->m_lpLLStm) {
            OleStdRelease((LPUNKNOWN)lpOleDoc->m_lpLLStm);
            lpOleDoc->m_lpLLStm = NULL;
        }
        if (lpOleDoc->m_pStg) {
            OleStdRelease((LPUNKNOWN)lpOleDoc->m_pStg);
            lpOleDoc->m_pStg = NULL;
        }

        hrErr = pStgNew->lpVtbl->OpenStream(
                pStgNew,
                "LineList",
                NULL,
                STGM_READWRITE | STGM_SHARE_EXCLUSIVE,
                0,
                &lpOleDoc->m_lpLLStm);
        if (hrErr != NOERROR) {
            goto error;
        }
        lpOleDoc->m_pStg = pStgNew;

        // OLE2NOTE: to hold onto IStorage* pointer, we must AddRef it
        pStgNew->lpVtbl->AddRef(pStgNew);
    }

    return NOERROR;

error:
    return ResultFromScode(E_OUTOFMEMORY);
}
```

See Also **OleSave**, **IStorage::CopyTo**, **IStorage::Commit**

IPersistStorage::SaveCompleted

HRESULT IPersistStorage::SaveCompleted(*pStgNew*)
LPSTORAGE *pStgNew*

IPersistStorage::SaveCompleted terminates both the no scribble and the hands off mode, returning the object to normal storage mode.

Parameter

pStgNew
Points to the **IStorage** instance in which the object was saved. It is NULL in no scribble storage mode and is never NULL in hands off storage mode.

Return Values

Value	Meaning
S_OK	Normal storage mode was re-entered successfully.
E_OUTOFMEMORY	The required streams cannot be opened. The container is left in the hands off state.
E_UNEXPECTED	Neither **IPersistStorage::Save** nor **IPersistStorage::HandOffStorage** was previously called.
E_INVALIDARG	**IPersistStorage::HandOffStorage** was called previously and *pStgNew* is NULL.
E_FAIL	The object could not be saved due to errors other than lack of memory.

Comments

In the hands off storage state, *pStgNew* is never NULL. If the current mode is hands off, the data in *pStgNew* depends on how the mode was entered:

- If the hands off state was entered from the normal state, *pStgNew* is the replacement for the one revoked by **IPersistStorage::HandsOffStorage**. The bits in *pStgNew* are the same as those that were in the revoked storage.
- If the hands off state was entered from the no scribble state, the bits in *pStgNew* are the same as those last saved. If **IPersistStorage::Save**(*pStgSave*, FALSE) was used, the bits in *pStgNew* are different than the ones in the **IStorage** instance being held onto and that was revoked in **IPersistStorage::HandsOffStorage**.

In the no scribble state, *pStgNew* might or might not be NULL. If it is NULL, the object is allowed to scribble to the storage it has. If it is non-NULL, the object should internally simulate receiving a call to **HandsOffStorage**, then proceed as in that case. Containers must be prepared for objects that refuse to do this (meaning, return an error, such as E_UNEXPECTED) and take responsibility for calling **HandsOffStorage** themselves.

As with **IPersistStorage::Save** and **IPersistStorage::HandsOffStorage**, **SaveCompleted** is a call that recurses to all currently loaded or running nested objects.

If **SaveCompleted** returns an error, the object should not return to the normal storage state. It should act as though **IPersistStorage::SaveCompleted** was never called in order to give the container the opportunity to try an alternate save strategy. **IOleObject::Close** can be called if necessary.

When **IPersistStorage::SaveCompleted** is called, often the object will clear the dirty flag reported by **IPersistStorage::IsDirty**. For more information on the various states an object can be in during a save operation and the effect it has on **SaveCompleted**, see "Structured Storage Overview," earlier in this chapter.

Example

The following implementation of **SaveCompleted** returns the **IStorage** back to normal storage state, after which **SaveCompleted** clears the object's dirty flag and sends an OnSave notification to all registered advise sinks.

```
HRESULT IPersistStg_SaveCompleted(LPPERSISTSTORAGE lpThis,
                                  LPSTORAGE pStgNew)
{
    LPDOC lpDoc =
            ((struct CDocPersistStorageImpl FAR*)lpThis)->lpDoc;
    HRESULT hrErr;

    lpDoc->m_dwStorageMode = STGMODE_NORMAL;

    /* OLE2NOTE: It is only legal to perform a Save or SaveAs operation
    **    on an embedded object. If the document is file-based,
    **    it cannot be changed to an IStorage-based object.
    **
    **      fSameAsLoad   pStgNew     Type of Save     Send OnSave
    **    ---------------------------------------------------------
    **         TRUE        NULL        SAVE              YES
    **         TRUE        ! NULL      SAVE *            YES
    **         FALSE       ! NULL      SAVE AS           YES
    **         FALSE       NULL        SAVE COPY AS      NO
    **
    **    * This is a strange case that is possible. It is inefficient
    **    for the caller; it would be better to pass pStgNew==NULL for
    **    the Save operation.
    */
```

```
if ( ((lpDoc->m_fSaveWithSameAsLoad && pStgNew==NULL) || pStgNew)
        && (lpDoc->m_docInitType != DOCTYPE_EMBEDDED) ) {
    return ResultFromScode(E_INVALIDARG);
}

/* OLE2NOTE: Inform any linking clients that the document has been
**    saved. In addition, any currently active pseudo objects
**    should also inform their clients. We should only broadcast an
**    OnSave notification if a Save or SaveAs operation was
**    performed. We do NOT want to send the notification if a
**    SaveCopyAs operation was performed.
*/
if ((lpDoc->m_fSaveWithSameAsLoad && pStgNew==NULL) || pStgNew) {

    // Clear dirty flag upon save or saveAs
    ServerDoc_SetModified(lpDoc, FALSE, FALSE, FALSE);

    ServerDoc_SendAdvise (
            lpDoc,
            OLE_ONSAVE,
            NULL,    /* lpmkDoc -- not relevant here */
            0);      /* advf -- not relevant here */
}

/*    Pre-open and hold open streams to guarantee that a
**    subsequent save will be successful in low-memory. If we fail
**    to open these streams, we want to force ourselves to close
**    to make sure that we cannot make editing changes that cannot
**    be saved later.
*/
if ( pStgNew && !lpDoc->m_fSaveWithSameAsLoad ) {

    hrErr = pStgNew->lpVtbl->OpenStream(
            pStgNew,
            "LineList",
            NULL,
            STGM_READWRITE | STGM_SHARE_EXCLUSIVE,
            0,
            &lpDoc->m_lpLLStm);

    if (hrErr != NOERROR) {
        goto error;
    }

    if (hrErr != NOERROR) {
        goto error;
    }

    lpDoc->m_pStg = pStgNew;
```

```
            // OLE2NOTE: Hold onto IStorage* pointer by calling AddRef on it
            pStgNew->lpVtbl->AddRef(pStgNew);
        }

        return NOERROR;

error:
        return ResultFromScode(E_OUTOFMEMORY);
}
```

See Also **IPersistStorage::IsDirty, IPersistStorage::Save**

IPersistStorage::HandsOffStorage

HRESULT IPersistStorage::HandsOffStorage()

IPersistStorage::HandsOffStorage causes the object to release its storage object and enter the hands off storage state.

Return Value

Value	Meaning
S_OK	S_OK is returned in all cases.

Comments

The hands off storage state is terminated when **IPersistStorage::SaveCompleted** is called. **SaveCompleted** passes a pointer to the storage object taking the place of the one released in **HandsOffStorage**.

IPersistStorage::HandsOffStorage is called from either the no scribble or the normal storage state. Between the time **HandsOffStorage** is called to initiate hands off storage state and **IPersistStorage::SaveCompleted** is called to terminate it, callers cannot expect the object to respond in any predictable manner.

Example

In the following implementation, **IPersistStorage::HandsOffStorage** sets the object's storage state to hands off, meaning the storage object is off limits to everyone until **IPersistStorage::SaveCompleted** is called.

```
HRESULT IPStg_HandsOffStorage(LPPERSISTSTORAGE lpThis)
{
    LPDOC lpDoc =
            ((struct IPersistStorageImpl FAR*)lpThis)->lpDoc;

    lpDoc->m_dwStorageMode = STGMODE_HANDSOFF;

    // release previous streams
    if (lpDoc->m_lpLLStm) {
          OleStdRelease((LPUNKNOWN)lpOleDoc->m_lpLLStm);
          lpDoc->m_lpLLStm = NULL;
```

```
    }
    if (lpDoc->m_pStg) {
          OleStdRelease((LPUNKNOWN)lpDoc->m_pStg);
          lpDoc->m_pStg = NULL;
    }

    return NOERROR;
}
```

See Also **IPersistStorage::SaveCompleted**

IPersistStream Interface

The **IPersistStream** interface is implemented and used by OLE to support persistent objects that use a simple serial stream for their storage needs (monikers are an example of objects that use **IPersistStream**). Containers might have a need to implement this interface in support of new moniker types.

Unlike the **IStorage** instances used in the implementation of **IPersistStorage**, the **IStream** instances used in **IPersistStream** are valid only during the call in which they are passed; the object *cannot* retain them after the call completes.

The **IPersistStream** interface contains the following methods (see also OLE2.H):

```
DECLARE_INTERFACE_(IPersistStream, IPersist)
{
  // *** IUnknown methods ***
 HRESULT QueryInterface (THIS_ REFIID riid, LPVOID FAR* ppvObj);
 ULONG AddRef (THIS);
 ULONG Release (THIS);

  // *** IPersist methods ***
 HRESULT GetClassID (THIS_ LPCLSID pclsid);

  // *** IPersistStream methods ***
 HRESULT IsDirty (THIS);
 HRESULT Load (THIS_ LPSTREAM pStm);
 HRESULT Save (THIS_ LPSTREAM pStm, BOOL fClearDirty);
 HRESULT GetSizeMax (THIS_ ULARGE_INTEGER FAR * pcbSize);
};
```

IPersistStream::IsDirty

HRESULT IPersistStream::IsDirty()

IPersistStream::IsDirty checks an object for changes since it was last saved.

Return Values

Value	Meaning
S_OK	The object has changed since the last save.
S_FALSE	The object has not changed since the last save.
E_OUTOFMEMORY	Memory constraints prohibit the successful determination of whether the object has changed.
E_FAIL	It was not possible to determine whether or not the object has changed due to errors other than lack of memory.

Comments

Calling **IPersistStream::IsDirty** determines whether any changes have occurred to an object that requires **IPersistStream::Save** being called to avoid losing information. The dirty flag is conditionally cleared in the implementation of **IPersistStream::Save**.

See Also

IPersistStream::Save

IPersistStream::Load

HRESULT IPersistStream::Load(*pStm***)**
LPSTREAM *pStm*

IPersistStream::Load initializes an object previously stored with **IPersistStream::Save**.

Parameters

pStm
Points to the stream from which the object should load itself.

Return Values

Value	Meaning
S_OK	The object was successfully loaded.
E_FAIL	The object was not successfully loaded.
E_OUTOFMEMORY	Memory constraints prohibit the successful loading of the object.

Comments

On entry, the stream is logically positioned just as it was in the call to **IPersistStream::Save**. The **IPersistStream::Load** method can both read and seek data from the stream but it cannot write to the stream.

Upon returning, the stream should be left in the same position as it was on exit from the call to **IPersistStream::Save**, which is just past the end of the data.

See Also

IPersistStream::Save

IPersistStream::Save

HRESULT IPersistStream::Save(*pStm, fClearDirty***)**
LPSTREAM *pStm*
BOOL *fClearDirty*

IPersistStream::Save saves the state of an object to the indicated stream.

Parameters

pStm
Points to the stream into which the object should be stored.

fClearDirty
Specifies whether or not the object's dirty flag should be cleared; TRUE clears the internal dirty flag after the save operation and FALSE leaves it alone.

Return Values

Value	Meaning
S_OK	Stream was successfully saved.
STG_E_MEDIUMFULL	**IStream::Write** returned STG_E_MEDIUMFULL.
STG_E_CANTSAVE	**IStream::Write** returned STG_E_CANTSAVE or if the object cannot currently be serialized.

Comments

The object does not write its CLSID to the stream because this is done by the caller. This permits the caller, in appropriate situations, to more efficiently store homogeneous collections of objects.

On entry, the stream is positioned to where the object should write its data, at which point the object can immediately invoke **IStream::Write** calls. The object can read and seek about in the stream, but the object must not seek the stream before the position at which it was on function entry. On exiting from this function, the stream should be positioned immediately past all the persistent data of the object.

If the object contains other objects that cannot be serialized, the object itself cannot be serialized. **IPersistStream::Save** returns STG_E_CANTSAVE and the position of the seek pointer is undefined.

See Also

IPersistStream::Load, IStream::Write

IPersistStream::GetSizeMax

HRESULT IPersistStream::GetSizeMax(*pcbSize***)**
ULARGE_INTEGER FAR * *pcbSize*

IPersistStream::GetSizeMax determines an upper boundary for the size of the stream that would be needed to save this object with **IPersistStream::Save**.

Parameters

pcbSize
Points to where to return the size boundary.

Return Value

Value	Meaning
S_OK	The size was successfully returned.

Comments

The returned value can be used to set buffer sizes for immediate and subsequent calls to **IPersistStream::Save**. This value must be a conservative estimate of the size required because the caller of **IPersistStream::Save** can choose to provide a non-growable buffer.

See Also

IPersistStream::Save

Storage Creation Functions

The functions described in the following sections deal with the creation of **IStorage**, **IStream**, and **ILockBytes** objects.

```
CreateILockBytesOnHGlobal (HGLOBAL hGlobal, BOOL fDeleteOnRelease,
    LPLOCKBYTES FAR* ppLkbyt);
CreateStreamOnHGlobal (HGLOBAL hGlobal, BOOL fDeleteOnRelease, LPSTREAM FAR* ppStm;
StgCreateDocfile(const char FAR* pwcsName, DWORD grfMode, DWORD dwReserved,
    LPSTORAGE FAR *ppStgOpen);
StgCreateDocfileOnILockBytes(LPLOCKBYTES pLkbyt, DWORD grfMode, DWORD dwReserved,
    LPSTORAGE FAR *ppStgOpen);
```

CreateILockBytesOnHGlobal

HRESULT CreateILockBytesOnHGlobal(*hGlobal*, *fDeleteOnRelease*, *ppLkbyt***)**
HGLOBAL *hGlobal*
BOOL *fDeleteOnRelease*
LPLOCKBYTES FAR* *ppLkbyt*

CreateILockBytesOnHGlobal returns an OLE-provided instance of the **ILockBytes** interface whose data is stored in the specified memory handle allocated by **GlobalAlloc**.

Parameters

hGlobal
Contains the memory handle allocated by **GlobalAlloc**. The handle must have been allocated as moveable and nondiscardable. If the handle is to be shared between processes, it must also have been allocated as shared. New handles should be allocated with a size of zero. If *hGlobal* is NULL, **CreateILockBytesOnHGlobal** internally allocates a new shared memory block.

fDeleteOnRelease
Indicates whether the underlying handle for this stream should be automatically freed when the stream is released.

ppLkbyt
Points to where to put the newly created **ILockBytes** instance.

Return Values

Value	Meaning
S_OK	The **ILockBytes** instance was created successfully.
E_INVALIDARG	An invalid value was specified for *hGlobal*.
E_OUTOFMEMORY	Not enough memory to create an **ILockBytes** instance.

Comments

The returned **ILockBytes** instance can be the basis for a compound file. A call to **StgCreateDocfileOnILockBytes** builds a compound file on top of the **ILockBytes**. **GlobalReAlloc** is called by the **ILockBytes** implementation to grow the memory block as needed.

The current contents of the memory block are undisturbed by the creation of the **ILockBytes**. The caller can use **StgOpenStorageOnILockBytes** to reopen a previously existing storage object already contained in the memory block.

Note Freeing the handle that **GetHGlobalFromILockBytes** returns invalidates the **ILockBytes** instance. Therefore, *ppLkbyt*->**Release** must be called *before* freeing the handle.

See Also

StgOpenStorageOnILockBytes

CreateStreamOnHGlobal

HRESULT CreateStreamOnHGlobal(*hGlobal*, *fDeleteOnRelease*; *ppStm*)
HGLOBAL *hGlobal*
BOOL *fDeleteOnRelease*
LPSTREAM FAR* *ppStm*

CreateStreamOnHGlobal returns an OLE-provided **IStream** instance where data is stored inside a global memory handle.

Parameters

hGlobal
Contains the memory handle allocated by **GlobalAlloc**. The handle must have been allocated as moveable and nondiscardable. If the handle is to be shared between processes, it must also be allocated as shared. New handles should be allocated with a size of zero. If *hGlobal* is NULL, **CreateStreamOnHGlobal** internally allocates such a shared new memory block.

fDeleteOnRelease
Specifies whether the handle to the memory is automatically freed when the stream is released.

ppStm
Points to where to return the stream. It cannot be NULL.

Return Values

Value	Meaning
S_OK	The stream was successfully created.
E_OUTOFMEMORY	The stream could not be created due to lack of memory.
E_INVALIDARG	Invalid value for one of the parameters.

Comments

The returned stream supports both reading and writing, is not transacted, and does not support locking. The initial contents of the stream are the current contents of the memory block provided in *hGlobal*. If hGlobal is NULL, **CreateStreamOnHGlobal** internally allocates a handle. The current contents of the memory block, therefore, are undisturbed by the creation of the stream and the user can call **CreateStreamOnHGlobal** to open a stream on an existing memory block.

The initial size of the stream is the size of the memory handle returned by **GlobalSize**. Because of allocation granularity rounding, this is not necessarily the same size as the handle originally allocated. If the logical size of the stream is important, the caller should follow the call to **CreateStreamOnHGlobal** with a call to **IStream::SetSize**.

See Also

CreateStreamOnHGlobal, GlobalSize, IStream::SetSize

StgCreateDocfile

HRESULT StgCreateDocfile(*pwcsName, grfMode, dwReserved, ppStgOpen***)**
const char FAR* *pwcsName*
DWORD *grfMode*
DWORD *dwReserved*
IStorageFAR* FAR* *ppStgOpen*

StgCreateDocfile creates a new root compound file in the file system.

Parameters

pwcsName
Points to the pathname of the compound file to create. Passed uninterpreted to the file system. This can be a relative name or NULL. If NULL, a temporary compound file is allocated with a unique name.

grfMode
Specifies the access mode to use when opening the new compound file. For more information, see the following comments.

dwReserved
Reserved for future use; must be zero.

ppStgOpen
If the operation is successful, it points to where the opened storage object is placed (**ppStgOpen*).

Return Values

Value	Meaning
S_OK	The compound file was successfully created.
STG_E_ACCESSDENIED	The calling process does not have sufficient access. Attempt to open file with conflicting permissions to a simultaneous open.
STG_E_FILEALREADYEXISTS	The compound file already exists and *grfMode* is set to STGM_FAILIFTHERE.
STG_S_CONVERTED	The compound file was successfully converted to Storage format.
STG_E_INSUFFICIENTMEMORY	Out of memory.
STG_E_INVALIDNAME	Bad name in *pwcsName*.
STG_E_INVALIDPOINTER	Bad pointer in *pwcsName* or *ppStgOpen*.
STG_E_INVALIDFLAG	Bad flag combination in *grfMode*.
STG_E_TOOMANYOPENFILES	Out of file handles.
File System Errors	Any file system error.

Comments

The name of the open compound file can be retrieved by calling **IStorage::Stat**.

StgCreateDocfile creates the file if it does not exist. If it does exist, the use of the STGM_CREATE, STGM_CONVERT, and STGM_FAILIFTHERE flags in *grfMode* indicate how to proceed:

Flag Values for *grfMode*	Meaning
STGM_CREATE	If the compound file exists, destroy it and replace it with the new name *pwcsName*.
STGM_CONVERT	If the compound file exists, replace it with the new file *pwcsName*, saving any data in the old file to a stream named **CONTENTS** in the new compound file. This stream contains the same data that was in the old file before the conversion.
STGM_DELETEONRELEASE	Indicates that the compound file is to be automatically destroyed when it is released. This capability is most useful with temporary files.
STGM_FAILIFTHERE	If the compound file exists, fail and return STG_E_FILEALREADYEXISTS.

If the compound file is opened in transacted mode (*grfMode* specifies STGM_TRANSACTED) and a file with this name already exists, the existing file is not altered until all outstanding changes are committed. If the calling process lacks write access to the existing file (because of access control in the file system), *grfMode* can only specify STGM_READ and *not* STGM_WRITE or STGM_READWRITE. The resulting new open compound file can still be written to, but a commit operation will fail (in transacted mode, write permissions are enforced at commit time).

If *grfMode* specifies STGM_TRANSACTED and no file yet exists with the name specified by *pwcsName*, the file is created immediately. In an access controlled file system, the caller must have write permissions in the file system directory in which the compound file is created.

The absence of STGM_TRANSACTED in *grfMode* indicates the file is to be created and opened in direct access mode. Any existing file is destroyed before creating the new file.

StgCreateDocfile can be used to create a temporary compound file by passing a NULL value for *pwcsName*. However, these files are temporary only in the sense that they have a system-provided unique name–likely one that is meaningless to the user. The caller is responsible for deleting the temporary file when finished with it, unless STGM_DELETEONRELEASE was specified for *grfMode*.

Note By default, a Windows application can have 20 file handles open at one time. Each open **IStorage** in transacted mode uses three file handles. To increase the number of file handles the application has available, applications often call the Windows **SetHandleCount** API. However, **SetHandleCount** impacts C run-time libraries (those statically linked to the application) that are hard-coded to expect only 20 file-handles. There is no check on overflow, so if the application already has a few compound files open and it then uses a C run-time library (for example, **fopen** or **sopen**), the application trashes memory past the end of the file-handle array (low in its data segment) if the library gets a file handle above 20.

To solve this problem, applications should reserve some number of file handles on start up, making them available to the components that might be based on C run-time libraries. If your application does not use any dynamic link libraries that use the C run-time libraries, there is no need for any special file-handle reservation code.

See Also **StgCreateDocFileOnILockBytes**

StgCreateDocfileOnILockBytes

HRESULT StgCreateDocfileOnILockBytes(*pLkbyt*, *grfMode*, *dwReserved*, *ppStgOpen*)
LPLOCKBYTES *pLkbyt*
DWORD *grfMode*
DWORD *dwReserved*
LPSTORAGE FAR* *ppStgOpen*

StgCreateDocfileOnILockBytes creates and opens a new compound file on top of an **ILockBytes** instance provided by the caller.

Parameters

pLkbyt
Points to the underlying byte array on which to create a compound file.

grfMode
Specifies the access mode to use when opening the new compound file. For more information, see the following comments.

dwReserved
Reserved for future use; must be zero.

ppStgOpen
If the operation is successful, This parameter points to where the opened storage object is placed (**ppStgOpen*).

Return Values

Value	Meaning
S_OK	The compound file was successfully created.
STG_E_ACCESSDENIED	The calling process does not have sufficient access. Attempt to open **ILockBytes** with conflicting permissions to a simultaneous open.
STG_E_FILEALREADYEXISTS	The compound file already exists and *grfMode* is set to STGM_FAILIFTHERE.
STG_S_CONVERTED	The compound file was successfully converted. The original **ILockBytes** was successfully converted to **IStorage** format.
STG_E_INSUFFICIENTMEMORY	Out of memory.
STG_E_INVALIDPOINTER	A bad pointer was in *pLkbyt* or *ppStgOpen*.
STG_E_INVALIDFLAG	A bad flag combination in *grfMode*.
STG_E_TOOMANYOPENFILES	Out of file handles.
File System Errors	Any file system error.
ILockBytes Errors	Any **ILockBytes** error.

Comments

StgCreateDocfileOnILockBytes can be used to store a document in a relational database. The byte array indicated by *pLkbyt* is used for the underlying storage in place of a disk file.

StgCreateDocfileOnILockBytes has almost exactly the same semantics as **StgCreateDocfile**. For more information, see the discussion of **StgCreateDocfile**.

The newly created compound file is opened according to the access modes in *grfMode*. For conversion purposes, the file is always considered to already exist. As a result, it is not useful to use the STGM_FAILIFTHERE value, because it always causes an error to be returned. However, STGM_CREATE and STGM_CONVERT are both still useful.

The ability to build a compound file on top of an **ILockBytes** instance is provided to support having the data (underneath an **IStorage** and **IStream** tree structure) live in persistent space, space that does not ultimately reside in the file system. Given this capability, there is nothing preventing a document that *is* stored in a file from using this facility. For example, a container might do this to minimize the impact on its file format caused by adopting OLE. However, it is recommended that OLE documents adopt the **IStorage** interface for their own outer-level storage. This has the following advantages:

- The storage structure of the document is the same as its storage structure when it is an embedded object, reducing the number of cases the application needs to handle.

- Outside tools can be written to access the embeddings and links within the document without special knowledge of the document's file format. An example of such a tool is a copy utility that copies a whole a web of linked documents. It needs access to the contained links to determine the extent of the web.
- The **IStorage** instance addresses the problem of how to commit the changes to the file. An application using the **ILockBytes** byte array must handle these issues itself.
- Future file systems will likely implement **IStorage** and **IStream** as their native abstractions, rather than layer on top of a byte array as is done in compound files. Such a file system could be built so documents using the **IStorage** interface as their outer level containment structure would get an automatic efficiency gain by having the layering flattened when files are saved on the new file system.

See Also **StgCreateDocfile**

Storage Query Functions

The functions included in this section test whether a file represents a valid **IStorage** object or if a pointer to an **ILockBytes** instance contains a **IStorage** object.

```
StgIsStorageFile(const char FAR* pwcsName);
StgIsStorageILockBytes(LPLOCKBYTES pLkbyt);
```

StgIsStorageFile

HRESULT StgIsStorageFile(*pwcsName*)
const char Far* *pwcsName*

StgIsStorageFile determines whether a particular disk file contains an **IStorage** object.

Parameter

pwcsName
Points to the name of the disk file be examined. The *pwcsName* parameter is passed uninterpreted to the underlying file system.

Return Values

Value	Meaning
S_OK	The file contains an **IStorage**.
S_FALSE	The file does not contain an **IStorage** object.

Value	Meaning
STG_E_INVALIDFILENAME	A bad name was passed in.
STG_E_FILENOTFOUND	The *pwcsName* parameter could not be determined.
File System Errors	Any file system error.

Comment

At the beginning of the disk file underlying an **IStorage** object is a signature distinguishing an **IStorage** object from other file formats. The **StgIsStorageFile** function is useful to applications whose documents use a disk file format that might or might not use storage objects.

StgIsStorageILockBytes can be used in a similar manner, testing an **ILockBytes** byte array to see whether it contains an **IStorage** object.

See Also

StgIsStorageILockBytes

StgIsStorageILockBytes

HRESULT StgIsStorageILockBytes(*pLkbyt***)**
LPLOCKBYTES *pLkbyt*

StgIsStorageILockBytes determines whether or not a given **ILockBytes** byte array contains an **IStorage** object.

Parameters

pLkbyt
Points to the **ILockBytes** byte array to be examined.

Return Value

Value	Meaning
S_OK	The *pLkbyt* parameter contains an **IStorage** object.
S_FALSE	The *pLkbyt* parameter does not contain an **IStorage** object.

Comment

At the beginning of the **ILockBytes** byte array underlying an **IStorage** object is a signature distinguishing an **IStorage** object from other file formats. **StgIsStorageILockBytes** is useful to applications whose documents use an **ILockBytes** byte array format that might or might not use storage objects.

StgIsStorageFile can be used in a similar manner, testing a disk file to see whether it contains a storage object.

See Also

StgIsStorageFile

Input/Output Storage Functions

The following functions support the retrieval of data from an **IStorage**, **IStream**, or **ILockBytes** object or the saving of data to objects of those types.

```
GetClassFile (LPCSTR szFilename, LPCLSID pclsid);
GetHGlobalFromILockBytes (LPLOCKBYTES pLkbyt, HGLOBAL FAR* phglobal);
GetHGlobalFromStream (LPSTREAM pstm, HGLOBAL FAR* phglobal);
ReadClassStg(LPSTORAGE pStg, LPCLSID pclsid);
ReadClassStm(LPSTREAM pStm, LPCLSID pclsid);
ReadFmtUserTypeStg (LPSTORAGE pStg, CLIPFORMAT FAR* pcf, LPSTR FAR* lplpszUserType);
StgOpenStorage(const char FAR* pwcsName, LPSTORAGE pstgPriority, DWORD grfMode,
   SNB snbExclude, DWORD dwReserved, LPSTORAGE FAR *ppStgOpen);
StgOpenStorageOnILockBytes(LPLOCKBYTES pLkbyt, LPSTORAGE pstgPriority,
   DWORD grfMode, SNB snbExclude, DWORD dwReserved, LPSTORAGE FAR *ppStgOpen);
StgSetTimes(char const FAR* lpszName, FILETIME const FAR* pctime,
   FILETIME const FAR* patime, FILETIME const FAR* pmtime);
WriteClassStg(LPSTORAGE pStg, REFCLSID rclsid);
WriteClassStm(LPSTREAM pStm, REFCLSID rclsid);
WriteFmtUserTypeStg (LPSTORAGE pStg, CLIPFORMAT cf, LPSTR lpszUserType);
```

GetClassFile

HRESULT GetClassFile(*lpszFileName*, *pclsid***)**
LPCSTR *lpszFileName*
LPCLSID *pclsid*

GetClassFile returns the CLSID associated with the given filename.

Parameters

szFileName
Points to the filename from which the CLSID is to be retrieved.

pclsid
Points to where to return the CLSID.

Return Values

Value	Meaning
S_OK	The CLSID was successfully returned.
MK_E_CANTOPENFILE	Unable to open the specified filename.
MK_E_INVALIDEXTENSION	The specified extension in the registration database is invalid.
File System Errors	Any file system error.

Comments

GetClassFile locates the CLSID for the code that can work with the specified file. For example, when a link to a file-based document is activated, the file moniker uses the returned CLSID to locate the link source's application.

The following strategies are used to determine an appropriate CLSID:

1. If the file is a storage object (call **StgIsStorageFile** to determine whether a file is a storage object), **GetClassFile** returns the CLSID written with **IStorage::SetClass**.
2. If the file is not a storage object, **GetClassFile** attempts to match various bits in the file against a pattern. The registration database contains a (possibly empty) series of entries that are logically of the form:

   ```
   regdb key = offset, cb, mask, value
   ```

   The entries *offset* and *cb* denote, with a zero-origin offset and length, a particular byte range in the file (negative values for *offset* are interpreted from the end of the file). *mask* is a bitmask "AND-ed" with that set of bytes, and the result is compared with *value*. If *mask* is omitted, it is assumed to be all-ones.

   These entries are pattern matched in the file in the order in which they are found in the database. The first entry that matches, if any, is used as the class of the file. For example, the following entries require that the first four bytes be AB CD 12 34 and that the last four bytes be FE FE FE FE:

   ```
   0 = 0, 4, FFFFFFFF, ABCD1234
   2 = -4, 4,, FEFEFEFE
   ```

3. If the above strategies fail, the file extension is consulted in the registration database. If the value under the key ".EXT" is a valid CLSID, it is used.
4. Otherwise, MK_E_INVALIDEXTENSION is returned.

See Also

WriteClassStg

GetHGlobalFromILockBytes

HRESULT GetHGlobalFromILockBytes(*pLkbyt*, *phglobal***)**
LPLOCKBYTES *pLkbyt*
HGLOBAL FAR* *phglobal*

GetHGlobalFromILockBytes returns a global memory handle to an **ILockBytes** instance created using **CreateILockBytesOnHGlobal**.

Parameters

pLkbyt
Points to the **ILockBytes** instance for which the handle is being returned.

phglobal
Points to the current memory handle used by this **ILockBytes** instance.

Return Values

Value	Meaning
S_OK	The handle was returned successfully.
E_INVALIDARG	Invalid value specified for *pLkbyt*. It can also indicate that the **ILockBytes** passed in is not one created by **CreateILockBytesOnHGlobal**.

Comments

The handle returned might be different from the original handle due to intervening calls to **GlobalRealloc**. The contents of the returned memory can be written to a clean disk file, and opened as a storage object using **StgOpenStorage**.

See Also

StgOpenStorage

GetHGlobalFromStream

HRESULT GetHGlobalFromStream(*pStm*, *phglobal*)
LPSTREAM *pStm*
HGLOBAL FAR* *phglobal*

GetHGlobalFromStream returns a global memory handle to a stream created using **CreateStreamOnHGlobal**.

Parameters

pStm
Points to the stream created by **CreateStreamOnHGlobal**.

phglobal
Points to the current memory handle used by this stream.

Return Value

Value	Meaning
S_OK	The handle was successfully returned.
E_INVALIDARG	Invalid value for *pstm*. In addition to the usual E_INVALIDARG cases, if the **IStream** passed in is not one created by **CreateStreamOnHGlobal**.

Comments

The returned handle might be different than the original handle due to intervening **GlobalRealloc** calls.

See Also

CreateStreamOnHGlobal, **GlobalRealloc**

ReadClassStg

HRESULT ReadClassStg(*pStg*, *pclsid*)
LPSTORAGE *pStg*
LPCLSID *pclsid*

ReadClassStg returns the CLSID retrieved from a previous call to **IStorage::Stat**.

Parameters

pStg
Points to the **IStorage** instance containing the CLSID to be returned.

pclsid
Points to where to return the CLSID. May return CLSID_NULL.

Return Values

Value	Meaning
S_OK	The CLSID was returned successfully.

E_OUTOFMEMORY

See Also **OleLoad, WriteClassStg**

IStorage::Stat errors.

ReadClassStm

HRESULT ReadClassStm(*pStm, pclsid*)
LPSTREAM *pStm*
CLSID FAR * *pclsid*

ReadClassStm returns an object's CLSID from the stream.

Parameters

pStm
Points to the stream from which the CLSID is to be read.

pclsid
Points to where to return the CLSID.

Return Values

Value	Meaning
S_OK	The CLSID was successfully returned.
STG_E_READFAULT	End of file was reached.
IStream::Read errors.	Can return any of the error codes from **IStream::Read**.

Comments

The returned CLSID must have been previously written to the stream with **WriteClassStm**.

Most applications do not call **ReadClassStm**. OLE calls it before making a call to an application's **IPersistStream::Load** implementation.

See Also **WriteClassStm, ReadClassStg, WriteClassStg**

ReadFmtUserTypeStg

HRESULT ReadFmtUserTypeStg(*pStg*, *pcf*, *lplpszUserType***)**
LPSTORAGE *pStg*
CLIPFORMAT FAR * *pcf*
LPSTR * *lplpszUserType*

ReadFmtUserTypeStg returns the clipboard format and user type saved with **WriteFmtUserTypeStg**.

Parameters

pStg
Points to the object's **IStorage** instance from which the information is to be read.

pcf
Points to where to return the clipboard format. Itcan be NULL, indicating the format is of no interest to the caller.

lplpszUserType
Points to where to return the user type. It can be NULL, indicating the user type is of no interest to the caller.

Return Values

Value	Meaning
S_OK	The information was read successfully.
E_OUTOFMEMORY	Out of memory.
E_FAIL	**WriteFmtUserTypeStg** was never called on the object.
IStream::Read errors.	Can return any of the error codes from **IStream::Read**.

Comments **WriteClassStg** must have been previously called before calling **ReadFmtUserTypeStg**.

See Also **WriteFmtUserTypeStg**

StgOpenStorage

HRESULT StgOpenStorage(*pwcsName, pstgPriority, grfMode, snbExclude, dwReserved, ppStgOpen***)**
const char FAR* *pwcsName*
LPSTORAGE *pstgPriority*
DWORD *grfMode*
SNB *snbExclude*
DWORD *dwReserved*
LPSTORAGE FAR* *ppStgOpen*

StgOpenStorage opens an existing **IStorage** object in the file system.

Parameter

pwcsName
: Points to the path of the **IStorage** object to open. If *ppStg* is non-NULL, *pwcsName* is ignored. In this case, the name is inferred from the location of *pstgPriority.*

pstgPriority
: Points to a previous opening of a root **IStorage** object (usually, one that was opened in priority mode) or NULL, which is most often the case.

  If *pstgPriority* is non-NULL, the **IStorage** object is closed and reopened according to *grfMode*. After **StgOpenStorage** returns, the **IStorage** contained in *pstgPriority* on function entry is invalid, and can no longer be used. The caller should use *ppStgOpen* instead.

grfMode
: Specifies the access mode to use to open the **IStorage** object. For more information, see the following comments.

snbExclude
: A non-NULL *snbExclude* points to a block of elements in this **IStorage** to be emptied as the **IStorage** is opened. This exclusion occurs independently of whether a snapshot copy happens on the open **IStorage** object. It can be NULL, indicating nothing is to be excluded.

dwReserved
: Reserved for future use; must be zero.

ppStgOpen
: If the operation is successful, *ppStgOpen* points to where the opened **IStorage** is placed (**ppStgOpen*).

Return Values

Value	Meaning
S_OK	The storage object was successfully opened.
STG_E_FILENOTFOUND	The file does not exist.
STG_E_ACCESSDENIED	Insufficient access to open file. Exclusions specified without read-write permissions or attempt to open file with conflicting permissions to a simultaneous open.
STG_E_FILEALREADYEXISTS	The file exists but is not a storage object.
STG_E_TOOMANYOPENFILES	Cannot open another file.
STG_E_INSUFFICIENTMEMORY	Out of memory.
STG_E_INVALIDNAME	Bad name in *pwcsName* or *snbExclude*.
STG_E_INVALIDPOINTER	Bad pointer in *snbExclude*, *pwcsName*, *pstgPriority* or *ppStgOpen*.
STG_E_INVALIDFLAG	Bad flag combination in *grfMode*.
STG_E_INVALIDFUNCTION	STGM_DELETEONRELEASE specified in *grfMode*.
STG_E_TOOMANYOPENFILES	Out of file handles.
STG_E_OLDDLL	The DLL being used to open this Storage is a version prior to the one used to create it.
STG_E_OLDFORMAT	The storage being opened was created by the Beta 1 **IStorage** provider. This format is no longer supported.
File System Errors	Any file system error.

Comments

Opening a storage object in read and/or write mode without denying write permission to others (*grfMode* set to STGM_SHARE_DENY_WRITE) can be expensive because **StgOpenStorage** must make a snapshot copy of the entire storage object.

Applications often try to open storage objects with the following access permissions:

```
STGM_READWRITE | STGM_SHARE_DENY_WRITE
        // transacted vs. direct mode omitted for exposition
```

If the call is successful, a snapshot copy need never be made. If it fails, the application can either revert to using STGM_READWRITE and have a snapshot copy made or use the following permissions:

```
STGM_READ | STGM_SHARE_DENY_WRITE
        // transacted vs. direct mode omitted for exposition
```

In the former case, the application should prompt the user before doing an expensive copy. In the latter case, if the call succeeds, a snapshot copy will not have been made because STGM_SHARE_DENY_WRITE was specified, denying others write access.

To reduce the expense of making a snapshot copy, applications can use priority mode (*grfMode* set to STGM_PRIORITY).

The *snbExclude* parameter specifies a set of element names in the storage object to be emptied as the storage object is opened. Streams are set to a length of zero and storage objects have all their elements removed. By excluding certain streams, the expense of making a snapshot copy can be significantly reduced. Almost always, this paradigm is used after first opening the storage object in priority mode, after which the now-excluded elements are read into memory. This earlier priority mode opening of the storage object should be passed through *pstgPriority* so the exclusion implied by priority mode is now removed. The caller is responsible for rewriting the contents of excluded items before committing. This technique is only useful for applications whose documents do not require constant access to their **IStorage** while they are active.

See Also **StgOpenStorageOnILockBytes**

StgOpenStorageOnILockBytes

HRESULT StgOpenStorageOnILockBytes (*pLkbyt, pstgPriority, grfMode, snbExclude, dwReserved, ppStgOpen*)
LPLOCKBYTES *pLkbyt*
LPSTORAGE *pstgPriority*
DWORD *grfMode*
SNB *snbExclude*
DWORD *dwReserved*
LPSTORAGE FAR* *ppStgOpen*

StgOpenStorageOnILockBytes opens an existing **IStorage** object that does not reside in a disk file, but instead lives in an **ILockBytes** instance provided by the caller.

Parameters

pLkbyt
: Points to the underlying byte array that contains the **IStorage** in which the compound file lives.

pstgPriority
Most often NULL. A non-NULL *pstgPriority* points to a previous opening of a root **IStorage** object, most often one that was opened in priority-mode. Refer to the description of *pstgPriority* under **StgOpenStorage** for more information.

grfMode
Specifies the access mode to use to open the **IStorage** object.

snbExclude
A non-NULL *snbExclude* points to a block of elements in this **IStorage** to be emptied as the **IStorage** is opened. This exclusion occurs independently of whether a snapshot copy happens on the open **IStorage** object. It can be NULL, indicating nothing is to be excluded.

dwReserved
Reserved for future use; must be zero.

ppStgOpen
If the operation is successful, the *ppStgOpen* parameter points to where the opened **IStorage** is placed (**ppStgOpen*).

Return Values

Value	Meaning
S_OK	**IStorage** object successfully opened.
STG_E_FILENOTFOUND	Byte array does not contain a storage object.
STG_E_ACCESSDENIED	Insufficient access. Exclusions specified without read-write permissions or attempt to open file with conflicting permissions to a simultaneous open.
STG_E_TOOMANYOPENFILES	Cannot open another file.
E_OUTOFMEMORY	Not enough memory to open **IStorage** object.
STG_E_INSUFFICIENTMEMORY	Out of memory.
STG_E_INVALIDNAME	Bad name in *snbExclude*.
STG_E_INVALIDPOINTER	Bad pointer in *snbExclude*, *pLkbyt*, *pstgPriority*, or *ppStgOpen*.
STG_E_INVALIDFLAG	Bad flag combination in *grfMode*.
STG_E_INVALIDFUNCTION	STGM_DELETEONRELEASE specified in *grfMode*.
STG_E_TOOMANYOPENFILES	Out of file handles.
STG_E_OLDDLL	The DLL being used to open this **IStorage** is a version prior to the one used to create it.

Value	Meaning
STG_E_OLDFORMAT	The **IStorage** being opened was created by the Beta 1 **IStorage** provider. This format is no longer supported.
File System Errors	Any file system error.
ILockBytes Errors	Any **ILockBytes** error.

Comments

The **IStorage** object must have been previously created by calling **StgCreateDocfileOnILockBytes**. If *pLkbyt* currently contains an **IStorage**, that object is opened according to the access modes in *grfMode* and returned through *ppStgOpen.*

The semantics of **StgOpenStorageOnILockBytes** are almost exactly the same as those of **StgOpenStorage**. For more information, see the discussion about **StgOpenStorage**.

See Also

StgOpenStorage

StgSetTimes

HRESULT StgSetTimes(*lpszName*, *pctime*, *patime*, *pmtime***)**
char const FAR* *lpszName*
FILETIME const FAR* *pctime*
FILETIME const FAR * *patime*
FILETIME const FAR * *pmtime*

StgSetTimes sets the creation, access, and modification times of the indicated file, if supported by the underlying file system.

Parameters

lpszName
Points to the name of the file to change.

pctime
Points to the new creation time.

patime
Points to the new access time.

pmtime
Points to the new modification time.

Return Values

Value	Meaning
S_OK	Time values successfully set.
STG_E_FILENOTFOUND	Element does not exist.
STG_E_INVALIDNAME	Bad name passed in *lpszName*, or a file system error.
STG_E_ACCESSDENIED	Insufficient permissions to access storage.
File System Errors	Any file system error

Comments

Each of the time value parameters can be NULL, indicating no modification should occur.

It is possible that one or more of these time values are not supported by the underlying file system. **IStorage::SetElementTimes** sets the times that can be set and ignores the rest.

WriteClassStg

HRESULT WriteClassStg(*pStg*, *rclsid***)**
LPSTORAGE *pStg*
REFCLSID *rclsid*

WriteClassStg writes the specified CLSID to the specified **IStorage** instance.

Parameters

pStg
Points to the object's **IStorage** instance.

rclsid
Points to the CLSID to be stored with the object.

Return Values

Value	Meaning
S_OK	CLSID returned successfully.
STG_E_MEDIUMFULL	CLSID could not be set due to lack of memory.
IStorage::SetClass errors.	Can return any of the error codes from **IStorage::SetClass**.

Comments

Containers typically call **WriteClassStg** before calling **IPersistStorage::Save**.

See Also

OleSave, ReadClassStg

WriteClassStm

HRESULT WriteClassStm(*pStm, clsid*)
LPSTREAM *pStm*
REFCLSID *rclsid*

WriteClassStm writes the indicated CLSID to the stream.

Parameters

pStm
Points to the stream into which the CLSID is to be written.

clsid
Specifies the CLSID to write to the stream.

Return Values

Value	Meaning
S_OK	CLSID successfully written.
STG_E_MEDIUMFULL	No space left on device.
IStream::Write errors.	Can also return any of the error codes from **IStream::Write**.

Comments

WriteClassStm writes the CLSID in a way that it can be retrieved by **ReadClassStm**.

Most applications do not call **WriteClassStm**. OLE calls it before making a call to an application's **IPersistStream::Save** implementation.

See Also

ReadClassStm, WriteClassStg, ReadClassStg

WriteFmtUserTypeStg

HRESULT WriteFmtUserTypeStg(*pStg, cFormat, lpszUserType*)
LPSTORAGE *pStg*
CLIPFORMAT *cFormat*
LPSTR *lpszUserType*

WriteFmtUserTypeStg writes the specified clipboard format and current user type to the specified **IStorage** instance.

Parameters

pStg
Points to the **IStorage** instance where the information is to be written.

cFormat

Specifies the clipboard format that describes the structure of the native area of the **IStorage** instance. The format tag includes the policy for the names of streams and substorages within this **IStorage** and rules for interpreting data within those streams.

lpszUserType

Points to the object's current user type. It cannot be NULL. This is the type returned by **IOleObject::GetUserType**. If this function is transported to a remote machine where the object class does not exist, this persistently stored user type can be shown to the user in dialog boxes.

Return Values

Value	Meaning
S_OK	The information was written successfully.
STG_E_MEDIUMFULL	Information could not be written due to lack of space on the storage medium.
	IStream::Write errors.

Comments

WriteClassStg must be called before calling **WriteFmtUserTypeStg**.

WriteFmtUserTypeStg must be called in an object's implementation of **IPersistStorage::Save** and by document-level objects that use structured storage for their persistent representation in their save sequence.

To read the information saved, applications call **ReadFmtUserTypeStg**.

See Also

IPersistStorage::Save, **ReadFmtUserTypeStg**

Compound Document Storage Functions

The helper functions described in this section support the loading of storages and streams and the saving of data to those storages and streams.

```
OleLoad(LPSTORAGE pStg, REFIID riid, LPOLECLIENTSITE pClientSite,
    LPVOID FAR* ppvObj);
OleLoadFromStream( LPSTREAM pStm, REFIID riid, LPVOID FAR* ppvObj);
OleSave(LPPERSISTSTORAGE pPS, LPSTORAGE pStg, BOOL fSameAsLoad);
OleSaveToStream( LPPERSISTSTREAM pPStm, LPSTREAM pStm );
```

OleLoad

HRESULT OleLoad (*pStg, riid, pClientSite, ppvObj*)
LPSTORAGE *pStg*
REFIID *riid*
LPOLECLIENTSITE *pClientSite*
LPVOID FAR * *ppvObj*

OleLoad loads an embedded or linked object into memory.

Parameters

pStg
Points to the **IStorage** instance from which to load the object.

riid
Identifies the interface to use when talking to the object.

pClientSite
Points to the object's client site.

ppvObj
Points to the newly loaded object.

Return Values

Value	Meaning
S_OK	Object loaded successfully.
E_OUTOFMEMORY	Object could not be loaded due to lack of memory.
E_NOINTERFACE	Object does not supported the specified interface.

IPersistStorage::Load errors.

Comments

OLE containers load objects into memory by calling the **OleLoad** function. When calling **OleLoad**, the application passes in a pointer to the open **IStorage** object in which the object's data is stored. This is usually a child storage object to the container's root **IStorage** object. Using the OLE information stored with the object, the object handler (usually, the default handler) attempts to load the object. On completion of the **OleLoad** function, the object is said to be in the loaded state, its object application is not running.

Some applications load all of the document's native data. Containers often defer loading the document's contained objects until required to do so. For example, until an object is scrolled into view and needs to be drawn, it does not need to be loaded.

OleLoad does the following steps as part of its functionality:

1. Checks to see whether an auto-conversion of the object is necessary (see **OleDoAutoConvert**).
2. Gets the CLSID from the open **IStorage** by calling **IStorage::Stat**.

3. Calls **CoCreateInstance** to create an instance of the handler. If the handler code is not available, the default handler is used (see **OleCreateDefaultHandler**).
4. Calls **IOleObject::SetClientSite**(*pClientSite*)to inform the object of its client site.
5. Calls **QueryInterface**, asking for **IPersistStorage**. If successful, IPersistStorage::Load is invoked.
6. Queries and returns the interface identified by *riid*.

See Also **ReadClassStg, IClassFactory::CreateInstance, IPersistStorage::Load**

OleLoadFromStream

HRESULT OleLoadFromStream(*pStm, riid, ppvObj*)
LPSTREAM *pStm*
REFIID *riid*
LPVOID* *ppvObj*

OleLoadFromStream loads an object from the stream.

Parameter

pStm
Points to the stream from which the object is to be loaded.

riid
Specifies the interface that the caller wants to use to talk to the object.

ppvObj
Points to where to return the object.

Return Values

Value	Meaning
S_OK	Object successfully loaded.
E_OUTOFMEMORY	Out of memory.
E_NOINTERFACE	Interface not supported.
ReadClassStream errors.	Can return any of the error codes from **ReadClassStream**.
CoCreateIntance errors.	Can return any of the error codes from **CoCreateInstance**.
IPersistStream::Load errors.	Can return any of the error codes from **IPersistStream::Load**.

Comments

OleLoadFromStream can be used to load an object that supports the **IPersistStream** interface. The CLSID of the object must immediately precede the object's data in the stream.

If the CLSID for the stream is CLSID_NULL, *ppvObj* is set to NULL.

See Also

OleSaveToStream

OleSave

HRESULT OleSave (*pPS*, *pStg*, *fSameAsLoad*)
LPPERSISTSTORAGE *pPS*
LPSTORAGE *pStg*
BOOL *fSameAsLoad*

OleSave saves an object opened in transacted mode into the storage object pointed to by *pStg*.

Parameters

pPS
Points to the object to be saved.

pStg
Points to the destination storage object.

fSameAsLoad
Indicates whether or not *pStg* is the same storage object from which the object was loaded or created; TRUE indicates that the storage is the same and FALSE indicates a different storage object.

Return Values

Value	Meaning
S_OK	Object was successfully saved.
STG_E_MEDIUMFULL	Object could not be saved due to lack of disk space.
IPersistStorage::Save errors	Can return any of the error codes from **IPersistStorage::Save**.

Comments

OleSave handles the common scenario in which an object uses the compound file implementation for its storage and is open in transacted mode. More customized or sophisticated scenarios can be handled with the **IPersistStorage** and **IStorage** interfaces directly.

OleSave does the following:

1. Calls **IPersistStorage::GetClassID** to get the CLSID.
2. Writes the CLSID to the storage object.
3. Calls **IPersistStorage::Save** to save the object.
4. If there were no errors on the save, calls **IPersistStorage::Commit** to commit the changes.

Note Static objects are saved into a stream called CONTENTS. Static metafile objects get saved in "placeable metafile format" and static DIB data gets saved in "DIB file format." These formats are defined to be the OLE standards for metafile and DIB. All data transferred using an **IStream** or a file (that is, via **IOleObject::GetDataHere**) must be in these formats. Also, all objects whose default file format is a metafile or DIB must write their data into a CONTENTS stream using these standard formats.

See Also

IStorage Interface, IPersistStorage Interface

OleSaveToStream

HRESULT OleSaveToStream(*pPStm, pStm***)**
LPPERSISTSTREAM *pPStm*
LPSTREAM *pStm*

OleSaveToStream saves an object to the stream.

Parameters

pPStm
Points to the object to be saved to the stream, preceded by its serialized CLSID. It can be NULL, which has the effect of writing CLSID_NULL to the stream.

pStm
Points to the stream in which the object is to be saved.

Return Values

Value	Meaning
S_OK	Object successfully saved.
STG_E_MEDIUMFULL	No space left on device.
WriteClassStm errors	Can return any of the error codes from **WriteClassStm**.
IPersistStream::Save errors	Can return any of the error codes from **IPerisistStream::Save**.

Comments

OleSaveToStream can be used to save an object that supports the **IPersistStream** interface. It does the following steps:

1. Calls **IPersistStream::GetClassID** to get the object's CLSID.
2. Writes the CLSID to the stream with **WriteClassStm**.
3. Calls **IPersistStream::Save** with *fClearDirty* set to TRUE.

See Also

OleLoadFromStream

CHAPTER 10

Drag and Drop Interfaces and Functions

An OLE drag and drop operation allows for the transfer of data within a document, between documents, or between applications. Drag and drop provides the same functionality as the OLE clipboard copy and paste but adds visual feedback and eliminates the need for menus. In fact, if an application supports clipboard copy and paste, little extra is needed to support drag and drop.

During and OLE drag and drop operation, the following three separate pieces of code used:

Drag and Drop Code Source	Implementation and Use
IDropSource interface	Implemented by the object containing the dragged data, referred to as the *drag source*.
IDropTarget interface	Implemented by the object that might potentially accept the drop, referred to as the *drop target*.
DoDragDrop API function	Implemented by OLE and used to initiate a drag and drop operation. Once the operation is in progress, it facilitates communication between the drag source and the drag target.

The **IDropSource** and **IDropTarget** interfaces can be implemented in either a container or in an object application. The role of being a drop source or drop target is not limited to any one type of OLE application.

The OLE API function, **DoDragDrop**, implements a loop that tracks mouse and keyboard movement until such time as the drag is canceled or a drop occurs. **DoDragDrop** is the key function in the drag and drop process, facilitating communication between the drag source and drop target.

During a drag and drop operation, there are three types of feedback that can be displayed to the user:

Type of Feedback	Description
Source feedback	Provided by the drag source, source feedback indicates the data is being dragged and does not change during the course of the drag. Typically, the data is highlighted to signal it has been selected.
Pointer feedback	Provided by the drag source, the pointer feedback indicates what happens if the mouse is released at any given moment. Pointer feedback changes continually as the user moves the mouse and/or presses a modifier key. For example, if the mouse pointer is moved into a window that cannot accept a drop, the pointer changes to the "not allowed" symbol.
Target feedback	Provided by the drop target, the target feedback indicates where the drop is to occur.

The Windows File Manager is an example of an application that is both a drag source and drop target that provides all three types of feedback. When a user selects a file to copy, File Manager supplies source feedback by indicating the selection. As the selection is being dragged and modifier keys are pressed, the pointer changes. For example, if the user presses the CTRL key, a plus sign is added, indicating that the drop would result in a copy rather than in the default move. When the file is dragged over an area that is not a drop target, the pointer changes appropriately. Target feedback, a line drawn around a file or directory, is provided when the pointer is over an area that is a drop target.

DROPEFFECT Enumeration

DoDragDrop and many of the drag and drop interface methods pass information about the effects that a drag source allows in a specific drag operation and the effect a potential drop will have on a target window. Valid drop effect values are the result of or-ing together values contained in the **DROPEFFECT** enumeration:

```
typedef enum tagDROPEFFECT {
    DROPEFFECT_NONE   = 0,       \\only lower three bits are significant
    DROPEFFECT_COPY   = 1,
    DROPEFFECT_MOVE   = 2,
    DROPEFFECT_LINK   = 4,
    DROPEFFECT_SCROLL = 0x80000000,
    }DROPEFFECT;
```

These values have the following meaning:

DROPEFFECT Name	Value	Description
DROPEFFECT_NONE	0	Drop target cannot accept the data.
DROPEFFECT_COPY	1	Drop results in a copy. The original data is untouched by the drag source.
DROPEFFECT_MOVE	2	Drag source should remove the data.
DROPEFFECT_LINK	4	Drag source should create a link to the original data.
DROPEFFECT_SCROLL	0x80000000	Scrolling is about to start or is currently occurring in the target. This value is used in addition to the other values.

Presently, only four of the 32 bit positions in a **DROPEFFECT** have meaning. In the future, more interpretations for the bits will be added. Drop sources and drop targets should carefully mask these values appropriately before comparing. They should never compare a **DROPEFFECT** against, say, DROPEFFECT_COPY by

```
if (dwDropEffect == DROPEFECT_COPY)...
```

Instead, the application should always mask for the value or values being sought:

```
if (dwDropEffect & DROPEFFECT_COPY) == DROPEFFECT_COPY)...
```

or

```
if (dwDropEffect & DROPEFFECT_COPY)...
```

Doing this allows new drop effects to be defined, while preserving backwards compatibility with existing code.

IDropSource Interface

The **IDropSource** interface is implemented by all applications containing data that can be dropped into another application. **IDropSource** contains the following methods (see also OLE2.H):

```
DECLARE_INTERFACE_(IDropSource, IUnknown)
{
  // *** IUnknown methods ***
 HRESULT QueryInterface (THIS_ REFIID riid, LPVOID FAR* ppvObj);
 ULONG AddRef (THIS);
 ULONG Release (THIS);

  // *** IDropSource methods ***
 HRESULT QueryContinueDrag (THIS_ BOOL fEscapePressed, DWORD grfKeyState);
```

```
    HRESULT GiveFeedback (THIS_ DWORD dwEffect);
};
```

Drag Source Responsibilities

The drag source is responsible for the following tasks:

- Providing the drop target with a data transfer object that exposes the **IDataObject** and **IDropSource** interfaces.
- Generating pointer and source feedback.
- Determining when the drag has been canceled or a drop has occurred.
- Performing any action on the original data caused by the drop operation, such as deleting the data or creating a link to it.

The main task is creating a data transfer object that exposes the **IDataObject** and **IDropSource** interfaces. The drag source might or might not include a copy of the selected data. Including a copy of the selected data is not mandatory, but it safeguards against inadvertent changes and allows the clipboard operations code to be identical to the drag and drop code.

Creating the data transfer object is dependent on the set of clipboard formats supported and whether the drag source is a container or server. Many drag sources use the same type of object that is the source of the selected data. When doing so, however, it is important to be aware of the areas that are treated differently.

The following table lists the areas in which the data transfer object and data source object differ:

Data Transfer Object	Data Source Object
Invisible.	Visible.
Stores a pointer to the data source document.	Does not need to store a data source document pointer.
Stores a pointer to a temporary moniker for the data selection.	Does not need to store a temporary moniker pointer.
Exposes only **IDataObject** and **IDropSource**.	Exposes **IDataObject** and other interfaces needed for linking and embedding, such as **IOleObject**. **IDropSource** not exposed.
SetData, **Advise**, **Unadvise**, and **EnumAdvise** methods in **IDataObject** are not supported.	If drag source is a server, all **IDataObject** methods are supported. If drag source is a container, **SetData**, **Advise**, **Unadvise**, and **EnumAdvise** are not supported.
Embedded Object, Embed Source, and Link Source formats are offered.	Embedded Object, Embed Source, and Link Source formats are not offered.

For more information on creating a data transfer object, see the chapter "Data Transfer/Caching Interfaces and Functions."

While a drag operation is in progress, the drag source is responsible for setting the pointer and, if appropriate, for providing additional source feedback to the user. The drag source cannot provide any feedback that tracks the mouse position other than by actually setting the real pointer (see the Windows **SetCursor** function). This rule must be enforced to avoid conflicts with the feedback provided by the drop target. (A drag source can also be a drag target. When dropping on itself, the source/target can, of course, provide target feedback to track the mouse position. In this case, however, it is the drop target tracking the mouse, not the source.)

Based on the feedback offered by the drop target, the source sets an appropriate pointer. Drop sources should use a variation on the standard northwest-pointing arrow, as shown in Figure 10-1.

Figure 10-1. Default drag and drop pointers representing an illegal action, move, and copy.

For more information on the recommended user interface considerations for a drag and drop operation, see the chapter "User Interface Guidelines."

Drag Distance and Delay Values

Dragging occurs when the drag pointer has been moved a specified minimum distance and a specified amount of time has passed since that distance was achieved. The default minimum distance, or radius, for pointer movement is 2 pixels and the default delay before dragging begins is 200 milliseconds, as defined in OLE2.H:

```
#define DD_DEFDRAGMINDIST 2          //the minimum distance before
                                     //dragging begins
#define DD_DEFDRAGDELAY 200          //the delay before dragging begins
```

Overriding values for the minimum distance and the drag delay time can be stored in WIN.INI. These values can then be retrieved during application initialization using the Windows **GetProfileInt** function, as follows:

```
GetProfileInt("windows", "DragMinDist", DD_DEFDRAGMINDIST);
GetProfileInt("windows", "DragDelay", DD_DEFDRAGDELAY);
```

The drag delay value can be used when an application detects a left button down message to determine when to begin the drag operation. When the mouse enters the region in which dragging can be done for the first time, a timer can be set to the amount of time specified by DD_DEFDRAGDELAY. The drag operation can begin after the timer expires if the mouse is still within the region in which dragging is allowed.

The minimum distance setting is used when a mouse move is detected. If the mouse has entered the region in which dragging can be done, each movement can be examined to determine whether the mouse position has changed sufficiently.

Generating Drag Feedback

IDropSource contains two methods, **QueryContinueDrag,** and **GiveFeedback**. **QueryContinueDrag** is called by **DoDragDrop** at the beginning of its loop to check whether the drag has been canceled, whether a drop is to occur, or whether the drag should continue.

The following table shows each state, listing the condition that determines the state and the designated return value.

User Action	Effect on Drag Operation	Return Value
ESCAPE key is pressed	Cancel the drag	DRAGDROP_S_CANCEL
Left mouse button released	Perform a drop	DRAGDROP_S_DROP
Absence of the other two conditions.	Continue the drag	S_OK

For every mouse move, **DoDragDrop** calls the drop target's **IDropTarget::DragOver**, which sets the drop effect. **DoDragDrop** passes the drop effect to **IDropSource::GiveFeedback,** which sets the pointer according to the feedback value. The drag source can either set its pointers manually or return DRAGDROP_S_USEDEFAULTCURSORS to ask OLE to use standard pointers defined for drag and drop operations. The standard pointers include the black brush to indicate scrolling, the plus sign (+) to indicate the copy effect, and a circle with a diagonal line across it to indicate an attempt to drop in an invalid region.

Ending the Drop Operation

When **DoDragDrop** returns, either the drop has occurred or the operation was canceled. The drag source uses the **HRESULT** returned from **DoDragDrop** to determine what to do with the data—delete it or leave it as is. If the data is to be deleted, as is the case with a move operation, the drag source must disable the sending of any data change notifications until the delete operation has been completed.

IDropSource::QueryContinueDrag

HRESULT IDropSource::QueryContinueDrag(*fEscapePressed*, *grfKeyState*)
BOOL *fEscapePressed*
DWORD *grfKeyState*

IDropSource::QueryContinueDrag determines whether a drag operation should continue.

Parameter

fEscapePressed
Specifies TRUE if the ESCAPE key has been pressed by the user since the previous call to **IDropSource::QueryContinueDrag** (or the call to **DoDragDrop** if **IDropSource::QueryContinueDrag** has not been called);otherwise, it is FALSE.

grfKeyState
Identifies the present state of the modifier keys on the keyboard. This is a combination of any of the flags MK_CONTROL, MK_SHIFT, MK_ALT, MK_BUTTON, MK_LBUTTON, MK_MBUTTON, and MK_RBUTTON.

Note that MK_ALT is the ALT key.

Return Value

Value	Meaning
S_OK	The drag operation should continue.
DRAGDROP_S_DROP	The drop operation should occur.
DRAGDROP_S_CANCEL	The drop operation should be canceled.
E_OUTOFMEMORY	Out of memory.
E_UNEXPECTED	An unexpected error occurred.

Comments

To determine whether the drag operation should continue, **IDropSource::QueryContinueDrag** checks whether the mouse button that started the drag operation has been released, causing a drop operation to occur, and/or whether the ESCAPE key has been hit, causing a cancel. The former case can be handled by examining the flags in the *grfKeyState* parameter, while the latter can be done by examining the *fEscapePressed* flag.

Example

In the following example, **IDropSource::QueryContinueDrag** checks both the value of *fEscapePressed* and the key state to see whether the drag and drop operation should be canceled, a drop should occur, or whether the drag operation should continue.

```
HRESULT     IDropSource_QueryContinueDrag (
    LPDROPSOURCE            lpThis,
    BOOL                    fEscapePressed,
    DWORD                   grfKeyState)
{
```

```
    if (fEscapePressed)
        return ResultFromScode(DRAGDROP_S_CANCEL);
    else if (!(grfKeyState & MK_LBUTTON))
        return ResultFromScode(DRAGDROP_S_DROP);
    else
        return ResultFromScode(S_OK);
}
```

See Also **DoDragDrop**

IDropSource::GiveFeedback

HRESULT IDropSource::GiveFeedback(*dwEffect***)**
DWORD *dwEffect*

IDropSource::GiveFeedback enables a source application to provide feedback during a drag and drop operation.

Parameter

dwEffect
Specifies the **DROPEFFECT** value returned by the most recent call to **IDropTarget::DragEnter** or **IDropTarget::DragOver**. For a list of values, see the section "DROPEFFECT Enumeration," earlier in this chapter.

Return Value

Value	Meaning
S_OK	The function completed its task successfully.
DRAGDROP_S_USEDEFAULTCURSORS	OLE should use the default pointer (cursor) to provide feedback to the user.
E_OUTOFMEMORY	Out of memory.
E_INVALIDARG	One or more arguments are invalid.
E_UNEXPECTED	An unexpected error occurred.

Comments

IDropSource::GiveFeedback is called by **DoDragDrop** once for every time it calls **IDropTarget::DragEnter** or **IDropTarget::DragOver**. This action enables the drop source to provide appropriate feedback in the source data. Unless a new target is immediately entered (in which case the call is omitted), **IDropSource::GiveFeedback** is called with *dwEffect* set to DROPEFFECT_NONE when **IDropTarget::DragLeave** is called.

There are two kinds of source feedback: appropriate changes to the pointer, and changes in the display of the original dragged data. The different feedback provided by the mouse pointer in the Windows 3.1 File Manager, with regard to a copy versus a move operation, is a good example of both kinds of source feedback.

The *dwEffect* parameter can include DROPEFFECT_SCROLL, indicating the source should put up the drag-scrolling variation of the appropriate pointer.

OLE defines a set of recommended pointers that can be used for each of the different drop effects. For more information on these pointers, see the chapter "User Interface Guidelines." For consistency across OLE applications, the drop source should use the recommended pointers.

IDropSource::GiveFeedback can return DRAGDROP_S_USEDEFAULTS, which causes **DoDragDrop** to put up the standard pointer appropriate for *dwEffect*. Other source feedback can be provided in addition to this standard feedback.

Example

Two example implementations are shown below. In the first example, **IDropSource::GiveFeedback** tells OLE to use its default drag and drop pointers by returning DRAGDROP_S_USEDEFAULTCURSORS (see "Drag Source Responsibilities," earlier in this chapter):

```
HRESULT IDropSource_GiveFeedback(LPDROPSOURCE lpThis, DWORD dwEffect)
{
    return ResultFromScode(DRAGDROP_S_USEDEFAULTCURSORS);
}
```

The next example shows how to provide application-specific feedback. **IDropSource_GiveFeedback** checks first to determine whether the application is currently scrolling and if it is, the special scroll pointer is used. If scrolling is not occurring, the appropriate pointer is loaded and set based on the value of *dwEffect*.

```
HRESULT IDropSource_GiveFeedback(LPDROPSOURCE lpThis, DWORD dwEffect)
{
    HCURSOR hcursor;
    SCODE sc;

    if (dwEffect & DROPEFFECT_SCROLL)  {
        hcursor = LoadCursor(NULL, IDC_IBEAM);
    } else  {
        switch (dwEffect)
        {
            case DROPEFFECT_NONE:
                hcursor = LoadCursor(NULL, IDC_ARROW);
                break;
            case DROPEFFECT_COPY:
```

```
                hcursor = LoadCursor(vhInstApp, "PlusCursor");
                break;
            case DROPEFFECT_MOVE:
                hcursor = LoadCursor(vhInstApp, "DragCursor");
                break;
            case DROPEFFECT_LINK:
                hcursor = LoadCursor(vhInstApp, "PlusCursor");
                break;
            default:
                hcursor = LoadCursor(NULL, IDC_ARROW);
                break;
        }
    }
    SetCursor(hcursor);
    sc = S_OK;
    return ResultFromScode(sc);
}
```

See Also **RegisterDragDrop**, **DoDragDrop**, **IDropTarget::DragLeave**, **IDropTarget::DragOver**

IDropTarget Interface

The **IDropTarget** interface is implemented by all applications that can accept dropped data. Every application window that can be a drop target registers as such by calling **RegisterDragDrop**, passing an **IDropTarget** interface pointer as an argument.

IDropTarget contains the following methods (see also OLE2.H):

```
DECLARE_INTERFACE_(IDropTarget, IUnknown)
{
  // *** IUnknown methods ***
 HRESULT QueryInterface (THIS_ REFIID riid, LPVOID FAR* ppvObj);
 ULONG AddRef (THIS);
 ULONG Release (THIS);

  // *** IDropTarget methods ***
 HRESULT DragEnter (THIS_ LPDATAOBJECT pDataObject, DWORD grfKeyState, POINTL pt,
  LPDWORD pdwEffect);
 HRESULT DragOver (THIS_ DWORD grfKeyState, POINTL pt, LPDWORD pdwEffect);
 HRESULT DragLeave (THIS);
 HRESULT Drop (THIS_ LPDATAOBJECT pDataObject, DWORD grfKeyState, POINTL pt,
  LPDWORD pdwEffect);
};
```

Drop Target Responsibilities

The drop target is responsible for the following tasks:

- Registering and revoking each drop target window.
- Determining what the effect on the drag source is at any given time.
- Implementing drag scrolling.
- Providing target feedback.
- Integrating the data if a drop occurs or if the drag is cenceled.

Registering as a Drop Target

Before they can accept dropped data, applications that have implemented the **IDropTarget** interface must register their class identifier (CLSID) and object handler in the registration database as potential drop targets. Applications must call the OLE API function **RegisterDragDrop** for every window that can accept dropped data.

Passed to **RegisterDragDrop** is a handle to the window and a pointer to the **IDropTarget** interface. **RegisterDragDrop** creates a stream to hold the **IDropTarget** interface pointer so the interface can be remoted across processes to support drag and drop from one application to another.

Note Drop targets must be externally locked in memory by calling **CoLockObjectExternal**. This lock ensures that the drop target is not prematurely released during a drag and drop operation. However, for applications using the visible document object to expose the **IDropTarget** interface, an additional call to **CoLockObjectExternal** is not required. Objects visible to the user typically already have an external lock.

If IDropTarget is not exposed through an object visible to the user, a call to **CoLockObjectExternal**(...,TRUE,...) is necessary before **RegisterDragDrop** is called. To free the locked drop target, call **CoLockObjectExternal**(...,FALSE,...) before calling **RevokeDragDrop**. For more information on locking objects and applications in memory, see the discussion of the **CoLockObjectExternal** function.

Typically, when the window is no longer available to accept drops, the drop target calls **RevokeDragDrop** to remove the registration. It is important to call **RevokeDragDrop** rather than relying on destroying the window to remove the registration. Neglecting to call **RevokeDragDrop** can result in a memory leak.

In the case where the desktop is registered as a drop target along with windows belonging to applications running on the desktop, revoking the application windows might not be sufficient to block a potential drop. If the desktop is still a valid registered drop target when the user drags across the application window, the cursor might reflect that a drop can be accepted. This is misleading to the user, who might think the data is to be dropped onto the application window when it is really to be dropped onto the desktop. To guard against this effect, application windows should stay registered and return an appropriate cursor when a drop cannot be accepted.

Determining Drop Effect Values

The drop target determines the effect of a potential drop in every **IDropTarget::DragEnter** and **IDropTarget::DragOver** call. **IDropTarget::DragEnter** is called when the mouse pointer initially enters the drop target window and is always called before **IDropTarget::Drop** or **IDropTarget::DragLeave** is called. **IDropTarget::DragOver** is called for every mouse move while the pointer is positioned over the drop target window. **DragLeave** is called when the pointer leaves the drop target window.

IDropTarget::DragEnter and **IDropTarget::DragOver** are passed parameters that identify the location of the mouse, the modifier key state, and a list of drop effects. **DragEnter** also receives a pointer to the data transfer object's **IDataObject** interface so it can enumerate the available formats. The drop target uses the list of available formats, the mouse pointer position, and the modifier key state to determine the appropriate drop effect value to return.

The following modifier keys affect the result of the drop:

Key Combination	User-Visible Feedback	Drop Effect
CTRL + SHIFT	=	DROPEFFECT_LINK
CTRL	+	DROPEFFECT_COPY
No keys	None	DROPEFFECT_MOVE
SHIFT	None	DROPEFFECT_MOVE

Another factor in determining the drop effect value is whether the drag source and drop target are in the same window. Areas in which data can be dropped may be different if the drop is local.

Drag Scrolling and Related Values

Drag scrolling is supported solely by the drop target; however, the drag source is responsible for displaying the scroll pointer. Objects that want to support drag scrolling should register themselves in the normal way through **RegisterDragDrop**.

Scrolling occurs when the pointer has been in an area close to the window's edge for a specified time interval. As discussed in the "OLE User Interface Guidelines" chapter, there is a *hot zone* adjacent to the window's edge that triggers drag scrolling. The default size (inset width) of the hot zone is 11 pixels, the default delay before drag scrolling starts is 50 milliseconds, and the default scroll interval (the amount of time between the display of each scrolled-over element) is 50 milliseconds, as defined in OLE2.H:

```
#define DD_DEFSCROLLINSET 11          //inset width of hot zone
#define DD_DEFSCROLLDELAY 50          //drag scroll delay time
#define DD_DEFSCROLLINTERVAL 50       //drag scroll interval (speed)
```

When the pointer first enters the hot zone, the pointer changes to its drag-scrolling variation. The size and existence of the hot zone are controlled by the drop target. Some drop targets allow scrolling in both the horizontal and vertical directions while others allow only vertical scrolling.

As soon as the pointer enters the hot zone, the drop target informs the drag source that the pointer should change to its drag scrolling variation by returning DROPEFFECT_SCROLL, which is then passed to the drop source in **IDropSource::GiveFeedback**. As long as the pointer is in the hot zone, the drop target should keep returning DROPEFFECT_SCROLL.

The drop target determines the scroll delay time the pointer must remain in the hot zone before scrolling is to begin. Timers are not needed to compute this delay; it is simpler to use the Windows **GetTickCount** function. Drop targets should first set an internal variable when the hot zone is first entered and compare that variable against the current **GetTickCount** in each subsequent call to **IDropTarget::DragOver**.

Overriding values for the inset width of the hot zone, the drag scroll delay time, and the drag scroll speed (interval) can be stored in WIN.INI. These values can then be retrieved using the Windows **GetProfileInt** function, as follows:

```
GetProfileInt("windows", "DragScrollInset", DD_DEFSCROLLINSET);
GetProfileInt("windows", "DragScrollDelay", DD_DEFSCROLLDELAY);
GetProfileInt("windows", "DragScrollInterval", DD_DEFSCROLLINTERVAL);
```

Ending the Drag Operation

A particular drag operation is ended when either the user clicks outside of the drop target window or releases the mouse while inside the window. **DoDragDrop** calls **IDropTarget::DragLeave** in the first case, **IDropTarget::Drop** in the second case. The implementation of **IDropTarget::DragLeave** involves releasing the data transfer object and, if appropriate, killing the drag scrolling timer.

The tasks involved in a drop operation are similar to the tasks involved in a clipboard paste. Depending on the order and type of formats passed with the data transfer object, the data is integrated statically, as an embedded object, or as a linked object.

IDropTarget::DragEnter

HRESULT IDropTarget::DragEnter(*pDataObject, grfKeyState, pt, pdwEffect***)**
LPDATAOBJECT *pDataObject*
DWORD *grfKeyState*
POINTL *pt*
LPDWORD *pdwEffect*

IDropTarget::DragEnter determines whether the target window can accept the dragged object and what effect the dragged object will have on the target window.

Parameter

pDataObject
Points to an instance of the **IDataObject** interface, through which the dragged data is accessible.

grfKeyState
Specifies a combination of the MK_CONTROL, MK_SHIFT, MK_ALT, MK_LBUTTON, MK_MBUTTON, and MK_RBUTTON flags that identifies the present state of the keyboard modifier keys.

pt
Points to a structure containing the current mouse/cursor coordinates in screen coordinates.

pdwEffect
Points to where to return the effect of this drag operation to the caller. The value for *pdwEffect* is from the **DROPEFFECT** enumeration. For a list of values, see the section "**DROPEFFECT** Enumeration," earlier in this chapter.

Return Value

Value	Meaning
S_OK	The function completed its task successfully.
E_OUTOFMEMORY	Out of memory.
E_INVALIDARG	One or more arguments are invalid.
E_UNEXPECTED	An unexpected error occurred.

Comments

During calls to **IDropTarget::DragEnter** and **IDropTarget::DragOver**, the target should provide appropriate target feedback to the user. During a drop operation, as the mouse passes over the unobscured portion of the window associated with this drop target, **IDropTarget::DragEnter**, **IDropTarget::DragOver**, and **IDropTarget::DragLeave** are called as the mouse first enters, moves around within, then leaves each drop target.

The first time the mouse enters the screen region for a given target, **IDropTarget::DragEnter** is called. As long as the drag operation continues and the target remains the same, **IDropTarget::DragOver** is called. When the target changes or the drag operation is canceled, **IDropTarget::DragLeave** is called. When the drop finally happens, **IDropTarget::Drop** is called. **IDropTarget::Drop** is never called without first calling **IDropTarget::DragEnter** on the given drop target.

IDropTarget::DragEnter determines whether the dragged object is acceptable by examining the clipboard formats available for the object, the values pointed to by the *pdwEffect* parameter, and the state of the modifier keys, as indicated in the *grfKeyState* parameter. If the dragged object can be dropped, **IDropTarget::DragEnter** determines the corresponding effect on the drop source.

The drop target indicates its decision through the *pdwEffect* parameter. The *pdwEffect* parameter is an OR-ing together values contained in the **DROPEFFECT** enumeration. Typically, DROPEFFECT_COPY is passed in *pdwEffect*, although DROPEFFECT_LINK can be passed to create a link to the source data. Whether the source allows the dragged data to be permanently moved from the source application is indicated by the presence or absence of DROPEFFECT_MOVE.

The value returned in *pdwEffect* is passed through the **DoDragDrop** function to **IDropSource::GiveFeedback** so the source can change the pointer appropriately and provide feedback to the user.

To provide appropriate target feedback, the drop target can pull data from *pDataObject*. (For example, a drop operation into a spreadsheet might want to know the size of the table being dropped is so it can highlight an appropriate set of cells.)

Example

The following implementation of **IDropTarget::DragEnter**, first checks for a valid **IDataObject** pointer parameter and then sets several state variables that relate to drag scrolling. Two OLE API functions, **OleQueryCreateFromData** and **OleQueryLinkFromData**, are called to determine if the data transfer object offers data in an acceptable format for embedding or linking.

The state of the modifier keys influences the drop effect. The absence of a modifier indicates the drop will result in a move operation, the CTRL key indicates a copy operation, and the CTRL and SHIFT key combination indicates a link operation.

The contents of *pdwEffect* is set to DROPEFFECT_NONE under the following conditions:

- There are no acceptable formats available from the data transfer object.
- The data selection being dragged in a selection from the drop target's current document.
- The modifier keys imply that the drop effect is to be either a move or a copy operation, but **OleQueryCreateFromData** returned an error, indicating that no appropriate formats were available from the data transfer object.
- The modifier keys imply that the drop effect is to be a link operation, but **OleQueryLinkFromData** indicated that the formats required to create a linked object were not available.

DoDragScroll is called to determine whether the pointer has been in the scrollable region for the specified amount of time and, if so, sets *dwDropEffect* to DROPEFFECT_SCROLL. If the resulting drop effect is a move, copy, or link operation, the value of *dwScrollEffect* is or-ed into the value of *pdwEffect* before **IDropTarget_DragEnter** returns.

```
HRESULT IDropTarget_DragEnter (
    LPDROPTARGET            lpThis,
    LPDATAOBJECT            pDataObject,
    DWORD                   grfKeyState,
    POINTL                  pointl,
    LPDWORD                 pdwEffect)
{
    if (pDataObject == NULL)
        return (ResultFromScode (E_INVALIDARG);

    LPDOC lpDoc = ((struct CDocDropTargetImpl FAR*)lpThis)->lpDoc;
    lpDoc->m_fDragLeave              = FALSE;
    lpDoc->m_dwTimeEnterScrollArea   = 0;
    lpDoc->m_lastdwScrollDir         = SCROLLDIR_NULL;
    lpDoc->m_dwScrollInset = (INT)GetProfileInt ("windows",
                                 "DragScrollInset",
                                 DD_DEFSCROLLINSET);
    lpDoc->m_dwScrollDelay = (INT)GetProfileInt ("windows",
                                 "DragScrollDelay",
                                 DD_DEFSCROLLDELAY);

    HRESULT hRes = OleQueryCreateFromData(pDataObject);
```

```
        sc = GetScode (hRes);
        if ((sc == S_OK) || (sc == OLE_S_STATIC))
            lpDoc->m_fCanDropCopy = TRUE;
        else
            lpDoc->m_fCanDropCopy = FALSE;

        if ( (OleQueryLinkFromData(pDataObject)) == NOERROR)
            lpDoc->m_fCanDropLink = TRUE;
        else
            lpDoc->m_fCanDropLink = FALSE;

        if (! lpDoc->m_fCanDropCopy && ! lpDoc->m_fCanDropLink)  {
            *lpdwDropEffect = DROPEFFECT_NONE;
            return NOERROR;
        }

        if (lpDoc->m_fLocalDrag) {
            if (SelectionLocal (pointl,lpDoc))  {
                *lpdwDropEffect = DROPEFFECT_NONE;
                return NOERROR;
            }
        }

        if (grfKeyState & MK_CONTROL) {
            if (grfKeyState & MK_SHIFT)
                *pdwEffect = DROPEFFECT_LINK;
            else
                *pdwEffect = DROPEFFECT_COPY;
        } else
            *pdwEffect = DROPEFFECT_MOVE;

        if ( (*pdwEffect == DROPEFFECT_COPY      ||
              *pdwEffect == DROPEFFECT_MOVE)        &&
             ! lpDoc->m_fCanDropCopy )  {
                *pdwEffect = DROPEFFECT_NONE;
                return NOERROR;
        }
        if ( *pdwEffect == DROPEFFECT_LINK && ! lpDoc->m_fCanDropLink )  {
            *pdwEffect = DROPEFFECT_NONE;
            return NOERROR;
        }
        if (DoDragScroll (lpDoc, pointl))
            dwScrollEffect = DROPEFFECT_SCROLL;

        *pdwEffect |= dwScrollEffect;
        return NOERROR;
    }
```

See Also **DoDragDrop, IDropSource::GiveFeedback**

IDropTarget::DragOver

HRESULT IDropTarget::DragOver(*grfKeyState, pt, pdwEffect***)**
DWORD *grfKeyState*
POINTL *pt*
LPDWORD *pdwEffect*

IDropTarget::DragOver provides feedback to the user and to **DoDragDrop** about the state of the drag operation within a drop target application.

Parameter

grfKeyState
A combination of the MK_CONTROL, MK_SHIFT, MK_ALT, MK_LBUTTON, MK_MBUTTON, and MK_RBUTTON flags that identifies the present state of the keyboard modifier keys.

pt
Structure containing the current mouse/cursor coordinates in screen coordinates.

pdwEffect
Points to where to return the effect of this drag operation to the caller. The return value is a combination of **DROPEFFECT** values. For a list of values, see the section "DROPEFFECT Enumeration," earlier in this chapter.

Return Value

Value	Meaning
S_OK	State information returned successfully.
E_OUTOFMEMORY	Out of memory.
E_INVALIDARG	One or more arguments are invalid.
E_UNEXPECTED	An unexpected error occurred.

Comments

After the pointer initially enters the target window, **IDropTarget::DragOver** is called each time the pointer (mouse) moves until the drag operation is canceled or a drop occurs. For efficiency reasons, no clipboard data object is passed. The clipboard data object passed in the most recent call to **IDropTarget::DragEnter** is used.

IDropTarget::DragOver determines whether the dragged object is acceptable by examining the clipboard formats available for the object, the values pointed to by the *pdwEffect* parameter, and the state of the modifier keys, as indicated in the *grfKeyState* parameter. If the dragged object can be dropped, **IDropTarget::DragOver** determines the corresponding effect on the drag source application.

The target application indicates its decision through the *pdwEffect* parameter.

To provide appropriate target feedback, the drop target can pull data from *pDataObject* (as was passed in the most recent call to **IDropTarget::DropEnter**).

Example

In the following implementation, **IDropTarget::DragOver** first checks whether it is time to begin scrolling before calling **QueryDrop** to determine whether a drop could happen at the current mouse position. **IDropTarget_DragOver** changes its feedback based on the return value from **QueryDrop**.

```
HRESULT IDropTarget_DragOver (
    LPDROPTARGET            lpThis,
    DWORD                   grfKeyState,
    POINTL                  pointl,
    LPDWORD                 pdwEffect)
{
    LPDOC   lpDoc = ((struct CDocDropTargetImpl FAR*)lpThis)->lpDoc;
    BOOL    fDragScroll;

    fDragScroll = DoDragScroll ( lpDoc, pointl );
    if (QueryDrop(lpDoc,grfKeyState,pointl,fDragScroll,pdwEffect))
        ChangeFeedback();
    else
        RestoreFeedback();

    return ResultFromScode(S_OK);
}
```

See Also

IDropTarget::DragEnter, IDropSource::GiveFeedback, DoDragDrop

IDropTarget::DragLeave

HRESULT IDropTarget::DragLeave()

IDropTarget::DragLeave causes the drop target to remove its feedback. This method is called when the mouse leaves the area of a given target while a drag is in progress or when the drag operation is canceled.

Return Value

Value	Meaning
S_OK	Drop target feedback was removed.
E_OUTOFMEMORY	Out of memory.

Comments

The data transfer object passed to the most recent call to **IDropTarget::DragEnter** is implied.

The drop target should remove any target feedback it currently has showing. If the drop target is currently holding on to the data transfer object passed to **IDropTarget::DragEnter**, it should release it at this time.

Example

The following example of **IDropTarget::DragLeave** sets a flag to indicate that a drag and drop operation has terminated and then restores the window to its previous state if the last known drop effect was a move, copy, or link.

```
HRESULT IDropTarget_DragLeave ( LPDROPTARGET lpThis)
{
    LPDOC lpDoc = ((struct CDocDropTargetImpl FAR*)lpThis)->lpDoc;
    HDC hdc;

    lpDoc->m_fDragLeave = TRUE;
    if (lpDoc->dwLastEffect != DROPEFFECT_NONE) {
        hdc = GetDC(lpDoc->hwnd);
        HighlightRect(lpDoc->hwnd, hdc, &lpDoc->rcDrag);
        ReleaseDC(lpDoc->hwnd, hdc);
    }
    return ResultFromScode(S_OK);
}
```

See Also

IDropTarget::DragEnter

IDropTarget::Drop

HRESULT IDropTarget::Drop(*pDataObject, grfKeyState, pt, pdwEffect***)**
LPDATAOBJECT *pDataObject*
DWORD *grfKeyState*
POINTL *pt*
LPDWORD *pdwEffect*

IDropTarget::Drop drops the source data, indicated by *pDataObject*, on this target application.

Parameter

pDataObject
Points to an instance of the **IDataObject** interface, through which the data is accessible.

grfKeyState
A combination of the MK_CONTROL, MK_SHIFT, MK_ALT, MK_LBUTTON, MK_MBUTTON, and MK_RBUTTON flags that identifies the present state of the keyboard modifier keys.

pt
Structure containing the current mouse/cursor coordinates in screen coordinates.

pdwEffect
Points to where to return the effect of this drag operation to the caller. The return value is a combination of **DROPEFFECT** values. For a list of these values, see "DROPEFFECT Enumeration," earlier in this chapter.

Return Value

Value	Meaning
S_OK	The function completed its task successfully.
E_OUTOFMEMORY	Out of memory.
E_INVALIDARG	One or more arguments are invalid.
E_UNEXPECTED	An unexpected error occurred.

Comments

The data being dropped is accessible through *pDataObject*. The formats available through the **IDataObject** interface should be used in conjunction with the state of the modifier keys to determine the semantics of what should happen on the drop. Appropriate information is passed back through *pdwEffect*. The caller can only use *pDataObject* for the duration of this call. By the time **IDropTarget::Drop** returns, the drop operation should have obtained everything it needs from *pDataObject*.

Example

The following implementation of **IDropTarget::Drop** determines the effect of the drop by examining *grfKeyState* and other variables internal to the data transfer object, *lpDoc*. If the drop results in a move, copy, or link operation, the same code used to paste and paste link a compound document object (**PasteFromData**) is called to complete the drop operation.

```
HRESULT    IDropTarget_Drop (
    LPDROPTARGET            lpThis,
    LPDATAOBJECT            pDataObject,
    DWORD                   grfKeyState,
    POINTL                  pointl,
    LPDWORD                 pdwEffect)
{
    LPDOC  lpDoc = ((struct CDocDropTargetImpl FAR*)lpThis)->lpDoc;
    lpDoc->m_fDragLeave = TRUE;
    lpDoc->m_fLocalDrop = TRUE;

    if (fDragScroll)
        dwScrollEffect = DROPEFFECT_SCROLL;

    if ( (! lpDoc->m_fCanDropCopy && ! lpDoc->m_fCanDropLink) ||
         ((lpDoc->m_fLocalDrag) && (DataInLocalSelection(lpDoc)))  {
            *pdwEffect = DROPEFFECT_NONE;
    }
    else if (grfKeyState & MK_CONTROL)  {
        if (grfKeyState & MK_SHIFT)  {
            if (lpDoc->m_fCanDropLink)
                *pdwEffect = DROPEFFECT_LINK;
```

```
                else
                    *pdwEffect = DROPEFFECT_NONE;
            }
            else if (lpDoc->m_fCanDropCopy)
                *pdwEffect = DROPEFFECT_COPY;
            else
                *pdwEffect = DROPEFFECT_NONE;

        } else if (lpDoc->m_fCanDropCopy)
            *pdwEffect = DROPEFFECT_MOVE;

        *pdwEffect |= dwScrollEffect;
        if (*pdwEffect != DROPEFFECT_NONE)  {
            BOOL fLink     = (*pdwEffect == DROPEFFECT_LINK);
            BOOL fStatus;

            fStatus = PasteFromData (lpDoc, pDataObject,
                lpDoc->m_fLocalDrag, fLink);

            // If the drop was unsuccessful, restore the original focus
            // line.
            if (! fStatus)
                ResetFocus( lpLL, (WORD)iFocusLine );

            // Do not enable redraw for a local drag/drop move until the
            // source is done deleting the moved object.
            if (! (lpDoc->m_fLocalDrag
                && (*pdwEffect & DROPEFFECT_MOVE) != 0 ))
                DisableRedraw ( (LPDOC)lpDoc );
        }

        return ResultFromScode(S_OK);
    }
```

See Also **IDropTarget::DragEnter, IDropSource::GiveFeedback, DoDragDrop**

Drag and Drop API Functions

The following API functions are used in drag and drop operations (see also COMPOBJ.H):

RegisterDragDrop(HWND hwnd, LPDROPTARGET pDropTarget);
RevokeDragDrop(HWND hwnd);
DoDragDrop(LPDATAOBJECT pDataObject, LPDROPSOURCE pDropSource, DWORD dwEffect, LPDWORD pdwEffect);

RegisterDragDrop

HRESULT RegisterDragDrop(*hwnd, pDropTarget***)**
HWND *hwnd*
LPDROPTARGET *pDropTarget*

RegisterDragDrop registers an application window as being able to accept dropped objects. This function only registers the window specified by the *hwnd* parameter.

Parameter

hwnd
Specifies the handle to the window that is the target for the drop.

pDropTarget
Points to the **IDropTarget** implementation through which information about the *hwnd* is communicated while the drag and drop operation is in progress.

Return Values

Value	Meaning
S_OK	The application was registered successfully.
DRAGDROP_E_INVALIDHWND	Invalid *hwnd*.
DRAGDROP_E_ALREADYREGISTERED	This window has already been registered as a drop target.
E_OUTOFMEMORY	Out of memory.

Comments

To accept drop operations, an application registers the applicable window(s) as potential drop targets. **RegisterDragDrop** *must* be called for each window capable of accepting dropped objects.

The *pDropTarget* parameter points to an instance of the **IDropTarget** interface, through which communication is made with the target application during a drag and drop operation. During a drag and drop operation, as the mouse passes over unobscured portions of the target window(s), the passed **IDropTarget::DragOver** is called. When a drop operation actually occurs in a given window, **IDropTarget::Drop** is called.

See Also

RevokeDragDrop

RevokeDragDrop

HRESULT RevokeDragDrop(*hwnd*)
HWND *hwnd*

RevokeDragDrop revokes an application window previously registered for drag/drop operations.

Parameter

hwnd
Specifies the handle to the window that is the target for the drop.

Return Values

Value	Meaning
S_OK	Window was revoked successfully.
DRAGDROP_E_INVALIDHWND	Invalid *hwnd*.
DRAGDROP_E_NOTREGISTERED	An attempt was made to revoke a drop target that has not been registered.
E_OUTOFMEMORY	Out of memory.

Comments

To revoke a window's ability to accept dropped objects, an application calls the **RevokeDragDrop** function on the window previously registered with the **RegisterDragDrop** function.

If an application wants to ensure that an object is kept alive during a call to **RevokeDragDrop**, it should preserve the lock count of the object. Instead of simply calling **RevokeDragDrop**, the applications should do the following:

```
CoLockObjectExternal(pUnk, TRUE, FALSE);
RevokeDragDrop(hwnd);
CoLockObjectExternal(pUnk, FALSE, FALSE);
```

This guarantees the object will be available after the **RevokeDragDrop** call.

See Also

RegisterDragDrop

DoDragDrop

HRESULT DoDragDrop(*pDataObject*, *pDropSource*, *dwEffect*, *pdwEffect*)
LPDATAOBJECT *pDataObject*
LPDROPSOURCE *pDropSource*
DWORD *dwEffect*
LPDWORD *pdwEffect*

DoDragDrop initiates a drag and drop operation and facilitates communication between the drop source and the drop target.

Parameter

pDataObject
Points to an instance of the **IDataObject** interface, which provides the data being dragged.

pDropSource
Points to an instance of the **IDropSource** interface, which is used to communicate with the source during the drag operation.

dwEffect
Determines the effects the drag source allows in the drag operation. Most significant is whether it permits a move. The *dwEffect* and *pdwEffect* parameters obtain values from the **DROPEFFECT** enumeration. For a list of values, see the section "DROPEFFECT Enumeration," earlier in this chapter.

pdwEffect
Points to a value that indicates how the drag operation affected the source data. The *pdwEffect* parameter is set only if the operation is not canceled.

Return Value

Value	Meaning
S_OK	The drop operation was initiated successfully.
DRAGDROP_S_DROP	The drop operation was successful.
DRAGDROP_S_CANCEL	The drop operation was canceled.
E_OUTOFMEMORY	Out of memory.
E_UNSPEC	An unexpected error occurred.

Comments

When a user starts to drag data, the drag source calls **DoDragDrop**, passing it pointers to the data transfer object's **IDataObject** and **IDropSource** interfaces and a place holder for a value indicating the effect of a potential drop. When the mouse pointer passes over a window that is a registered drop target, **DoDragDrop** calls **IDropTarget::DragEnter**.

The modifier key state, location of the mouse, and the **IDataObject** interface pointer are passed as parameters to **IDropTarget::DragEnter**. This information is used by **IDropTarget::DragEnter** to return a drop effect—a value that represents what the effect of a drop would be on the drag source. From the perspective of the drag source, the result is that the data is either removed or unchanged. For a list of valid drop effects, see "DROPEFFECT Enumeration," earlier in this chapter.

For each iteration of its loop, **DoDragDrop** calls **IDropSource::QueryContinueDrag** to check whether to continue or cancel the drag. The return value from **IDropSource::QueryContinueDrag** determines which **IDropTarget** method is called next.

IDropSource::QueryContinueDrag Return Value	Resulting Interface Method Call(s)
DRAGDROP_S_CANCEL	**IDropTarget::DragLeave**
DRAGDROP_S_DROP	**IDropTarget::Drop**
S_OK	**IDropTarget::DragOver** **IDropSource::GiveFeedback**

IDropTarget::DragOver and **IDropSource::GiveFeedback** are paired so that as the mouse moves across the drop target, the user is given the most up-to-date feedback on the mouse's position. **DoDragDrop** continues to loop until such time that the user cancels the drag or drops the data. Depending on the user action, **IDropSource::GiveFeedback** returns DRAGDROP_S_CANCEL for a canceled drag and DRAGDROP_S_DROP for a successful drop.

The values for *pdwEffect* and *dwOKEffect* are based on an or-ing of the values in the **DROPEFFECT** enumeration.The *pdwEffect* parameter determines the effect the drag and drop operation had on the source data. Typically, DROPEFFECT_COPY is passed in *dwEffect*, although DROPEFFECT_LINK can be passed to create a link to the source data. The presence or absence of DROPEFFECT_MOVE indicates whether the source allows the dragged data to be permanently moved from the source application.

See Also **IDropSource::GiveFeedback**

CHAPTER 11

In-Place Activation Interfaces and Functions

This chapter describes the interfaces that are implemented and used by containers and object applications that support activating embedded objects in place, within the context of their containing document.

This chapter is divided into two parts: the first part provides an overview and procedural information on implementing in-place activation. The second part describes the in-place interfaces and API functions.

Implementing In-Place Activation

In order for the user to work with an active embedded object in OLE 1 applications, the object has to be opened in its own top-level document window within the object application's process space. Although this model is still supported by OLE 2, a new process—called *in-place activation*—enables users to interact with an object without leaving the open compound document in which the object is embedded.

While an object is active in place, the container shares its process and user interface space with the active object. A *composite menu bar*, composed of menu groups from both the container and in-place object's object application, replaces the container's main menu bar during an in-place activation session. This makes commands and features from both applications available to the user, including context-sensitive help on behalf of the active object.

The user is often unaware of the interaction happening between the active object and its container. The underlying OLE interprocess communication system allows the active embedded object to interact with its container in response to user input.

Note In-place activation is sometimes referred to as "in-place editing" or "visual editing." However, not all objects support editing as their primary verb action (for example, a video clip might have play as its only verb of choice). Therefore, in-place activation is used to include any action associated with the object's primary verb.

Basic Approach to In-Place Activation

In-place activation is always initiated by the object in response to an **IOleObject::DoVerb** call, usually because the user double-clicked on the object or because the user selected a verb from the Edit menu.

Activating an embedded object in place causes the following sequence of events to happen:

- The object should request its container to show the object and continue using the embedding site pointer for its activation in place of the **IOleClientSite**. (This is only done if the selected verb implies making changes to the object (rather than just showing it) and the pointer to the object's **IOleClientSite** (passed to **DoVerb)** is not the same as the object's embedding site.)
- An in-place window is created by the activated object. This window is a child of the container window containing the object's view. The window might or might not belong to the container's process—this depends on whether the embedded object's object application is a DLL or an EXE implementation.
- The container's menu bar is replaced by a composite menu bar consisting of some menus from the container along with some menus from the object's object application.
- The in-place activation window is given a shaded border, following the recommendations in the chapter, "OLE User Interface Guidelines."
- The embedded object can request space from the container to display one or more toolbars, formula bars, rulers, or other frame adornments.
- The in-place activation window is activated and takes the keyboard focus.

The in-place window receives keyboard and mouse input while the embedded object is active. When the user selects commands from the composite menu bar, the command and associated menu messages are sent to the container or object application, depending on which application owns the particular drop-down menu selected (the object application does not receive WM_INITMENU). Input through the object's rulers, toolbars and/or frame adornments go directly to the embedded object because these windows belong to it.

An embedded object remains active until it voluntarily gives up the active state or until the container deactivates the object—for example, the user clicks the mouse inside the client area of the container but outside the in-place activation window.

In particular, the object is not deactivated if the user clicks on the menu bar, the title bar, or a scroll bar belonging to the container application. However, clicking on another OLE object embedded in the same document deactivates the in-place object.

The code implementing an embedded object can be either a DLL or a stand-alone EXE file. In both cases, the composite menu bar contains items (typically drop-downs) from both processes. In the case of a DLL object application, the in-place activation window is just another child window in the container's window hierarchy, receiving its input through the container application's message pump.

In the EXE case, the in-place activation window belongs to the embedded object's object application process, but its parent is a window in the container's window hierarchy. The input for the in-place window appears in the object application's message queue and is dispatched by the message loop in the object application. The OLE libraries are responsible for making sure that menu commands and messages are dispatched correctly.

In-Place Window Hierarchy

When an object is active in place, it has access to the following windows in the window hierarchy:

In-place Window Hierarchy	Description
Frame window	The outermost main window where the container application's main menu resides.
Document window	The window in which the compound document containing the embedded object is shown to the user.
Pane window	In an application that has split-pane windows, this is a subwindow of the document window that contains the object's view.
Parent window	The container's window that contains the object's view. It is in this window that the in-place window is to be created.
In-place window	The window containing the active in-place object. It is a child of the parent window.

With the exception of the in-place window, these are often the same window. For example, an SDI container's frame window is the same as its document window. Figure 11-1 is an example in which a simple container without split-pane views or complex window structures has its document, pane, and parent windows all in the the same window. (In these cases, the container returns NULL for the redundant **IOleInPlaceUIWindow** interface pointers in response to the in-place object calling the container's **IOleInPlaceFrame::GetWindowContext** method.)

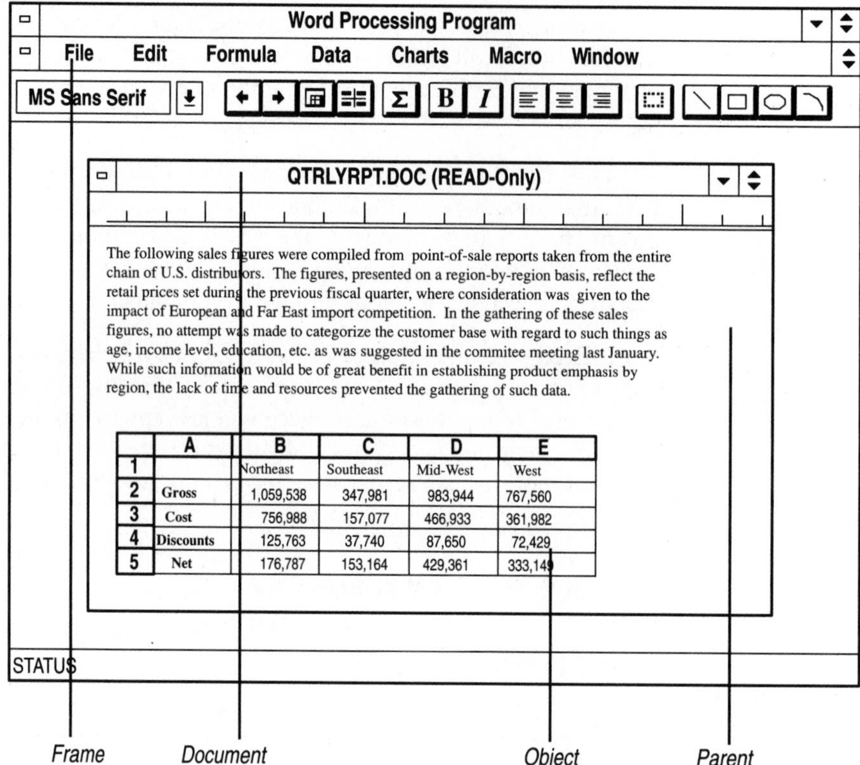
Word Processing Program
File Edit Formula Data Charts Macro Window
MS Sans Serif
QTRLYRPT.DOC (READ-Only)
The following sales figures were compiled from point-of-sale reports taken from the entire chain of U.S. distributors. The figures, presented on a region-by-region basis, reflect the retail prices set during the previous fiscal quarter, where consideration was given to the impact of European and Far East import competition. In the gathering of these sales figures, no attempt was made to categorize the customer base with regard to such things as age, income level, education, etc. as was suggested in the commitee meeting last January. While such information would be of great benefit in establishing product emphasis by region, the lack of time and resources prevented the gathering of such data.
A B C D E
1 Northeast Southeast Mid-West West
2 Gross 1,059,538 347,981 983,944 767,560
3 Cost 756,988 157,077 466,933 361,982
4 Discounts 125,763 37,740 87,650 72,429
5 Net 176,787 153,164 429,361 333,149
STATUS
Frame
Document
Object
Parent

Figure 11-1. In-place activation window hierarchy for a simple container.

More complex cases involve MDI applications, split-pane and structured views, and nested objects (where the parent is not the same as the pane). In these cases, the object creates its in-place window as a child of the parent window, and uses the other windows to place the composite menu bar and optional toolbars and/or frame adornments.

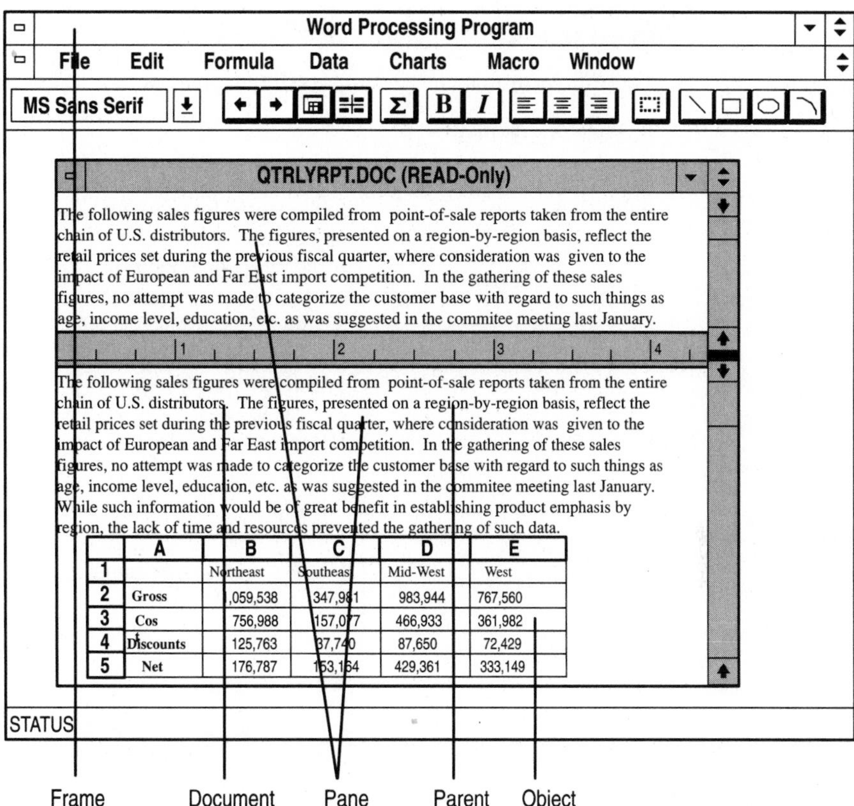
Word Processing Program
File Edit Formula Data Charts Macro Window
MS Sans Serif
QTRLYRPT.DOC (READ-Only)
The following sales figures were compiled from point-of-sale reports taken from the entire chain of U.S. distributors. The figures, presented on a region-by-region basis, reflect the retail prices set during the previous fiscal quarter, where consideration was given to the impact of European and Far East import competition. In the gathering of these sales figures, no attempt was made to categorize the customer base with regard to such things as age, income level, education, etc. as was suggested in the commitee meeting last January.
The following sales figures were compiled from point-of-sale reports taken from the entire chain of U.S. distributors. The figures, presented on a region-by-region basis, reflect the retail prices set during the previous fiscal quarter, where consideration was given to the impact of European and Far East import competition. In the gathering of these sales figures, no attempt was made to categorize the customer base with regard to such things as age, income level, education, etc. as was suggested in the commitee meeting last January. While such information would be of great benefit in establishing product emphasis by region, the lack of time and resources prevented the gathering of such data.
A B C D E
1 Northeast Southeast Mid-West West
2 Gross 1,059,538 347,981 983,944 767,560
3 Cos 756,988 157,077 466,933 361,982
4 Discounts 125,763 37,740 87,650 72,429
5 Net 176,787 153,164 429,361 333,149
STATUS
Frame
Document
Pane
Parent
Object

Figure 11-2. In-place activation window hierarchy for a more complex application.

An in-place object can request space for the toolbars on the frame, document, or pane windows. The object can also add adornments, expanding the in-place window as needed to make room. These latter adornments overlay the other contents in the container.

In-Place Activation Interfaces

The following interfaces support the in-place activation of an embedded object:

In-Place Activation Interface	Implementation	Purpose
IOleWindow	Inplemented by every in-place object and container, **IOleWindow** contains the methods used to obtain the handle to the in-place window and for support of context-sensitive help. All other in-place interfaces are derived from **IOleWindow**.	Used to return the window handle to the various windows associated with in-place activation (frame, document, parent and in-place object). Also used to enter and exit context-sensitive help mode.
IOleInPlaceObject	Implemented by the in-place object's object application, **IOleInPlaceObject** contains the methods used to activate and deactivate an in-place object.	Used by the object's immediate container to activate and deactivate the object.
IOleInPlaceActiveObject	Implemented by the in-place object's object application, **IOleInPlaceActiveObject** provides a direct channel of communication between the in-place object and the frame and document windows.	Used by the in-place object's top-level container to manipulate the object while it is active.
IOleInPlaceUIWindow	Implemented by the container, **IOleInPlaceUIWindow** provides the methods used to manipulate the container's document window.	Used by the in-place object to negotiate borders on a document window.
IOleInPlaceFrame	Implemented by the container, **IOleInPlaceFrame** provides the methods used to control the application's top-level frame window.	Used by the in-place object to control the top-level container's menus, status line display, keystroke accelerator translation, help mode, and modeless dialogs.
IOleInPlaceSite	Implemented by the container, **IOleInPlaceSite** provides the methods used to interact with the object's in-place client site.	Used by the in-place object to control in-place activation from the container.

Hierarchical Relationship Between In-Place Interfaces

The arrangement of objects and connections between their interfaces is shown in Figure 11-3. The nesting of objects makes it possible for several levels of embedded objects to be active. However, no more than one object can share the top-level container's main menu. Calls that install user interface menus and tools, activate and switch between windows, and dispatch menu and keystrokes go directly between the active in-place object and the top-level container. The calls that support activating, deactivating, scrolling, or clipping objects go through the containment hierarchy so that each object level can perform the correct actions.

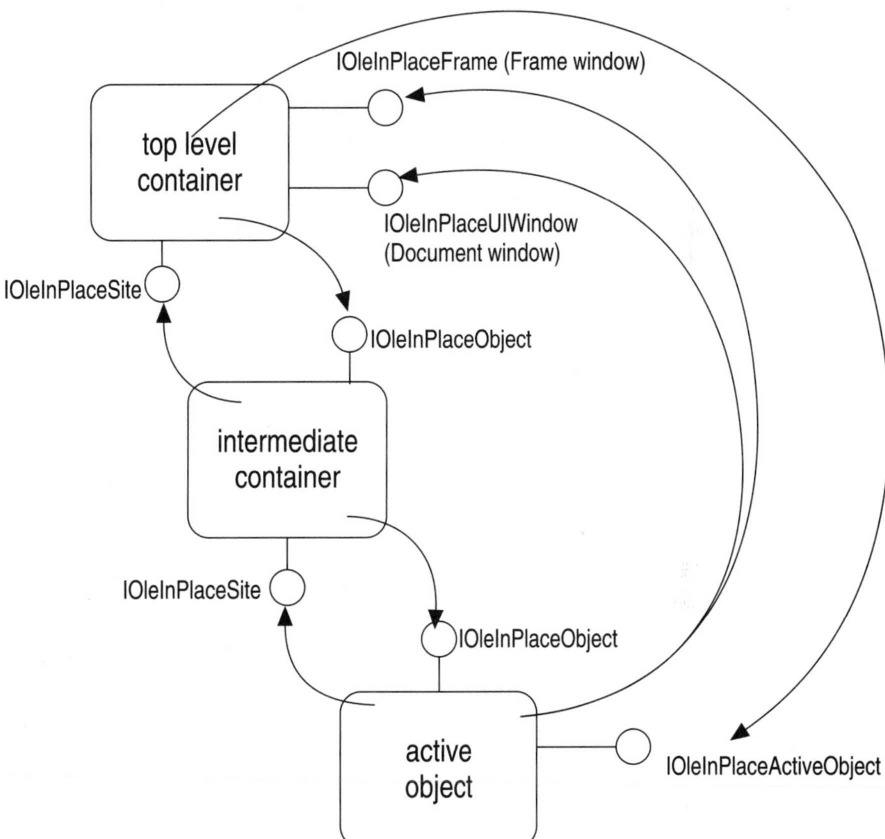

Figure 11-3. Relationship of object, container, and frame interfaces.

The **IOleWindow** interface is implemented by both objects and containers. All the other in-place activation interfaces are derived from **IOleWindow**. Calling **IOleInPlaceSite::GetWindowContext** returns the handle to the parent window in which the in-place active window is created.

An in-place object talks to its immediate container using the container's exposed **IOleInPlaceSite** interface. The active in-place object interacts with objects higher up in the containment hierarchy by using the top-level container's implementation of the **IOleInPlaceFrame** and **IOleInPlaceUIWindow** interfaces. Pointers to these interfaces are obtained by calling the container's **IOleInPlaceSite::GetWindowContext** method. If the container itself is an in-place object, it returns its immediate container's **IOleInPlaceFrame** and **IOleInPlaceUIWindows** interface pointers through **GetWindowContext** rather than through its own implementation.

A container uses the **IOleInPlaceObject** interface to talk to its embedded objects. Upper-level objects at the document- and frame-level windows use the **IOleInPlaceActiveObject** interface talk to the active in-place object.

Object States and Transitions

An active in-place object is modal with respect to the document in which it is contained. Other than through the container menu commands available on the composite menu bar, the user is not able to edit other objects or data in the same document.

Clicking outside the active in-place window deactivates the user interface for the active in-place object. When deactivating, the in-place object removes the composite menu bar, toolbars and/or frame adornments before removing the hatched shading around itself. The new selection state determines the container's user interface.

The in-place object's object application is not actually shut down at this point. Instead, it is in a ready state that allows for quick reactivation should the user activate the object again or choose to undo changes made to the object while it was active in place. The object is fully deactivated when the user invokes some other command that causes the object to lose the ability to undo changes.

While an object is active in place, the user can switch to other windows, leaving the object and its containing document in a dormant state. SDI and MDI applications handle user interface changes differently when switching between windows. When the user switches to a top-level window in another SDI container application, the frame window is shown to have an inactive border and title. The menu bar and any toolbars or other editing controls remain visible but are inactive. On switching back to the in-place window, the titles are made active and focus is returned to the object's in-place window.

If the user switches to a top-level window in a different MDI container, the behavior is the same as in the SDI case. If, however, the user switches to another document window in the same MDI workspace, the containing document window is drawn as inactive, the composite menu bar is replaced by the menu bar appropriate for the document being activated, and any frame-level or pop-up user interface toolbars shown by the object application are hidden. On switching back to the in-place window, the composite menu is restored and focus is returned to the object's in-place window so the control bars are shown and the document window is shown as active.

Activating the Object

At the time an object is activated in place, it will have already been created and embedded in the container and there will be an associated client site in the container. In-place activation is always initiated by the object in response to an **IOleObject::DoVerb** call (usually, the result of the user double-clicking on the object or selecting one of the object's verbs from the Edit menu).

The **IOleObject::DoVerb** method takes an *lpmsg* parameter and a *lindex* parameter (to tell which of the extended-layout rectangles containing the object have been activated). The object uses these active layout rectangles to either activate an object it contains (thus implementing inside out activation) or to determine why the **IOleObject::DoVerb** function was called (in response to the user double-clicking or selecting a verb from the Edit menu).

The following list summarizes the implementation of **IOleObject::DoVerb** to support in-place activation:

- The object uses results from the most recent layout negotiation to determine whether it can activate in place or not. For example, a view scale other than 100% might make it impossible to activate in place. In this case, the object should open a new top-level document window (as in OLE 1).

  Layout negotiation is always done in client coordinates and is performed in the coordinate space of the target device, usually a printed page. On activation, the object assumes that the negotiated space is mapped onto the window coordinates supplied in the *lprcChildPos* parameter passed to the **IOleInPlaceSite::GetWindowContext** method. The coordinates enable the object to determine the prevailing view scaling and to properly perform its drawing.
- The object calls the container's **IOleClientSite::QueryInterface** to obtain **IOleInPlaceSite** interface. If the container supports in-place activation, it returns a referenced pointer to the **IOleInPlaceSite** interface; otherwise, it returns NULL.

After getting the pointer to the **IOleInPlaceSite** interface, the object calls **IOleInPlaceSite::CanInPlaceActivate** to see whether the container is willing to activate the object. At this stage of the activation, the container can refuse to activate the object (as indicated by a return value other than S_OK), even though it supports in-place activation. If the container does not support in-place activation, the object should instead open a new document window in which to activate the object (as in OLE 1). If **CanInPlaceActivate** returns S_OK, the object calls **IOleInPlaceSite::OnInPlaceActivate** to notify the container that the object is about to be activated.

- The object calls **IOleInPlaceSite::GetWindowContext** to get the interface pointers to the container's frame and document windows. **IOleInPlaceFrame** is returned for the frame window and **IOleInPlaceUIWindow** is returned for the document window. This pointer might be NULL depending on whether the container supports the document window.

  In addition, **GetWindowContext** fills in the **OLEINPLACEFRAMEINFO** structure with the container's accelerator table and the container MDI flag. It also returns the object's *posRect* and *clipRect* rectangles in the container's document.
- The object calls **IOleInPlaceSite::OnUIActivate** to alert the container that it is about to activate the in-place user interface menu.

After getting pointers to the **IOleInPlaceFrame** and **IOleInPlaceUIWindow** interfaces, the object should:

1. Calculate the required size needed for the in-place window, which is the intersection of the *posRect* and *clipRect* rectangles passed in *lprcClipRect.*
2. Create an in-place window of the right size as a child of the parent window. The object creates the window so that the object application can use the window classes it defined and so the in-place object can receive the input messages directly from the system queue. The in-place window border should be shaded, following the recommendations listed in the chapter "OLE User Interface Guidelines."
3. Call the container's **IOleInPlaceSite::GetWindow** method to get the handle to the object's parent window. After getting the parent window, the object calls **SetParent** (*hWndEditWindow*, *hWndParent*) to change the in-place window's parent.
4. To add titlebars, palettes, toolbars, or adornments of any type, negotiate with the container to position them, as described in, "Installing Toolbars and Other Frame Adornments," later in this chapter.

   Should the container refuse to accept any adornments, the object can choose to cancel the in-place activation and instead open a new document window in the object application's process space, as is done in OLE 1 applications (see "Opening Compound Documents," in the chapter, "Programming Considerations").

5. Create an empty menu by calling the **CreateMenu** function. The object then calls the container's **IOleInPlaceFrame::InsertMenus** method with the new composite menu bar to allow the container to insert any necessary menu elements. Upon the return from **InsertMenus**, the object adds its own menu elements to the menu bar.

   After adding its menu elements, the object calls the **OleCreateMenuDescriptor** API function to create a **HOLEMENU** descriptor of the shared menu, which OLE uses when dispatching menu messages and commands. The object passes to **OleCreateMenuDescriptor** the handle to the composite menu and a pointer to the **OLEMENUGROUPWIDTHS** structure, which contains an array of values showing the number of elements in each menu group. For more information on creating this composite menu, see "Merging User Interface Components," later in this chapter.

6. To give the container a pointer to its **IOleInPlaceActiveObject** interface and its name, the object calls **IOleInPlaceFrame::SetActiveObject**, as well as **IOleInPlaceUIWindow::SetActiveObject** for the document window, if it is non-NULL. The object must make calls to the **SetActiveObject** methods before calling **IOleInPlaceFrame::SetMenu**. This is the only way the container is given a pointer to the object's **IOleInPlaceActiveObject** interface and that the container can ask OLE to provide the F1 accelerator support.

7. To set the composite menu on the container's frame window, the object calls the container's **IOleInPlaceFrame::SetMenu** method. The object should take the focus if it is activating by calling the Windows **SetFocus** API function. The container can fail on **SetMenu**, in which case the object must pop up its menu.

   It is important that no visual changes take place until *after* the object has decided to activate in place (that is, after the decision in step 4 has been made).

8. At this point, the object can proceed with any standard processing for **IOleObject::DoVerb**.

Shading an Object's Active Window

The active object should be surrounded by a black diagonal hatch border as an indication of the active state and to suggest the area of focus. The hatch pattern border consists of right-ascending diagonal lines with transparent pixels between the lines. The default size for the hatch border is defined in OLE2.H to be four pixels:

```
#define INPLACE_DEFBORDERWIDTH 4
```

The default size of the hatch border can be overridden by adding an "OleInPlaceBorderWidth" entry to the WIN.INI file. The overriding value can be obtained by calling the Windows **GetProfileInt** function, as follows:

```
GetProfileInt("windows", "OleInplaceBorderWidth",
INPLACE_DEFBORDERWIDTH);
```

For more information on the user interface recommendations for shading an object, see the chapter "User Interface Guidelines."

Merging User Interface Components

An object that is active in-place shares the user interface menu with its container. On being activated, the object's object application creates a composite menu bar that is then filled in and used by both the container and the object while the object is active in place.

On the composite menu, the container optionally supplies menu groups for the File, Container, and Window menus (only if the container is an MDI application). The in-place object supplies the Edit, Object, and Help menu groups for the composite menu. These menu groups are then combined to create a composite menu in the following order:

File	Edit	Container	Object	Window	Help

As an example, consider the following container and object application menu groups that are combined to create an in-place composite menu:

Container menu groups:

Menu Group:	*File*	*Container*	*Window*
Contents:	**File**	empty	**Window**

Object application menu groups:

Menu Group:	*Edit*	*Object*			*Help*
Contents :	**Edit**	**DataSeries**	**Chart**	**Format**	**Help**

Composite menu bar:

File	Edit	DataSeries	Chart	Format	Window	Help
container menu	object application menu				container menu	object application menu

To illustrate a more complex example, consider the composite menu comprising the following container and object application menu groups:

Container menu groups:

Menu Group:	*File*	*Container*	*Window*
Contents:	**File**	**View**	**Window**

Object application menu groups:

Menu Group:	*Edit*	*Object*	*Help*
Contents:	**Edit**	**Gallery** **Format**	**Help**

Composite menu bar:

File	Edit	View	Gallery	Format	Window	Help
container menu	object applica-tion menu	container menu	object applica-tion menus		container menu	object application menu

Resource Ownership

The individual drop-down menus are referenced, *not copied*,to the composite menu. This means that the container or object application can use the **HMENU** of their individual drop-down menus to check, gray, or draw menu items. Similarly, the container can use the same drop-down menus for multiple-object menus, provided it ensures that the lifetime of the drop-down menus exceeds that of any object application menu that refers to them.

The object application creates the top-level composite menu and destroys it when the in-place activation session is finished. This means that the object application can create several such menus, and switch among them, depending on editing mode or viewing state. The container does not have this ability: it can only supply one set of drop-down menus for the duration of an active in-place session.

Figure 11-4 shows the flow of control in constructing the composite menu. Notice that the create/destroy and set/unset calls are paired. Each nested group of calls can be repeated as necessary, although usually only the calls to the container's **IOleInPlaceFrame::SetMenu** method are repeated to set the menu when the focus changes and task switching occurs.

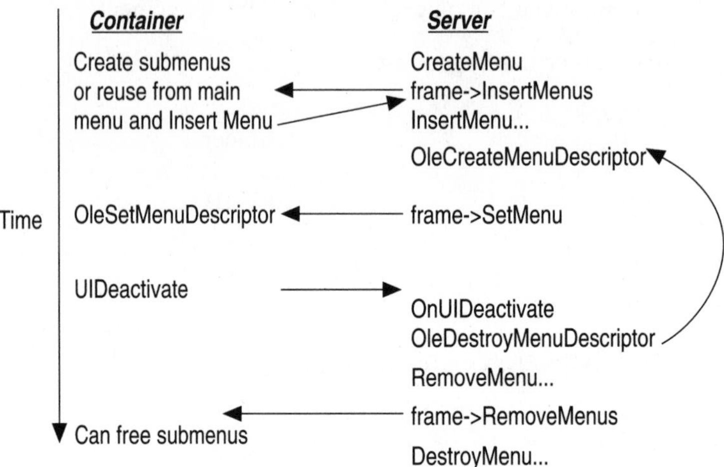

Figure 11-4. Flow of control in creating a composite menu bar.

The object creates an empty menu bar by calling the Windows **CreateMenu** API function. After creating the new menu bar, the object calls the container's **IOleInPlaceFrame::InsertMenus** method to have the container insert its menu groups. The container inserts its drop-down menus so that the object's menu bar contains references to them but not copies. The container might create these submenus on demand, or reuse submenus of its main menu. The container returns the number of items in each of its three menu groups in the **OLEMENUGROUPWIDTHS** structure. The object inserts its menus into the menu at positions offset by the **OLEMENUGROUPWIDTHS** values and then adds its counts to the **OLEMENUGROUPWIDTHS** structure.

Creating the Composite Menu

To create a composite menu, a container and object application perform the following tasks:

- To create a blank composite menu, the object application calls the Windows **CreateMenu** function. After creating the blank menu, the in-place object tells the container to insert its menus by calling the **IOleInPlaceFrame::InsertMenus** method, passing it a handle to the composite menu and a pointer to the **OLEMENUGROUPWIDTHS** structure.
- Given the handle to the composite menu by the in-place object, the container inserts its menus such that the composite menu contains references to the container's drop-down menus instead of copies. The container can create these submenus on demand or reuse submenus of its main menu. The container should store the number of menus it inserted in menu groups zero, two, and four in the **OLEMENUGROUPWIDTHS** structure and return it to the object.
- The object application calls the Windows **InsertMenu** function to insert its menus into the composite menu. The object application uses the information provided by the container in the **OLEMENUGROUPWIDTHS** structure to determine where to place its menu groups in the composite menu. The object application then calls the **OleCreateMenuDescriptor** function, passing in the handle to the composite menu and the pointer to the **OLEMENUGROUPWIDTHS** structure. Using the information provided, OLE builds a menu descriptor to dispatch commands to the appropriate container or object application window. OLE returns the handle to the menu descriptor in the **HOLEMENU** handle.
- To install the composite menu on the frame window, the object application calls the container's **IOleInPlaceFrame::SetMenu** method, passing in the handle to the composite menu, a pointer to the OLE menu descriptor, and the handle to the object's in-place window (to which menu messages and commands are to be sent). To install the menu, an SDI container calls the Windows **SetMenu** API function. An MDI container should send the WM_MDISETMENU message, using the handle to the composite menu as the menu to install. To install the OLE dispatching code, the container calls the **OleSetMenuDescriptor** function.

Creating A Menu Descriptor

To build a menu descriptor used by OLE to dispatch commands to the appropriate window (container or object), the object calls the **OleCreateMenuDescriptor** API function, passing in the handle to the composite menu and a pointer to the **OLEMENUGROUPWIDTHS** structure. To set the menu on the container's frame windows, the object calls the **IOleInPlaceFrame::SetMenu** method, passing in the handle to the composite menu, the main menu descriptor, and the window handle for the object (to which menu messages and commands are to be sent).

When deactivating, the object calls **IOleInPlaceSite::OnUIDeactivate** method to alert the container. The container then calls **IOleInPlaceFrame::SetMenu** (NULL) to remove the composite menu from its frame (removing the menu is done by the container to minimize window repaints). After the container has removed the composite menu, the in-place object calls **OleDestroyMenuDescriptor** to free the menu descriptor. The object then removes its menus and asks the container to remove its menus from the composite menu bar by calling the **IOleInPlaceFrame::RemoveMenus** method to actually remove the menu. The object must call **OnUIDeactivate** *before* calling **RemoveMenus**. This alerts the container that the composite menu no longer refers to the container's drop-down menus, which might allow the container to free them. Finally, the object frees the menu by calling the Windows **DestroyMenu** API function. The container must have called the Windows **RemoveMenu** API function to remove its menus; otherwise, the call to **DestroyMenu** frees them.

Using Status Lines

Many applications display a status line to give brief informative help to the user. Examples are feedback on the effect of a menu selection (before the user selects it), or hints about what the selection is and what can be done with it, such as "Double-click to edit this chart object."

During an in-place session, the container owns the status line. When an object is activated in place, it can ask to display information in the container's status line (if there is one), by calling the **IOleInPlaceFrame::SetStatusText** method.

When switching between menus owned by the container and the object, the status bar text is not reflected properly if the in-place object does not call the container's **IOleInPlaceFrame::SetStatusText** method. For example, if, during an in-place session, the user selected the File menu, the status bar would reflect what would occur if the user selected this menu. If the user then selected the Edit menu (which is owned by the in-place object), the status bar text would not change unless **IOleInPlaceFrame::SetStatusText** was called. This is because there is no way for the container to tell that one of the object's menus has been made active because all the messages the container would trap are now going to the object.

To avoid problems, an in-place object should process the WM_MENUSELECT message and call **IOleInPlaceFrame::SetStatusText**—even if the object does not usually provide status information (in which case the object can just pass a NULL string for the requested status text).

Installing Toolbars and Other Frame Adornments

While it is active in place, the object can supply auxiliary windows to the container. These windows can include toolbars, status lines, palettes, and formula bars. The container provides space for these windows. The size of the tool area is the result of negotiation between the container, which knows how much space is available, and the object, which knows the contents of the windows. If the container does not provide space for the windows, the object can either do without them, display them as pop-up windows, or refuse to activate in place. In general, containers should remove or disable their own toolbars during an in-place activation session because their commands might not be available.

Objects can display controls (such as row and column headings for tables) around their borders while active. Gluing attachments to objects should not affect the layout of the surrounding container objects. If necessary, the attachments can overlap the surrounding container contents. These attachments exist only during the in-place activation process and are not part of the object.

To ask other windows in the containment hierarchy to allocate space along their borders, the object does the following tasks:

1. To get the outer rectangle, the object calls **IOleInPlaceUIWindow::GetBorder**.
2. To get the space defined by the inner rectangle, the object calls **IOleInPlaceUIWindow::RequestBorderSpace**, passing it the width of space needed by its tools. The container can either grant or refuse this request.
3. If the container grants the request in step 2, the object calls **IOleInPlace UIWindow::SetBorderSpace** to actually allocate the border space.

Figure 11-5 shows this relationship between the active object and the window hierarchy.

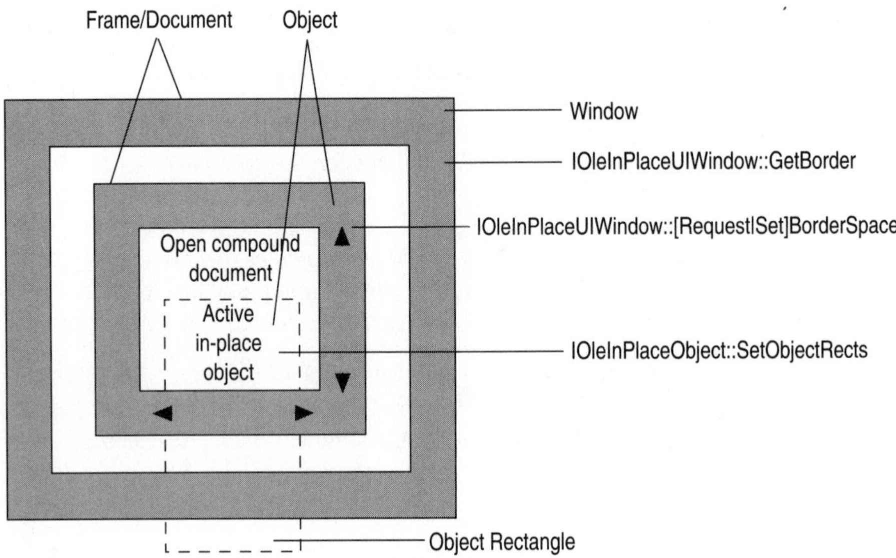

Figure 11-5. Active object negotiating space for control bars and frame adornments.

When the object asks the container for more space, the container can either grant the space requested or do nothing. The container determines whether the user interface object lies over part of the container's contents or whether the layout of the container's contents is shifted to make room for the user interface object. Commonly, the container draws scroll bars inside any border attachments, next to the content of the document. If the container refuses to provide space to the object, the object can show the tool as a popup—if it decides to show it at all. The choice is up to the object.

While an object is active in place, the container needs to be aware of the user interface objects that are being displayed by the active object:

- The container should not move the embedded object when it is displaying or hiding toolbars, palettes or frame adornments for the active object (most likely the user has double-clicked on the object and moving it could mean that it is no longer under the mouse cursor).
- If the container scrolls, causing the active in-place object to move, the container must ensure that the object's in-place window gets the correct move and/or size messages. This is done by calling **IOleInPlaceObject::SetObjectRects**.

- If the container's window(s) change size, the container must renegotiate with the object over the space assigned for the object's tools, in case the object wants to wrap instead of clip. Floating palettes are not affected by this, only windows attached as children of the frame and document windows. To negotiate new space requirements, the container calls the object's **IOleInPlaceActiveObject::ResizeBorder** method.

Because the container can move or resize the object's in-place window, the object must take notice of these move and size messages to maintain any necessary relationships, such as aligning a ruler on the document border with the object.

Note During in-place activation and MDI activation, it is possible to have an MDI client window intersect with an object application-supplied toolbar. If the object application's frame adornment window is not created using WS_CLIPSIBLINGS, then when the MDI client window is moved to its appropriate space during a **SetWindowPos** or **DeferWindowPos** operation Windows will incorrectly copy bits from the object application's toolbar for the intersection of the MDI client window.

Applications that support repositioning of toolbars (for example, by dragging) can reinvoke the negotiation at any time. Usually the object remembers the space allocated it by the container. If it needs more space, it can call **IOleInPlaceUIWindow::SetBorderSpace** with the new space needed. If that request fails, the object can engage in a full negotiation sequence for the needed space.

Containers can alter the border within which the object's tools are placed. Before altering any document space, the container should call the object's **IOleInPlaceActiveObject::ResizeBorder** method to force the object to renegotiate the placement and size of its toolbars.

Floating palettes are simply popup windows owned by the object window. The container need not be aware of their existence. The object is responsible for hiding and showing these windows on activation and deactivation.

Deactivating In-Place Objects

Deactivating an in-place object is done at the request of the container or the embedded object. The container usually deactivates the object when the user clicks in the client area of the container but outside the embedded object's in-place window. To deactivate the in-place object user interface, the container calls **IOleInPlaceObject::UIDeactivate**, which removes the user interface.

To fully deactivate the in-place object (but not take it out of the running state) the container calls **IOleInPlaceObject::InPlaceDeactivate**. The object remains in the running state until the container explicitly calls **IOleObject::Close**.

When deactivating from an in-place session, the object should:

- Destroy or hide any toolbars, floating palette, and/or any other frame adornments.
- Destroy or hide the in-place activation window.
- Ask the container to reinstall its own user interface by calling the the container's **IOleInPlaceSite::OnUIDeactivate** method.
- Free the menu descriptor by calling the **OleDestroyMenuDescriptor** function.
- Remove the drop-down menus from the composite menu bar using the Windows **RemoveMenu** API.
- Ask the container to remove its drop-down menus from the composite menu bar by calling the **IOleInPlaceFrame::RemoveMenus** method. This indicates that the composite menu no longer refers to the container's drop-down menu, which might allow the container to free them.
- Free the composite menu by calling the **DestroyMenu** function. (The container must have used **RemoveMenu** to remove its drop-down menus, otherwise the call to **DestroyMenu** frees them.)

Note On being deactivated, the embedded object should not discard its undo state, nor save changes to its **IStorage** object. Instead, the object should hold onto its undo state until the container calls the object's **IOleInPlaceObject::InPlaceDeactivate** method, at which time the Undo state can be discarded. Along the same lines, the container should separately ask the object to save its state to storage.

Implementing In-Place Containers and Objects

This section describes the pseudo code for in-place containers and object applications. Support for inside-out activation is also included.

An in-place object can be inside out or outside in. Outside-in objects hide and destroy their windows at the time the user interface is deactivated. Inside-out objects have an additional state, which is in between the time the UI is deactivated and the active inplace object is deactivated. The object reaches the inside-out state when it's UI is deactivated. In this state the object has its window visible in place, but its adornments, hatch border, and frame- and document-level tools are not visible.

Containers can support inside-out objects (single-clickable) or they can deal with all the objects as outside-in objects (double-clickable).

Figure 11-6 shows the state diagram for an outside-in object, and the methods that can be called to transition an object from one state to another.

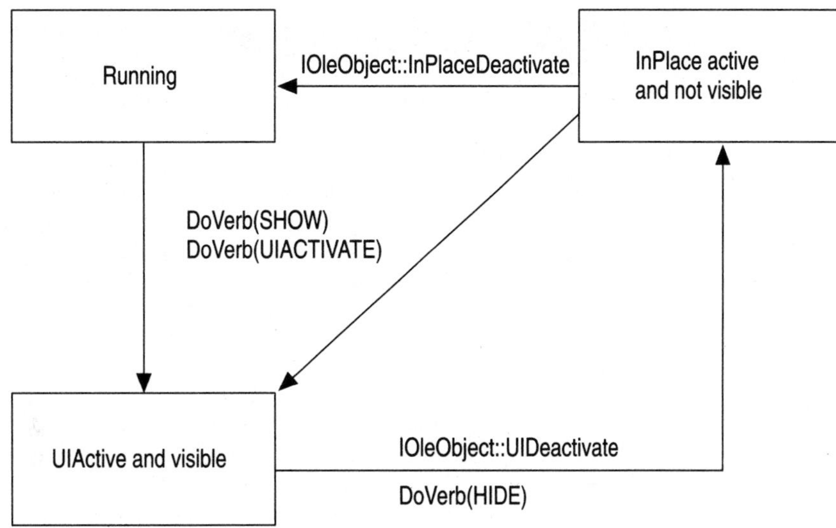

Figure 11-6. In-place state transition diagram for outside-in objects.

The state diagram for an inside-out object is shown in Figure 11-7.

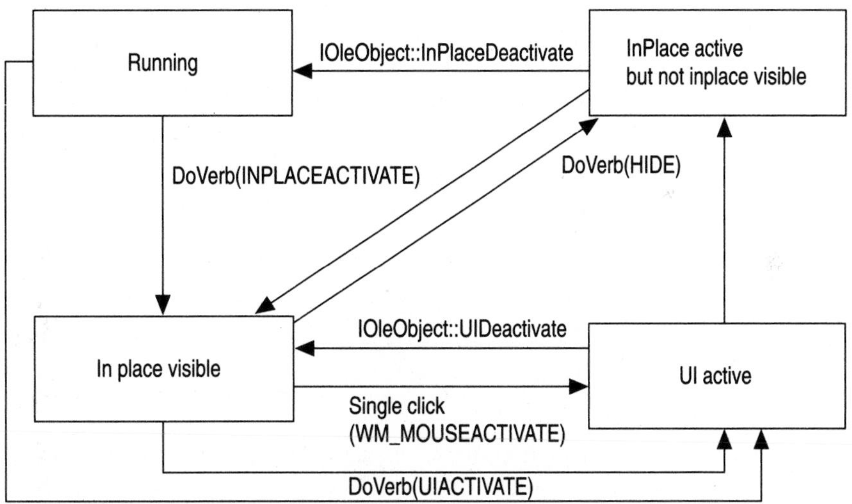

Figure 11-7. In-place state transition diagram for inside-out objects.

To support inside-out activation, **IOleObject::DoVerb** supports the predefined verbs OLEIVERB_UIACTIVATE and OLEIVERB_INPLACEACTIVATE. When the object receives either of these verbs it should try to bring itself into the appropriate in-place state. If it is not able to activate in place, it must fail the **DoVerb** call rather than doing normal activation. The verb OLEIVERB_DISCARDUNDOSTATE is also supported by **DoVerb**, which the container can use to tell the object to discard its undo state. This gives the containers finer control over the objects. For example, the container can make the object discard its undo state without hiding its window.

Notice that **IOleInPlaceObject::InPlaceDeactivate** completely removes the in-place state (including the undo state) and takes the object back to running state.

Also added were the miscellaneous status bits OLEMISC_INSIDEOUT and OLEMISC_ACTIVATEWHENVISIBLE. All of the inside-out object applications must register and return OLEMISC_INSIDEOUT. The OLEMISC_ACTIVATEWHENVISIBLE bit is usually registered and returned by light-weight inside-out objects.

Containers that do not support inside-out activation never look at these miscellaneous status bits. Instead, they call **DoVerb**(OLEIVERB_HIDE) immediately after calling **IOleInPlaceObject::UIDeactivate**. This makes sure that the window of the inside-out object is hidden on UI deactivation. The **DoVerb**(OLEIVERB_HIDE) call does not have any effect on outside-in objects, because they would have hidden their window as part of UI deactivation.

Containers that want to support inside-out objects must look at these miscellaneous status bits and make a decision on whether to deal with the objects as inside-out or outside-in objects. Some containers might want to handle all the objects that have the OLEMISC_INSIDEOUT miscellaneous bit set as inside-out objects, even if the OLEMISC_ACTIVATEWHENVISIBLE bit is not set. Other containers look for the OLEMISC_ACTIVATEWHENVISIBLE bit (in addition to the OLEMISC_INSIDEOUT bit) before making that decision. If the OLEMISC_INSIDEOUT is not set, the object does not support inside-out activation. In this case, it must be dealt with as outside-in object.

Containers that support inside-out objects *must* in-place activate (using OLEIVERB_INPLACEACTIVATE) all the objects they have identified as inside-out objects whenever those objects become visible. This is so they can be single-clicked all the time in that container. All other objects can be double-clicked all the time. Note that the same object can behave differently in different containers but it *must* behave the same way in the same container all the time.

When **IOleInPlaceObject::UIDeactivate** is called, inside-out objects remove and hide their toolbars, menu bar, adornments and hatch border, but leave their window visible in place. On the other hand, outside-in objects remove and hide their window in addition to doing what inside-out objects do. Because this type of behavior is what the container wants, the container would only call the **UIDeactivate** method of the objects (not **DoVerb**(OLEIVERB_HIDE)).

In containers that support inside-out objects, there can be more than one object that is in-place active with its window visible. In these cases, the container is supposed to call **IOleInPlaceObject::SetObjectRects** on all of those objects when the document window size changes, in addition to calling **IOleInPlaceActiveObject::ResizeBorder**.

Pseudo Code Examples

In order that in-place activation works properly, it is very important that container and object application developers follow the guidelines described in the following pseudo code examples. Following the guidelines ensures that the objects are activated and deactivated correctly, as well as avoiding excessive movement and repaints of the windows, toolbars, menu bar, and so forth.

The following list describes some of the in-place activation scenarios where excessive repaints can happen, especially if the guidelines described in the pseudo code are not followed:

- Switching between two MDI documents, both of which have UI active objects.
- Switching from one MDI document that has a UI active object, to another document that has no object UI active.
- Double-clicking on an in-place object in a document, while there is another UI active object in the same document.
- Activating nested in-place objects.

In each of these situations, the goal is to reach the final state with minimal repaints.

Pseudo Code for Object Applications

The following pseudo code shows the activation/deactivation steps for object applications:

```
// Activation.....
IOleObject::DoVerb (LONG lVerb, ...)
{
    switch (lVerb) {
    case OLEIVERB_SHOW:
        if (already in open mode)
            show object in window
        else
```

```
                if (DoInPlaceActivate(lVerb) == error)
                    do normal activation.
            break;

#ifdef INSIDEOUT
        case OLEIVERB_INPLACEACTIVATE:
#endif
        case OLEIVERB_UIACTIVATE:
            if (aready in open mode)
                return error.
            return DoInPlaceActivate(lVerb);
            // Must not do normal activation if in-place activation fails

        case OLEIVERB_DISCARDUNDOSTATE:
            if (!m_fInPlaceActive)
                return OLE_E_NOT_INPLACEACTIVE;
            discard undo state if you have any;
            break;

        case OLEIVERB_HIDE:
            if (m_fInPlaceActive) {
                DeactivateUI();
                DoInPlaceHide();
            } else
                Hide object window
            break;

        case OLEIVERB_OPEN:
            if (m_fInPlaceActive)
                object->InPlaceDeactivate();
            Show object window
            break;

        ..... deal with your other application specific verbs

        default:
            if (lVerb < 0)  // return error for other negative
                            // (pre-defined) verbs
                return error;
        }
}

DoInPlaceActivate(LONG lVerb)
{
        if (! m_fInPlaceActive) {
            QueryInterface for inplacesite pointer.
            if (inplacesite == NULL || inplacesite->CanInPlaceActivate ==
                error)
                return error;
            inplacesite->OnInPlaceActivate
```

```
            m_fInPlaceActive = TRUE;
        }

        if (! m_fInPlaceVisible) {
            m_fInPlaceVisible = TRUE;
            inplacesite->GetWindow  // parent window
            inplacesite->GetWindowContext
            create/re-parent object window as a child of inplace site's window
            AssembleMenus
#ifdef INSIDEOUT
            // Outside-in object applications do not support this verb.
            if (lVerb == OLEIVERB_INPLACEACTIVATE) {
                Show object without adornments and border shading
                return NOERROR;
            }
#endif
        }

        // object window is visible....
        if (! m_fUIActive) {
            m_fUIActive = TRUE;
        #ifdef CNTR_SVR
            if (m_lpUIActiveObject)
                UIDeactivateContainedObject()
            else
        #endif
                inplacesite->OnUIActivate
            SetFocus to the object window
            Show object with adornments and border shading
            frame->SetActiveObject(my IOleInPlaceActiveObject*, lpsznames);
            if (doc)
                doc->SetActiveObject(my IOleInPlaceActiveObject*, lpsznames);

            AddFrameLevelUI  // set menu and show tools
        }
}

IOleInPlaceActiveObject::OnDocWindowActivate
{
        if (activating )
            AddFrameLevelUI
        else
            remove frame level tools (toolbars etc); //do not call
                                                    // SetBorderSpace(NULL);
}
#ifdef INSIDEOUT
// An outside-in object does not have its window visible when in UI
// deactivated state. Hence it would not receive the
// mouse-click/activation.
// The inside-out object, after it receives mouse activation, must
```

```
// notify its inplacesite that it is going to display its UI and then
// display the frame/document level tools, adornments, and hatch border.
// This gives its container a chance to UI deactivate, if there is
// another object that is UI active in it.
// This UI activation must be done on WM_LBUTTONUP.

// Add the following code to your WNDPROC.
{
    static BOOL fUIActivateOnLButtonUP = FALSE;

    WM_MOUSEACTIVATE:
        if (m_fInPlaceActive && !m_fUIActive)
            m_fUIActivateOnLButtonUp = TRUE;

    WM_LBUTTONUP:
        if (m_fInPlaceActive && !m_fUIActive &&
m_fUIActivateOnLButtonUP) {
            m_fUIActivateOnLButtonUp = FALSE;
            DoInPlaceActivate(OLEIVERB_UIACTIVATE);
        }
        .... Do other stuff;
}
#endif

AssembleMenus()
{
    HMENU   m_hmenuShared = NULL;

#ifdef  PARTICIPATE_IN_MENU_MERGING
    m_hmenuShared = CreateMenu();
    if (frame->InsertMenus(hmenuShared, &menugroupwidths) == NOERROR)
    {
        Insert my menus...
        update menugroupwidths structure.
    } else {
        DestroyMenu(hmenuShared);
        m_hmenuShared = NULL;
    }
#endif

// It is critical to create the "hOleMenu" and call
// IOleInPlaceFrame::SetMenu even if either the object or the top-level
// container does not participate in menu merging. This is the only way
// that the top-level container can let OLE subclass the frame window.
// The subclassing is necessary to deal with Alt-Tab, Alt-Esc, or user
// pulling down menus using menu-mnemonics when the in-place object has
// the focus.

    m_hOleMenu= OleCreateMenuDescriptor(m_hmenuShared,&menugroupwidths);
}
```

```
AddFrameLevelUI()
{
    frame->SetMenu(m_hOleMenu, m_hmenuShared);
    negotiate for space and show frame level tools
}

// Deactivation.....

IOleObject::Close
{
    if (m_fInPlaceActive)
        object->InPlaceDeactivate();

    ... Do other stuff
}

IOleInPlaceObject::InPlaceDeactivate
{
    if (! m_fInPlaceActive)
        return NOERROR;
    m_fInPlaceActive = FALSE;

    DeactivateUI()
    DoInPlaceHide()
    discard Undo state
    inplacesite->OnInPlaceDeactivate()
}


DoInPlaceHide()
{
    if (! m_fInPlaceVisible)
        return NOERROR;
    m_fInPlaceVisible = FALSE;

#ifdef CNTR_SVR
    InPlaceDeactivateContainedObjects();
#endif
    re-parent back to object app's window
    DisassembleMenus
    frame->Release
    if (doc) doc->Release
}


IOleInPlaceObject::UIDeactivate
{
    DeactivateUI();
#ifndef  INSIDEOUT
```

```
    DoInPlaceHide(); // the outside-in server hides its window at
UIDeactivate time
#endif
}

DeactivateUI()
{
    if (! (m_fUIActive || m_lpUIActiveObject))
        return NOERROR;
    if (m_fUIActive) {
        m_fUIActive = FALSE;
        remove border shading and adornments
        if (doc)   doc->SetActiveObject(NULL, NULL)
        frame->SetActiveObject(NULL, NULL)
        hide frame level tools
    }
#ifdef CNTR_SVR
    else
        UIDeactivateContainedObject();
#endif

    inplacesite->OnUIDeactivate
}

DisassembleMenus()
{
    OleDestroyMenuDescriptor(m_hOleMenu);
    if (m_hmenuShared) {
        Remove my menus
        frame->RemoveMenus
        destroy the composite menu;
    }
}

#ifdef (CNTR_SVR || CNTR_ONLY)
// The following 2 routines get used in the in-place container
// application's pseudo code.

UIDeactivateContainedObject()
{
    if (m_lpUIActiveObject) {
        m_fDeactivating = TRUE;
        m_lpUIActiveObject->UIDeactivate();
#ifndef INSIDEOUT
        m_lpUIActiveObject->DoVerb(OLEIVERB_HIDE)
#endif
        m_lpUIActiveObject = NULL;
        m_fDeactivating = FALSE;
    }
}
```

```
InPlaceDeactivateContainedObjects()
{
    m_fDeactivating = TRUE;
    while (lpInPlaceObject = GetNextInPlaceObject())
        lpInPlaceObject->InPalceDeactivate();
    m_fDeactivating = FALSE;
}
#endif
```

Pseudo Code for Container Applications

If the active in-place object does not want any tool space, the top-level container must leave its tools displayed (if it has any) on the frame and/or document window.

The following pseudo code shows the activation/deactivation steps for the container application. In the pseudo code, the blocks of code that need to be implemented by either the container/object application application and/or MDI application are contained within the **#ifdef** and **#endif** declarations. The container defines the following variables in its document object:

```
BOOL    m_fAddMyUI;
BOOL    m_fMyToolsOnFrame; // Needed only if you have frame-level tools
BOOL    m_fMyToolsOnDoc; // Needed only if you have document-level tools
BOOL    m_fDeactivating;
HWND    m_hwnd;

# ifdef CNTR_SVR
HMENU       m_hSharedMenu;      // NULL if it is the top level container
HOLEMENUm_hOleMenu;     // NULL if it is the top level container
#endif

#ifdef  INSIDEOUT
LPOLEINPLACEOBJECT      m_lpUIActiveObject;
#endif

LPOLEINPLACEFRAME           m_lpTopFrame;
LPOLEINPLACEUIWINDOW m_lpTopDoc;

RECT    nullRect = {0, 0, 0, 0};

// For a container-only application or the top-level container,
// m_lpTopFrame and m_lpTopDoc are pointers to the container's frame
// and document-level object pointers.

IOleInPlaceSite::OnInPlaceActivate()
{
    QueryInterface() for IOleInPlaceObject pointer and remember it
}
```

```
IOleInPlaceSite::OnInPlaceDeactivate()
{
    Release() the IOleInPlaceObject pointer that you remembered.
}

IOleInPlaceSite::OnUIActivate()
// Can be top-level container or intermediate container in a
// nested chain.
{
    if (m_lpUIActiveObject ) {
        UIDeactivateContainedObject();
        // No need to propagate OnUIActivate() in this case, because
        // from the parent's point of view it is already UI active.
    } else {
        lpMyDoc->m_fAddMyUI = FALSE;

    #ifdef   HAVEFRAMETOOLS
        lpMyDoc->RemoveFrameLevelTools();
    #endif

    #ifdef   HAVEDOCTOOLS
        lpMyDoc->RemoveDocLevelTools();
    #endif

    #ifdef CNTR_SVR
        if (inplacesite)
            inplacesite->OnUIActivate(); // propagate activation
                                         // information.
    #endif
    }
}

IOleInPlaceSite::OnUIDeactivate(BOOL fUndoAvailable)
{
    if (fUndoAvailable) {
        if (do not need the undo state) {
#ifdef INSIDEOUT
            call DoVerb(OLEIVERB_DISCARDUNDOSTATE), if you don't want it
#else
            lpInplaceObject->InPlaceDeactivate()
#endif
        } else
            remember that object has undo state
    }

    if (m_fDeactivating)
        return NOERROR;

    PeekMessage for double-click;
    if (no double-click message for this doc) {
```

```
#ifdef  (CNTR_SVR ||  MDI)
        lpMyDoc->AddDocLevelTools();
#endif
        lpMyDoc->AddFrameLevelUI();
    }
    else {
#ifdef  (CNTR_SVR || MDI)
        // If you are an intermediate container  in a nested chain or
        // top level MDI container, you can not
        // do menu optimization because windows MDI code dynamically
        // adds/removes menus when
        // the MDI child window gets maximized/minimized. So, you must
        // put your menu back .
        lpTopFrame->SetMenu(m_hSharedMenu, m_hOleMenu, m_hwnd);

        // In all cases the toolbar optimizations can be done
#endif

        lpMyDoc->m_fAddMyUI = TRUE;
    }
    .... Do the other stuff
}

IOleInPlaceFrame::SetMenu(hmenuShared, hOleMenu, hwndActiveObj)
// Top-level container's SetMenu method.
{

// If the container does not participate in menu sharing, it would
// indicate that by failing the IOleInplaceFrame::InsertMenus call, but
// the container must honor this (SetMenu) call. Even when menu
// sharing is not taking place, the object creates the hOleMenu by
// calling OleSetMenuDescriptor and passing it on to this routine. And
//the container is required to call OleSetMenuDescriptor(),
//so that OLE can subclass the container's frame window. The subclassing
//is necessary to deal with Alt-Tab, Alt-Esc, or user pulling down menus
//using menu-mnemonics, when the in-place object has the focus.
//
// If the container does not participate in menu merging, it must fail
// this call if "hmenuShared" is not NULL.
//
#ifdef  PARTICIPATE_IN_MENU_MERGING
    HMENU hmenu;
    if (hOleMenu && hmenuShared)
        hmenu = hmenuShared;
    else
        hmenu = hmenuMyMenu; // container's normal menu
    if (SDI application)
        SetMenu(hwndFrame, hmenu)    //windows api
    else// MDI case
        SendMessage(hwndFrame, WM_MDISETMENU, ...);
```

```
#else
    if (hmenuShared != NULL)
        return error;
#endif

    return OleSetMenuDescriptor(hOleMenu, hwndFrame, hwndActiveObj,
....);
}

MyDocClass::DoubleClickHandler()
{
    ... Do the normal stuff (DoVerb, etc)
    if (m_fAddMyUI) {
#ifdef (CNTR_SVR || MDI)
        AddDocLevelTools();
#endif
        AddFrameLevelUI();
    }
}

 #ifdef  HAVEFRAMETOOLS
MyDocClass::RemoveFrameLevelTools()
{
    if (m_fMyToolsOnFrame)
        m_fMyToolsOnFrame = FALSE;
        Hide frame-level tools   // Do not call SetMenu(NULL) or
                                 // SetBorderSpace(NULL)
    }
}
#endif

#ifdef  HAVEDOCTOOLS
MyDocClass::RemoveDocLevelTools()
//Removing toolbars from the document-level window:
{
    if (lpMyDoc->m_lpTopDoc && m_fMyToolsOnDoc)  {
        m_fToolsOnDoc = FALSE;
        Hide my doc-level tools;     // Don't call SetBorderSpace(NULL).
    }
}
#endif

MyDocClass::AddFrameLevelUI()
//Adding a composite menu bar to the top-level container's frame window
{
#ifdef  CNTR_SVR
    // Frame will not be your frame if you are an intermediate container
    // in a nested chain.
    lpTopFrame->SetMenu(m_hSharedMenu, m_hOleMenu, m_hwnd);
```

```
#else
    lpTopFrame->SetMenu(NULL, NULL, NULL);
#endif
    AddFrameLevelTools();
}

MyDocClass::AddFrameLevelTools()
//Adding toolbars and/or frame adornments to the frame-level window
{
#ifdef   HAVEFRAMETOOLS
    if (!m_fMyToolsOnFrame) {
        Negotiate with m_lpTopFrame for border space.
        Place frame tools and make them visible.
        m_fMyToolsOnFrame = TRUE;
    }
#else
#ifdef  CNTR_SVR
    if (I am not the top level container)
        m_lpTopFrame->SetBorderSpace(NULL);
                // Note: container must pass a NULL pointer
    else
#endif
        m_lpTopFrame->SetBorderSpace(&nullRect);
#endif
}


#ifdef  (CNTR_SVR  ||  MDI)
MyDocClass::AddDocLevelTools()
//Adding toolbars and/or adornments to the document-level window
{
    // Document will not be your document if you are an intermediate
    // container in a nested chain.
    if (!m_lpTopDoc)
        return;
#ifdef  HAVEDOCTOOLS
    if (!m_fMyToolsOnDoc) {
        Negotiate with m_lpTopDoc for border space.
        Place doc tools  and make them visible.
        m_fMyToolsOnDoc = TRUE;.
    }
#else
#ifdef   CNTR_SVR
    if (I am not the top level container)
        m_lpTopDoc->SetBorderSpace(NULL);
                // Note: container must pass NULL pointer
    else
#endif
    m_lpTopDoc->SetBorderSpace(&nullRect);
```

```
#endif
}
#endif
#ifdef  MDI
WM_MDIACTIVATE Message handler(BOOL fActivate)
// Top level container document's WM_MDIACTIVATE handler routine
{
    if (lpInPlaceActiveObject in this document) {
        if  (fActivate)
            lpFrame->SetActiveObject(lpInPlaceActiveObject, NULL);
        else
            lpFrame->SetActiveObject(NULL, NULL);

        lpInPlaceActiveObejct->OnDocWindowActivate(fActivate);
    }
    else if (fActivate)
        lpMyDoc->AddFrameLevelUI();
}
#endif

IOleInPlaceFrame::SetBorderSpace(lpBorderWidths)
// Top-level container's frame's method
{
    // Note: check for NULL pointer (not for rect with NULLs) is made
    if (lpBorderWidths == NULL) {
        lpActiveDoc = GetActiveDocument();
        lpActiveDoc->AddFrameLevelTools();
    }
     else {
        validate widths
        remember the widths, and size your window
    }
}

#ifdef   MDI
IOleInPlaceUIWindow::SetBorderSpace(lpBorderWidths)
// Top-level container document's method
{
    // Note: check for NULL pointer (not for rect with NULLs) is made
    if (lpBorderWidths == NULL)
        this->AddDocLevelTools();
    else {
        validate widths
        remember the widths, and size your window
    }
}
#endif
```

Displaying Modeless Dialogs

When an object is active in place, it is possible for one application to display a modal dialog at the same time the other application has modeless dialogs visible. To get the right enable/disable behavior, the application that wants to display the modal dialog must first call **EnableModeless** (FALSE). After completion of the dialog, it must call **EnableModeless** (TRUE). The object calls **IOleInPlaceFrame::EnableModeless** and the container calls **IOleInPlaceActiveObject::EnableModeless**.

Providing Context-Sensitive Help

Many applications use an accelerator key (usually SHIFT+F1) to allow the user to obtain help on some visible control or item. On receipt of this key, the application enters a modal state, and the next mouse click determines the help topic. The active in-place object receives the accelerator and determines whether the help mode is to be entered. The object application calls the container's **IOleInPlaceSite::ContextSensitiveHelp** method to notify the container to enter the mode. If the user exits the help mode (for example, with the ESC key), the object application calls **IOleInPlaceSite::ContextSensitiveHelp** to tell the container to leave the help mode.

When the user clicks on something owned by the object, the object calls the container's **IOleInPlaceSite::ContextSensitiveHelp** method and provides help to the user. When the user clicks on something owned by the container, the container calls the object application's **IOleInplaceObject::ContextSensitiveHelp** method to tell the object to exit the mode so the container can provide the help.

There are two ways a user can invoke context-sensitive help:

1. Press SHIFT+F1 and then click on the topic for which help is needed.
2. To get help on a particular menu item, press the F1 key when that menu item is selected.

Not all applictions provide context-sensitive help. Even if the OLE application does not provide help, it must follow the guidelines described in the following sections so those applications that do provide help are able to do so while an object is active in place.

To support context-sensitive help, the **ContextSensitiveHelp** (**Bool** *fEnterMode*) method is part of the **IOleWindow** interface implementation. Because all the other in-place interfaces inherit from **IOleWindow**, the **IOleInPlaceFrame**, **IOleInPlaceUIWindow**, **IOleInPlaceSite**, **IOleInPlaceObject** and **IOleInPlaceActiveObject** have the same method.

As shown in Figure 11-8, the top-level container implements the **IOleInPlaceFrame** interface in association with its frame window. In addition to **IOleInPlaceFrame**, MDI container applications must implement **IOleInPlaceUIWindow** in conjunction with their document windows.

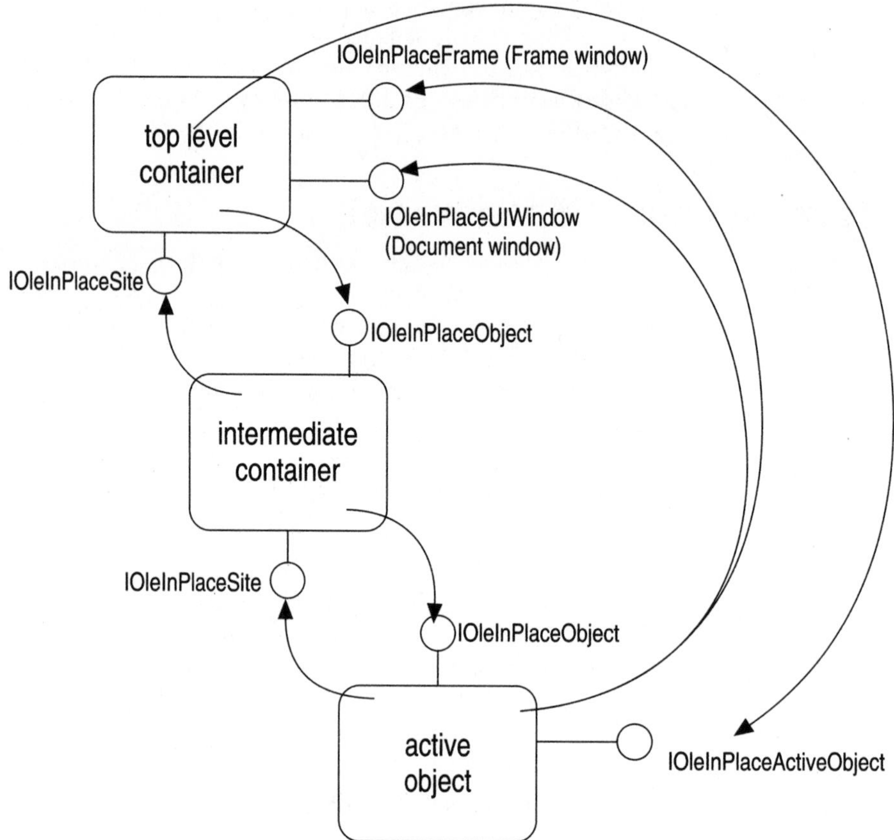

Figure 11-8. Relationship of object, container, and frame interfaces.

Within this window hierarchy, at any given moment objects can be active in place in more than one document. However, at the most, *only* one object can share the frame window's user interface. Each one of these active in-place objects can receive mouse clicks directly without the other active objects knowing about those events. Because of this, it is important that all of the in-place active objects know about the context-sensitive help modal state. If they do, when the mouse click is made on their windows, they can either provide the help or ignore the click (if they don't have help for that context or if they don't support context-sensitive help), instead of deactivating the in-place objects active in them.

SHIFT + F1

When an object is active in place, it shares the top-level container's main menu and shares the frame-level real estate. In this state, the keyboard focus is with the object's in-place window. When the user selects SHIFT+F1, either the frame or the active in-place object can receive the keystrokes.

When the top-level container receives the keystrokes, it calls its containing documents' **IOleInPlaceUIWindow::ContextSensitiveHelp** method with *fEnterMode* TRUE.

The following pseudo code for the various in-place interface implementations of the **ContextSensitiveHelp** method shows how the state is propagated from the top-level container to all the in place objects so that they can take the appropriate action when they receive the mouse click or WM_COMMAND.

```
Frame's private ContextSensitiveHelp (BOOL fEnterMode)    // FRAME window
// NOTE: This is not the implementation of
// IOleInPlaceFrame:ContextSensitiveHelp that gets used in giving CSH
// when the F1 key is pressed while menu processing is going on.
{
    if (m_fCSHMode != fEnterMode) {
        m_fCSHMode = fEnterMode;  // remember the state
        if this application is an MDI application
            call IOleInPlaceUIWindow::ContextSensitiveHelp(fEnterMode)
            on all of the documents;
        if this is an SDI application & an object is UI active,
            callIOleInPlaceObject::ContextSensitiveHelp(fEnterMode)
    }
}

// only if MDI app
IOleUIWindow::ContextSensitiveHelp(BOOL fEnterMode)  // Document window
{
    if (m_fCSHMode != fEnterMode) {
        m_fCSHMode = fEnterMode;
        if (I have an object active in place)
            call IOleInPlaceObject::ContextSensitiveHelp(fEnterMode);
    }
}

IOleInPlaceObject::ContextSensitiveHelp(BOOL fEnterMode)
{
    if (m_fCSHMode != fEnterMode) {
        m_fCSHMode = fEnterMode;
        if (I have an object active in place)
            call  IOleInPlaceObject::ContextSensitiveHelp(fEnterMode);
    }
}
```

The following pseudo code shows how the state propagates in the other direction from the active in-place object (the one with keyboard focus) to all the in-place objects in the container tree of which the frame window is the root. If the in-place object receives the SHIFT+F1 keystroke, it must recognize that it has entered the help mode and it must call **IOleInPlaceSite::ContextSensitveHelp** (TRUE).

```
IOleInPlaceSite::ContextSensitiveHelp (BOOL fEnterMode)
{    if (m_fCSHMode != fEnterMode) {
          m_fCSHMode = fEnterMode;
          if (I have an in-place parent)
               IOleInPlaceSite::ContextextSensitiveHelp(fEnterMode);
          else {
               if (my window is a doc window)        //Only if MDI
                    call my frame's private CSH method;
                    //not IOleInPlaceFrame::ContextSensitiveHelp(fEnterMode)
          }
     }
}
```

As shown in the preceding pseudo code example, each in-place site calls, in turn, its in-place parent site recursively. The top-level container site is associated with the document only if it is an MDI application. In that case, it should call the frame's private **ContextSensitiveHelp** function, which in turn calls the **ContextSensitiveHelp** method of each of its documents. Otherwise, it is associated with the frame and the propagation stops there.

By means of the preceding mechanism, all the active in-place objects enter the context-sensitive help mode when the SHIFT+F1 is pressed. In this state, any of the visible windows can receive the mouse click. Iin addition, the frame and active in-place object can receive WM_COMMAND.

All applications that can activate an object in place must provide support for context-sensitive help, as follows:

1. Implement code for the **ContextSensitiveHelp** method in all the relevant interfaces, as described in the preceding pseudo code examples.
2. While in the context-sensitive help mode, if the object receives the mouse click, it can either ignore the mouse click (if it does not provide context-sensitive help), or it can tell the other objects to exit the context-sensitive help mode and then provide help for that context.
3. While in context-sensitive help mode, if the object receives a WM_COMMAND, it should tell all the other objects to exit context-sensitive help mode and then, if it can, provide help for the command, although not executing it.

To tell the other objects to exit the context-sensitive help mode, the object should do the following:

```
{
    m_fCSHMode = FALSE;

    // call Down....
    if (I have any objects inplace active in me)
        IOleInPlaceObject::ContextSensitiveHelp(FALSE);

 // call Up.....
 call my implementation of IOleInPlaceSite::ContextSensitiveHelp(FALSE);
{
```

F1 Accelerator

When an application enters the menu-processing mode, Windows **USER** code takes control, executing **GetMessage** and **Dispatch** calls on some messages and throwing away the remaining ones. This poses a problem when a menu item is selected and the user presses the F1 key. Because the **USER** code throws messages away, the application might not receive the keystroke. To provide context-sensitive help on menu items, applications typically install their own message filters so that they can intercept the F1 key and provide help on the currently selected menu item.

Recall that the active in-place object calls **IOleInPlaceFrame::SetMenu** to have the container set the composite menu on the menu bar. The container in turn calls the **OleSetMenuDescriptor** function, at which time OLE subclasses the frame window of the application so that it can do the proper menu dispatching.

Usually, the application determines whether to provide context-sensitive help on menu item or not. However, if the application is to be a container for in-place objects, it must do one of the following:

- Add its own keyboard message filter, so it can intercept the F1 key (see "Writing a Keyboard Message Filter," later in this chapter).
- Ask the OLE default object handler to add a message filter by passing valid, non-NULL values for the **IOleInPlaceFrame** * *lpFrame* and **IOleInPlaceActiveObject** * *lpActiveObj* parameters of **OleSetMenuDescriptor**.

Referring to the diagram shown in Figure 11-9, Box 1 must be present when an object is being activated in place and the menu processing is in progress, whether the container has support for F1-based context-sensitive help or not. Box 2 exists as long as menu processing is going on. Box 3 exists only if the application is an in-place container and there is currently an object active in place in it.

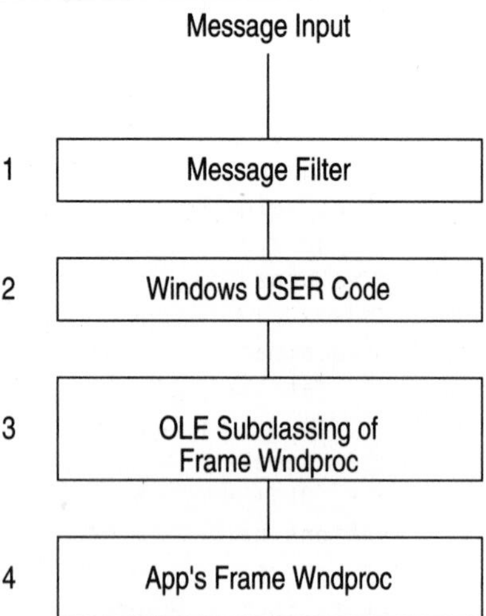

Figure 11-9. Message hierarchy for context-sensitive help.

Writing a Keyboard Message Filter

If the application is going to write its own message filter, it should be written as follows. (There could be some other mechanism through which the container can find out that the F1 key is pressed while menu processing is going on. Even in that case, most of the following would still be relevent.)

```
MessageFilterProc(int nCode, WPARAM wParam, LPARAM lParam)
{
    LPMSG   lpMsg = (LPMSG) lParam;

    // If it is not the F1 key then let the message (without
    // modification) go to the next proc in the message filter chain.
    if (lpMsg  &&  lpMsg->message == WM_KEYDOWN  &&
        lpMsg->wParam == VK_F1) {
        HMENU   hmenuPopUp;

        // Container app cannot know what the current menu selection is
        // if an object is getting in-place edited in it, because the
        // menu bar is shared and the menu messages are intercepted and
        // dispatched to the appropriate process by OLE's frame window
        // sub-classing (see Box 3).  So, when the container sends the
        // OM_POST_WM_COMMAND:
        //
        //      if (an object is getting in-place edited)
        //          it will go to Box 3, and OLE posts WM_COMMAND to the
        //          right process.
        //      else
        //          it will go to Box 4, which is app's own frame wnd
        //          proc, and its OM_POST_WM_COMMAND code can post the
```

```
//          WM_COMMAND for the current selection (that the app
//          maintains).
//
// With this scheme the same message filter proc can be used
// whether the object is getting activated in place or not.
// NOTE 1: If the current selection is a popup menu,
// WM_COMMAND cannot be generated, so the code for
// OM_POST_WM_COMMAND returns the handle of the popup menu;
// otherwise, it returns NULL
// NOTE 2: Do  uOmPostWmCommand = RegisterWindowMessage
// ("OM_POST_WM_COMMND") at startup.

if (hmenuPopup = (HMENU) SendMessage(hwndFrame,
    uOmPostWmCommand, 0, 0L)) {
    // Now the applications have 4 options:
    // 1. Give help for the popup menu and cancel the menu mode
    //    as well as the CSH mode (WORD does this).
    // 2. Change the cursor to question mark cursor
    //    (== SHIFT+F1), and do not disturb the menu state, and
    //    enter the CSH mode.
    // 3. Remove the CSH mode and cancel the menu mode.
    // 4. Leave the menu state as it is and ignore the F1 key
    //    (ie. do not pass the F1 key down the  msg filter
    //    chain).
    //
    // OLE recommends option 4; if the container app wants OLE
    // to install the message filter, OLE will. In this
    // sample code, OLE is going for option 4.

    return TRUE;     // let the system know that we have handled
                     // the message
}
else {
    // call the frame and active in-place object's
    // ContextSensitiveHelp() methods.
    lpFrame->ContextSensitiveHelp(TRUE);     //
IOleInPlaceFrame.
    lpInPlaceActiveObj->ContextSensitiveHelp(TRUE);
    // IOleInPlaceActiveObject

    // when either of these 2 objects receive the WM_COMMAND
    // they will call the other one's ContextSensitiveHelp()
    // method. Note that the tree walk does not happen if the
    // CSH mode has been entered because of F1 on selected
    // menu.
}

// Change message value to be WM_CANCELMODE and then call the
// next proc in the message filter chain. When windows
// USER's menu processing code sees this message it will bring
```

```
        // down menu  state and come out of its menu processing loop.

        lpMsg->message = WM_CANCELMODE;
        lpMsg->wParam   =  NULL;
        lpMsg->lParam     =  NULL;
    }
    return CallNextHookEx (hMsgHook, nCode, wParam, lParam);
}
```

As shown in the following example, the code for the **ContextSensitiveHelp** method in the **IOleInPlaceFrame** and the **IOleInPlaceActiveObject** interfaces is as simple as remembering the flag passed in:

```
IOleInPlaceFrame::ContextSensitiveHelp(BOOL fEnterMode)
{
    m_fMenuMode = fEnterMode;
}

IOleInPlaceActiveObject::ContextSensitiveHelp(BOOL fEnterMode)
{
    m_fMenuMode = fEnterMode;
}
```

The following pseudo code shows what the application should do when it receives either a WM_COMMAND or mouse click.

```
WM_COMMAND:
    if (m_fMenuMode || m_fCSHMode)  {
        if (m_fCSHMode) {
            m_fMenuMode  = FALSE;
            call parents ContextSensitiveHelp(FALSE), if I have any
            call children's ContextSensitiveHelp(FALSE), if I have any
        }

        if (m_fMenuMode) {
            m_fMenuMode = FALSE;
            call IOleInPlaceFrame::ContextSensitiveHelp(FALSE);
            //instead call IOleInPlaceActiveObject::ContextSensitiveHelp
            //(FALSE) if this is the top-level container
        }
        call WinHelp if you provide help.
        return;
    }
    do the normal thing.

Mouse click:
    if (m_CSHMode) {
         if (I provide context-sensitive help) {
            m_fMenuMode  = FALSE;
            call parent's ContextSensitiveHelp(FALSE), if  I have any
```

```
            call children's ContextSensitiveHelp(FALSE), if  I have any
        } else {
            ignore the click.
        }
        return;
    }
```

Undoing Changes During In-Place Activation

When an object is active in place, the object's immediate container should preserve its undo state and let the activating object know whether or not the immediate container has undo state (by calling the object's **IOleInPlaceSite::GetWindowContext** method). If, after being made active, the userls first action is to request Undo, the object should deactivate by calling the **IOleInPlaceSite::OnUIDeactivate** method and then ask the container to undo the previous changes.

On being deactivated, an object can have undo state. The object informs its container of the undo state by calling the container's **IOleInPlaceSite::OnUIDeactivate** method. Should the user's next request be to undo the changes made to the in-place object, the container calls **IOleInPlaceObject::ReactivateandUndo** to reactivate the object so the user can undo the changes.

Clipping Objects

Objects can be clipped, either by the window boundary, frame adornments, or some containing object or document. The object's immediate container calls the in-place object's **IOleInPlaceObject::SetObjectRects** method to inform the object of the accumulated clipping. Intermediate objects (that are both contained and a container) are responsible for computing the intersection of the clipping rectangles.

Defining Accelerator Tables

When object is active in place, its container should not respond to commands (menu, toolbar, or keyboard) that apply to or affect the selection since at that point the selection is under control of the object. The container can respond to commands that affect the document as a whole (for example, scrolling, zooming and printing).

The following recommendations should be followed when defining accelerator keys around an in-place active object. Remember that even though a container may keep keys active, the in-place object may intercept them since it has always has the first chance at translating them.

- The container should not have alpha-numeric characters (with or without SHIFT) as accelerators.
- The container should disable any accelerator keys (CTRL+, ALT+) that affect the selection. Accelerator keys that affect the whole document or, in rare cases, affect the object (but which wouldn't disable the object), may remain active.
- The arrow, INSERT, DELETE, and TAB keys should be disabled in the container since these directly affect the selection.
- The PAGE UP and PAGE DOWN keys should remain enabled since these affect up and down movement within a page of the document.
- The container can enable the HOME and END keys if they are used to scroll the document (to the top or bottom). These keys should be disabled if they relocate the selection (or insertion point) to the beginning or end of a structure (such as a line in a text container).

So that they will work properly with object applications that do their own accelerator keystroke translations, accelerator tables for containers should be defined as follows:

```
nCode, wID, VIRTKEY, [,NOINVERT] [,SHIFT] [,CONTROL] [,ALT]
```

This is the most common way for describing keyboard accelerators. Failure to do so can result in keystrokes being lost or sent to the wrong object during an in-place session.

Dispatching Accelerator Keys

How an object application is implemented affects the message processing of the active in-place window. When the object application is implemented as a DLL, the in-place window is created as a child window in the container's window tree. In this case, the in-place object uses the container's message queue and message loop to receive and dispatch messages.

In a stand-alone EXE object application, the in-place window belongs to the object application but is a child of the container's window tree. The input messages for the in-place window appear in the object application's message queue and are dispatched by the object application's message loop. In both cases, the composite menu bar consists of menu groups (typically drop-down menus) from both the container and object application.

Note The rule for translating accelerator keys is that the EXE object application *always* has the first chance of translating. If the object does not want the message, it lets the container attempt to translate the message. There is a similar requirement on the container when the embedded object is created by a DLL object application. The portion of code that owns the message loop has an obligation to allow the other piece of code to translate messages (in this case through the object application's **IOleInPlaceActiveObject::TranslateAccelerator** method).

When the object application is a DLL, the container must dispatch all the messages sent to the in-place activation window. To aid in this message processing, the container should maintain a flag that indicates whether or not an embedded object is active in place; the **IOleInPlaceSite::OnUIActivate** and **IOleInPlaceSite::OnUIDeactivate** methods are useful for setting and clearing the flag. If the container generally processes messages from the message queue based on the message type, it should suspend this special processing while an object is active in place.

When the object application is a stand-alone EXE and the in-place active object gets a keystroke message that is not an accelerator that it recognizes, the object must check to see whether the message is one that the container recognizes. The object should first check its own accelerators. If the keystroke is not for the object the object should pass the keystroke on to the container by calling the **OleTranslateAccelerator** function *before* calling the **TranslateMessage** and **DispatchMessage** functions. If the container does not want the keystroke, the **OleTranslateAccelerator** function returns FALSE. In this case, the object should continue using its normal **TranslateMessage** and **DispatchMessage** code.

Should the object's call to **TranslateAccelerator** fail, the object will not know whether the translation failed because the keystroke is not one of its accelerators or because the menu item corresponding to that keystroke is disabled (grayed). Usually when the object's attempt to translate the keystroke message fails, it calls **OleTranslateAccelerator** to give the container a chance to translate the message. This can result in inconsistant behavior when both the object and container have the same accelerator. If the menu item is enabled, the object's command gets executed. If it is disabled, the container's command gets executed.

To guard against this, the object must not call **OleTranslateAccelerator** when the keystroke is one of its accelerators—no matter what happens in the call to **TranslateAccelerator**. An application that translates its own accelerator can easily detect the accelerator and does not need to call **OleTranslateAccelerator**.

If the container accepts the keystroke, OLE calls the container's **IOleInPlaceFrame::TranslateAccelerator** method to translate the message. The container can call the Windows **TranslateAccelerator** and/or **TranslateMDISysAccel** functions to process the accelerator key or do its own special processing.

Note Windows has no state associated with the message (such as key state or extra message information), because the message has been transferred from the object's object application to the object's container. Containers should therefore choose accelerators that can be encoded into the accelerator tables used when an object is active in place.

Usually, a Windows application processes messages either by calling the **GetMessage**, **WaitMessage**, and **PeekMessage** functions or when another application sends it a message by using **SendMessage** (the application can also send itself a message with **SendMessage**). When the in-place object's object application is an EXE, the in-place window is created as a child in the container's process. This can lead to reentrancy problems when calling **SendMessage** between the two process boundaries. To guard against these problems, the container can call the Windows **InSendMessage** function to determine whether it is being called from another process.

The following interface methods are dispatched using the Windows **SendMessage** function. While executing these methods, the application cannot call the **Yield**, **Peek**, or **GetMessage** functions, display a dialog box, or call any other interface method or OLE function—other than those in this list.

IOleWindow::GetWindow

IOleInPlaceActiveObject::OnFrameWindowActivate
IOleInPlaceActiveObject::OnDocWindowActivate
IOleInPlaceActiveObject::ResizeBorder

IOleInPlaceUIWindow::GetBorder
IOleInPlaceUIWindow::RequestBorderSpace
IOleInPlaceUIWindow::SetBorderSpace

IOleInPlaceFrame::SetMenu
IOleInPlaceFrame::SetStatusText

IOleInPlaceObject::SetObjectRects

A reasonable strategy, especially for new OLE applications that are implementing in-place activation, is to develop the object application in two pieces. The first piece is a relatively small executable file containing the code to manage the frame window, the File menu, the Window menu (only if it is an MDI application), and the message pump. The second piece is an object handler to support the OLE 2 interfaces. Only the object handler is needed to support embedded objects. When the object application is run as a stand-alone application, it provides the functionality necessary to embed a single instance of the embedded object type in the client area of its top-level frame window or in its top-level MDI windows. (This strategy of using an object handler to handle the embedded object is more feasible in the Win32 APIs, given the level of support for per-instance data segments and that SS always equals DS).

In-Place Data Structures

This section describes the data structures that support in-place activation.

OLEINPLACEFRAMEINFO

The **OLEINPLACEFRAMEINFO** structure provides data needed by OLE to dispatch keystroke accelerators to a container (frame) while an object is active in place. The structure is defined as follows:

```
typedef struct tagOIFI          //OleInPlaceFrameInfo
{
    UINT     cb;                //Size of OleInPlaceFrameInfo structure
                                //provided by the object application
    BOOL     fMDIApp;           //TRUE if an MDI app; otherwise, FALSE
    HWND     hwndFrame;         //Handle to the container's frame window
    HACCEL   haccel;            //Handle to container's accelearator table
    int      cAccelEntries;     //Number of entries in container's
                                //accelerator table
} OLEINPLACEFRAMEINFO, FAR* LPOLEINPLACEFRAMEINFO;
```

Object applications must fill in the *cb* field with the correct size of the **OLEINPLACEFRAMEINFO** structure. If the container receives an **OLEINPLACEFRAMEINFO** structure with an uninitialized *cb* field, it should assume that the structure is defined for OLE 2. If the *cb* field is not the size that the container expects, it is assumed to be in the uninitialized state.

The *hAccel* member is a handle to the container-supplied accelerator table. The number of entries in the table is in *cAccelEntries*.

To have the container fill in the fields to the **OLEINPLACEFRAMEINFO** structure, the object application calls the container's **IOleInPlaceSite::GetWindowContext** method.

OLEMENUGROUPWIDTHS

The **OLEMENUGROUPWIDTHS** structure keeps track of the number of menus in each menu group. The structure is defined as follows:

```
typedef struct tagOleMenuGroupWidths {
    LONGwidth[6];
} OLEMENUGROUPWIDTHS, FAR * LPOLEMENUGROUPWIDTHS;
```

The container supplies values for elements 0, 2, and 4, and the object supplies values for elements 1, 3 and 5. To create the in-place composite menu, the object application first creates an empty menu and then passes the handle of the menu to the container in the call to the **IOleInPlaceFrame::InsertMenus** method. The container adds its menu groups to the composite menu and fills in the fields to the **OLEMENUGROUPS** structure, which is then passed back to the object application. The object application then adds its menu groups to the shared menu before creating a shared menu descriptor with **OleCreateMenuDescriptor**.

To activate the shared menu, the object application calls **IOleInPlaceFrame::SetMenu**, which in turn should call **OleSetMenuDescriptor**, so that OLE can install the dispatching code.

For more information on creating the composite menu, see "Merging User Interface Components," earlier in this chapter.

```
typedef HANDLE HOLEMENU;
```

HOLEMENU is a handle to a data structure that OLE uses to dispatch menu messages and commands to containers and objects as appropriate.

BORDERWIDTHS

The **BORDERWIDTHS** structure contains four integer widths for determining border space on the frame- and document-level windows for displaying toolbars and optional frame adornments.

```
typedef RECT    BORDERWIDTHS;
typedef LPRECT  LPBORDERWIDTHS;
typedef LPCRECT LPCBORDERWIDTHS;
```

Each member of the structure is the width in pixels being requested or set for the top, bottom, left, and right sides of the window, as shown in Figure 11-10:

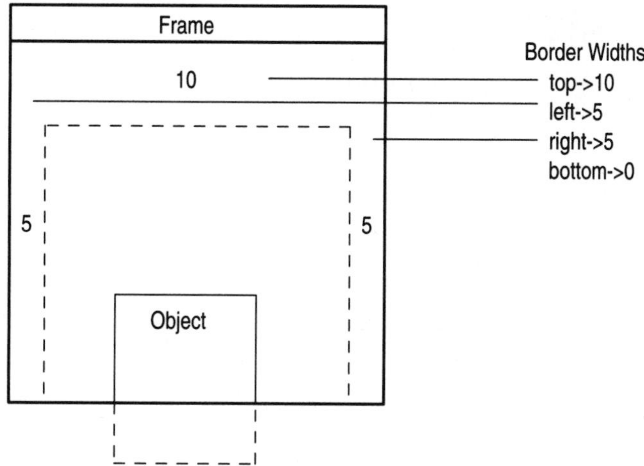

Figure 11-10. Negotiating space for frame adornments.

To negotiate space, the object fills in the **BORDERWIDTHS** structure and passes it to **RequestBorderSpace** and **SetBorderSpace** methods on the frame or document window, depending on which window the space is being requested.

IOleWindow Interface

The **IOleWindow** interface, defined in OLE2.H, is implemented and used by both container and object applications. The **IOleWindow** interface contains methods that allow an application to obtain the handle to the various windows participating in in-place activation and also to enter and exit context-sensitive help mode.

All other in-place activation interfaces are derived from the **IOleWindow** interface.

```
DECLARE_INTERFACE_(IOleWindow, IUnknown)
{
   // *** IUnknown methods ***
  HRESULT QueryInterface (THIS_ REFIID riid, LPVOID FAR* ppvObj);
  ULONG AddRef (THIS);
  ULONG Release (THIS);

   // *** IOleWindow methods ***
  HRESULT GetWindow (THIS_ HWND FAR* lphwnd);
  HRESULT ContextSensitiveHelp (THIS_ BOOL fEnterMode);
};
```

IOleWindow::GetWindow

HRESULT IOleWindow::GetWindow(*lphwnd***)**
HWND * *lphwnd*

IOleWindow::GetWindow returns the window handle to one of the various windows participating in the in-place activation (frame, document, parent, or in-place object window).

Parameter

lphwnd
Points to where to return the window handle.

Return Value

Value	Meaning
S_OK	The window handle was successfully returned.
E_INVALIDARG	One or more invalid arguments.
E_UNEXPECTED	An unexpected error happened.
E_FAIL	There is no window handle currently attached to this object.

Example

The following **IOleWindow::GetWindow** example returns the handle to the window that currently contains the focus of the active object.

```
HRESULT InPlaceWindow_GetWindow(
        LPOLEINPLACEOBJECT  lpThis,
        HWND FAR*           lphwnd)
{
    LPSERVERDOC lpServerDoc =
            ((struct CDocOleObjectImpl FAR*)lpThis)->lpServerDoc;
    *lphwnd = ((LPSERVERDOC) lpServerDoc)->m_hWndDoc;
    return S_OK;
}
```

IOleWindow::ContextSensitiveHelp

HRESULT IOleWindow::ContextSensitiveHelp(*fEnterMode***)**
BOOL *fEnterMode*

IOleWindow::ContextSensitiveHelp determines whether the context-sensitive help mode should be entered during an in-place activation session.

Parameter

fEnterMode
Specifies TRUE if help mode should be entered; FALSE if it should be exited.

Return Value

Value	Meaning
S_OK	The help mode was entered or exited successfully, depending on the value passed in *fEnterMode*.
E_UNEXPECTED	An unexpected error happened.

Comments

Applications can invoke context-sensitive help in either of the following user situations:

- SHIFT+F1 is pressed, then a topic is clicked on.
- F1 key is pressed when a menu item is selected.

When SHIFT+F1 is done, either the frame or the active object can receive the keystrokes. If the container's frame receives the keystroke, it calls its containing document's **IOleWindow::ContextSensitiveHelp** with *fEnterMode* TRUE. This propagates the help state to all of its in-place objects so they can correctly handle the mouse click or WM_COMMAND.

If an active object receives the SHIFT+F1 keystroke, it calls the container's **IOleInPlaceSite::ContextSensitiveHelp** with *fEnterMode* TRUE, which then recursively calls each of its in-place sites until there are no more to be notified. The container then calls its document's or frame's **ContextSensitiveHelp** method with *fEnterMode* TRUE.

When in context-sensitive help mode, an object that receives the mouse click can either:

1. Ignore the click if it does not support context-sensitive help, or
2. Tell all the other objects to exit context-sensitive help mode (**ContextSensitiveHelp**(FALSE)) and then provide help for that context.

An object in context-sensitive help mode that receives a WM_COMMAND should tell all the other in-place objects to exit context-sensitive help mode and then provide help for the command.

If a container application is to support context-sensitive help on menu items, it must either provide its own message filter so that can intercept the F1 key or ask the OLE library to add a message filter by calling the **OleSetMenuDescriptor** function and passing valid, non-NULL values for the *lpFrame* and *lpActiveObj* parameters.

For more detailed information on implementing context-sensitive help, see "Providing Context-Sensitive Help," earlier in this chapter.

See Also

OleSetMenuDescriptor

IOleInPlaceObject Interface

The **IOleInPlaceObject** interface is implemented by object applications and is used by containers to activate and deactivate an in-place object. A pointer to the **IOleInPlaceObject** interface can be obtained by calling **QueryInterface** on the **IOleObject** interface.

The **IOleInPlaceObject** interface contains the following methods (see also OLE2.H):

```
DECLARE_INTERFACE_(IOleInPlaceObject, IOleWindow)
{
  // *** IUnknown methods ***
 HRESULT QueryInterface (THIS_ REFIID riid, LPVOID FAR* ppvObj);
 ULONG AddRef (THIS);
 ULONG Release (THIS);

  // *** IOleWindow methods ***
 HRESULT GetWindow (THIS_ HWND FAR* lphwnd);
 HRESULT ContextSensitiveHelp (THIS_ BOOL fEnterMode);

  // *** IOleInPlaceObject methods ***
 HRESULT InPlaceDeactivate (THIS);
 HRESULT UIDeactivate (THIS);
 HRESULT SetObjectRects (THIS_ LPCRECT lprcPosRect,
   LPCRECT lprcClipRect);
 HRESULT ReactivateAndUndo (THIS);
};
```

IOleInPlaceObject::InPlaceDeactivate

HRESULT IOleInPlaceObject::InPlaceDeactivate()

IOleInPlaceObject::InPlaceDeactivate deactivates an active in-place object and discards the object's undo state.

Return Value

Value	Meaning
S_OK	The object was successfully deactivated.
E_UNEXPECTED	An unexpected error happened.

Comments

Before deactivating, the object application should give the container a chance to put its user interface back on the frame window.

On return from **IOleInPlaceObject::InPlaceDeactivate**, the object discards its undo state. The object application should not shut down immediately after this call. Instead, it should wait for an explicit call to **IOleObject::Close** or for the object's reference count to reach zero.

If the in-place user interface is still visible during the call to **InPlaceDeactivate**, the object application should call its own **IOleInPlaceObject::UIDeactivate** method to hide the user interface. The in-place user interface can be optionally destroyed during calls to **IOleInPlaceObject::UIDeactivate** and **IOleInPlaceObject::InPlaceDeactivate**. If the user interface has not already been destroyed when the container calls **IOleObject::Close**, the user interface *must* be destroyed during the call to **IOleObject::Close**.

During the call to **IOleObject::Close**, the object should check to see whether it is still in-place active. If so, it should call **InPlaceDeactivate**.

Example

In the following **IOleInPlaceObject::InPlaceDeactivate** example, the object application checks to see whether the object is still active, in which case the object and its UI is hidden (but available for quick reactivation should the user again double-click the object). If the object is being closed, the in-place UI will be destroyed as will the in-place window hierarchy.

```
HRESULT InPlaceObj_InPlaceDeactivate(LPOLEINPLACEOBJECT lpThis)
{
    LPSERVERDOC lpServerDoc =
            ((struct CDocOleObjectImpl FAR*)lpThis)->lpServerDoc;
    HRESULT hrErr;

    hrErr = ServerDoc_DoInPlaceDeactivate(lpServerDoc);
    return hrErr;
}
HRESULT ServerDoc_DoInPlaceDeactivate(LPSERVERDOC lpServerDoc)
{
    LPINPLACEDATA  lpIPData = lpServerDoc->m_lpIPData;

    // object still active?
    if (!lpServerDoc->m_fInPlaceActive)
        return S_OK;

    lpServerDoc->m_fInPlaceActive = FALSE;

    SvrDoc_IPObj_UIDeactivate(
            (LPOLEINPLACEOBJECT)&lpServerDoc->m_OleInPlaceObject);

    /* OLE2NOTE: an inside-out style in-place server will
    **    NOT hide its window in IPObj::UIDeactive (an outside-in
    **    style object will hide its window in UIDeactivate).
    **    thus, an inside-out server must explicitly hide
    **    its window in InPlaceDeactivate. it is ALSO important for an
```

```
    **    outside-in style object to call ServerDoc_DoInPlaceHide here
    **    BEFORE freeing the InPlaceData structure. it is common
    **    for in-place containers to call IOleInPlaceObject::
    **    InPlaceDeactivate in their IOleInPlaceSite::OnUIDeactiate
    **    implementation.
    */
    ServerDoc_DoInPlaceHide(lpServerDoc);

    lpIPData->lpSite->lpVtbl->OnInPlaceDeactivate(lpIPData->lpSite);

    OleStdRelease((LPUNKNOWN)lpIPData->lpSite);
    lpIPData->lpSite = NULL;

    ServerDoc_FreeInPlaceData(lpServerDoc);

    return NOERROR;
}
HRESULT ServerDoc_DoInPlaceHide(LPSERVERDOC lpServerDoc)
{
    LPINPLACEDATA   lpIPData = lpServerDoc->m_lpIPData;
    LPOUTLINEDOClpOutlineDoc = (LPOUTLINEDOC)lpServerDoc;
    LPOLEAPP        lpOleApp = (LPOLEAPP)g_lpApp;
    HWND        hWndApp = OutlineApp_GetWindow(g_lpApp);

    if (! lpServerDoc->m_fInPlaceVisible)
        return NOERROR;

    // Set the parent back to server app's window
    OleDoc_HideWindow((LPOLEDOC)lpServerDoc, FALSE /* fShutdown */);

    /* we need to enusure that our window is set to normal 100% zoom.
    **    If the window is next shown in open mode, it should start out
    **    at normal zoom factor. Our window might have been set to a
    **    different zoom factor while it was in-place active.
    */
    OutlineDoc_SetCurrentZoomCommand(lpOutlineDoc,IDM_V_ZOOM_100);

    lpServerDoc->m_fInPlaceVisible = FALSE;

    lpServerDoc->m_hWndParent = hWndApp;
    SetParent(
        lpOutlineDoc->m_hWndDoc,
        lpServerDoc->m_hWndParent
    );

    // make sure App busy/blocked dialogs are parented to our
    // own hWndApp
    OleStdMsgFilter_SetParentWindow(lpOleApp->m_lpMsgFilter, hWndApp);

    // Hide the in-place hatch border window.
```

```
    ShowWindow(lpServerDoc->m_hWndHatch, SW_HIDE);

    ServerDoc_DisassembleMenus(lpServerDoc);

    /* we no longer need the IOleInPlaceFrame* or the doc's
    ** IOleInPlaceWindow* interface pointers.
    */
    if (lpIPData->lpDoc) {
        OleStdRelease((LPUNKNOWN)lpIPData->lpDoc);
        lpIPData->lpDoc = NULL;
    }

    if (lpIPData->lpFrame) {
        OleStdRelease((LPUNKNOWN)lpIPData->lpFrame);
        lpIPData->lpFrame = NULL;
    }

    ((LPSERVERAPP)g_lpApp)->m_lpIPData = NULL;

    return NOERROR;
}
```

See Also **IOleInPlaceSite::OnInPlaceDeactivate, IOleObject::Close**

IOleInPlaceObject::UIDeactivate

HRESULT IOleInPlaceObject::UIDeactivate()

IOleInPlaceObject::UIDeactivate deactivates and removes the user interface that supports in-place activation.

Return Value

Value	Meaning
S_OK	The in-place UI was deactivated and removed.
E_UNEXPECTED	An unexpected error happened.

Comments Resources such as menus and windows can be either cleaned up or kept around in a hidden state until **IOleInPlaceObject::InPlaceDeactivate** or **IOleObject::Close** is called to completely deactivate the object. The object application must call **IOleInPlaceSite::OnUIDeactivate** before doing anything with the composite menus so that the container is first detached from the frame window. On deactivating the in-place object's user interface, the object is left in a ready state for quick reactivation. The object stays in this state until the undo state of the document changes. The container should then call **IOleInPlaceObject::InPlaceDeactivate** to tell the object to discard its undo state.

If the container has called **IOleInPlaceObject::UIDeactivate**, it should later call the **IOleInPlaceObject::InPlaceDeactivate** method to properly clean up resources. The container can assume that stopping or releasing the object cleans up resources if necessary. The object must be prepared to do so if **IOleInPlaceObject::InPlaceDeactivate** has not been called at these points.

Example

In the following **IOleInPlaceObject::UIDeactivate** example for an inside-out object, the object application first notifies the document and frame windows that the object's UI is being deactivated. The object then removes its frame adornments and in-place tools and menus. Although the object's menus and tools are removed from the screen, the object does not call the container's **IOleInPlaceFrame::SetBorderSpace** or **IOleInPlaceFrame::SetMenu** if there is another object that is going to be activated in place.

For more information on handling UI deactivation, see "Deactivating In-Place Objects," earlier in this chapter.

```
HRESULT InPlaceObj_UIDeactivate(LPOLEINPLACEOBJECT lpThis)
{
    LPSERVERDOC       lpServerDoc =
                ((struct CDocOleObjectImpl FAR*)lpThis)->lpServerDoc;
    LPSERVERAPP       lpServerApp = (LPSERVERAPP)g_lpApp;
    LPCONTAINERDOC        lpContainerDoc = (LPCONTAINERDOC)lpServerDoc;
    LPINPLACEDATA     lpIPData = lpServerDoc->m_lpIPData;
    LPOBJLIST         lpObj = (LPOBJLIST)&((LPCONTAINERDOC)lpServerDoc)-
>m_ObjList;
    HWND              hWndApp = OutlineApp_GetWindow(g_lpApp);

if (!lpServerDoc->m_fUIActive)
        return NOERROR;

    lpServerDoc->m_fUIActive = FALSE;

    // Clip the hatch window to the size of pos rect so that the object
    // adornments and hatch border is not visible.
    ServerDoc_ResizeInPlaceWindow(lpServerDoc,
            (LPRECT)&(lpServerDoc->m_lpIPData->rcPosRect),
            (LPRECT)&(lpServerDoc->m_lpIPData->rcPosRect));

    // Notify document and frame that active object is going to be
    // UI deactivated
    if (lpIPData->lpDoc)
        lpIPData->lpDoc->lpVtbl->SetActiveObject(lpIPData->lpDoc, NULL, NULL);

    if (lpIPData->lpFrame) {
        lpIPData->lpFrame->lpVtbl->SetActiveObject(
            lpIPData->lpFrame,
            NULL,
            NULL);
```

```
    }

    /* OLE2NOTE: The object must hide its frame tools here but NOT call
    **    IOleInPlaceFrame::SetBorderSpace(NULL) or SetMenu(NULL).
    **    The object must also hide its tools BEFORE calling
    **    IOleInPlaceSite::OnUIDeactivate. The container then puts
    **    its menus and tools back when OnUIDeactivate is called.
    */
    ServerDoc_RemoveFrameLevelTools(lpServerDoc);

    lpIPData->lpSite->lpVtbl->OnUIDeactivate(lpIPData->lpSite, FALSE);

    /* Reset to use our normal application's accelerator table */
    g_lpApp->m_hAccelApp = lpServerApp->m_hAccelBaseApp;
    g_lpApp->m_hAccel = lpServerApp->m_hAccelBaseApp;
    g_lpApp->m_hWndAccelTarget = hWndApp;

#if !defined(SVR_INSIDEOUT)
    /* OLE2NOTE: An outside-in style in-place server would hide its
    **    window here. An inside-out style server leaves its window
    **    visible when it is UIDeactivated (it would only hide its
    **    window when InPlaceDeactivated). This application is an
    **    inside-out style server. It is recommended for most objects
    **    to support inside-out behavior, if possible.
    */
    ServerDoc_DoInPlaceHide(lpServerDoc);
#endif

    return NOERROR;
}

void ServerDoc_RemoveFrameLevelTools(LPSERVERDOC lpServerDoc)
{
    LPCONTAINERDOC lpContainerDoc = (LPCONTAINERDOC)lpServerDoc;

    FrameTools_Enable(lpContainerDoc->m_lpFrameTools, FALSE);
}

HRESULT ServerDoc_DoInPlaceHide(LPSERVERDOC lpServerDoc)
{
    LPINPLACEDATA   lpIPData = lpServerDoc->m_lpIPData;
    LPCONTAINERDOC  lpContainerDoc = (LPCONTAINERDOC)lpServerDoc;
    LPOLEAPP        lpOleApp = (LPOLEAPP)g_lpApp;
    HWND        hWndApp = ContainerApp_GetWindow(g_lpApp);

    if (! lpServerDoc->m_fInPlaceVisible)
        return NOERROR;

    // Set the parent back to server app's window
    OleDoc_HideWindow((LPOLEDOC)lpServerDoc, FALSE /* fShutdown */);
```

```
    /* We need to enusure that our window is set to normal 100% zoom.
    **    If the window is next shown in open mode, it should start out
    **    at normal zoom factor. Our window might have been set to a
    **    different zoom factor while it was in-place active.
    */
    ContainerDoc_SetCurrentZoomCommand(lpContainerDoc,IDM_V_ZOOM_100);

    lpServerDoc->m_fInPlaceVisible = FALSE;

    lpServerDoc->m_hWndParent = hWndApp;
    SetParent(
        lpContainerDoc->m_hWndDoc,
        lpServerDoc->m_hWndParent);

    // make sure App busy/blocked dialogs are parented to our own hWndApp
    OleStdMsgFilter_SetParentWindow(lpOleApp->m_lpMsgFilter, hWndApp);

    // Hide the in-place hatch border window.
    ShowWindow(lpServerDoc->m_hWndHatch, SW_HIDE);

    ServerDoc_DisassembleMenus(lpServerDoc);

    /* we no longer need the IOleInPlaceFrame* or the doc's
    **    IOleInPlaceWindow* interface pointers.
    */
    if (lpIPData->lpDoc) {
        OleStdRelease((LPUNKNOWN)lpIPData->lpDoc);
        lpIPData->lpDoc = NULL;
    }
    if (lpIPData->lpFrame) {
        OleStdRelease((LPUNKNOWN)lpIPData->lpFrame);
        lpIPData->lpFrame = NULL;
    }

    ((LPSERVERAPP)g_lpApp)->m_lpIPData = NULL;

    return NOERROR;
}
```

See Also **IOleInPlaceObject::InPlaceDeactivate, IOleInPlaceSite::OnUIDeactivate, IOleInPlaceObject::ReactivateAndUndo, IOleObject::Close**

IOleInPlaceObject::SetObjectRects

HRESULT IOleInPlaceObject::SetObjectRects(*lprcPosRect, lprcClipRect*)
LPCRECT *lprcPosRect*
LPCRECT *lprcClipRect*

IOleInPlaceObject::SetObjectRects indicates how much of the in-place object is visible.

Parameters

lprcPosRect
Points to the rectangle containing the position of the in-place object in the client coordinates of its parent window.

lprcClipRect
Points to the outer rectangle containing the in-place object's position rectangle (*PosRect*). This rectangle is relative to the client area of the object's parent window.

Return Value

Value	Meaning
S_OK	Operation was successful.
E_INVALIDARG	One or more invalid arguments.
E_UNEXPECTED	An unexpected error happened.

Comments

The container should call **IOleInPlaceObject::SetObjectRects** whenever the window position of the in-place object and/or visible part of the in-place object changes. The object must size its in-place window to match the intersection of *lprcPosRect* and *lprcClipRect*. The object must also draw its contents into the object's in-place window so that proper clipping takes place.

The object should compare its width and height with those provided by its container (conveyed through *lprcPosRect*). If the comparison does not result in a match, the container is applying either scaling or zooming to the object. The object must then decide whether it should continue the in-place editing in the scale/zoom mode or deactivate.

It is possible for *lprcClipRect* to change without the *lprcPosRect* changing. The size of an in-place object's rectangle is *always* calculated in pixels. This is different from other OLE objects visualizations, which are in HIMETRIC.

Note While executing **IOleInPlaceObject::SetObjectRects**, an application *cannot* call the Windows **Yield**, **Peek**, or **GetMessage** functions or display a dialog box. There are further restrictions on which OLE interface methods and functions can be called from within **SetObjectRects.** For more information, see "Dispatching Accelerator Keys" earlier in this chapter.

Example

The following example shows the object's **IOleInPlaceObject::SetObjectRects** method, in which the object resizes its in-place window. Because the object must size itself to the intersection of *lprcPosRect* and *lprcClipRect*, it saves the new values passed in. If the object is not UI active, the object clips itself to just the size of its content before hiding its hatch and frame adornments. The object then calls **ServerDoc_ResizeInPlaceWindow** to redraw the window. **ResizeInPlaceWindow** then calculates the space needed to display the object's frame adornments and then draws the object within the new *lprcClipRect* space.

```
HRESULT InPlaceObj_SetObjectRects(
        LPOLEINPLACEOBJECT  lpThis,
        LPCRECT             lprcPosRect,
        LPCRECT             lprcClipRect)
{
    LPSERVERDOC  lpServerDoc =
                ((struct CDocOleObjectImpl FAR*)lpThis)->lpServerDoc;
    LPINPLACEDATA lpIPData = lpServerDoc->m_lpIPData;
    LPOBJLIST lpObj = ContainerDoc_GetObjList((LPCONTAINERDOC)lpServerDoc);

    // save the current PosRect and ClipRect
    lpIPData->rcPosRect = *lprcPosRect;
    lpIPData->rcClipRect = *lprcClipRect;

    if (! lpServerDoc->m_fUIActive)  // object's hatch and adornaments
                                     // must not be drawn
        lprcClipRect = lprcPosRect;

    ServerDoc_ResizeInPlaceWindow(
            lpServerDoc, (LPRECT)lprcPosRect, (LPRECT)lprcClipRect);

    return NOERROR;
}
/* ServerDoc_ResizeInPlaceWindow
** -----------------------------
**    Resize the in-place ServerDoc windows according to the
**    PosRect and ClipRect allowed by the in-place container.
**
**    OLE2NOTE: the PosRect rectangle that the in-place container tells
**    us is always the rectangle required for the object to display
**    itself. It does NOT include the space we require for object frame
**    adornments.
*/
void ServerDoc_ResizeInPlaceWindow(
        LPSERVERDOC         lpServerDoc,
        LPCRECT             lprcPosRect,
        LPCRECT             lprcClipRect)

{
    LPSERVERDOC lpServerDoc = (LPSERVERDOC)lpServerDoc;
```

```
    LPOBJLIST   lpObj = (LPOBJLIST)&lpServerDoc->m_ObjList;
    SCALEFACTOR  scale;
    RECT         rcDoc;
    POINT        ptOffset;

    /* OLE2NOTE: Calculate the space needed for our object frame
    **    adornments. Our in-place container tells us the size our
    **    object should take in window client coordinates
    **    (lprcPosRect). The rectangle corresponds to the size our
    **    LineList ListBox should be. Our document window must the
    **correct amount larger to accomodate our row/column headings.
    **    Then move all windows into position.
    */
    ServerDoc_CalcInPlaceWindowPos(
            lpServerDoc,
            (LPRECT)lprcPosRect,
            (LPRECT)&rcDoc,
            (LPSCALEFACTOR)&scale);

    /* OLE2NOTE: The object needs to honor the lprcClipRect specified by
its
    **    in-place container. Object must NOT draw outside of the
    **    ClipRect.In order to achieve this, the object will size
    **    the hatch window to be exactly the size that should be visible
    **    (rcVisRect). The rcVisRect is defined as the intersection of
    **    the full size of the in-place server window and the
    **    lprcClipRect. The ClipRect could, in fact, clip the HatchRect
    **    on the right/bottom and/or on the top/left. If it is clipped
    **    on the right/bottom, it is sufficient to simply resize the
    **    hatch window. If the HatchRect is clipped on the top/left,
    **    the object must "move" the ServerDoc window (child of
    **    HatchWindow) by the delta that was clipped. The window origin
    **    of the ServerDoc window will then have negative coordinates
    **    relative to its parent HatchWindow.
    */
    SetHatchWindowSize(
            lpServerDoc->m_hWndHatch,
            (LPRECT)&rcDoc,
            (LPRECT)lprcClipRect,
            (LPPOINT)&ptOffset);

    // shift Document window to account for the hatch frame being drawn
    OffsetRect((LPRECT)&rcDoc, ptOffset.x, ptOffset.y);

    // move/size/set scale factor of ServerDoc window.
    ServerDoc_SetScaleFactor(
            lpServerDoc, (LPSCALEFACTOR)&scale, (LPRECT)&rcDoc);

}
```

See Also **IOleInPlaceSite::OnPosRectChange**

IOleInPlaceObject::ReactivateAndUndo

HRESULT IOleInPlaceObject::ReactivateAndUndo()

IOleInPlaceObject::ReactivateAndUndo reactivates a previously deactivated object, undoing the last state of the object.

Return Value

Value	Meaning
S_OK	The object was successfully reactivated.
E_NOTUNDOABLE	Called when the Undo state is not available.
E_INVALIDARG	One or more invalid arguments.
E_UNEXPECTED	An unexpected error happened.

Comments

If the user chooses the Undo command before the Undo state of the object is lost, the object's immediate container calls **IOleInPlaceObject::ReactivateAndUndo** to activate the user interface, carry out the Undo operation, and return the object to the active state.

For more information on undoing changes, see "Undoing Changes During In-Place Activation" earlier in this chapter.

IOleInPlaceActiveObject Interface

The **IOleInPlaceActiveObject** interface is implemented by object applications to provide a direct channel of communication between the in-place object and the frame and document windows. The container uses the interface methods to manipulate an object while it is active in place.

The **IOleInPlaceActiveObject** interface contains the following methods (see also OLE2.H):

```
DECLARE_INTERFACE_(IOleInPlaceActiveObject, IOleWindow)
{
   // *** IUnknown methods ***
  HRESULT QueryInterface (THIS_ REFIID riid, LPVOID FAR* ppvObj);
  ULONG AddRef (THIS);
  ULONG Release (THIS);

   // *** IOleWindow methods ***
  HRESULT GetWindow (THIS_ HWND FAR* lphwnd);
  HRESULT ContextSensitiveHelp (THIS_ BOOL fEnterMode);
```

```
    // *** IOleInPlaceActiveObject methods ***
    HRESULT TranslateAccelerator (THIS_ LPMSG lpmsg);
    HRESULT OnFrameWindowActivate (THIS_ BOOL fActivate);
    HRESULT OnDocWindowActivate (THIS_ BOOL fActivate);
    HRESULT ResizeBorder (THIS_ LPCRECT lprectBorder, LPOLEINPLACEUIWINDOW lpUIWindow,
      BOOL fFrameWindow);
    HRESULT EnableModeless (THIS_ BOOL fEnable);
};
```

IOleInPlaceActiveObject::TranslateAccelerator

HRESULT IOleInPlaceActiveObject::TranslateAccelerator(*lpMsg*)
LPMSG *lpMsg*

IOleInPlaceActiveObject::TranslateAccelerator translates messages from the active object's message queue.

Parameter

lpMsg
Points to the message that might need to be translated.

Return Value

Value	Meaning
S_OK	The message was translated successfully.
S_FALSE	The message was not translated.
E_INVALIDARG	One or more invalid arguments.
E_UNEXPECTED	An unexpected error happened.

Comments

IOleInPlaceActiveObject::TranslateAccelerator is called by the container's message loop when an embedded object is active in place. While active in place, an active object *always* has the first chance at translating the messages. Therefore, **IOleInPlaceActiveObject::TranslateAccelerator** should be called before any other translation. The container should apply its own translation only if this function returns S_FALSE.

The **IOleInPlaceActiveObject::TranslateAccelerator** function is only be invoked for an object created by a DLL object application. An object created by an EXE object application gets keystrokes from its own message pump so the container does not get those messages.

If the container calls **IOleInPlaceActiveObject::TranslateAccelerator** for an object that is not created by a DLL object application, the default object handler returns S_FALSE.

An object application can call the Windows **TranslateAccelerator** API function for its implementation of **IOleInPlaceActiveObject::TranslateAccelerator**.

Example

The following example shows a simple implementation of **IOleInPlaceActiveObject::TranslateAccelerator** for an EXE object application. Because the application is an EXE, all incoming accelerator messages are received first by the object. Therefore, there is no need to provide an implementation. (Had the object been implemented as a DLL, the messages would have been first received by the container which would have called **OleTranslateAccelerator** to send the message to the object.)

For more information on translating accelerator messages, see "Dispatching Accelerator Keys" earlier in this chapter.

```
HRESULT InPlaceActiveObj_TranslateAccelerator(
        LPOLEINPLACEACTIVEOBJECT    lpThis,
        LPMSG                       lpmsg)
{
    // This will never be called because this object application is
    // implemented as an EXE
    return NOERROR;
}
```

See Also

OleTranslateAccelerator

IOleInPlaceActiveObject::OnFrameWindowActivate

HRESULT IOleInPlaceActiveObject::OnFrameWindowActivate(*fActivate***)**
BOOL *fActivate*

IOleInPlaceActiveObject::OnFrameWindowActivate notifies the object when the container's top-level frame window gains or loses activation.

Parameter

fActivate
Indicates the state of the container's top-level frame window. It is TRUE if the window is activating; FALSE if it is deactivating.

Return Value

Value	Meaning
S_OK	The method completed successfully.

Comments

IOleInPlaceActiveObject::OnFrameWindowActivate is called when the container's top-level frame window is either being activated or deactivated and the object is the current active object for the frame.

Note While executing **IOleInPlaceActiveObject::OnFrameWindowActivate**, an application *cannot* call the Windows **Yield**, **Peek**, or **GetMessage** functions or display a dialog box. There are further restrictions on which OLE interface methods and functions can be called from within **OnFrameWindowActivate**. For more information, see "Dispatching Accelerator Keys" earlier in this chapter.

Example

In the following **IOleInPlaceActiveObject::OnFrameWindowActivate** example, the object application sends a **PostMessage** to itself to update its toolbar (because it cannot call any OLE functions to do this work while **OnFrameWindowActivate** is executing).

```
HRESULT InPlaceActiveObj_OnFrameWindowActivate(
        LPOLEINPLACEACTIVEOBJECT    lpThis,
        BOOL                        fActivate)
{
    LPSERVERDOC lpServerDoc = (LPSERVERDOC)
            ((struct CDocOleObjectImpl FAR*)lpThis)->lpServerDoc;

    //Get the window handle of the document.
    HWND hWndDoc = ServerDoc_GetWindow(lpServerDoc);

    /* OLE2NOTE: This is a notification of the container application's
    **    WM_ACTIVATEAPP status. Some applications might find this
    **    important. We need to update the enable/disable status of our
    **    toolbar buttons.
    */

    // OLE2NOTE: We cannot call ServerDoc_UpdateFrameToolButtons
    //           until this call completes because that would
    //           generate some OLE calls (and eventually
    //           WM_ACTIVATEAPP), which would form a loop. Therefore, we
    //           delay the frame tool initialization until
    //           WM_ACTIVATEAPP is finished by posting a message
    //           to ourselves.

    /* Update enable/disable state of buttons in toolbar */
    if (fActivate)
        PostMessage(hWndDoc, WM_U_INITFRAMETOOLS, 0, 0L);

    return NOERROR;
}

HWND ServerDoc_GetWindow(LPSERVERDOC lpServerDoc)
{
    if(! lpServerDoc) return NULL;
    return lpServerDoc->m_hWndDoc;
}
```

IOleInPlaceActiveObject::OnDocWindowActivate

HRESULT IOleInPlaceActiveObject::OnDocWindowActivate(*fActivate*)
BOOL *fActivate*

IOleInPlaceActiveObject::OnDocWindowActivate notifies the active in-place object when the container's document window gains or loses activation.

Parameter

fActivate
Indicates the state of the MDI child document window. It isTRUE if the window is activating; FALSE if it is deactivating.

Return Value

Value	Meaning
S_OK	The method completed successfully.

Comments

IOleInPlaceActiveObject::OnDocWindowActivate is called when the MDI child document window is activated or deactivated and the object is the current active object for the document.

If activating, the object should install frame-level tools (including the shared composite menu and/or optional toolbars and frame adornments), and take focus. When deactivating, the object should remove the frame-level tools, but not call **IOleInPlaceUIWindow::SetBorderSpace** (NULL).

Note While executing **IOleInPlaceActiveObject::OnDocWindowActivate**, an application *cannot* call the Windows **Yield**, **Peek**, or **GetMessage** functions or display a dialog box. There are further restrictions on which OLE interface methods and functions can be called from within **OnDocWindowActivate**. For more information, see "Dispatching Accelerator Keys" earlier in this chapter.

Example

In the following example for **IOleInPlaceActiveObject::OnDocWindowActivate**, the object installs its frame-level tools and UI if it is active in place. If the object is not active in place, it simply hides the tools from the user.

For more information on implementing **IOleInPlaceActiveObject::OnDocWindowActivate**, see "Pseudo Code for Object Applications" earlier in this chapter.

```
HRESULT InPlaceActiveObj_OnDocWindowActivate(
        LPOLEINPLACEACTIVEOBJECT    lpThis,
        BOOL                        fActivate)
{
    LPSERVERDOC lpServerDoc =
            ((struct CDocOleObjectImpl FAR*)lpThis)->lpServerDoc;
    LPINPLACEDATA lpIPData = lpServerDoc->m_lpIPData;
```

```
    if (fActivate) {
        ServerDoc_AddFrameLevelUI(lpServerDoc);  //add tools
    }
    else {
        ServerDoc_RemoveFrameLevelTools(lpServerDoc); //remove tools
    }
    return NOERROR;
}
```

IOleInPlaceActiveObject::ResizeBorder

HRESULT IOleInPlaceActiveObject::ResizeBorder(*lprectBorder, lpUIWindow, fFrameWindow***)**
LPCRECT *lprectBorder*
LPOLEINPPLACEWINDOW *lpUIWindow*
BOOL *fFrameWindow*

IOleInPlaceActiveObject::ResizeBorder is called to alert the object that it needs to resize its border space.

Parameters

lprectBorder
Points to a **RECT** structure containing the new outer rectangle within which the object can request border space for its tools.

lpUIWindow
Points to the frame or document window object whose border has changed.

fFrameWindow
Specifies TRUE if the frame window object is calling **ResizeBorder**; otherwise, it is FALSE.

Return Value

Value	Meaning
S_OK	The method completed successfully.
E_INVALIDARG	One or more invalid arguments.
E_UNEXPECTED	An unexpected error happened.

Comments

The **IOleInPlaceActiveObject::ResizeBorder** function is called by the top-level container's document or frame window object when the border space allocated to the object should change. Because the active in-place object is unaware of which window has changed (the frame- or document-level window), **IOleInPlaceActiveObject::ResizeBorder** needs to be passed the pointer to the window's **IOleInPlaceUIWindow** interface.

In most cases, the resize just requires the object to grow, shrink, or scale the frame adornments. However, for more complicated adornments, the object might need to renegotiate the border space with calls to **IOleInPlaceUIWindow::RequestBorderSpace** and **IOleInPlaceUIWindow::SetBorderSpace**. For more information on negotiating border space, see "Installing Toolbars and Other Frame Adornments" earlier in this chapter.

Note While executing **IOleInPlaceActiveObject::ResizeBorder**, an application *cannot* call the Windows **Yield**, **Peek**, or **GetMessage** functions or display a dialog box. There are further restrictions on which OLE interface methods and functions can be called from within **ResizeBorder**. For more information, see "Dispatching Accelerator Keys" earlier in this chapter.

Example

In the following example, the top-level container calls **ResizeBorder** to tell the object that it needs to renegotiate its border space on the newly resized frame window. In its implementation of **ResizeBorder**, the object application calls FrameTools_NegotiateForSpaceAndShow to negotiate frame space for displaying the object's toolbars and/or frame adornments. Should the container not make any space available to the object, the object displays its tools as pop ups.

```
HRESULT InPlaceActiveObj_ResizeBorder(
        LPOLEINPLACEACTIVEOBJECT     lpThis,
        LPCRECT                      lprectBorder,
        LPOLEINPLACEUIWINDOW         lpIPUiWnd,
        BOOL                      fFrameWindow)
{
    LPSERVERDOC lpServerDoc =
            ((struct CDocOleObjectImpl FAR*)lpThis)->lpServerDoc;
    LPOUTLINEDOC lpOutlineDoc = (LPOUTLINEDOC)lpServerDoc;

    if (fFrameWindow) {
        FrameTools_NegotiateForSpaceAndShow(
                lpOutlineDoc->m_lpFrameTools,
                (LPRECT)lprectBorder,
                (LPOLEINPLACEFRAME)lpIPUiWnd);
    }
    return NOERROR;
}

void FrameTools_NegotiateForSpaceAndShow(
        LPFRAMETOOLS              lpft,
        LPRECT                    lprcFrameRect,
        LPOLEINPLACEFRAME         lpTopIPFrame)
{
    BORDERWIDTHS    borderwidths;
    RECT            rectBorder;
    HRESULT         hrErr;
```

```
    if (lprcFrameRect)
        rectBorder = *lprcFrameRect;
    else {
        /* OLE2NOTE: By calling GetBorder, the server can find out the
        **    size of the frame window. It can use this information to
        **    make decisions about how to orient/organize it tools
        **    (for example, if window is taller than wide put tools
        **    vertically at the left edge).
        */
        hrErr = lpTopIPFrame->lpVtbl->GetBorder(
                lpTopIPFrame,
                (LPRECT)&rectBorder);
    }
    /* Try SetBorderSpace() with the space you need. If it fails,
    ** you can negotiate for space and then do the SetBorderSpace().
    */
    FrameTools_GetRequiredBorderSpace(lpft,(LPBORDERWIDTHS)&borderwidths);
    hrErr = lpTopIPFrame->lpVtbl->SetBorderSpace(
            lpTopIPFrame,
            (LPCBORDERWIDTHS)&borderwidths);

    if (hrErr != NOERROR) {
        // Frame did not give the tools space that we want. So negotiate

        hrErr = lpTopIPFrame->lpVtbl->RequestBorderSpace(
                lpTopIPFrame,
                (LPCBORDERWIDTHS)&borderwidths);

        if (hrErr == NOERROR) {
            hrErr = lpTopIPFrame->lpVtbl->SetBorderSpace(
                    lpTopIPFrame,
                    (LPCBORDERWIDTHS)&borderwidths);
        }
    }
    if (hrErr == NOERROR) {
        FrameTools_Move(lpft, (LPRECT)&rectBorder); // we got what we wanted
    } else {
        /* We did not get tool space, so display them as pop up.
        /* OLE2NOTE: Because we are popping up our tools, we MUST inform
        **    the top-level frame window that we need NO tool space
        **    BUT that it should NOT put its own tools up. If we were
        **    to pass NULL instead of (0,0,0,0), the container
        **    would have the option to leave its own tools up.
        */
        hrErr = lpTopIPFrame->lpVtbl->SetBorderSpace(
                lpTopIPFrame,
                (LPCBORDERWIDTHS)&g_rectNull);
        FrameTools_PopupTools(lpft);
    }
}
```

See Also **IOleInPlaceUIWindow::GetBorder**

IOleInPlaceActiveObject::EnableModeless

HRESULT IOleInPlaceActiveObject::EnableModeless(*fEnable***)**
BOOL *fEnable*

IOleInPlaceActiveObject::EnableModeless is called to enable or disable modeless dialog boxes when the container creates or destroys a modal dialog.

Parameter

fEnable
Specifies TRUE to enable modeless dialog windows; FALSE to disable them.

Return Value

Value	Meaning
S_OK	The method completed successfully.

Comments

IOleInPlaceActiveObject::EnableModeless is called by the top-level container to enable and disable modeless dialogs that the object displays. To display a modal dialog, the container first calls the **IOleInPlaceActiveObject::EnableModeless** method, specifying FALSE to disable the object's modeless dialog windows. After completion, the container calls **IOleInPlaceActiveObject::EnableModeless** (TRUE) to reenable the object's modeless dialog boxes.

For more information on enabling and disabling the display of modal dialogs, see "Displaying Modeless Dialogs" earlier in this chapter.

See Also **IOleInPlaceFrame::EnableModeless**

IOleInPlaceUIWindow Interface

The **IOleInPlaceUIWindow** interface is implemented by container applications and is used by object applications to negotiate border space on the document or frame window. The document window might not exist in all applications. If this is the case, NULL is returned for **IOleInPlaceUIWindow** by **IOleInPlaceSite::GetWindowContext**.

The **IOleInPlaceUIWindow** interface contains the following methods (see also OLE2.H):

```
DECLARE_INTERFACE_(IOleInPlaceUIWindow, IOleWindow)
{
  // *** IUnknown methods ***
  HRESULT QueryInterface (THIS_ REFIID riid, LPVOID FAR* ppvObj);
```

```
    ULONG AddRef (THIS);
    ULONG Release (THIS);

    // *** IOleWindow methods ***
    HRESULT GetWindow (THIS_ HWND FAR* lphwnd);
    HRESULT ContextSensitiveHelp (THIS_ BOOL fEnterMode);

    // *** IOleInPlaceUIWindow methods ***
    HRESULT GetBorder (THIS_ LPRECT lprectBorder);
    HRESULT RequestBorderSpace (THIS_ LPCBORDERWIDTHS lpborderwidths);
    HRESULT SetBorderSpace (THIS_ LPCBORDERWIDTHS lpborderwidths);
    HRESULT SetActiveObject (THIS_ LPOLEINPLACEACTIVEOBJECT lpActiveObject,
     LPCSTR lpszObjName);
};
```

IOleInPlaceUIWindow::GetBorder

HRESULT IOleInPlaceUIWindow::GetBorder(*lprectBorder*)
LPRECT *lprectBorder*

IOleInPlaceUIWindow::GetBorder returns a **RECT** structure in which the object can put toolbars and similar controls while an object is active in place.

Parameter

lprectBorder
Points to a **RECT** structure where the outer rectangle is to be returned. The **RECT** structure is relative to the window being represented by the interface.

Return Value

Value	Meaning
S_OK	The rectangle was successfully returned.
E_NOTOOLSPACE	The object cannot install toolbars in this window object
E_INVALIDARG	One or more invalid arguments.
E_UNEXPECTED	An unexpected error happened.

Comments

The **IOleInPlaceUIWindow::GetBorder** function, when called on a document or frame window object, returns the outer rectangle (relative to the window) where the object can put toolbars or similar controls. If the object is to install these tools, it should negotiate space for the tools within this rectangle using **IOleInPlaceUIWindow::RequestBorderSpace** and then call **IOleInPlaceUIWindow::SetBorderSpace** to get this space allocated.

Note While executing **IOleInPlaceUIWindow::GetBorder**, an application *cannot* call the Windows **Yield**, **Peek**, or **GetMessage** functions or display a dialog box. There are further restrictions on which OLE interface methods and functions can be called from within **GetBorder**. For more information, see "Dispatching Accelerator Keys" earlier in this chapter.

Example

In the following example, the container's **IOleInPlaceUIWindow::GetBorder** implementation returns a **RECT** structure to the in-place object. Within the space of this returned **RECT**, the object can then negotiate space for the display of its toolbars and/or frame adornments.

```
HRESULT InPlaceUIWindow_GetBorder(
          LPOLEINPLACEFRAME lpThis,
          LPRECT lprectBorder)
{
    LPOUTLINEAPP lpOutlineApp = (LPOUTLINEAPP);

    CntrApp_GetFrameRect(g_lpApp, lprectBorder);

    return NOERROR;
}

void CntrApp_GetFrameRect(LPCONTAINERAPP lpContainerApp,
                          LPRECT lprcFrameRect)
{
    GetClientRect(lpContainerApp->m_hWndApp, lprcFrameRect);

    lprcFrameRect->bottom -= STATUS_HEIGHT;
}
```

See Also

IOleInPlaceUIWindow::RequestBorderSpace, **IOleInPlaceUIWindow::SetBorderSpace**

IOleInPlaceUIWindow::RequestBorderSpace

HRESULT IOleInPlaceUIWindow::RequestBorderSpace(*lpborderwidths***)**
LPCBORDERWIDTHS *lpborderwidths*

IOleInPlaceUIWindow::RequestBorderSpace determines whether tools can be installed around the object's window frame while the object is active in place.

Parameter

lpborderwidths
Points to a **BORDERWIDTHS** structure containing the requested widths (in pixels) needed on each side of the window for the tools.

Return Value

Value	Meaning
S_OK	The requested space could be allocated to the object.
E_NOTOOLSPACE	The object cannot install toolbars in this window object, or there is insufficient space to install the toolbars.
E_INVALIDARG	One or more invalid arguments (for example, an invalid pointer or parameter). All methods, except those that take no parameters or only BOOLEAN parameters, can return this error code.
E_UNEXPECTED	An unexpected error happened.

Comments

The object calls **IOleInPlaceUIWindow::RequestBorderSpace** to ask if tools can be installed inside the window frame. These tools would be allocated between the rectangle returned by **IOleInPlaceUIWindow::GetBorder** and the **BORDERWIDTHS** structure specified in the argument to this call.

The space for the tools is not actually allocated to the object until it calls **IOleInPlaceUIWindow::SetBorderSpace**, allowing the object to negotiate for space (such as while dragging toolbars around), but deferring the moving of tools until the action is completed.

If the object wants to install these tools, it should pass the width in pixels that is to be used on each side. For example, if the object wanted 10 pixels on the top, 0 pixels on the bottom, and 5 pixels on the left and right sides, it would pass the following **BORDERWIDTHS** structure to **IOleInPlaceUIWindow::RequestBorderSpace**:

```
lpbw->top       = 10
lpbw->bottom    =  0
lpbw->lLeft     =  5
lpbw->right     =  5
```

For more information on negotiating border space, see the description of the **BORDERWIDTHS** structure earlier in this chapter.

Note While executing **IOleInPlaceUIWindow::RequestBorderSpace**, an application *cannot* call the Windows **Yield**, **Peek**, or **GetMessage** functions or display a dialog box. There are further restrictions on which OLE interface methods and functions can be called from within **RequestBorderSpace**. For more information, see "Dispatching Accelerator Keys" earlier in this chapter.

Example

If the container does not care how much space the active object uses for its toolbars, it can simply return NOERROR as shown in the following **IOleInPlaceUIWindow::RequestBorderSpace** example. It is recommended that containers not unduly restrict the display of tools by the active in-place object. For more information on the user interface considerations related to in-place activation, see the chapter "User Interface Guidelines."

```
HRESULT InPlaceUIWindow_RequestBorderSpace(
    LPOLEINPLACEFRAME   lpThis,
    LPCBORDERWIDTHS     lpWidths)
{
    /* Container allows the object to have as much border space as it
    ** wants.
    */
    return NOERROR;
}
```

See Also

IOleInPlaceUIWindow::GetBorder, IOleInPlaceUIWindow::SetBorderSpace

IOleInPlaceUIWindow::SetBorderSpace

HRESULT IOleInPlaceUIWindow::SetBorderSpace(*lpborderwidths***)**
LPCBORDERWIDTHS *lpborderwidths*

IOleInPlaceUIWindow::SetBorderSpace allocates space for the border requested in the call to the **IOleInPlaceUIWindow::RequestBorderSpace** method.

Parameter

lpborderwidths
Points to a **BORDERWIDTHS** structure containing the requested width (in pixels) of the tools. It can be NULL, indicating the object does not need any space.

Return Value

Value	Meaning
S_OK	The requested space has been allocated to the object.
OLE_E_INVALIDRECT	The rectangle does not lie within that returned by **IOleInPlaceUIWindow::GetBorder**.
E_INVALIDARG	One or more invalid arguments.
E_UNEXPECTED	An unexpected error happened.

Comments

The object calls the **IOleInPlaceUIWindow::SetBorderSpace** method to allocate the space on the border.

The **BORDERWIDTHS** structure used in this call generally would have been passed in a previous call to **IOleInPlaceUIWindow::RequestBorderSpace**, which must have returned S_OK.

If an object needs to renegotiate space on the border, it can just call **SetBorderSpace** again with the new widths. If the call to **SetBorderSpace** fails, the object can do a full negotiation for border space with calls to **GetBorder**, **RequestBorderSpace**, and **SetBorderSpace**.

Note While executing **IOleInPlaceUIWindow::SetBorderSpace**, an application *cannot* call the Windows **Yield**, **Peek**, or **GetMessage** functions or display a dialog box. There are further restrictions on which OLE interface methods and functions can be called from within **SetBorderSpace**. For more information, see "Dispatching Accelerator Keys" earlier in this chapter.

Example

In the following **IOleInPlaceUIWindow::SetBorderSpace** example, the container checks to see whether an active object needs any tool space. If not (*lpBorderWidths* is NULL), the container displays its own tools on the frame window. Otherwise, the container gives the active object the space needed for its tools.

```
HRESULT InPlaceUIWin_SetBorderSpace(
    LPOLEINPLACEFRAME   lpThis,
    LPCBORDERWIDTHS     lpBorderWidths)
{
    LPCONTAINERAPP lpContainerApp =
            ((struct COleInPlaceFrameImpl FAR*)lpThis)->lpContainerApp;

    if (lpBorderWidths == NULL) {

        /* OLE2NOTE: IOleInPlaceSite::SetBorderSpace(NULL) is called
        **    when the in-place active object does NOT want any tool
        **    space. In this situation, the in-place container should
        **    put up its tools.
        */
        LPCONTAINERDOC lpContainerDoc;

        lpContainerDoc =(LPCONTAINERDOC)ContainerApp_GetActiveDoc(lpContainerAp
        ContainerDoc_AddFrameLevelTools(lpContainerDoc);
    } else {

        ContainerApp_SetBorderSpace(
                (LPCONTAINERAPP) lpContainerApp,
                (LPBORDERWIDTHS)lpBorderWidths);
    }
    return NOERROR;
}
```

See Also **IOleInPlaceUIWindow::GetBorder**, **IOleInPlaceUIWindow::RequestBorderSpace**

IOleInPlaceUIWindow::SetActiveObject

HRESULT IOleInPlaceUIWindow::SetActiveObject (*lpActiveObject, lpszObjName*)
LPOLEINPLACEACTIVEOBJECT *lpActiveObject*
LPCSTR *lpszObjName*

IOleInPlaceUIWindow::SetActiveObject is called by the object to provide each of the frame and document windows a direct channel of communication with the active in-place object.

Parameters

lpActiveObject
Points to the active in-place object's **IOleInPlaceActiveObject** interface.

lpszObjName
Points to a string containing the document title.

Return Value

Value	Meaning
S_OK	The method completed successfully.
E_INVALIDARG	One or more invalid arguments.
E_UNEXPECTED	An unexpected error happened.

Comments

An object calls **IOleInPlaceUIWindow::SetActiveObject** to establish a direct communication link between itself and the document and frame windows.

When deactivating, the object calls **IOleInPlaceUIWindow::SetActiveObject**, passing NULL for the *lpActiveObject* and *lpszObjName* parameters.

An object *must* call **IOleInPlaceUIWindow::SetActiveObject** before calling **IOleInPlaceFrame::SetMenu** to give the container the pointer to the active object. The container then uses this pointer in the processing of **IOleInPlaceFrame::SetMenu** method and to pass to the **OleSetMenuDescriptor** function.

Example

In the following **IOleInPlaceUIWindow::SetActiveObject** example, the container first checks to see whether there is an object already active in place. If there is, the container releases the current active object before it sets a pointer to the new in-place active object.

```
HRESULT InPlaceUIWindow_SetActiveObject(
    LPOLEINPLACEFRAME           lpThis,
    LPOLEINPLACEACTIVEOBJECT    lpActiveObject,
    LPCSTR                      lpszObjName)
```

```
{
    LPCONTAINERAPP lpContainerApp =
            ((struct COleInPlaceFrameImpl FAR*)lpThis)->lpContainerApp;

    if (lpContainerApp->m_lpIPActiveObj)
        lpContainerApp->m_lpIPActiveObj->lpVtbl->
        Release(lpContainerApp->m_lpIPActiveObj);

    if (lpContainerApp->m_lpIPActiveObj = lpActiveObject)
        lpContainerApp->m_lpIPActiveObj->lpVtbl->
        AddRef(lpContainerApp->m_lpIPActiveObj);

    return NOERROR;
}
```

See Also **IOleInPlaceFrame::SetMenu, OleSetMenuDescriptor**

IOleInPlaceFrame Interface

The **IOleInPlaceFrame** interface is implemented by container applications and is used by object applications to control the display and placement of the composite menu, keystroke accelerator translation, context-sensitive help mode, and modeless dialog boxes.

The **IOleInPlaceFrame** interface contains the following methods (see also OLE2.H):

```
DECLARE_INTERFACE_(IOleInPlaceFrame, IOleInPlaceUIWindow)
{
  // *** IUnknown methods ***
  HRESULT QueryInterface (THIS_ REFIID riid, LPVOID FAR* ppvObj);
  ULONG AddRef (THIS);
  ULONG Release (THIS);

  // *** IOleWindow methods ***
  HRESULT GetWindow (THIS_ HWND FAR* lphwnd);
  HRESULT ContextSensitiveHelp (THIS_ BOOL fEnterMode);

  // *** IOleInPlaceUIWindow methods ***
  HRESULT GetBorder (THIS_ LPRECT lprectBorder);
  HRESULT RequestBorderSpace (THIS_ LPCBORDERWIDTHS lpborderwidths);
  HRESULT SetBorderSpace (THIS_ LPCBORDERWIDTHS lpborderwidths);
  HRESULT SetActiveObject (THIS_ LPOLEINPLACEACTIVEOBJECT lpActiveObject,
   LPCSTR lpszObjName);

  // *** IOleInPlaceFrame methods ***
  HRESULT InsertMenus (THIS_ HMENU hmenuShared,
   LPOLEMENUGROUPWIDTHS lpMenuWidths);
  HRESULT SetMenu (THIS_ HMENU hmenuShared, HOLEMENU holemenu,
```

```
    HWND hwndActiveObject);
   HRESULT RemoveMenus (THIS_ HMENU hmenuShared);
   HRESULT SetStatusText (THIS_ LPCSTR lpszStatusText);
   HRESULT EnableModeless (THIS_ BOOL fEnable);
   HRESULT TranslateAccelerator (THIS_ LPMSG lpmsg, WORD wID);
};
```

IOleInPlaceFrame::InsertMenus

HRESULT IOleInPlaceFrame::InsertMenus(*hmenuShared, lpMenuWidths*)
HMENU *hmenuShared*
LPOLEMENUGROUPWIDTHS *lpMenuWidths*

IOleInPlaceFrame::InsertMenus is called by the object application to allow the container to insert its menu groups in the composite menu that is to be used during the in-place session.

Parameters

hmenuShared
Specifies a handle to an empty menu.

lpMenuWidths
Points to an **OLEMENUGROUPWIDTHS** array of six LONG values. The container fills in elements 0, 2, and 4 to reflect the number of menus elements it provided in the File, View, and Window menu groups.

Return Value

Value	Meaning
S_OK	The menu groups were inserted successfully.
E_INVALIDARG	One or more invalid arguments.
E_UNEXPECTED	An unexpected error happened.

Comments

The object application asks the container to add its menus to the menu specified in *hmenuShared* and to set the group counts in the **OLEMENUGROUPWIDTHS** array pointed to by *lpMenuWidths*. The object application then adds its own menus and counts. Objects can call **IOleInPlaceFrame::InsertMenus** several times to build several composite menus. The container should reuse the same menu handles for the drop-downs and use the same handles as on the normal menu bar.

For more information on installing a composite menu for the in-place object, see "Merging User Interface Components" earlier in this chapter.

Example

In the following **IOleInPlaceFrame::InsertMenus** example, the container calls the Windows **AppendMenu** API to add its menus to the in-place menu passed in by the object through *hMenu*. After adding its menus, the container sets the group counts for these menus in **OLEMENUGROUPWIDTHS**.

```
HRESULT InPlaceFrame_InsertMenus(
    LPOLEINPLACEFRAME       lpThis,
    HMENU                   hMenu,
    LPOLEMENUGROUPWIDTHS    lpMenuWidths)
{
    LPCONTAINERAPP lpContainerApp = (LPCONTAINERAPP)g_lpApp;
    BOOL     fNoError = TRUE;

fNoError &= AppendMenu(hMenu, MF_POPUP, (UINT)lpContainerApp->m_hMenuFile,
                         "&File");
fNoError &= AppendMenu(hMenu, MF_POPUP, (UINT)lpContainerApp->m_hMenuView,
                         "O&utline");
fNoError &= AppendMenu(hMenu, MF_POPUP,(UINT)lpContainerApp->m_hMenuDebug,
                         "DbgI&Cntr");
   lpMenuWidths->width[0] = 1;
   lpMenuWidths->width[2] = 1;
   lpMenuWidths->width[4] = 1;

 return (fNoError ? NOERROR : ResultFromScode(E_FAIL));
}
```

IOleInPlaceFrame::SetMenu

HRESULT IOleInPlaceFrame::SetMenu(*hmenuShared, holemenu, hwndActiveObject*)
HMENU *hmenuShared*
HOLEMENU *holemenu*
HWND *hwndActiveObject*

IOleInPlaceFrame::SetMenu installs the composite menu into the window frame containing the object being activated in place.

Parameters

hmenuShared
Specifies a handle to the composite menu constructed by calls to **IOleInPlaceFrame::InsertMenus** and the Windows **InsertMenu** function.

holemenu
Specifies the handle to the menu descriptor returned by the **OleCreateMenuDescriptor** function.

hwndActiveObject
Specifies a handle to a window owned by the object and to which menu messages, commands, and accelerators are to be sent.

Return Value

Value	Meaning
S_OK	The method completed successfully.
E_INVALIDARG	One or more invalid arguments.
E_UNEXPECTED	An unexpected error happened.

Comments

The object calls **IOleInPlaceFrame::SetMenu** to ask the container to install the composite menu. An SDI container should call the Windows **SetMenu** function. An MDI container should send a WM_MDISETMENU message, using *hmenuShared* as the menu to install. The container should call **OleSetMenuDescriptor** to install the OLE dispatching code.

When deactivating, the container *must* call **IOleInPlaceFrame::SetMenu**(NULL) to remove the shared menu. This is done to help minimize window repaints. The container should also call **OleSetMenuDescriptor** (NULL) to unhook the dispatching code. Finally, the object application calls **OleDestroyMenuDescriptor** to free the data structure.

For more information on installing a composite menu for the in-place object, see "Merging User Interface Components" earlier in this chapter.

Note While executing **IOleInPlaceFrame::SetMenu**, an application *cannot* call the Windows **Yield**, **Peek**, or **GetMessage** functions or display a dialog box. There are further restrictions on which OLE interface methods and functions can be called from within **SetMenu**. For more information, see "Dispatching Accelerator Keys" earlier in this chapter.

Example

In the following **IOleInPlaceFrame::SetMenu** example, the container either puts up the shared in-place menu (passed in through *hMenuShared*) or its normal menu if the object specifies NULL for *hMenu* (usually in response to a **IOleInPlaceSite::OnUIDeactivate** call). The menu is set in place by calling the Windows **SetMenu** API. For more information on setting the menu, see the pseudo code examples for the container and the object earlier in this chapter.

```
HRESULT InPlaceFrame_SetMenu(
    LPOLEINPLACEFRAME   lpThis,
    HMENU               hMenuShared,
    HOLEMENU            hOleMenu,
    HWND                hwndActiveObject)
{
    LPOUTLINEAPP lpContainerApp = (LPOUTLINEAPP)g_lpApp;
    HMENU   hMenu;
    HRESULT hrErr;
```

```
    if (hOleMenu && hMenuShared)
        hMenu = hMenuShared;
    else
        hMenu = lpContainerApp->m_hMenuApp;

    /* OLE2NOTE: SDI apps put menu on frame by calling Windows SetMenu.
    ** MDI apps would send WM_MDISETMENU message instead.
    */
    SetMenu (lpContainerApp->m_hWndApp, hMenu);
    hrErr = OleSetMenuDescriptor (hOleMenu, lpContainerApp->m_hWndApp,
                    hwndActiveObject, NULL, NULL);

    return hrErr;
}
```

See Also **IOleInPlaceFrame::InsertMenus, OleSetMenuDescriptor, OleDestroyMenuDescriptor**

OleInPlaceFrame::RemoveMenus

HRESULT IOleInPlaceFrame::RemoveMenus(*hmenuShared***)**
HMENU *hmenuShared*

IOleInPlaceFrame::RemoveMenus is called by the object application to give the container a chance to remove its menu elements from the in-place composite menu.

Parameter

hmenuShared
Specifies a handle to the in-place composite menu which was constructed by calls to **IOleInPlaceFrame::InsertMenus**and the Windows **InsertMenu** function.

Return Value

Value	Meaning
S_OK	The method completed successfully.
E_INVALIDARG	One or more invalid arguments.
E_UNEXPECTED	An unexpected error happened.

Comments

The object should always give the container a chance to remove its menu elements from the composite menu before deactivating the shared user interface.

For more information on removing the shared menu, see “Deactivating In-Place Objects” earlier in this chapter.

Example

In the following **IOleInPlaceFrame::RemoveMenus** example, the object asks the container to remove its menu items from the shared in-place menu as part of the normal tear down of an in-place session.

```
HRESULT InPlaceFrame_RemoveMenus(
    LPOLEINPLACEFRAME   lpThis,
    HMENU               hMenu)
{
    LPCONTAINERAPP lpContainerApp = (LPCONTAINERAPP)g_lpApp;
    BOOL fNoError = TRUE;

    /* Remove container group menus */
    while (GetMenuItemCount(hMenu))
        fNoError &= RemoveMenu(hMenu, 0, MF_BYPOSITION);

    return (fNoError ? NOERROR : ResultFromScode(E_FAIL));
}
```

See Also

IOleInPlaceFrame::SetMenu

IOleInPlaceFrame::SetStatusText

HRESULT IOleInPlaceFrame::SetStatusText(*lpszStatusText***)**
LPCSTR *lpszStatusText*

IOleInPlaceFrame::SetStatusText sets and displays status text about the in-place object in the container's frame window status line.

Parameter

lpszStatusText
Points to a null-terminated character string containing the message to display.

Return Value

Value	Meaning
S_OK	The text was displayed.
S_TRUNCATED	Some text was displayed but the message was too long.
E_INVALIDARG	One or more invalid arguments.
E_UNEXPECTED	An unexpected error happened.
E_FAIL	The text could not be displayed.

Comments

The object calls **IOleInPlaceFrame::SetStatusText** to ask the frame to display object text in the frame's status line, if it has one. Because the status line is owned by the container's frame window, calling **IOleInPlaceFrame::SetStatusText** is the *only* way an object can display status information. If the container refuses the object's request, the object application can negotiate for border space to display its own status window.

When switching between menus owned by the container and the in-place active object, the status bar text is not reflected properly if the object does not call the container's **IOleInPlaceFrame::SetStatusText** method. For example, if, during an in-place session, the user were to select the File menu, the status bar would reflect the action that would occur if the user selected this menu. If the user then selected the Edit menu (which is owned by the in-place object), the status bar text would not change unless the **IOleInPlaceFrame::SetStatusText** happened to be called. This is because there is no way for the container to recognize that one of the object's menus has been made active because all the messages that the container would trap are now going to the object.

To avoid potential problems, all objects being activated in place should process the WM_MENUSELECT message and call **IOleInPlaceFrame::SetStatusText** —even if the object does not usually provide status information (in which case the object can just pass a NULL string for the requested status text).

For more information on displaying status lines during an in-place session, see "Using Status Lines" earlier in this chapter.

Note While executing **IOleInPlaceFrame::SetStatusText**, an application *cannot* call the Windows **Yield**, **Peek**, or **GetMessage** functions or display a dialog box. There are further restrictions on which OLE interface methods and functions can be called from within **SetStatusText**. For more information, see "Dispatching Accelerator Keys" earlier in this chapter.

Example

In the following **IOleInPlaceFrame::SetStatusText** example, the container displays *lpszStatusText* for the object in the frame's status line. Because *lpszStatusText* is only guaranteed to be valid during the duration of this call, the container must hold a copy of *lpszStatusText* if it will need to do anything with it later.

```
HRESULT InPlaceFrame_SetStatusText(
   LPOLEINPLACEFRAME   lpThis,
   LPCSTR              lpszStatusText)
{
   LPCONTAINERAPP   lpContainerApp = (LPCONTAINERAPP)g_lpApp;

   //Save a copy of the string for future use
   if(lpContainerApp->m_szMessageHold)
        delete lpcontainerApp->m_szMessageHold;
   lpContainerApp->m_szMessageHold = new char [strlen(lpszStatusText) +1];
   strcpy(lpcontainerApp->szMessageHold, lpszStatusText);

   ContainerApp_SetStatusText(lpContainerApp, (LPCSTR)lpszStatusText);

   return ResultFromScode(S_OK);
}
```

```
void ContainerApp_SetStatusText(LPCONTAINERAPP lpContainerApp,
                                LPSTR lpszMessage)
{
    SetStatusText(lpContainerApp->m_hWndStatusBar, lpszMessage);
}
```

IOleInPlaceFrame::EnableModeless

HRESULT IOleInPlaceFrame::EnableModeless(*fEnable***)**
BOOL *fEnable*

IOleInPlaceFrame::EnableModeless enables or disables a frame's modeless dialog boxes.

Parameter

fEnable
Specifies whether the modeless dialogs are to be enabled (TRUE) or disabled (FALSE).

Return Value

Value	Meaning
S_OK	The dialog was eiter enabled or disabled successfully, depending on the value for *fEnable*.
E_UNEXPECTED	An unexpected error happened.

Comments

IOleInPlaceFrame::EnableModeless is called by the active in-place object to manage enabling and disabling modeless dialogs that the container might be displaying. To display a modal dialog, the object first calls the **IOleInPlaceFrame::EnableModeless** method, specifying FALSE to disable the container's modeless dialog windows. After completion, the object calls **IOleInPlaceFrame::EnableModeless** (TRUE) to reenable them.

For more information on displaying modal dialogs, see "Displaying Modeless Dialogs" earlier in this chapter.

See Also

IOleInPlaceActiveObject::EnableModeless

IOleInPlaceFrame::TranslateAccelerator

HRESULT IOleInPlaceFrame::TranslateAccelerator(*lpmsg, wID***)**
LPMSG *lpmsg*
WORD *wID*

IOleInPlaceFrame::TranslateAccelerator translates accelerator keystrokes intended for the container's frame while an object is active in place.

Parameters

lpmsg
Points to an **MSG** structure containing the keystroke message.

wID
Contains the command identifier value corresponding to the keystroke in the container-provided accelerator table. Containers can use this value in preference to translating again.

Return Value

Value	Meaning
S_OK	The keystroke was used.
S_FALSE	The keystroke was not used.
E_INVALIDARG	One or more invalid arguments.
E_UNEXPECTED	An unexpected error happened.

Comments

IOleInPlaceFrame::TranslateAccelerator is called indirectly by **OleTranslateAccelerator** when a keystroke accelerator intended for the container (frame) is received. The container application should perform its normal accelerator processing, or use *wID* directly, and then return, indicating whether the keystroke accelerator was processed. If the container is an MDI application and the Windows **TranslateAccelerator** call fails, the container can call the Windows **TranslateMDISysAccel** API function, just as it does for its normal message processing.

When an object is implemented by a DLL object application, the object receives messages from the container's message queue. In this case, the container should always call **IOleInPlaceActiveObject::TranslateAccelerator** before doing its own accelerator translation, giving the in-place object the first chance at translating the message. Conversely, an executable object application should call **OleTranslateAccelerator** after calling **TranslateAccelerator,** calling **TranslateMessage** and **DisplatchMessage** only if both translation functions fail.

Note So that they will work properly with object applications that do their own accelerator keystroke translations, accelerator tables for containers should be defined as follows:

```
"char", wID, VIRTKEY, CONTROL
```

This is the most common way for describing keyboard accelerators. Failure to do so can result in keystrokes being lost or sent to the wrong object during an in-place session.

Example

In the following **IOleInPlaceFrame::TranslateAccelerator** example, the container calls the Windows **TranslateAccelerator** API to translate the accelerator message sent to it by the in-place object (by using an earlier call to **OleTranlateAccelerator**).

```
HRESULT InPlaceFrame_TranslateAccelerator(
    LPOLEINPLACEFRAME   lpThis,
    LPMSG               lpmsg,
    WORD                wID)
{
    LPCONTAINERAPP lpContainerApp = (LPCONTAINERAPP)g_lpApp;
    SCODE sc;

    if (TranslateAccelerator (lpContainerApp->m_hWndApp,
                              lpContainerApp->m_hAccelIPCntr, lpmsg))
        return ResultFromScode(S_OK);

#if defined(MDI_VERSION)
    else if (TranslateMDISysAccel(lpContainerApp->m_hWndMDIClient, lpmsg))
        return ResultFromScode(S_OK);
#endif

    else
        return ResultFromScode(S_FALSE);
}
```

See Also

OleTranslateAccelerator

IOleInPlaceSite Interface

The **IOleInPlaceSite** interface is implemented by container applications and is used by object applications to interact with the object's in-place client site.

The **IOleInPlaceSite** interface contains the following methods (see also OLE2.H):

```
DECLARE_INTERFACE_(IOleInPlaceSite, IOleWindow)
{
  // *** IUnknown methods ***
  HRESULT QueryInterface (THIS_ REFIID riid, LPVOID FAR* ppvObj);
  ULONG AddRef (THIS);
  ULONG Release (THIS);

  // *** IOleWindow methods ***
  HRESULT GetWindow (THIS_ HWND FAR* lphwnd);
  HRESULT ContextSensitiveHelp (THIS_ BOOL fEnterMode);

  // *** IOleInPlaceSite methods ***
  HRESULT CanInPlaceActivate (THIS);
```

```
    HRESULT OnInPlaceActivate (THIS);
    HRESULT OnUIActivate (THIS);
    HRESULT GetWindowContext (THIS_ LPOLEINPLACEFRAME FAR* lplpFrame,
      LPOLEINPLACEUIWINDOW FAR* lplpDoc, LPRECT lprcPosRect, LPRECT lprcClipRect,
      LPOLEINPLACEFRAMEINFO lpFrameInfo);
    HRESULT Scroll (THIS_ SIZE scrollExtent);
    HRESULT OnUIDeactivate (THIS_ BOOL fUndoable);
    HRESULT OnInPlaceDeactivate (THIS);
    HRESULT DiscardUndoState (THIS);
    HRESULT DeactivateAndUndo (THIS);
    HRESULT OnPosRectChange (THIS_ LPCRECT lprcPosRect);
};
```

The **IOleInPlaceSite** interface pointer is obtained by calling **QueryInterface** on the object's **IOleClientSite** interface.

IOleInPlaceSite::CanInPlaceActivate

HRESULT IOleInPlaceSite::CanInPlaceActivate()

IOleInPlaceSite::CanInPlaceActivate is called by the object to determine whether the container can activate the object in place.

Return Value

Value	Meaning
S_OK	The container allows in-place activation for this object.
S_FALSE	The container does not allow in-place activation for this object.
E_INVALIDARG	One or more invalid arguments.
E_UNEXPECTED	An unexpected error happened.

Comments

IOleInPlaceSite::CanInPlaceActivate is called by the client site's immediate child object when this object wants to activate in place. This function allows the container application to accept or refuse the activation request.

Only objects being displayed as DVASPECT_CONTENT can be activated in-place.

Example

In the following example for **IOleInPlaceSite::CanInPlaceActivate**, the container returns S_FALSE if the object requesting to be activated is in any format other than DVASPECT_CONTENT; otherwise, the container returns NOERROR.

```
HRESULT InPlaceSite_CanInPlaceActivate(LPOLEINPLACESITE lpThis)
{
    LPCONTAINEROBJ lpContainerObj =
```

```
            ((struct COleInPlaceSiteImpl FAR*)lpThis)->lpContainerObj;

    /* OLE2NOTE: The container canNOT allow in-place activation if it
    **    is currently displaying the object as an ICON (DVASPECT_ICON).
    **    It can ONLY do in-place activation if it is displaying the
    **    DVASPECT_CONTENT of the OLE object.
    */
    if (lpContainerObj->m_dwDrawAspect == DVASPECT_CONTENT)
        return NOERROR;
    else
        return ResultFromScode(S_FALSE);
}
```

IOleInPlaceSite::OnInPlaceActivate

HRESULT IOleInPlaceSite::OnInPlaceActivate()

IOleInPlaceSite::OnInPlaceActivate notifies the container that one of its objects is being activated in place.

Return Value

Value	Meaning
S_OK	The container allows the in-place activation.
E_UNEXPECTED	An unexpected error happened.

Comments

IOleInPlaceSite::OnInPlaceActivate is called by the client site's immediate child object when it is activated in-place for the first time. The container should note that the object is becoming active.

A container that supports linking to embedded objects must properly manage the running of its in-place objects when they are UI inactive and running in the hidden state. To reactivate the in-place object quickly, a container should *not* call **IOleObject::Close** until the container's **IOleInPlaceSite::DeactivateAndUndo** method is called. To safeguard against the object being left in an unstable state should a linking client do a silent update, the container should call **OleLockRunning** to lock the object in the running state. This prevents the hidden in-place object from shutting down before it can be saved in its container.

Example

In the following **IOleInPlaceSite::OnInPlaceActivate** example for an outside-in container, only one object can be in-place active at one time. If another object is in-place activated, the container calls **ContainerDoc_ShutDownLastInPlaceObjectIfNotNeeded** to close the previously activated object application if it is not needed.

Because the container supports links to embedded objects, it guards the in-place object from being prematurely closed should a link client need to do a silent update against the object while it is UI deactivated and in a hidden, unlocked state. To lock the object in a running state (thus guaranteeing that it is to be saved later), the container calls **OleLockRunning** on the active object.

```
HRESULT InPlaceSite_OnInPlaceActivate(LPOLEINPLACESITE lpThis)
{
  LPCONTAINEROBJ lpContainerObj =
        ((struct COleInPlaceSiteImpl FAR*)lpThis)->lpContainerObj;
  LPCONTAINERDOC lpContainerDoc = lpContainerObj->m_lpDoc;
  SCODE sc = S_OK;

  if (lpContainerDoc->m_lpLastIpActiveObj) {
      ContainerDoc_ShutDownLastInPlaceObjectIfNotNeeded(
           lpContainerDoc, lpContainerObj);
  }
      lpContainerDoc->m_lpLastIpActiveObj = lpContainerObj;

    /* OLE2NOTE: To avoid LRPC problems, it is important to cache the
    **    IOleInPlaceObject* pointer and NOT call QueryInterface
    **    each time it is needed.
    */
  lpContainerObj->m_lpOleIPObj = (LPOLEINPLACEOBJECT)
     ContainerObj_GetOleObject(lpContainerObj,&IID_IOleInPlaceObject);

  if (! lpContainerObj->m_lpOleIPObj) {
  return ResultFromScode(E_FAIL);    // ERROR: refuse to in-place activate
   }
   lpContainerObj->m_fIpActive       = TRUE;
   lpContainerObj->m_fIpVisible      = TRUE;

   // Lock the object running to prevent problems if a link client does
   // a silent update when our in-place object is UI deactivated and
   // running in a hidden state.
   if (! lpContainerObj->m_fIpObjRunning) {
       lpContainerObj->m_fIpObjRunning = TRUE;
       OleLockRunning((LPUNKNOWN)lpContainerObj->m_lpOleIPObj, TRUE, 0);
   }

    lpContainerObj->m_lpDoc->m_cIPActiveObjects++;

    return NOERROR;
}

void ContainerDoc_ShutDownLastInPlaceServerIfNotNeeded(
      LPCONTAINERDOC          lpContainerDoc,
      LPCONTAINEROBJ         lpNextActiveObj)
{
   LPCONTAINEOBJ lpLastIpActiveObj =
```

```
            lpContainerDoc->m_lpLastIpActiveObj;
BOOL fEnableServerShutDown = TRUE;
LPMONIKER lpmkLinkSrc;
LPMONIKER lpmkLastActiveObj;
LPMONIKER lpmkCommonPrefix;
LPOLELINK lpOleLink;
HRESULT hrErr;

if (lpLastIpActiveObj != lpNextActiveObj) {
    if (lpLastIpActiveObj) {

   /* OLE2NOTE: If the object which is about to be activated is
   **    actually a link to the last activated object,
   **    we do NOT want to shut down the last activated
   **    object because it is about to be used. When activating
   **    a linked object, the source of the link gets .
   **    activated
    */
    lpOleLink = (LPOLELINK)ContainerObj_GetOleObject(
            lpNextActiveObj,
            &IID_IOleLink);
    if (lpOleLink) {
        lpOleLink->lpVtbl->GetSourceMoniker(
                lpOleLink,
                (LPMONIKER FAR*)&lpmkLinkSrc);
        if (lpmkLinkSrc) {
            lpmkLastActiveObj = ContainerObj_GetFullMoniker(
                    lpLastIpActiveObj,
                    GETMONIKER_ONLYIFTHERE);
            if (lpmkLastActiveObj) {
                hrErr = lpmkLinkSrc->lpVtbl->CommonPrefixWith(
                        lpmkLinkSrc,
                        lpmkLastActiveObj,
                        &lpmkCommonPrefix);
                if (GetScode(hrErr) == MK_S_HIM ||
                        GetScode(hrErr) == MK_S_US) {
                    /* The link source IS to the object
                    **    contained in the last activated
                    **    object of the document. Disable the
                    **    attempt to shut down the last
                    **    running in-place object application.
                    */
                    fEnableServerShutDown = FALSE;
                }
                if (lpmkCommonPrefix)
                    OleStdRelease((LPUNKNOWN)lpmkCommonPrefix);
                OleStdRelease((LPUNKNOWN)lpmkLastActiveObj);
            }
            OleStdRelease((LPUNKNOWN)lpmkLinkSrc);
        }
```

```
                }
                OleStdRelease((LPUNKNOWN)lpOleLink);
            }

            /* If it is OK to shut down the previous in-place object
            **    and one is still running, shut it down. Shutting
            **    down the object application is done by forcing the OLE
            **    object to close. This forces the object to transition
            **    from running to loaded. If the object is actually
            **    only loaded, this is an NOP.
            */
            if (fEnableServerShutDown &&
                    lpLastIpActiveObj->m_fIpServerRunning) {

                ContainerObj_CloseOleObject(
                        lpLastIpActiveObj, OLECLOSE_SAVEIFDIRTY);

                // we can now forget this last in-place active object.
                lpContainerDoc->m_lpLastIpActiveObj = NULL;
            }
        }
    }
}
```

IOleInPlaceSite::OnUIActivate

HRESULT IOleInPlaceSite::OnUIActivate()

IOleInPlaceSite::OnUIActivate notifies the container that the object is about to be activated in-place and that the object is going to replace the container's main menu with that of the in-place composite menu.

Return Value

Value	Meaning
S_OK	The container allows the in-place activation.
E_UNEXPECTED	An unexpected error happened.

Comments

IOleInPlaceSite::OnUIActivate is called by the in-place object just prior to activating its user interface. The container should remove any user interface associated with its own activation. If the container is itself an embedded object, it should remove its document-level user interface.

If there is already an object active in place in the same document, the container should call **IOleInPlaceObject::UIDeactivate** before calling **OnUIDeactivate**.

Example

The following **IOleInPlaceSite::OnUIActivate** code example is for an inside-out container. In **OnUIActivate**, the container is notified that another in-place object has become UI active. As an inside-out style container, the container must deactivate the current object's UI when a new object becomes UI active. (Because inside-out objects have their own windows visible, it is possible that a click directly in another server window can cause it to become UI active. Therefore, the container must deactivate the other object's UI because at most only one object can have its UI active at a time.)

```
HRESULT InPlaceSite_OnUIActivate (LPOLEINPLACESITE lpThis)
{
    LPCONTAINEROBJ lpContainerObj =
            ((struct COleInPlaceSiteImpl FAR*)lpThis)->lpContainerObj;
    LPCONTAINERDOC lpContainerDoc = lpContainerObj->m_lpDoc;
    LPCONTAINEROBJ lpLastUIActiveObj = lpContainerDoc->m_lpLastUIActiveObj;
    HWND hWndNewUIActiveObj;

    lpContainerObj->m_fUIActive        = TRUE;
    lpContainerDoc->m_fAddMyUI          = FALSE;
    lpContainerDoc->m_lpLastUIActiveObj = lpContainerObj;

    lpContainerObj->m_lpOleIPObj->lpVtbl->GetWindow(
            lpContainerObj->m_lpOleIPObj,
            (HWND FAR*)&hWndNewUIActiveObj);
    //UI deactivate the object
    if (lpLastUIActiveObj && (lpLastUIActiveObj!=lpContainerObj)) {
       ContainerObj_UIDeactivate(lpLastUIActiveObj);

       // Make sure new UIActive window is on top of all others
       SetWindowPos(
          hWndNewUIActiveObj,
          HWND_TOPMOST,
          0,0,0,0,
          SWP_NOMOVE | SWP_NOSIZE);

       return NOERROR;
    }
    lpContainerDoc->m_hwndUIActiveObj = hWndNewUIActiveObj;

    ContainerDoc_RemoveFrameLevelTools(lpContainerDoc);

    return NOERROR;
}
```

See Also

IOleInPlaceObject::UIDeactivate

IOleInPlaceSite::GetWindowContext

HRESULT IOleInPlaceSite::GetWindowContext(*lplpFrame, lplpDoc, lprcPosRect, lprcClipRect, lpFrameInfo***)**
LPOLEINPLACEFRAME * *lplpFrame*
LPOLINPLACEUIWINDOW * *lplpDoc*
LPRECT *lprcPosRec*
LPRECT *lprcClipRect*
LPOLEINPLACEFRAMEINFO *lpFrameInfo*

IOleInPlaceSite::GetWindowContext enables the in-place object to retrieve the window interfaces that form the window object hierarchy, and the position in the parent window where the object's in-place activation window should be placed.

Parameters

lplpFrame
Points to where the pointer to the frame interface is to be returned.

lplpDoc
Points to where the pointer to the document window interface is to be returned. NULL is returned through *lplpDoc* if the document window is the same as the frame window. In this case, the object can only use *lplpFrame* or border negotiation.

lprcPosRect
Points to the rectangle containing the position of the in-place object in the client coordinates of its parent window.

lprcClipRect
Points to the outer rectangle containing the in-place object's position rectangle (*PosRect*). This rectangle is relative to the client area of the object's parent window.

lpFrameInfo
Points to an **OLEINPLACEFRAMEINFO** structure that the container is to fill in with appropriate data.

Return Value

Value	Meaning
S_OK	The method completed successfully.
E_INVALIDARG	One or more invalid arguments (for example, an invalid pointer or parameter). All methods, except those that take no parameters or only BOOLEAN parameters, can return this error code.
E_UNEXPECTED	An unexpected error happened.

Comments

The **OLEINPLACEFRAMEINFO** structure provides data needed by OLE to dispatch keystroke accelerators to a container frame while an object is active in place. For more information on this structure, see "In-Place Data Structures" earlier in this chapter. For more information on dispatching keystrokes, see "Dispatching Accelerator Keys" earlier in this chapter.

When an object is activated, it calls the **GetWindowContext** method from its container. The container returns the handle to its in-place accelerator table through the **OLEINPLACEFRAMEINFO** structure. Before calling **GetWindowContext**, the object must fill in the *lpFrameInfo->cb* member.

Example

The following example shows the container's **IOleInPlaceSite::GetWindowContext** method. The example is written for an SDI container application. When the object calls **GetWindowContext**, it passes in pointers to its *PosRect* and *ClipRect*, which the container uses to calculate the object's position in the window hierarchy. The container returns a pointer to its implementation of the **OLEINPLACEFRAMEINFO** structure and NULL for *lplpDOC*, indicating that its document window is the same as its frame window.

```
HRESULT InPlaceSite_GetWindowContext(
    LPOLEINPLACESITE             lpThis,
    LPOLEINPLACEFRAME FAR*       lplpFrame,
    LPOLEINPLACEUIWINDOW FAR*    lplpDoc,
    LPRECT                       lprcPosRect,
    LPRECT                       lprcClipRect,
    LPOLEINPLACEFRAMEINFO        lpFrameInfo)
{
    LPCONTAINERAPP lpContainerApp = (LPCONTAINERAPP)g_lpApp;
    LPCONTAINEROBJ lpContainerObj =
            ((struct COleInPlaceSiteImpl FAR*)lpThis)->lpContainerObj;

    //Get pointer to OLEINPLACEFRAME structure
   *lplpFrame = (LPOLEINPLACEFRAME)&lpContainerApp->m_OleInPlaceFrame;

    // must return AddRef'ed ptr
    (*lplpFrame)->lpVtbl->AddRef(*lplpFrame);


    *lplpDoc  = NULL;  // An MDI app would have to provide *lplpDoc

    // Get the extent of the object in client coordinates(after scaling)
    ContainerObj_GetOleObjectRectInPixels(lpContainerObj, lprcPosRect);

    //Get the ClipRect in client coordinates
    ContainerDoc_GetClipRect(lpContainerObj->m_lpDoc, lprcClipRect);


    lpFrameInfo->hwndFrame        = lpContainerApp->m_hWndApp;
    lpFrameInfo->haccel           = lpContainerApp->m_hAccelIPCntr;
```

```
    lpFrameInfo->cAccelEntries  = NUM_INPLACE_ACCELS;

    return NOERROR;
}
```

IOleInPlaceSite::Scroll

HRESULT IOleInPlaceSite::Scroll(*scrollExtent***)**
SIZE *scrollExtent*

IOleInPlaceSite::Scroll is called by an in-place object to tell the container to scroll the object by the number of pixels specified by *scrollExtent.*

Parameter

scrollExtent
Contains the number of pixels by which to scroll in the *X* and *Y* directions. Positive *X* values mean to move *X* pixels to the left (scroll to the right).

Return Value

Value	Meaning
S_OK	The method completed successfully.
E_INVALIDARG	One or more invalid arguments.
E_UNEXPECTED	An unexpected error happened.

Comments

As a result of scrolling, the object's visible rectangle can change. If that happens, the container should give the new *ClipRect* to the object by calling **IOleInPlaceObject::SetObjectRects**. The intersection of the *ClipRect* and *PosRect* rectangles gives the new visible rectangle.

See Also

IOleInPlaceObject::SetObjectRects

IOleInPlaceSite::OnUIDeactivate

HRESULT IOleInPlaceSite::OnUIDeactivate(*fUndoable***)**
BOOL *fUndoable*

On deactivation, **IOleInPlaceSite::OnUIDeactivate** notifies the container that it should reinstall its user interface and take focus.

Parameter

fUndoable
Specifies whether the object can undo changes. It is TRUE if the object can undo, FALSE if it cannot.

Return Value

Value	Meaning
S_OK	The method completed successfully.
E_UNEXPECTED	An unexpected error happened.

Comments

IOleInPlaceSite::OnUIDeactivate is called by the site's immediate child object when it is deactivating to notify the container that it should reinstall its own user interface components and take focus. The container should wait for the call to **IOleInPlaceSite::OnUIDeactivate** to complete before fully cleaning up and destroying any composite submenus.

The object indicates whether it can undo changes through the *fUndoable* flag. If the object can undo changes, the container can (by the user invoking the Edit Undo command) call the **IOleInPlaceObject::ReactivateAndUndo** method to undo the changes.

Example

The following **IOleInPlaceSite::OnUIDeactivate** example was written to support an outside-in container that supports Undo state. When called, the container first checks to see whether there is a DBLCLK message waiting in its message queue. If there is, the container calls **ContainerDoc_AddFrameLevelUI** to put its normal tools and menu back. Otherwise, the container sets the *fAddMyUI* flag to TRUE to indicate that it needs to restore its tools later. (If another object is being activated, the container clears *fAddMyUI* in its implementation of **IOleInPlaceSite::OnUIActivate**.)

Before handling any Undo state, the container takes focus of the frame window and forces a redraw of the object to remove the in-place hatched border. If the object has Undo state that needs to be saved, the container call **IOleObject::DoVerb**(OLEIVERB_HIDE) to hide the running object from the user. Otherwise, the container calls **IOleInPlaceObject::InPlaceDeactivate** to release the object.

```
HRESULT InPlaceSite_OnUIDeactivate(
    LPOLEINPLACESITE    lpThis,
    BOOL                fUndoable)
{
    LPCONTAINEROBJ lpContainerObj =
          ((struct COleInPlaceSiteImpl FAR*)lpThis)->lpContainerObj;
  LPCONTAINERDOC lpcontainerDoc = (LPCONTAINERDOC)lpContainerObj->m_lpDoc;
  LPCONTAINERAPP lpContainerApp = (LPCONTAINERAPP) g_lpApp;
  LPOBJLIST lpObj;
  int nIndex;
    MSG msg;
  HRESULT hrErr;

  lpContainerObj->m_fUIActive = FALSE;
  lpContainerObj->m_fIpChangesUndoable = fUndoable;
  lpContainerObj->m_lpDoc->m_hwndUIActiveObj = NULL;
```

```
    if (lpContainerObj == lpContainerObj->m_lpDoc->m_lpLastUIActiveObj) {

        lpContainerObj->m_lpDoc->m_lpLastUIActiveObj = NULL;

        /* See if there is a DBLCLK in our message queue.
        **    NOTE: MDI containers and nested-level container/servers
        **    may NOT do this menu optimization. The nested-level
        **    containers MUST ALWAYS directly put back their menus. MDI
        **    containers MUST put back their menus if the MDI child
        **    window is maximized. This is due to the fact that the MDI
        **    child window system menu has been added to the menu bar.
        */
        if (! PeekMessage(&msg, lpContainerDoc->m_hWndDoc,
                WM_LBUTTONDBLCLK, WM_LBUTTONDBLCLK,
                PM_NOREMOVE | PM_NOYIELD)) {
            ContainerDoc_AddFrameLevelUI(lpContainerObj->m_lpDoc);
        } else {
            lpContainerObj->m_lpDoc->m_fAddMyUI = TRUE;
        }

        /* OLE2NOTE: The in-place object application window previously had
        ** the focus. Because this window has just been removed, we should
        ** take focus.
        */
        SetFocus(ContainerDoc_GetWindow(
                (LPCONTAINERDOC)lpContainerObj->m_lpDoc));

        // force the object to redraw to remove in-place active hatch
        lpObj = ContainerDoc_GetObject(lpContainerDoc);
        ForceObjectRedraw(lpLL, nIndex, TRUE);
    }
    /* OLE2NOTE: An outside-in style container that supports UNDO
    **    calls IOleObject::DoVerb(OLEIVERB_HIDE) to make the in-place
    **    object go invisible. When it wants the in-place active object
    **    to discard its undo state, it calls
    **    IOleInPlaceObject::InPlaceDeactivate. There is no need for an
          outside-in style container to call
    **    IOleObject::DoVerb(OLEIVERB_DISCARDUNDOSTATE). If either the
    **    container or the object do not support UNDO, the
    **    container can immediately call InPlaceDeactivate
    **    instead of calling DoVerb(HIDE).
    */
    if (lpContainerObj->m_fIpChangesUndoable) {
        ContainerObj_DoVerb(lpContainerbj,OLEIVERB_HIDE,NULL,FALSE,FALSE);
        return NOERROR;
    } else {
            return ResultFromScode(lpContainerObj->m_lpOleIPObj->
                    lpVtbl->InPlaceDeactivate(lpContainerObj->m_lpOleIPObj));
    }
}
```

```
void ContainerDoc_AddFrameLevelUI(LPCONTAINERDOC lpContainerDoc)
{
    LPCONTAINERDOC lpContainerDoc = (LPCONTAINERDOC)lpContainerDoc;
    LPOLEINPLACEFRAME lpTopIPFrame = ContainerDoc_GetTopInPlaceFrame(
            lpContainerDoc);
    HMENU           hSharedMenu;            // combined obj/cntr menu
    HOLEMENU        hOleMenu;               // returned by OleCreateMenuDesc.

    ContainerDoc_GetSharedMenuHandles(
            lpContainerDoc,
            &hSharedMenu,
            &hOleMenu);
    lpTopIPFrame->lpVtbl->SetMenu(
            lpTopIPFrame,
            hSharedMenu,
            hOleMenu,
            lpContainerDoc->m_hWndDoc);
    /* OLE2NOTE: Even if our application does NOT use FrameTools, we
    ** must still call IOleInPlaceFrame::SetBorderSpace.
    */
    ContainerDoc_AddFrameLevelTools(lpContainerDoc);
}
void ContainerDoc_AddFrameLevelTools(LPCONTAINERDOC lpContainerDoc)
{
    LPOLEINPLACEFRAME lpTopIPFrame = ContainerDoc_GetTopInPlaceFrame(
            lpContainerDoc);
    LPCONTAINERAPP lpContainerApp = (LPCONTAINERAPP)g_lpApp;
    LPCONTAINERDOC lpContainerDoc = (LPCONTAINERDOC)lpContainerDoc;

    FrameTools_Enable(lpContainerDoc->m_lpFrameTools, TRUE);

    FrameTools_NegotiateForSpaceAndShow(
            lpContainerDoc->m_lpFrameTools,
            NULL,
            lpTopIPFrame);
}
void FrameTools_Enable(LPFRAMETOOLS lpft, BOOL fEnable)
{
    lpft->m_fToolsDisabled = !fEnable;
    if (lpft->m_fToolsDisabled) {
        ShowWindow(lpft->m_hWndPopupPalette, SW_HIDE);
        ShowWindow(lpft->m_ButtonBar.m_hWnd, SW_HIDE);
        ShowWindow(lpft->m_FormulaBar.m_hWnd, SW_HIDE);
    }
}
void FrameTools_NegotiateForSpaceAndShow(
        LPFRAMETOOLS            lpft,
        LPRECT                  lprcFrameRect,
        LPOLEINPLACEFRAME       lpTopIPFrame)
{
```

```
    BORDERWIDTHS     borderwidths;
    RECT             rectBorder;
    HRESULT          hrErr;

    if (lprcFrameRect)
        rectBorder = *lprcFrameRect;
    else {
        /* Object can call GetBorder to find out the
        **    size of the frame window. it can use this information to
        **    make decisions about how to orient/organize it tools (eg.
        **    if window is taller than wide put tools vertically at
        **    left edge).
        */
        hrErr = lpTopIPFrame->lpVtbl->GetBorder(
                lpTopIPFrame,
                (LPRECT)&rectBorder);
    }
    /* Try SetBorderSpace() with the space that you need. If it fails,
    ** negotiate for space and then call SetBorderSpace().
    */
    FrameTools_GetRequiredBorderSpace(lpft,(LPBORDERWIDTHS)&borderwidths);
    hrErr = lpTopIPFrame->lpVtbl->SetBorderSpace(
            lpTopIPFrame,
            (LPCBORDERWIDTHS)&borderwidths);
    if (hrErr == NOERROR) {
        FrameTools_Move(lpft, (LPRECT)&rectBorder);   // got what we wanted
    } else {
        /* We did not get tool space, so POP them up.
        /* OLE2NOTE: Because we are popping up our tools, we MUST inform
        **    the top in-place frame window that we need NO tool space
        **    BUT that it should NOT put its own tools up. If we were
        **    to pass NULL instead of (0,0,0,0), the container
        **    would have the option to leave its own tools up.
        */
        hrErr = lpTopIPFrame->lpVtbl->SetBorderSpace(
                lpTopIPFrame,
                (LPCBORDERWIDTHS)&g_rectNull);
        FrameTools_PopupTools(lpft);
    }
}
```

See Also **IOleInPlaceObject::ReactivateAndUndo**

IOleInPlaceSite::OnInPlaceDeactivate

HRESULT IOleInPlaceSite::OnInPlaceDeactivate()

IOleInPlaceSite::OnInPlaceDeactivate notifies the container that the object is no longer active in place.

Return Value

Value	Meaning
S_OK	The method completed successfully.
E_UNEXPECTED	An unexpected error happened.

Comments

IOleInPlaceSite::OnInPlaceDeactivate is called by an in-place object when it is fully deactivated. This function notifies the container that the object has been deactivated, and it gives the container a chance to run code pertinent to the object's deactivation. In particular, **IOleInPlaceSite::OnInPlaceDeactivate** is called as a result of **IOleInPlaceObject::InPlaceDeactivate** being called. Calling **IOleInPlaceSite::OnInPlaceDeactivate** indicates that the object can no longer support Undo.

If the container is holding pointers to the **IOleInPlaceObject** and **IOleInPlaceActiveObject** interface implementation, it should release them after the **IOleInPlaceSite::OnInPlaceDeactivate** call.

Example

In the following **IOleInPlaceSite::OnInPlaceDeactivate** example, the container clears the flags that it internally maintained on the object while it was active in place before releasing its pointer to **IOleInPlaceObject**.

```
HRESULT InPlaceSite_OnInPlaceDeactivate(LPOLEINPLACESITE lpThis)
{
    LPCONTAINEROBJ lpContainerObj =
            ((struct COleInPlaceSiteImpl FAR*)lpThis)->lpContainerObj;
    lpContainerObj->m_fIpActive             = FALSE;
    lpContainerObj->m_fIpVisible            = FALSE;
    lpContainerObj->m_fIpChangesUndoable    = FALSE;

    OleStdRelease((LPUNKNOWN) lpContainerObj->m_lpOleIPObj);
    lpContainerObj->m_lpOleIPObj = NULL;

    return NOERROR;
}
```

See Also

IOleInPlaceObject::InPlaceDeactivate

IOleInPlaceSite::DiscardUndoState

HRESULT IOleInPlaceSite::DiscardUndoState()

IOleInPlaceSite::DiscardUndoState is called by the active object while performing some action that would discard the Undo state of the object. **IOleInPlaceSite::DiscardUndoState** tells the container to discard its Undo state.

Return Value

Value	Meaning
S_OK	The method completed successfully.
E_UNEXPECTED	An unexpected error happened.

Comments

If an object is activated in place and the object's object application maintains only one level of undo stack, there is no need to have more than one entry on the undo stack. That is, once a change has been made to the active object that invalidates its Undo state saved by the container, there is no need to maintain this Undo state in the container. The in-place object calls **IOleInPlaceSite::DiscardUndoState** to notify the container to discard the object's last saved Undo state.

IOleInPlaceSite::DeactivateAndUndo

HRESULT IOleInPlaceSite::DeactivateAndUndo()

IOleInPlaceSite::DeactivateAndUndo is called by the active object when the user invokes Undo in a state just after activating the object.

Return Value

Value	Meaning
S_OK	The method completed successfully.
E_UNEXPECTED	An unexpected error happened.

Comments

Upon completion of this call, the container should call **IOleInPlaceObject::UIDeactivate** to remove the user interface for the object, activate itself, and Undo.

IOleInPlaceSite::OnPosRectChange

HRESULT IOleInPlaceSite::OnPosRectChange(*lprcPosRect***)**
LPCRECT *lprcPosRect*

IOleInPlaceSite::OnPosRectChange is called by an in-place object when the object's extents have changed.

Parameter

lprcPosRect
Points to the rectangle containing the position of the in-place object in the client coordinates of its parent window.

Return Value

Value	Meaning
S_OK	The method completed successfully.
E_INVALIDARG	One or more invalid arguments.
E_UNEXPECTED	An unexpected error happened.

Comments

When the in-place object calls **IOleInPlaceSite::OnPosRectChange**, the container *must* call **IOleInPlaceObject::SetObjectRects** to specify the new position of the in-place window and the *ClipRect*. Only then does the object resize its window.

In most cases, the object grows to the right and/or down. There could be cases where the object grows to the left and/or up, as conveyed through *lprcPosRect*. It is also possible to change position without changing the size of the object.

Example

The following **IOleInPlaceSite::OnPosRectChange** example is for an inside-out container. When an in-place object's size changes, the object calls **OnPosRectChange** to notify the container of its new extents. When called, the container calls **IOleObject::GetExtent** to get the new extents for the object before updating the object's position in the in-place frame. The container then calls **ContainerDoc_UpdateInPlaceObjectRects** to update the extents of all objects below this object in the container.

```
HRESULT InPlaceSite_OnPosRectChange(
    LPOLEINPLACESITE    lpThis,
    LPCRECT             lprcPosRect)
{
    LPCONTAINEROBJ lpContainerObj =
            ((struct COleInPlaceSiteImpl FAR*)lpThis)->lpContainerObj;
    LPCONTAINERDOC lpContainerDoc = (LPCONTAINERDOC)lpContainerObj->m_lpDoc;
    LPSCALEFACTOR lpscale = ContainerDoc_GetScaleFactor(lpContainerDoc);
    LPOBJ lpObj = (LPOBJ)lpContainerObj;
    LPOBJLIST lpObj;
    int nIndex;
    RECT rcClipRect;
    RECT rcNewPosRect;
    SIZEL sizelPix;
    SIZEL sizelHim;
    int nIPObjHeight = lprcPosRect->bottom - lprcPosRect->top;
    int nIPObjWidth = lprcPosRect->right - lprcPosRect->left;
    HRESULT hrErr;
```

```
    /* Get the new extents of the in-place object.
    ** The call to IOleObject::GetExtent will be delegated to the
    ** running object to retrieve the actual current extents in the
    ** object application. Do NOT call IViewObject2::GetExtent
    ** as that would retrieve the extents from the last cached picture.
    ** At this point, the cache has not been updated.

    hrErr = lpContainerObj->m_lpOleObj->lpVtbl->GetExtent(
                lpContainerObj->m_lpOleObj,
                lpContainerObj->m_dwDrawAspect,
                (LPSIZEL)&sizelHim);

    ContainerObj_UpdateExtent(lpContainerObj, &sizelHim);
    ContainerObj_GetOleObjectRectInPixels(
            lpContainerObj, (LPRECT)&rcNewPosRect);

    ContainerDoc_GetClipRect(lpContainerObj->m_lpDoc, (LPRECT)&rcClipRect);

    lpContainerObj->m_lpOleIPObj->lpVtbl->SetObjectRects(
            lpContainerObj->m_lpOleIPObj,
            (LPRECT)&rcNewPosRect,
            (LPRECT)&rcClipRect);

    lpObj = ContainerDoc_GetObjList(lpContainerDoc);
    nIndex = ObjList_GetObjIndex(lpObj, (LPOBJ)lpContainerObj);
    if (g_InsideOut)
       // Need to call SetObjectRects for all of the in-place active
       // objects that are below this object in the document
       ContainerDoc_UpdateInPlaceObjectRects(lpContainerObj->
               m_lpDoc, nIndex);

    return NOERROR;
}

/* ContainerDoc_UpdateInPlaceObjectRects
** -------------------------------------
**    Update the PosRect and ClipRect of the currently in-place active
**    object. If there is no object active in place, do nothing.
**
**    OLE2NOTE: This function is called when an action occurs
**    that changes either the position of the object in the document
**    (for example, changing document margins changes PosRect) or the
**    clipRect changes (for example, resizing the document window
**    changes the ClipRect).
*/
void ContainerDoc_UpdateInPlaceObjectRects(LPCONTAINERDOC
lpContainerDoc, int nIndex)
{
    LPOBJLIST lpObj = &((LPCONTAINERDOC)lpContainerDoc)->m_ObjList;
    int i;
```

```
    LPOBJ lpObj;
    RECT rcClipRect;

    if (g_fInsideOutContainer) {

        if (lpContainerDoc->m_cIPActiveObjects) {

            /* OLE2NOTE: As an INSIDE-OUT CONTAINER, we must update the
            **    PosRect/ClipRect for all in-place active objects
            **    starting from the object "nIndex".
            */
            ContainerDoc_GetClipRect(lpContainerDoc, (LPRECT)&rcClipRect);

            for (i = nIndex; i < lpObj->m_nNumObjs; i++) {
                lpObj=ObjList_GetObj(lpObj, i);

                if (lpObj && (Obj_GetObjType(lpObj)==CONTAINEROBJTYPE)) {
                    LPCONTAINEROBJ lpContainerObj = (LPCONTAINEROBJ)lpObj;
                    ContainerObj_UpdateInPlaceObjectRects(
                            lpContainerObj, &rcClipRect);
                }
            }
        }
    }
    else {
        /* OLE2NOTE: (OUTSIDE-IN CONTAINER) If there is a currently
        **    UIActive object, we must inform it that the
        **    PosRect/ClipRect has now changed.
        */
        LPCONTAINEROBJ lpLastUIActiveObj =
                lpContainerDoc->m_lpLastUIActiveObj;
        if (lpLastUIActiveObj && lpLastUIActiveObj->m_fUIActive) {
            ContainerDoc_GetClipRect(lpContainerDoc, (LPRECT)&rcClipRect);

            ContainerObj_UpdateInPlaceObjectRects(
                    lpLastUIActiveObj, &rcClipRect);
        }
    }
}
```

See Also **IOleInPlaceObject::SetObjectRects**

In Place Activation Functions

OLE provides the following API functions, which can be used to support in-place activation (see also OLE2.H).

```
OleCreateMenuDescriptor(HMENU hmenuCombined, LPOLEMENUGROUPWIDTHS
 lpMenuWidths);
OleDestroyMenuDescriptor(HOLEMENU holemenu);
OleSetMenuDescriptor(HOLEMENU holemenu, HWND hwndFrame,
  HWND hwndActiveObject, LPOLEINPLACEFRAME lpFrame,
  LPOLEINPLACEACTIVEOBJECT lpActiveObject);
OleTranslateAccelerator(LPOLEINPLACEFRAME lpFrame,
  LPOLEINPLACEFRAMEINFO lpFrameInfo, LPMSG lpmsg);
```

OleCreateMenuDescriptor

HOLEMENU OleCreateMenuDescriptor(*hmenuCombined, lpMenuWidths*)
HMENU *hmenuCombined*
LPOLEMENUGROUPWIDTHS *lpMenuWidths*

OleCreateMenuDescriptor creates and returns a descriptor for OLE to use when dispatching menu messages and commands.

Parameters

hmenuCombined
Specifies a handle to the combined menu created by the object.

lpMenuWidths
Points to an array of six LONG values giving the number of menus in each group.

Return Value

Returns the handle to the descriptor, or NULL if insufficient memory is available.

Comments

OleCreateMenuDescriptor can be called by the object to create a descriptor for the composite menu. OLE then uses this descriptor to dispatch menu messages and commands.

OleDestroyMenuDescriptor

void OleDestroyMenuDescriptor(*holemenu*)
HOLEMENU *holemenu*

OleDestroyMenuDescriptor is called by the container to free the shared menu descriptor allocated by the **OleCreateMenuDescriptor** API function.

Parameter

holemenu
Specifies a handle to the shared menu descriptor that was returned by **OleCreateMenuDescriptor**.

Return Value

None. (This function cannot indicate failure.)

See Also

OleCreateMenuDescriptor

OleSetMenuDescriptor

HRESULT OleSetMenuDescriptor(*holemenu, hwndFrame, hwndActiveObject, lpFrame, lpActiveObj*)
HOLEMENU *holemenu*
HWND *hwndFrame*
HWND *hwndActiveObject*
LPOLEINPLACEFRAME *lpFrame*
LPOLEINPLACEACTIVEOBJECT *lpActiveObj*

OleSetMenuDescriptor installs or removes dispatching code from the container's frame window.

Parameters

holemenu
Specifies the handle to the composite menu descriptor returned by **OleCreateMenuDescriptor**. If NULL, the dispatching code is unhooked.

hwndFrame
Specifies the handle to the container's frame window where the in-place composite menu is to be installed.

hwndActiveObject
Specifies the handle to the object's in-place activation window. OLE dispatches menu messages and commands to this window.

lpFrame
Points to the container's frame window.

lpActiveObj
Points to the active in-place object.

Return Value

Value	Meaning
S_OK	The menu was installed correctly.
E_FAIL	A Windows function call failed,indicating a resource allocation failure or improper arguments.

Comments

OleSetMenuDescriptor should be called by the container to install the dispatching code on *hwndFrame* when the object calls **IOleInPlaceFrame::SetMenu**, or to remove the dispatching code by passing NULL as the value for *holemenu* to **OleSetMenuDescriptor**.

OLE installs the context-sensitive help F1 message filter for the application if both the *lpFrame* and *lpActiveObj* parameters are non-NULL. Otherwise, the application must supply its own message filter.

See Also

OleCreateMenuDescriptor, **IOleInPlaceFrame::SetMenu**

OleTranslateAccelerator

HRESULT OleTranslateAccelerator(*lpFrame, lpFrameInfo, lpmsg*)
LPOLEINPLACEFRAME *lpFrame*
LPOLEINPLACEFRAMEINFO *lpFrameInfo*
LPMSG *lpmsg*

OleTranslateAccelerator is called by the object application, allowing the container to translate its accelerators pointed to by *lpFrameInfo*.

Parameters

lpFrame
Points to the **IOleInPlaceFrame** interface where the keystroke might be sent.

lpFrameInfo
Points to an **OLEINPLACEFRAMEINFO** structure containing the accelerator table obtained from the container.

lpmsg
Points to an **MSG** structure containing the keystroke.

Return Value

Value	Meaning
S_OK	The keystroke was processed.
S_FALSE	The object should continue processing this message.

Comments

While active in place, the object *always* has first chance at translating any messages received. If the object does not want to translate the message, it calls **OleTranslateAccelerator** to give the container a chance.If the message matches one found in the container-provided accelerator table, **OleTranslateAccelerator** passes the message and its command identifier on to the container through the **IOleInPlaceFrame::TranslateAccelerator** method, which returns the accelerator table from the container.

Note So that they will work properly with object applications that do their own accelerator keystroke translations, accelerator tables for containers should be defined as follows:

```
"char", wID, VIRTKEY, CONTROL
```

This is the most common way for describing keyboard accelerators. Failure to do so can result in keystrokes being lost or sent to the wrong object during an in-place session.

Objects can call **IsAccelerator** to see whether the accelerator keystroke belongs to it or the container. For more information on handling accelerator keystrokes during in-place activation, see "Dispatching Accelerator Keys" earlier in this chapter.

See Also

IsAccelerator, IOleInPlaceFrame::TranslateAccelerator

IsAccelerator

BOOL IsAccelerator(*hAccel*, *cAccelEntries*, *lpMsg*, *lpwCmd***)**
HACCEL *hAccel*
INT *cAccelEntries*
LPMSG *lpMsg*
WORD FAR * *lpwCmd*

IsAccelerator can be called to determine whether the keystroke maps to an accelerator in the given accelerator table.

Parameters

hAccel
Specifies the handle to the accelerator table.

cAccelEntries
Specifies the number of entries in the accelerator table.

lpMsg
Points to the keystroke message that is to be translated.

lpwCmd

Points to where to return the corresponding command ID if there is an accelerator for the keystroke. It may be NULL.

Return Value

alue	Meaning
TRUE	The message is for the object application.
FALSE	The message is not for the object and should be forwarded on to the container.

Comments

While active in-place, the object *always* has first chance to translate the keystrokes into accelerators. If the keystroke corresponds to one of its accelerators, then the object must *not* call **OleTranslateAccelerator**—even if its call to the Windows **TranslateAccelerator** API fails. Failure to process keystrokes in this manner can lead to inconsistant behaviour.

If the keystroke is not one of object's accelerators then the object must call **OleTranslateAccelerator** to let the container try its accelerator translation.

The object application can call **IsAccelerator** to determine if the accelerator message belongs to it. Some object applications do accelerator translation on their own and do not call **TranslateAccelerator**. Those applications will not call **IsAccelerator**, because they already know the answer.

For more information on processing accelerator messages,see "Pseudo Code for Object Applications," earlier in this chapter.

See Also

OleTranslateAccelerator

CHAPTER 12

Compatibility with OLE 1

Note In moving from OLE 1 to OLE 2, the following changes in terminology were made:

- The OLE 1 term "server application" has been changed to "object application."
- The OLE 1 term "client application" has been changed to "container application."

Compatibility implies that an OLE 1 client application can contain OLE 2 embedded and linked objects and that an OLE 1 server application can create objects to be embedded in and linked to by OLE 2 containers. OLE provides these capabilities by means of a built-in compatibility layer in the core code, that includes a set of API functions for conversion.

Figure 12-1 illustrates how communication between OLE 1 and OLE 2 applications is achieved. OLE 1 applications makes calls to other OLE 1 applications and to OLE 2 applications using DDE.

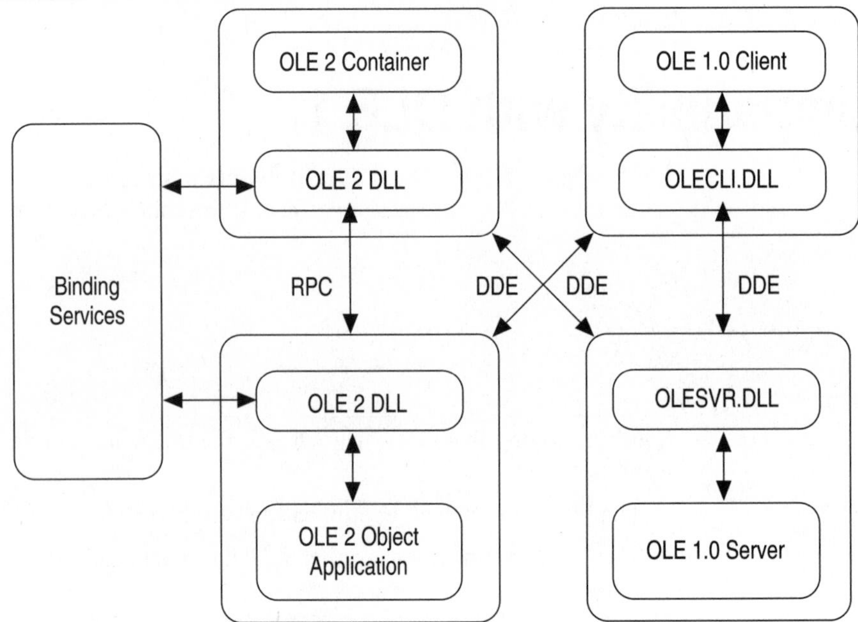

Figure 12-1. Communication between OLE 1 and OLE 2 applications.

Compatibility between OLE 2 and OLE 1 applications is achieved through the implementation of two special remoting objects, called a stub and proxy. The stub is instantiated on the object, or server, application's side of the process; the proxy is instantiated on the container, or client, application's side. These special stubs and proxies use DDE to communicate rather than LRPC. When an OLE 2 object makes a call to a function in an OLE 1 client application, for example, the stub intercepts the call and responds appropriately. For the most part, this response simulates the response that an OLE 2 object or container would make. However, in a few cases the behavior is different or special **HRESULT** values are returned.

This chapter discusses the issues that affect applications that need to be compatible with an earlier or more recent version of OLE and describes the API functions that promote this compatibility.

Working with OLE 1 Clients

This section describes some of the known idiosyncrasies of working with OLE 1 clients.

A successful call to **IOleClientSite::GetContainer** returns a pointer to the container's **IOleContainer** interface. If the container does not support **IOleContainer**, OLE_E_NOT_SUPPORTED is returned. All OLE 1 clients fall in this category as do OLE 2 containers that do not support linking to their embedded objects.

IOleClientSite::ShowObject, a request to make the embedded or linked object visible, always returns OLE_E_NOT_SUPPORTED when called on an OLE 1 client. The purpose of this method is to help make the user model work smoothly; its failure does not effect OLE functionality.

When an OLE 1 client contains an OLE 2 object and the object is activated or **OleUpdate** is called, the aspect of the data returned will always be DVASPECT_CONTENT. This is because OLE 1 clients have no concept of a **FORMATETC** data structure. This situation may occur when an iconic OLE 2 object is pasted from an OLE 2 container into an OLE 1 container. When the object is first pasted, its presentation remains iconic. With the next update, however, the object's content picture is returned.

OLE 1 clients can link to OLE 2 objects only if the link source:

- is represented by a file moniker or a generic composite moniker consisting of a file moniker and one item moniker.
- is not an embedded OLE 2 object.

An OLE 1 client can contain an incompatible link when a linked object is pasted from an OLE 2 container into the OLE 1 client or when an OLE 2 container, to allow the OLE 1 version of the application access to its data, saves the data to an OLE 1 file. When the OLE 1 client loads the incompatible link, the link is converted to an embedded object and assigned the class name "Ole2Link." The OLE 1 client cannot connect to the link source. However, if the newly created embedded object is then pasted into an OLE 2 container using the clipboard or converted to an OLE 2 object using **OleConvertOLESTREAMToIStorage**, it will be converted back to its original state as an OLE 2 linked object.

When the link source for an OLE 1 linked object changes its name, the link can remain intact only if the file moniker for the link source has changed. That is, if the link source is a range of cells within an OLE 2 spreadsheet application and the name of the file that contains the cell range changes, OLE will track the link. However, if the name of the cell range changes, the link will be broken.

Pasting an OLE 2 linked object into an OLE 1 client document and then calling **OleCopyFromLink** to convert it to an embedded object will fail if the data transfer object provided by the link source does not support **IPersistStorage**. Creating an embedded object always requires native data and **IPersistStorage** provides access to native data.

Working with OLE 1 Servers

This section describes some of the known idiosyncrasies of embedding or linking OLE 1 objects.

As is the case with OLE 2 objects, either **IPersistStorage::InitNew** or **IPersistStorage::Load** must be called to properly initialize a newly instantiated OLE 1 object before any other OLE calls are made. The **InitNew** method should be called to initialize a newly created object; the **Load** method should be called for existing objects. If one of the **OleCreate** helper functions or **OleLoad** is being used, these functions make the **IPersistStorage** call, thus eliminating the need to make the call directly. When an OLE 2 container with an OLE 1 embedded or linked object calls **IDataObject::GetData** or **IDataObject::GetDataHere**, the container can expect support for a smaller set of formats and storage mediums than would be supported for an OLE 2 object. The following table lists the combinations that can be supported.

Tymed Formats	Data Formats
TYMED_MFPICT	CF_METAFILEPICT
TYMED_GDI	CF_BITMAP
TYMED_HGLOBAL	cfNative, CF_DIB, and other OLE 1 server formats

For the aspect value of DVASPECT_ICON, only TYMED_MFPICT with CF_METAFILEPICT is supported. The icon returned from the **IDataObject::GetData** or **IDataObject::GetDataHere** call will always be the first icon (index 0) in the executable object application.

Several methods typically called by containers have unique implementations for OLE 1. **IPersistStorage::IsDirty** is defined to return S_OK if the object has changed since its last save to persistent storage; S_FALSE if it has not changed. When an OLE 2 container with an OLE 1 embedded object calls **IPersistStorage::IsDirty**, the compatibility code always returns S_OK when the server is running because there is no way to determine if the object has in fact changed until the File Close or File Update command is selected. S_FALSE is returned when the server is not running.

An OLE 2 implementation of **IOleObject::IsUpToDate** can return either S_OK if the object is up-to-date, S_FALSE if it is not up-to-date, or OLE_E_UNAVAILABLE if the object cannot determine whether the it is up-to-date. The OLE 1 implementation always returns either E_NOT_RUNNING, if the object is in the loaded state, or S_FALSE, if the server is running.

The OLE 1 implementation of **IOleItemContainer::EnumObjects** always returns OLE_E_NOTSUPPORTED because it is not possible for an OLE 1 server to enumerate its objects.

IOleObject::Close takes a save option as a parameter that indicates whether the object should be saved before the close occurs. For OLE 2 objects, there are three possible save options: OLECLOSE_SAVEIFDIRTY, OLECLOSE_NOSAVE, and OLECLOSE_PROMPTSAVE. The OLE 1 implementation of **IOleObject::Close** treats OLECLOSE_PROMPTSAVE as equivalent to OLECLOSE_SAVEIFDIRTY because it is not possible to require an OLE 1 server to prompt the user.

OLE 2 containers cannot expect an OLE 1 object to activate in-place; all OLE 1 objects support activation in a separate, open window.

OLE 1 servers do not support linking to their embedded objects. It is up to OLE 2 containers with OLE 1 embedded objects to prevent a possible link from occurring. Containers can call **CoIsOle1Class** to determine at clipboard copy time if a data selection being copied is an OLE 1 object. If **CoIsOle1Class** returns TRUE, indicating that the selection is an OLE 1 object, the container should not offer the Link Source format. Link Source must be available for a linked object to be created.

OLE 2 containers can store multiple presentations for an OLE 1 object. However, only the first presentation format is sent to the container when the OLE 1 server closes. After that, the server is in the process of closing down and cannot honor requests for any more formats. Therefore, only the first presentation cache will be updated. The rest will be out of date (perhaps blank) if the object has changed since the last update.

Because OLE 1 servers do not update the cache for every change to an embedded object, until the user selects the File Update command, an OLE 2 container cannot assume it is obtaining the latest data from the server. By calling **IOleObject::Update,** the container can obtain the latest object data.

An OLE 1 embedded (not linked) object does not notify its container that its data has changed until the user does a File Update or File Close. Therefore, if an OLE 2 container registers for a data change notification on an OLE 2 object in a particular format, it should be aware that it will not be notified immediately when the data changes.

When an OLE 1 object is inserted into a container document and then closed without an update being invoked, a save will not occur and the correct streams for the object are not written into storage. Any subsequent loading of the object by the container will fail. To protect against this potential condition, containers that want data to be available after the object closes without updating can implement the following:

```
OleCreate();                      \\ to insert the object
OleRun();                         \\ if OLERENDER_NONE was specified
IOleObject::Update();             \\ to get snapshot of data
OleSave();
IOleObject::DoVerb();
```

Upgrading Applications

When an OLE 1 server is being upgraded to an OLE 2 object application, several issues arise. A primary issue is whether the OLE 2 application will replace the OLE 1 application or both versions will coexist. If only the newer version will be available to the user, it is desirable to have objects from the older version of the application be converted automatically to the new version format. Objects can be converted on a global basis, where all objects of a specific class are converted, or on a more selective basis, where only some objects are converted. Conversion can be either automatic, under programmatic control, or under the control of a user.

Being able to detect whether an object is from an OLE 1 server is helpful for implementing conversion functionality. The OLE 2 implementation of **IPersistStorage::Load** can check for a stream named "\1Ole10Native." The "\1Ole10Native" stream contains a DWORD header whose value is the length of the native data that follows. The existence of this stream indicates that the data is coming from an OLE 1 server. Applications can check if a storage object contains an object in an OLE 1 format by calling **ReadUserFmtTypeStg** (*pStg*, *pcfFormat*, *lplpszUserType*) and examining the contents of *pcfFormat*. This is where the OLE 1 class name would appear.

In **IPersistStorage::Save,** objects that are being permanently converted should be written back to storage in the new format and the "\1Ole10Native" stream should be deleted. The conversion bit in the storage should also be cleared once the conversion to the new format is complete.

To allow manual conversion of an old OLE 1 object to the new OLE 2 version, the OLE 2 object application must put the OLE 1 server's ProgID (OLE 1 server class name) into the registration database under **CLSID\{...}\Conversion\Readable\Main**. This entry indicates that the OLE 2 application is able to read its OLE 1 data format; the 'clipboard format' of the OLE 1 data is the ProgID (that is, the class name) of the OLE 1 object.

To get a CLSID for an OLE 1 server, **CLSIDFromProgId** or **CLSIDFromString** must be called. That is, an OLE 1 application cannot be assigned a CLSID from an OLE 2 application with **guidgen.exe**, **CoCreateGuid**, or by using a GUID from a range assigned by Microsoft. Because all OLE 1 CLSIDs are expected to fall in a specific range, OLE 1 CLSIDs are assigned with **CLSIDFromProgId**.

Refer to the chapter called "Registering Object Applications" for detailed information on the required registration database entries for upgraded applications.

Functions to Support Compatibility

The API functions described in this section enable an application to determine whether an object class is from OLE 1 and support conversion between OLE 1 and OLE 2 storage formats.

CoIsOle1Class

BOOL CoIsOle1Class(*rclsid***)**
REFCLSID *rclsid*

CoIsOle1Class determines whether a given CLSID represents an OLE 1 object.

Parameters

rclsid
Reference to the CLSID to check.

Return Values

Value	Meaning
S_TRUE	CLSID refers to an OLE 1 object.
S_FALSE	CLSID does not refer to an OLE 1 object.

Comments

CoIsOle1Class is useful for preventing linking to embedded OLE 1 objects within a container. Once a container has determined that copied data represents an embedded object, **CoIsOle1Class** can be called to determine whether the embedded object is an OLE 1 object. If **CoIsOle1Class** returns S_TRUE, the container does not offer Link Source.

OleConvertIStorageToOLESTREAM

HRESULT OleConvertIStorageToOLESTREAM(*pStg*, *pOleStm***)**
LPSTORAGE* *pStg*
LPOLESTREAM *pOleStm*

OleConvertIStorageToOLESTREAM converts the storage of an OLE object from OLE 2 structured storage to OLE 1 storage.

Parameters

pStg
Points to the object's OLE 2 **IStorage** instance to be converted to an OLE 1 **OLESTREAM** storage.

pOleStm
Points to the object's **OLESTREAM** storage.

Return Values

Value	Meaning
CONVERT10_E_STG_NO_STD_STREAM	Object cannot be converted because its storage is missing a stream.
E_INVALIDARG	Invalid value for *pStg* or *pOleStm*.

Comment

OleConvertIStorageToOLESTREAM is useful for converting an OLE 2 document to the OLE 1 format. The OLESTREAM code implemented for OLE 1 must be available.

On entry, the stream pointed to by *pOleStm* should be created and positioned just as it would be for an OLE 1 **OleSaveToStream** call. On exit, the stream contains the persistent representation of the object using OLE 1 storage.

Paintbrush objects are dealt with differently from other objects because their native data is in DIB format. When converting Paintbrush objects using **OleConvertIStorageToOLESTREAM**, no presentation data will be added to the OLESTREAM.

See Also

OleConvertOLESTREAMToIStorage

OleConvertIStorageToOLESTREAMEx

HRESULT OleConvertIStorageToOLESTREAMEx (*pStg, cfFormat, lWidth, lHeight, dwSize, pmedium, pOleStm*)
LPSTORAGE *pStg*
CLIPFORMAT *cfFormat*
LONG *lWidth*
LONG *lHeight*
DWORD *dwSize*
LPSTGMEDIUM *pmedium*
LPOLESTREAM *pOleStm*

OleConvertIStorageToOLESTREAMEx converts the storage of an embedded object from OLE 2 structured storage to OLE 1 storage. This function differs from **OleConvertIStorageToOLESTREAM** in that the presentation data to be written to the OLE 1 storage is passed in.

Parameters

pStg
Points to the object's OLE 2 **IStorage** instance to be converted to an OLE 1 **OLESTREAM** storage.

cfFormat
The format of the presentation data. May be NULL, in which case the *lWidth, lHeight, dwSize,* and *pmedium* parameters are ignored.

lWidth
The width of the object presentation data in HIMETRIC units.

lHeight
The height of the object presentation data in HIMETRIC units.

dwSize
The size of the data to be converted, in bytes.

pmedium
Points to the **STGMEDIUM** structure for the serialized data to be converted.

pOleStm
Points to the object's **OLESTREAM** storage.

Return Values

Value	Meaning
S_OK	The conversion was completed successfully.
DV_E_STGMEDIUM	*pmedium->hGlobal* is NULL.
E_INVALIDARG	*dwSize* is NULL or *pStg* or *pOleStm* is invalid.
DV_E_TYMED	*pmedium->tymed* is not TYMED_HGLOBAL or TYMED_ISTREAM.

Comments

Since **OleConvertIStorageToOLESTREAMEx** can specify which presentation data to convert, it can be used by applications that do not use the OLE default caching resources but do use OLE's conversion resources.

The value of *pmedium->tymed* may only be TYMED_HGLOBAL or TYMED_ISTREAM. The medium will not be released by **OleConvertIStorageToOLESTREAMEx.**

See Also

OleConvertOLESTREAMToIStorageEx, OleConvertIStorageToOLESTREAM.

OleConvertOLESTREAMToIStorage

HRESULT OleConvertOLESTREAMToIStorage(*pOleStm, pStg, ptd*)
LPOLESTREAM *pOleStm*
LPSTORAGE *pStg*
const DVTARGETDEVICE FAR* *ptd*

OleConvertOLESTREAMToIStorage converts the storage of an embedded object from OLE 1 **OLESTREAM** storage to OLE 2 structured storage.

pOleStm
Points to the OLE 1 **OLESTREAM** storage for the object.

pStg
Points to the OLE 2 **IStorage** instance of the object.

ptd
Points to a target device.

Return Values

Value	Meaning
CONVERT10_S_NO_PRESENTATION	Object either has no presentation data or uses native data for its presentation.
DV_E_DVTARGETDEVICE or DV_E_DVTARGETDEVICE_SIZE	Invalid value for *ptd*.
E_INVALIDARG	Invalid value for *pOleStm*.

Comments

OleConvertOLESTREAMToIStorage can be used to convert an application document that supported OLE 1 to one that supports OLE 2. The *pOleStm* pointer contains the current OLE 1 persistent storage of the embedded object.

On entry, *pOleStm* should be created and positioned just as it would be for an **OleLoadFromStream** function call. On exit, *pOleStm* is positioned just as it would be on exit from **OleLoadFromStream**, and *pStg* now contains the uncommitted persistent representation of the object using the OLE 2 storage model.

For OLE 1 objects that use native data for their presentation, **OleConvertOLESTREAMToIStorage** returns CONVERT10_S_NO_PRESENTATION. Upon receiving this return value, callers should call **IOleObject::Update** to get the presentation data so that it can be written to storage.

The following steps illustrate the conversion process using C:

1. Create a root **IStorage** object by calling **StgCreateDocfile**(..., *&pStg*).
2. Open the OLE 1 file (using **OpenFile** or another OLE 1 technique).
3. Using the OLE 1 procedure for reading files, read from the file until an OLE object is encountered.
4. Allocate an **IStorage** object from the root **IStorage** created in step 1:

```
pStg->lpVtbl->CreateStorage(...&pStgChild);
hRes = OleConvertIStorageToOLESTREAM(pOleStm, pStgChild);
hRes = OleLoad(pStgChild, &IID_IOleObject, pClientSite, ppvObj);
```

5. Repeat step 3 as often as is necessary until the file is completely read.

Example

To get native data from an OLE 1 stream that has been converted to OLE 2 storage, use the following code, where *kszOle10Native* is set to "\1Ole10Native":

```
HGLOBAL GhGetNativeData(LPSTORAGE pStg)
{
    LPSTREAM    lpstmNative = NULL;
    HGLOBAL     gh = NULL;
    HRESULT     hrErr;

    /* call IStorage::OpenStream on Ole10Native stream */
    hrErr = pStg->lpVtbl->OpenStream(pStg, kszOle10Native, NULL,
        STGM_READWRITE | STGM_SHARE_EXCLUSIVE, 0, &lpstmNative);

    // this is an OLE 1 object: its native data is in the stream
    if (SUCCEEDED(hrErr) && lpstmNative)  {
        DWORD       dwSize = 0;
        LPSTR       lpb = NULL;

        /* call IStream::Read on native stream */
        hrErr = lpstmNative->lpVtbl->Read
            (lpstmNative, &dwSize, sizeof(DWORD), NULL);
        if (FAILED(hrErr) || !dwSize)
            return gh;
```

```
            gh = GlobalAlloc(GMEM_DDESHARE | GMEM_MOVEABLE, dwSize);
            if (!gh || !(lpb = GlobalLock(gh)))  {
                if (gh && lpb)
                    GlobalUnlock(gh);
                if (gh && (!lpb || FAILED(hrErr)))  {
                    GlobalFree(gh);
                    gh = NULL;
            }
            else hrErr = lpstmNative->lpVtbl->Read  (lpstmNative, lpb,
                                    dwSize, NULL);
        }
        return gh
    }
```

OleConvertOLESTREAMToIStorageEx

HRESULT OleConvertOLESTREAMToIStorageEx(*pOleStm, pStg, pcfFormat, lWidth, lHeight, dwSize, pmedium***)**
LPOLESTREAM *pOleStm*
LPSTORAGE *pStg*
CLIPFORMAT * *pcfFormat*
LONG * *plWidth*
LONG * *plHeight*
DWORD * *pdwSize*
LPSTGMEDIUM *pmedium*

OleConvertOLESTREAMToIStorageEx converts the storage of an embedded object from OLE 1 **OLESTREAM** storage to OLE 2 structured storage. This function differs from **OleConvertOLESTREAMToIStorage** in that the presentation data that is read from **OLESTREAM** is passed out and the newly created IStorage does not contain a presentation stream.

Parameters

pOleStm
Points to the OLE 1 **OLESTREAM** storage for the object.

pStg
Points to the OLE 2 **IStorage** instance of the object.

pcfFormat
Points to where to return the format of the presentation data. May be NULL, indicating the absence of presentation data.

plWidth
Points to where to return the width value (in HIMETRIC) of the presentation data.

plHeight
Points to where to return the height value (in HIMETRIC) of the presentation data.

pdwSize
Points to where to return the size in bytes of the converted data.

pmedium
Points to where to return the **STGMEDIUM** structure for the converted serialized data.

Return Values

Value	Meaning
S_OK	The conversion was completed successfully.
DV_E_TYMEDI	The value of *pmedium->tymed* is not TYMED_ISTREAM or TYMED_NULL.

Comments

Since **OleConvertOLESTREAMToIStorageEx** can specify which presentation data to convert, it can be used by applications that do not use OLE's default caching resources but do use the conversion resources.

The *tymed* member of **STGMEDIUM** can only be TYMED_NULL or TYMED_ISTREAM. If TYMED_NULL, then the data will be returned in a global handle through the *hGlobal* member of **STGMEDIUM,** otherwise data will be written into the *pstm* member of this structure.

See Also

OleConvertIStorageToOLESTREAMEx, OleConvertIStorageToOLESTREAM

CHAPTER 13

Concurrency Management

Concurrency management facilitates handling a variety of demands placed on OLE applications in any typical session. OLE applications must be able to correctly deal with user input while processing one or more calls from OLE or the operating system. OLE calls, when made between processes, fall into three categories:

- Synchronous calls
- Asynchronous notifications
- Input-synchronized calls

Most of the communication that takes place within OLE is synchronous. When making *synchronous calls,* the caller waits for the reply before continuing and, if preferred, can receive incoming messages while waiting. OLE enters into a modal loop to wait for the reply, receiving and dispatching other messages in a controlled manner. When OLE is running on Windows platforms, OLE makes synchronous calls by using **PostMessage**. When OLE is running on Macintosh platforms, a high-level event is posted in place of the **PostMessage** call.

When sending *asynchronous notifications,* the caller does not wait for the reply. OLE uses **PostMessage** or high level events to send asynchronous notifications, depending on the platform. OLE defines five asynchronous methods:

- **IAdviseSink::OnDataChange**
- **IAdviseSink::OnViewChange**
- **IAdviseSink::OnRename**
- **IAdviseSink::OnSave**
- **IAdviseSink::OnClose**

While processing an asynchronous call, synchronous calls cannot be made. For example, a container application's implementation of **IAdviseSink::OnDataChange** cannot contain a call to **IPersistStorage::Save**.

When making *input-synchronized calls,* the callee must complete the call before yielding control. This ensures that focus management works correctly and that data entered by the user is processed appropriately. These calls are made by OLE through the Windows **SendMessage** function. A modal loop is not entered. While processing an input-synchronized call, the callee must not call any function or method (including synchronous methods) that might yield control.

The following methods are input synchronized:

- **IOleWindow::GetWindow**
- **IOleInPlaceActiveObject::OnFrameWindowActivate**
- **IOleInPlaceActiveObject::OnDocWindowActivate**
- **IOleInPlaceActiveObject::ResizeBorder**
- **IOleInPlaceUIWindow::GetBorder**
- **IOleInPlaceUIWindow::RequestBorderSpace**
- **IOleInPlaceUIWindow::SetBorderSpace**
- **IOleInPlaceFrame::SetMenu**
- **IOleInPlaceFrame::SetStatusText**
- **IOleInPlaceObject::SetObjectRects**

Figure 13-1 is a high-level view of the communication that occurs between a caller, OLE, and a callee on a Windows platform when each of these types of calls are sent.

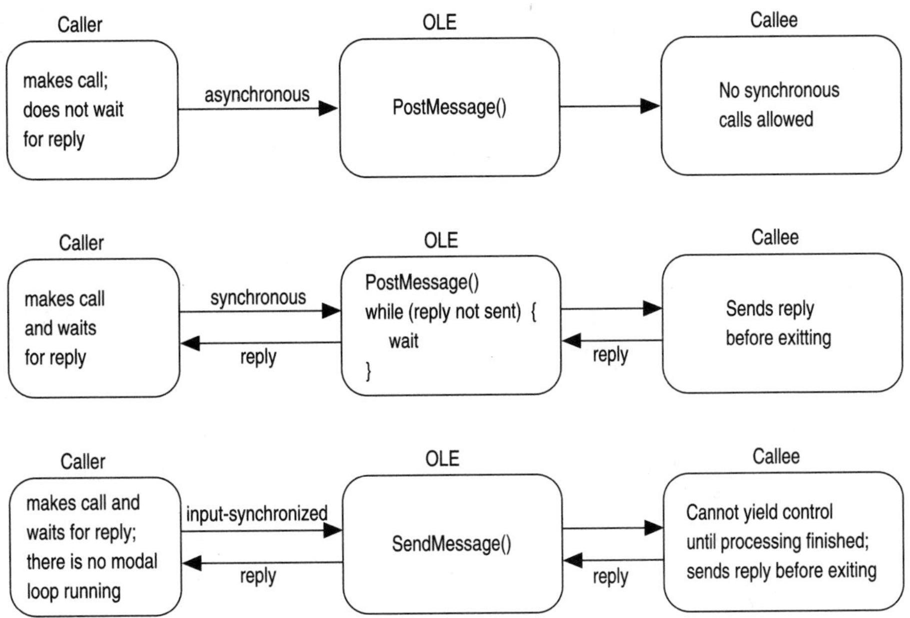

Figure 13-1. Communication between caller, callee, and OLE.

To minimize problems that can arise from asynchronous message processing, the majority of OLE method calls are synchronous. With synchronous communication, there is no need for special code to dispatch and handle incoming messages. When an application makes a synchronous method call, OLE enters a modal wait loop that handles the required replies and dispatches incoming messages to applications capable of processing them.

OLE manages method calls by assigning an identifier called a *logical thread ID*. A new one is assigned when a user selects a menu command or when the application initiates a new OLE operation. Subsequent calls that relate to the initial OLE call are assigned the same logical thread ID as the initial call.

Application Shutdown with WM_QUERYENDSESSION and WM_ENDSESSION

When the user exits Windows, such as by choosing File Exit Windows from the Program Manager, each open application receives a WM_QUERYENDSESSION message following by a WM_ENDSESSION message if the exit is not canceled. These messages are invoked with **SendMessage**, which unfortunately restricts the initiation of all outgoing RPC calls. This situation is problematic for those container applications receiving a shutdown request that have open embedded objects. RPC is needed to close those objects.

Container or container/object applications with open documents typically display a message box upon receipt of the WM_QUERYENDSESSION message that asks the user if he or she wants to save changes. A positive response is usually the default. The recommendation for dealing with the situation described above is for the application to display an alternate message box asking the user if he or she wants to discard changes; a negative response should be the default. If the user chooses to discard the changes, TRUE should be returned for WM_QUERYENDSESSION, a signal to Windows that it can terminate. If the user does not want to discard the changes, FALSE should be returned. No attempt should be made to close or release running embeddings.

Object applications should return TRUE for WM_QUERYENDSESSION without prompting the user.

Upon receipt of a WM_ENDSESSION message, all OLE applications should execute the normal close sequence for each of the application's documents and/or objects. During this time, any errors that occur from the close sequence(s) should be ignored. All storage pointers (**IStorage** and **IStream** interface pointers) need to be released to properly flush any temporary files maintained by the compound file implementation of structured storage.

IMessageFilter Interface

Applications can selectively handle incoming or outgoing messages while waiting for responses from synchronous calls by implementing the **IMessageFilter** interface. The ability to filter messages is often useful when a dialog box is being displayed or a lengthy operation is in progress. Performance can be improved when applications handle some messages and defer others.

IMessageFilter contains the following methods (see also COMPOBJ.H):

```
DECLARE_INTERFACE_(IMessageFilter, IUnknown)
{
  // *** IUnknown methods ***
  HRESULT QueryInterface (THIS_ REFIID riid, LPVOID FAR* ppvObj);
  ULONG AddRef (THIS);
  ULONG Release (THIS);

  // *** IMessageFilter methods ***
  DWORD HandleInComingCall (THIS_ DWORD dwCallType,
   HTASK htaskCaller, DWORD dwTickCount, LPINTERFACEINFO lpInterfaceInfo);
  DWORD RetryRejectedCall (THIS_
   HTASK htaskCallee, DWORD dwTickCount, DWORD dwRejectType );
  DWORD MessagePending (THIS_
   HTASK htaskCallee, DWORD dwTickCount, DWORD dwPendingType );
};
```

For applications that do not implement **IMessageFilter**, OLE provides default behaviors for each of the conditions that would be handled by an **IMessageFilter** method. For incoming calls, OLE dispatches all calls, regardless of their logical thread ID. For incoming Windows messages or Macintosh events, the default behavior is as if **IMessageFilter::MessagePending** had returned PENDINGMSG_WAITDEFPROCESS. This means that task switching and window activation messages are dispatched, WM_PAINT and WM_TIMER messages are left in the queue, and all other input messages are discarded. OLE continues to wait for the reply.

IMessageFilter::HandleIncomingCall

DWORD IMessageFilter::HandleIncomingCall(*dwCallType*, *htaskCaller*, *dwTickCount*, *lpInterfaceInfo*)
DWORD *dwCallType*
HTASK *htaskCaller*
DWORD *dwTickCount*
LPINTERFACEINFO *lpInterfaceInfo*

IMessageFilter::HandleIncomingCall is called when an incoming OLE message is received. **IMessageFilter::HandleIncomingCall** provides the application with a single entry point for all incoming calls.

Parameters

dwCallType
Indicates the kind of incoming call that has been received; valid values are from the enumeration **CALLTYPE**:

```
typedef enum tagCALLTYPE
{
    CALLTYPE_TOPLEVEL                 = 1,
    CALLTYPE_NESTED                   = 2,
    CALLTYPE_ASYNC                    = 3,
    CALLTYPE_TOPLEVEL_CALLPENDING     = 4,
    CALLTYPE_ASYNC_CALLPENDING        = 5
    } CALLTYPE;
```

The following table describes the CALLTYPE values:

Value	Meaning
CALLTYPE_TOPLEVEL	A call has arrived with a new logical thread ID. The application is not currently waiting for a reply from an outgoing call. Calls of this type should always be handled.

Value	Meaning
CALLTYPE_NESTED	A call has arrived with the same logical thread ID as that of an outgoing call for which the application is currently waiting for a reply. Calls of this type should always be handled.
CALLTYPE_ASYNC	An synchronous call has arrived; calls of this type cannot be rejected. OLE always delivers them.
CALLTYPE_TOPLEVEL_CALLPENDING	A call has arrived with a new logical thread ID. The application is currently waiting for a reply from an outgoing call. Calls of this type may be handled or rejected.
CALLTYPE_ASYNC_CALLPENDING	An asynchronous call has arrived with a new logical thread ID. The application is currently waiting for a reply from an outgoing call. Calls of this type cannot be rejected.

htaskCaller
Specifies the handle of the task that is calling this task.

dwTickCount
Specifies the elapsed tick count since the outgoing call was made if *dwCallType* is not CALLTYPE_TOPLEVEL. If *dwCallType* is CALLTYPE_TOPLEVEL, *dwTickCount* should be ignored.

lpInterfaceInfo
Points to an **INTERFACEINFO** structure that contains information about the incoming call. Can also be NULL. The **INTERFACEINFO** structure is defined as follows:

```
typedef struct tagINTERFACEINFO
{
    LPUNKNOWN           pUnk;
    IID                 iid;
    WORD                wMethod;
} INTERFACEINFO, FAR * LPINTERFACEINFO;
```

Return Values

Value	Meaning
SERVERCALL_ISHANDLED	The application might be able to process the call.
SERVERCALL_REJECTED	The application cannot handle the call due to an unforeseen problem, such as network unavailability.
SERVERCALL_RETRYLATER	The application cannot handle the call at this time. For example, an application might return this value when it is in a user-controlled modal state.

Comments

Depending on the application's current state, the call can be either accepted and processed or rejected (permanently or temporarily). The return value SERVERCALL_ISHANDLED indicates that the application might be able to process the call. Whether processing is successful might depend on the interface for which the call is destined. OLE rejects or processes the call, returning RPC_E_CALL_REJECTED if the call could not be processed.

Input-synchronized calls and asynchronous calls are dispatched even if the application returns SERVERCALL_REJECTED or SERVERCALL_RETRYLATER.

IMessageFilter::HandleIncomingCall should not be used to hold off updates to objects during operations such as band printing. **IViewObject::Freeze** should be used for that purpose.

IMessageFilter::HandleIncomingCall can also be used to set up the application's state so that the call can be processed in the future.

Example

OLE provides a standard implementation of **IMessageFilter** in its user interface library. The OLESTDMESSAGEFILTER object, shown below, tracks the state of the application and stores, in addition to a pointer to the **IMessageFilter** interface VTBL, pointers to several callback functions. The function pointed to by *m_lpfnHandleInComingCallback* is called in the implementation of **IMessageFilter::HandleInComingCall** to override the current call status. Applications can instantiate the OLESTDMESSAGEFILTER object to access the standard **IMessageFilter** implementation.

```
typedef struct tagOLESTDMESSAGEFILTER {
    IMessageFilterVtbl FAR* m_lpVtbl;
    UINT                    m_cRef;
    HWND                    m_hWndParent;
    DWORD                   m_dwInComingCallStatus;
    HANDLEINCOMINGCALLBACKPROC m_lpfnHandleInComingCallback;
    BOOL                    m_fEnableBusyDialog;
    BOOL                    m_fEnableNotRespondingDialog;
    MSGPENDINGPROC          m_lpfnMessagePendingCallback;
    LPFNOLEUIHOOK           m_lpfnBusyDialogHookCallback;
    LPSTR                   m_lpszAppName;
    HWND                    m_hWndBusyDialog;
    BOOL                    m_bUnblocking;
 }OLESTDMESSAGEFILTER, FAR* LPOLESTDMESSAGEFILTER;
```

The following method is the sample implementation of **IMessageFilter::HandleInComingCall.** **OleStdMsgFilter_HandleInComingCall** accepts or rejects the incoming call depending on the value of *dwCallType*. If the call is a top-level call (pending or otherwise) or an unrecognized type, the current incoming call status is returned. SERVERCALL_ISHANDLED is returned when *dwCallType* is CALLTYPE_NESTED, CALLTYPE_ASYNC, or CALLTYPE_ASYNC_PENDING because these calls must be handled. The current call status, stored in *m_dwInComingCallStatus*, is set initially to SERVER_ISHANDLED and changed when necessary.

```
DWORD OleStdMsgFilter_HandleInComingCall (
        LPMESSAGEFILTER     lpThis,
        DWORD               dwCallType,
        HTASK               htaskCaller,
        DWORD               dwTickCount,
        DWORD               dwReserved
)
{
   LPOLESTDMESSAGEFILTER lpStdMsgFilter = (LPOLESTDMESSAGEFILTER)lpThis;

    // Call HandleInComingCallbackProc if it exists.
    if (lpStdMsgFilter->m_lpfnHandleInComingCallback && !IsBadCodePtr
        ((FARPROC)lpStdMsgFilter->m_lpfnHandleInComingCallback)){
        return lpStdMsgFilter->m_lpfnHandleInComingCallback
            (dwCallType, htaskCaller, dwTickCount,
            (LPINTERFACEINFO)dwReserved);
    }

    switch (dwCallType) {
        case CALLTYPE_TOPLEVEL:
            return lpStdMsgFilter->m_dwInComingCallStatus;

        case CALLTYPE_TOPLEVEL_CALLPENDING:
            return lpStdMsgFilter->m_dwInComingCallStatus;

        case CALLTYPE_NESTED:
            return SERVERCALL_ISHANDLED;

        case CALLTYPE_ASYNC:
            return SERVERCALL_ISHANDLED;     // value doesn't matter

        case CALLTYPE_ASYNC_CALLPENDING:
            return SERVERCALL_ISHANDLED;     // value does not matter

        default:
            return lpStdMsgFilter->m_dwInComingCallStatus;
    }
}
```

IMessageFilter::RetryRejectedCall

DWORD IMessageFilter::RetryRejectedCall(*htaskCallee*, *dwTickCount*, *dwRejectType*)
HTASK *htaskCallee*
DWORD *dwTickCount*
DWORD *dwRejectType*

IMessageFilter::RetryRejectedCall is called by OLE immediately after it receives SERVERCALL_RETRYLATER or SERVERCALL_REJECTED from **HandleInComingCall. IMessageFilter::RetryRejectedCall** gives the application a chance to display a dialog box so the user can either retry or cancel the call, or switch to the task identified by *hTaskCallee*.

Parameters

hTaskCallee
Specifies the handle of the server task that rejected the call.

dwTickCount
Specifies the number of elapsed ticks since the call was made.

dwRejectType
Specifies either SERVERCALL_REJECTED or SERVERCALL_RETRYLATER, as returned by the server application.

Return Values

Value	Meaning
-1	The call should be canceled. OLE then returns RPC_E_CALL_CANCELLED from the original method call.
Value between 0 and 100	The call is to be retried immediately.
Value > 100	OLE will wait for this many milliseconds and then retry the call.

Comments

If an application task rejects a call, OLE checks to determine whether there are incoming calls (possibly from the application this task tried to call). If so, OLE processes the calls after checking the return from **IMessageFilter::HandleIncomingCall**, and retries. If not, the application is probably in a state where it cannot handle such calls, perhaps temporarily. **IMessageFilter::RetryRejectedCall** is called when the latter condition occurs.

Applications should silently retry calls that have returned SERVERCALL_RETRYLATER and show a dialog box only after a reasonable amount of time has passed, such as five seconds. The callee may momentarily be in a state where calls can be handled. This option to wait and retry is provided for special kinds of calling applications such as background tasks executing macros or scripts, so that they can retry in a nonintrusive way.

If, after a dialog box is displayed, the user chooses to cancel, the call will appear to fail with RPC_E_CALL_REJECTED.

Example

The following example of **IMessageFilter::RetryRejectCall** puts up the standard OLE dialog box to alert the user that the called application is too busy to process the call. Only when the callee has responded with SERVERCALL_RETRYLATER is the dialog box displayed using the user interface library function **OleUIBusy**. If the dialog box cannot be displayed, -1 is returned. This indicates that the call should be canceled. If the value of *htaskCallee* is invalid, the call is tried again after a predefined amount of time. For this application, the call is retried after 5000 milliseconds.

```
DWORD OleStdMsgFilter_RetryRejectedCall (
        LPMESSAGEFILTER     lpThis,
        HTASK               htaskCallee,
        DWORD               dwTickCount,
        DWORD               dwRejectType
)
{
    LPOLESTDMESSAGEFILTER lpStdMsgFilter =
        (LPOLESTDMESSAGEFILTER)lpThis;
    DWORD dwRet = 0;
    UINT uRet;

    if (dwRejectType == SERVERCALL_RETRYLATER &&
            lpStdMsgFilter->m_fEnableBusyDialog) {

        OLEUIBUSY bz;
        bz.cbStruct = sizeof(OLEUIBUSY);
        bz.dwFlags = 0L;
        bz.hWndOwner = lpStdMsgFilter->m_hWndParent;
        bz.lpszCaption = lpStdMsgFilter->m_lpszAppName;
        bz.lpfnHook = lpStdMsgFilter->m_lpfnBusyDialogHookCallback;
        bz.lCustData = 0;
        bz.hInstance = NULL;
        bz.lpszTemplate = NULL;
        bz.hResource = 0;
        bz.hTask = htaskCallee;
        bz.lphWndDialog = NULL; // We don't need the hDlg for this call
        uRet = OleUIBusy(&bz);

        switch (uRet) {
            case OLEUI_BZ_RETRYSELECTED:
                dwRet = 0;                  // Retry immediately
                break;

            case OLEUI_CANCEL:
                dwRet = OLESTDCANCELRETRY;
                break;

            case OLEUI_BZERR_HTASKINVALID:
                dwRet = OLESTDRETRYDELAY;
```

```
                break;
            }
        } else {
            dwRet = OLESTDCANCELRETRY;
        }
        return dwRet;
    }
```

IMessageFilter::MessagePending

DWORD IMessageFilter::MessagePending(*htaskCallee*, *dwTickCount*, *dwPendingType*)
HTASK *htaskCallee*
DWORD *dwTickCount*
DWORD *dwPendingType*

IMessageFilter::MessagePending is called if a Windows message or Macintosh event appears in the queue while OLE is waiting to reply to a remote call.

Parameters

hTaskCallee
Specifies the task handle of the called application that has not yet responded.

dwTickCount
Specifies the elapsed time since the call was made. It is calculated either from the Windows function, **GetTickCount**, or the Macintosh function, **TickCount**.

dwPendingType
Indicates the type of call made during which a message or event was received. Valid values are from the enumeration PENDINGTYPE:

```
typedef enum tagPENDINGTYPE {
    PENDINGTYPE_TOPLEVEL    = 1,
    PENDINGTYPE_NESTED      = 2,
} PENDINGTYPE;
```

Return Values

Value	Meaning
PENDINGMSG_CANCELCALL	Cancel the outgoing call. This should be returned only under extreme conditions. Canceling a call that has not replied or been rejected can create orphan transactions and lose resources. OLE fails the original call and return RPC_E_CALL_CANCELLED.

Value	Meaning
PENDINGMSG_WAITNOPROCESS	Continue waiting for the reply and do not dispatch the message. A subsequent message will trigger another call to **IMessageFilter::MessagePending**. Leaving messages or events in the queue enables them to be processed normally if the outgoing call is completed.
PENDINGMSG_WAITDEFPROCESS	Invoke OLE default message handling and dispatch only the activation messages. WM_PAINT, WM_TIMER, and WM_MOUSEMOVE remain in the queue. Discard input messages other than task switching, then continue waiting.

Comments

IMessageFilter::MessagePending is called by OLE after an application has made an OLE method call and, for example, while waiting for the reply, the user selects a menu command or double-clicks an object. Before OLE makes the **IMessageFilter::MessagePending** call, it calculates the elapsed time since the original OLE method call was made to pass in *dwTickCount*. In the meantime, OLE does not remove the message from the queue.

Windows messages or Macintosh events that appear in the caller's queue should remain in the queue until sufficient time has passed. A two or three second delay is recommended to ensure that the messages are probably not the result of typing ahead but are, instead, an attempt to get attention. If the amount of time has passed and the call has not been completed, the messages should be flushed from the queue, and a dialog box displayed offering the user the choice to retry (keep waiting) or switch to the task identified by *hTaskCallee*.

The above rule ensures that:

- if calls are completed in a reasonable amount of time, type ahead will be treated correctly.
- if the callee does not respond, type ahead is not misinterpreted and the user is able to act to solve the problem. For example, OLE 1.0 servers can queue up requests without responding when they are in modal dialogs.

Handling input while waiting for an outgoing call to finish can introduce complications. The application should determine whether to process the message without interrupting the call, continue waiting, or cancel the operation.

When there is no response to the original OLE call, the application can cancel the call and recover the OLE object to a consistent state by calling **IStorage::Revert** on its storage. The object can be released if and when the container is to shut down. However, canceling a call can create orphaned operations and resource leaks. Canceling should be used *only* as a last resort It is strongly recommended that applications not allow it at all.

Caution Returning PENDING_WAITNOPROCESS can cause the message queue to fill.

Example

The following example of **IMessageFilter::MessagePending** displays the standard dialog box provided in the OLE user interface library if the tick count for this call exceeds the retry delay (in this case, 5000) and if the user has issued a significant event such as a mouse click or keyboard event. A simple mouse move does not trigger this dialog box. Once in the dialog box message loop, there is a possibility that another call will be initiated and that the dialog box procedure will be reentered. The *m_bUnblocking* variable is used to prevent the display of two dialog boxes simultaneously.

All mouse and keyboard input messages are removed from the queue because these messages were generated by the user while the application was waiting for a response to its OLE call.

If the dialog box cannot be displayed because the application is blocked, the message must be rejected and PENDINGMSG_WAITDEFPROCESS is returned.

If there is a callback function set up for the message filter, the function pointed to by *m_lpfnMessagePendingCallback* is called by using the current message. However, if there is no callback function, the default behavior takes over and OLE is told to automatically apply default message handling.

```
DWORD IMessageFilter_MessagePending (
        LPMESSAGEFILTER     lpThis,
        HTASK               htaskCallee,
        DWORD               dwTickCount,
        DWORD               dwPendingType
)
{
    LPOLESTDMESSAGEFILTER lpStdMsgFilter =
        (LPOLESTDMESSAGEFILTER)lpThis;
   DWORD                dwReturn = PENDINGMSG_WAITDEFPROCESS;
    MSG                  msg;
    BOOL                 fIsSignificantMsg = IS_SIGNIFICANT_MSG(&msg);
    UINT                 uRet;

    if (dwTickCount > (DWORD)OLESTDRETRYDELAY
        && (! lpStdMsgFilter->m_bUnblocking) && fIsSignificantMsg)
    {
```

```
            if (lpStdMsgFilter->m_fEnableNotRespondingDialog)  {
                OLEUIBUSY bz;
                lpStdMsgFilter->m_bUnblocking = TRUE;
                while (PeekMessage(&msg, NULL, WM_MOUSEFIRST, WM_MOUSELAST,
                    PM_REMOVE | PM_NOYIELD));

                while (PeekMessage(&msg, NULL, WM_KEYFIRST, WM_KEYLAST,
                    PM_REMOVE | PM_NOYIELD));

                // Set up "not responding" OLEUIBUSY dialog */
                bz.cbStruct = sizeof(OLEUIBUSY);
                bz.dwFlags = BZ_NOTRESPONDINGDIALOG;
                bz.hWndOwner = lpStdMsgFilter->m_hWndParent;
                bz.lpszCaption = lpStdMsgFilter->m_lpszAppName;
                bz.lpfnHook = lpStdMsgFilter->m_lpfnBusyDialogHookCallback;
                bz.lCustData = 0;
                bz.hInstance = NULL;
                bz.lpszTemplate = NULL;
                bz.hResource = 0;
                bz.hTask = htaskCallee;
                bz.lphWndDialog =
                    (HWND FAR *)&(lpStdMsgFilter->m_hWndBusyDialog);
                uRet = OleUIBusy(&bz);
                lpStdMsgFilter->m_bUnblocking = FALSE;
                return PENDINGMSG_WAITNOPROCESS;
            }
        }

        if (lpStdMsgFilter->m_bUnblocking)
            return PENDINGMSG_WAITDEFPROCESS;

        if (lpStdMsgFilter->m_lpfnMessagePendingCallback && !IsBadCodePtr
              ((FARPROC)lpStdMsgFilter->m_lpfnMessagePendingCallback)){
                MSG msg;

            if (PeekMessage(&msg, NULL, 0, 0, PM_NOREMOVE | PM_NOYIELD)) {
                if (lpStdMsgFilter->m_lpfnMessagePendingCallback(&msg)) {
                    // Message was processed; can remove it from queue.
                    PeekMessage(&msg, NULL, msg.message, msg.message,
                                PM_REMOVE | PM_NOYIELD);
                    dwReturn = PENDINGMSG_WAITNOPROCESS;
                } else {
                    // Message not processed; let OLE take default action.
                    dwReturn = PENDINGMSG_WAITNOPROCESS;
                }
            }
        }
        return dwReturn;
    }
```

CoRegisterMessageFilter

HRESULT CoRegisterMessageFilter(*lpMessageFilter* , *lplpMessageFilter*)
LPMESSAGEFILTER *lpMessageFilter*
LPMESSAGEFILTER FAR* *lplpMessageFilter*

CoRegisterMessageFilter registers, with OLE, the instance of an EXE application's **IMessageFilter** interface to be used for handling concurrency issues. DLL object applications cannot register a message filter.

Parameters

lpMessageFilter
Points to an **IMessageFilter** interface supplied by the application. Can be NULL, indicating that the current **IMessageFilter** registration should be revoked.

lplpMessageFilter
Returns a pointer,if this parameter is non-NULL, to the previously registered **IMessageFilter** instance. If NULL, indicates no previous **IMessageFilter** instance was registered.

Return Values

Value	Meaning
S_OK	**IMessageFilter** instance registered or revoked successfully.
S_FALSE	An error registering or revoking **IMessageFilter** instance.

PART 3

Appendixes

APPENDIX A

Object Handlers

In OLE, an object handler is nothing more than a piece of code that implements the interfaces expected by a container when an object is in its loaded state. OLE includes a default object handler, OLE2.DLL.

This chapter discusses the following types of object handlers:

Types of object handlers	Description
Default object handler	OLE2.DLL is the default object handler provided with the OLE libraries. It is used to cache presentation data and to render objects using data from the OLE default data cache. In most cases, the default handler/cache provides the level of functionality needed for container applications.
Custom handler	A custom handler is typically used with the OLE default object handler and an EXE object application to do special rendering. A custom handler can be written to supplement or replace some or all of the functionality offered by the OLE default object handler. Custom handlers are registered in the registration database in place of the OLE2.DLL default object handler using the keyword **InprocHandler**.
DLL object application	An object application can be written as a DLL to directly reside in the container's process space. DLL object applications replace not only the functionality of an EXE object application, but that of the default object handler and/or custom object handler. DLL object applications are registered in the registration database using the keyword **InprocServer**, which leads to their often being referred to as an *in-process server*.

OLE Default Object Handler

Note Object handlers provide services on behalf of OLE object applications while an object is in its *loaded* state, thus avoiding the process time of starting the object applications. The OLE default object handler is always used unless a custom handler or DLL object application is written and registered for an object class.

Figure A-1 shows a representation of the OLE default object handler and its aggregation of the default data cache. The illustration shows only the interface implementations exposed externally; internal implementations are not shown. For example, the data cache has internal implementations of **IDataObject** and **IPersistStorage** that are made available to the default handler through its aggregation with the cache.

As shown, the default handler is used as the intermediary between the container application and an object application. If the default handler is unable to handle a request by the container or the object needs to be put into its running state, the handler passes the call on to the object application for processing. Through the exposed **IOleClientSite** interface, the object application is able to obtain the services offered by the container application.

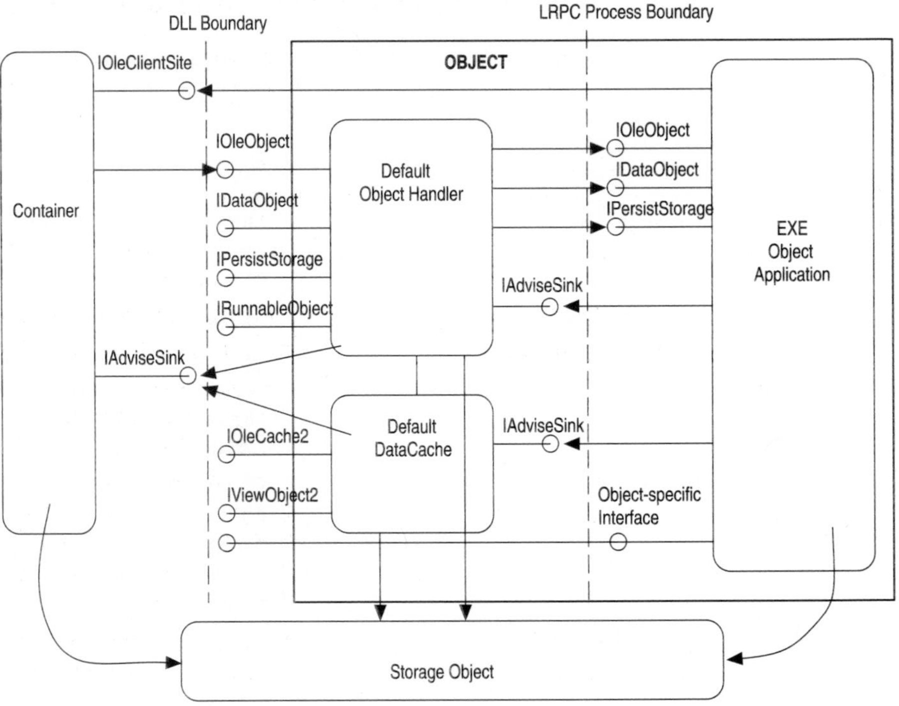

Figure A-1. OLE default object handler, OLE2.DLL.

The container makes interface method calls to what it interprets to be the object application. In reality, the calls are intercepted by the default object handler, which provides services on behalf of the object in its loaded state.

The OLE default handler and data cache are often thought of as being one object; in reality, they are two separate objects; the cache is aggregated with the handler. The default handler (through **IViewObject2**) is responsible for drawing the requested object using the data maintained in the data cache. Drawing is always done locally, never by remoting the call to the object application.

The object handler transparently converts the cached data for drawing purposes as the object is moved from one platform to another platform (for example, from Windows to the Macintosh). OLE, through its implementation of the **IOleCache2** interface, can convert between the presentation formats it knows about: metafiles, bitmaps and DIB on Windows and PICTs on the Macintosh.

The default handler is also responsible for transitioning the object from the loaded state to the running state and for keeping the data cache up to date against changes made to the running object. As an object enters its running state, the handler sets up appropriate advisory connections on the running object by passing an **IAdviseSink** of itself to the running object. When the object changes, **OnDataChange** is invoked on the handler's sink, at which point the handler updates the cache. After updating the cache, the handler sends **OnDataChange** and/or **OnViewChange** notifications to the advisory sink in the container.

Through the default handler, the following interface implementations are exposed for use by the container while an object is in its loaded state:

Default Handler's Interface Implementations	Purpose
IDataObject	Uses the cached presentation data to enumerate and retrieve data from the registration database and to be notified when an object's data has changed.
IPersistStorage	Saves and loads presentation/data caches.
IViewObject2	Enables the container to render an object, using one of three standard data formats obtained from the object's cached data. These formats include metafile, bitmap, and DIB.
IOleObject	Enumerates the list of verbs (using entries from the registration database) that the container makes available to the user for a given object. **IOleObject::DoVerb** puts the object into its running state.
IOleCache2	Caches, uncaches, and selectively updates an object's presentation data.

Interfaces Implemented by the Default Handler

To better understand how the default handler works with an object in its loaded and running states, the following sections describe the interfaces implemented by the default handler.

IOleObject Interface

The default handler's implementation of the **IOleObject** interface is minimal in that only the **DoVerb** and **Update** methods put the object in the running state; the remainder of the **IOleObject** methods either return an HRESULT or save the information for future use.

The following table lists the **IOleObject** methods along with a description of how the default handler's implementation affects an object when it is in its loaded and running states.

IOleObject Method	Object in Loaded State	Object in Running State
Advise	Remembers and forwards to the object application at the appropriate time.	Remembers the **Advise** and delegates to the running object.
EnumAdvise	Enumerates the remembered advises.	Enumerates the remembered advises.
Unadvise	Delegates the call to the advise holder object in order to remove the advise from the list.	Delegates the call to the advise holder object in order to remove the advise from the list and tells the object to do an unadvise.
Close	Returns NOERROR. Containers can safely call **Close**, but it is meaningless while an object is in its loaded state.	Delegates the call to the running object.
DoVerb	Puts the object in its running state and delegates the call to the running object.	Delegates the call to the object.
EnumVerbs	Searches the verb entries in the registration database to create the needed enumeration; returns NOERROR.	Delegates the call to the running object; if the object returns OLE_YES_USEREG, the object searches the registration database.

IOleObject Method	Object in Loaded State	Object in Running State
GetClientSite	Returns the last **IOleClientSite** (as remembered by **SetClientSite**) and returns NOERROR.	Delegates the call to the running object.
GetClipboardData	Cannot be called unless the object is running; returns OLE_E_NOTRUNNING.	Delegates the call to the running object.
GetExtent	If available, returns the size of the requested aspect from the cache. Otherwise, returns NOERROR if aspect not found.	Delegates the call to the running object.A successful call returns to the container while an error forces object to get the extents from the cache.
GetMiscStatus	Searches the MiscStatus entries in the registration database for the specified CLSID and returns NOERROR.	Delegates the call to the running object. If the object returns OLE_YES_USEREG, searches the registration database.
GetMoniker	Calls **IOleClientSite::Get-Moniker** if **SetClientSite** has been called with a valid **IOleClientSite** pointer. Otherwise, returns E_UNSPEC.	Calls **IOleClientSite::Get-Moniker** if **SetClientSite** has been called with a valid **IOleClientSite** pointer. Otherwise, returns E_UNSPEC.
GetUserClassID	Returns the CLSID remembered from creation time and returns NOERROR.	
GetUserType	Retrieves a string from the CLSID's AuxUserType entry in the registration database and returns NOERROR.	Delegates the call to the running object; if the object returns OLE_YES_USEREG, searches the registration database.
InitFromData	Returns OLE_E_NOTRUNNING.	Delegates the call to the running object.
IsUpToDate	Returns OLE_E_NOTRUNNING.	Delegates the call to the running object.
SetClientSite	Save the **IOleClientSite** pointer for future use and returns NOERROR.	Remembers and delegates the call to the running object.

IOleObject Method	Object in Loaded State	Object in Running State
SetColorScheme	Returns OLE_E_NOTRUNNING.	Delegates the call to the running object.
SetExtent	Returns OLE_E_NOTRUNNING.	Delegates the call to the running object.
SetHostNames	Saves the string for future use and returns NOERROR.	Saves the string and delegates the call to the running object.
SetMoniker	Returns NOERROR (object can obtain later from object's client site.	Delegates the call to the running object.
Update	Runs and delegates the call to the object; if the object was not previously running, it stops the object after the update. Updates the OnSave caches.	Delegates the call to the running object. Updates the OnSave caches.

IDataObject Interface

The default handler's **IDataObject** implementation depends on what is in the cache. In the loaded state, the handler delegates **GetData**, **GetDataHere**, and **QueryGetData** method calls to the cache's **IDataObject** implementation.

The default handler's **IDataObject** implementation is as follows:

IDataObject Methods	Object in Loaded State	Object in Running State
DAdvise	Remembers and forwards to the object application at the appropriate time.	Remembers the **Advise** and delegates the call to the running object.
EnumDAdvise	Enumerates the remembered advises.	Enumerates the remembered advises.
DUnadvise	Delegates the call to the advise holder object in order to remove the advise from the list.	Delegates the call to the advise holder object in order to remove the advise from the list and tells the object to do an unadvise.
EnumFormatEtc	Creates an enumerator from the object's DataFormats and GetSet entries in the registration database. The cache returns E_NOTIMPL.	Delegates the call to the running object; if the object returns OLE_YES_USEREG, searches the registration database.

IDataObject Methods	Object in Loaded State	Object in Running State
GetCanonicalFormatEtc	Returns OLE_E_NOTRUNNING.	Delegates the call to the running object.
GetData	Calls the cache. If the data is not cached, the handler returns OLE_E_NOTRUNNING.	Calls the cache. If the data is not cached, the handler delegates the call to the running object and returns the data from the object. (A subsequent call to **IOleCache::Cache** is needed to cache the data.)
GetDataHere	Calls the cache. If the data is not cached, the handler returns OLE_E_NOTRUNNING.	Calls the cache. If the data is not cached, delegates the call to the running object and returns the data from the object.
QueryGetData	Calls the cache. If the data is not cached, the handler returns OLE_E_NOTRUNNING.	Calls the cache. If the data is not cached, delegates the call to the running object and returns the data from the object.
SetData	Returns OLE_E_NOTRUNNING.	Delegates the call to the running object.

IPersistStorage Interface

In the loaded state, the default handler (after performing some action) delegates all **IPersistStorage** method calls to the cache. The default handler never tries to run the object as the result of an **IPersistStorage** call; the handler works exclusively with the cached data and never with the object's native data.

The default handler's implementation of **IPersistStorage** works as follows for when an object is in both the loaded and running state:

IPersistStorage Methods	Object in Loaded State	Object in Running State
GetClassID	Returns the remembered CLSID or what is in the object's **IStorage**.	Delegates the call to the running object and then to the cache.
IsDirty	Delegates the call to the cache.	Delegates the call to the running object; if the object is dirty, it returns immediately. If the object is not dirty, it asks the cache if it is dirty, returning whatever from the cache.

IPersistStorage Methods	Object in Loaded State	Object in Running State
InitNew	Increments the object's **IStorage** reference count and delegates the call to the cache.	Delegates the call to the running object and then to to the cache.
Load	Increments the object's **IStorage** reference count and delegate the call to the cache.	Delegates the call to the running object and then to the cache.
Save	Save the OLE private data stream and then delegate the call to the cache, which will write the presentation data stream.	Delegates the call to the running object and then to the cache.
SaveCompleted	Clears the internal state saved with the **Save** method and delegates the call to the cache.	Delegates the call to the running object and then to the cache.
HandsOffStorage	Releases the object's **IStorage** and delegates the call to the cache.	Delegates the call to the running object and then to the cache.

Interfaces Implemented by the Cache

This section describes the interfaces implemented by the OLE default data cache. The cache implements the **IPersistStorage**, **IDataObject**, **IViewObject2**, and **IOleCache2** interfaces, as described in the following sections.

IPersistStorage Interface

The following table describes the cache's **IPersistStorage** implementation and the effect of calling its methods on an object in both the loaded and running state:

IPersistStorage Methods	Object in Loaded State
GetClassID	Returns the CLSID passed to **OleCreateDefaultHandler. GetClassId** is not usually called because the default handler already knows the CLSID
IsDirty	Returns NOERROR if the cache is dirty; otherwise, it returns S_FALSE.
InitNew	Saves and increments the object's new **IStorage** reference count and returns NOERROR.

IPersistStorage Methods	Object in Loaded State
Load	Saves and increments the object's **IStorage**; reference count. Does demand loading of the presentation streams available in the cache as required by the cache's **IDataObject** implementation. Regardless of the running state of the object application, an error code may be returned.
Save	Saves all presentation data that have changed since the call to **Load** along with information about what was cached. Regardless of the running state of the object application, an error code may be returned.
SaveCompleted	Releases the **IStorage** pointer and returns NOERROR.
HandsOffStorage	Releases the **IStorage** pointer that the cache had previously remembered.

IDataObject Interface

The following table lists the cache's **IDataObject** implementation and the effect of calling its methods on an object in the loaded state. The cache does not make any **IDataObject** method calls on the object in its running state; in the running state, the cache delegates all calls to the default handler.

IDataObject Methods	Object in Loaded State
DAdvise	Returns OLE_E_ADVISENOTSUPPORTED.
EnumDAdvise	Returns OLE_E_ADVISENOTSUPPORTED.
DUnadvise	Returns OLE_E_NOCONNECTION.
EnumFormatEtc	Returns E_NOTIMPL.
GetCanonicalFormatEtc	Returns E_NOTIMPL.
GetData	Returns the data if the requested presentation was cached before this call, otherwise, returns OLE_E_BLANK. **GetData** supports TYMED_HGLOBAL, TYMED_METAPICT, and TYMED_GDI.
GetDataHere	Returns the data if the requested presentation was cached before this call, otherwise, returns OLE_E_BLANK. **GetDataHere** supports TYMED_ISTREAM and TYMED_HGLOBAL.
QueryGetData	If the requested **FORMATETC** was cached, then it returns NOERROR; otherwise, the cache returns S_FALSE or OLE_E_BLANK.
SetData	

IViewObject2 Interface

The cache's **IViewObject2** implementation is used to render objects using data from the cache. The cache tries to perform the requested action based on a presentation in the cache. At no time does the cache try to run the object application. If you plan to implement the **IViewObject2** interface in a handler, you must implement the entire interface method set. However, in your implementation you can delegate method calls as needed to the cache's **IViewObject**.

The cache's **IViewObject2** interface implementation is as follows when an object is in the loaded state (**IViewObject2** is an extension of **IViewObject**; as such, it inherits all of the **IViewObject** methods):

IViewObject2 Methods	Effect on Object in Loaded State
Draw	Attempts to draw the object using a presentation from the cache; otherwise, it returns OLE_E_BLANK.
GetColorSet	Tries to determine the color set from the Metafile or DIB in the cache. Returns OLE_E_BLANK if there is no presentation; otherwise, it returns NOERROR or S_FALSE, depending on the success of the method.
Freeze	Adds the aspect to an internal list that affects the behavior of **Draw** and returns NOERROR if successful. It returns OLE_E_BLANK if not. Returns If this is a repeat request, it returns VIEW_S_ALREADY_FROZEN.
UnFreeze	Removes an entry from the internal list of frozen aspects and returns OLE_E_NOCONNECTION if the aspect was not frozen, otherwise, it returns NOERROR.
SetAdvise	Saves the **IAdviseSink** so that the cache itself will call its OnViewChange when the object application notifies the cache (through the cache's **IAdviseSink**). It returns NOERROR.
GetAdvise	Returns the last **IAdviseSink** and the last aspect from which the advise happened (from **SetAdvise**) and returns NOERROR.
GetExtent	Returns the view extents of an object using data from the cache.

IOleCache2 Interface

The cache only works with an object in its loaded state; when an object is in the running state, the cache delegates all calls to the default handler.

The following table summarizes the calling the **IOleCache2** methods, and the effect that call has on an object in its loaded state. (**IOleCache2** is an extension of **IOleCache** and, as such, it inherits all of the **IOleCache** methods.)

IOleCache2 Methods	Effect on Object in the Loaded State
Cache	Tries to create a cache for the requested **FORMATETC**. Returns the cache connection ID and OLE_S_SAMECACHE if the **FORMATETC** is already cached. If the **FORMATETC** is already cached but a new set of Advise flags are passed in to **Cache**, then **Cache** overwrites the old Advise flags with the new ones before returning CACHE_S_SAMECACHE. (Note that these flags are advisory only. The cache may be updated more frequently, depending on the state of the running object.) In the running state, **Cache** checks to see if the object supports the specified **FORMATETC**. Even if the **FORMATETC** is not supported, the cache creates the cache node and returns CACHE_S_FORMATNOTSUPPORTED. There might be cases in which you get a cache connection ID of zero but no error. This implies that the **FORMATETC** is implicitly cached by the object as part of its native data and need not be explicitly cached (thus reducing storage space for the object).
UnCache	Invalidates the cache connection ID returned by **Cache**.
EnumCache	Returns an enumerator that enumerates all implicit and explicit cache nodes. For more information, see "Strategies for Caching Data with Custom Handlers."
InitCache	Using the **IDataObject** as the source, **InitCache** updates each of the associated cache nodes. NOERROR is returned if one or more nodes are updated; otherwise, CACHE_S_NOTUPDATED is returned.
SetData	Using the **IDataObject** as its source, **SetData** determines whether there are any associated cache nodes that need to be updated.
UpdateCache	Selectively updates the various cache nodes according to the control flag(s) passed in to the method. Semantically, **UpdateCache** is similar to **InitCache**.

Strategies for Caching Data

The default cache supports two types of data caching: implicit and explicit. *Implicit caching* refers to when an object directly supports the data formats needed to render itself in the container, thus saving the overhead of storing these data formats in the object's **IStorage**. *Explicit caching* means that the data formats required to render the object are physically cached and saved with the object.

To illustrate the use of implicit caching, consider the case of a custom handler being used to render objects. In this case, the handler is able to render the object directly from the object's native data in **IStorage**. When the container asks the handler to cache the data format for an object, the handler first checks to see if the object supports the specified data format. If it does, the handler returns a cache connection ID of zero and returns CACHE_S_SAMECACHE. A connection ID of zero indicates that the object directly supports the data format and an explicit cache of the data format is not required. This behavior is always true for objects created by DLL object applications.

In contrast, there are only two cases that require an explicit cache of the data:

- The container asks to cache an iconic representation of the object (DVASPECT_ICON), or
- The container specifies ADVFCACHE_FORCEBUILTIN to forcefully cache the data.

In these cases, the handler delegates the call to the default cache to explicitly create a cache node for the data format.The handler must remember the connection ID returned by **IOleCache::Cache** and support enumerating the connection ID in **IOleCache::EnumCache**.

Typically, handlers have an array of **STATDATA**s that they use for enumeration:

```
typedef struct tagSTATDATA
{
    FORMATETC formatetc;
    DWORD advf;
    IAdviseSink FAR* pAdvSink;
    DWORD dwconnection;
} STATDATA
```

The number of entries in the array will be equal to the number of **FORMATETC**sthat the object supports. The array is initialized with the supported **FORMATETC**s and zero for connection IDs. An explicit cache against one of the supported **FORMATETC**s results in a nonzero cache connection ID being stored in the corresponding **STATDATA** entry. At load time, the explicit caches must be enumerated and the connection IDs stored in the appropriate location in the **STATDATA** array.

Of note about handlers that render objects directly by using the object's native data: even if the handler is told explicitly to cache the presentation data (through ADVFCACHE_FORCEBUILTIN), the handler will not use the cached representation for drawing; it continues to draw using the native data from the object's **IStorage**.

Custom Object Handlers

A custom handler is simply a class-specific handler, something other than the default handler provided with OLE. Custom handlers typically implement one or more interfaces in a different manner than does the default handler. Most often the custom handler uses the features provided by the default handler, either through aggregation or delegation. Delegation can be done against an entire interface implementation or on an individual method basis. If the custom handler delegates based on methods, it must implement all of the methods in that interface. In almost all cases, a custom handler delegates caching to the OLE default cache.

Currently, a custom handler *must* aggregate the default handler, because this is the only means by which the object can be transitioned into and out of the running state. Figure A-2 shows a common integration point for a custom object handler, between the container application and the OLE default object handler, OLE2.DLL. As shown, the custom handler acts like a filter between the container application and the default handler and object application. (The drawing shown is representative of how the sample object handler (shipped with the OLE SDK) is designed to work.

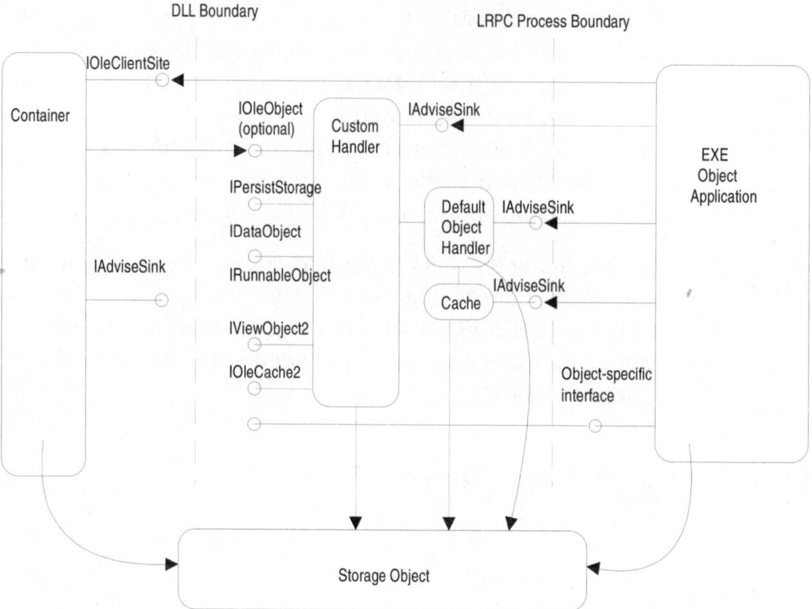

Figure A-2. Relationship between a custom handler and the default handler.

More complex handlers can be created that not only replace the functionality offered by the default handler, but that of the object application also. In these cases, the handler is acting as a DLL object application. For more information on DLL object applications, see "Considerations for DLL Object Applications," later in this chapter.

In general, it is unlikely that writing a custom handler to totally replace the functionality offered by the default object handler would be to your advantage. Before you set out to write an object handler, first determine your needs. As a first step, look at the support offered by the OLE default object handler and ask yourself what is needed beyond the support offered by the default handler.

Some of the reasons you might consider writing a custom object handler are listed below:

- Custom handlers can be written to handle data formats beyond the Metafile, Bitmap, and DIB formats supported by the default object handler.
- Custom handlers can be used for special resizing while an object is in its loaded state. The handler can be designed to trap the incoming **IOleObject::SetExtent** calls and use the object's native data to render the object instead of starting the object application.
- Custom handlers reside in the container application's process space and are much faster than object applications.

- Custom handlers provide very fast services for display and print operations; however, because they typically do not have a user interface, they are generally not suitable for tasks requiring an object to be in its running state (for example, editing). Because they often reduce or eliminate the need to run an EXE object application; this makes certain tasks in container applications much faster.
- Custom handlers can support any class of object, as does the default object handler. An object handler can be designed to work with just a specific class of object(s), as is discussed later in this appendix.
- Custom handlers can support unique interface implementations; implementing them in a handler avoids the LPRC overhead associated with providing the **IMarshal** interface needed for marshaling the methods to and from an object application.
- Custom handlers lend themselves more readily to licensing for redistribution than do EXE applications.

Rendering Handlers

Rendering handlers are the most common type of custom object handler. Rendering handlers provide better drawing functionality than that offered by the default handler and they save disk storage space. Because the object can draw directly from its native data, no data cache is needed.

Rendering handlers can be written to support both embedded and linked objects; this section describes supporting embedded objects. For information on rendering linked objects, see the section "Custom Link Source Format" in the "Data Transfer/Caching Interfaces and Functions" chapter.

Rendering Objects from Native Data

Rendering an object from its native data requires the object application to first write the data to storage. The handler then draws the object from the data in storage. This requires that the handler and EXE object application coordinate the use of object's **IStorage**. Elements within an **IStorage** must be opened in STG_SHARE_EXCLUSIVE mode. Hence the storage cannot be opened by the object application and the handler at the same time.

The following list outlines the coordination of storage between the object application and the rendering handler:

- The handler sets up an ADV_NODATA advise with the object application.
- The object application writes its data into the data streams and releases the streams before sending an **OnDataChange** to the handler. Note that the object must not commit the changes to **IStorage**.

- When the handler receives the **OnDataChange** notification, it generates an **OnViewChange** notification and sets a flag to indicate it needs to get the object's new extents in a subsequent call to **IViewObject2::GetExtent**.
- When the container calls **IViewObject::Draw** or **IDataObject::GetData**, the handler opens the stream, reads the data, and releases the stream immediately.

Interfaces Implemented by Rendering Handlers

A rendering handler needs to implement the **IPersistStorage**, **IOleCache2**, **IViewObject2**, and **IDataObject** interfaces. For a description of these interfaces and their role when implemented in a handler, see "Interfaces Implemented by the Default Handler," earlier in this appendix.

In addition, a rendering handler needs to implement the **IAdviseSink** interface as follows:

- The **IAdviseSink** must have a different object identity than the rendering handler, meaning that it must be implemented as a separate object.
- The handler and sink objects cannot share a common **QueryInterface** method.
- When **QueryInterface** is called on the sink, the sink must not return pointers to the handler object's interface implementations.
- The sink object typically supports only **IUnknown** and **IAdviseSink**. In the **IAdviseSink** implementation, only the **OnDataChange** method need be implemented; the remaining methods can be coded to return NOERROR. In the **OnDataChange** method, the sink sets the flag indicating a need to get the new extents on the object and send the **OnViewChange** notification for the appropriate aspects to the container.

Writing a Custom Object Handler

Writing an object handler is fairly straightforward; the level and complexity of implementation is directly related to the functionality required. To write a custom object handler, you must do the following tasks:

1. Implement the **IClassFactory** interface and the **DllGetClassObject** and **DllCanUnloadNow** functions.
2. Determine the additional OLE interfaces preferred for the object handler, then implement them into the handler's code.
3. Aggregate the OLE default handler with the custom object handler.
4. Register the object handler in the registration database, using the key **InprocHandler**.

In addition to these steps, all those common to any OLE application apply, including program initialization and termination, interface negotiation, object loading, and so forth, as discussed earlier in this book.

Required Interface Implementations

An object handler *must* implement the **IClassFactory** interface and **DllGetClassObject**. **IClassFactory** enables the object handler to create objects of a specific class while the exported **DllGetClassObject** function returns a pointer to the handler's **IClassFactory** interface implementation. In addition to these, you can implement any of the other OLE interfaces, depending on the level of functionality needed. Once implemented, an interface's methods are used just as they would be when interacting with the OLE default object handler or an object application. For example, you might include an implementation of the **IOleObject** interface, in which **DoVerb** executes certain verbs on behalf of the loaded object (for example, play) while delegating all other supported verbs to the object application. Or you could decide to implement a custom **IViewObject2** and **IOleCache2** to support data formats other than those supported by the default handler (metafile, bitmap, and DIB formats).

Note A custom object handler can instantiate any class of objects, just as the default object handler does. On the other hand, an object handler can be designed to work specifically with a certain class of object(s). This can be done by testing for a certain CLSID of an object and rejecting all others in the **IClassFactory::CreateInstance** implementation.

The following code example shows the implementation of the **DllGetClassObject** function and the **IClassFactory::CreateInstance** method, as they were written for the sample object handler that is shipped with the OLE tool kit. The implementation of **DllGetClassObject** is quite simple: when the container application calls one of the OLE object-creation functions, OLE first searches in the registration database for the keyword **InprocHandler** and loads the associated object handler into memory. When the object handler is loaded , OLE then calls **DllGetClassObject** to return an instance of the **IClassFactory** interface. OLE can then use the **IClassFactory** pointer to call **IClassFactory::CreateInstance** to instantiate the object for the container application.

```
STDAPI DllGetClassObject(REFCLSID rclsid, REFIID riid, LPVOID FAR* ppv)
//-------------------------------------------------------------------
// Exported DLL initialization is run in context of running application
// ------------------------------------------------------------------
{
    HRESULT hRes;
    CClassFactory *pClassFactory = new CClassFactory(rclsid);
    if (pClassFactory != NULL) {
        hRes = pClassFactory->QueryInterface(riid, ppv);
        pClassFactory->Release(); //OK to release ptr since
                                  //container now responsible for
                                  //releasing the instantiated
                                  //class factory object
    }
```

```
    return hRes;
} //DLLGetClassObject()

CClassFactory::CClassFactory(REFCLSID rclsid)
{
    m_dwRefs = 1;
    m_ClsId = rclsid;


}   // CClassFactory()

CClassFactory::~CClassFactory()
{
}   // ~CClassFactory()

STDMETHODIMP CClassFactory::CreateInstance(IUnknown FAR* pUnkOuter,
                                           REFIID riid,
                                           LPLPVOID ppunkObject)
{
    HRESULT hRes;
    CHandlerObject* pObject;

    if (ppunkObject)
    {
        *ppunkObject = NULL; //NULL-out return parameters
    }

    if (pUnkOuter != NULL)
    {
    //Custom handler doesn't support being an aggregate object (although
    //it aggregates the default handler)

        hRes = ResultFromScode(E_NOTIMPL);
        goto errReturn;
    }

    pObject = new CHandlerObject(NULL); //create memory for object
    //Create object
    if ((hRes = pObject->CreateObject(m_ClsId,riid,ppunkObject)) != NOERROR)
    {
        delete pObject;
    }

    errReturn:
        return hRes;
}
```

Aggregating the OLE Default Object Handler

In writing a custom object handler, you *must* make the default object handler an aggregate object of your custom handler. By aggregating the default handler, you expose the features offered by the OLE default object handler, including the ability to cache the presentation data for an object and to launch the object application when an object needs to be put into its running state. In this way, you are still able to write only those interface implementations needed to support your class of object(s), while delegating other interface implementations to the default handler.

The custom handler processes all calls within its capabilities, delegating requests it does not support to the default object handler (such as cache updating). It can delegate either on a method-by-method basis or it can delegate on a complete interface implementation.

The default handler launches the object application when an object needs to be put in its running state. In the running state, calls from the object application to the container are first passed to the custom handler, which might process them, depending on in its interface implementations. Depending on the call, the container is then notified of changes made to an object.

To aggregate the default handler, the custom handler calls **OleCreateDefaultHandler**, passing in its CLSID (as registered in the registration database) and a pointer to the its **IUnknown** interface. The CLSID is used by the default handler to locate certain entries in the registration database for that object, the **IUnknown** is the controlling Unknown which ensures that the custom handler always gets first chance at any call. After aggregating the default handler, the custom handler can call **QueryInterface** to get pointers to the default handler's interface implementations so it can later delegate calls to them.

The following example illustrates how to create a custom handler that aggregates the default handler. **CreateObject** calls **OleCreateDefaultHandler** to instantiate a default handler. If the call is successful, the default handler's QueryInterface method is called to retrieve pointers to each of the interfaces to which the custom handler may delegate future calls.

```
HRESULT CHandlerObject::CreateObject(REFCLSID rclsid, REFIID riid,
                                      LPVOID FAR* ppv)
//--------------------------------------------------------------------
// CreateObject:
//--------------------------------------------------------------------
{
    HRESULT hRes = ResultFromScode(E_FAIL);
    ULONG dwRefs;

    m_ClsId = rclsid;
    //Create instance of default handler as an aggregate object
    hRes = OleCreateDefaultHandler(m_ClsId, &m_Unknown, IID_IUnknown,
```

```
                                        (LPVOID FAR*) &m_pDefHandler);
    if (hRes != NOERROR)
    {
        return hRes;
    }
    //Cache pointers to interfaces of default handler; note that these
    //are non-Addref'd pointers.
    hRes = m_pDefHandler->QueryInterface(IID_IOleObject,
                                        (LPVOID FAR*)&m_pOleObject);
    if (hRes == NOERROR)
    {
    //OK to  release because OleCreateDefaultHandler keeps object
    //alive
        dwRefs = m_pOleObject->Release();
    }

    hRes = m_pDefHandler->QueryInterface(IID_IDataObject,
                                        (LPVOID FAR*)&m_pDataObject);
    if (hRes == NOERROR)
    {
        dwRefs = m_pDataObject->Release();
    }

    hRes = m_pDefHandler->QueryInterface(IID_IViewObject,
                                        (LPVOID FAR*)&m_pViewObject);
    if (hRes == NOERROR)
    {
        dwRefs = m_pViewObject->Release();
    }

    hRes = m_pDefHandler->QueryInterface(IID_IOleCache,
                                        (LPVOID FAR*)&m_pOleCache);
    if (hRes == NOERROR)
    {
        dwRefs = m_pOleCache->Release();
    }

    hRes = m_pDefHandler->QueryInterface(IID_IPersistStorage,
                                        (LPVOID FAR*) &m_pPersistStorage);
    if (hRes == NOERROR)
    {
        dwRefs = m_pPersistStorage->Release();
    }
    //Get interface for whoever is creating the object
    if ((hRes =  m_Unknown.QueryInterface(riid, ppv)) == NOERROR)
    {
        ULONG dwRefs = ((LPUNKNOWN)*ppv)->Release();
    }

    return hRes;

}
```

Registering Object Handlers

Object handlers must be registered in the registration database. The registration process is the same as for registering object applications, except that the keyword **InprocHandler** is used as the registration key.

The registration database contains, by default, the following entry set belonging to the OLE default handler, OLE2.DLL.

```
HKEY_CLASSES_ROOT\CLSID\{00000402-0000-0000-c000-000000000046}\InprocHandler = OLE2.DLL
```

To register a custom handler, this entry must be set to the CLSID the handler is associated with and the name of the DLL, as shown in the following entry (the entry shown is for the OLE sample object handler):

```
HKEY_CLASSES_ROOT\CLSID\{00000402-0000-0000-c000-000000000046}\InprocHandler = DBGHNDLR.DLL
```

Whenever a container application calls one of the OLE object-creation functions, OLE uses the CLSID specified for the object and the **InprocHandler** key to search the registration database. If an object handler is found for the CLSID, it is loaded and initialized. Because handlers are usually designed to work with a particular object application, the registration database entry should be included with the entries for the related object application. When installing a custom handler with an object application, the above registration entry can be placed in the .REG file used to install the object application.

For more information on registering object handlers, see the chapter on "Registering Object Applications."

Loading Object Handlers

Object handlers get loaded when the container application calls one of the following OLE object-creation functions or **IClassFactory::CreateInstance**:

OleCreate	**OleCreateLink**
OleCreateLinkToFile	**OleCreateFromData**
OleCreateLinkFromData	**OleCreateFromFile**
OleLoad	**CoCreateInstance**
CoGetClassObject	

Once the object handler has been loaded, the container can call **QueryInterface** for any interface pointer, just as it usually does. If the custom object handler has implemented that interface, it returns a pointer to it; otherwise, it passes **QueryInterface** on to the default handler for processing.

Unloading Object Handlers

Object handlers, being DLLs, are at the mercy of the container process that instantiated them. This means that they remain in the container's process space until the container frees them, usually at application shutdown. To optimize the freeing of an object handler from memory, the object handler can optionally implement and export the **DllCanUnloadNow** function. Containers call **DllCanUnloadNow** to find out whether there are any existing instances of an object class remaining for which the object handler is responsible. If there are no objects loaded, **DllCanUnloadNow** returns TRUE, indicating that the handler can be safely freed from memory. To take advantage of this optimization, the container must call **CoFreeUnusedLibraries**.

Whether or not the object handler implemented **DllCanUnloadNow**, the object handler is forcefully unloaded when the container application calls **OleUninitialize** to uninitialize the OLE libraries. **DllCanUnloadNow** is optional and can be used to better manage memory resources.

DLL Object Applications

Figure A-3 shows how an object application can be implemented as a DLL object application. An object handler implemented in this manner *always* replaces the functionality offered by the OLE default handler and/or custom object handler. Obviously, process time is going to be much faster, given that there is no LRPC overhead or startup time. It's much easier to expose a new interface in a DLL object application because LRPC remoting is not required, hence there is no need to write custom marshaling code (see the **IMarshal** interface, earlier in this book). The downside of a DLL object application is that it has full responsibility for an object, in any and all of its states.

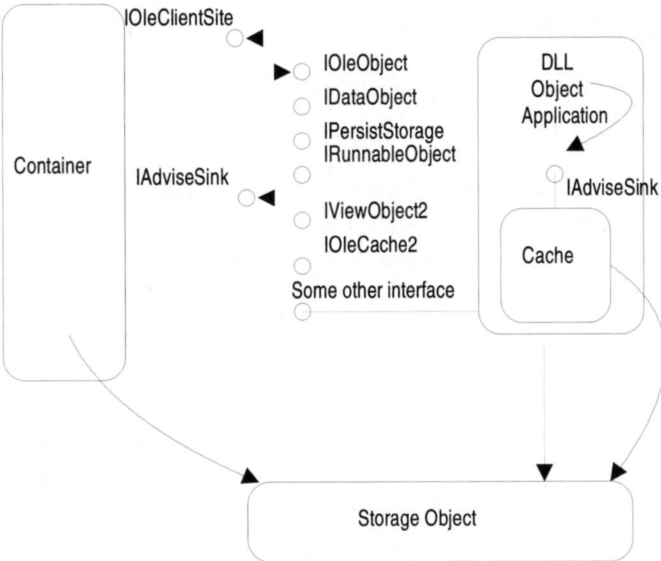

Figure A-3. Object application implemented as a DLL.

While OLE provides a default data cache, DLL object applications must expose their own implementation of the **IOleCache2** interface, delegating method calls as needed to the default cache. Because a DLL object application replaces the default handler (which exposes the default cache), DLL object applications need to call the **CreateDataCache** function to get an instance of the default cache.

The following factors should be considered before writing a DLL object application.

- DLL object applications are responsible for handling an object in *any and all* of its states. This implies that a DLL object application has a user interface for editing objects.
- DLL object applications cannot register a message filter for handling concurrency issues (by using the **IMessageFilter** interface); only EXE object applications can register message filters.
- DLL object applications are never "single use," they are always "multiple-use."
- Currently, the OLE libraries are not able to load a DLL object; therefore, DLL object applications *cannot* support links to file-based objects.
- DLL object applications are registered in the registration database using the keyword **InprocServer**. Other than using the required keyword, register DLL object applications just as you would register a custom object handler (see "Registering Object Handlers," earlier in this appendix).

- The **DllCanUnloadNow** function can be implemented by the DLL object application and called by the container application to see whether there are any existing objects in memory for which the DLL object application is responsible. If there are no objects, the DLL object application can be safely freed.
- DLL object applications can be written to support any of the OLE interfaces, including those that handle in-place activation and drag and drop operations. Support of in-place activation implies there is a user interface.
- Currently, DLL object applications are not compatible with OLE 1 applications because there is no way for the OLE 1 application to load the OLE 2 DLL. One work around is to create a small stub EXE that handles the loading and unloading of the OLE 2 DLL.
- DLL object applications being written for both 16- and 32-bit platforms must be compiled against both platforms because OLE does not automatically support interoperability across these platforms.
- DLL object applications have no message loop for processing Windows messages. In the case of in-place activation, where the active object is sharing a menu, the object handler needs to rely on the container application calling **IOleInPlaceActiveObject::TranslateAccelerator** before calling the Windows **TranslateAccelerator** API. The DLL object handler can then call **TranslateAccelerator** with the appropriate table and HWND. If the DLL object application has an open edit window, there is no way to get accelerators translated properly. One solution to this problem is to set a message hook when the open window has the focus.
- Because object handlers do not have a message processing loop, they cannot perform background processing during idle message processing. However, the object handler can implement a timer loop during which it processes any background tasks to work around this problem.

Required Interfaces for DLL Object Applications

A DLL object application must implement all of the interfaces required of a custom handler as well as the **IExternalConnection**, **IRunnableObject**, and **IOleObject** interfaces. In addition, a DLL object application is free to implement any of the other OLE interfaces. Generally, a DLL object application implements at least **IDataObject** and **IPersistStorage**. DLL object applications typically don't implement the **IAdviseSink** interface.

The implementation of **IDataObject**, **IPersistStorage**, and **IOleObject** should be similar to that for an EXE object application, with one exception:

The handler's **IPersistStorage::Save** and **IOleObject::Update** methods need to call **IOleCache2::UpdateCache** to update all cache nodes created with ADVFCACHE_ONSAVE.

The **IOleCache2** implementation should be similar to that implemented for a rendering handler; for more information, see "Rendering Handlers," earlier in this appendix.

The following sections describe the implementation aspects behind the **IRunnableObject** and **IExternalConnection** interfaces. For information on the other interfaces required of a custom handler, see "Interfaces Implemented by the Default Handler," earlier in this appendix.

IRunnableObject Interface

IRunnableObject is also implemented by DLL object applications to transition the object in and out of the running state.

IRunnableObject Interface Methods	Object in Running State
GetRunningClass	Returns the object's CLSID.
Run	If the object is running, it returns NOERROR. Otherwise, the object sets the run flag to TRUE and registers itself in the Running Object Table.
IsRunning	Returns the run flag previously set in **Run**.
LockRunning	Calls **CoLockObjectExternal** to create or release a strong external connection to the object.
SetContainedObject	Returns NOERROR; can be ignored.

IExternalConnection Interface

The **IExternalConnection** interface must be implemented to support silent updates of linked objects.

IExternalConnection Interface Methods	Object in Running State
AddConnection	Creates an external connection to the running object.
ReleaseConnection	Releases an external connection previously created by **AddConnection** and, if this is the last connection to the object, closes the object.

APPENDIX B

OLE Property Sets

Property sets are used to store information in such a way that any conforming program can later manipulate the information. Examples of property sets are the character formatting properties in a word processor or rendering attributes of an element in a drawing program. OLE does not provide any code or interfaces for manipulating property sets, it only specifies a standard data format structure.

Structure of Property Sets

Property sets are made up of tagged sections of values, each section uniquely identified by a name, a CLSID, and and a Format Identifier (FMTID). Every property consists of a *property identifier* and a *type indicator* that represents a *value*. Each value stored in a property set has a unique property identifier that is used to name the property. The type indicator describes the representation of the data in the value. For example, if a specific property in a property set was to hold an animal's scientific name, that name would be stored as a zero-terminated string. Stored along with the name would be a type indicator to indicate the value is a zero-terminated string. The representation of properties is shown below:

Property Identifier	Type Indicator	Value Represented
PID_ANIMALNAME	VT_LPSTR	Zero-terminated string
PID_LEGCOUNT	VT_I2	WORD

Any application that recognizes the property set format would be able to look at the property with an ID of PID_ANIMALNAME, determine it is a zero-terminated string, and read and write the value. Of course, the given application might not know anything about the property. The standard structure defined by OLE for property sets is generic as it relates to the semantics of the properties being represented; it says nothing about what they mean.

Examples of Using Property Sets

To illustrate the diverse functionality of property sets, this section describes two samples. The first uses the OLE Documentary Summary Information property set to show how property sets can be stored within files to allow common access to the information represented. The second example shows how property sets can be transferred between applications or OLE objects as an effective means of communication.

Storing Document Summary Information

The Document Summary Information property set is one of the simplest and most commonly used property sets. Most documents created by applications have a common set of attributes that are useful to users of those documents. These attributes include the name of the document's author, the subject of the document, when it was created, and so on.

In Windows 3.1, each application has a different way of storing this information within its documents. To examine the summary information for a given document, the user has to run the application that created the document, open it, and invoke the application's Summary Information dialog box. For example, the summary information dialog boxes that Microsoft Word displays for its documents are shown in Figure B-1:

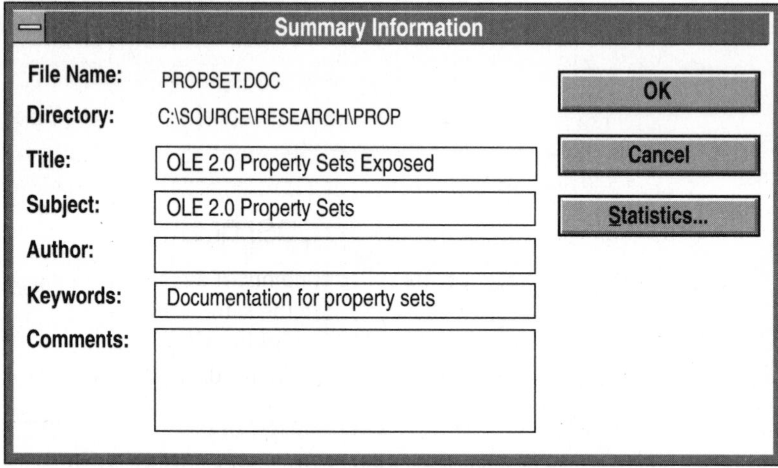

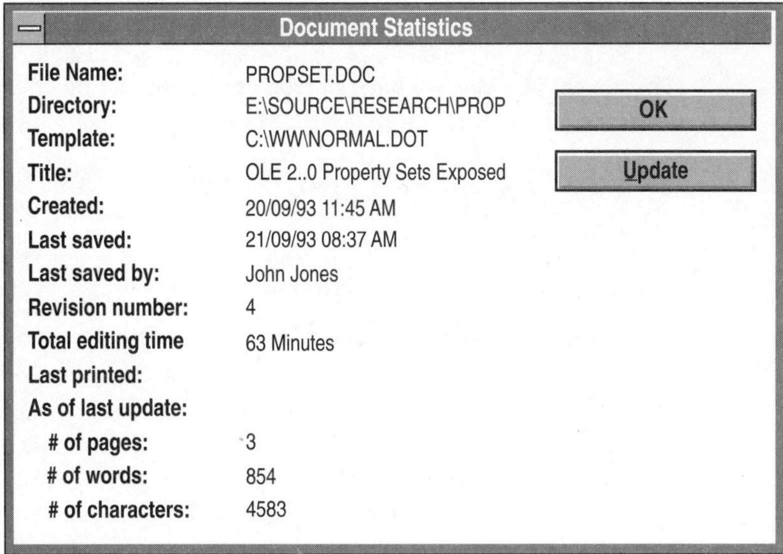

Figure B-1. Sample Summary Information dialog boxes.

Unfortunately, no application but Word can display the summary information for the document. Eventually, the OLE Document Summary Information Property Set will likely help remove this limitation. Any application that understands the data format for property sets will be able to access the summary information contained in any document created by an OLE application that also understands the format.

For more information about the Document Summary Information property set and implementing it in your applications, see "The Document Summary Information Property Set" later in this appendix.

Transferring Data Contained in Property Sets

Storing information about the contents of a document is useful, and a standard that would allow all files to share the same information with all applications would be even better. However, working with this type of information is only one example of how property sets can be used.

Another use for them is in the transfer of data between OLE objects or applications. To illustrate the process of transferring data between two OLE objects, consider the following example. A trader on Wall Street relies on large amounts of data to make important financial decisions regarding trades of securities. This market data must be delivered to the trader's workstation in real time (or at least very soon after it was generated).

Assume that, at any given moment during an open day on Wall Street, the trader is interested in the opening, high, low, current, and last closing price of an instrument (a specific stock), and the volume of trading on that stock so far that day.

As noted earlier, a property in a property set has three attributes: the property identifier, a value type indicator, and a value. In this example, the following properties can be defined:

Property Identifier	Type Indicator	Value Represented
PID_SYMBOL	VT_LPSTR	Zero-terminated string
PID_OPEN	VT_CY	Currency value
PID_CLOSE	VT_CY	Currency value
PID_HIGH	VT_CY	Currency value
PID_LOW	VT_CY	Currency value
PID_LAST	VT_CY	Currency value
PID_VOLUME	VT_I4	32-bit unsigned integer

Without worrying about how the data is transferred between the data server and the trader's application, think about what data is transferred and its format. Every property set must have a FMTID associated with it.

A single data element representing the stock of XYZ during the day might look like this:

```
PID_SYMBOL  contains "XYZ"
PID_OPEN    contains 42-3/4
PID_CLOSE   contains 42-3/4
PID_HIGH    contains 49-1/8
PID_LOW     contains 40-7/8
PID_LAST    contains 47-3/8
PID_VOLUME  contains 123,032
```

During a trading day on Wall Street only a few of the properties of a single instrument change. The opening price doesn't change all day, and the low price may go unchanged for several hours. Using property sets as the data transfer format allows applications to transfer only the data that has changed. For example, at some point during the day the Data Server may update the Traders Application by transferring the following StockQuote property set:

```
PID_SYMBOL      contains "XYZ"
PID_HIGH        contains 49-1/8
PID_LAST        contains 49-1/8
PID_VOLUME      contains 23,321
```

This example demonstrates how property sets can be used as a data transfer format, allowing sparse data representation. By transferring only the changed data, the overall performance of the trader's workstation is enhanced. Using property sets as a data transfer format has many uses beyond this example.

Notes on Using Property Sets

OLE property sets were designed to store data that is suited to representation as a collection of fine-grained values. Furthermore, it is assumed that the entire stream containing the property set would be read and/or written as a whole. Data sets that are too large for this to be feasible should be broken into separate streams and/or storages. The OLE property set data format was not meant to provide a substitute for a database of millions of tiny objects.

OLE Property Set Specification

All data elements within a property set are stored in Intel representation (byte order).

OLE defines a standard, serialized data format for property sets, which gives them the following characteristics:

- Property sets may be stored in a single **IStream** instance or in an **IStorage** instance containing multiple streams.
- Property sets can be transmitted using the **IDataObject** interface and/or the clipboard. Because property sets are self-identifying, they are ideal for transferring data between applications.
- Property sets are open-ended. Additional type identifiers can be published allowing new data types to be represented; for more information, see "Defining New Type Indicators," later in appendix.
- Property sets allow for extensibility. A property set may be defined as an extension of an existing property set, allowing readers to skip over unknown extensions, and preserve them, while still extracting information from the properties that they do know.
- Property sets allow for a dictionary of human-readable names to be included to further describe the contents. For more information on this optional dictionary, see "Property Set Dictionaries" later in this appendix.

Figure B-2 shows the overall structure of a property set:

Stream containing a serialized property set

Byte-order Indicator (WORD)	Format Version (WORD)	Originating OS Version (DWORD)	Class Identifier (CLSID (16 bytes))	Count of Sections *(n)* (DWORD)

Format ID for Section 1 (FMTID (16 bytes))	Offset 1 (DWORD)
Format ID for Section 2 (FMTID (16 bytes))	Offset 2 (DWORD)
m Entries	
Format ID for Section n (FMTID (16 bytes))	Offset n (DWORD)

Section 1 Header

Size of section (DWORD)	Count of Properties *(m)* (DWORD)

Property ID	Offset
Property ID for Property 1 (DWORD)	Offset 1 (DWORD)
Property ID for Property 2 (DWORD)	Offset 2 (DWORD)
m Entries	
Property ID for Property n (DWORD)	Offset n (DWORD)

Type Indicator 1 (DWORD)	Property Value 1 (Variable Length)
Type Indicator 2 (DWORD)	Property Value 2 (Variable Length)
m Entries	
Type Indicator n (DWORD)	Property Value n (Variable Length)

n Sections

Property Set Header | Format ID/Offset Pairs | Sections | Property ID/Offset Pairs | Type Indicators

Figure B-2. Serialized format for property sets.

The following sections describe the individual components that make up the property set data format shown in Figure B-2.

Property Set Header

The property set stream can be divided into three major parts. At the beginning of the first part is a header. It consists of a byte-order indicator, a format version, the originating operating system version, the CLSID, and a count of sections within the property set (there must be at least one). Each offset is the distance in bytes from the start of the whole stream to where the section begins.

The following pseudo-structures illustrate the header:

```
typedef struct tagPROPERTYSET
{
    // Header
    WORD      wByteOrder ;     // Always 0xFFFE
    WORD      wFormat ;        // Always 0
    WORD      dwOSVer ;        // System version
    CLSID     clsID ;          // Application CLSID
    DWORD     cSections ;      // Number of sections (must be at least 1)

    // Format ID/Offset pairs
    FORMATIDOFFSET  rgFIDO[cSections] ;

    // Sections
    PROPERTYSECTION rgSections[cSections] ;
} PROPERTYSET, FAR * LPPROPERTYSET ;
```

Byte-Order Indicator

The byte-order indicator is a WORD and should always hold the value 0xFFFE. This is the same as the Unicode byte-order indicator. When written in Intel byte order, this appears in the file or stream as 0xFe (0). The presence of the byte order indicator allows generic tools to determine whether the file or stream is written in Intel byte order.

Format Version

The Format Version is a WORD used to indicate the format version of this stream. It should always be zero. The format-version indicator should be checked when reading the property set. If it is not zero, then the stream was written to a different specification and cannot be read by code developed according to the OLE 2 specification.

Originating OS Version

This DWORD should hold the kind of operating system in the high word and the version number of the operating system in the low word. Possible values for the operating system are:

Operating System	Value
16-Bit Windows (Win16)	0x0000
Macintosh	0x0001
32-Bit Windows (Win32)	0x0002

For Windows, the operating system version is the low order word of **GetVersion**. On Windows, the following code would correctly set the version of the originating operating system:

```
#ifdef WIN32
dwOSVer = (DWORD)MAKELONG( LOWORD(GetVersion()), 2 ) ;
#else
dwOSVer = (DWORD)MAKELONG( LOWORD(GetVersion()), 0 ) ;
#endif
```

CLSID

The CLSID is that of a class that can display and/or provide programmatic access to the property values. If there is no such class, this value should be CLSID_NULL.

Count of Sections

This DWORD indicates how many sections exist in the stream. A property set can consist of any number of sections. Readers must be able to handle the case where there are zero sections.

Format Identifier/Offset Pairs

The second part of the property set stream contains Format Identifier (FMTID)/Offset Pairs. Each of these pairs both names and points to a section within a property set. The FMTID uniquely identifies how to interpret the contents of a section. The Offset is the distance of bytes from the *start of the whole stream* to where the section begins.

The following structure is helpful in dealing with Format Identifier/Offset Pairs:

```
typedef struct tagFORMATIDOFFSET
{
    GUID    FormatID ;
    DWORD   dwOffset ;
} FORMATIDOFFSET, FAR * LPFORMATIDOFFSET;
```

Format Identifiers

To allow for extension of property sets over time, while still permitting older clients to access the properties that they do understand, the values are stored in a sequence of sections, each tagged with a unique FMTID. Each property set FMTID indicates the meaning of the properties in the section, and succeeding sections are assumed to be defined as extensions of the preceding one so that property identifiers do not conflict.

For example, the FMTID for the OLE Document Summary Information property set is:

```
F29F85E0-4FF9-1068-AB91-08002B27B3D9
```

To define a FMTID for the Document Summary Information property set, you would use the **DEFINE_GUID** macro in an include file for the code that manipulates the property set:

```
DEFINE_GUID(FormatID_SummaryInformation, 0xF29F85E0, 0x4FF9, 0x1068,
0xAB, 0x91, 0x08, 0x00, 0x2B, 0x27, 0xB3, 0xD9);
```

Anywhere in your code you need to use the FMTID for the Document Summary Information property set, you can access it through the FormatID_SummaryInformation variable.

Allocating Format Identifiers

FMTIDs are created and represented in the same way as OLE CLSIDs and interface IDs. To create a unique FMTID, use the GUIDGEN.EXE program included in the OLE SDK.

Sections

This is the third part of the property set stream, as shown in Figure B-2. Property sets can contain many sections to allow for the extension of property sets over time. To allow older clients to access the properties that they do understand, property values are stored in a sequence of sections. The oldest definition would be found in the first section, with newer or extended definitions following. Because each section is tagged with a unique FMTID and succeeding sections are defined as extensions to the preceding ones, property identifiers do not conflict.

Each section contains:

- A byte count for the section (which is inclusive of the byte count itself)
- A count of the property values in the section
- An array of 32-bit Property ID/Offset pairs
- An array of property Type Indicators/Value pairs

The two arrays must be in corresponding order. Offsets are the distance from the start of the section to the start of the property (type, value) pair. This allows sections to be copied as an array of bytes without any translation of internal structure.

The following pseudo-structure illustrates the format of a section:

```
typedef struct tagPROPERTYSECTION
{
    DWORD    cbSection ;      // Size of Section
    DWORD    cProperties ;    // Count of Properties in section

    // Property ID/Offset Pairs
    PROPERTYIDOFFSET    rgPropIDOffset[cProperties] ;

    // Type/Value Pairs
    PROPERTY            rgTypeValue[cProperties] ;
} PROPERTYSECTION, FAR *LPPROPERTYSECTION ;
```

Size of Section

This DWORD indicates the size of the section. Because the section size is the first four bytes, you can copy sections as an array of bytes.

For example, an empty section (one with zero properties in it) would have a byte count of eight (the DWORD byte count and the DWORD count of properties). The section itself would contain the eight bytes:

```
08 00 00 00 00 00 00 00
```

Count of Properties

This DWORD gives a count of the property values in the section. A property set may contain any number of property values. Readers must be able to handle the case where there are zero properties.

Property ID/Offset Pairs

Following the Count of Properties is an array of Property ID/Offset Pairs. Property IDs are 32-bit values that uniquely identify a property within a section. The Offsets indicate the distance from the start of the section to the start of the property Type/Value Pair. By having the offsets relative to the section, sections can be copied as an array of bytes.

Property IDs are not sorted in any particular order. Properties can be omitted from the stored property set; readers must not rely on a specific order or range of property IDs.

Property ID/Offset Pairs can be described by the following structure:

```
typedef struct tagPROPERTYIDOFFSET
{
    DWORD   PropertyID;
    DWORD   dwOffset;
} PROPERTYIDOFFSET, FAR * LPPROPERTYIDOFFSET;
```

Type Indicators

After the table of Property ID/Offset Pairs comes the actual properties. Each property is stored as a DWORD type followed by the data value.

```
typedef struct tagPROPERTY
{
    DWORD   dwType;
    BYTE    rgbValue[ /*size of value*/ ];
} PROPERTY, FAR * LPPROPERTY;
```

Type indicators and their associated values are defined in the header file VARIANT.H.

All Type/Value pairs must begin on a 32-bit boundary. Thus values may be followed with null bytes to align the subsequent pair on a 32-bit boundary. Given a count of bytes, the following code will calculate how many bytes are needed to align on a 32-bit boundary:

```
cbAdd = (((cbCurrent + 3) >> 2) << 2) - cbCurrent ;
```

Within a vector of values, each repetition of value must align with its natural alignment rather than with a 32-bit alignment. In practice, this is only significant for types VT_I2 and VT_BOOL (which have two-byte natural alignment). All other types have four-byte natural alignment. Therefore, a property value with type indicator VT_I2 | VT_VECTOR would be:

- A DWORD element count, followed by
- A sequence of packed two-byte integers with no padding between them.

A property value of type identifier VT_LPSTR | VT_VECTOR would be:

- A DWORD element count (**DWORD** *cch*), followed by
- A sequence of strings (**char** *rgch*[]), each of which may be followed by null padding to round to a 32-bit boundary.

The following table lists the standard OLE-defined property type indicators and their meaning:

Type Indicator	Code	Value Representation
VT_EMPTY	0	None. A property set with a type indicator of VT_EMPTY has no data associated with it; that is, the size of the value is zero.
VT_NULL	1	None. This is like a pointer to NULL.
VT_I2	2	Two bytes representing a WORD value. This value will be zero-padded to a 32-bit boundary.
VT_I4	3	Four bytes representing a DWORD value.
VT_R4	4	Four bytes representing a 32-bit IEEE floating point value.
VT_R8	5	Eight bytes representing a 64-bit IEEE floating point value.
VT_CY	6	Eight-byte two's complement integer (scaled by 10,000). This type is commonly used for currency amounts.
VT_DATE	7	Time format used by many applications, it is a 64-bit floating point number representing seconds since January 1, 1900. This is stored in the same representation as VT_R8.
VT_BSTR	8	Counted, zero-terminated binary string; represented as a DWORD byte count (including the terminating null character) followed by the bytes of data.
VT_BOOL	11	Two bytes representing a Boolean (WORD) value containing 0 (FALSE) or -1 (TRUE). This type must be zero-padded to a 32-bit boundary.
VT_VARIANT	12	Four-byte indicator followed by the corresponding value. This is only used in conjunction with VT_VECTOR.
VT_I8	20	Eight bytes representing a signed integer.
VT_LPSTR	30	Same as VT_BSTR; this is the representation of most strings.
VT_LPWSTR	31	A counted and zero-terminated Unicode string; a DWORD character count (where the count includes the terminating null character) followed by that many Unicode (16-bit) characters. Note that the count is not a byte count, but a WORD count.

Type Indicator	Code	Value Representation

VT_FILETIME	64	64-bit **FILETIME** structure, as defined by Win32:
		`typedef struct_FILETIME{`
		`DWORD dwLowDateTime;`
		`DWORD dwHighDateTime;`
		`}FILETIME;`

VT_BLOB	65	DWORD count of bytes, followed by that many bytes of data. The byte count does not include the four bytes for the length of the count itself; an empty BLOB would have a count of zero, followed by zero bytes. This is similar to VT_BSTR but does not guarantee a null byte at the end of the data.
VT_STREAM	66	A VT_LPSTR (DWORD count of bytes followed by a zero-terminated string that many bytes long) that names the stream containing the data. The real value for this property is stored in an **IStream**, which is a sibling to the CONTENTS stream. This type is only valid for property sets stored in the CONTENTS stream of an **IStorage**.
VT_STORAGE	67	A VT_LPSTR (DWORD count of bytes followed by a zero-terminated string that many bytes long) that names the storage containing the data. The real value for this property is stored in an **IStorage**, which is a sibling to the CONTENTS stream that contains the property set. This type is only valid for property sets stored in the CONTENTS stream of an **IStorage**.
VT_STREAMED_OBJECT	68	Same as VT_STREAM, but indicates that the **IStream** named in this property contains a serialized object, which is a CLSID followed by initialization data for the class. The named **IStream** is a sibling to the CONTENTS stream that contains the property set. This type is only valid for property sets stored in the CONTENTS stream of an **IStorage**.
VT_STORED_OBJECT	69	Same as VT_STORAGE, but indicates that the **IStorage** named in this property contains an object. This type is only valid for property sets stored in the CONTENTS stream of an **IStorage**.

Type Indicator	Code	Value Representation
VT_BLOB_OBJECT	70	An array of bytes containing a serialized object in the same representation as would appear in a VT_STREAMED_OBJECT (VT_LPSTR). The only significant difference between this type and VT_STREAMED_OBJECT is that VT_BLOB_OBJECT does not have the system-level storage overhead as VT_STREAMED_OBJECT. VT_BLOB_OBJECT is more suitable for scenarios involving numerous small objects.
VT_CF	71	An array of bytes containing a clipboard format identifier followed by the data in that format. That is, following the VT_CF identifier is the data in the format of a VT_BLOB. This is a DWORD count of bytes followed by that many bytes of data in the following format: a LONG followed by an appropriate clipboard identifier and a property whose value is plain text should use VT_LPSTR, not VT_CF to represent the text. Notice also that an application should choose a single clipboard format for a property's value when using VT_CF. For more information on clipboard format identifiers, see "Clipboard Format Identifiers," later in this appendix.
VT_CLSID	72	A CLSID, which is a DWORD, two WORDs, and eight bytes.
VT_VECTOR	0x1000	If the type indicator is one of the previous values in addition to this bit being set, then the value is a DWORD count of elements, followed by that many repetitions of the value. When VT_VECTOR is combined with VT_VARIANT (VT_VARIANT *must* be combined with VT_VECTOR) the value contains a DWORD element count, a DWORD type indicator, the first value, a DWORD type indicator, the second value, and so on. Examples: VT_LPSTR | VT_VECTOR has a DWORD element count, a DWORD byte count, the first string data, a DWORD byte count, the second string data, and so on. VT_I2 | VT_VECTOR has a DWORD element count followed by a sequence of two-byte integers, with no padding between them.

Defining New Type Indicators

There is no provision in the OLE specification for adding new type indicators to the list above. Property sets are designed to be partially self-describing so that code that does not recognize everything about the property set can at least tell the types of values contained in it. If new VT tags were allowed to be defined, it would be impossible for code to skip over values that are not understood. However, new types can be defined by using the VT_VARIANT type combined with the VT_VECTOR flag. For example, assume you want to store the following packed structure in a property set:

```
typedef struct tagPACKED
{
    DWORD   dwValue1 ;      // 32 bit value
    WORD    wFlag ;         // 16 bits of flags
    WORD    wValue2 ;       // 16 bit value
} PACKED ;
```

This 64-bit structure could be stored using VT_VARIANT | VT_VECTOR as follows:

```
DWORD   // dwTypeIndicator = VT_VARIANT | VT_VECTOR ;
DWORD   // dwElementCount = 3 ;
DWORD // dwTypeIndicator = VT_I4 ;
DWORD   // dwValue1 ;
DWORD // dwTypeIndicator = VT_I2 ;
WORD// wFlag ;
DWORD // dwTypeIndicator = VT_I2 ;
WORD// wValue2 ;
```

Extending an Existing Property Set

A property set can be defined as an extension to an existing property set. To do this, allocate a new FMTID using the GUUID.EXE utility. Then define property identifiers for your extension that do not conflict with the identifiers in the set you are extending.

Extensions defined in this manner allow clients of the property set to skip over extensions they do not know, but still access properties in the original definition. The serialized data format for property sets stores both the base and extension FMTIDs in the property set.

Reserved Property IDs

As a designer of property sets you can use any Property ID for your properties except 0 and 1, which are reserved for use by applications as follows:

Property ID Zero

To enable users of property sets to attach meaning to properties beyond those provided by the type indicator, property ID zero is reserved for an optional dictionary of human-readable names for the property set.

The value will be an array of Property ID/String pairs, where the first ID is zero and its corresponding string is the name of the property set. The remaining entries are the IDs and corresponding names of the properties. The dictionary is stored as a VT_BLOB | VT_VECTOR value. Each BLOB in the vector contains the prerequisite **DWORD** count of bytes followed by a **DWORD** indicating the Property ID followed by the name (a zero-terminated string).

Property ID zero must be in the following format:

- A DWORD count of the number of following pairs
- An unsorted sequence of pairs of the form:

  ```
  DWORD propertyID, LPSTR propertyName
  ```

Not all the names of the properties in the set need to appear in the dictionary. The dictionary in property ID zero can omit entries for properties assumed to be universally known by clients that manipulate the property set. Typically, names for the base property sets for widely accepted standards are omitted, but extensions or special purpose sets may include dictionaries for use by browsers.

Property Set Dictionaries

Property sets may contain an optional dictionary of human readable names that describe the properties in the set. The property set dictionary is stored in property ID zero.

The dictionary is stored as a list of Property ID/String pairs. This can be illustrated using the following pseudo-structure definition for a dictionary entry (it's a pseudo-structure because the sz[] member is variable in size):

```
typedef struct tagENTRY
{
    DWORD   dwPropID ;  // Property ID
    DWORD   cb ;    // Count of characters in the string
    charsz[cb];         // Zero-terminated string.
} ENTRY ;
```

```
typedef struct tagDICTIONARY
{
    DWORD   cbEntries ; // Count of entries in the list
    ENTRY   rgEntry[ cbEntries ] ;
} DICTIONARY ;
```

Note the following about property set dictionaries:

- Property ID Zero does not have a type indicator. The DWORD that indicates the count of entries sits in the type indicator position.
- If the dictionary exists, the first entry in this list must contain a property ID (*dwPropID*) of zero, and a string that names the property set. In other words, the name of the property set is stored using property ID zero and is always the first element in the list.
- The count of characters in the string (cb) includes the zero character that terminates the string.
- The dictionary is entirely optional. However, if it does exist, it must contain at least one entry (the name of the property set). As already pointed out, not all the names of properties in the set need to appear in the dictionary. The dictionary may omit entries for properties assumed to be universally known by clients that manipulate the property set.

Example Dictionary

The stock market data transfer example (see "Transferring Data Contained in Property Sets," earlier in this chapter) might include a human readable name of "Stock Quote" for the entire set, and "Ticker Symbol" for PID_SYMBOL. If a property set contained just a symbol and the dictionary, the property set section would have a byte stream that looked like the following:

```
Offset  Bytes
; Start of section
000043 01 00 00              ; DWORD size of section
000402 00 00 00              ; DWORD number of properties in section

; Start of PropID/Offset pairs
000800 00 00 00              ; DWORD Property ID (0 == dictionary)
000C18 00 00 00              ; DWORD offset to property ID
001003 00 00 00              ; DWORD Property ID (i.e. PID_SYMBOL)
001400 00 00 00              ; DWORD offset to property ID

; Start of Property (Type/Value Pair, which is really the dictionary
; because it has Property ID 0)
001808 00 00 00              ; DWORD Number of entries in dictionary
                                 ; (NOTE: No type indicator!!)
```

```
001C00 00 00 00              ; DWORD dwPropID = 0
002000 00 00 00              ; DWORD cb = strlen("Stock Quote")+1 == 12
0024"Stock Quote\0"          ; char sz[12]
003003 00 00 00              ; DWORD dwPropID = 3 (PID_SYMBOL)
003400 00 00 00              ; DWORD cb = strlen("Ticker Symbol")+1 == 14
0038"Ticker Symbol\0"        ; char sz[14]
... ; dictionary would continue, but may not contain entries for
  ; every possible entry. Also entries do not need to be in order
  ; (except dwPropID == 0 must be first).

; Start of Property (Type/Value Pair)
013B1E 00 00 00              ; DWORD type indicator (VT_LPSTR == 1E)
013F05 00 00 00              ; DWORD count of bytes
0143"MSFT\0"                 ; char sz[5]
```

Property ID One

Property ID One is reserved as an indicator of which code page (Windows) or Script (Macintosh) any strings in the property set originated from. All values must be stored with the same code page. If an application cannot understand this indicator, it should not modify the property. When an application that is not the author of a property set changes a property of type string in the set, it should examine the code page property and either write its values out to that code page or rewrite all other string values in the property set to the new code page and modify the code page's property ID value. Possible values are given in the Window 32 API (see the **GetACP** function) and *Inside Macintosh Volume VI, §14-111*. If the code page indicator is not present, the prevailing code page on the reader's machine must be assumed. Property ID one begins with a VT_I2 type indicator.

Clipboard Format Identifiers

There are five kinds of clipboard FMTIDs that can occur in VT_CF values: Windows Clipboard Format Values, Macintosh Format Values, Format Identifiers, Clipboard Format Names, and No Format Name. The following table illustrates the representation of each of these five types:

First Four Bytes	Following Value Size	Meaning
-1L	4 bytes (DWORD)	Windows built-in Clipboard Format Value (CF_TEXT).
-2L	4 bytes (DWORD)	Macintosh Format Value (4-byte tag).
-3L	16 bytes (Format ID)	FMTID.

First Four Bytes	Following Value Size	Meaning
Length of String	Variable	Clipboard format name that has been registered by **RegisterClipboardFormat** (or some Macintosh equivalent, if any).
0L	Zero	No format name.

Therefore, the format of a VT_CF value is:

```
DWORD cb ;                  // count of bytes that follow (4 + cbTag +
                            // cbData)
DWORD cftag ;               // contains one of the five cftag values
                            // (0,-1,-2,-3, or positive)
BYTE rgcftag[ cbTag ] ;  // cbTag bytes representing the FMTID
BYTE rgData[ cbData ] ;  // clipboard data in the specified format
```

For example, if a VT_CF property contained a 4235 byte bitmap that was stored in the Windows CF_DIB (0x08) clipboard format, the count of bytes would be 4243 (4235 + 4 + 4) or 0x1093. The following stream of bytes would be stored:

```
93 10 00 00 FF FF FF FF 08 00 00 00 ?? ?? ?? ?? ?? ?? ...
|--- cb ---|-- cftag --|- rgcftag -|--- rgData (4235 bytes )...
```

Storing Property Sets

Applications can expose some of the state of their documents so that other applications can locate and read that information. Some examples are a property set describing the author, title, and keywords of a document created with a word processor, or the list of fonts used in a document. This facility is not restricted to documents; it can also be used on embedded objects.

Note If you are storing a property set that is internal to your application, you might not want to follow the guidelines described below. On the other hand, if you want to expose your property set to other applications, you need to follow the guidelines.

To store a property set in a compound file:

1. Create an **IStorage** or **IStream** instance in the same level of the storage structure as its data streams. Prepend the name of your **IStorage** or **IStream** with "\0x05." Stream and storage names that begin with 0x05 are reserved for common property sets that can be shared among applications. The names can be selected from either published names and formats or by creating a new name and assigning the property set a CLSID and FMTID.
2. A property set may be stored in a single **IStream** instance or in an **IStorage** instance containing multiple streams. In the case of an **IStorage**, the contained stream named "CONTENTS" is the primary stream containing property values, where some values may be names of other streams or storage instances within the storage for this property set.
3. Specify the CLSID of the object class that can display and/or provide programmatic access to the property values. If there is no such class, the the CLSID should be set to CLSID_NULL. For a property set that uses an **IStorage** instance, either set the CLSID of the **IStorage** to be the same as that stored in the CONTENTS stream or to CLSID_NULL (the value in a newly created **IStorage**).
4. Define the property set, assigning it unique format and property IDs. A property set can be defined as an extension of an existing property set by allocating a new format ID and property IDs that do not conflict with the base set. The serialized representation includes the base set and the extension, and both format IDs. As noted earlier, this allows readers to skip over unknown extensions while still extracting information from the properties that they do understand.
5. Optionally, the human-readable names that form the contents of the dictionary can be specified.

Some applications only know how to read implementations of property sets stored as **IStream** instances. Applications should be written to expect that a property set may be stored in either an **IStorage** or **IStream**, unless the property set definition indicates otherwise. For example, the Document Summary Information property set's definition says that it can only be stored in a named **IStream**. In cases where you are searching for a property set and you don't know whether it is a storage or stream, it is suggested that you look for an **IStream** with your property set name first. If that fails, look for an **IStorage**.

To illustrate storing property sets in an **IStorage** implementation, suppose there is a class of applications that edit information about animals. First, a CLSID (CLSID_AnimalApp) is defined for this set of applications so they can indicate that they understand property sets containing animal information (FormatID_AnimalInfo) and others containing medical information (FormatID_MedicalInfo).

```
IStorage (File): "C:\OLE\REVO.DOC"
    IStorage: "\005AnimalInfo", CLSID = CLSID_AnimalApp
        IStream: "CONTENTS"
            WORD dwByteOrder, WORD wFmtVersion, DWORD dwOSVer,
            CLSID CLSID_AnimalApp, DWORD cSections...
            ...
            FormatID = FormatID_AnimalInfo
            Property: Type = PID_ANIMALTYPE, Type = VT_LPSTR, Value = "Dog"
            Property: Type = PID_ANIMALNAME, Type = VT_LPSTR, Value = "Revo"
            Property: Type = PID_MEDICALHISTORY, Type = VT_STREAMED_OBJECT,
                            Value = "MedicalInfo"
            ...
        IStream: "MedicalInfo"
            WORD dwByteOrder, WORD wFmtVersion, DWORD dwOSVer,
            CLSID CLSID_AnimalApp, DWORD cSections...
            ...
            FormatID = CLSID_MedicalInfo
            Property: Type = PID_VETNAME, Type = VT_LPSTR, Value = "Dr. Woof"
            Property: Type = PID_LASTEXAM, Type = VT_DATE, Value = ...
```

Note that the class IDs of the **IStorage** and both property sets is CLSID_AnimalApp. This identifies any application that can display and/or provide programmatic access to these property sets. Any application can read the information within the property sets (the point behind property sets), but only applications identified with the class ID of CLSID_AnimalApp can understand the meaning of the data in the property sets.

The Document Summary Information Property Set

OLE defines a standard common property set for storing summary information about documents. The Document Summary Information property set must be stored in an **IStream** instance off of the root **IStorage**; it is not valid to store the property set in the "CONTENTS" stream of a named **IStorage**.

All shared property sets are identified by a stream or storage name prepended with "\005" (or 0x05) to show it is a property set shareable among applications and the Document Summary Information property set is no exception.

The name of the stream that contains the Document Summary Information property set is:

```
"\005SummaryInformation"
```

The FMTID for the Document Summary Information property set is:

```
F29F85E0-4FF9-1068-AB91-08002B27B3D9
```

Use the DEFINE_GUID macro to define the FMTID for the property set:

```
DEFINE_GUID(FormatID_SummaryInformation, 0xF29F85E0, 0x4FF9, 0x1068,
0xAB, 0x91, 0x08, 0x00, 0x2B, 0x27, 0xB3, 0xD9);
```

On an Intel byte-ordered machine, the FMTID has the following representation:

```
E0 85 9F 4F 68 10 AB 91 08 00 2B 27 B3 D9
```

The following table shows the property names for the Document Summary Information property set, along with the respective property IDs and type indicators.

Property Name	Property ID	Property ID Code	Type
Title	PID_TITLE	0x00000002	VT_LPSTR
Subject	PID_SUBJECT	0x00000003	VT_LPSTR
Author	PID_AUTHOR	0x00000004	VT_LPSTR
Keywords	PID_KEYWORDS	0x00000005	VT_LPSTR
Comments	PID_COMMENTS	0x00000006	VT_LPSTR
Template	PID_TEMPLATE	0x00000007	VT_LPSTR
Last Saved By	PID_LASTAUTHOR	0x00000008	VT_LPSTR
Revision Number	PID_REVNUMBER	0x00000009	VT_LPSTR
Total Editing Time	PID_EDITTIME	0x0000000A	VT_FILETIME
Last Printed	PID_LASTPRINTED	0x0000000B	VT_FILETIME
Create Time/Date*	PID_CREATE_DTM	0x0000000C	VT_FILETIME
Last saved Time/Date*	PID_LASTSAVE_DTM	0x0000000D	VT_FILETIME
Number of Pages	PID_PAGECOUNT	0x0000000E	VT_I4
Number of Words	PID_WORDCOUNT	0x0000000F	VT_I4
Number of Characters	PID_CHARCOUNT	0x00000010	VT_I4
Thumbnail	PID_THUMBNAIL	0x00000011	VT_CF
Name of Creating Application	PID_APPNAME	0x00000012	VT_LPSTR
Security	PID_SECURITY	0x00000013	VT_I4

* Some methods of file transfer (such as a download from a BBS) do not maintain the file system's version of this information correctly.

Guidelines for Implementing the Document Summary Information Property Set

The following guidelines pertain to the Document Summary Information property set described in the preceding section:

- PID_TEMPLATE refers to an external document containing formatting and styling information. The means by which the template is located is implementation defined.
- PID_LASTAUTHOR is the name stored in User Information by the application. For example, suppose Mary creates a document on her machine and gives it to John, who then modifies and saves it. Mary is the author, John is the last saved by value.
- PID_REVNUMBER is the number of times the File/Save command has been called on this document.
- PID_CREATE_DTM is a read-only property; this property should be set when a document is created, but should not be subsequently changed.
- For PID_THUMBNAIL, applications should store data in CF_DIB or CF_METAFILEPICT format. CF_METAFILEPICT is recommended.
- PID_SECURITY is the suggested security level for the document. By noting the security level on the document, an application other than the originator of the document can adjust its user interface to the properties appropriately. An application should not display any information about a password protected document or allow modifications to enforced read-only or locked-for-annotations documents. Applications should warn the user about read-only recommended if the user attempts to modify properties:

Security Level	Value
None	0
Password protected	1
Read-only recommended	2
Read-only enforced	3
Locked for annotations	4

APPENDIX C

Creating Distribution Disks

This appendix discusses issues related to the distribution of your OLE application. It continues with a description of the files that must be included on your distribution disk(s), discusses special considerations for OLE application distribution, and concludes with a discussion of special considerations for distribution of OLE server applications.

Disk Contents

In addition to the files you need to ship with your application you must distribute the files listed below if your application is OLE 2 aware. When installing your application on the end user's system your install/setup program *must* copy the following files to the user's xxxx\SYSTEM directory (where xxxx is the directory where Windows 3.1 is installed:

COMPOBJ.DLL

OLE2.DLL

OLE2PROX.DLL

OLE2DISP.DLL

OLE2NLS.DLL

OLE2CONV.DLL

OLE2.REG

STDOLE.TLB

STORAGE.DLL

TYPELIB.DLL

Since OLE 2 requires all of these files in order to run correctly, your setup/installation program must install **all of them** regardless of whether or not the application itself uses the files.

Installation Issues

Where to Install

The install/setup program MUST check the user's xxxx\system (where xxxx is the directory where Windows 3.1 is installed) subdirectory to verify if copies of the OLE 2 files are already present. **If the files are already present in the user's system, the version information of *each* file MUST be checked to make sure that newer versions of the OLE 2 files will not be overwritten by older versions.**

You can use the File Installation Library, VER.DLL, supplied with Microsoft Windows Version 3.1 to extract a version string from the application. For more information on VER.DLL, see the *Microsoft Windows Programmer's Reference, Volume 1: Overview* in Version 3.1 of the Microsoft Windows Software Development Kit.

Additionally, the application should copy its registration entry file

YYYY.REG (YYYY is determined by the object application)

into the directory that the application installs its executable (.exe file). This will allow the user to double click on the YYYY.REG file and re-register the application in the case the registration database (REG.DAT) gets corrupted. For the content and creation of the registration files, see "Registering Object Applications."

Things to Check During the Installation

TEMP Entry

The setup of an application should detect if the user's TEMP= entry points to a removable media and prompt the user to change it to point to a local hard drive. (If the application is doing AUTOEXEC.BAT modification, it should make the modification for the TEMP= entry also).

SHARE.EXE

In order to function, the OLE 2 Compound File implementation requires that file range-locking be enabled. If range-locking is not already installed on the machine, then the MS-DOS command

SHARE.EXE

needs to be added to AUTOEXEC.BAT. Use of SHARE.EXE is the common way that range-locking is supported on Microsoft Windows 3.1. On Microsoft Windows for Workgroups, the range locking is part of the system and SHARE.EXE should not be installed.

Caution The SHARE.EXE entry should follow the PATH statement in AUTOEXEC.BAT, but precede any statement that starts Windows or otherwise prevents SHARE.EXE from being executed.

To determine if range locking is installed, open a local file and attempt to acquire a range lock on it. If an error is returned, then range locking is not supported (see MS-DOS Int 21h Function 5Ch for further details.) AUTOEXEC.BAT is a suggested local file to use for this purpose.

If range-locking is not supported, then SHARE.EXE needs to be added to AUTOEXEC.BAT. If range-locking is in fact currently supported, then AUTOEXEC.BAT may still need to be modified. You need to scan AUTOEXEC.BAT looking for SHARE.EXE. If it is not found, do nothing; if it is found, then ensure that it's /L and /F options are at least as large as outlined below.

The /L option on the MS-DOS SHARE command indicates the number of locks that can be placed on files. The /F parameter allocates file space (in bytes) for the MS-DOS storage area used to record file sharing information. The default setting for the /L option is 20 locks; the default setting for the /F option is 2048. Each open OLE 2 Compound File requires for its own use 4 (or less) dedicated locks. A small number (less than 5) of additional locks are needed by the Compound File implementation, independent of how many files are open. Each lock reserved by /L requires 18 bytes.

It is recommended that a /L setting of at least /L:500 and a /F setting of at least /F:5100 be used:

```
SHARE /L:500 /F:5100
```

If the /L or the /F setting to SHARE has a larger value than listed here, installation programs should leave the setting as it is rather than reducing it.

Note Be sure to add the necessary copyright notice to the copyright notice(s) for your application. See the SDK documentation for information on copyright notices.

Glossary

A

activation The process of binding an object in order to put it into its running state. Also refers to invoking a particular operation on an object. *See Binding.*

advisory sink An object that implements **IAdviseSink** and optionally **IAdviseSink2**; these interfaces enable the object to receive notifications of changes in the embedded object or link source.

aggregate object A component object that is made up of one or more other component objects. One of the objects in the aggregate is designated the controlling unknown; this object has the implementation of **IUnknown** to which the other implementations forward their calls.

aggregation A composition technique for implementing component objects whereby a new object can be built using one or more existing objects that support some or all of the new object's required interfaces.

artificial reference counting The technique of incrementing an object's reference count to safeguard the object prior to making a potentially destructive function call. After the function returns, the reference count is decremented.

asynchronous call A function call whereby the caller does not wait for the reply. OLE defines five asynchronous methods, all within the **IAdviseSink** interface: **OnDataChange**, **OnViewChange**, **OnRename**, **OnSave**, and **OnClose**.

automation A way to manipulate an application's objects from outside the application to enable programmability.

B

binding The process of getting an object into the running state so that operations supplied by the object's application (such as editing and play) can be invoked.

C

cache An object provided by OLE that stores presentation data for embedded objects.

cache initialization state The stage where an embedded object's cache is filled using the data formats provided on the clipboard or from a drag and drop operation.

class factory table A task table that stores the registered class identifier (CLSID) of a class object. Every OLE object application (or container that allows linking to its embedded objects) must register a CLSID for each supported class of object. *See also Class identifier.*

class identifier (CLSID) A unique identification tag associated with an OLE object. An object registers its CLSID in the registration database to enable clients to locate and load the executable code associated with the object(s).

class object An object that implements the **IClassFactory** interface, allowing it to instantiate an instance of an object of a specific class. Object implementors implement one class object for each object class they support.

client A component that is requesting services from another component. *See also Container.*

client site The display site for an embedded or linked object within the compound document. The client site is used to provide positional and conceptual information about the object.

component object An object that conforms to the component object model. Component objects implement and use the set of interfaces that support object interaction.

composite moniker *See Generic composite moniker.*

commit The act of persistently saving any changes made to an object since its storage was opened or since the last time changes were saved. *See also Revert.*

component object model An object-oriented programming model that defines how objects interact within a single application or between applications.

composite menu A shared menu bar composed of menu groups from both the in-place container and the in-place object application. The object application is responsible for installing and removing the menu from the container's frame window.

compound document A document that contains data of different formats, such as sound clips, spreadsheets, text, and bitmaps, created by different applications. Compound documents are stored by container applications.

compound document object A component object that is used specifically in compound documents. Compound document objects are either linked or embedded.

compound file An OLE-provided implementation of the interfaces that support the structured storage model. Compound files are disk-based files and are sometimes referred to as *Docfiles.*

container *See Container application.*

container application An application that is the consumer of a compound document object. Container applications provide storage for the object, a site for display, and access to this display site.

Container/Object An application that has implemented OLE interfaces such that the application supports the features and capabilities of both a container and object application.

Container/Server *See Container/Object.*

D

data transfer object An object that implements the **IDataObject** interface for the purpose of transferring data via the clipboard and drag and drop operations.

default object handler An object handler that is provided with the OLE 2 SDK. The default object handler performs tasks on behalf of the loaded object, such as rendering an object from its cached state when the object is loaded into memory.

direct access mode One of two access modes in which a storage object can be opened. In direct mode, all changes are immediately committed to the root storage object. *See also Transacted access mode.*

docfile *See Compound file.*

drag and drop The act of using the mouse, or other pointing device, to drag data from one window and drop it into the same window or another window.

E

embedded object An compound document object that physically resides with the container, but is initially created and subsequently edited by its object application.

explicit caching One of two ways an object can cache its presentation data; explicit caching requires the physical creation of the cache nodes needed to save the data formats of the object. *See also Implicit caching.*

F

file moniker An object that implements the **IMoniker** interface for the file class. Representing a file-based link source, a file moniker is a wrapper for a pathname in the native file system and is always the left-most part of a generic composite moniker.*See also Item moniker and Generic composite moniker.*

G

global memory *See Shared application memory.*

generic composite moniker An object that implements the **IMoniker** interface for the composite class. The generic composite moniker is a sequenced collection of other types of monikers, starting with a file moniker to provide the document-level pathname and continuing with one or more item monikers. *See also Item moniker and File moniker.*

H

handler *See Object handler.*

helper function A function that encapsulates functionality that is publicly available with the OLE SDK. That is, a caller can choose the implement the tasks included in the helper function or just call the helper function.

HRESULT An opaque result handle defined to be zero for a successful return from a function and non-zero if error or status information is to be returned. To convert an HRESULT into the more detailled SCODE, applications call **GetScode**(). *See SCODE.*

I

implicit caching The "implied" caching of presentation data by an object that is capable of rendering itself using its native data. Cache nodes are not created with implicit caching. *See also Explicit caching.*

in parameter A parameter that is allocated, set, and freed by the caller of a function.

In/Out parameter A parameter that is initially allocated by the caller of a function and set, freed, and reallocated if necessary by the callee.

in-place editing *See In-place activation.*

in-place activation The ability to activate an object within the context of its container document and to associate a verb with that activation (for example, edit, play, change); not all applications support in-place activation. Sometimes referred to as in-place editing or visual editing (from a user's viewpoint).

in-process server An object application that is run in the container's process space.

input synchronized call A function call whereby the callee must complete the call before yielding control. This ensures that focus management works correctly and that data entered by the user is processed appropriately. Many of the methods used for in-place activation are input synchronized:

instance An in-memory instantiation of an object.

instantiate The process of allocating and initializing an object's data structures in memory.

interface A grouping of semantically related functions through which one application accesses the services of another. Interfaces are the binary standard for component object interaction.

interface identifier (IID) A unique identification tag associated with each interface; applications use the IID to reference the interface in function calls.

interface negotiation The process by which a server or container can query an object about a specified interface and have the object return a pointer to that interface if it is supported. *See also Reference counting.*

item moniker An object that implements the **IMoniker** interface for the item class. Item monikers contain an application-defined string to represent a link source. *See also File moniker and Generic composite moniker.*

L

link object A component object that is instantiated when a linked compound document object is created or loaded. The link object implements the IOleLink interface and is provided by OLE.

linked object A compound document object whose source data physically resides where it was initially created. Only a moniker that represents the source data and the appropriate presentation data is kept with the compound document. Changes made to the link source are automatically reflected in the linked compound document object in the container(s).

link source The data that is the source of a linked compound document object. A link source may be a file, an embedded object, or either a portion of a file or an embedded object (also called pseudo objects).

loaded state The state of a compound document object after its data structures created by the object handler have been loaded into container memory. *See also Passive state and Running state.*

local application memory Memory that is allocated by OLE (or an optional object handler) using an application-supplied memory allocator.

local server An object application implemented as an EXE that is not run in the container's process space.

lock OLE defines two types of locks that can be held on an object: *strong* and *weak*. A strong lock will keep an object in memory, a weak lock will not.

LRPC (Lightweight remote procedure call) OLE's RPC-based protocol for interprocess communication. LRPC is "lightweight" in that it handles communication between processes on one machine only.

M

marshaling The processing of packaging and sending interface parameters across process boundaries.

member function *See method.*

method One of a group of semantically related functions that make up a specific interface, providing a specific service.

mini server A mini server is a object application that cannot run stand-alone; it is always run from another application. An object created by a mini server is stored as part of the container document.

moniker An object that implements the IMoniker interface and provides a conceptual handle to the source of a linked object. There are several types of moniker classes, each with a different implementation of IMoniker. *See also File moniker, Item moniker, and Generic composite moniker.*

Multiple Document Interface (MDI) Application An application that can support multiple documents from one application instance. MDI object applications can simultaneously service a user and one or more embedding containers. *See also Single Document Interface (SDI) application.*

Multiple object application An application that is capable of supporting more than one class of object; for example, a spreadsheet program might support charts, spreadsheets, and macros.

N

nested object An object that is contained within another object; OLE objects can be arbitrarily nested to any level.

native data Data provided by an object that is used to edit the object.

O

object A unit of information that resides in a container's compound document and whose behavior is constant no matter where it is located; the object's behavior is defined by the object rather than by the compound document that holds it.

object application An application that is capable of creating compound document objects that can then be embedded in or linked to by containers.

object class A type of object that is registered in the registration database and that is serviced by a particular object application. *See Class object.*

object handler A piece of object-specific code that is dynamically loaded into the address space of its container. Object handlers process requests for specific class or classes of objects, enabling single process communication rather than remote messaging.

object state The description of the relationship between a compound document object in its container and the application responsible for the object's creation. There are three compound document object states: *passive*, *loaded*, and *running*.

object type name A unique identification string that is stored as part of the information available for an object in the registration database—for example, Acme Drawing.

OLE An acronym for Object Linking and Embedding.

out parameter A parameter that is allocated and set by the callee of a function and freed by the caller.

P

passive state The state of a compound document object when it is in its stored state (on disk or in a database). The object is not selected or active. *See also Loaded state and Running state.*

persistent storage Storage of a file or object in an **IStorage**-based medium such as a file system or database.

primary verb The action associated with the most common, preferred operation users perform on an object; the primary verb is always defined as verb zero in the system registration database. An object's primary verb is executed by double-clicking on the object.

presentation data Data provided by an object that is used to render the object on an output device.

programmability The ability for an application to define a set of properties and commands and make them accessible to other applications. *See Automation.*

proxy An interface-specific object that packages parameters for that interface in preparation for a remote method call. A proxy runs in the address space of the sender and communicates with a corresponding stub in the receiver's address space. *See also Stub, Marshaling, and Unmarshaling.*

pseudo object A selection of data within a document or embedded object that can be the source for a compound document object.

R

reference counting Keeping a count of each interface pointer instance to ensure that an object is not destroyed before all references to it are released.

revert The act of discarding any change(s) made to an object since the last time the changes were committed or the object's storage was opened. *See Commit.*

Root IStorage object The outermost **IStorage** instance in a document; also called the root storage object. Compound document objects are always saved as children of a root **IStorage** object.

running state The state of a compound document object when the object application is running and it is possible to edit the object, access its interfaces, and receive notification of changes. *See also Loaded state and Passive state.*

running object table A globally accessible lookup table that is used to store running objects and their monikers. Registering an object in the running object table results in a reference count being made on behalf of the object; before the object can be destroyed, its moniker must be released from the running object table.

S

SCODE A DWORD value that is used to pass detailed information to the caller of an interface method or API function. *See also HRESULT.*

server *See object application.*

shared application memory Memory that is primarily used between processes to optimize the data copying that occurs in LPRC calls.

Single Document Interface (SDI) Application
An application that can support only one document at a time. Multiple instances of an SDI application must be started to service both an embedded object and a user. *See also Multiple Document Interface (MDI) application.*

single object application An application that is capable of creating and manipulating one class of object. *See also Multiple object application.*

stand-alone object application An object application that was implemented as an executable (EXE) program, as opposed to a DLL object application.

state *See Loaded state, Passive state, and Running state.*

static object A picture that is provided a compound document object wrapping by OLE. This wrapping makes it possible for containers to treat them as though they were linked or embedded objects with one exception: static objects cannot be edited.

storage object An object that implements the **IStorage** interface. The storage of a compound document object is always relative to a root **IStorage** object. *See also Root IStorage object.*

stream object An object that implements the **IStream** interface. Objects can create as many data streams (**IStream** objects) as needed in which to save an object's data.

structured storage model A specification that defines a hierarchical method of storing objects. OLE provides an implementation of the structured storage model called Compound Files. *See Compound file and Docfile.*

stub An interface-specific object that unpackages the parameters for that interface marshaled across the process boundary and makes the required method call. The stub runs in the address space of the receiver and communicates with a corresponding proxy in the sender's address space. *See Proxy, Marshaling, and Unmarshaling.*

synchronous call A function call whereby the caller waits for the reply before continuing. Most OLE interface methods are synchronous calls.

T

transacted access mode One of two access modes in which a storage object can be opened. When opened in transacted mode, changes are stored in temporary buffers until the root **IStorage** object commits its changes.

U

uniform data transfer A model for transferring data via the clipboard, drag and drop, or through automation. Objects conforming to the model implement the **IDataObject** interface. This model replaces DDE. *See Data transfer object.*

unmarshaling The processing of unpackaging parameters that have been sent across process boundaries.

V

Virtual Table (VTBL) An array of function pointers that point to interface method implementations.

visual editing A marketing term that refers to the user being able to interact with a compound document object in the context of its container; the term most often used by developers is in-place activation. *See also In-place activation.*

Index

Symbols

A

E

F

K

L

N

O

S

W